AD NUMBER
AD088221

LIMITATION CHANGES

TO:

Approved for public release; distribution is unlimited. Document partially illegible.

FROM:

Distribution: Further dissemination only as directed by Office of the Chief of Naval Operation, Navy Department, Washington, DC 20301, 10 JUN 1947, or higher DoD authority. Document partially illegible.

AUTHORITY

USFF ltr dtd 14 Feb 2013

UNCLASSIFIED

AD NUMBER
AD088221

CLASSIFICATION CHANGES

TO:

UNCLASSIFIED

FROM:

CONFIDENTIAL

AUTHORITY

CNO ltr, dtd 13 Jan 1955

THIS PAGE IS UNCLASSIFIED

DISCLAIMER NOTICE

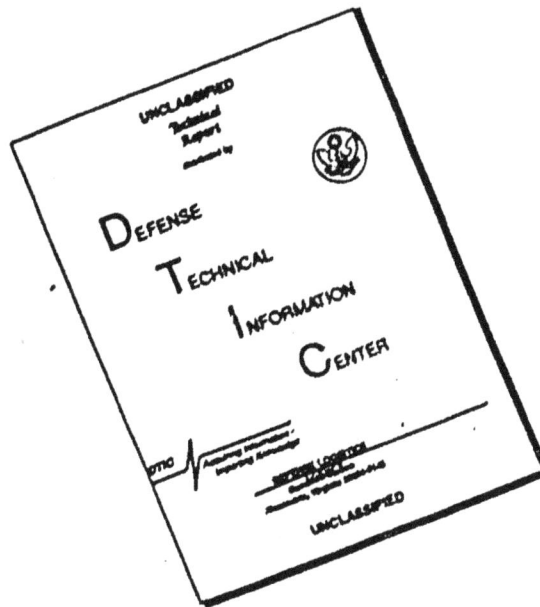

THIS DOCUMENT IS BEST QUALITY AVAILABLE. THE COPY FURNISHED TO DTIC CONTAINED A SIGNIFICANT NUMBER OF PAGES WHICH DO NOT REPRODUCE LEGIBLY.

R.A. Butler.

REPORT OF
OPERATION HIGHJUMP

FC

U.S. NAVY
ANTARCTIC DEVELOPMENT
PROJECT 1947

56A4   13751

AD 88221

Armed Services Technical Information Agency

Reproduced by

REPORT OF
OPERATION HIGHJUMP

FC

U. S. NAVY ANTARCTIC
DEVELOPMENT PROJECT 1947

56AA 12751

CONFIDENTIAL

UNITED STATES ATLANTIC FLEET

CARE F. P. O., NEW YORK, N.Y.

CONFIDENTIAL

14 JUL 1947

FIRST ENDORSEMENT on
TF 68 conf. ltr CTF 68/
A9/rdk Serial 0184 of
10 June 1947

From: Commander in Chief, United States Atlantic Fleet.
To: Chief of Naval Operations.
Via: Officer-in-Charge, Antarctic Developments Project, 1947.

Subject: Report of Antarctic Developments Project, 1947, (Operation HIGHJUMP).

    1.   Forwarded.

    2.   The Commander in Chief, U.S. Atlantic Fleet considers that all reasonable measures were taken, in the relatively short period available, to adequately prepare the units assigned to the Task Force for the subject operation.

    3.   It is noted that all major objectives were accomplished except the construction, at Little America, of a matted (marston mat) airstrip. The construction of such an airstrip was intended to provide the means for determining the feasibility of maintaining and operating wheel type aircraft thereon. The existing unusually severe ice conditions precluded accomplishing this project. However, considerable experimental work was conducted and the Task Force Commander believes that an acceptable technique was developed for constructing such an airstrip on snow (neve) covered glacial ice permitting the operation thereon of aircraft using conventional wheel type landing gear.

    4.   Due to the assignment of such a relatively large task force, the Navy now has available a large reservoir of polar-conditioned personnel. In view of the increasing strategic importance of the Arctic, this comparatively large number of cold-weather-trained officers and men might, at some future date, prove most valuable to the naval service.

    5.   The Commander in Chief, U.S. Atlantic Fleet concurs with the Task Force Commander in the conviction that very real and definite advantages have accrued to the United States and to the naval service as a result of the conduct of subject operation. It is recommended that a definite program of naval operations be carried out annually in either the Arctic or the Antarctic regions. The Arctic region would be preferable in view of the much shorter distance from U.S. ports.

W. H. P. BLANDY

Copy to:
  CTF 68

56AA   12751

In reply refer to Initials
and No.

A9/BYRD/rdk

NAVY DEPARTMENT
OFFICE OF THE CHIEF OF NAVAL OPERATIONS
WASHINGTON 25, D. C.

for PEACE
SAVINGS
BONDS

4 August 1947

CONFIDENTIAL

SECOND ENDORSEMENT on
TF 68 Conf. ltr CTF 68/
A9/rdk Serial 0184 of
10 June 1947.

From: Officer-in-Charge, Antarctic Developments Project,
            1947.
To :   Chief of Naval Operations.

Subject: Report of Antarctic Developments Project, 1947,
            (Operation HIGHJUMP).

1.   Forwarded.

2.   It is thought that the next large Antarctic Expedition
should be a joint Army and Navy Project, and it is so recommended.

R. E. BYRD.

UNITED STATES ATLANTIC FLEET

CARE F. P. O., NEW YORK, N.Y.

14 JUL 1947

FIRST ENDORSEMENT on
TF 68 conf. ltr CTF 68/
A9/rdk Serial 0184 of
10 June 1947

From: Commander in Chief, United States Atlantic Fleet.
To: Chief of Naval Operations.
Via: Officer-in-Charge, Antarctic Developments Project, 1947.

Subject: Report of Antarctic Developments Project, 1947, (Operation
            HIGHJUMP).

1.   Forwarded.

2.   The Commander in Chief, U.S. Atlantic Fleet considers that all
reasonable measures were taken, in the relatively short period available, to
adequately prepare the units assigned to the Task Force for the subject
operation.

3.   It is noted that all major objectives were accomplished except
the construction, at Little America, of a matted (marston mat) airstrip.
The construction of such an airstrip was intended to provide the means for
determining the feasibility of maintaining and operating wheel type aircraft
thereon. The existing unusually severe ice conditions precluded accomplishing this project. However, considerable experimental work was conducted and
the Task Force Commander believes that an acceptable technique was developed
for constructing such an airstrip on snow (neve) covered glacial ice permitting the operation thereon of aircraft using conventional wheel type
landing gear.

4.   Due to the assignment of such a relatively large task force,
the Navy now has available a large reservoir of polar-conditioned personnel.
In view of the increasing strategic importance of the Arctic, this comparatively large number of cold-weather-trained officers and men might, at some
future date, prove most valuable to the naval service.

5.   The Commander in Chief, U.S. Atlantic Fleet concurs with the
Task Force Commander in the conviction that very real and definite advantages
have accrued to the United States and to the naval service as a result of the
conduct of subject operation. It is recommended that a definite program of
naval operations be carried out annually in either the Arctic or the Antarctic
regions. The Arctic region would be preferable in view of the much shorter
distance from U.S. ports.

W. H. P. BLANDY

Copy to:
    CTF 68

NAVY DEPARTMENT

OFFICE OF THE CHIEF OF NAVAL OPERATIONS

WASHINGTON 25, D. C.

A9/BYRD/rdk

for PEACE
SAVINGS
BONDS

4 August 1947

SECOND ENDORSEMENT on
TF 68 Conf. ltr CTF 68/
A9/rdk Serial 0184 of
10 June 1947.

From: Officer-in-Charge, Antarctic Developments Project,
           1947.
To :   Chief of Naval Operations.

Subject: Report of Antarctic Developments Project, 1947,
           (Operation HIGHJUMP).

   1.   Forwarded.

   2.   It is thought that the next large Antarctic Expedition
should be a joint Army and Navy Project, and it is so recommended.

R. E. BYRD.

UNITED STATES ATLANTIC FLEET

CARE F. P. O. NEW YORK, N.Y..

CONFIDENTIAL

14 JUL 1947

<u>FIRST ENDORSEMENT</u> on
TF 68 conf. ltr CTF 68/
A9/rdk Serial 0184 of
10 June 1947

From: Commander in Chief, United States Atlantic Fleet.
To: Chief of Naval Operations.
Via: Officer-in-Charge, Antarctic Developments Project, 1947.

Subject: Report of Antarctic Developments Project, 1947, (Operation HIGHJUMP).

1.   Forwarded.

2.   The Commander in Chief, U.S. Atlantic Fleet considers that all reasonable measures were taken, in the relatively short period available, to adequately prepare the units assigned to the Task Force for the subject operation.

3.   It is noted that all major objectives were accomplished except the construction, at Little America, of a matted (marston mat) airstrip. The construction of such an airstrip was intended to provide the means for determining the feasibility of maintaining and operating wheel type aircraft thereon. The existing unusually severe ice conditions precluded accomplishing this project. However, considerable experimental work was conducted and the Task Force Commander believes that an acceptable technique was developed for constructing such an airstrip on snow (neve) covered glacial ice permitting the operation thereon of aircraft using conventional wheel type landing gear.

4.   Due to the assignment of such a relatively large task force, the Navy now has available a large reservoir of polar-conditioned personnel. In view of the increasing strategic importance of the Arctic, this comparatively large number of cold-weather-trained officers and men might, at some future date, prove most valuable to the naval service.

5.   The Commander in Chief, U.S. Atlantic Fleet concurs with the Task Force Commander in the conviction that very real and definite advantages have accrued to the United States and to the naval service as a result of the conduct of subject operation. It is recommended that a definite program of naval operations be carried out annually in either the Arctic or the Antarctic regions. The Arctic region would be preferable in view of the much shorter distance from U.S. ports.

W. H. P. BLANDY

Copy to:
   CTF 68

NAVY DEPARTMENT

OFFICE OF THE CHIEF OF NAVAL OPERATIONS

A9/BYRD/rdk   WASHINGTON 25, D. C.

4 August 1947

CONFIDENTIAL

SECOND ENDORSEMENT on
TF 68 Conf. ltr CTF 68/
A9/rdk Serial 0184 of
10 June 1947.

From: Officer-in-Charge, Antarctic Developments Project,
          1947.
To :   Chief of Naval Operations.

Subject: Report of Antarctic Developments Project, 1947,
          (Operation HIGHJUMP).

1.   Forwarded.

2.   It is thought that the next large Antarctic Expedition
should be a joint Army and Navy Project, and it is so recommended.

R. E. BYRD.

UNITED STATES ATLANTIC FLEET

CARE F. P. O., NEW YORK, N.Y.

CONFIDENTIAL

14 JUL 1947

FIRST ENDORSEMENT on
TF 68 conf. ltr CTF 68/
A9/rdk Serial 0184 of
10 June 1947

From: Commander in Chief, United States Atlantic Fleet.
To: Chief of Naval Operations.
Via: Officer-in-Charge, Antarctic Developments Project, 1947.

Subject: Report of Antarctic Developments Project, 1947, (Operation
            HIGHJUMP).

1.   Forwarded.

2.   The Commander in Chief, U.S. Atlantic Fleet considers that all
reasonable measures were taken, in the relatively short period available, to
adequately prepare the units assigned to the Task Force for the subject
operation.

3.   It is noted that all major objectives were accomplished except
the construction, at Little America, of a matted (marston mat) airstrip.
The construction of such an airstrip was intended to provide the means for
determining the feasibility of maintaining and operating wheel type aircraft
thereon. The existing unusually severe ice conditions precluded accomplishing this project. However, considerable experimental work was conducted and
the Task Force Commander believes that an acceptable technique was developed
for constructing such an airstrip on snow (neve) covered glacial ice permitting the operation thereon of aircraft using conventional wheel type
landing gear.

4.   Due to the assignment of such a relatively large task force,
the Navy now has available a large reservoir of polar-conditioned personnel.
In view of the increasing strategic importance of the Arctic, this comparatively large number of cold-weather-trained officers and men might, at some
future date, prove most valuable to the naval service.

5.   The Commander in Chief, U.S. Atlantic Fleet concurs with the
Task Force Commander in the conviction that very real and definite advantages
have accrued to the United States and to the naval service as a result of the
conduct of subject operation. It is recommended that a definite program of
naval operations be carried out annually in either the Arctic or the Antarctic
regions. The Arctic region would be preferable in view of the much shorter
distance from U.S. ports.

W. H. P. BLANDY

Copy to:
    CTF 68

NAVY DEPARTMENT

OFFICE OF THE CHIEF OF NAVAL OPERATIONS

WASHINGTON 25, D. C.

A9/BYRD/rdk

for PEACE
SAVINGS
BONDS

4 August 1947

SECOND ENDORSEMENT on
TF 68 Conf. ltr CTF 68/
A9/rdk Serial 0184 of
10 June 1947.

From: Officer-in-Charge, Antarctic Developments Project,
          1947.
To :   Chief of Naval Operations.

Subject: Report of Antarctic Developments Project, 1947,
          (Operation HIGHJUMP).

    1.   Forwarded.

    2.   It is thought that the next large Antarctic Expedition
should be a joint Army and Navy Project, and it is so recommended.

R. E. BYRD.

TASK FORCE SIXTY EIGHT
CTF68/A9/rdk   U. S. Atlantic Fleet
Serial 0184   10 June 1947

From: Commander Task Force SIXTY EIGHT.
To :   Chief of Naval Operations.
Via :   Commander-in-Chief, U. S. Atlantic Fleet.
         Officer-in-Charge, Antarctic Developments Project, 1947.

Subject: Report of Antarctic Developments Project, 1947, (Operation HIGHJUMP).

Reference: (a) C.T.F. 68 Op-plan 2-46 dated 20 Nov. 1946.

Enclosure: (A) CNO conf. serial 065P33 dated 26 August 1946.
           (B) CinCLantFlt conf. serial 0568 dated 15 October 1946 .

1.   The Antarctic Developments Project, 1947, identified by the codeword "IGHJUMP", was established by the Chief of Naval Operations by Enclosure (A) dated 26 August 1946. This directive charged the Commander-in-Chief, U. S. Atlantic Fleet with the operational and administrative control of the project. Technical control was retained by the Chief of Naval Operations and was exercised with the assistance of Rear Admiral Richard E. Byrd, U.S.N. (Retired), who was designated as Officer-in-Charge of the Project and who locally exercised technical control while present in the Antarctic.

2.   Operational and administrative instructions for the conduct of the Project were issued to the Task Force Commander by the Commander in Chief, U. S. Atlantic Fleet in a letter of instructions dated 15 October, 1946, Enclosure (B).

3.   Prior to the departure of Task Force SIXTY EIGHT for the conduct of "Operation NANOOK" in the Arctic, July-September 1946, the Task Force Commander was informed that preliminary discussions were being held regarding an operation to be held in the Antarctic during the forthcoming winter. As a result some preliminary planning was done by the staff during the operational period of "NANOOK" and, during the latter part of the operation some of the key members of the staff were returned by air to augment the planning staff which was being assembled with the Rear Echelon at the Navy Department. However, full scale planning did not begin until the latter part of September, upon the return of the Task Force from the Arctic.

4.   As eventually organized the Task Force consisted of 13 ships; 7 ships from the Atlantic Fleet plus the U.S. Coast Guard ice breaker NORTHWIND on loan from the Coast Guard, and 5 ships from the Pacific Fleet. Aircraft assigned were: - 6 PBM, 6 R4D, 2 J2F, 2 SOC,

CONFIDENTIAL

Subject: Report of Antarctic Developments Project, 1947, (Operation HIGHJUMP).

- -

1 JA plus 4 HO3S-1 and 2 HOS helicopters. Total naval and marine personnel participating was slightly in excess of 4700 officers and men. In addition 8 U.S.Army observers, 25 civilian observers from various agencies of the U. S. Government and 11 radio and press correspondents participated in the operation.

5.   The short period available for planning and preparation required strenuous work on the part of all. Many of the ships were in an inactive status and all were below peace time complements. All aircraft required winterization and some alterations. Little time was available for the training and indoctrination of the hastily assembled crews of the ships and aircraft. Much specialized equipment had to be assembled and modified for the special conditions to be encountered, especially that for the base at Little America. The departure date of 2 December 1946 could not have been met except for the splendid cooperation of the various Bureaus and agencies of the Navy Department and of numerous commands afloat and ashore.

6.   The objectives of the operation as specified by the Commander-in-Chief, U. S. Atlantic Fleet were:

(a) Training personnel and testing equipment in frigid zones.

(b) Consolidating and extending United States sovereignty over the largest practicable area of the Antarctic continent.

(c) Determining the feasibility of establishing, maintaining and utilizing bases in the Antarctic and investigating possible base sites.

(d) Developing techniques for establishing, maintaining and utilizing air bases on ice, with particular attention to later applicability of such techniques to operations in interior Greenland where conditions are comparable to those in the Antarctic.

(e) Amplifying existing stores of knowledge of hydrographic, geographic, geological, meteorological and electro-magnetic propagation conditions in the area.

(f) Supplementary objectives of the 1946 NANOOK Operation.

CONFIDENTIAL

Subject: Report of Antarctic Developments Project, 1947,
              (Operation HIGHJUMP).
- -

7.   To accomplish these objectives the Task Force was
organized and tasks assigned as follows:

(a) TG 68.1 Central Group, Rear Admiral Cruzen.
             MOUNT OLYMPUS (TFF)   1 AGC
             NORTHWIND (USCG)   1 WAG
             BURTON ISLAND   1 AG
             YANCEY, MERRICK   2 AKA
             SENNET   1 SS

        TASK: To establish a temporary base and airstrip
        in the vicinity of Little America, Antarctica,
        transporting and landing required material and
        personnel. To conduct systematic long range air
        exploration and associated operations, and to
        carry out assigned projects for training naval
        personnel, testing materials and amplifying
        existing scientific knowledge of the Antarctic.

(b) TG 68.2 Western Group, Captain Bond.
             CURRITUCK (TGF)   1 AV
             CACAPON   1 AO
             HENDERSON   1 DD

        TASK: To conduct systematic air exploration of
        assigned areas of Antarctica, stressing delinea-
        tion of unknown or improperly charted portions of
        the coast line, with ships remaining outside of
        the main continental ice pack. To initiate opera-
        tions in the vicinity of the Balleny Islands, and
        to continue operations to westward along the conti-
        nental perimeter.

(c) TG 68.3 Eastern Group, Captain Dufek.
             PINE ISLAND (TGF)   1 AV
             CANISTEO   1 AO
             BROWNSON   1 DD

        TASK: Same as for the Eastern Group, except to
        initiate operations in the vicinity of Peter I
        Island and to continue operations to eastward
        along the continental perimeter.

- 3 -

Subject: Report of Antarctic Developments Project, 1947,
             (Operation HIGHJUMP).
- -

    (d) TG 68.4   Carrier Group, Captain Cornwell.
              PHILIPPINE SEA   1 CV

           TASK: To transport 6 R4D airplanes to a position
           north of Little America and to northward of the
           main continental ice pack and to launch these air-
           craft for flight to Little America.

    (e) TG 68.5   Base Group, Commander Campbell.
              Air Unit, Commander Hawkes
              Temporary Construction Unit, Commander Reinhardt
              Emergency Base Unit, Lieutenant Wagner.

           TASK: To establish and maintain during the Antarctic
           summer a temporary base for approximately 400 person-
           nel, and an airstrip on the Ross Shelf Ice in the
           vicinity of Little America. To conduct systematic
           outward radial air exploration of assigned areas
           of the Antarctic continent. To establish an emer-
           gency winter camp to accommodate 35 personnel for
           a period of fifteen months, for the conduct of res-
           cue operations for aviation personnel forced down
           in the interior of the continent after evacuation
           of the temporary base and withdrawal of all ships.
           (Note:- This emergency camp was constructed and
           equipped, but not activated)

8.   The operational phase began on 2 December 1946, with
the departure of the majority of the ships from ports on the East
and West coasts of the United States, and was considered terminated
with the return of the Task Force flagship to Washington, D. C. on
14 April 1947. Details of operations are contained in the narratives
of the Task Group Commanders and of the Commanding Officers of the
ships participating, annexed hereto.

9.   Had circumstances permitted, a departure date approximately two weeks earlier would have been advantageous, particularly
for the Eastern and Western Groups. This would have permitted them
to profit by the comparatively favorable flying conditions that prevail in the Antarctic during the latter half of December. Under the
unusually severe ice conditions existing this year in the Ross Sea
it is doubtful if the ships of the Central Group could have reached
Little America at a materially earlier date. However, had the icebreaker

CTF68/A9/rdk
Serial 0184

Subject: Report of Antarctic Developments Project, 1947,
             (Operation HIGHJUMP).
- -

started a reconnaissance of the passage into the Ross Sea some two
weeks earlier it is quite probable that the passage of the unprotected
ships through the pack ice to the Bay of Whales would have been facilitated.

10.   Operations of the Eastern and Western Groups in the
Antarctic were continued as long as practicable. They were terminated at approximately the date anticipated by the approach of the
winter season, with accompanying bad weather and shorter periods of
daylight. The Central Group was forced to withdraw from the base
at Little America two to three weeks earlier than anticipated, due to
the unusually heavy pack ice in the Ross Sea, with the consequent
danger of the ships being beset by consolidation of the ice floes
during an early freeze of the Ross Sea.

11.   All ships of the Central Group suffered damage of
varying degree to hulls and propellers, none of which was serious
except for the loss of the MERRICK's rudder. This accident occurred
while the MERRICK was manoeuvering in heavy pack ice with a wind of
approximately 40 knots and while withdrawing from the Ross Sea. The
PINE ISLAND's propeller was damaged by ice and was replaced by an on-
board spare upon return to Panama. One PBM Seaplane and two HO3S-1
helicopters crashed and were lost. In addition one PBM seaplane
was lost overboard from the flight deck of the CURRITUCK during heavy
weather.

12.   There were seven deaths during the operation. Three
members of the crew of the PBM seaplane which crashed and burned on
EIGHT's Peninsula were killed. In addition one of the survivors of
this accident had both legs amputated below the knee as the result
of injuries during the crash and subsequent frostbite. One man from
the YANCEY was killed as the result of an unloading accident at the
Bay of Whales. Two men from the Western Group were killed in an
automobile accident while on liberty in Sydney, Australia, and one
man from the MOUNT OLYMPUS was drowned in Panama. This latter man
was overleave and was attempting to avoid detection by swimming
back to the ship.

13.   With one exception, the major objectives of the operation were accomplished. Initial plans contemplated construction, at
Little America, of a matted air strip (marston mat) for use by aircraft on wheels. This project was not initiated due to the delay in
reaching Little America and early realization that the severe ice
conditions encountered in the Ross Sea would require evacuation of all
personnel and ships from Little America at a considerably earlier date

- 5 -

CTF68/A9/rdk
Serial 0184

<u>CONFIDENTIAL</u>

Subject: Report of Antarctic Developments Project, 1947,
             (Operation HIGHJUMP).
- -

than originally hoped. However, considerable experimental work was
done along this line and it is believed that an acceptable technique
has been developed for the construction of an airstrip on snow (nevé)
covered glacial ice, for the use of aircraft on wheels.

14.   Much information of value to the naval service and of
scientific interest was obtained. Details of observations and results
are contained in various annexes to this report and in separate reports
made directly to the various Bureaus and agencies of the Navy Department and commands afloat. All data relative to geographical discoveries
and mapping, together with certain scientific data, have been turned
over to the Hydrographic Office, Washington, D. C., for evaluation
and processing. It is estimated two years will be required to complete
this work and until this is done it is not possible to assess accurately
the results or extent of this work. It is presently estimated that
1,500,000 square miles of the Antarctic continent were sighted, about
700,000 square miles of which were previously unexplored. Much of
this area was covered by aerial photographs. These figures are approximate only and are subject to revision upon completion of the work now
in progress in the Hydrographic Office. Ships' track charts and flight
tracks of aircraft from the various Task Groups are contained in annexes
to this report and give the general location of the areas covered.

15.   Strictly speaking this was not a cold weather operation
for severe temperatures were not encountered. The lowest temperature
recorded aboard ship was minus 2 degrees Fahrenheit; at the base at
Little America minus 23 degrees Fahrenheit; and by aircraft in flight
minus 40 degrees Fahrenheit. However the ability of naval forces,
with only limited special preparation, to operate in the polar regions
was demonstrated, and much information was obtained and recorded regarding that type of operations. The scientific program was curtailed due
to the short period available in the Antarctic plus the fact that, of
necessity, priority had to be given to operational requirements. However, this was recognized prior to departure and the scientific programs
were adjusted accordingly.

16.   The Task Force Commander is convinced that very real and
definite advantages have accrued to the United States and to the naval
service from this operation. However many of these advantages will be
lost if there is no follow-up. It is recommended that a definite program of naval operations be carried out yearly in the Antarctic.

- 6 -

CTF68/A9/rdk
Serial 0184

<u>CONFIDENTIAL</u>

Subject: Report of Antarctic Developments Project, 1947,
               (Operation HIGHJUMP).

- -

The size of the force employed and the scope of operations, of necessity, must depend upon many factors, both naval and national. A small operation next year employing only the available ice breaker and possibly utilizing some by the facilities which were left at the base at Little America would be profitable and relatively inexpensive.

17.   The strategic importance of the Arctic is today generally recognized, and naval forces must be prepared to operate in the Arctic. The capabilities and limitations of operations in the Arctic, of forces, ashore and afloat, must be determined by actual operations in polar areas. The Antarctic is not now, and probably will not be in the near future, strategically important. However, it does provide a valuable testing ground where naval operations may be carried out with a minimum of international complications.

18.   The Task Force Commander wishes to express his appreciation of the outstanding work of the U. S. Coast Guard Cutter NORTHWIND, and the fine service and loyal cooperation of the U. S. Marine Corps flight crews and other Marine Corps personnel participating in the operation. It is also desired to thank the observers from the U. S. Army, U. S. Geological Survey, U. S. Weather Bureau, U. S. Fish and Wildlife Service and the U. S. Coast and Geodetic Service for their splendid cooperation and help.

19.   The recommended distribution list for this report is attached.

R. H. CRUZEN

NAVY DEPARTMENT

OFFICE OF THE CHIEF OF NAVAL OPERATIONS

WASHINGTON 25, D. C.

Op33/hcc
QG4
Serial No: 065P33

for PEACE
OF
MIND
BUY
SAVINGS
BONDS

CONFIDENTIAL   26 August 1946

From: Chief of Naval Operations.
To :   Commander-in-Chief, U. S. Atlantic Fleet.
            Commander-in-Chief, U. S. Pacific Fleet.

Subject: Antarctic Developments Project, 1947.

    1.   An Antarctic Developments Project, to be carried out
during the Antarctic summer (January to March) of 1947 is hereby
established. This project will be identified by the code word,
"HIGHJUMP".

    2.   The Antarctic continent covers an estimated area of
6,000,000 square miles. Geological opinion is that this area com-
prises a vast reservoir of natural resources.

    3.   Purposes of the Antarctic Developments Project, 1947,
supplement those of the 1946 Arctic Project, and include:

        (a) Training personnel and testing material in the frigid
            zones.
        (b) Consolidating and extending United States sovereignty
            over the largest practicable area of the Antarctic
            continent.
        (c) Determining feasibility of establishing, maintaining
            and utilizing bases in the Antarctic, and investi-
            gating possible base sites.
        (d) Developing techniques for establishing, maintaining
            and utilizing air bases on ice, with particular atten-
            tion to later applicability of such techniques to opera-
            tions in interior Greenland where conditions are com-
            parable to those in the Antarctic.
        (e) Amplifying existing stores of knowledge of hydrographic,
            geographic, geological, meteorological and electro-
            magnetic propagation conditions in the area.

    4.   Tentative plans for the project contemplate the establish-
ment of a base on the Ross Sea Shelf Ice in the vicinity of Little
America earliest practicable after navigation opens, the systematic
outward radial expansion of air exploration from this base, and inward radial air exploration by ship based aircraft from ships operating around the continental perimeter. Preliminary estimates indicate that three task groups will be required, one composed of 1 AG
(Ice Breaker ,"Wind" class), 2 AK or AKA, 1 AV and two groups of 1 AV

Encl. (A)   - 1 -

Op33/hcc
4G4
Serial No: 065P33

<u>CONFIDENTIAL</u>

Subject: Antarctic Developments Project, 1947.
- -

(with PBM winterized aircraft) 1 DD and 1 AO. It will be necessary
that a part of the above be supplied by each the Atlantic and Pacific
Fleet. For planning purposes consider that the AG and AN will be
provided by the Atlantic Fleet, one half remainder by each fleet. The
first group will be required in position on 180th meridian at the
Antarctic Circle by about 1 January, 1947; other two groups about
two weeks later. Coordination with cold weather operations of other
fleet units is also a possibility.

        5.   Technical control of this project will be retained by
the Chief of Naval Operations and will be exercised with the assistance
of Rear Admiral Richard E. Byrd, U.S.N. (Retired), who will be designated
as officer-in-charge of the Project. The actual expedition will comprise
a task force of the U.S. Atlantic Fleet under the command of Captain
Richard H. Cruzen, now commanding Task Force 68 in the Arctic. The
Officer-in-Charge of the Project may participate in the actual expedition and locally exercise technical control, but tactical command will
continue to be vested in the Task Force Commander.

        6.   Commanders-in-Chief, Atlantic and Pacific Fleet are re-
quested to submit earliest practicable comment and specific recommendations for any coordination desired with fleet cold weather operations.

        7.   Commands addressed in the distribution list submit by
15 September 1946, list of technical and scientific projects desired
to be undertaken, giving:

        (a) Character and scope of project.
        (b) Personnel to be accommodated on board ship and at base.
        (c) Weight and space requirements for special equipment to
            be installed on board ship.
        (d) Weight and space requirements of material to be trans-
            ported to base.
        (e) Priority.

        8.   Action addressees and distribution list are directed to
implement detailed plans as later promulgated.

        9.   The Chief of Naval Operations only will deal with other
governmental agencies. Direct dealing between subordinate naval compo-
nents is authorized. No diplomatic negotiations are required. No
foreign observers will be accepted.

Encl. (A)
                              - 2 -

Op33/hcc
QG4
Serial No; 065P33

<u>CONFIDENTIAL</u>

Subject: Antarctic Developments Project, 1947.
- -

10.   Available information indicates that one U.S.S.R.
government sponsored expedition is being organized for work in the
sub-Antarctic during the 1947 season and that one or more civilian
sponsored expeditions of other nationalities may also be present.

11.   This project as a whole is classified CONFIDENTIAL,
but sub-projects will be more highly classified if substance warrants.
Special precautions are enjoined to the end that knowledge of purpose,
scope and destination is limited to naval distribution and within
naval jurisdiction to those who need to know.

                                        /s/ D. C. RAMSEY
                                  Vice Chief of Naval Operations

Encl. (A)

CinCLant File
A1/A2-12/(0568)
Care F.P.O., New York, N. Y.
15 October 1946

CONFIDENTIAL

From: Commander-in-Chief, United States Atlantic Fleet.
To :   Captain R. H. CRUZEN, U.S.N., Commander HIGHJUMP
          Force (CTF-68).

Subject: Instructions for Operation HIGHJUMP.

Reference: (a) CNO conf. ltr. serial 065P33 of 26 August 1946.
           (b) CNO restr. ltr. serial 444P33 of 24 April 1946.

1.   Under the technical control of CNO, plan and conduct
operations of Antarctic Development Project, 1947, identified by the
codeword "HIGHJUMP".

2.   The objectives of Operation HIGHJUMP are:

     (a) Training personnel and testing equipment in frigid zones.

     (b) Consolidating and extending United States sovereignty
         over the largest practicable area of the Antarctic
         continent.

     (c) Determining the feasibility of establishing, maintaining
         and utilizing bases in the Antarctic and investigating
         possible base sites.

     (d) Developing techniques for establishing, maintaining and
         utilizing air bases on ice, with particular attention
         to later applicability of such techniques to operations
         in interior Greenland where conditions are comparable
         to those in the Antarctic.

     (e) Amplifying existing stores of knowledge of hydrographic,
         geographic, geological, meteorological and electro-mag-
         netic propagation conditions in the area.

     (f) Supplementing objectives of the 1946 NANOOK operation.

3.   Upon activation of the HIGHJUMP Task Force or at an
appropriate time, ships designated to participate will be ordered to
report to you for operational control. Release Pacific Fleet ships
to CinCPac and Atlantic Fleet ships to appropriate Atlantic Fleet
Type Commanders when no longer required or when directed by me. You
are authorized to deal directly with CinCPac regarding matters concerning ships from the Pacific Fleet designated to participate in the

- 1 -

Encl. (B)

CinCLant File
A1/A2-12/(0568)

CONFIDENTIAL

Subject: Instructions for Operation HIGHJUMP.
- -

operations; keeping CinCLant informed.

4.   Make dates of departure and return such as to take maximum advantage of the navigable season in the Antarctic. Operations are to be terminated when weather and ice conditions render further operations unprofitable. It is not intended that any ship or aircraft remain in the Antarctic during the winter months.

5.   Utilize personnel, vessels, aircraft and equipment placed at your disposal to best advantage and as directed by CinCLant or CNO.

6.   Consistent with facilities available and the general conduct of operations, it is desired that you afford the maximum opportunity to Naval, and other government agencies as may be approved by CNO, for carrying out approved projects which will be of immediate or potential value to the naval operating forces.

7.   CinCLant desires that the exploration of the Antarctic be pursued aggressively, having due regard for the safety of personnel.

8.   Logistic support as required will be furnished primarily by ComServLant. Additional support may be requested from ComServPac.

9.   No diplomatic arrangements are required. No foreign observers will be accepted.

10.   Keep CinCLant informed of the general progress of operations and of any unusual conditions encountered. Submit your final report to CNO via CinCLant, together with a recommended distribution.

11.   This project as a whole is classified CONFIDENTIAL, but subjects will be more highly classified as substance warrants. Special precautions are enjoined to the end that knowledge of the purpose, scope and destination is limited to Naval distribution and within Naval jurisdiction to those who need to know.

MARC A. MITSCHER

Copy to:
  CNO   ComServLant   ComMinLant
  ComAirLant   ComOpDevFor   ComTraComdLant
  ComServPac   ComDesLant   ComPhibLant
  ComBatCruLant   ComSubLant   CinCPac

Encl. (B)

DISTRIBUTION LIST

	No. Copies	Total
SecNav	1	1
Asst. SecNav for Air	1	2
CNO Op-01	1	3
Op-02 (3 for Op-20)	5	8
Op-03	5	13
Op-04	5	18
Op-05	5	23
BuAer	5	28
BuShips	5	33
BuOrd	5	38
BuPers	2	40
BuMed	5	45
BuSandA	5	50
BuDocks	5	55
Hydrographic Office	5	60
CinCLantFlt.	5	65
ComAirLant	4	69
ComBatCruLant	2	71
ComPhibsLant	2	73
ComTraComLant	1	74
ComDesLant	2	76
ComServLant	2	78
ComMinLant	1	79
LantFlt Weather Central, Norfolk, Va.	1	80
ComSubLant	2	82
ComGenFMFLant	1	83
ComGenAirFMFLant	1	84
CinCPacFlt	5	89
ComAirPac	4	93
ComPhibsPac	2	95
ComTraComPac	1	96
ComDesPac	2	98
ComServPac	2	100
ComSubPac	2	102
ComBatCruPac	2	104
PacFltWeather Central	1	105
ComGenFMFPac	1	106
ComGenAirFMFPac	1	107
ComFirst Task Fleet	5	112
ComSecond Task Fleet	5	117
ComNavEastLant	3	120
Comdt. USCG	4	124
Comdt. USMC	4	128

	No. Copies	Total
Commanding General Army Air Forces	5	133
Commanding General Army Ground Forces	5	138
Adjutant General, U.S. Army	5	143
ComEasSeaFron	1	144
ComWesSeaFron	1	145
ComCaribSeaFron	1	146
ComPanamaSeaFron	1	147
ComHawSeaFron	1	148
ComAlaskaSeaFron	1	149
ComONE	1	150
ComTHREE	1	151
ComFIVE	1	152
ComELEVEN	1	153
ComTWELVE	1	154
ComFOURTEEN	1	155
ComFIFTEEN	1	156
ComSEVENTEEN	2	158
ComNOBArgentia	1	159
ComNavBase, Norfolk, Va.	1	160
ComNOB, Coco Solo	1	161
OinC, ABD, Port Hueneme, Calif.	1	162
ComNATS	1	163
ComNATSLant	1	164
ComNATSPac	1	165
ComAirTestCen, Patuxent, Md.	2	167
ComNavAirShipTraandExp.,Lakehurst, N. J.	1	168
ComHelDevRons, Lakehurst, N. J.	1	169
OinC Aerographer's School, Lakehurst, N. J.	1	170
ComOpDevFor	2	172
ComCarDivONE	1	173
ComCarDivTWO	1	174
ComCarDivTHREE	1	175
ComCarDivFOUR	1	176
ComCarDivFIVE	1	177
ComCarDivSIX	1	178
ComCarDivFOURTEEN	1	179
ComCarDivFIFTEEN	1	180
ComCarDivSEVENTEEN	1	181
ComFairWestPac	1	182
ComFairWestCoast	1	183
ComFairSeattle	1	184
ComFairAlameda	1	185
ComFairQuonset	1	186
ComFairWingONE	1	187
ComFairWingTWO	1	188
ComFairWingTHREE	1	189
ComFairWingFOUR	1	190
ComFairWingELEVEN	1	191
ComFairWingFOURTEEN	1	192

	No. Copies	Total
Chief of Naval Intelligence	2	194
Director Public Information	1	195
Dir USN Photo Service	1	196
USN Photo Science Lab.	1	197
NavMed Institute	1	198
U.S. Naval Observatory	1	199
President Nav War College	2	201
Post Graduate School, Annapolis, Md.	1	202
David Taylor Model Basin	1	203
OinC Antarctic Dev. Project (RAdm. Byrd)	1	204
CTF 68 (RAdm Cruzen)	1	205
Gen Line School, Newport, R.I.	1	206
Office of Naval Research	2	208
Naval Research Laboratory	2	210
NavOrdLab, NGF, Wash., D.C.	1	211
Nav. Electronics Lab., San Diego	2	213
U.S. Marine Corps School, Quantico, Va.	1	214
U.S. Dept. of State	2	216
U.S. Dept. Commerce	2	218
U.S. Dept. Interior	2	220
National Bureau of Standards	1	221
Naval Liaison Officer, Eglin Field, Fla.	1	222
Armed Forces Staff College	1	223
National War College	1	224
JRDB, 1712 "G" St., N.W. Wash. D.C.	1	225
Sen. Member Joint War Plans Committee	1	226
Rm. 5216 New War Dept., Wash., D.C.		
Central Intelligence Group	1	227
Rm. 2161, New War Dept., Wash., D.C.		
Woods Hole Oceanographic Institute, Mass.	1	228
Scripps Oceanographic Institute, La Jolla, Cal.	1	229
ComNorLantPat (via Comdt. U.S.C.G.)	1	230
U.S.S. MOUNT OLYMPUS	1	231
U.S.S. BURTON ISLAND	1	232
U.S.S. EDISTO	1	233
U.S.S. SENNET	1	234
U.S.S. PINE ISLAND	1	235
U.S.S. HENDERSON	1	236
U.S.S. BROWNSON	1	237
U.S.S. PHILIPPINE SEA	1	238
U.S.L. New London, Conn.	1	239
Industrial College Armed Forces	1	240
Files CTF 68	10	250

INDEX TO ANNEXES

OF

OPERATION HIGHJUMP

(c) Communication Electronics
(d) Airborne Electronics
(e) Radar
(f) Sonar

ANNEX SEVEN - AEROLOGY

ANNEX EIGHT - SURFACE NAVIGATION

ANNEX NINE - AMPHIBIOUS AND ICE OPERATIONS

ANNEX TEN - CAMP CONSTRUCTION

ANNEX ELEVEN - CARGO HANDLING

ANNEX TWELVE - CLOTHING

ANNEX THIRTEEN - SURVIVAL EQUIPMENT

ANNEX FOURTEEN - DEMOLITION OPERATIONS IN
                 ICE FIELDS.

ANNEX FIFTEEN - LOGISTICS

ANNEX SIXTEEN - PUBLIC RELATIONS

ANNEX SEVENTEEN - TRANSPORTATION AND CON-
                  STRUCTION EQUIPMENT

ANNEX EIGHTEEN - TESTS OF STANDARD NAVY
                 SHIPBOARD EQUIPMENT

ANNEX NINTEEN - MEDICAL

ANNEX TWENTY - DENTAL

ANNEX TWENTY-ONE - NAVY RATIONS

ANNEX TWENTY-TWO - EXPERIMENTAL AIR STRIP

ANNEX TWENTY-THREE - PERSONNEL

ANNEX TWENTY-FOUR - SUMMARY OF SCIENTIFIC
                    AND TECHNICAL PROJECTS

ANNEX ONE - (a)

COMMANDER TASK GROUP 68.1

NARRATIVE

Elements of the Central and Eastern Groups of Task Force Sixty-Eight departed Norfolk, Virginia in company on the afternoon of the 2nd of December 1946. This force consisted of the following ships:

CENTRAL GROUP

USS MOUNT OLYMPUS (AGC-8) - Task Force Flag (Rear Admiral R. H. Cruzen, USN)
USCGC NORTHWIND (WAG-282) - U. S. Coast Guard Ice Breaker

EASTERN GROUP

USS PINE ISLAND (AV-12) - T.G. 68.3 Flag (Captain G. J. Dufek, USN)
USS BROWNSON (DD-868)

The trip to Panama was uneventful except for an unusually high number of breakdowns enroute, nearly all of which were due to inexperienced engineering personnel. Upon reaching Colon, Canal Zone, on 7 December 1946, the ships passed through the Canal and remained in Balboa, Canal Zone for two days in order to provide a last liberty for all hands. At Balboa the USS CANISTEO (AO-99) and the USS SENNET (SS-408) joined the Eastern and Central Groups, respectively.

All ships departed Balboa 10 December 1946, and course was set for Antarctica. The following day the ships were deployed in line, distance 50 miles, in order to obtain soundings along the maximum number of tracks.

Upon arrival at the 100th meridian west longitude on the 17th of December both groups, with the exception of the NORTHWIND, fueled from the CANISTEO. After fueling, the Eastern Group was detached and directed to proceed to the vicinity of Peter I Island to commence operations in accordance with the operation plan. The CANISTEO, although part of the Eastern Group, remained with the Central Group and continued with this group to Scott Island. The same afternoon that the Eastern Group left for Peter I Island, the SENNET and the NORTHWIND discovered and developed a previously unreported bank having a least depth of approximately 167 fathoms. This bank was centered in position Latitude 25° 10' S., Longitude 100° 50' W.

The Central Group continued on to Scott Island, fueling from the CANISTEO once again while enroute. The first iceberg was sighted the day after Christmas in position Latitude 62° 15' S., Longitude 141° 22' W., and for the next two days the group passed through an area of many icebergs. Scott Island was sighted on the 30th of December and a rendezvous was made with the YANCEY and the MERRICK. These two ships had departed from the west coast of the United States in company with the Western Group. They had been detached by CTG 68.2 two weeks previously and directed to proceed to Scott Island independently to rendezvous with the Central Group. Enroute they passed through the

Annex I-(a)   - 1 -

reported position of the Nimrod Islands (Latitude 56° 30' S., Longitude 158° 30' W.) in excellent weather. There was no evidence that these islands existed in or near their reported position.

After the rendezvous on the 30th, both the YANCEY and the MERRICK were fueled from the CANISTEO. While the fueling was in progress, the NORTHWIND proceeded southward independently to reconnoiter the ice pack. The NORTHWIND, ballasted down, stood south along the 180th meridian, passed through approximately 100 miles of moderate, broken ice pack and then scouted 30 additional miles by helicopter. Two well defined leads to the southward were discovered. These extended as far to the southward as the eye could see.

As a result of this reconnaissance and due to the fact that evidence from all previous successful passages through the pack indicated the most advantageous position to enter the pack was along the 180th meridian or a little to the westward, it was decided to follow the route indicated by the NORTHWIND's reconnaissance.

Upon completion of fueling, the Task Force Commander transferred to the NORTHWIND, and the Central Group headed south into the ice pack. The CANISTEO was ordered to join the Eastern Group. About 20 miles south of Scott Island, the first pack ice was encountered on the 31st of December 1946, in position, Latitude 67° 49' S., Longitude 180°. At that time the formation was in column in the following order: NORTHWIND, MERRICK, YANCEY, MOUNT OLYMPUS, and SENNET. All that "night" and the following day this group continued its passage southward with the pack ice getting steadily heavier. The ice changed from loose, scattered pack about two feet thick and free of bergs to close, heavy pack ranging from six to ten feet thick and containing large pieces of shelf ice; through all this a winding, twisting course had to be chosen. Large tabular icebergs were passed with increasing frequency. The speed of the group was reduced to about three knots and the unprotected ships suffered some damage. The MOUNT OLYMPUS bent 10 frames (forward, on the starboard side), sprang a leak in the bow, and bent two blades of her propeller. The leak was soon stopped and the frames shored. The MERRICK opened a seam which let in 120 gallons of water per minute but the leak was soon brought under control. The YANCEY sustained minor damage.

The second of January, 1947 found the NORTHWIND, MERRICK, YANCEY, MOUNT OLYMPUS and SENNET lying to in a pool of water formed by surrounding ice in position, Latitude 69° 18' S., Longitude 179° 49' W. A conference of all Commanding Officers was called aboard the NORTHWIND. It was decided to push ahead into the pack rather than wait for a possible lead to open in the ice ahead, as the position of the ships was precarious due to the presence of large bergs in the immediate vicinity. As soon as the conference was terminated, the ships got underway on a southerly course and headed into the ice pack. It was impossible to steer a steady course; only a general direction could be maintained. Finally, about midnight, a small pool was reached where the ships remained until the next morning, when a generally southerly course was resumed.

Progress during the morning of the 3rd of January was difficult, the ships frequently became stuck in the pack and had to be broken out by the NORTHWIND. Ice began drifting up on the deck of the SENNET and it became apparent that to continue further southward with her, would seriously handicap progress of the large ships. It was therefore decided to return her to the north of the pack. The NORTHWIND took the SENNET in tow, returned her to the pool of open water that had harbored the formation the previous day, and proceeded to rejoin the remainder of the ships to escort them to a safe position where they could be left while the NORTHWIND was escorting the SENNET northward clear of the pack.

Upon joining the large ships it was found that they were fast in the ice. Considerable time was required to break them out and reform the column. The formation had not proceeded far southward when word was received from the SENNET that the pool in which she was lying was closing rapidly and that she required assistance. The NORTHWIND left the formation and rejoined the SENNET. After extricating her from the ice, the SENNET was taken in tow and course set to northward.

As the rest of the ships seemed to be in a comparatively good position with some open water and no icebergs in their immediate vicinity, it was decided to continue northward with the SENNET to open water.

Some twelve hours later, on the morning of 4 January, word was received from the administrative staff aboard the MOUNT OLYMPUS that the wind had increased to twenty knots, that the open water was closing, and that two icebergs had drifted into the immediate vicinity of the ships. However, there was no open water in which the SENNET could be safely left, so the NORTHWIND continued northward with the SENNET in tow. Messages concerning the seriousness of the situation of the other ships continued to arrive. By 1000 a pool of open water was reached which would afford at least temporary shelter for the SENNET. She was cast loose and the NORTHWIND set course to rejoin the other ships at best speed.

NORTHWIND made contact with the ships late on the afternoon of 4 January. All ships were fast in the ice and unmaneuverable, with the YANCEY and MERRICK in an uncomfortable and potentially dangerous position. Considerable difficulty was encountered in extricating the three ships and reforming the column, but by midnight all ships were enroute southward and escorted to an area free of icebergs and heavy ice floes in Latitude 69° 04' S., Longitude 179° 46' W.

The NORTHWIND again headed north to rejoin the submarine SENNET. Shortly before noon, the SENNET was sighted and again taken in tow. Soon thereafter the pack became loose enough for her to proceed independently astern of the icebreaker and she was cast loose. The NORTHWIND escorted the SENNET as far north as 67° 30' S. where the SENNET was detached, that area being clear of all pack. Upon being detached, the SENNET was ordered to remain in the vicinity of Scott Island to carry out her tests and await further orders. The NORTHWIND then headed south at best speed to rejoin the other ships.

On the 6th of January 1947, at 0200 (XRAY) the NORTHWIND rejoined the other three ships and an hour later the formation got underway and headed southwest. At 0600 a clear area or pool (Latitude 70° 11' S., Longitude 178° 23' W.) was reached and it was decided that the NORTHWIND would proceed southward for futher reconnaissance. The NORTHWIND departed alone, leaving the other ships in the pool. She made her way to the southeast through heavy pack at best speed, 6 knots. During the remainder of the day and following night, six reconnaissance flights were made by helicopter. Later that night, the NORTHWIND rejoined the other three ships and the formation headed southward.

The NORTHWIND continued steaming south with MERRICK, MOUNT OLYMPUS and YANCEY. At 0405 on the 7th the pack became quite heavy with evidence of considerable pressure building up between the floes, so course was reversed to the north. Shortly thereafter the MERRICK became stuck in the ice. The NORTHWIND soon broke her out and the force continued northward. At 0620 the MOUNT OLYMPUS was stopped by the heavy ice and again the NORTHWIND came to the rescue. Finally, at 0801 the large lake (70-11S, 178-23 W) that the formation had left the previous day was reached and it was decided to wait there until further air reconnaissance could be undertaken.

That afternoon the J2F, a single engine Grumman Amphibian, was hoisted out and a reconnaissance flight was made to the southeast with Captain Thomas, Commanding Officer of the USCGC NORTHWIND, as observer.

At this point, Task Group 68.2 was ordered to steam eastward and make long range reconnaissance flights in order to find out the best possible way for Task Group 68.1 to continue southward.

The next morning, two more flights were made with the J2F, one to the southeast and one to the southwest. Both of these flights extended over one hundred miles to the southward and failed to disclose any leads.

The NORTHWIND headed southward independently, to test ice conditions. After proceeding 17 miles and making one helicopter reconnaissance flight it was obvious that the formation could not proceed southward, and the NORTHWIND returned to the lake arriving there about 1130, January 9, 1947.

In the meantime, CTG 68.2 was having little or no luck in getting off a reconnaissance flight. His position was to the northwest of Scott Island and the weather had been unfavorable for flying. Since the NORTHWIND had found the weather around Scott Island to be good a few days before, CTG 68.2 was ordered to close Scott Island and try to get his flights off from there. The SENNET was ordered to take station 200 miles east of Scott Island and act as a weather station and alternate airdrome for the PBM's of TG 68.2.

Later that afternoon, the pool in which the formation was lying to, started to close in. It was necessary to find a new pool so the NORTHWIND got underway about 1800 and steamed five miles to the south where a new pool was found. It was intended to move the formation to the new pool but the MOUNT OLYMPUS was unable to get underway. She still had two leaks to repair and this could not be accomplished in less than 12 hours. As a result of this, the formation remained in the old pool until the following morning.

At 0800 on the 10th of January 1947, the USCGC NORTHWIND got underway. During the night the ice had closed in around the formation to such an extent that it was necessary to break the ships out. By 0930 this had been accomplished and course was set for the south to the pool that the NORTHWIND had found the day before. The going was difficult and it was not until 1300 that all ships were safely in the new pool – an average speed of less than 1½ knots had been made.

That afternoon, the NORTHWIND made another reconnaissance trip to the southward, leaving the rest of the formation in the pool. The going was very difficult and by the time the NORTHWIND had proceeded 10 miles to the south the weather had taken a turn for the worse so course was reversed to head back for the formation. When the NORTHWIND rejoined the formation there were two PBM aircraft from Task Group 68.2 circling overhead. The weather grew steadily worse. The ceiling closed in to about 400 feet and it started to snow. Both planes reported icing and were dispatched for home, the USS CURRITUCK. At 2030 word was received of their safe arrival.

On 9 January, the USS PHILIPPINE SEA flying the flag of Rear Admiral R. E. Byrd, USN (Retired) Officer-in-Charge, Antarctic Development Project, departed from Balboa and reported to the Commander Task Force 68 for duty.

At 0600, January 11th, the NORTHWIND got underway and headed south leaving the other ships in the formation in order to find the best route southward. The going had improved since the previous day and by 0830 a distance of 18 miles had been made good. It was then decided to return to the other ships and bring them south.

Task Group 68.1 continued steaming southward until the 14th. Each succeeding day found the going a little easier. By the morning of the 14th there were large strips of open water in which a fairly good speed could be made. Unfortunately, the speed had to be kept below 13 knots due to the MOUNT OLYMPUS' bent propeller.

At 1300 on the 14th of January 1947, the Task Force Commander shifted his flag from the NORTHWIND to the MOUNT OLYMPUS. The NORTHWIND remained guide but the order of the column was changed to NORTHWIND, MOUNT OLYMPUS, MERRICK and YANCEY. The course of the formation was changed from due south to 140° T, heading for the Bay of Whales. Occasional patches of ice were encountered and also an occasional iceberg. That evening, about 2200, Captain Thomas, USCGC NORTHWIND, made a helicopter flight and sighted the barrier ice bearing 140° T, distance 20 miles from the formation.

Shortly after midnight, the NORTHWIND and the MOUNT OLYMPUS were off Discovery Inlet; the YANCEY and the MERRICK were ordered to remain where they were and await the return of the other two ships. After a brief reconnaissance of Discovery Inlet, the NORTHWIND and MOUNT OLYMPUS returned and the formation steamed eastward along the northern edge of the Barrier. At 0615 Lindbergh Inlet was passed abeam to starboard and shortly thereafter the entrance to the Bay of Whales was reached. The entrance to the Bay of Whales had changed from 1½ miles wide, as found by the last expedition, to about 300 yards. From the outside it seemed to be clogged with unbroken bay ice. At 1000, the Task Force Commander shifted his flag to the NORTH-WIND and proceeded into the Bay of Whales itself, the rest of the ships remaining outside. Once inside, it was found that the Bay of Whales itself had grown considerably smaller and that ice conditions there were bad. In its present state, the AKA's would not be able to enter and unload. It was necessary to have the NORTHWIND break the bay ice in the bay. The force would have to wait for a southerly wind to empty the loose broken ice into the Ross Sea. A conference was called of all Commanding Officers and they were informed as to the conditions in the Bay of Whales.

While all this was taking place, back in San Diego the USS BURTON ISLAND was getting underway for Antarctica. Construction had been speeded up so she was ready about two weeks ahead of schedule. As she was urgently needed, it was necessary that she forego her shakedown cruise and depart at once for Little America. It was expected that she would join Task Group 68.1 in the Bay of Whales about 9 February.

On the 16th of January, the Commanders of Task Groups 68.2 and 68.3 were ordered to direct the destroyer BROWNSON and the tanker CACAPON to proceed in time to rendezvous with the PHILIPPINE SEA prior to 1300 (XRAY) on the 25th. Upon arrival they were to report for duty, transfer mail and supplies and the CACAPON was to fuel the ships at the rendezvous. All day the 16th and the 17th, the NORTHWIND proceeded to break ice in the Bay of Whales. At 0145 on the 18th of January the YANCEY proceeded inside the Bay of Whales and tied up to the ice. By 0345, she was secured and had commenced to unload her cargo.

The entrance to the Bay of Whales in January 1947 was a narrow opening in the barrier ice about 300 yards wide. The barrier ice on either side of the opening varied between approximately 70 and 100 feet high. About two hundred yards inside the entrance, the western shore line of the barrier receded sharply for a distance of about a mile. The eastern shore line continued in almost a straight line to the very southern extremity of the Bay. After receding about a mile, the barrier ice gave way to the bay ice which commenced to close the eastern shore line in a gentle curve, giving the entire Bay the form of a lopsided ellipse about a mile wide and a mile and a half long. Ships were moored at the southern end of the bay. This ice continued southward for about 2 miles where it gave way to barrier ice, which to the layman resembled rolling foothills of snow. Between this shelf ice and the barrier were a series of pressure ridges that had to be crossed before getting onto the barrier. The party that had gone ashore on the 16th of January had laid out the site of the new camp and the route that would have to be followed to get to it. The new camp site was on the barrier ice, about 1½ miles from the water and to the southeast of the bay. The route to it had been chosen over that part of the pressure ridges that was easiest to cross. In order to cross the main pressure ridge, it was necessary for the seabees to build a bridge capable of bearing the weight of the heavy equipment of the expedition. This bridge was completed by the morning of the 17th and by the time it was completed, the YANCEY had most of its transportation equipment on the shelf ice.

At 1930 on the 19th of January, the MERRICK headed into the Bay of Whales, and by 2200 was moored alongside the ice, astern of the YANCEY. Unloading operations were started immediately. The following day, the 20th, the NORTHWIND departed from the Bay of Whales enroute to rendezvous with the carrier PHILIPPINE SEA in the vicinity of Scott Island. The PHILIPPINE SEA which had left Panama on the 9th of January was due at the rendezvous point on the 26th.

While the YANCEY and MERRICK were unloading and the MOUNT OLYMPUS was lying to outside, the construction detail under Commander Reinhardt (CEC), USN, was busy laying out the temporary tent camp and surveying for the airstrip.

On 22 January the MOUNT OLYMPUS entered the Bay of Whales and moored. The Norseman airplane was unloaded onto the bay ice and towed to the Base Camp. That day and the next, all three ships continued to unload as quickly as possible. The morning of the 22nd, Vance Woodall, S2, of Louisville, Kentucky, age 17, was killed while engaged in the unloading supplies for the air strip. He was riding on the yoke by which a sheepsfoot roller was pulled, when the roller lurched due to the rough surface and threw his hand against one of the teeth. He was pulled in between the roller and yoke and crushed. Memorial services were held at 1400 on Thursday the 23rd.

To the northward, both the NORTHWIND and SENNET were steadily steaming toward the rendezvous position in Latitude 67S, Longitude 175W.

About the time that the MERRICK was tying up in the Bay of Whales, the NORTHWIND and the SENNET arrived at the rendezvous. Three hours later, the destroyer BROWNSON which had been proceeding from the Eastern Group, joined them and at two o'clock in the morning the CACAPON from the Western Group, came over the horizon. As soon as the CACAPON joined the other ships, she commenced fueling the SENNET. While in the midst of fueling operations, the carrier PHILIPPINE SEA, flying the flag of Rear Admiral R. E. Byrd (Ret.) USN, arrived. All ships were now at the rendezvous position as planned. The weather which had forced the PHILIPPINE SEA to slow from her previous 20 knots two days prior to the rendezvous, had not improved and it was impossible to launch the six R4D aircraft that day. While waiting for the weather to improve, all ships with the exception of the PHILIPPINE SEA were fueled from the CACAPON. The SENNET was dispatched to scout the northern limits of the ice pack between 165° W. and 175° W., and provisions and mail were transferred between ships.

Suddenly, during the morning watch on the 27th of January, the ice in the Bay of Whales started to crack. During the night the wind had increased to 20 knots from the east south east. By 0700 there were occasional gusts up to 45 knots and snow started to fall. The recall signal was sounded and once again the ships put out to sea. While getting underway, the wind forced the MOUNT OLYMPUS against the bay ice with such force that she sheered two rivets and opened a seam, starboard side frame #86, letting in about 200 gallons of water per minute. This was soon brought under control. Once outside they steamed slowly into the driving snow, maintaining position off the entrance to the Bay of Whales.

On the 28th of January the weather abated somewhat, enough so that the YANCEY was able to stand into the Bay of Whales. Once inside, the YANCEY found that conditions were not favorable so she hove to in the bay to transfer men and supplies to the Base Camp. As soon as this was done, she again stood out to sea. The following day, weather conditions improved still more and the MERRICK was ordered into the bay, to moor to the ice, which she did at midnight. Meanwhile, the Commanding Officer of the Base Camp reported that conditions on the airstrip were suitable for landing aircraft. To the north, the PHILIPPINE SEA had been lying to in the vicinity of Scott Island waiting for favorable conditions to launch the R4D's. At 2330 (XRAY) on 29 January 1947, the first two R4D's took off from the carrier bound for Little America. Not only was it the first time that a plane as large as an R4D had taken off from a carrier but it was the first time that any airplane had ever taken off from a carrier with a combination wheel-ski arrangement. In the first plane, the Officer-in-Charge of the Antarctic Development Project, Rear Admiral R. E. Byrd, USN (Ret.) was flying as observer. The take-offs of the first two planes were successful and for five and a half hours they continued their way southward. They passed over the ice breaker NORTHWIND which had been stationed at the midpoint of the flight. Strong head winds were encountered all the way down. Finally at 0500 on January 30th, they were sighted from Little America and at 0528 the first plane landed.

As soon as the news of the success of the first flight was received aboard the carrier, preparations were made to launch the remaining four planes. The first plane of this group took off at 0800 and shortly thereafter all the remaining three were airborne. The same strong headwinds were encountered enroute. About 200 miles from Little America, the last plane ran into trouble. First its gyro failed and it had to rely on its magnetic compass. The weather had started to close in and the sun was no longer visible so the astro compass was of no use. A short while later its radio stopped functioning and many anxious moments were spent by those listening both at Little America and in the PHILIPPINE SEA. At about 1332, the first three planes of this group landed on the snow strip at Little America. The fourth plane still had not been heard from. It was a great relief when a few minutes after the second plane had landed, radio contact with the fourth plane was made. They had been set to the west, and the radar in the MOUNT OLYMPUS picked them up to the westward, and at 1406 they landed.

While the planes were enroute to Little America, the MOUNT OLYMPUS stood into the Bay of Whales and moored to the ice. As the last plane landed, the barometer was dropping rapidly. By 1600 the visibility had changed from unlimited, an hour before, to a thousand yards with intermittent snow. At 1650 the MOUNT OLYMPUS sounded the recall and an hour later once more put to sea. It was necessary to leave the MERRICK inside to weather out the storm as best she could as she was in the midst of unloading. By the time the MOUNT OLYMPUS cleared the entrance to the Bay of Whales, the barometer had dropped to 28"30.

The storm died down almost as quickly as it came up. Later that evening the YANCEY was ordered to re-enter the bay, moor and continue unloading. The next day, the 31st of January, the MOUNT OLYMPUS entered the Bay of Whales to transfer personnel, and stood out again. All that day and the next, she lay to outside and finally about noon on the 2nd of February she re-entered and moored along the portside of the MERRICK. From the 2nd of February until the 6th the ships of the Central Group stayed moored to the ice in the Bay of Whales.

On the 6th of February it was agreed that the time had arrived for the ships of the Central Group to start their way back through the ice pack. If the departure were delayed longer, it might mean that the entire Central Group would be caught in the ice and have to winter over, which they were not prepared to do. All day on the 6th, last minute transfers of personnel and material were made. At 1700 the Task Force Commander shifted his flag to the NORTHWIND and shortly thereafter, Admiral Byrd left the MOUNT OLYMPUS and took up his quarters at the Base Camp at Little America. There he stayed, taking part in the exploration flights and assuming active charge of base operations. At 1930 the ships of the Central Group, NORTHWIND (Flag), MOUNT OLYMPUS, YANCEY and MERRICK got underway and stood out of the Bay of Whales. After clearing the entrance, the formation headed for Scott Island.

To the north, the USS BURTON ISLAND was steaming steadily southward to join the Central Group. The evening of the 6th in Latitude 68° 38' S., Longitude 175° 30' W., she had her first baptism of ice. There she continued to the southwest encountering loose pack. The pack did not change much on the following day but on the 8th in Latitude 69° 48' S., Longitude 178° 17' E., she encountered solid pack ice. From there until clear of the pack to the south the going was difficult.

The Central Group, steaming northward, found conditions in the Ross Sea considerably improved, but with much new ice forming. Progress, however, was not difficult. Rendezvous with the BURTON ISLAND was made at 0005 (XRAY) on the 10th, in Latitude 70° 14' S., Longitude 179° 02' E. After the BURTON ISLAND joined, the Central Group entered heavy pack, still on a northerly course with the two icebreakers in the lead clearing the way. For the next three days, Task Group 68.1 made steady progress through close but well broken heavy pack. There were occasional pools of open water but very few open leads. The weather during this period was generally bad, with frequent snow fall and low to very low visibility.

On 12th of February, when almost within sight of open water, Task Group 68.1 suffered its worst ship casualty. That morning found the group lying to in a small pool of open water, while the NORTHWIND and BURTON ISLAND scouted for leads. By late afternoon, both ice breakers had returned and all ships proceeded through a well defined lead, first to southwest and then to northwest. The wind increased to about 30 knotw with gusts up to 45 knots. While proceeding through the pack, the MERRICK was forced to shear out of column to avoid some heavy ice in the channel. By this maneuver the ships astern were also forced out of column and became stuck in the ice. While manoeuvering to free the ships from this position, a strong gust forced the MERRICK's stern down upon a heavy floe, breaking her rudder stock. She was taken in tow by the NORTHWIND. With no steering control in the ice and high wind, she became unmanageable and was cast off. During the night the MERRICK drifted northward with the wind, while the NORTHWIND, operating to leeward, cleared the ice from her path. In the morning the wind abated and she was again taken in tow. The MOUNT OLYMPUS and YANCEY after being extricated from the ice, continued northward with the BURTON ISLAND in the lead. These three vessels arrived in clear water on the morning of the 12th, at which time the BURTON ISLAND reversed course to rejoin the NORTHWIND and MERRICK.

By 1100 the following morning, all ships of the Cental Group were clear of the pack.

As soon as the Chief of Naval Operations received the report of the loss of the MERRICK's rudder, the fleet tug CHOWANOC was ordered to proceed from Pago Pago, Samoa to the Antarctic and report to CTF 68. By 20 February, it was apparent that this vessel could not intercept the NORTHWIND and MERRICK before these ships would arrive in New Zealand. Consequently, the CHOWANOC was ordered by CTF 68 to return to Pago Pago.

From this time on, the Central Group ceased to act as a concerted group. The NORTHWIND towed the MERRICK to Port Chalmers, New Zealand, accompanied by the YANCEY. Enroute, a storm with winds of 70 knot velocity and very heavy seas was encountered. Further damage and possible disaster was averted only by the superior seamanship of the Commanding Officers of the NORTHWIND and MERRICK. Finally on the 22nd of February 1947, the three vessels arrived at Port Chalmers, where installation of a temporary rudder on the MERRICK's old rudder stock was undertaken. Repairs were completed on the 21st of March, 1947, at which time she departed for San Diego, California. The MERRICK arrived in San Diego and reported to her type commander on 12 April 1947.

The MOUNT OLYMPUS remained in the vicinity of Scott Island while the BURTON ISLAND, with the Commander Task Force 68 on board, steamed southward to McMurdo Sound. Drygalski Ice Tongue was reached the morning of the 16th of February and McMurdo Sound entered that night. Once in the Sound, the weather became unfavorable and the ice-breaker was forced to lie to for two days until it moderated. On the 20th, the BURTON ISLAND's helicopter made a flight to Cape Armitage and landed near the hut that Scott had built there in 1901. The hut was in remarkably good condition and after spending a short time there, the helicopter returned to the BURTON ISLAND. That afternoon, a second flight was made to photograph Scott's camp site. While making a landing near the hut, the tail rotor of the helicopter was damaged and the plane was unable to take off again. The crew of the helicopter found in the hut a sledge that Scott had used some 45 years before. The sledge was still in good condition. Using it, the crew returned to the BURTON ISLAND over ten miles of ice, obtained the parts necessary to repair the tail rotor, and returned. Once back at the hut, the repairs were made, and the helicopter flown back to the BURTON ISLAND. That same afternoon, the J2F aircraft took off and an ice reconnaissance flight of approximately 100 miles was made. The BURTON ISLAND departed McMurdo Sound for Little America on 20 February.

The morning of 22 February 1947 the BURTON ISLAND arrived at the Bay of Whales and commenced evacuating personnel of the base camp. The evacuation was completed and departure taken for Scott Island on 23 February 1947. The pack was cleared on the 25th, and on the 26th rendezvous was made with the MOUNT OLYMPUS which had remained in the immediate area since clearing the pack on the 13th of February. The Officer-in-Charge, Antarctic Developments Project, the Task Force Commander and the majority of base camp personnel, transferred to the MOUNT OLYMPUS. The BURTON ISLAND then headed for

Wellington via Port Chalmers, New Zealand, and the MOUNT OLYMPUS for Wellington direct.

On the 5th of March, the MOUNT OLYMPUS was joined by the NORTHWIND. This vessel had been engaged in the collection of oceanographic data since her departure from Port Chalmers. As many stations as possible were occupied and a survey of the Antipodes Islands was made. Later on the 5th, the BURTON ISLAND got underway at Port Chalmers and joined the formation the next day. The three ships arrived in Wellington on the 7th of March, 1947.

The MOUNT OLYMPUS, NORTHWIND, and BURTON ISLAND departed Wellington, New Zealand, on 14 March, 1947. The MOUNT OLYMPUS sailed direct to Panama and then to Washington, D. C. She arrived in Washington on the 14th of April. The NORTHWIND and BURTON ISLAND proceeded in company as far as Pago Pago, Samoa. From there, the NORTHWIND sailed to Seattle, Washington, by way of Pearl Harbor, arriving in Seattle on 6 April. The BURTON ISLAND sailed direct to San Pedro and reported to her type commander on 31 March.

The YANCEY left Port Chalmers, New Zealand on 5 March, 1947 and arrived at Pago Pago, Samoa on the 11th of March, where she picked up cargo and a tow. She departed Pago Pago towing the YTL-153 on the 27th and arrived in Pearl Harbor on 14 April. At Pearl Harbor, she discharged her tow and her cargo and sailed for Port Hueneme, Calif., arriving there 2 May, 1947 and reporting to her type commander on 15 May 1947.

INTRODUCTION:

This narrative is quite long. It is taken from a detailed diary which tried to cover every form of operation as it affected the command. It is intended especially to show the importance of weather in such operations -- in <u>any</u> naval operation, and perhaps aid the reader to understand a little more clearly, some of the intricacies involved in carrying out this most interesting assignment.

Task Group 68.2 started to take shape in late November 1946 on the West Coast, when U.S.S. CURRITUCK (AV 7) and U.S.S. HENDERSON (DD 785) reported for duty in San Diego, and the U.S.S. CACAPON (AO 52) reported in San Pedro, all on the 20th. I reported on board CURRITUCK on 27 November. The ships were busy over a holiday period getting gear on board and trying until the last moment to fill the ships complement. Personnel were obtained much in the fashion of more ancient sailing ship days, although the crews were not recruited from grog shops and jails, but on bended knee in staff personnel offices. The only incident occurred when the HO3S helicopter almost cracked up when landing on board. The pilot slid the plane off the edge of the platform. Fortunately the wheel caught in the netting. The netting paid 200% dividend in 30 seconds.

We all cleared harbor independently on 2 December, between fog banks. Our group also included U.S.S. YANCEY (AKA 93) which sailed from Port Hueneme. The U.S.S. MERRICK (AKA 97) was delayed until 5 December to load more pierced plank matting for the air strip. All vessels proceeded expeditiously to their assigned tracks, 50 miles apart on the great circle course to the Marquesas Islands and did not sight each other until that rendezvous. Enroute all vessels were to sound the ocean bottom to increase our hydrographic knowledge of little known areas. The MERRICK and YANCEY could sound only to a depth of 250 fathoms. This was a definite limitation and emphasizes the necessity for equipping such ships properly and sailing them on separate routes if we are ever to properly chart unfrequented water areas and eliminate many "existence or position doubtful" notes now on hydrographic charts.

On 3 December received a dispatch from VX-3, advising against installing skis on helicopters. The ski was prompted by imagining what would happen if a 2½ ton helicopter were to sit down, with its small wheels, on a bit of inaccessible shelf ice and have a wheel go through, cant the plane, and wreck a rotor blade. We decided to make plywood boards to place under the wheels if a landing was attempted on the shelf ice. The rotors would be kept swinging until these boards were placed by one of the crew.

When opportunity presented we flew the HO3S; the pilots' skill improved with each landing. When we went through the TUAMOTUS, it flew for four hours, the pilot watching for coral reefs in the relatively unknown area. This scouting gave a comfortable feeling to the navigators and was of great aid.

On 4 December CACAPON wiped a main shaft bearing and slowed to 4 knots, but was able to regain position by the time we reached the Marquesas. Worked out an operation plan for this group. The bathythermographs in CACAPON and HENDERSON were doing well. On 8 December the CURRITUCKS' starboard main circulator bearing wiped, and slowed the ship to 9½ knots for several hours until it was repaired. Also Davy Jones came up the port hawse pipe and initiated crossing-the-line ceremonies, and goings-on commenced. Crossed the equator at 0840, 9 December. Straightened out communication problems with the flagship. On 11 December HENDERSON fueled from CACAPON.

The advent of electronics has changed atoll navigation considerably. Four ships all equipped with radars, a helicopter pilot talking reassuringly, fathometers and sound gear, made it look easy. We picked up the Marquesas' high mountains many miles at sea. The flat atolls of the Tuamotus were a little closer before the radars bounced their waves off the coconuts. It took the sonar equipment of the DD to pick up reefs and beaches which were visually indicated only by green water when uncomfortably close. With electronic gear these islands are navigable at night or in thick weather. The minimum depth through the Tuamotus was 630 fathoms. Entering the Marquesas we raised a sea-mountain "hogback" heretofore undiscovered, whose soundings rose from 1800 to 360 fathoms in a half hour and then gradually went down to 1800 fathoms.

On 12 December all four ships rendezvoused and passed through the Tuamotus in fine weather. We noted an obvious seven mile error in local charts and passed the information to MERRICK now 2 days behind us. That afternoon we held tactical drills. The results were not too impressive, but not bad considering green crews and different type ships. Detached YANCEY to join MERRICK, and TG 68.2 fanned out once more on separate tracks to continue soundings. CURRITUCK and CACAPON remained together during the night and fueled in driving rain and rough seas next morning.

On 14 December picked up Tubuai Island 26 miles away on radar. Somewhat to the navigator's surprise he was right in position even after no sights for two days. On 15 December our barometer readings of 30.15 indicated that we were in the south Pacific high. Temperatures started to drop, the days got longer, and we started to prepare for the roaring forties. Received dispatches from TFC advising that more survival gear (including skis) was coming to us, and establishing limiting ranges of operations for our utility aircraft.

RESTRICTED

By 17 December we were at 40° south, sunrise was at 0410, the barometer 30.40, and temperature 61°F. The tender and destroyer fueled from the tanker. The tanker was then released to fuel MERRICK and YANCEY. The CURRITUCK and HENDERSON once more fanned out on assigned tracks and bravely entered the fearsome forties. The weather, however, continued most agreeable. The barometer gradually dropped; there was rain and fog; the wind shifted to west; all temperatures continued downward. We began to realize that the Australian and South African weather reports would mean a lot more to us than had believed probable. Data were quite good and very extensive. We regretted we couldn't help them with our weather reports (orders from CNO). Incidentally, we had good weather maps all the way across the Pacific.

On 19 December CACAPON was released by MERRICK to us. Task Force Commander directed that all operational reports were to be classified. When his attention was invited to the fact that if this included aircraft it would hamper their operations considerably, he later altered his original despatch to allow faster communications and yet preserve security.

On 20 December CURRITUCK's steering compass took off, going on a rampage for one hour, then settled down again. This was the first sign of magnetic pole 1400 miles southwest. We crossed the date line and skipped 21 December. The barometer was 29.55, temperature 47°F, more fog occurred but no gales. The next day (the 22nd) the glass dropped from 29.50 to 29.00 and we couldn't help steeling ourselves for a heavy blow. The weather continued nice, and the aerologists were tearing their hair out. Apparently we went through a front that moved at 45 knots. This isn't aerological cricket where we come from. They shortly developed into 45 knot aerologists and the relative motion was zero, ie., they licked the weather.

On the 23rd, more strange weather - and here in the Antarctic, weather is everything - weather and ice. The wind suddenly whipped around from 16 knots out of the West to 40 knots from SSE, and as suddenly died down. The barometer rose from 29 to 29.70 but with hardly any other climatic changes. Meanwhile the temperature hit freezing and the injection dropped from 40° to 30°F. The magnetic compasses were now almost useless. They were not calibrated properly in the first place and wouldn't help too much anyway 800 miles from the pole. The HENDERSON rendezvoused and the tender checked her RDF - and found it almost useless. (Several days later we learned an old lesson all over again; our scientists had rigged a wire closed-loop hoisting arrangement from the foreyard to the upper deck; when this was replaced with lanyard, the RDF behaved once more - and became invaluable.) At 1330 we sighted our first iceberg. From then until early March, they were our constant companions. I don't believe the radar screen was ever perfectly free of these "silent sentinels of

RESTRICTED

of the snowy south". They were as much a part of the scenery as sky
and water. Held a TBS conversation with CO of DD before parting to
take up stations; talked on the subject of good operating areas; how
to scout the pack; fuel, etc. (I wish we could have made a wire
recording of that conversation between a couple of Antarctic tender-
feet, just before meeting the pack. Not a person in the entire task
group had ever been in the Antarctic before, and very few of us had
ever seen an iceberg or pack ice - and then only from a distance.)
It no longer became dark at "night". The sun set at 2241 and stayed
just under the horizon. That meant no more star sights for many a
moon. Meanwhile the CACAPON had to slow down in joining us because
of a blown boiler gasket.

The sun rose soon after midnight. Not much sleep this night;
it was all too interesting and spectacular - actually I believe this
was the most interesting period on the entire trip. It was calm and
clear. The red sunlight striking the chalk-like tabular icebergs,
with their green and blue caves and waterlines, made a color display
that was beyond description. We were to learn that this weather was
the exception and not the rule; we had beginner's luck. At 0100 we
"met the pack"; the situation looked like duck soup. We were hardly
rolling. We could throw the barometer over the side as any relation
between it and weather was a coincidence. No roaring of the forties,
nor screaming of the fifties and sixties, and now sunlight all day,
and perfect calm! It was too good to be true. We detached the
destroyer to proceed to station 300 miles west and scout the pack
enroute. Then we headed west ourselves, as we were still far from the
Balleny Islands, and the pack was further north than we'd been led to
believe it would be.

At 0730 the day before Christmas we commenced our first operation. It was like taking candy from a baby; but we had no weather
stations to our westward yet and so we made no grandiose plans. It
was a pretty rusty job - getting that first plane over the side. A
little practice on the way south would have helped considerably. It
took until 1215 to get our first plane into the air. By this time it
was getting overcast and we sent the plane to the Northwest to investigate this weather. In an hour he ran into icing, snow and low ceiling,
and returned to the ship. On the way he photographed an iceberg with
a lake on top, in which floated some "little" icebergs. The ship
rolled 2° while hoisting in the plane which was almost catastrophic
to a beginner. By March this condition would be considered almost
ideal. Our pilot tested his equipment and we learned that the Sperry
electric gyro, upon which we depended so heavily for our navigation,
was precessing badly. In the afternoon, to our surprise, along came
the HENDERSON from the east. She had been caught in a cul-do-sac- and
we had passed her during the morning. She now, almost sheepishly,
continued westward. We also flew our HO3S this first day. As the overcast moved in we got our first view of the iceblink over the pack

(without low cloud layer there is no iceblink). By supper time, all hands were somewhat exhausted; it had been a long and exciting day. Now it was Christmas Eve, and we rigged trees, arranged presents, and the Chaplain held divine services in a very cold hangar. At 2234 the sun set; there was a low overcast; whales spouted all about us; there were many silent snowy petrels flying about. Thus ended our first day in the Antarctic.

On Christmas Day the barometer dropped from 29.50 to 29.10. Snow, fog, and low ceilings closed in. We spoke a Jap whalechaser, FUMI MARU #3, who came silently out of the fog from the west. This was our first contact for quite a while. She was about 400 tons, wooden, and flying the "MacArthur flag", something new on the high seas. Shortly thereafter we intercepted a weather report on 500 Kcs, and learned it was from the Jap whale factory; from then on we intercepted and forwarded these reports to the Task Force. They proved to be quite accurate and invaluable aids to us. The fog formed clear ice on our rigging. The destroyer is getting a little worried about her fuel - she is down to 112000 gallons. I believe she feels rather lonesome.

The CACAPON reported her port pinion gear bearing wiped, and is making 6 knots. We had a bit of a scare with our HO3S today when we were shrouded by a heavy fog bank shortly after he had taken off. We recovered him, but we learned (1) you can't spot a helicopter over the icepack on radar, (therefore we decided to install IFF in it) (2) It is **not** an instrument flyer (3) It should have an astral compass (4) It cannot land on these ice floes - they aren't large enough; (an iceberg might be used, but none were in sight just then). Therefore, the "eggbeater" should be used only in contact weather.

We put the other PBM over for test flight in 26 December; rendezvoused with the CACAPON, and started to repair her radar which was broken down. The PBM rehearsed the controlled approach system. The hoisting operations were greatly improved. Next day, continued fog and low overcast. The tanker's radar and bearings were repaired. Meanwhile I had called the destroyer in, and had a bad time finally making the rendezvous. The RDF had to be used and soon became most endeared to us. Navigation, with a moving ice pack, unknown currents, low overcasts and fog, is a guessing game. We started using bubble octants with some success. We learned that in case of a rendezvous, establishing it at the edge of the ice pack eliminated much guesswork. We used the PBM RDF's on the fantail to check the ship's RDF - and they were quite accurate. At this time we discovered the aforementioned closed loop on the foreyard, and its removal restored normal RDF operations. To make sure, the AV compensated her RDF on the DD as it came over the horizon, through the solid fog, checking against the radar. The DD finally arrived in our vicinity in the late afternoon with whistles blowing. She was ordered by TBS to fuel from the AO.

This was done entirely by electronics, as she did not sight the tanker until she was several hundred yards away. Fueling was accomplished by the alongside method. We tracked this entire display of electronic seamanship by radar. The only trick is to be able to distinguish a tanker from an iceberg. I ordered the DD to lend an ETM to the AO for a month, and a good thing it was.

On 28 December led the CACAPON in toward the pack for fueling. About this time we calculated our needs for fuel. Informed TFC that it would be a close call as our oiler would have to fuel the PHILIPPINE SEA later. Our radar can now pick up the pack at 4000 yards, and improving. By this time we realized the tremendous importance of radar - ALL radars - and sufficient expert men to keep them running. We were beginning to learn all manners of things about our planes. I wrote up a new air annex to my Op Plan, to agree with TFC's instructions on operating PBM's over the continent. Our weather ships (the DD and AO) were sending in nice weather reports every 3 hours; things were shaping up.

We learned that the pack was receding, and that it changes its outline continually while moving westward because of SE prevailing wind and current.

One question puzzled us; how much light is necessary for photography? In other words, how low may the sun get before we must turn off the cameras. This governs the time of planes taking off and staying on station. At present we weren't worried at the ship, for we could operate 24 hours a day.

Sent a dispatch to my group with pointers on "boating in the Antarctic": how to equip boat if a danger exists of separation in fog or storm; course to steer to reach ice pack; recall signals; radio; duties of the boat officer, etc.

The fog persisted from the first beautiful day of our arrival for the rest of 1946. At first we thought this was general weather for that area; later we learned that we were located all this time in a very large ice bay - we were surrounded on three sides by ice pack, and the fog was advected over the water after being formed by cooling of the air over the icepack. Had we moved north, east, or west some 20 miles we'd have found much better weather and probably been able to fly.

By this time we had learned that our operations were limited by: (a) icebergs and pack ice (b) brash ice (c) swells (d) wind chop (e) visibility (f) ice-forming precipitation. Our means of getting a plane home from a flight were (a) RDF bearings (b) ADF in the planes (c) radar (d) YE/YG (e) visual sighting of edge of pack and following east or west until meeting ship. If there is a high overcast, the sun (or astral) compass is useless; if there is a very low undercast or fog, drift cannot be taken and the ice pack may be missed, unless spotted by plane's radar. With our Sperry gyro compasses precessing badly and the magnetic compasses useless the situation was none too good. Our plans tried to anticipate every emergency, and as a last resort, in case planes returned in bad weather, they could (a) land by GCA (controlled approach) (b) land in the clear near to ship as possible and ship steam toward plane (c) land at alternate airdromes (destroyer or tanker, both of which were equipped to fuel, care for, and tow PBM's). If the water became very rough, it was planned that the plane (a) land in lee of ice pack or large berg (b) land in a slick prepared by the tender steaming at 16 knots (c) use alternate airdrome.

Other questions to decide were: whether the PBM's should fly above or below the overcast, and what to do about icing on the planes. We learned quickly that it was best to go right up through the clouds, which are usually relatively thin layers, accept the icing - for which the plane is equipped - and get on top where the accumulated ice evaporates and the astral compass can be used.

The ship is covered with ice, all over the rigging, lines and antenna. It has to be broken off the helicopter rotor blades and the PBM's. As the old year closed out we got news that the Eastern Group had lost George One.

The new year found us in latitude 64-17S, 161-14E. Here we really got our first operational flight into the air. Our first "wedge" of cold air moved in on us, between lows. At 1100 decided to move east, where it looked better. The ceiling lifted. We sounded flight quarters, and at 1317 hove to and began launching operations. The first plane got off but the second plane was rammed by boat and had to be hoisted back on board. We then again moved east. This was our first lesson on how to find good weather - move east with it when it comes. The communications with the plane were very poor - it was still required to encode weather reports and positions. The plane was tracked out 120 miles on SK radar. Also our RDF tracked to within 1°. At about 1945 we met snow flurries, then light scud at 300'-400'. Since the sun was getting too low for good photography, the plane was recalled. At 2030 hove to and received plane. The plane reported heavy precessing of all directional gyros. Found the Balleny's half exposed and photographed them and almost reached the continent before it was recalled. This flight helped restore pilots' confidence, which had been shaken by the loss of George One.

A new angle to weather reporting; the aerologists reported that the New Zealand and almost all Australian stations shut down weather reports apparently as a result - or in anticipation of New Year's celebration. They simply said "We're shutting down" and that was all.

RESTRICTED

Launched the HO3S for a flight of several hours to investigate the pack. He reported great difficulty seeing us from 900' while we saw him plainly at all times.

CACAPON sent in a careless weather report and omitted another report. This threw our aerologists into a spin. We informed him of the necessity for accurate reports. From then on they were fine.

We flew the next day. Both planes got into the air. The first one tried to go in under the overcast, and had to return. He was going to land, but I ordered him through the overcast. Once both planes finally went up through, (after some coaching) the situation straightened out, and everyone felt much happier. Both planes flew to the Ballenys and from there they proceeded to the coastline. The coast was souped over and no photos of value were taken. The instruments are still not doing too well; so no flying was done inland. Many new mountains were seen and the boys are beginning to get the spirit of exploration. I sent a dispatch to HENDERSON to reduce fuel expenditures as far as possible without discomfort. He answered that he would cut out another boiler and steam on just one at three knots when not too near the ice pack.

When the pilots saw the photos they got over the Ballenys, their enthusiasm picked up still more, and they took a great deal more interest in their job.

On the 3rd, HENDERSON reported an acute appendicitis case and started for the CACAPON which also started toward the DD. Each ship was ignorant of the other's position and had to do a little communicating to find this out. Hereafter all posits were made info of the rest of the task group. The two ships met during the night in foggy calm and transferred the patient. Then the DD refueled from the tanker, and returned to her station.

We noticed some strange light effects about us. Under certain conditions icebergs look exactly like land. This occurs not only when the berg is silhouetted but also under certain conditions of overcast and direction of the light. The caves look precisely like earth. Time and again whale spouts were reported by lookouts as black smoke.

We decided to keep the time on minus twelve zone; thus as we move west this should keep sunrise just about right for hoisting out aircraft.

At various times we were surprised to find penguins many miles from the ice pack. Several times we saw them on bergs apparently floating to the northward, and our hearts bled for the little beasts which, we figured, would eventually be reduced to fighting for parking area on a piece of ice the size of an orange crate somewhere well to the north. We learned later that these remarkable creatures can exist

Annex I-(b)   - 8 -

happily hundreds of miles from the closest piece of "dry" ice, or land. They are truly more fish than fowl.

The electric gyros are even more disturbing. On a bench test one precessed 32° in one hour. Examination revealed that the leads were apparently reversed. A check with the same gyros on the SOC's wiring disclosed that they functioned perfectly. The leads were corrected on the bench tests and the gyros ran properly. This handy bit of information was sent to the Eastern Group, all our leads were corrected, and our troubles ended. BuAer was informed of this mistake which was apparently made at A&R Norfolk.

Another bubble of polar air overtook us on the afternoon of the 4th, and we launched planes. Another lesson was learned at this time - if there is a chance of flying the planes should be kept warmed up. When we finally decided to fly, it took two hours after flight quarters were sounded to get the first plane warmed up and over the side. This time it was souped up over the Ballenys and the planes went directly to the continent, and started mapping in earnest. On this trip we started the reference point system of position reporting. A point was selected on the map as point "Y" or "Z" and the plane simply sent in his bearing and distance from this point along with his course and speed. This was very simple and rapid, was easy to plot and convert to latitude and longitude, and transmit in code to the rest of the Task Force.

The planes reported some new troubles on this flight. For one thing the altitude was giving them trouble. Even with oxygen, flying at 13000' is very uncomfortable. The PhoM's are all thumbs in changing magazines. The pilots seemed to be more than ordinarily fatigued. Communications were poor-apparently the assigned frequencies are not good. The frequent posits and weather reports seem to take all the attention of one pilot. The navigators are unhappy about the gyros which are still uncorrected and give them trouble thus requiring frequent astral sights to compensate for the Sperry. But we're down here partly to find out these very things.

On the 5th I decided to make the flight with Lt. Comdr. Bunger. Every item I carried on that trip, from flying boots to parka and hood, was government issue - even including bridge work. Everything was good stuff. The flight was a routine affair outwardly, but it was hard to forget the tremendous strides between the Wilkes Expedition of a hundred years ago and this comfortable flight with all the enjoyments of home. The acme of the experience came when I bit off a piece of nicely cooked steak, looked over the side, and discovered a brand new glacier, never before sighted by man.

Along the Continent we noticed an "inland waterway" extending as far as the eye could see. Sometimes it was a few hundred feet wide, sometimes several miles wide. This suggested an easy looking

means of surveying the coast by icebreaker. It was most difficult to
tell where land began and sea ice ended. Sometimes a tidal crack
would show up some distance inside of where the coast was thought
to run. The radar altimeter was not able to differentiate the rise
of terrain under us too well, due to its small scale reading and
because of change of barometer affecting the pressure altimeter, as
we get away from the ship. I'm afraid it will be a difficult task
to determine the position of this coast line with any accuracy less
than several miles at best. A magnetometer survey may eventually, be
necessary, as well as close-in coastal survey by ship.

The charts furnished on this trip were practically useless
for navigation. They were used only as plotting charts. All flights
were plotted only by positions determined by dead reckoning from the
ship and by occasional celestial lines of position in flight. In
some cases when the ship was close to the coastline, the ship's radar
tracked planes over the coastline a limited distance and thus determined their positions somewhat more accurately. Benchmarks along the
coast of Antarctica are very few and far between.

The visibility here is phenomenal. It was usual to see one
hundred miles of "coast" in each direction, and with glasses we
could see mountain ranges 200 or 300 miles away. Yet as a whole, the
terrain was featureless; to seaward was the loose pack, water and ice,
with occasional large in-ice lakes; the amount of ice thickened as it
approached the continent, until it reached the "inland waterway"; then
large fields of solid ice occurred; then perhaps some tidal cracks;
old icebergs scattered over the sea area, surrounded by various types
of pack ice; then the doubtful area where the surface rose gradually.
Not until a nunatak or mountain was sighted were you sure it was actually
land. The ice cap rose gradually, and we never were able to determine
where or if it stopped rising. We penetrated to places where the
altitude of the icecap was 9500' and still rising.

With such a landscape, it was difficult to determine where one
had flown on the reverse track along the coast; we were supposed to fly
on tracks 20 miles apart, but it was virtually impossible to tell when
one was 20 miles from either the coast or the previous track. In fact,
it was hard to tell where we first started our coastal mapping flight.
On this flight, it was merely a matter of dead reckoning navigation
and noting a certain distinctive grounded iceberg obstructing part of
the inland waterway, noticed several hours previously, near the
commencement.

The wind shifts were not apparent and were somewhat unexpected;
these threw off our navigation a bit. The effects of katabatic winds
were noticed on the surface as rolling puffs of snow, and soon the
surface began to become quite indistinct as the wind built up, and snow
began to fly far below us. Then it got a little turbulent aloft, and
a drift sight indicated a big change in drift.

All hands were very busy in the plane; no place for duds in this business. There was hardly time to eat or cook. To add to the excitement, the relief tube froze up for one crew number, in the very middle of its use. This was not funny.

Upon return the Ballenys seemed pretty clear. Although the sun's elevation was only 3 degrees we decided to photograph the islands. By the time we'd completed the last island (we shot only half of the group) the sun was a bit lower, and some of the shots were directly into the sun. The pictures all came out beautifully, with plenty good long shadows. The moon was just above the horizon to the north at this time.

At the ship the plane descended through a layer of icing cloud and landed in the relative darkness beneath, at 25 minutes past midnight. We had now mapped the coast from Smith Inlet to within sight of Mawson's explorations near INNIS glacier.

The communications problems are approaching solution, especially since CTF 68 in a dispatch, allowed us to use some better frequencies.

Here TFC ordered us not to proceed westward, as we had planned, as he might require us to scout the ice pack for his group, which was locked in the Ross Sea ice pack. Also he told us to conduct operations with greater fuel economy. We had recently instituted these measures, and fuel expenditures henceforth dropped rapidly. We lay to, awaiting further instructions.

At 0830 6 January we headed eastward at 10 knots to be available in case TFC needs us. At this time we started giving thought to the possibility of a PBM losing an engine while over the icecap well inland. This was discussed with pilots, and it was decided that the best procedure would be: (1) to keep plane's chart marked with mountain passes, glaciers and other low areas, so as to be able to avoid flying over mountains on return; (2) note open water near coast for emergency landings; then if in trouble, pilots can head for nearest water; (3) keep high altitude over the ice cap, to give plenty time for jettisoning, feathering, dumping gas, and thus get over coastal mountain ranges; (4) dump just enough gas to reach coast, if necessary, and land in open water; (5) use radar to locate water, if there is an undercast; (6) if landing in coastal waters taxy up to large solid floe, facing east to get lee from prevailing winds, pad the bow well, get lines out to dead men on ice; drain oil and keep warm; watch out for drifting ice; rig engine warmers (if available); locate engine trouble and radio base so as to effect repairs; set up antenna on ice for communications. A rescue plane could land and secure to same floe; repair engine if possible; load JATO's; transfer gasoline by handy-billy; bring a boat if necessary for work, and bring also engine heaters.

RESTRICTED

Each plane carried single engine performance curves, and a jettison bill was made up and kept posted, so crew would know what to dump, and in what order.

Pilots were instructed to study glaciers as they flew over them to ascertain if their crevasses would indicate the direction of flow - in case plane had to follow the glacier down to the sea in low visibility.

As our aircraft radarmen pick up proficiency, they get some fine results with their sets. They are able to pick up not only land as distinguished from ice pack, but open water lakes and large leads. Later they were able to discern the edge of the ice pack, and finally to distinguish ships from icebergs. They were also able, to a certain degree, to tell if a water area were free from growlers.

At 1355 on 7 January we crossed the Antarctic circle at 171°E steaming southeast at 10 knots, still awaiting orders to assist central group. Made all preparations for this work. Both tanker and destroyer were left on their previous stations, well to westward, to conserve fuel. Just when it was too late to fly that day we received a dispatch from TFC to launch planes to determine depth of ice pack along 180th meridian, make summary of ice conditions, locate open leads, and if possible look at Bay of Whales. Upon receipt of this message we raised speed to 15 knots. The aerologist estimated a cold front to lie to southward of us, and advised that we cross this front before launching. Requested weather from MOUNT OLYMPUS and SENNET, and stated "We will launch earliest". TFC stated no urgency for recco, be sure conditions were favorable. We stayed to westward of SENNET so as to spread our weather stations apart and have an alternate seadrome. The SENNET's weather reports were initially unsatisfactory. Their importance to us was pointed out and from then on their reports were perfect, much better than we expected a submarine could do.

By now we had learned that best aircraft communications were obtained by using 444 kcs out to 350 miles, then shifting to 6430. After this system was adopted we rarely lost touch with planes.

We received a dispatch from BuAer which corroborated our findings that the Sperry gyro leads were reversed. The gyros had been turning backward all this time. A very heartening "well done" was received from Admiral Byrd, for surveying coastline. This was passed on to Task Group. No sunset tonight.

Comments on requirements for future meteorological aids to flying here: (a) complete weather service from Australia, New Zealand, etc. to track incoming lows and fronts (b) local ships' weather reports used to maximum including whalers (c) In-flight weather reports from aircraft (d) Steaming toward good, or away from bad, weather - usually eastward (e) Weather recco plane in direction of oncoming weather - usually to the northwest.

About 1500 8 January, things looked up. Good weather was reported over central group. It was decided to launch planes. The first plane made a recco flight to NW. He very quickly ran into lowering ceilings and scud. The wind shifted to north. B-1 remained in the vicinity for a further look at the weather. Meanwhile B-3 popped an oil seal as a result of starting up too cold and threw oil over everything. It took ½ hour to replace this oil seal. This caused a revision in our warming up process which resulted in smoother work in the future. The SOC was launched to act as weather recco plane in case PBM's were sent ove the ice pack. All equipment including gyros is now working well and pilot confidence mounting.

The CURRITUCK was able to talk with MOUNT OLYMPUS at times on 3265 voice, over 200 miles of ice pack. The decision to keep the PBM near the ship was fortunate. Hoisted him on board at 2015 and very shortly the ceiling was almost on the water. The pilot reported that the magnetic compass was behaving quite normally since we had moved away from the magnetic pole a few hundred miles.

The weather continued foul all day Thursday with a solid soup from 200 feet to 10000 and plenty of ice therein. The front is hanging right over or near us. We received a dispatch from TFC aggressively to reconnoitre the ice pack, as prudence dictates, between 170 E and 170 W, to establish North and South limits of the pack, and to investigate a possible route for his group. Plans to comply with these instructions required one flight of 1085 miles and another of 1150 miles. Equipped planes to take high altitude trimetrogon pictures with very little overlap and to use radar photography in case of fog or very low undercast.

Meanwhile the HENDERSON had her weekly medical case and started a dash for the CACAPON. He was ordered to fuel once more, and return at most economical speed.

We received a dispatch from BuOrd that our JATO's are not to be used for cold weather operation. Since this would simply mean no more operations, I sent back a dispatch explaining our position, our care in mounting JATO's and requested permission to continue their use - and meanwhile continued using them.

It was noted that boats in the water cause some interference with radio. They need spark suppressors. Radio sonde is also on the same frequency as TBS and causes interference. Incidentally, we used radio sonde to determine the thickness of cloud layers above us so as to know how much icing our aviators could expect in climbing through.

Lt. Comdr. Clarke, the bull aerologist, mentioned a Jap device that measures light intensity. Cloud layers and thickness are thus determined more accurately than they can be by using radio sonde. Several of our radio sondes froze up on us, reaching a low maximum altitude. The boats also interfered with radio sonde.

TFC advised that we move over to Scott Island, some 150 miles to eastward if we were having weather difficulties. This we did. It now became apparent that the situation for his group was becoming urgent. The weather is still bad - fog, rain, low visibility and ceilings. The SENNET was in the clear, more or less. I requested TFC to move SENNET 200 miles eastward for weather reporting and to serve as an alternate seadrome. This was done. All arrangements were made for weather reports by MOUNT OLYMPUS, for manning CIC, and for a local emergency landing in a large lake near TG 68.1, etc. The weather continued bad all day of 10 January.

At 0400 of the 11th sounded flight quarters. Patchy fog surrounded the CURRITUCK, and SENNET was clear. Locally it looked worse than on the three previous days but now we were ready to use the slightest excuse to fly. At 0602 the first plane was off. The only JATO failure of entire trip occurred on this take off. Next plane took off at 0707 between fogbanks. At 0845 TFC ordered the planes to return to base. The CURRITUCK headed north in low visibility and light snow. Both planes were aboard by 1130. It had been quite a thrilling show. B-3 came in over the flagship, on top, but got bad weather dope, and found bad icing and low ceilings over the pack. The MOUNT OLYMPUS gave out an erroneous ship's heading, which put our planes some 15° off course when returning to base. Communications were good, and the planes were on ship's radar from beginning to end.

We had on board with us Ensign HURD, USNR, who has been trained to get accurate positions ashore, as well as take magnetic observations. The problem was, how to use his capacities. We certainly needed some ground control along that coast to anchor our aerial surveys. It was decided to use the HO3S to land him on ice tongues or shore when - and if - we got close enough. (We never did!). I had him drill in embarking in HO3S with all equipment, and then practice, for speed, in disembarking and setting up equipment, while HO3S kept rotors turning or even returned to the ship. We estimated the weight and planned the storage of survival gear he should have with him. He would also have to train an assistant. Another projected method for establishing ground control was to land a PBM in the inland waterway and take reasonably good sights with sextant while sitting on the water. If there were large inland bays this method would be fine. They were rather scarce however, and there was also the thought "what to do if the PBM couldn't take off again? is it worth taking the chance?" Not knowing what the future held we planned for all eventualities.

In a talk with the aerologists I learned they are simply fore-
casting "contact" or "Closed" conditions - no "instrument". I pointed
out that we can start flying under instrument conditions, as our planes
and pilots are now well qualified for it. We had to learn to combat
icing and low ceilings, use alternate airdromes, etc. The pilots, I
learned, are still feeling the effects of the PINE ISLAND lost plane,
and it affects their work directly, even though they may not notice it
themselves.

BuOrd concurred in our request for continued use of JATO and
recommended continuance of present method of use.

TFC sent dispatch requiring data after each flight to be sent
him in a prescribed form for uniformity, record, and photogrammetry.
This standardization was sorely needed and is a great improvement.

I requested MOUNT OLYMPUS to manufacture for us some aerological
maps of greater scope than the present ones since those issued to us
did not extend far enough north.

Baker 3 used one roll of tri-met film in scouting the ice pack
ahead of MOUNT OLYMPUS. However, it was from very low altitudes, sometimes 400', and was primarily interesting in showing that this method
of scouting is possible, as there was very little blurring. The pilot
intended to drop the exposed film on MOUNT OLYMPUS by parachute, but
they (wisely) wouldn't let him as it might foul their complicated
rigging or necessitate sending men off over the pack ice - and the
ships were then underway.

TFC answered my dispatch on low fuel situation. He ordered us
to use diesel, of which there were some 16,000 barrels in CACAPON. I
hadn't realized this could be done. TFC assumed we'd remain on station
until 15 March and that the ships would arrive in Sydney with reserve
fuel on board, and that CURRITUCK would burn diesel. The present
average daily fuel consumption is: CACAPON 5260 gallons; CURRITUCK
10,000 gallons; HENDERSON 6700 gallons; total 22,060 gallons. The
CACAPON has a total of 66,000 bbls. cargo on board.

On Sunday, 12 January, sounded flight quarters at 0800. At
the same time we received the wonderful news of the finding of George
One and 6 survivors. After weather report from MOUNT OLYMPUS showed
improving weather we put the planes over the side. Both were in air
at 1240 after a small engine casualty. Followed planes for 90 miles
on radar. Flew HO3S for 1½ hours to obtain low altitude temperatures and humidity readings for our two scientists. Also flew SOC to
scout ice pack and weather to westward.

The planes returned by 1837, with another slightly wild tale.
The ceiling over MOUNT OLYMPUS was supposed to be 2000'; it turned
out to be 500'. They flew south ten miles apart to 73° S, ran into
loose ice and practically open sea, but overcast forced them almost

to water and heavy icing began. They turned back and asked TFC if they were to also scout east and west. He ordered them to return to base. TG 68.1 had 60 miles of tough pack to traverse yet. The Sperry gyros are now almost perfect. The SOC Sperry precesses somewhat, as it was never calibrated for extreme southern latitudes.

At 0410 on the 13th TFC radioed "No further need for ice recco, return to station and carry out primary mission." We immediately started to westward somewhat slowed up by bad visibility, a course clear of ice pack to make greater speed and avoid fog area and growlers. Radioed DD and AO to take new stations at most economical speed and advised them that we were heading west to commence operations. They were instructed to start burning diesel oil instead of black. In the afternoon the sun came out for the first time in a long while, and we saw many whales spouting. That night we had our first sunset since 6 January.

In the evening of 15 January we passed a huge dead whale. It was green and smooth. The seas breaking over it made it look precisely like a mass of rocks. If it hadn't been for the fathometer we'd have gotten the jitters; passed it 500 yards abeam.

We received a dispatch from Admiral Byrd that the following cold weather trail items were in the PHILIPPINE SEA, for us: skis (complete with gear), 15 sleds, 30 sleeping bags and covers, mittens, mukluks, insoles, socks, crampons, parkas, pants, tents, and a quantity of Byrd cloth. He recommended using rubberized tents. We began to realize we had inadequately outfitted our plane crews.

We received a negative from MOUNT OLYMPUS on our request to make new aerological charts so requested them from PHILIPPINE SEA. They in turn said their press was too small and suggested that we try the MOUNT OLYMPUS. We replied that we had already been turned down and requested them to make us the map in two pieces. This was done, and proved most beneficial to us.

Some pertinent notes on operating off the ice pack: (a) a southerly, or straight-off ice pack wind gives best weather and calmest sea (b) operations too close to ice pack may give danger of brash ice (c) a high wind off the ice pack seems to pack the brash ice close to pack and gives a sharper edge, although the reason for this is not clear (d) when winds leaves pack at a small angle fog is frequently found 2 to 5 miles from ice, then the ceiling lifts and possible snow showers occur beyond ten miles (e) large icebergs don't give much lee unless one is dangerously close to them, if then (f) ice bays may calm the seas down somewhat, but large ones are liable to produce fog or snow (g) weather ships should remain 5 to 10 miles off the pack and not in an ice bay, in order to give more representative weather reports.

We reached our new operating area on the morning of 16 January. Bad weather continued all day - with fog, drizzle, snow, heavy swell, and low ceilings. The magnetic compasses are all AWOL as the south magnetic pole is only a short distance to the southwest. Our noon position was 64°-54'S, 148°-34'E.

CACAPON had another engineering casualty. This time it is apparently to the steering engine, as she is steering with her main engines.

I wrote a letter to the Naval Attache, Melbourne, Australia, regarding our prospective visit to that country, and gave some facts on our Task Group to help us both in our planning.

A radio blackout existed all day due to ionospheric disturbance. We can only hear the Japs and our Task Group, but are able to copy NSS continuously on 18 Kcs.

We are only 88 miles from MERTZ Glacier.

While lying to in fog and broadside to wind, we noted that the ship's heat dried the fog and left an outline of the ship in the fog to leeward for as much as a mile. An albatross landed on our fantail for a blow.

Next day was a heartbreaker. The fog broke up about 0600, for no reason at all. Then it became evident that a wedge that had broken out from the continent had become a "bubble" or small high. It became a beautiful day, but bad swells from NW made operations too risky. We noticed a heavy concentration of shrimps about the ship. We'd drifted down upon a great mess of them. They turned the water reddish brown, and were packed almost solidly. They averaged $1\frac{1}{2}$" long, were reddish and transparent, with 2 beady black little eyes. This apparently is the staple whale food. We noticed great schools of shrimp all over the surface.

Instructions issued to the oiler on fueling the Group, collecting mail, etc., preparatory to rendezvousing with the PHILIPPINE SEA.

TFC ordered us to increase PBM crew rations from the 30 days we are now carrying to 2 months' supply. He also directed planes to return to the ship when low visibility over the target area obviated the possibility of a successful mission.

By 2100 17 January, communications were returning to normal, and traffic was getting cleared.

We scouted the pack to eastward in search of an ice bay, but none was sighted.

At this time sunset was at 0026 next morning, and sunrise 0438.

The weather continued bad all of the 18th and 19th. Our current is setting us 240° at 1.4 knots, as determined by radar fixes on icebergs inside the ice pack. However, we don't know what the icebergs are doing. They are apparently affected by a different force than the one that sets ice floes and ships. The weather reports gave the faintest indication of a "wedge" (of good weather) forming to westward.

TG 68.3 lost their helicopter. We shall be even more careful to. fly only in contact weather, and pay lots of attention to carburetor air heat, which may have been the cause of their accident.

CACAPON started toward DD on first leg to Scott Island.

TFC suggested we move west to break weather jinx. We believed this area to be the best area for hundreds of miles in either direction, both from past performance (there were 4 perfect days just before we arrived here, as determined by destroyer and Jap weather) and because it is the nearest point to a large stretch of uncharted coast. I'd hate to miss this piece of coastline. Also, there is no reason why this should be a continually bad area; it is not one of those "catch-basins" for the lows, such as the Ross and Bellingshausen Sea areas. However, we moved west at 13 knots to find that wedge which was definitely taking shape, and then we planned to move east with it. The swells were still bad here, although both the other ships reported calm seas. The ship was covered with ice and icicles, and this caused our anemometers to read 10 knots low. Already our course was 30 to 40 miles inside of the position of the pack as reported by the DD a week ago. Either someone's navigation is way out, or the pack is melting very rapidly. The planes were heated and $\frac{1}{2}$" of ice was removed. At 1700 the swell was still prohibitive and a strong SE wind was kicking up, so flying was cancelled for the day. The "wedge" arrived, and it was merely a question of whether the swell would die down so that we could use the good weather.

On 21 January the destroyer fueled 300 miles to westward, and the tanker headed toward us. We made all preparations for early hoisting. There was some swell but it was not too bad. Things looked good. Then, after getting a boat in the water preparatory to hoisting out, the port crane broke down. We couldn't hoist out any more so we hoisted in the other boat. We started eastward to stay with the good weather. Instead of one hour, it took three hours to repair the crane. By that time a strong wind from ESE had sprung up and in addition, the swell began to build up again. As the wind was almost parallel to the edge of the pack, we had to tuck in close to the ice to get a lee, but there we found bad brash ice. We couldn't outguess the weather again. At 1112 we headed north to see if the wind would abate; it

got worse. Meanwhile, when we came about at 1225 to head south, and
bucked a 40 knot relative wind, a rotor-tip boot and securing line
chafed through and allowed one helicopter blade to flip up to a
position past vertical. This broke a couple of brackets, bent some
other parts, and caused possible unseen damage to the internal gear
box. Our #1 eggbeater was out of commission for a long while.

The wind kept up strong all afternoon and at 1600 we finally
gave up all thought of flying. Apparently the pack was breaking up
rapidly for we were far south of the edge of the pack reported by the
HENDERSON 10 days ago and there was brash ice for several miles from
the main pack. The storm must have broken up the pack pretty much,
and the wind blown it north for rapid melting.

The HENDERSON was instructed to relocate herself 300 miles
bearing 300° from us while the CACAPON was gone, instead of remaining
west of us, along the pack; and to be prepared to make 15 knots on
½ hours' notice during flight operations.

TFC told us to get the CACAPON to rendezvous 24 hours early
if practicable as PHILIPPINE SEA was arriving early. We issued orders
to CACAPON information of interested parties, for proceeding to this
most important of rendezvouses - for it brings us mail!

Next morning TFC sent us a very encouraging dispatch, that it
was a good thing that the crane busted down yesterday. We hadn't
looked at it that way, and just then realized what a blessing it was
that we were prevented from flying, as it would have been a bloody
mess if we'd have tried to recover a plane in that rough open sea.
What a lot of good a well-worded dispatch can do - especially when
one was trying hard to deliver the goods, as our boys were doing.

Things looked up today, light winds from ESE, smooth sea,
nice flying weather; we even saw some blue sky once. Flight quarters
were sounded at 0519. All planes were in the air at 0815. The first
plane took off with 1600 gallons of gasoline in a fairly rough sea.
This take off was so rapid and smooth that the next plane took 1800
gallons and took off in an incredibly short run. The CACAPON came
into sight at 0530 and transfers of mail and passengers were effected.
At 0930 with all boats on board, CURRITUCK got underway due north at
8 knots and fueled from the CACAPON, taking 145,000 gallons of diesel
oil. At 1005, changed course to due west while fueling. Then, as with
other fuelings from this ship, the weather turned bad and we experienced
heavy snowfall. We recalled the planes, as the weather seemed to be
generally deteriorating. By 1300 fueling had been completed and
CACAPON proceeded eastwards at 15 knots for rendezvous. In a conversation with C.O., I asked him to see if he could swipe some fresh vegetables from the PHILIPPINE SEA (he got one stalk of celery, and ate
that himself). He said he'd been blown 80 miles off station without

knowing it, due to his light draft, heavy winds and no sights. This accounted for several strange weather reports from her that seemed inexplicable to our meteorologists.

By 1330 we were again lying to off the pack, and by 1600 all planes were aboard. One plane was slightly damaged when one of the crew dropped a wing line which allowed the plane to swing into the ship. It was touch and go, as a northerly swell had set in ½ hour before hoisting and the wind had picked up from the east. There was also some brash ice.

I noted that all operations between tender and tanker were slow, but safe. At this distance from the nearest friendly navy yard, it was very probably the smartest way to handle things.

Many penguins were sighted swimming around the ship, and the first seal was sighted.

Our planes had encountered icing going through cloud layers, and were forced up to 11000'. There were also severe and unknown wind shifts. Baker 3 had headed due south from the ship. The radar tracked him out on a course 160°T, thus showing the value of CIC's radar acting as a drift sight. Several hundred miles of coast were mapped by this plane, but it was most difficult to tell where the coastline was, as it was flat with no mountains and only ice cliffs and some water. The gas consumption rose as the temperature dropped and the interior of the plane was coated with frost (the heater didn't work in this plane; it will if I have to ride in it!). The other plane flew 380 miles inland through much cloud. His radar altimeter was out, and he was too low over the ice cap for both safety and photography (9500' by the low radio altimeter). I issued orders that no planes should hereafter go inland more than 50 miles over an undercast. One plane took a sunsight and got an intercept of 120 miles but didn't believe it. Later it was found to be right on. Planes were set well to westward.

We removed a lot of extra gear from planes, including bomb bay tanks - which we'll reinstall later when they are needed for really long flights. The gear removed from the plane more than compensated for the 534 pounds of added survival food we were ordered to carry.

CACAPON reported to CTG 68.4 (PHILIPPINE SEA) for duty. TFC ordered quick releasing safety belts for helicopters. I sent a dispatch to BuAer describing our HO3S mishap and asked for advice on how to handle it, as our helicopter unit was relatively inexperienced.

On the morning of the 23rd we were engaged in trying to find a lee so that it would be possible to shift planes, thus repairing the damaged wing tip on B-3. About 1150 it shoaled rapidly to 45 fathoms -

and we discovered "CURRITUCK shoal". The Captain stopped quickly;
ordered the hand lead to verify the fathometer and get a bottom
sample. This was quite a surprise after our long time at sea with
average soundings over 1000 fathoms. It took some time to man the
chains. By that time the leadsman found 55 fathom and recovered a
small bottom sample of mud and sand. It was strange that there were
no grounded icebergs in the vicinity. It took a little time to
recover from the surprise as we had just come to assume that the last
thing to worry about off the ice pack is running aground. We followed
the 100 fathom curve at 5 knots to eastward, for some time, looking for
a lee. The icepack was certainly breaking up rapidly now. The wind
stayed pretty high all day, east 18 to 29 knots.

At 0900 on the 24th we passed a small Jap whaler, perhaps 85'
long, 150 tons, harpoon gun and all, with MacArthur flag flying. At
0955 we passed two Jap whale factories. Had I known then that there
were several United Nations representatives on board keeping the Japs
in line (they were notoriously rotten whalers) I'd have sent a cheery
message – which they'd probably have needed. As it was I maintained
a properly stand-offish silence. The factory ship had a stern ramp
and twin stacks – an ugly affair. The other seemed to be a fleet
oiler type, and was probably the oiler for the group as well as the
whale oil storage ship.

BuAer passed all our questions on the HO3S right on to BAR
Stratford, and there our pitiful wail seemed to die a natural death.

I sent a dispatch to TFC complaining about poor raobs and
rawins from Central Group as only 7 observations were received out of
the 20 required.

The weather kept slowly building up. By night the wind was
33 knots from ESE and the barometer was down to 29.10, the sea was
getting pretty rough. At 2015 we turned west once more. We are still
crippled by that one plane having a crushed wingtip and torn-up deicer
boot. The plagued wingtip sticks 20 feet or so over the side where
we can't work on it, although we tried many rigs.

Learned that the PHILIPPINE SEA lost her HO3S.

The Captain of the CURRITUCK offered a prize to the enlisted
man giving information leading to the taking of the best photograph
of the cruise. He set a continuous daylight photographer's mate watch
to be sure we didn't miss anything.

On the 25th, being well fed up with this weather (the wind
was now 41 knots from ESE) I decided to move westward to 130°E, and
abandon plans for magnetic and navigational surveys near the magnetic
pole. We would try to complete mapping the coast from 138 to 151 East
from the new location.

Annex L-(b)   - 21 -

I requested information from the PHILIPPINE SEA as to the cause of her HO3S crash and data on the rescue. I also requested all helicopter spares she brought down which were not needed by other units.

CACAPON made her rendezvous on time.

We received another congratulatory dispatch from Admiral Byrd on our last two flights.

The rough weather continues all day. We headed toward the ice pack to be sure we don't miss any large ice bays while moving west. Our track took us as far south as any ship has ever sailed without entering the ice pack itself. That afternoon at 2215 we located a likely looking bay, in which the swells decreased remarkably after going through a mile of pack ice. The remaining swell came around the corner. It looked so nice we decided to stay there in case things looked better in the morning. Our position was 65°-09'N 137°-05E. There was a great collection of large and weather beaten bergs just south of us. The wind was now 16 knots from ESE, and the sea was considerably smoother.

Next day, Sunday, things looked good and we put out our boats and made all ready to fly. We steamed into our bay (we'd laid to off the entrance during night) to find it had largely broken up, and filled with brash, and the swell was again too high. Here we noticed a strange thing. The ship lay broadside to a 17 knot breeze a little ways west of the edge of the pack but instead of drifting away from the pack, the pack caught up with us. In other words, the pack was drifting before the wind faster than we were. Last night at sundown a peculiarly shaped berg was located several miles west of us, outside the pack; by breakfast time this morning it had smacked through our ice bay and was now buried in the pack a mile south of us. The large concentration of bergs which were south of us last night had moved to the southeast. In other words, we were rapidly drifting westward, as sights later proved. This explains the straight clean-cut edge of pack on the westward edge. Here we had noticed a seal sleeping on an ice floe a hundred yards from the edge, and several killer whales cruising slowly around looking for breakfast.

At 0715 we headed west once more. The wind died down considerably. We touched the 100 fathom curve several times. The sea bottom shelves from 100 to 700 fathom very sharply.

Our mistake of the preceeding night was in not staying inside the bay, or observing its breakup on radar, so as to be able to make westing as soon as the breakup was apparent. However, we didn't know these bays broke up so rapidly.

Water sky well inside the pack indicated the presence of large inland, or "in-ice", lakes that would make wonderful operating areas - if we had an icebreaker to get us in and out. These lakes were later confirmed by our planes flying over them. The water sky versus ice blink also indicated, in certain instances, the presence of ice bays, 10 or 12 miles away. While I was still pondering this interpretation, we ran right into an excellent ice bay, at 1600, and sounded flight quarters. Baker one was in the air by 1758 and we quickly relocated our other plane to work on that blasted wingtip. (I've never realized one man dropping a line could cause so much trouble!).

Baker one made a fairly good flight clear to Commonwealth Bay, where he got some excellent shots of high winds (katabatic) blowing snow well out to seaward over Mawson's old camp site. The plane was back on board by 0021.

What was supposed to be a minor repair job on Baker One's wingtip took us until 0500 Monday morning. This indicates how repair work drags out in cold weather. Cold weather slows everything down except optimism. A jury rig hangar of wood and canvas along with good hot air would have speeded up the work.

Monday morning found our old ice bay breaking up and a new one forming slightly to eastward. We got some interesting radar pictures of this. Flight quarters were sounded at 0500, all planes were airborne at 0826 (delay caused by having to respot one plane after repairs).

Upon viewing planes' radar-scope photographs, I learned that they had not been handling the scope for best hydrographic purposes. I directed planes to change range scale, log picture times, etc; in this way we hoped to fill in missing sections of coast when the trimets are shooting through clouds. They may also help to distinguish land, water, and ice, even when photographed. I also saw some radar pictures taken of a PBM scope while the plane was sitting on the water. The picture showed icebergs 5 miles away.

By 1630 our ice bay had so filled with brash that we had to move into the open sea to recover Baker One in a two degree roll. One plane had scouted 100 miles westward looking for a suitable lee, but found none. At 1730 decided to move west anyway as there was no lee locally. As a low was moving in on us from the west and the local area was pretty well mapped, we'd have to forego connecting our recco to Commonwealth Bay with Cook Bay which was our furthest westward flight from near the Ballenys.

After investigating "single engine performance on inland flights" we decided to send pilots in at high altitudes to a position where they could clear a 7500' ice cap, (this would allow a 500' clearance for wives and children) while on single engine, after jettisoning all gear mentioned previously. In other words, I proposed sending planes in at 12000'-15000' and have them proceed 50 miles or so beyond the 7500' contour. This will get them back to open water. After arriving at the coast, they would have to decide whether to land in a lake or inland waterway, or jettison more food, etc, and make a run for the ship. I requested approval (in condensed form) of this policy by TFC.

Baker three's flight inland was a little disappointing. The pilot took a literal interpretation of my instructions and turned back at the 7500' contour, which was only 110 miles from the coast. When he arrived at the coast again - after going 60 miles westward, he attempted to photograph west of Porpoise Bay but encountered a dense haze, our first one. He could see the ground -(or what passes for "ground" in these parts) in a narrow cone directly under him. This was much like our typical southern California hazes, but he couldn't see a mile ahead, and went completely on instruments. Since it was no use trying to photograph, he flew out to seaward and scouted the ice pack 100 miles to westward of the ship. He saw occasional large collections of icebergs, which were probably grounded, and lakes in the pack, about 3 X 15 miles in size. The pack was 60 miles wide. The plane was back on board at 1330.

Baker One's flight was not much more successful. This flight got to 68°-18'S, at which position the elevation of the ice cap was 8500'. He came out to the coast near Commonwealth Bay. Since it was CAVU, he started taking pictures to eastward. While he was getting the cameras set, it closed in completely within 10 minutes. He did photograph the coast to Mertz glacier, which showed up dimly in his radar pictures. Pilot stated that it was hard to see the horizon although the weather was CAVU. Baker One was hoisted on board at 1730 in a 2° roll. Underway soon to westward, looking for a better operating area.

Celestial sights indicated that we, ice bay and all, had been drifting on course 290 at .8 knot. We were not sure what the icebergs were doing.

Admiral Byrd asked us how we navigated in the vicinity of the magnetic pole on flight 9. I used this as an opportunity to elaborate on all lessons we had learned so far, for the benefit of pilots just arriving in Central Group. The main points discussed were: magnetic compasses were not used; used Sperry electrical directional gyro with Mark II astral compass for navigation and vacuum directional gyro for auto pilots; utilized ship's radar and rarely RDF near ship; computed frequent sun lines and occasional moon sight. We expected the flux-gate compass to behave soon. We stressed over - the - top flying so

as to use the sun, determining drift occasionally by dropping under the
clouds. The clouds were never too high but icing could be expected in
them. We emphasized the importance of checking the course carefully
before leaving the ship.

The nights are getting longer. Sunset tonight is 0055 and
sunrise is 0628 on Tuesday 28 January. Our noon position was 64°-58'S
124°-51'E that date. Temperature dropped a little more to 27°F. The
weather was beautiful all day although overcast at 2000'. This is
apparently another polar wedge which is strangely moving westward. The
sun is shining from rare blue skies and there's a cold 15 to 20 knot
breeze from off the pack. We raised our speed to find an icebay as it
was too rough to operate in the open sea. And at 1400 we found a fair
lee, but with much brash. Both planes were airborne at 1631, each with
1800 gallons gas. The SOC was launched at 1745 to scout the ice pack
to westward.

Both helicopters are now out of commission. The HOS starter
broke, meshing teeth with engine. This requires an engine change. I
ordered all speed to repair the HO3S.

This morning we sighted the "appearance of land" as stated in
BA Chart 3172. Our plane, in flying over this area yesterday, found
a dense collection of apparently grounded and domed icebergs, and the
ship's radar corroborated this. It surely did look like land and was
a perfect deception.

The aerologists' explanation of "haze" seen yesterday by Baker
3 is that it was actually haze, thought to be formed by condensation
or sublimation, on salt particles, at relative humidity of 60-70%
which caused scattering of light when one looked toward the sun (west,
in this case). It could have been penetrated somewhat by using amber
filters in cameras and polaroid or amber glasses for the pilot. The
visibility was much better, looking away from the sun.

Tracked the planes today by ship's radar while they flew along
coastline. We were thus able to plot in the coastline to an accuracy
of 3 miles. The aircraft radar pictures of Mertz glacier, taken
yesterday, show the outlines of ice tongue only where an ice tongue
cliff or barrier faced the plane, as the ice tongue is completely
surrounded by heavy sea-ice and old icebergs. Apparently our airborne
radar pictures discern the coastline, distinguishing ground from
water, although this is indistinguishable from plane. This can only
be definitely confirmed after a rather painful and thankless study
by the photogrammetrists.

The SOC landed and was hoisted on board at 2009. This plane
has received practically a complete overhaul since being received on
board, and is now fairly safe. But nobody loves it any more. In

heavy winter flying clothes only smallish people can be shoe-horned into its cockpit.

The navigator got his first star sight today since 7 January. Our drift was 240° at 1.1 knot. The sunset was beautiful tonight; a solid overcast left a few degrees of open sky to southward over the ice pack and the sun, very red, turned everything else red along with it.

By now we are getting used to have the sun to the north at noon, and having the lows and highs circulating in the "wrong" directions.

Both PBM's landed and were aboard by 0005. Baker 3 covered the coast from 122° to 130° E and got an inland segment to 68°-25'S where he turned back as his gas was getting low. He experienced our first camera trouble of consequence, which caused much useless circling for repair. The Gremlin camera (which photographs pressure altitude, time, and turn and bank for each exposure of tri-met) had to be repaired. One tri-met camera had to be replaced. The radar camera didn't work all day. Ice cap maximum altitude was 6500' when the plane was only a moderate distance inland. (68-25S at 125°E.) The plane experienced a "white out"; although the weather was CAVU there was no horizon and the ice cap under the plane was absolutely featureless. It seems like a terrible waste of film photographing featureless sections of this ice cap, however, I suppose one day someone may want to know what this surface looked like. It was hard to distinguish the coast. No mountains were sighted; just some ice cliff.

Baker One's flight was excellent; it covered the coast from 112° to 125°E. This flight observed radical changes in this coast, 2 new glaciers and a deep new bay never before seen by man. Budd Coast was open for 15 miles to seaward, which was as far as the pilot could see. The magnetic compasses settled down somewhat on this trip. Part of engine cowling was lost after takeoff but he continued his flight anyway. Our pilots are getting enthusiastic. This plane now goes into check. That sounds as though we're flying.

The lovely weather continued on the 29th, but the winds continued too high for operations, ESE 17 to 21 knots, finally dying down to 12 knots. There was brash ice everywhere. We lay to, awaiting more favorable conditions.

I viewed some photos taken over the ice cap by the tri-mets using an amber filter. These pictures show the surface in great detail although the pilots reported seeing absolutely nothing, even with polaroid and all other types of Navy glasses. Since the surface must be seen in case of forced landing, this phenomenon would bear a little research.

By 1600, secured from flight condition III - planes had been warmed up by heaters enough to considerably shorten the warm up period . This has been our finest day, plenty of sunshine - and plenty swells and brash ice. We could have accomplished wonders from an aircraft carrier.

Our photographers rigged their cameras at sunset (0104) to get a picture of the "green flash", that phenomenon of the setting sun in a clear atmosphere. There was a brief green flash, but it didn't show up in the colored stills; perhaps it was caught in the movies.

Next morning the fine weather continued, although a big low was passing to the north of us. We have moved slowly westward along the pack; now we are moving at 10 knots, as the weatherman says the swell will drop and good weather continue. The storm is moving rapidly eastward. I told HENDERSON to move west, that we expect to operate from 115°E tomorrow.

A school of whales - at least 4 - got on a collision course from starboard and finally passed, just ahead of the ship, moving slowly from starboard to port, about 100 yards ahead of us. No wonder they're easy to knock off. We could easily see their spout mechanism working; quite noisy, too.

The 0800 cloud report was symbolized by a blank circle, which means that there wasn't a cloud in the sky. Meanwhile the wind came around to the south, the temperature dropped to 24°, and the barometer took a plunge from 29.10 to 28.35 by midnight. The weather remained perfect, with only scattered good weather cumuli clouds even at midnight. The very tight low is to the east of us now, the Japs reported force 8 winds. The air, ordinarily moisture laden, had been swept over the high and cold continent, then pushed out to sea and dried in the descent.

Sounded flight quarters at 1310. The ship was dead in the water, and plane B-3 was almost in the water, when brash ice was noticed moving in quite rapidly from astern. The CURRITUCK hoisted in the plane and moved further from the pack. The behavior of this ice was at times a little too unpredictable for us. Baker three finally got into the air with 2000 gallons at 1520. Baker One is still in 120 hour check. By 2000 we found a nice turn in the ice pack to Northwest which gave us an excellent lee from SW winds. The swell was down now; we lay to.

Flight 15, Baker 3, covered the coast from 115° to 127°E to rephotograph coastal areas missed due to faulty tri-met camera operations of the previous run. He also made a run inland along 115°E to

68° south, where the ice cap rose to an elevation of 4500'. At this point he received orders from me to go in on 118°E. He started over but met clouds and returned to the ship. (This indicates once more the fallacy of changing orders in the air - in this case the apparent need for a change was due to a garble in his position report). He reported that while proceeding inland along 115°E the ice cap to the west of him rose to a considerable height and that he seemed to be in a valley or at the foot of a slope. This was corroborated by flights to the westward later, although we couldn't explore this area as well as I wanted to. The pilot stated that an icebreaker could have reached the coast at any point, as the pack was very loose. I instructed pilots to get pictures of the pack on the way in and out. There were few bergs in the pack. Magnetic compasses were improving. The pilot saw the edge of the ice pack when it was 100 miles away and sighted the CURRITUCK 80 miles away with the naked eye.

The barometer dropped like a rock and by midnight levelled off at 28"30, there were scattered tropical-appearing good weather cumuli at 1000 feet, wind was 15 knots from WSW, temperature was 25°, humidity was 75% and a rippled sea from NW. Incidentally I don't know how much to trust this humidity business, for with the temperature at 25°F I don't see how there is such a thing as a "wet bulb". It seemed that the air was much drier at times than 60%, which is our lowest recorded humidity. The humidity in the ship is low enough to start a fire by rubbing two toothpicks together, due to the heaters raising the temperature of the cold air from 25° to 75°F.

On the 31st, after such a previous auspicious day, the weather again acted strangely in a reverse direction and we lay to all day without flying. The barometer rose to normal during the day (29.20). The wind shifted to NW 12 knots, it became warmer, and the fog should have come in - but didn't. The snow-makers prescribed heavy cloud over the continent, especially the coast-line. Although we had another cloudless sky early in the morning, and it remained calm all day, a good solid overcast gradually formed, and we even had a touch of snow around midday.

Yesterday's peculiar weather still had the weather -wise talking. The combination of very low barometer and extraordinarily fine weather, they say, can occur only here in Antarctica and west of Greenland when a low is positional over that great ice cap of the north. We estimate the pressure at the center of this low to be 28"03. In the west Pacific we wouldn't ask questions, just dive for the bilges or cellar, as the case may be.

First two planes from CV 47 arrived at Little America. We were greatly cheered (1) to see the Central Group get started (2) to know that soon our mail would start this way. Later we heard that all six planes had arrived at L. A.

On yesterday's flight the pilot tested out everything we had over the ice cap to see if he could pick up details of the surface better. He found smoked glasses plus Wratten filters "A-25 red" the best, and "K-1 filter #6 yellow" the next best. I sent dispatches to other groups with this information and asked for any data they might have.

CACAPON reported for duty, rejoining us.

The C.O. and I discussed the CURRITUCK's compass situation; he had quite a battle to get his small additional ship's gyro put in, (not even hooked up with ship's repeaters). We were thinking what a "sad sack" it would be now to have an overcast (and no sun) with ship's magnetic compasses useless, and now the ship's main gyro broken down. The only thing on board to indicate any accurate direction is that auxiliary gyro in the I. C. room.

Still lying to off our ice cove, on 1 February in latitude 64°-57'S, 119°-52'E, with southeast breezes. We had flight 16 airborne at 0807, but at 0935 the same piece of engine cowling blew off and Baker One returned. He didn't want to stretch his horse shoe too far. This time we didn't just replace the cowling by dzus fittings; we bolted or welded it on, I forget which. He had been unable to fly his assigned mission due to solid "undercast" (a phrase I believe we coined, as we never heard it before), and the pilot started an inland segment further to westward when the cowling blew off. Meanwhile a swell had started up from the northwest. By the time Baker One was hoisted on board at 1130 it was bad enough so that he was damaged in hoisting,so that he was decommissioned for the rest of the day. The swell stayed with us. I'm afraid we're pretty fortunate! The pilot also said he had clouds all over the landscape and the pictures wouldn't have been good. The other plane was still in 120 hour check. The maintenance crews are taking a pretty good licking, making their checks and knocking off each time we hoist out or in - for they all have duplicate jobs.

Today the AV sent a recreation party into the pack to get some seals. The men got a tremendous kick out of it and brought back a dead seal and live one (probably crab-eaters). The dead one left a little blood dribbling over the stern and the men stated a killer whale followed them back to the ship. Had they known of this beast's habit of diving, then smashing up under a thick ice floe on which a seal is basking, shattering the floe and practically catching the seal on the rebound - I'm sure they'd have been a little more cautious in flirting with these scoundrels. This dead seal was cut up and served. Captain Clark seemed to enjoy some of the liver.

RESTRICTED

The live seal brought a good deal more interest to the crew.
It was brought aboard in the cargo net, lay about on deck for the crew
to examine and be photographed with. When faced with the problem of
feeding it, it was decided to return it to the "beach".

At 1545 underway to westward at 10 knots to avoid the swell and
prepare for 2-plane operations. We had pretty well examined this area
anyway. CACAPON ran into bad weather and lay to - with our mail on
board.

Finally got an answer from BuAer to our dispatch of the 22nd
on the HO3S and its repair.

Continued steaming westward all night. Sunset was at 0128
and sunrise was at 0739. Sunrise was getting pretty late, so we
changed from time zone (-)12 to (-)11 today.

The swell decreased gradually. We're getting closer to the
coast all the time - just about as close as free ships have ever gotten.
Every once in a while we stopped and tested the swell, but it was too
much. Meanwhile we had entered the very center of a "bubble", which
in local parlance is a "wedge" that finally broke off from the main
Antarctic high and is now on its way northward. This is one of the
main ways in which this polar air gets detached and gets itself into
circulation, to eventually form a high. A front had formed to south
of us, over the coast, clouding it up. Anything could happen. The
sea was calm but there was much brash ice. It was clearing to northward. One of the very rare occasions when it was dead calm,was noted
today.

CACAPON enlivened things by suggesting he turn around and go
directly to BURTON ISLAND, to get a shaft bearing sent down by ServPac.
In other words, being half way back to us, he wanted to turn around
and go back to Scott Island. This started a series of dispatches, some
explosive, which cleared the atmosphere, brought a communication garble
to light, and kept the CACAPON coming westward. He was able to avoid
giving the PHILIPPINE SEA any oil. This was most fortunate, as will be
seen later.

At 1540 it was decided that we could fly, the wind shifting to
south. With some swell and no wind the gas load would have to be light.
Both planes were airborne at 1723. Then a fog bank appeared to the
west, approaching very slowly. Headed east at 10 knots.

Baker Three didn't do so well. He flew over almost solid
undercast and obtained very few photos. However, he recorded some
interesting altitudes of the ice cap. This plane confirmed the
existence of the valley in the ice cap noted in a previous flight.

Annex I-(b)   - 30 -

The pilots also noted the looseness and navigability of the ice pack. The plane was talked down in a power landing on a glassy sea by another pilot on the ship's bridge. After recovery at 2048 the ship got underway to eastward again, keeping ahead of the fog bank. B-1 landed in a clear area and was aboard at 2310. Baker One mapped the coast from 114° to 105°E although he was forced down to 4000' at the westward end of his flight. This new coast, never before sighted and up until today just a dotted line on the map was very different from what had been expected. Four new glaciers were found. The most spectacular and larger one had a jagged ice tongue and a 1000' sheer drop. It was on a large, open, and glassy calm bay, with many skerries or rocky islets. The pilot also found new nunataks, and land out-croppings. Apparently this land formed dust that discolored the glacier and icebergs in the vicinity. The pilot found what he considered an excellent landing field site on the shore of this open bay. He came down to 1000' and thoroughly photographed the area. The results were some of our most spectacular and amazing photographs. He stated that this area would be easily accessible to ships once they were through the ice pack. He also confirmed the large dome - shape of Budd Land promontory. I consider this as one of our most successful flights, and I proposed that this large and beautiful bay be named Kreitzer Bay after the pilot who discovered it and immediately recognized its potentiality. On his return to the ship, this plane experienced "reciprocal bearing trouble" with his ADF until near the ship. Why a direction finder should act so cantankerous in the Antarctic is some-thing I can't understand.

We lay to, and at 0300, Monday morning, 3 February, the fog caught up to us. We expected it to last three days.

By now we were far enough to westward of the Japs so we couldn't intercept their 500 Kcs weather reports which we missed greatly. I ordered CACAPON to intercept them as best she could and forward them to CTF 68, who could use them more than we could.

This morning in the fog we got heavy hoar-frost all over the rigging to windward. By the time the fog had drifted across the ship a few feet it had become so heated and dried that it left no frost. The hoar-frost grew in spikes a good half inch long. It was crystaline, brittle and light,and powdered easily.

Since this was non-flying weather, the CACAPON was stopped by similar weather,and the HENDERSON running low on fuel, I ordered the latter to rendezvous the CURRITUCK for provisioning.

I believe a special rule could be used in the Antarctic where-by only vessels underway and making an appreciable speed would be required to sound fog signals. The CURRITUCK, lying to in fog near the pack, has not been sounding the international signal for "underway and no way on". This would allow no sleep for some of us. With radar going 24 hours a day a growler moving 300 feet would be detected, you might say, and we're positive we're the only ship within 300 miles, so all this noise seemed rather superficial.

At 1340 headed NW to clear the local east-west frontal area for better rendezvous weather in which to meet the HENDERSON.

Another little local phenomenon of the local so-called "fog". was observed. The water is 32°F. The air temperature 3 feet above water is 26°F, 100' up it is 25°F, and at 1100' it is 43°F. This means that a radical inversion exists commencing at 100'. These temperatures were provided by our two scientists, Doctors Hopkins and Gibbs, who were out in all kinds of weather getting temperatures and other data. They used wire-sonde, with an aerological balloon. The wire became covered with ice crystals and they had intermittent static discharge from the lower end of the wire. Accurate humidity was unobtainable. There was an extremely large-crystal-type light snow-fall, which indicated a high super-saturation (relative ice). In other words, this wasn't real fog; but was cumulus cloud resting on the surface of the ocean and being held down by the inversion.

CURRITUCK learned a simple lesson in cold weather fueling when the Chief Engineer was notified at 1700 that he was to fuel the HENDERSON tomorrow. He notified the Captain that he needed 24 hours to heat the oil before fueling.

We are sending reports to CTF delineating the new coastline. Didn't realize how interesting it was to the boss to get first hand information on brand-new geography - unrolling the last secret of the world's coastlines.

By 1900 we were lying to in good local weather, although the continent was still souped over. The HO3S was back in commission but not yet flight tested, as the new brackets, which were being made out of steel, were not ready yet. The HO3S was ready for emergency use on the old rewelded brackets. That crew had been working on straight shifts to get this job done, in all but the roughest weather. These kids can take it.

Tuesday 4 February, lying to awaiting rendezvous with the DD. The CACAPON had been slowed down more by running into heavy streamers of pack ice reaching north to 63°-15'. (The position reports of Jap whalers indicate that they are located well south of him. He's headed right for a tight low.

There are two operations which I hope to accomplish sometime soon while lying to (1) investigate operations in the lee of a large

RESTRICTED

iceberg (2) check the possibility of making slicks in rough water for
PBM's - i.e. - similar to cruiser's cast recovery. We planned to use
the helicopter to fly around a berg to check underwater projections.
I wish that we had more data on what happens when a big chunk of tabular
berg decides to set up business for himself. I can't blame the ship's
captain for not wanting to get too close to the berg, especially when
reading that calving makes a noise simulating the sound of gunfire; that
sounds rather dangerous to us. Today we put a boat over to take lead
soundings around a medium berg; no bottom at 30 fathoms anywhere.

HENDERSON came into sight at 1430 and we were soon loading
personnel and supplies. They have had no fresh vegetables or fruits
for 30 days and had been rolling heavily, steaming at 3 knots to keep
from broaching. He reported that he had rolled 25° continuously for
one week. He reported excellent sonar results - apparently better
than radar for detecting small ice. He took this occasion to send
over a "liberty party" - or rather, a visiting party.

At 2008 CURRITUCK commenced fueling her on course 125°at 6
knots, swell from ahead, 20 knot wind from 110°T, and very comfortable.
At 0025 completed fueling and set course back to the pack at 5 knots,
until darkness made it prudent to lie to for a while. It is now dark
enough to make growlers dangerous in a seaway. This factor of darkness versus growlers should be considered carefully in planning ship
operations in ice areas.

At 1050 Wednesday the 5th we found a nice ice bay and lay to.
The weather was not good. Wind up to 28 knots from ESE. At 1230 the
wind decreased to 14 knots. We started flight operations but hesitated
due to lack of good weather stations (HENDERSON too close), and still
a little too much roll. Shortly thereafter the wind picked up and held
at 20 knots.

Current 275°, drift .8 knot.

Our lessons on "How to fly in the Antarctic" can be summarized,
and some of the limitations set down as follows:

(a) Winds over 17 knots make hoisting hazardous due to wind
getting under PBM wings.
(b) Swells cause the ship to roll and pitch; (sometimes the
latter is more dangerous); this causes the plane to start swinging
and hit the ship or other planes.
(c) A bad chop or wind swell will put a bad strain on the
hoisting sling, as well as making boating alongside the PBM hazardous.
(d) Poor combinations of swell and wind makes take-off hazardous for loaded PBM.
(e) Brash ice, growlers, or pack in line of take-off is a constant danger.

Annex I-(b)   - 33 -

(f) Heavy icing, low ceiling, or other weather phenomena are limiting factors.

(g) Nights are getting longer, and it becomes colder, slowing up operations and limiting times of takeoff.

(h) After all the above, the mapping areas may be clouded over, even though all other conditions good.

Outside of this, flying is easy down here.

Another observation: There should be some definite research done in the way of producing an icebreaker for naval purposes; one large, broad, and powerful enough to break the toughest ice we may expect to operate in, capable of arctic camouflage, armed and armored. Perhaps an OBB could be converted along this line. It should be able to take a CV right through all this stuff with ease.

Thursday morning we went to flight condition II, but a 29 knot wind changed our plans. Our aerologists - not waiting for prompting any longer - advised us to run west for lower winds. We did, at 15 knots.

There was a "double sun" at sunrise today, although the mock sun was not very clear cut.

1325 sighted Norwegian whale chasers headed westward making heavy weather into seas. At 1400 the wind abated, as per forecast, but heavy swells remained. Met 6 whalechasers altogether. Every now and then we'd hear their harpoon guns booming. At 1800 found an ice bay; lay to, heavy swell still running. At 2200 we met the NORHVAL, Norwegian whale factory, a twin stacker. (athwartships). He asked us for whale information and information on Japs. We answered only that Japs broadcast their position and weather on 500 Kcs. Asked him for his weather broadcasts, which he said he would furnish on 500 Kcs if requested. Told him there were more whales here than seen elsewhere - they were in sight in all directions.

One thing strikes us clearly: If we were a CV operating a few R4D's from our deck (obviously impossible at present) and could move from west to east, with the weather, we could easily map the entire Antarctic coastline and much interior in one season, by starting in December from the Weddell Sea. Just find some good "wedges" and move east with them.

The CACAPON reported a 50 knot wind, gusts to 60 and increasing seas.

New ice is forming in the glassy water in the shadow of the ship. The temperature went down to $24^{\circ}F$, the seawater is $30^{\circ}F$.

Friday the 7th was a fine day. At 0700 we sounded flight condition I, put the boats over; then suddenly the ship rolled 4 and 5°. This was a new one. For ten minutes the maximum roll was 2° - then suddenly a whopper, and no way to see it coming. It was most puzzling. We checked trim, draft, and all, but could not explain it. It probably was simply that the fast moving low to the north of us produced swells from several directions, and occasionally they got into phase; so would the CURRITUCK, and away she went.

New ice formed in little transparent cakes, even as one watched the calm water. The temperature dropped to 23°. At 1600 secured from flight quarters. Current 255°, 3/4 knot - ice pack, ice bay, and all.

CACAPON was having more trouble; her telemotor line broke, and she shifted to trick wheel. All this occurred in "mountainous waves which ship rode like surfboard..... no damage."

Our weather men say they see signs of "autumn" setting in - more lows and more intense ones, further north, and the air getting colder. The swells go right through the pack, rolling us frequently as much as 7°. We hope this beautiful weather will last another day. There is plenty of sunshine today.

Saturday morning we found our ice bay considerably decomposed. The swells were still wicked and we began to wonder if we were just sitting in an area where the swells are just a built-in part of the landscape. Perhaps they were reflected by a shoal to the SE.

At 0800 we gave up all thoughts of flying and headed eastward at 13 knots to rendezvous CACAPON, to expedite fueling. CURRITUCK is down to 50% fuel.

The HENDERSON rolled 45° last night (we learned this by operator's signals); advised him to move south toward pack for calmer water, but he explained later we were too late as it later calmed down all by itself.

We sighted the CACAPON at 1240 after some difficulty rendezvousing due to navigation; fueled on course 275°, speed 8 knots, with wind and swell almost dead astern. The wind built up to 30-35 knots from astern; the ships handled fine, no yawing. It was a pretty sight to see our mail coming aboard. At 2023 fueling was completed and CACAPON headed west to fuel HENDERSON. Told him to try to intercept South African weather on his teletype, as he'll be 400 miles closer to Africa than we will - and we have no teletype in the CURRITUCK. Incidentally, it would have been a blessing to have had one, so as to be able to get orders to officers and more press.

At 2100 came east at 5 to 7 knots, barely making headway in high winds. We will remain in this area for one more good weather period then move west, regardless of results, in order to do some work.

Sunday morning, sunrise at 0730, found us riding out a 45 knot gale, and very comfortable. CACAPON preparing to fuel HENDERSON to westward. The barometer has dropped from 29.20 yesterday to 28.85 and is now rising again slowly.

Our weather wizards put together the reports and stated that a large wedge of good weather was breaking out well to the west of the Shackleton Shelf Ice and moving east behind the low. It was now even clearer that the ideal situation would be to move east with the weather. Instead of this we had to "surfboard" with a wedge, then back-track through two or three lows to the westward, then scoot eastward again with the next wedge. This used oil. By now we're getting wise to the way of the Antarctic. We're getting very little benefit from Australian weather because (1) the information is garbled due to distance (2) their weather is getting more past than future. To the northwest we have only a big open chunk of Indian Ocean, with very incomplete data upon which to guess what is happening. In other words, we were now just about completely on our own for this vitally important stuff.

Monday 10 February we were still battling the ESE gale. At 0720 we headed west, running for good weather. At 1650 we headed south to close the pack and soon sighted iceblink. We also met a nest of 8 to 10 whalechasers and the British whale factory BALEANA; noted two totally flensed whales on the BALEANA, complete in outline, and all bright red and white. These whale factories are ugly ships, but very efficient looking. There was a great structure near the stern which resembled nothing so much as a complete cement factory. Steam was issuing from odd places. As the ship passed we noted the stern ramp, and above it a respectable appearing aircraft hangar. We've sighted no whaling aircraft. I couldn't help feeling sorry for whales after seeing this floating abattoir.

We turned westward upon sighting pack shortly afterward, looking for an operating area. Planes are all equipped now with skis, boots, crampons, mukluks, sleeping bags, tents, etc., received from PHILIPPINE SEA. The question came up - How to teach naval aviators to use skis? The aviators simply briefed themselves on all this new equipment from our library of books by Antarctic explorers, plus a few Army Training publications. But one thing was brought out: anyone flying in the Arctic, to be thoroughly prepared for it, must have not only food and equipment, but the know-how to use them. I would recommend that a course of pre-instruction include the use of a large enclosed space, in more temperate and accessible climes, which could reproduce every feature of the rawest Arctic weather, including bitter

cold and wind, from darkness to blinding glare. Then throw these
aviators in there for a straight 24 hour stretch with this equipment
and let them fight their way through - the comfortable and safe way.

Now that our pilots are well briefed, I instructed them, (on
the basis of what we've seen and read of the ice-cap), to start for
the coast at the earliest opportunity after a forced landing, if high
on the ice cap, leaving definite signs and direction of their departure at the wreck. My reasons for this are: (1) The Central Group is
too far away to assist in rescue operations from here to the west (2)
They would have to trek to the coast anyway, and the sooner the better
(3) Winter is approaching (4) If they had a forced landing it might
be weeks before they would be found, and they might as well keep
moving and make it easier to find them, being nearer the coast. The
only disadvantage in this procedure is the difficulty of finding a
party on the ice cap, but if they were to head due north from the
crash, they'd be relatively easy to find. They have recognition equipment and radio - and their morale would be good!

The next day was much better, a beautiful day, just scattered
clouds, and we found an excellent and large ice bay at 0700. Both
planes were in the air by 1000, each with 2200 gallons of gas. Wind
was WSW all day, 12 to 20 knots; temperature dropped to 24°.

CURRITUCK compensated her compasses during the day, and tested
her 5" battery, including successful 7 gun salute to no one in particular, but in preparation for our liberty port a month hence. HENDERSON
reported excellent ice bays to the westward of us. She fueled to the
hilt from CACAPON, who is now almost on weather station. HENDERSON is
on one engine, because of a condenser leak. They passed the British
whaler ARISTOPHANES during the night, headed east.

Received dispatch from TFC indicating his great interest in
the landing field site, discovered by Lt. Kreitzer at 109°E, and wants
all possible data. He can't send us an icebreaker now to get in there,
but might be able to after Little America is evacuated. If future
operations are desired now would be the best time to investigate it.

I ordered HENDERSON to send her position, course, and speed
when notified of impending flight operations so that planes could use
her position for homing or positioning.

Some confusion cropped up between the ship and the planes
today. Each day of flying I issue missions for one plane or for two,
specifying the priority of importance of missions. Usually planes are
ordered primarily to map the coast, and if unable to do that, to get
certain inland sectors up to the 8000' contour, with flight lines 60
miles apart (3°of longitude in this area). Today Baker One was to
map the coast to maximum westward with an inland segment as alternate.

Baker 3 had a small coastal sector plus an inland one. He weathered up and requested permission to change mission. I gave him a new sector and part of Baker One's coast to map, and then ordered Baker One to trace the northern limits of the Shackleton Shelf Ice on returning from the west. It was all finally accomplished with some duplication. There happened to be so much of interest to shoot that any duplication won't hurt. This again illustrates the difficulty of changing missions in the air.

By 1848 both planes were on deck. It was just too late to send out a third plane, considering the large area covered today and weather over the continent. Baker One followed the east cliff of the Shelf Ice in to the coast, discovered a 20 mile square area of brown conical hills, with little ice; large lakes of pea green, dark blue, chocolate, and light green water. Since no smoke was sighted all this is apparently caused by hot springs. They got some good colored photographs. B-1 also flew west and found Mt. Gauss right in position but most of the coast between the Shelf and this mountain is shown considerably out of position. A new glacier was discovered at 88°E. The Davis Sea was open but loose pack blocked the entrance. They saw an iceberg estimated 10 miles long. The pilot talked to the HENDERSON by VHF and used ADF on her. Colder temperatures are gradually increasing gas consumption. Pilots experienced some large wind shifts.

Baker 3 found DENMAN Glacier area quite different from that on the chart; found new nunataks east of there along the coast; went inland 75 miles to ice cap altitude of 6000'; found some 5000' mountains near the coast, and delineated new coastline to the east of the Shelf Ice.

I received a dispatch from the flagship asking for more information on our PBM flights. The flights have aroused keen public interest. So, getting publicity minded we dug up a young enlisted news correspondent who heretofore had carefully kept his light under a bushel. He began to interrogate the crews and brought the results in to me (at 0330) for release. From then on we had one eye glued onto our new public and moved into the fourth estate. (Upon completion of the expedition, I was much surprised to learn that our doings were of interest to anyone besides CTF 68. We got very little from the daily press news).

The ARISTOPHANES passed us to northward, headed east, in the late afternoon.

This has been a fine day.

Underway at 0000 Wednesday 12 February at 15 knots, moving west for the next area. Decreased visibility slowed us down at times. The sea was fine, but we ran into fog, and the ceiling dropped to the masthead. Apparently we were under some influence of the Shelf Ice, just to south of us. HENDERSON reported bad weather, fog, and snow, but water smooth as a mill pond. No flying today but prospects looked good for tomorrow.

Several bubbles of Cp (Polar continental) air broke off during the last few days in this locale. This caused some weird looking weather maps and gave our rain-prophets some bad times. There was no new low in sight to the westward. In fact, we're beginning to think this is a fine flying area. We passed one beautiful ice bay after another.

I told the AO and DD to move west at speeds up to 12 knots and to keep station on us. I have stationed the AO 400 miles northwest of us now, the DD is remaining 300 miles west. The Task group was instructed to keep whatever local time desired.

I sent a dispatch to TFC today giving a general plan for future operations. I plan to move westward at a good clip to 50°E, arriving there by 17 February. The primary mission will be to map the coast, getting the interior only if really good conditions exist and not to delay our movement. Then I shall return eastward at 150 miles per day to obtain continental penetration, re-photograph poorly mapped coastal regions, investigate Kreitzer Bay at 109°E, and arrive at 150°E by 7 March at which time depart for Australia. This plan offered the advantage of moving east with good weather, and allowed better judgment for departure from Antarctica. I also laid out my ideas on penetration of the continent.

This dispatch crossed an information dispatch from TFC mentioning a date for discontinuance of operations of 1 March, at which time this group was estimated to be at 50°E. We were instructed to conduct operations primarily to get the coastline; conserve fuel to maximum so as to reduce buying it in foreign ports; reduce number of fuelings to give the longest possible interval. TFC recommended that we arrive Sydney, Australia, on 14 March for 6 days visit.

By now the CACAPON was riding high, as she'd gotten rid of much cargo. Her present load consisted of 36136 barrels of black and 6646 of diesel. According to my best computations, we would burn 42000 gallons a day for 30 days and arrive in Sydney with just about reserve fuel, without burning the diesel oil.

Thursday the 13th: At 0700 we found an excellent operating area. The fog was patchy, but the aerologists said it would lift. The other two ships were in the clear. A "bubble" had broken off and was north of us. At 0845 Baker 3 was airborne, myself as passenger, with 2400 gallons. We flew into fog patches almost immediately upon take-off. We flew right up through fog layer, just after take off and then learned that the vacuum driven instruments were not functioning properly! We flew north for 50 miles to check our weather. It got clearer, as forecast. At 1030 Baker 1 which was waiting for our weather recco report, was airborne.

Baker 3 attempted to map the coast from 88°E to the westward, however, the coast was souped in and we headed south along 88°E passing Mt. Gauss close aboard. We photographed inland to the 8000' contour, at 69°-16'S, then headed west to 85°E, then north to the coast, swinging in to investigate and photograph a large nunatak 800' high somewhat between our two tracks. This nunatak was dark red and looked like sandstone or granite. It was picked up on the radar 20 miles away, and as we got closer the radarman noted two other blips nearby. When we got there we found what appeared to be rough spots in the otherwise smooth ice cap. From this we surmise there was some ground just under the surface. This indicated the value and future possibilities of radar in searching similar surfaces, in conjunction with magnetometer surveys.

My impression of the ice cap from an airplane is not startling, but it may be interesting. The surface is apparently quite smooth, but closer inspection indicates the ubiquitous sastrugi or long rolling snowdrifts in a SE-NW direction, which can make travel across them so miserable. Nearer the coast the cap is broken up into faintly discernible crevasses and ice falls, and the radar altimeter indicated broad and shallow valleys, or steps, over the entire surface. Around the nunatak's northeast corner was a large and deep pocket cut into the ice, caused by winds eddying around the rock slope above it. The horizon was relatively clear today but it was still hard to discern, as the sky appears yellowish-white as it approaches the ice cap. The sky itself was a simple matter-of-fact blue, without a cloud in it. The entire scene, you might say, was one of absolute and complete desolation - blue above, white below - period. The vastness of it all approaches the beauty of a desert or an open expanse of sea. My only thought was "May I never have to take a walk down there". While we can't say we photographed all this area, its' a cinch nothing important escaped us for 30 miles in any direction, as we ran our cameras about half the time. The return to the ship was uneventful; the coast was still covered.

Asked HENDERSON for straight information, from official sources, as to his "minimum fuel" situation and reasons therefore, in order to estimate properly his fuel situation. He replied that 85000 gallons was his minimum for safe operations, and this included ballasting all possible tanks. This is his lowest except in "extreme" emergency, when he then sacrifices his stability. He already ballasts tanks as emptied, as a routine procedure. It seems strange that a man-of-war can't go under 40 per cent of his fuel without running into extreme danger, even with ballasting.

I sent a dispatch to Hydro asking for information on how we could get weather broadcasts of Prince Edward, Kerguelen, and St. Paul's Islands, all in the South Indian Ocean; also frequency and time of schedules between these islands and the major broadcasting station. "It is urgently required for current operations".

Baker One, flight 21, flew over Drygalski Island (which souped up but was detected by radar altimeter under the clouds). He photographed south along 91°E to 69°S (the 8300' contour) then east to 94°E, and north to coast. He then flew eastward to get a strip of coast previously missed, and on this flight saw mountains on the southern horizon - probably 100 miles south. He then flew to what the flagship called "Bungers' Oasis" and, (as he later said) was "coaxed" into landing on one of the lakes by his crew. This event started quite a disturbance in the publicity line. We could not yet discern its news value - and scientific importance. More photographs were obtained, on the water and in the air. The rest is well known. By the time the furore over this simple piece of real estate had built up, I was rather glad that we had gotten as little information on it as we did. Now many people will be able to dream up all manner of ideas and schemes in connection with it, without having to be disappointed to learn later that there were no palm trees, Dorothy Lamours, and hungry fish within its boundaries. It formed a sort of release from all the other pessimistic world reports. All planes were aboard by 2000.

Clocks were set back one hour today to zone time (-)9.

At 2015 we were underway to the westward at 15 knots.

From operations to date, it is apparent that if the Navy is to operate extensively in Arctic regions, new terms will have to enter the vocabulary of the naval officer. An HO138 for arctic naval operations is necessary. The General Signal Book will have to take ice into account. Tactical publications must be reviewed in this new light. The simple subject "effect of pack ice and icebergs on naval strategy and tactics" would be a neat little project in itself.

The aerologists' crystal ball said "no flying for 36 hours." and we commenced our fast run to the west as planned. A low was beginning to take shape ahead of us. We're now in new frontiers. Not too much is known of meteorology in this area. "Is the MacKenzie Sea another low-collector like the Ross Sea?" is our biggest question among many others.

Friday 14 February, we steamed westward at 15 knots, when conditions would permit. CACAPON sent a dispatch in the middle of the night, worrying about hitting bergy bits in the dark, and wanting to know if he should maintain his present latitude. (I had pulled him south in yesterday's operations because I wanted my auxiliary seadrome closer considering the fog patches, "pulling in the ends"). I answered - in the night also - instructing him to take station 400 miles northwest of me, and to make up distance lost when visibility improved, that safety came first. I then issued instructions to both ships on how to move west, with the CURRITUCK as a guide. Our "fleet" really covered a lot of ocean area.

We ran into fog patches in the morning, but it cleared nicely in the afternoon. After dinner tonight we encountered the heaviest concentration of icebergs thus far; they simply covered the SG scope. There was a slight "corridor" on bearing 315°T, and that was where the wind was from. We then ran right into our densest fog. We eased along at 5 knots. Then we got an RDF on an unknown ship (I believe on 500 Kcs) behind us to the east and later picked it up on the radar, out of the innumerable bergs, so the CURRITUCK commenced fog signals. I felt sorry for whoever it was in this mess without radar. These bergs were much more weathered than previous ones and were breaking up into bergy bits. No large tabular bergs were seen. Some were very streaked with dirt and old ice, and most of them had capsized. We made 5 to 10 knots all night on southwesterly courses dodging bergs. HENDERSON reported crossing the Antarctic circle (entering the MacKenzie Sea) and that their morale was up 100%. There should be more and easier circles to cross. I was surprised that the pack was open that far south. It begins to make operations in that area begin to appear more feasible - weather permitting.

On Saturday the color of the water had changed to a distinct green, and it remained green with all sorts of light conditions and weather. We made 15 knots most of the day, even with occasional fog, snow and rain. The HENDERSON was in heavy fog, and I warned her not to get caught in the ice again - in that fog. The cause of this fog was not quite understood. We did know that the "old" low that might have given us good flying in this area had disappeared, and a new one had appeared without warning out of the northwest.

Hydro answered our plea for help on South African weather giving us no assistance, and suggested we contact Capetown. However, CNO has told us not to contact shore stations regarding weather. TFC asked for more information on "Bunger Oasis" and we exhausted every last drop of information we had on it, just remaining within the realm of truth.

Radio communications with TFC were out for 18 hours, apparently due to interference, distance, and much land (ice cap) between us, - not an ionospheric storm.

I told the destroyer that heavy weather was headed this way; and instructed her to get out of that ice pack and low visibility and to prepare for a gale. An hour later came the reply that she was riding out a heavy sea.

Meanwhile we had been making much preparation to send a size-able expedition over to Bunger Oasis upon our return eastward. We had scouted the task group for any person with geological experience, for flora and fauna experts, etc. We were getting the entire scheme shaped up to explore the several lakes using rubber boats with out-board motors, a rock sampler, a portable fathometer. Emergency recall signals, leaders, etc., had been designated. We were getting a bit interested ourselves, now.

Clocks were set back to minus 8 zone time on 15 February.

CTG 68.3 was dunked again, transferring between ships. It indi-cates that exposure suits should be used for transfer operations and all work over the side in very cold water areas. The CURRITUCK's crew has been well sermoned on falling overboard; I'm glad to see the stout lifelines on this vessel.

Sent a dispatch to BuAer describing our two helicopters' repairs, and asking for comments, if any, before sending these planes on distant missions. Our inexperience along these lines, and the price of carelessness, made us forget our pride in self-sufficiency.

The seas are getting rougher by the hour. The wind reached 35 knots from NE, the barometer dropped from 29.65 to 28.46 and the temperature rose from 33 to 36°F. The ship rolled 19° once, with a staccato of broken china. However, it was still quite comfortable. We were on a collision course with the center of the gale, but strangely enough, as our glass dropped precipitately and we were right in front of the center, the winds were much less than those experienced by the DD and AO who were 200 to 300 miles further out than we. Since there was a slight chance of flying tomorrow afternoon, I ordered the CURRITUCK to close the pack by noon tomorrow, making maximum westing meantime. If we can lick the swell....

By noon Sunday 16 February we were at 65°-09'S 67°-13'E. We had passed right through the eye of the storm and out of the western side of it. We encountered low winds, but a confused sea, caused some uncomfortable rolls. Meanwhile the speed of HENDERSON had been held down to 9 knots while we barrelled along at 15 and we had passed her, 60 miles to northward. CACAPON was fighting a force 7 to 8 wind and heavy seas, and also fell well behind her position. Her value as a weather station had fallen off considerably, (No fault of her own as in her latitude it was much rougher than in ours). The low had stalled and was filling up, and we could not fly under the existing conditions.

Held a conference of senior pilots, photographic and aerological officers on coming operations. Explained the priority of
operations with the coast coming first, and trying to learn the char-
acter of the interior at least 100 miles inland. We had expended
only 57% of our tri-met film. Therefore, we could afford to be a
little extravagant and change film magazines at more opportune times
during flight instead of waiting for the end of the magazine, and thus
avoid breaking up good photographic runs at the wrong time. It was
also decided that planes would carry extra film and rewind magazines
in the air, as we had insufficient magazines to properly outfit two
planes at once. Also directed pilots to start using and relying
more upon magnetic compasses, since we were quite distant from the
south magnetic pole - just in case they're caught under an overcast,
and need magnetic courses.

At 1215, flying was impossible locally, so we changed course
due west to clear the ice pack off Cape Borley on the Kemp Coast.
Clocks were set back one hour to zone time (-)7.

At 1838 our CQM figured we were exactly 180° from the turn-
stile on the nickel ferry in San Diego.

I told the DD to be prepared to fuel from us tomorrow as
she was now quite close to us and this would not delay operations.
It would also save another fueling later from the CACAPON.

At this point there arose some confusion in communications
with the Flag. The original dispatch outlining our present scheme to
run west to 50°E longitude had been inadvertently filed by the MOUNT
OLYMPUS, while TFC had shifted his flag (but not administration) to
the BURTON ISLAND. As a result, he was ignorant of this plan, its
changes, and its sweeping movements until an attendant matter was
brought to his attention. At this point our plan was "un fait accompli".
While he did not approve this deviation from the original plan, he
nevertheless released us from any culpability and praised our past
work. We realized that this had better be a darned good idea!

By nightfall the wind had settled down to 25 knots from east,
and we were definitely west of the low. We decided to shop around for
a good operating area and find some nice cold fresh air, right off the
continent. We kept running westward. The barometer was 28.60 and
rising.

TFC told TF 68 to be sure that no one got caught in the ice
pack during the remainder of the operations. We echoed his thought
on the matter. Some good bull sessions were used up wondering what
we'd do if we were faced with the prospect of a winter in the pack.
For instance, we would throw overboard all ammunition and other
spare gear, carefully fill all wing tanks with water (also the bottom

tanks and perhaps magazines) and allow them to freeze, thereby strength-
ening the ship against ice pressure to prevent rupturing the hull.
That would mean the elimination of extensive heat in the boiler and
engine spaces. We'd evacuate all the excess crew by helicopter or
what not, and keep just enough to fight the ice and get out in the
"spring thaw".

The MERRICK, with no rudder, and NORTHWIND are fighting out
an 80 mile gale.

At 1100 Monday 17 February we had our first glimpse of the
Antarctic continent, when we sighted Proclamation Island, and the
ice cap and mountain ranges of Kemp Coast, from over some 40 miles
of heaving pack. This is the first land sighted visually since we
passed through the Tuamotus in mid-December.

The wind continued from SE; a solid overcast came down to
700' by midnight. The weathermen said the present 30 knot wind would
decrease on the other side of Kemp Coast promontory; that this head-
land acted as a funnel to the prevailing easterly wind. So we continued
the fast westerly run all day. Sure enough, at 1300 the wind abated and
was down to 15 knots by 1500. But now the brash ice - and occasional
floes - extended well out to sea. There was also a NE swell, plus one
from NW, plus wind chop from SE. A few testing lay-to's disclosed an
occasional $3\frac{1}{2}°$ roll. Finally any thoughts of operations were given
up today.

Passed a large ice floe which was almost pitch black throughout.

At 1830 picked up HENDERSON on radar, astern of us, and soon
she was alongside and fueling from the CURRITUCK. Issued instructions
to the C.O. by fueling telephone for operations in the immediate future.
I learned that he had encountered no ice pack during his meanderings
in the MacKenzie Sea. It was really open! Fueled on course 320°T
(down-wind) at 6 knots; completed at 0041 and sent the destroyer on
mission assigned. Sunset was at 2347 and sunrise 0754; the nights are
steadily getting longer and blacker.

On Tuesday morning the CACAPON reported having fine weather -
the first in a long while. She's had a rough "summer" of it.

We kept heading SW at 5 knots, rounding Cape Ann, remaining
near the pack, ready to operate at dawn. It looked good, but the
remainder of the day was spent in trying to lick the swells, brash,
snow, etc. It was very disheartening. Our view of the continent
yesterday whetted our appetites for further exploration. Open sunshine over the pack towards the shore still showed under the overcast.
At 1700 we secured from a continuous flight condition II; the "wedge"

RESTRICTED

had sneaked past us somehow and was now to the east. It passed us
unnoticed, due to local weather effects. This seems to happen when-
ever we are near the lee of a large promontory; it happened at Budd
Land; now funny things are happening here too...and now, faint signs
of another low coming from the west.

In addition, we note with misgivings that HO 138 mentions the
heavy N or NE swell all along this section of coast, but we did'nt
take it too seriously, for there's no reason for more swell here than
elsewhere.

In the afternoon we lay to near 65-43S and 49E, in a slight
ice bay, rolling 3°, in good visibility and a solid overcast; we
should have been flying. About 2200 the weather map showed the
possibility of the wedge stopping to the east of us. We got underway at best speed to chase it.

Next morning we were steaming NE to round Cape Ann, looking for
this wedge. At sunrise we saw that the weather was not good. Lay to,
scratching our heads. Later, eased slowly south to look for a lee. By
sunset - back where we started from. The steady NW swell prohibits
hoisting; otherwise, it is excellent flying weather.

Kemp Coast is on the radar; determined current here at 222°,
¼ knot.

By sunset first signs of the low appeared locally; barometer
steady, but getting snowfall, and visibility deteriorating.

TFC orders us to map coast to westward to limit of safe operations before moving eastward, then fill in gaps coming east. He said
the oasis investigation is merely incidental, not to interfere with
coastal mapping; its use is for a possible future base of operations;
termination of operations depended upon operating conditions; and that
we are not committed to a date for visiting Australia.

Proceeding slowly westward along the pack, looking for a lee.

At 0630 Thursday morning we headed north, at 15 knots, to see
if swells might possibly decrease further from the pack. It was another
beautiful day for flying. Both of the other ships reported slight seas
and calms. The on-coming low doesn't seem to be doing much to us so
far unless it causes the NW swells.

We rolled just as much 100 miles north of the pack as anywhere
else. So we decided to head SW to 35°E, where HO 138 hints at a large
collection of bergs and a sharp turn of the pack - which might give us
a lee. I sent a dispatch to TFC explaining the swell situation - as

much asking for help as trying to alibi for recent lack of flying results.

It remained good weather all day. We are north of the east-west Antarctic front (the boundary between the polar air mass and the relatively "warm" maritime air mass). Hardly a sign of a breeze all day.

In the afternoon CURRITUCK tested the HO3S with 3 hovers for each pilot, with crash boat standing by in the water. Some bugs came to light; by tomorrow should have final test flight.

At 2200 cloud formations to southward were noted - the Antarctic front. It looked just like a tropical front, even to great vertical developments of cumulus, anvil and all. Took pictures of it, just to prove it.

Friday 21 February we steamed on course 230 all day at 15 knots, looking for that lee to eastward of Gunnerus Bank. At 1258 we crossed the Antarctic circle for the second time, at 37-53°E. Set clocks back one hour to (-)6 zone time.

TFC says if sea conditions don't improve within 24 hours, to move east.

At this time the necessity of weather information from South Africa, which was now getting to the northward of us, was forcibly brought to our attention. We accidentally intercepted weather reports from some sort of "Antarctic Weather Service" from a South African station. Apparently forecasts were made for the benefit of Norwegian and British whalers, from the whalers' reports. This forecast gave daily positions of lows passing through our area from as far west as Greenwich meridian, and gave their rate of movement. We found this data of some use in calculating chances of operating. No small bit of information is too unimportant down here. We often wished our weather service were more complete, our maps more extensive in area, and that we could exchange all manner of meteorological data with the several whalers in the Antarctic with us. I'm sure they would have willingly allowed us in on their circuit, as we had more to give than they did, and we were not competing with them - i.e. - no American whalers are operating in the Antarctic.

I asked the Scripps Institute oceanographers in the CACAPON for their opinion of this swell - where does it come from, why, etc. In reply they didn't feel they could hazard more than a guess, and thought them possibly caused by monsoons, and/or prevailing westerlies. There is also the matter of resonance. Again and again we would stop to test the swell; it would steady down... and suddenly a 5° roll, just when we were about to order "flight quarters".

At 1800 sighted ice blink, much further south than expected. Worked westward, found a big streamer of pack ice stretching to northeastward, which gave some protection from northwest. If the wind would shift so as to hold our stern or bow into the swell, we might be able to launch. At 2300, moved several miles NE and lay to. We were in the "lee of Gunnerus Bank", and there was some protection.

Washington's Birthday was jackpot day in the Antarctic. Our position was 67-42S, 34-15E. Variable light winds from SSW, SE, E, and ENE. Scattered and broken clouds, and excellent visibility. At 0700 we moved in toward the pack. At 0845 Baker Three's APU (auxiliary power unit) failed and had to be repaired before flight. 0955 Baker One airborne with 2600 gallons, flying to westward.

The temperature dropped suddenly from 28° to 19°F, and stayed there most of the day. The boats started having strainer trouble. Eventually all boats except the crash boat froze up; they were hoisted on board for melting. The ice is very hard. At 1014 launched the HO3S for a 1 hour test flight.

We probably place too much stress on the swell in this report. It would scarcely affect carrier operations, but it may, on the other hand, affect amphibious operations. The knowledge of cause, effect, and sizes of swell could stand some research. There aren't very good methods of measuring it, either. Our station ships report calm and smooth, when we get 3 or 4° rolls, several hundred miles down-swell from them. These swells are hardly perceptible to the eye. As they come from several directions at once, they probably do get into phase, build up momentarily and cause the 5° rolls.

By 1220 Baker 3 was airborne, flying to eastward. The HO3S got another hour in the air in the afternoon and is now in full commission. Current is north, .7 knot, rounding Gunnerus Bank, and may explain the large ice pack streamer, miles thick, reaching to NE.

A boating party went well into the pack and captured 3 Adelie penguins, which were crated on the CURRITUCK's fantail. A wood and canvas swimming pool was built for them adjoining the crate.

At 1500 Baker One radioed "Surrounded by high mountains. Having wonderful time. Wish you were here, CAVU WX" (Perfect Weather). He was really doing some discovery work!

A new low was picked up to westward by the CACAPON. We are now between two lows - the first one passed well to the north of us, giving us little else than swells. Meanwhile the swell was beginning to pick up almost imperceptibly here. The sky became overcast. The surface of the sea began forming new ice when the water became calm, and under the overcast, or in the ship's shadow.

At 2112 Baker One was on board, having mapped the coast from 34 to 15°E. He discovered that what has been taken for coast all this time is actually the edge of a great shelf ice, probably larger than the Shackleton Shelf Ice in area. The actual coast is 30 to 45 miles south of the present plotted position. Its presence was verified by radar altimeter. The true coast was marked by ice falls and a gradual rise in elevation. He also discovered a 13000' mountain range, with the ice cap piled up behind it, and glaciers spilling out to seaward through its passes. Another lower mountain range was discovered, and several nunataks. The weather was CAVU the entire trip. He expended 6 trimet magazines. Water froze on the plane on takeoff and landing.

At 2142 Baker 3 was on board. He had mapped the coast in general between 34 and 50E; some bad weather was encountered. He made a single flight line just inland from the coast between 40 and 50°E without seeing the coast line itself because of clouds, but getting radar pictures of it. At Amundsen Bay he photographed the western and southern shores and the mountains lining the edges of this bay, but the east coast and White Island (if existent) were obscured. He encountered heavy icing, climbed on top, and returned to the ship. He also discovered several new glaciers. Returned to the vicinity of the ship, he then mapped Prince Harald coast from 39 to 34°E, although again not sighting the coast line very much due to clouds. By strange coincidence the magnetic compasses on this flight remained within 2° of the grid course for the entire trip - in other words, the magnetic variation equalled the longitude.

As the success of these flight began to shape up, I ordered the DD and AO to steam eastward at 7 knots.

At 2215 we were underway to the NE, along the pack, at 13 knots. Thus, we will gain position on the other ships, who are somewhat to the east of their station. We hope to gain Kemp Coast by Tuesday morning, then reach back and photograph Amundsen Bay and intervening coast.

In hoisting a PBM on board tonight, we took a 3° roll at the critical time of lowering the plane onto the deck. The PBM's wing tip float swung well in between the wings of the SOC -- and didn't touch a thing.

On Sunday the visibility dropped steadily during the day, and snow set in. We left the pack, heading for Cape Ann. By 2000 the wind was 45 knots from dead ahead, and we slowed to 10 knots. The glass hardly moved from 29"00 all day. We are now in a "trough" as a result of the low to the NW, plus the antarctic wedge to the south. Much of the ship became coated with ice from spray and snow. We are in an area of "tightened gradients" - hence the high winds. These winds gradually loosened and wrecked the port aileron of the after PBM - and of course on the wing that projects over the side. Again we must move the plane inboard to repair this casualty with an estimated time of 4 hours.

Monday morning the wind moderated to 30 knots, but it still made rough steaming for us at 10 knots. The other two ships gained position on us due to our slowing down for the storm. This narrowed down our weather information, and illustrated the value of the "art" of stationing and using weather ships.

By 1630 we were headed east. There were signs of our passing through the front.

Learned that Little America had been evacuated.

Tuesday morning we steamed eastward at 7 knots into fairly rough seas. The HENDERSON was ordered to slow down as she was closing too much to be of value to us. Now that we were more or less homeward bound, she was more "eager beaver" than "reluctant dragon". In fact, we all were, somewhat.

Soon it calmed down a great deal; we sighted ice blink and closed the pack to the SE at 1230. Shortly thereafter Proclamation Island, the black mountains, and the ice cap of Enderby Land were in view once more, and the CURRITUCK commenced plotting in mountains by visual and radar, to verify the chart. A new method of surveying land over 40 miles of icepack!

By mid afternoon the weather became perfect. The NW swell died down, but still getting a prohibitive NE one. By sunset this was gone too - and so was the sunlight. Kept steaming eastward along the pack at best speed; in the meantime stopped the DD and slowed the AO. The Kemp Coast - or a mirage of it - was in sight at sunset into the setting sun, out of radar range. At 2320 lay to off the ice pack.

During the night a large iceberg came over the horizon and passed within 7 miles of CURRITUCK without slightest indications on SG radar scope, which was otherwise functioning perfectly. This was one of our major mysteries.

At 0750 Wednesday, Baker 3 was airborne in fine weather. However, all 3 boats froze up within 5 minutes of being water-borne - the temperature dropped to 14°F. It was necessary to use blow torches to keep the boats going. As soon as Baker 3 was gone, Baker 1 was shifted forward and athwartships to repair the aileron. With a great sigh of relief we learned that there was no internal damage, and repair would be simple. At 0932 we were steaming eastward at 15 knots to keep ahead of a low which seemed to be chasing us from the west.

RESTRICTED

Again I had to call HENDERSON, for moving eastward at 5 knots all night after having been ordered to lie to.

The penguins' salt water swimming pool on the fantail completely froze over; we broke up the ice and they hopped right in, got good and wet, then sat around the edge looking miserable.

There was much sunshine today through broken clouds.

Baker 3 was on the radar screen a good bit of the time and we were able to plot in much of the coast within 100 miles of the ship. He went west to 56°E where clouds stopped him, reversed course and mapped the coast to 70°E where he was again stopped by cloud. He used all his film. The plane took on an estimated 300-400 # of ice on takeoff, "making the plane sluggish". He also iced up his static tube which affected instruments for 3 hours or so. The plane was on board at 1610. Nothing startling was accomplished on this trip, as the coast is relatively well known - i.e. - several control points had already been established.

At 1640 again making 15 knots to eastward. All day we'd been keeping "in the Wedge" and ahead of a line of low clouds to the westward. It caught up to us while hoisting B-3 and stayed with us as we moved. However, there was a chance we could keep in good weather.

All planes on board CURRITUCK were now in commission.

At 1600, while lying to, a group of icebergs were noted to be aground exactly where 79 Fathom Shoal is indicated in the British Admiralty chart. These are excellent charts, by the way.

All ships were ordered to move eastward. By now I knew that the only way to keep the AO and DD in the proper weather station was to order them to move at certain speeds and in certain directions, otherwise they'd pass us going east in the rush to reach port. (While this was not the actual case, it seemed so at times to the aerologists, who would have liked them 500 miles out had they had their way!).

Thursday brought continued fine weather, easterly and southerly light winds, temperature from 25 to 20°F, and a smooth sea. It was now 3600 miles to Sydney.

The TFC was back in MOUNT OLYMPUS and heading for New Zealand.

Steamed eastward at 10 knots all last night, at dawn, 15 knots, except in snow. We started chasing good weather as seen from the ship and by 1124 decided the wedge was south of us, stationary, and we headed for it. At 1230 we met the pack, with streamers of new pancake

Annex I-(b)   - 51 -

ice; the wind was 19-20 knots with no swell. We were on or near Fram Bank, in 280 fathoms, and again within the Antarctic circle; our position was 66-40S, 71-27E. The date is Thursday 27 February.

At 1433 Baker One was airborne and by 1516 Baker Three was also in the air. Not too much was accomplished. No coast was mapped. Baker 3 went well inland of his area (southwest shore of the MacKenzie Sea) more than 60 miles from the coast, over solid undercast; the ice cap was found there to be 8000', a new mountain range was discovered as well as another group of small mountains. The tri-met magazines kept breaking down and the static tube froze up on takeoff. The pilot used radar over the ice cap to plot the mountain ranges. The other plane (Baker One) sighted no land at all, but learned that a small or secondary low was located to the east, which caused the eastern shore line of the MacKenzie Sea (his assigned area) to be souped over.

The boats froze up again - but not the crews; they surely can take it!

Plans were issued to AO and DD to rendezvous each other for provisioning, after which the oiler will fuel the tender.

Sighted our largest iceberg today - (7½ miles east-west alone, by radar) well to the southward. The area is full of magnificent bergs, probably stranded on Fram Bank.

The big low was passing to the north of us; we were under the protection of the Antarctic front to our north. We were indeed happy that this MacKenzie Sea area was not a "low collector" like the Ross Sea at this particular moment. Do not understand why we didn't get swells from this low.

Kept moving eastward, stopping only to recover aircraft, which were all aboard by 2134. Sunset was at 2047 and sunrise at 0525 (-6). Tonight we lay to. At 0630 the next morning we started moving eastward, but the wind rose to 23 knots. Still no swell. We estimated that coasts would be socked in until late afternoon.

About 1100 CURRITUCK stopped in the lee of an iceberg to test operating conditions. The berg didn't help too much - just wasn't large enough. The wind rolled over the top of the berg and caused all kinds of variable winds and eddies, to judge by the surface. However, it helped smooth down the chop. At 1650 lay to for the day, north of the pack. Many bergs were around us, the sky was clearing up and things looked good for tomorrow.

TFC ordered us to continue our high speed run to eastward, filling in gaps of coastline if weather permits; at 110°E to discontinue operations then proceed to Sydney via Bass Strait.

CACAPON reported arriving at her rendezvous - but no HENDERSON. Two hours later they met and started fueling. Another case for the RDF. Later the AO reported her gyro failed while fueling the destroyer, but fueling was completed. CACAPON proceeded eastward to meet us; HENDERSON remained 300 miles to NW.

About 2300 a brilliant display of Aurora Australis commenced in a cloudless sky. It showed as a long brilliant streamer, like a scarf of very gauzy material, from a northeasterly direction clear across the zenith to the other horizon, and changing shape every two or three minutes. At the same time I saw the clearest and brightest shooting star I've ever seen.

We were ready to go at the crack of dawn (Saturday 1 March). And as the dawn cracked, the wind unaccountably whipped up to 20 knots and the sky clouded over after a perfectly clear night. At 0410 headed west at 15 knots; the wind went up to 23 or 24 knots. At 0930 the wind was down to 17 knots and we headed for the pack for operations. Baker 3 was airborne at 1150. Baker One developed a defective gasoline pump and could not yet be hoisted over.

The helicopter was launched for a one hour flight in the morning and was flown again in the afternoon.

At 1255 underway to eastward at 13 knots. Shortly after, Baker 3 reported "discovering" another oasis, not as spectacular as Bunger Oasis, but along the same order. However, this was determined, as suspected, to be the Vestfold mountains, already delineated in HO138; it was the first time it was properly photographed, however. The plane got low level photos, but did not land.

By 1310 Baker One was repaired, and at 1507 he was airborne; however, he developed a serious gasoline leak, jettisoned gas, and came back aboard. Then we proceeded eastward again to meet Baker 3. By now we began to get just a little concerned about him. Sunset was at 2040 and he was a long ways off. The aerologists dug up a new one for me - a "precip shield" was moving down from the NW quite rapidly, which would give us 1/8 mile visibility. At 1735 ordered the plane to be back by 1930, and at 1805 told him to return now. Frankly, I believe it was a case where we'd gotten to the end of the season without any big mistakes and we all wanted to keep the record clear. We were beginning to be pursued by the spectre of "what would you do if you had a forced landing away off toward the continent NOW"!

Sent a "well done" to HENDERSON for her aerological personnel who took a rawin in heavy snow, seas, and wind - a difficult task and one which gave very valuable data.

Baker 3's flight was quite productive; the coast was mapped between 70 and 80°E. The "land" between THORSHAVN and SANDEFJORD Bays was actually a 60 X 120 mile shelf ice, and the true coast was at a range of mountains near where the previous flight discovered a new mountain range. The entire flight was in CAVU weather. The SORSDAL glacier was found to be much larger than charted. There is much open water in the south MacKenzie Sea. The coast from 80 to 88°E was all souped over, and the weather was closing in. Baker 3 landed at 1922, on board by 1943.

At 1900 sent the group "Heads up, tails over the dash board, homeward bound". Told the DD to move eastward. We headed north, securing for heavy weather. This was no place to run into a bad gale. We had used up a lot of bright shiny good fortune in the MacKenzie Sea.

During the night we met the "precip shield". It snowed heavily and we had some pretty good winds.

Sunday morning 2 March headed northeast. Began meeting much brash ice and growlers. At 1908 sighted CACAPON, who fell in astern. Issued the plan for our run to Australia. Roughly the scheme was for the CACAPON to take station well to NW; AV and DD to proceed eastward together to 105°E where AV would top off DD's fuel, then DD would continue east at 15 knots. When ordered, all ships would head on great circle course for Bass Strait. The purpose was for the heavy ships to form a weather screen for the destroyer, who would be prepared for a high speed crossing between gales.

The icebergs were pretty thick now and they were breaking up into bergy bits. Barometer dropped to 28.50. Temperature rose from 23 to 35°F. We apparently crossed several currents, as the injection jumped 4°.

Monday, 3 March, steamed east to avoid bergs and brash ice. At 0330 picked up HENDERSON on radar; used searchlight to help her locate us among icebergs. All three ships are now in company.

CTG 68.3 announced he had discontinued operations and was retiring. We still had a slight chance to map the only missing section of coast we could possibly get - from 80 to 88°E. This has been a tough nut to crack.

0800 CURRITUCK commenced fueling from CACAPON on course 110°T, speed 8 knots, dodging bergs and bergy bits. Fog and high winds had been forecast; actually it was perfect. The tender took 401217 gallons of black oil, the highest amount so far. Completed fueling at 1325.

At 1045 RDF'd Norwegian ships to southeastward. I am sold on keeping RDF in our ships.

HENDERSON wants to fuel again; can take 50000 gallons. He
had dumped a lot of "contaminated fuel" overboard. CACAPON called
him - why not use settling tanks or give "poor fuel" back to CACAPON
on next fueling? At any rate; HENDERSON fueled again from CACAPON,
who then departed for her position to northward for the crossing.

At 2000 changed course to southeast to close pack, in case
weather allows us to fly tomorrow. HENDERSON got a condenser leak;
steamed on 1 engine; repaired in 4 hours.

Tuesday, 4 March, and in a bad growler area. These babies
are something to give pause. They're hard to see and can't be picked
up on radar, especially in a rough sea. Searchlights help some if
there is no precipitation in the air. To get punched by a growler
or a floe at 15 knots is no joke; it probably means a hole, maybe a
big one, forward. They give the ship a distant jar at 5 knots. Trying
to make any speed at night, especially in darkened ship, is practically
impossible. Slightly amusing is the fact that the stewards' mates
living compartment is on the waterline, and when we first ran into
heavy brash or pack, it made such a racket in their compartment that
they made an almost dangerous exit for topside.

At 0430 with snow, swell, and signs of a low in the MacKenzie
Sea decided against flying today; headed east at 13 knots. Our noon
position was 62-41S, 94-19E.

We now have another ionospheric storm, with no communications
with TFC but receiving Washington Fox.

The 1600 weather map showed almost ideal conditions for
commencing the run for Bass Strait, although we were still west of
the longitude at which we were ordered to cease operations. Ordered
AV and DD (in company) to commence run at 16½ knots, came to course
080°; ordered CACAPON to make 17 knots. Requested permission from TFC
to cease operation now, giving circumstances.

While desirous of making best speeds, day and night, to clear
the Antarctic, the ships are dogged by having to slow down at night
because of growlers. It was suggested that a powerful searchlight,
located in the very stem of the ship, might be best used to illuminate
the ship's path without blinding the bridge watch and lookouts. Some
research along this line is indicated for this problem, so peculiar
to Arctic areas.

Our course of 072°T is taking us out of the Antarctic all too
slowly; however, the CACAPON is almost out of the ice belt and should
be making good speeds day and night soon.

Communicated plans to Task Group for titivating ship and making respectable entry into Sydney. Hope to anchor in Bass Strait to accomplish this. Ordered HENDERSON to proceed independently at maximum speed of 22 knots to latitude 50°S, on great circle course to Bass Strait, then await me inside the Strait. Discontinued weather reports to TFC. Issued a movement report "from Antarctica to Sydney".

The weather remained excellent; no "screeching sixties" so far. There is not a slight indication of a low to the northwest; it couldn't look better for a fast crossing.

Sent a dispatch to Alusna Melbourne on our movements, with ETA at Sydney. Learned later that this dispatch apparently went from us to MOUNT OLYMPUS (in New Zealand), who sent it to Samoa, who cabled it back to Alusna New Zealand (in same port with MOUNT OLYMPUS) where it died a natural death and was never received in Melbourne.

On Thursday 6 March set clocks ahead one hour to minus 8 zone time. We had some moonlight last night; this allowed us to make 10 knots during the night. Received approval from TFC for our dash across roaring forties; dispatch delayed by ionospheric storm.

CURRITUCK made a successful full power run, claiming 19.3 knots. Sighted our last ice berg this morning at 0500. At 1300 we were on course 056°T; a great circle course changes rapidly in these parts.

TFC requested complete information on our fuel situation, as I was somewhat apprehensive on this matter; I had requested permission either to fuel at Sydney or stop at Samoa enroute U.S., to make sure of sufficient fuel, without having to burn more expensive diesel.

On Friday morning 7 March, after maintaining a good speed all night due to full moon, we encountered a strong north wind blowing in toward a low that had whistled in from the west and passed to the south of us. We felt its effects a very short time, and the wind was soon down again to 14 knots from NNW. Barometer was now 29.20, temperature 45°F. It was now so "warm" that our Adelie penguins were gasping for breath (seemingly); they were placed in an unlighted chill box below decks and seemed much happier. The Antarctic winter had set in suddenly for them.

CACAPON reported her boilers to be in bad shape, and wanted to reduce speed to allow boiler repair and overhaul, and to proceed independently, meeting us outside Sydney. Warned him of approaching storm, now detected to NW; told him to hold his speed until tomorrow. Other two ships will maintain high speeds.

Computed our fuel situation as follows: There was just enough fuel left to get the CURRITUCK to Panama at 15 knots and the other two

ships to San Diego at 12 knots, and be just a little under reserve.
Conveyed this data to TFC. This used the diesel oil.

On Saturday set clocks ahead one hour to minus 9 time.

The low picked up to the west is approaching us at 45 knots.
This is "unfair to Antarctic Explorers". No storm should move that
fast. The wind was freshening from the north by noon. We crossed
the trough and the wind backed to NW, and by sunset we were rolling
under a 40 knot breeze, but still steaming at 15 knots. The low
rapidly passed to southward of us and we are now on course 041°T, to
get away from the center as fast as possible.

At 1720 we picked up the CACAPON on radar, dead ahead; she
crossed to starboard on course 090°, riding along with the storm.
We sent her the CURRITUCK's course and speed. CACAPON interpreted
this as an order to follow us, and at 1900, on course 035°T, she
reported she was taking too much water over the bow, and later that
she had lost her forward starboard life raft. Told her she was not
ordered to follow us; to pursue a safe course.

By midnight we had slowed to ten knots. There was a full
moon again. It was beginning to blow harder all the time. CACAPON
decided not to slow down for a while, for boiler work, but to get
out of this weather first.

At 0630 Sunday morning a cold front passed us from NW, with
gusts to 70 knots. The front was distinctly tracked on the radar as
a remarkably solid mass, a band 5000 yards thick, moving across the
radar scope at 40 knots. It was accompanied by torrential rain, and
the seas increased thereafter. Notified AO and DD of phenomenon.

Now we knew we were in a gale. The winds weren't too high -
40 to 45 knots, but they had a terrific fetch. This storm was
thousands of miles across. Strangely, these gales are not of high
intensity at the center with diminished winds at the edge; almost the
entire area had the same winds. If anything, as we learned previously
the winds might be lighter in the area just outside the eye. These
waves we were experiencing, had 1500 miles of straight open sea, with
an almost unvarying wind direction to build them up.

Fortunately, the destroyer was (relatively) comfortable the
entire time; his winds were consistently 8 to 10 knots lower than ours,
due to his comfortable distance ahead of us. She, as well as CACAPON,
was able to maintain 15 knots all the time. With our planes on the
fantail we had to select a course to reduce roll, keep seas off the
fantail, and yet get out of this blow - and the next one. It was
too big an order. The CURRITUCK rode comfortably at first but she
began to roll, and soon rolled just enough... at 1441 she took a 23°

roll to starboard that loosened the spare PBM on the very stern and rolled it lightly into Baker Three's nose, doing minor damage. Then the ship rolled 32°to port, and over the side went the PBM, leaving the beaching gears, all bent and crystallized, useless, and well tied down, on deck. The deck stayed dry. A few minutes before, 2 youngsters had been in the plane, helping to secure it even more. They were fortunate; the plane disappeared in 20 seconds. The spare SOC float was also wrecked in the ruckus. Most of this was caught by a movie camera held by Marine Warrant Officer Chapel.

By 1445 we were on course 010°T, at 9 knots, and gradually came around to 330°T. This steadied the ship down enough to replace worn out rocking blocks under the beaching gear.

About 2000 we rolled 35° again; slowed down to 7½ knots. It was wonderful to see those waves come in. The ones that did the heavy work formed up before one's very eyes; there was no watching them come over the horizon. They seemed to combine from two different directions and form a series of three or four very high, steep, and short waves, that would form for a matter of a minute or so, then decrease once more, to normal size. They were larger waves than ones I've seen in typhoons in the western Pacific in much higher wind velocities.

Early next morning, more damage was received by one of our other PBM's when the tail beaching gear fittings crystallized and parted. A jury rig saved the plane from further damage. Also the cables secured from the engine mounts to the deck had pulled 3 out of 4 engines out of line. This left us with only one flyable PBM. It seems that the lesson is to be able to cradle PBM's on deck for long and rough voyages.

By 0900 Monday 10 March, the low causing us all our misery had started moving SE again, and winds and seas began to abate. By now we were on course 055° at 16½ knots.

The destroyer rounded King Island and this evening anchored in the lee, in Bass Strait. Ordered the AO and DD to rendezvous and fuel, move east and await us. A storm warning of another low moving toward us was issued from PERTH. We're getting out just in time. Our barometer is steady at 29.60 and the temperature is 60°F.

As a passing observation, it is believed that more study and research should be put into automatic weather reporting stations. They must be made simpler, more complete and more reliable. It's the only way we'll ever really learn the weather in the Antarctic - the easy way.

On Tuesday 11 March, changed to zone time -10. Excellent weather today; heavy swell from port quarter, but riding comfortably.

At 1135 the SK radar picked up King Island at 80 miles. Entered Bass
Strait about sunset. HENDERSON fueled this morning. Received a dispatch from Alusna Melbourne wanting to know our ETA at Sydney, indicating he never received our dispatch of the 5th. Sent a tracer on this.

On Wednesday at 0453 the entire group was formed in column, and
early in the morning sortied east from Bass Strait, proceeded north,
and anchored on a bank several miles off the Australian coast, to clean
ship. While doing this a cold front caught up to us and we had to knock
off titivating. Held a conference of CO's on board to discuss our stay
in Sydney. Underway shortly for that port.

Thursday evening passed British cruiser and 3 destroyers
holding gunnery practice, and exchanged pleasantries.

0800 Friday 14 March entered Sydney harbor, firing 21 gun
national salute. Later fired 13 gun salute to RAdm Farncomb, RAN, in
HMAS HOBART. (Our saluting charges, I learned later, were guaranteed
20% misfires. The salutes were pretty ragged, but we got away with it.
We used 5" blank charges, with much burning cork and not too much noise).

All 3 ships moored in Woolloomooloo Bay; we sort of moored
accidentally, as there were no line handling parties ashore; had to
land our own men to help a few itinerant dock loafers do their work.

Moored at 0915. Alusnas Melbourne, Captain Tompkins and
Commander Moynahan came aboard. The fun began immediately. By sunset
I had called on Admiral Farncomb, RAN (also know as SACAS - Senior
Admiral Commanding Australian Squadron); then RAdm. G. D. Moore, RAN,
FOIC (Flag Officer in Charge) ashore at Naval Base Headquarters.
Shortly thereafter both calls were returned. At 1400 called on Consul-
General, Mr. Neilson; then the Lord Mayor; then Lieutenant-General
Berryman at Victoria Barracks; then Air Commodore Lachal at Bradfield
Park; then the premier of New South Wales, Mr. McGirr. At 1700 a
large cocktail party was held in Hotel Australia by the naval attache.
At this time I learned that the American Ambassador would call officially
on Wednesday, and stay for lunch, with some guests.

Here it is sad to note that two splendid young men of the
CURRITUCK's helicopter crew met instantaneous death this evening
in a motor accident, shortly after going ashore.

Next day, Saturday 15 March, I received an official call
from Consul-General Neilson. Then we both called officially on the
Governor, Lieutenant-General Northcutt. Also today our aviators
received briefing on local flying from Squadron Commander Kingsford -
Smith. (We requested permission to fly; the British said to just go
ahead and fly without asking, so they'll never be embarrassed if
someone else were to ask and they'd have to refuse permission. I
could not quite follow the logic.).

Received sailing orders from TFC on 16 March.

Monday 17 March received official calls from Lieut.-General Berryman and Air Commodore Lachal. Lieut-General Berryman remained for lunch.

Tuesday the HO3S took off, flew to Bradfield Park and flew the Air Commodore and several of his officers in it. The PBM made a JATO takeoff in the harbor. At 0930 received an informal call from Lt. Com. Smith, Royal Netherlands Navy. At 1000 Lt. Com. Powers and 4 officers of the RAN came aboard to get data on how to prepare ships for Antarctic work. Several CURRITUCK officers gave them data of non-classified nature and suggested they request more detailed data from the Navy Department via official channels. 1130 RAdm Moore gave cocktail party to 20 American officers at his mess; at 2000 he gave a dinner at his home for the commanding officers.

Wednesday, I told both Admirals of my intention to get underway tomorrow. HENDERSON fueled from CACAPON (alongside each other). At 1000 all CO's called on the American Ambassador, Mr. Butler, at Consulate-General. At 1130 the Ambassador called on us officially. We had quite a time about the gun salutes which were greatly desired; fortunately permission was denied by the port authorities, as it would have broken many windows of the warehouse alongside, and probably set fire to the stores inside. All went well, apparently, and a luncheon for 14, held after an inspection of the ship and viewing of photographs, went down successfully. At 1700 a cocktail party was held for us by the Governor, at Government House. The helicopter flew again today.

Thursday 20 March PBM flew again in the morning and was hoisted aboard. 1000 received official visit by Hon. C. R. Evatt, representing the premier, Mr. McGirr. HO3S flew again for the Aussies and finally landed on board while we were proceeding down the harbor channel. 1345 the destroyer was underway, followed by the tanker, and tender at 1500. Many messages went back and forth. When clear of harbor formed column and set course to clear north tip of New Zealand. Two negro steward'smates were left behind AOL.

We were unable to fuel next day because of high seas; besides, the tender shouldn't fuel until the latest practicable date, due to her long trip to Panama. In the evening CACAPON complained of "heavy seas breaking over ship, taking green water over bridge", in danger of losing 2 cadavers overboard (in caskets). I suggested he deballast and move caskets to a safe area. This he did and was able to remain in company. At 2220 changed course to bisect course between Panama and San Diego, as this rough weather may continue and prohibit fueling for some time, and I didn't want to take the AO and DD too far out of their way. Nor did I wish to reverse course for fueling.

Fueled CURRITUCK from CACAPON commencing 1022 Sunday 23 March. Upon completion, detached CACAPON and HENDERSON to proceed in company to West Coast.

TFC recommended we try to get to Panama a day early, that is, on 9 April. This will be pushing pretty hard, but CURRITUCK will try.

Crossed the date line at 2348 and repeated Monday 24 March 12 minutes later, which is pretty close timing. Early in the morning of this second date we passed through the KERMADECS, spotting these lonesome rocks on radar. Ran into a thick fog bank for several miles this afternoon.

Here are some thoughts on "the Ideal Composition of the Next Antarctic Expedition":

Composition: 1 CVE, with TBM's tri-met configured, and 2 R4D's, knocked down, for rescue purposes over ice cap. These planes would accurately map the coastline, being always on the radar of either CVE or icebreaker.

1 AV, equipped for passage through ice pack, including steel propellors and protected (anti-ice) belt, with 3 PBM's carrying MAD for long range interior recco; to operate in water inside ice pack.

1 Icebreaker, with 2 helicopters, to accurately benchmark coastline, sound coastal waters; for air sea rescue; horizontal coastal photography; soil samples, etc - and to get AV in and out of ice.

1 Tanker, for fuel, and weather reporting.

1 Fleet tug, for tow in case of damage, and for weather reporting.

And if necessary, 1 plane guard for CVE if she is unable to carry large enough boats for this purpose. Travel of this force should be from west to east.

On 25 March we raised our speed a knot, feeling pretty secure on fuel now. CURRITUCK instituted some very sound fuel economy measures, forgotten since engineering competition was eliminated. CACAPON offered to take passengers or mail from Samoa to U.S., but this was not required by ComNavBase. Our great circle course was now 086°T. HENDERSON fueled from CACAPON. Excellent weather continues.

At 0020 on Sunday 30 March CURRITUCK picked up Cadman Island on radar, 12 miles. This island is very low; no altitude of the land is given in chart or sailing directions.

Sighted MANGAREVA Island visually, distance 48 miles. Radar contact on only strange ship of voyage this morning, 16 miles north.

Monday 31 March HENDERSON proceeded to San Diego independently after a last fueling from CACAPON, whose bunkers are now dry. The CURRITUCK was thoroughly engaged in preparing to exchange personnel and material with PINE ISLAND at Balboa, writing up reports on HIGHJUMP, and preparing ship for inactivation in Naval Base, Philadelphia.

On 5 April corrected movement report to arrive Balboa 9 April instead of 10 April. I received orders for proceeding to Washington from Panama by air. Next day, radar contact on Galapagos Islands toward evening and passed them to southward during night. Crossed equator at 92-30 W. HENDERSON arrived San Diego and reported ComDesPac.

On 8 April launched Baker Three in open sea, with all 3 flight crews, to get in flight time and have plane off the ship for transit of canal. This was our last flight. It was rather strange to see a seaplane tender stop and launch a PBM in a very casual manner in the middle of the Pacific Ocean. It was perfect hoisting weather and the whole operation was "duck soup." The plane flew in to NAS Coco Solo. At 1715, "land ho!" the new way: Pt. Mariato, 73 miles away by radar. CACAPON reported for duty to ComServPac, having arrived San Pedro.

CURRITUCK arrived Balboa 0800 9 April and berthed at Balboa just outboard of the big drydock where PINE ISLAND was changing her propeller. Oversaw exchange of personnel and material which was completed that night, at which time I hauled down my burgee command pennant, making a movement report to that effect, and proceeded to Washington, D. C., via NATS on 11 April.

Another comment on this operation. It was proved many times that information on ships of the group was lacking to this command. This had to be either called for or assumptions made. A complete and up to date characteristic card was necessary, and procured after some delay. It is suggested that a card system be promulgated by which individual ships send out abbreviated cards on which is depicted the current military status of the ship as to her battery, electronics, engineering, etc. This would allow each command to have listed in its card index enough knowledge of each ship, at all times, to plan and conduct operations, even when unexpectedly thrown together with unfamiliar vessels.

ANNEX ONE - (c)

NARRATIVE

CTG 68.3

Task Group 68.3 was composed as follows:

Commander Task Group 68.3
    Captain George J. Dufek, U.S. Navy, 59616

U.S.S. PINE ISLAND (AV-12), Flagship
    Captain Henry Howard Caldwell, U.S. Navy, 61115

U.S.S. CANISTEO (AO-99)
    Captain Edward K. Walker, U.S. Navy, 59561

U.S.S. BROWNSON (DD-868)
    Commander Harry M. S. Gimber, Jr., U.S. Navy, 70077

Task Group 68.3, less CANISTEO, departed Norfolk, Virginia, in company with Task Group 68.1 on 2 December 1946.

The U.S.S. PINE ISLAND was equipped with the following aircraft:

(1) Three completely winterized PBM type aircraft on after deck. Two airplanes were completely assembled and ready to fly, while one PBM, carried as a spare, had its outer wing panels removed for stowage in the hangar.

PBM's were equipped with tri-metrogon camera installations.

Planes were stowed and equipped with two months supply survival equipment, as outlined in detail in U.S.S. PINE ISLAND Report of Operation HIGHJUMP.

The mission of these planes was to operate from the PINE ISLAND, stationed outside the Antarctic Ice Belt, and to fly in to the Antarctic Continent to discover and photograph the Antarctic coastline and continent.

The PBM's were chosen for this work rather than the PBY type, because of superior camera installation, greater load with long range capacity, and superior pilot position for take-off and landing. Their disadvantage lay in their size and weight, which made launching in a sea way with the tender rolling more than three degrees difficult and hazardous.

(2) Two Helicopters.

(a) One HO3S-1 (Sikorsky) four place helicopter with maximum range, 400 nautical miles; specially equipped with ZB (ARR-2) homing radio and ARC 1 VHF voice radio equipment; equipped as land plane; not winterized and not equipped with other special equipment. Stowed on forward platform.

(b) One HOS-1 (Sikorsky) two place helicopter with maximum range, 180 nautical miles; specially equipped with ZB (ARR-2) homing radio equipment; equipped as land plane; not winterized and not equipped with other special equipment. Stowed in hangar.

(c) The PINE ISLAND had a special platform rigged on her bow for landing and take-off.

(d) The helicopters were intended for:

(1) Ice reconnaissance which would enable the tender to enter sheltered waters for launching PBM's.

(2) Effecting landings on otherwise inaccessible islands and land areas.

(3) Air-Sea rescue.

(3) One SOC (Float Type).

This type plane was intended for ice reconnaissance and local exploration flights. It was used to advantage in the Arctic, but it had the disadvantage of poor navigational and radio equipment. Thus, her value in the Antarctic, where there are few or no known land masses in the intended operating area, indicates further reduction of her operational value.

The PINE ISLAND and BROWNSON arrived Cristobal, Canal Zone, 7 December 1946. As the PINE ISLAND could not transit the Canal with her PBM's aboard due to the extension of the wings over the side, she anchored and hoisted two airplanes over the side. These PBM's were tended by the Naval Air Station, Coco Solo, during the visit of the Task Force in the Canal Zone.

Task Groups 68.1 and 68.3 transited the Panama Canal on 7 December, and then berthed on the Balboa side for a three day period of leave and liberty, which would be their last before they received another--more than three months hence.

10 December 1946 Task Groups 68.1 and 68.3 got underway for the Antarctic Continent. The PINE ISLAND and BROWNSON stopped to recover the two PBM's that had been flown over from Coco Solo. The HO3S and SOC were flight tested and found to be in good operating condition, as were the two PBM's.

Launching and recovery operations were ragged. Due to the rapid demobilization of the Navy after the war, and the short period in which to prepare for Operation HIGHJUMP, there were many inexperienced hands in the

PINE ISLAND. It was with a feeling of "Hold your hats, boys, here we go again", that we rejoined formation and continued on the voyage, knowing full well that as in Operation NANOOK, the crew would have to be trained under the worst of operating conditions. There was a date to be met with the weather during the Antarctic summer, and we could not delay longer for training under favorable conditions.

The Group crossed the Equator at Longitude 82° 47' West on December 12th. The usual ceremonies and activities had been held, restricted somewhat by a deck load of aircraft and below deck spaces crowded with stores and equipment.

On the 17th of December the CANISTEO fueled the PINE ISLAND and BROWNSON, then set course to join Task Group 68.1. The PINE ISLAND and BROWNSON set course for PETER I Island to inaugurate operations in accordance with Commander Task Force 68 Operation Plan No. 2-46. PINE ISLAND and BROWNSON were designated Task Group 68.3.

Task Group 68.3 crossed the 40th parallel at approximately 1100 on December 20th. Instead of the anticipated "Roaring Forties", the ships proceeded through smooth seas, clear skies, and fair weather. Moving pictures and lectures of past Antarctic Expeditions were frequently held for officers and men to build up their enthusiasm to the key pitch necessary to conduct successfully the difficult operations ahead. Foul weather clothing was issued, and demonstrations of proper method of dressing for inclement weather were conducted, as well as drills in the use of survival equipment.

(Note: Hereinafter unless otherwise indicated all times will be local zone time.)

As the 50th parallel was passed, much interest was displayed in sighting the first icebergs. A fruit cake was offered as a prize to the first man sighting one. Indicative of modern improvements in Polar exploration, the first iceberg was picked up by radar at a range of 40,000 yards. This was on the 24th of December in Latitude 62° 41' S., Longitude 99° 30' W. This was our first indication that perhaps this was not a normal ice year, as ordinarily in this area in December, bergs may be met as far north as 45° South, while south of the 50th parallel the bergs should be very numerous.

Further, on this day PINE ISLAND fueled the BROWNSON during our first snowfall. BROWNSON was then ordered to take station 200 miles west of PINE ISLAND to act as weather reporting station, emergency seadrome, and to report ice conditions. During the next few days icebergs became more numerous and were gradually accepted as a part of the Antarctic panorama.

During the evening before Christmas, Divine Services were held in the hangar deck, followed by a program of community singing.

The Antarctic Circle was crossed at Longitude 100° 35' West at 0500, 25 December 1946. Continuing on course 180° True the open pack was met at Lat. 66° 57' S., Long. 101° 13' W. The helicopter (HO3S-1) was launched at 1100 for ice reconnaissance and landed on deck at 1200. It was determined that by moving the PINE ISLAND a few miles to the westward into an ice bay and in the lee of a large iceberg, launching of the PBM's would be feasible. Preparations were made for launching aircraft the morning of 26 December.

The first PBM was launched on the morning of 26 December. The wind increased to 17 knots, picking up a choppy sea. One of the boats tending the plane bumped into the port wing tip float, thereby rupturing it. The plane was hoisted aboard and the wing tip float repaired. The weather continued unfavorable for launching, and further flight operations for the day were cancelled.

The weather during 27 and 28 December continued bad with low ceiling and frequent snowstorms.

On Sunday, 29 December, the weather cleared, and at 0500 "flight quarters" were sounded. The first aircraft was hoisted over the side, and just as it was water-borne, a snowstorm began so that the airplane was taken back aboard.

The weather cleared in the late morning, and at noon No. 1 was again hoisted over the side. At 1335 Marine-George One was airborne, and after flight testing, at 1435 departed for the Antarctic Continent on the first exploration and photographic flight. This flight was highly successful, the plane making initial contact with the coast and mountain tops first discovered by the U.S.S. BEAR's airplane on 25 February 1940. The coastline was developed to the westward, and successful photographic runs made. The plane returned and landed at the ship at 2315--time of flight, 10 hours. Plane was refueled for the next flight.

Plane No. 2 departed from PINE ISLAND for the Antarctic Continent on the same day at 1633. This plane made contact with the same part of the coastline as No. 1, and continued development of the area. This plane returned and landed at the PINE ISLAND at 0533, 30 December, and was hoisted aboard. Time of flight was 13 hours.

Plane No. 1, refueled, departed for the Antarctic Continent with flight crew number three and the Commanding Officer, PINE ISLAND, at 0300. Estimated time of flight, ten hours. This was the ill-fated flight that crashed on the Noville Mountain Range of the Antarctic Continent.

CRASHED PLANE

On the morning of 30 December 1946, the weather began to deteriorate. The last weather report from Mariner George One in flight was at 301225Z, and is quoted, "CEILING 600 TO 1000 FEET SKY COMPLETELY OVERCAST OBJECTS NOT VISIBLE TWO MILES SNOW OR SLEET 29.32 INCHES WIND SOUTH 11 to 16 KNOTS".

The last radio transmission made by Mariner George One at 301310Z was, "TRACK REPORT NUMBER SEVEN TRUE COURSE 180 GROUND SPEED 118 KNOTS AIR SPEED 130 KNOTS DRIFT ZERO DEGREES".

As time passed and continued efforts to get into communication with the plane proved unsuccessful, the concern for the safety of the plane increased. It was hoped that the plane's radio had completely failed, a remote possibility, and that the plane would return on time.

Finally, when the plane's estimated time in flight had expired, the following message was sent to the Task Force Commander:

"PLANE NUMBER ONE CW AND VOICE CALL GEORGE ONE CAPTAIN CALDWELL AND FLIGHT CREW NUMBER THREE OVERDUE SINCE 301945Z X ACCORD-ANCE RESCUE DOCTRINE HAVE MADE PREPARATIONS FOR SEARCH AND RESCUE AS FOLLOWS X PLANE NUMBER TWO STANDING BY FOR FLIGHT SOON AS WEATHER PERMITS X PREPARATIONS UNDERWAY TO ASSEMBLE SPARE PBM BT....."

Then came a period of watchful waiting for the weather. The weather was bad. Snowstorms, high winds and poor visibility. If the ceiling lifted to 600 feet and visibility to four miles, a plane would be put over the side in hopes that when it was ready to take-off the weather would be sufficiently good for a try at a rescue flight.

In the meantime we tried to analyze the missing plane's situation, and what led to it. The weather was bad in her vicinity when the radio was last heard. The last message had been sent completely, and then the radio was never heard again. The plane's position was well fixed at the time of last transmission, Lat. 71° 22' S., Long. 99° 30' W., which was near the Antarctic coast. Open water safe for landing in this area had been observed on the first flight, and this was confirmed by photographs. Also, rising from the coast were mountain ranges 1800 feet high with wide open spaces of neve.

We reasoned that:

(1) The plane encountered bad flying weather and chose to land in the open water along the coast and wait for the weather to improve.

(2) The plane attempted to climb up over the weather, iced up, went out of control and crashed.

(3) The plane, flying over the continent, began icing, the ceiling kept lowering, and the plane made a forced landing on the neve. The occupants in this event could very well be alive, and the radio understandably damaged beyond use.

The first case seemed unlikely, as it would be possible to continue communications. We refused to consider the second case, and pinned all our hopes on the third. Events later disclosed that this was pretty close to what happened.

Extra survival equipment attached to cargo parachutes were stowed in the rescue planes. Messages of encouragement were broadcast hourly to the missing crew. Homing signals were sent for the first five minutes of every fifteen. We continued to wait for an improvement in the weather.

On 5 January, the first rescue flight went out in search of Mariner George One. Forty five minutes from the ship the plane was forced back by impossible flying weather.

On 6 January, Mariner George Three took off for search and rescue of the missing plane and succeeded in reaching the coast. The fog was down to the bottom on the coast and it was impossible to fly over land. The sea area of the search plan was covered, which had the advantage of eliminating the larger unlikely area from the search plan. During this flight of 11 hours, an area of 11,000 square miles was searched. It is interesting to note that this plane passed within fifteen miles of the crashed Mariner George One. Incidental to this search, one hundred more miles of unknown coastline were discovered and photographed.

(Note: From Captain Caldwell's diary, "Monday 6 January (8th day). The sky is down on us today. The ice and snow background merge into the fog and overcast without distinction. This is not flying weather. The breeze is from the WNW blowing the fog in from the sea and over us. For breakfast we had a half slice of bread covered thick with peanut butter. We ground the emergency radio like mad for a full half hour and then for the most part just sat around and talked.")

On the morning of 7 January, flight quarters were sounded, but before the first plane was waterborne, a snow blizzard set in. Flight operations were cancelled.

(Note: From Captain Caldwell's diary, "Tuesday 7 Jan (9th day). There is no flying on such a day as this so we have very little to look forward to. Such days really drag out interminably.")

On 7 January, CANISTEO had rejoined from the Central Group and now formed a part of Task Group 68.3. BROWNSON had been called in from her station and CANISTEO fueled both ships. CANISTEO was then positioned 200 miles west of PINE ISLAND for weather reporting and emergency seadrome. BROWNSON proceeded south into the open pack about 95 miles to facilitate aircraft navigation and communication, and to report weather.

During the afternoon of the seventh, both planes were put over the side for test flights. Weather again prevented flights to the Continent. Flight operations secured.

The officers and men had been working around the clock continuously since the day Mariner George One was lost. It could be seen that they were getting jumpy and irritable. Standby status was secured and movies held the evening of 7 January.

As the weather on the 8th of January (Wednesday) was not favorable for flying, holiday routine was declared at 0900. At 1335 flight quarters were sounded and preparations made for another search flight. At 1445 George Three was airborne. An hour later the plane returned, forced back again by bad weather.

(Note: From Captain Caldwell's diary, "Wed 8 Jan (10th day). The weather is still down on us. It is completely overcast with light snow. The air is light from the NW and visibility is 500 yards. We have put in our morning 30 minutes on the emergency radio. It does our morale good just to hear the grinder turning. We had our usual breakfast of a half slice of bread covered with peanut butter. This won't last much longer as we now are in our last loaf of bread. To date we have feasted on the plane flight rations. They are nearly used up and at that time we will be on pemmican alone. Not a very pleasing outlook.

"Kearns and Le Blanc are still improving. Kearns can move his right arm now and he has started sitting outside with the rest of us. He is coming along fast. Le Blanc seems to have passed the delirious stage now. He has full control of his senses and is improving steadily.")

The weather on the 9th started out favorably, and preparations for flight operations began at 0530. At 0900 Mariner George Two was airborne, but landed shortly thereafter due to bad weather, returned to the ship and was hoisted aboard. All during the afternoon it snowed heavily, and we wondered what sort of weather was holding in the area of the lost plane some 350 miles to the south of us.

(Note: From Captain Caldwell's diary, "Thursday, 9 Jan (11th day). Good day today. Visibility excellent, low broken clouds--much blue sky. The only mountains visible to date are off to the west. It is good flying weather here; if only it could be good weather at the ship's position. McCarty and I took a short walk this morning and now we are positive that if we get rescued it will be from this spot. None of us are in condition for any long hike.

"Le Blanc is taking a turn for the worse. We really could not endure much good weather such as this without something happening. Our spirits improve with the weather and this condition will continue until it is proved that good weather here will bring no AID. The wind has picked up to 15-18 knots from the west and we have the emergency radio antenna kite flying. I just finished 30 minutes on the grinder. Our best weather is in the morning. It clouds over and turns definitely much colder after 1700."

On the morning of 10 January, hoping to break the jinx of this damnable weather, the PINE ISLAND was moved to the westward, to position Lat. 66° 30' S., Long. 104° 30' W. In the late afternoon the helicopter was launched for ice reconnaissance. This flight made it possible to position the ship for launching PBM's. It also determined that this was as far south as it was possible to get the PINE ISLAND at this time because of the pack ice. Weather to the south was unfavorable for flight operations.

(Note: From Captain Caldwell's diary, "Friday 10 Jan. (12th day). What a day! I was the first one up and didn't say a word when asked the state of the weather. It was completely overcast, almost; off to the south horizon I saw a very thin rift of blue. I kept watching this blue, called all the others, and within two hours the SE wind had driven off all the clouds and we had CAVU.

"For breakfast we used our last bit of bread with peanut butter. We used the emergency radio and tapped out signals. Found and worked on the putt-putt but without success. Tried to rig a radio receiver with the emergency radio transmitter, but also without success.

"The five of us spent most of the day around our hull opening hangout just enthusing all over about our good prospects and the perfect weather.

"Robbins and Warr took a hike south and the result was additional information that pointed to our being on the north end of Fletcher Island.

"Supper--we had our usual stew but with beets rather than with beans tonight. Everyone ate heartily and between 7 and 8 turned in with the highest spirits to date.")

Early morning of 11 January brought fair weather. No time was lost in launching Mariner George Two, and she was airborne at 0641. Mariner George Two with F.P.C. Lt.(jg) J. L. Ball, USN, departed PINE

ISLAND on search and rescue mission at 0700. This was the first flight in the last five days not to be turned back by bad weather. Upon reaching the coast the plane was to take up the search plan as left off by Mariner George Three.

At 1116 the following message was received from Mariner George Two:

"MARINER GEORGE ONE BURNT WRECKAGE AND ALIVE MEN AT 71-03 SOUTH 98-47 WEST",

then a few minutes later: "FIVE MEN ALIVE BY OUR COUNT."

This was followed by: "LOPEZ HENDERSIN WILLIAMS DEAD. SIX OTHER MEN ALIVE AND ON FEET. PLANE DISINTEGRATED AND BURNED."

Mariner George Two then reported that the survivors were ten miles south of the coast and that along the coast there was sufficient open water to land and take off a PBM. Emergency survival gear was parachuted to the survivors. The trail from the crash to open water was marked, and additional survival gear dropped along this trail. The survivors were instructed to follow the trail to the coast.

Immediately upon receipt of the sighting despatch preparations were made to launch Mariner George Three. Mariner George Three with P.P.C. Lt. Comdr. John D. Howell, USN, was airborne at 1357 and departed for the scene of the crashed plane.

George Two due to low gas supply departed from the area of the survivors at 1620, and at 1750 George Three reported it had sighted the survivors, was dropping supplies and again marking the trail to the coast. The survivors had progressed about one quarter of the distance from the crash to open water on the coast. George Three requested permission to land in the area of the open water near the coastline, which was granted.

At 1835 George Two was over the ship, landed, and was hoisted aboard. The flight crew was interviewed and from the information gained, the following despatches were sent to Commander Task Force 68:

"MARINER GEORGE ONE FIRST SIGHTED BY LONG W.A. CPHM MONROE NCAROLINA ON THIRD LEG OF SEARCH X SIX MEN WERE FIRST SIGHTED STANDING AROUND FIRE WAVING FLAGS AND RUBBER LIFE RAFT X ON STBD WING TOP WAS PAINTED IN YELLOW QUOTE LOPEZ HENDERSIN WILLIAMS DEAD UNQUOTE X SURVIVORS WERE INFORMED WATER FOR SEA-PLANE LANDING EIGHT MILES NORTH AND PLANE WOULD MARK THE TRAIL AND IF MESSAGE UNDERSTOOD TO JOIN HANDS X MEN JOINED HANDS DANCED AND STOOD ON THEIR HEADS TO INDICATE THEY UNDERSTOOD X OPINION OF PLANE CREW NO APPARENT SERIOUS INJURY TO SURVIVORS ALTHOUGH ON TREK TO COAST FIVE MEN WALKED AND ONE RODE ON SLED X

WHEN MARINER GEORGE TWO DEPARTED AT 112220Z SURVIVORS HAD
MADE ONE QUARTER DISTANCE TO COAST BT.....120135Z

"MORE ON GEORGE TWO BRIEFING X GEORGE ONE CRASHED AND BURNED
PARTIALLY X PORT ENGINE 15 FT AHEAD FUSELAGE X STBD ENGINE
IN SNOW AHEAD OF PLANE X WINGS OFF X FUSELAGE BROKEN IN TWO
NEAR FWD BUNK ROOM X FUSELAGE 60 PERCENT BURNED AMIDSHIPS X
TAIL SECTION CRUMPLED X WING TIP FLOATS AND STRUTS SCATTERED
OVER RADIUS 150 YDS X SURVIVORS APPARENTLY LIVING IN FWD
COMPT OF FUSELAGE USING PARACHUTE SILK FOR ADDITIONAL TENT-
AGE X APPEARANCE OF SLED AND PAINTS INDICATES FOOD WAS SALV-
AGED X MANY OBLIQUE PHOTOGRAPHS TAKEN UNDER EXCELLENT CONDIT-
IONS X RADIOMEN BELIEVE NO RADIO EQUIPMENT SALVAGED THAT COULD
BE UTILIZED TO TRANSMIT OR RECEIVE MESSAGES BT.....120149Z

"THIS IS LAST OF GEORGE TWO BRIEFING X GEORGE ONE CRASHED ON
BARRIER OF EIGHTS PENINSULA AT ALTITUDE OF 1000 FEET ON APPROX
COURSE 130 TRUE MOUNTAIN TOPS SIGHTED ABOUT 25 MILES SOUTH OF
CRASH X CRASHED PLANE WAS VERY DIFFICULT TO SEE AND SIGHTING
WAS GREATLY ENHANCED BY SMOKE OF SURVIVORS FIRE BT....120204Z"

At 1920 George Three reported she was on the water, and Lt. Comdr.
Howell and PHOM1 R. R. Conger were rowing toward the ice barrier in a
rubber raft with sled, survival equipment, and food. Upon landing the
survivors were sighted four miles away. The parties met, and then made
their way with great difficulty over rugged terrain to the coast following the tracks left by the rescuers. In the meantime a heavy fog set
in, lasting throughout the night, rendering it impossible to embark in
the plane. Weather at the PINE ISLAND continued excellent.

Early the morning of 12 January the weather cleared along the
Ice Barrier. All were embarked in the plane and at 0819 the plane took
off and headed for the PINE ISLAND. At 1035 George Three landed and at
1120 was hoisted aboard. Medical aid was administered to those needing
immediate attention. Those suffering minor injuries were interviewed,
and the substance of their story was contained in the following despatch
to CTF 68:

"THIS PART ONE OF CAPTAIN CALDWELL AND FLIGHT CREW NUMBER THREE
BRIEFING X LAST WEATHER REPORT FROM MARINER GEORGE ONE IN
FLIGHT AT 301225Z QUOTE CEILING 500 TO 1000 FEET SKY COMPLETELY
OVERCAST OBJECTS NOT VISIBLE TWO MILES SNOW OR SLEET 29.32
INCHES WIND SOUTH 11 TO 16 KNOTS UNQUOTE LAST RADIO MESSAGE
RECEIVED FROM MARINER GEORGE ONE AT 301310Z QUOTE TRACK REPORT
NUMBER SEVEN TRUE COURSE 180 GROUND SPEED 118 KNOTS AIR SPEED
130 ZERO DEGREES DRIFT X ETA MARINER GEORGE THREE 121615Z BT"

"IMMEDIATELY UPON DISEMBARKING FROM RESCUE PLANE EACH SURVIVOR

WILL BE MET WITH A WRITER AND DISPATCH PAD AND AFFORDED
OPPORTUNITY TO SEND MESSAGE TO HIS FAMILY BT"

"THIS IS PART THREE X DRAWING OUT INFORMATION PIECEMEAL X
WILL SEND SOMETHING SOON"

"THIS IS PART FOUR X REPORT OF EVENTS LEADING TO CRASH X LTJG
KEARNS AT CONTROLS STATED X IMMEDIATELY AFTER NUMBER SEVEN
TRACK REPORT CAPE DART SIGHTED ONE POINT ON PORT BOW DISTANCE
ABOUT TWELVE MILES X RADAR UNRELIABLE X AFTER SIGHTING LAND
CHANGED COURSE FROM 180 TO 160 X ALTITUDE PLANE INCREASED
FROM 600 TO 1000 FEET X AT THIS POINT SIGHTED LAND DEAD AHEAD
AND ON STBD BOW WITH CEILING DOWN ON MOUNTAIN TOPS X FLYING
IN NUMEROUS SNOW SQUALLS X TO AVOID FLYING INTO MOUNTAINS CHANGED
COURSE TO 090 X ON HEADING EAST NO DISTINGUISHABLE HORIZON X
SNOW BLENDED UP INTO OVERCAST X MORE FOLLOWS"

"THIS IS PART FIVE X ON COURSE 090 IT APPEARED AS THOUGH PLANE
WERE FLYING INTO CLOUDS X PLANE WAS PUT INTO A SHALLOW LEFT
TURN AND SUDDENLY STRUCK A SNOW RIDGE X PLANE BOUNCED IN AIR
AND FULL POWER WAS APPLIED TO ENGINES X PLANE WAS THEN FLYING
AND UNDER CONTROL X PLANE WAS PUT INTO A FURTHER LEFT TURN TO
SET COURSE FOR PINE ISLAND WHEN SUDDENLY PLANE EXPLODED IN AIR
X TIME ELEMENT BETWEEN STRIKING RIDGE AND EXPLOSION ABOUT THREE
SECONDS X BELIEVE FRICTION OF BOTTOM OF HULL TANK IGNITED GAS-
OLINE IN HULL TANK X PLANE DISINTEGRATED IN THE AIR AS FOLLOWS
X ABLE X BOTH WINGS CONNECTED TOGETHER WERE SEPARATED FROM THE
FUSELAGE IN THE AIR FOLLOWING THE EXPLOSION OF THE HULL TANKS X
BAKER X FUSELAGE WAS BLOWN APART IN THE AIR AND SEPARATED AFT
OF APU DECK X AFTER SECTION HEADED SOUTH X FWD SECTION HEADED
NORTH 40 FEET WEST OF AFTER SECTION X CHARLIE X WINGS STILL
HELD TOGETHER LANDED 80 FEET WEST OF AFTER FUSELAGE IN A NE-SW
DIRECTION X DOG X PORT ENGINE LANDED 16 FEET AHEAD OF AFTER
SECTION FUSELAGE X EASY X STBD ENGINE LANDED 18 FEET WEST OF
WINGS X WING TIP FLOATS AND STRUTS SCATTERED ABOUT WINGS X
VARIOUS PARTS PLANE AND EQUIPMENT SCATTERED OVER AREA 100 YDS
DIAMETER X MORE FOLLOWS BT.....121545Z"

"THIS IS PART SIX X FOX GASOLINE FIRE ABOUT FWD SECTION BURNED
FOR ABOUT AN HOUR X WING TANKS BURNED X BOMB BAY TANKS SCORCHED
BUT DID NOT BURN X ABOUT SIX HUNDRED GALLONS GAS IN BOMB BAY
AVAILABLE AND LATER USED FOR COOKING BT.....121545Z"

"THIS IS PART SEVEN X REPORT OF INJURIES TO PERSONNEL X LT (JG)
R P LEBLANC USNR CRITICAL X MINOR INJURIES TO OTHER PERSONNEL
BT.....121545Z"

"THIS IS PART EIGHT X LT (JG) KEARNS COMMA MCCARTY AND WARR
DESCRIBED POSITIONS OF MEN IN PLANE AND WHAT HAPPENED TO THEM

WHEN PLANE CRASHED AS FOLLOWS X ABLE X CAPTAIN CALDWELL IN
BOW WAS THROWN BACKWARD BY THE IMPACT AND THEN THROWN CLEAR
OF PLANE X BAKER X LT (JG) LEBLANC WAS STRAPPED INTO SEAT AND
WAS RENDERED UNCONSCIOUS BY STRIKING HEAD AGAINST THROTTLES X
HE REMAINED IN BURNING COCKPIT UNTIL REMOVED BY LT (JG) KEARNS
COMMA ROBBINS AND WARR X LT LEBLANCS CLOTHING WAS ON FIRE AT
THIS TIME X ENTIRE PILOTS COCKPIT IN FLAMES X LT (JG) KEARNS
UNFASTENED LT LEBLANCS SAFETY BELT AND ROBBINS AND WARR DRAGG-
ED LT LEBLANC FROM THE BURNING PLANE X CHARLIE X LT (JG)
KEARNS IN CO-PILOTS SEAT AND IN CONTROL OF AIRCRAFT DID NOT
HAVE SAFETY BELT SECURED AND WAS THROWN CLEAR OF COCKPIT
THROUGH WINDSHIELD X DOG X ROBBINS ARM2 AT HIS POSITION BY
RADAR WAS THROWN CLEAR OF PLANE X EASY X ENS LOPEZ AT NAVIGAT-
ORS TABLE KILLED INSTANTLY X FOX X HENDERSIN ARM1 AT RADIO
PANEL KILLED INSTANTLY AND THROWN CLEAR OF PLANE X GEORGE X
WILLIAMS AMM1 STANDING AT FLIGHT ENGINEERS PANEL WAS THROWN
CLEAR BUT DIED FROM MULTIPLE INJURIES APPROXIMATELY TWO HOURS
LATER X HOW X WARR AMMAC2 WAS AT THE FLIGHT ENGINEERS CONTROL
PANEL COMMA SAFETY BELT NOT SECURED AND WAS THROWN CLEAR OF
PLANE X ITEM X MCCARTY CPHOM AT HIS STATION IN TUNNEL OF PLANE
WAS RENDERED SEMI CONSCIOUS BUT RECOVERED SUFFICIENTLY TO DRAG
HIMSELF FROM TUNNEL TO THE WAIST COMPARTMENT AFTER CRASH X
BRIEFING HAS JUST DISCLOSED THAT TOP OF FORWARD FUSELAGE
SECTION WAS BLOWN OFF BT.....121545Z"

"THIS IS PART NINE X GEAR LEFT AFTER CRASH X CAPTAIN CALDWELL
STATED THAT EVERY PART OF THE AIRCRAFT AND EVERYTHING IN IT
WAS UTILIZED DURING THEIR DAILY EXISTENCE ON THE ANTARCTIC
CONTINENT X CAPTAIN CALDWELL CARRIED THE NARRATIVE ASSISTED
BY ROBBINS FILLING IN X DURING THE FIRST TWO DAYS WEATHER
CONDITIONS WERE VERY BAD WITH SNOW STORMS AND HIGH WINDS FROM
THE SOUTH X VISIBILITY ZERO ZERO X ALL SURVIVORS LIVED IN THE
TUNNEL SECTION OF THE AFTER FUSELAGE SECTION X THIS WAS THE
ONLY PROTECTED COMPARTMENT AT THE TIME X ALL MEN WERE INJURED
OR SUFFERING FROM SHOCK X ALL THAT THE MEN WANTED WAS TO SLEEP
OR REST X NO EFFORT WAS MADE TO BREAK OUT SLEEPING BAGS WHICH
WERE NOT USED UNTIL THE THIRD DAY X NO ONE ATE ANYTHING FOR A
DAY AND A HALF X MEN JUST LAY AROUND IN A DAZE DURING THAT
PERIOD X PASSAGE OF TIME WAS NOT REALIZED X CORRECT TIME AND
DATE WAS LATER DETERMINED BY EIGHT DAY CLOCK ON PILOTS INSTRU-
MENT PANEL X ABOUT 312100Z ROBBINS STARTED MOVING AROUND AND
AROUSED WARR X THE TWO MEN HEADED FOR THE GALLEY IN THE FOR-
WARD SECTION OF THE FUSELAGE LOOKING FOR SOMETHING TO EAT X
FIRST FOOD FOUND WAS SOME CANNED GOODS X CAN CONTAINING
APRICOTS THAT WERE NOT FROZEN WAS OPENED AND TAKEN TO TUNNEL
SECTION AND SHARED WITH ALL REMAINING SURVIVORS X EACH MAN
HAD 2 AND ½ APRICOTS X NOTHING ELSE WAS EATEN THAT DAY OR
NIGHT X AT THIS TIME CAPTAIN CALDWELL ESTABLISHED RATION 2

MEALS A DAY X ALL HANDS RESTED AND SLEPT THAT NIGHT UNTIL
FOLLOWING MORNING WHICH WAS NEW YEARS DAY X ON NEW YEARS DAY
EVERYONE EXCEPT LT (JG) LEBLANC AND KEARNS AND MCCARTY GOT
UP AND MOVED ABOUT X EACH MAN HAD A CUP OF HOT SPINACH SOUP X
NEW YEARS DAY SUPPER CONSISTED OF 1 CUP HOT CHICKEN SOUP 1
SLICE BREAD AND PEANUT BUTTER PER MAN X MEN CONTINUED ON RE-
DUCED RATIONS X FIRST FIVE DAYS WERE PASSED JUST RESTING SLEEP-
ING EATING AND SEARCHING FOR MORE FOOD THAT WAS SCATTERED
THROUGHOUT THE AREA AND TAKING INVENTORY OF SURVIVAL GEAR X 90
PERCENT OF THE FOOD INITIALLY ABOARD WAS FOUND AND ALL USABLE
X DURING TWO WEEKS MEN SUBSISTED ENTIRELY ON CANNED GOODS
FRESH MEATS AND BREAD THAT WERE CARRIED IN THE PLANE X 180 LBS
PEMMICAN AND 350 CANS LIFE RAFT RATIONS WERE HELD IN RESERVE
AND USED ONLY EXPERIMENTALLY X MEN LIKED PEMMICAN WHEN MIXED
AS A HOT SOUP X MEATS POTATOES AND PEMMICAN WERE COOKED AS A
STEW AND PRONOUNCED EXCELLENT X EVERYTHING IN LIFE RAFT RATIONS
WAS LIKED X CIGARETTES AND CANDY IN PERSONAL BAGS CONSIDERED
A TREAT X ON THE SIXTH DAY (COUNTING 30 DEC FIRST DAY) TWO 2
MAN TENTS WERE ERECTED BETWEEN THE TWO SECTIONS OF THE FUSE-
LAGE X ROBBINS AND WARR SHARED ONE TENT X CAPTAIN CALDWELL
AND MCCARTY SHARED THE OTHER X LT KEARNS AND LT LEBLANC CON-
TINUED LIVING IN THE TUNNEL COMMA KEARNS ADMINISTERED TO THE
NEEDS OF LT LEBLANC WHO WAS NOT ABLE TO GET ABOUT X CONTINUED
IN PART TEN BT.....121545Z"

"THIS IS PART TEN X THE DEAD WERE BURIED UNDER THE SOUTH EDGE
OF THE WING ON THE SEVENTH DAY CMA AND AN AMERICAN FLAG WAS
ERECTED TO HONOR THEM X APPROPRIATE CEREMONIES LED BY CAPTAIN
CALDWELL WERE HELD WITH ALL SURVIVORS PRESENT X PARA X WATER
WAS OBTAINED BY MELTING ICE WHICH HAD FORMED ALONG THE FUSE-
LAGE X ICE WAS MELTED WHEN MEALS WERE COOKED X CANS OF SNOW
IN TENTS MELTED INTO WATER DURING THE DAY X EFFICIENCY OF
MELTING SNOW MUCH LESS THAN MELTING ICE X NO ONE SUFFERED FOR
LACK OF WATER OR FOOD BT.....121545Z"

"THIS IS PART ELEVEN X THIS PART ON COMMUNICATIONS X THE
GIBSON GIRL RADIO WAS PUT IN OPERATION WITHIN ONE HOUR AFTER
THE CRASH BY ROBBINS ARM2 ASSISTED BY CAPTAIN CALDWELL X THE
ANTENNA WAS ERECTED BY USING THE BOX KITE A PART OF THE RADIO
ASSEMBLY X THIS KITE WAS BLOWN AWAY DURING THE FIRST NIGHT BY
HIGH WINDS CMA IT HAVING BEEN LEFT FLYING LARGELY DUE TO THE
INABILITY OF THE MEN TO HAUL THE KITE IN X A NEW ANTENNA WAS
FASHIONED AND ERECTED BY ROBBINS AND STRETCHED BETWEEN THE
VERTICAL STABLIZER OF THE EMPENNAGE SECTION OF THE IFF STAB
ANTENNA ON THE STARBOARD WIND AND OPERATION OF THE GIBSON GIRL
CONTINUED X CAPTAIN CALDWELL REPEATEDLY OPERATED THE RADIO FOR
MORE THAN ONE HALF HOUR SEVERAL TIMES X TWO RAX TYPE RADIO
RECEIVERS WERE LOCATED IN THE CRASH AREA X ROBBINS CMA BY

CANNABALIZING ONE OF THE TWO RECEIVERS CMA SUCCEEDED IN
PLACING THE OTHER IN AN OPERATING CONDITION BUT DUE TO IN-
SUFFICIENT VOLTAGE FROM THE AIRCRAFT STORAGE BATTERIES THIS
PROJECT WAS DOOMED AT LEAST FOR THE PRESENT X WHEN THE MEN
WERE LOCATED CMA ROBBINS AND WARR HAD FOUND A QUANTITY OF
FLASH LIGHT BATTERIES AND WERE PREPARING TO ADD THESE TO THE
STORAGE BATTERIES IN ORDER TO GET THE ONE RECEIVER ON THE AIR
X ALL OTHER RADIO AND RADAR EQUIPMENT WAS ENTIRELY DESTROYED
X THE AUXILIARY POWER UNIT WAS DAMAGED TO THE EXTENT THAT IN
SPITE OF THE BEST EFFORTS OF ROBBINS AND WARR IT COULD NOT
BE USED X NO COMMUNICATIONS OTHER THAN VISUAL WERE EVER
ESTABLISHED X VISUAL SIGNALS WERE SENT FROM PLANE TO SURVIVORS
BY ALDIS LAMP WITH WHITE LIGHT WHICH WAS EFFICIENT X ALDIS
LAMP WITH RED LIGHT WAS INEFFICIENT X DROPPING MESSAGES WAS
EFFICIENT X BLINKER GUN WITH SUN REFLECTOR WAS NOT USED BY
SURVIVORS PROBABLY DUE TO EXCITEMENT AND REDUCED MENTAL AND
PHYSICAL CAPABILITIES X COMMUNICATIONS WERE ESTABLISHED BY
PLANE SENDING A MESSAGE REQUESTING AN ANSWER YES OR NO BY
ACTIONS TO BE PERFORMED BY SURVIVORS X RADAR REFLECTORS WERE
GENEROUSLY LAID OUT AND THESE COUPLED WITH SURFACE OF PLANE
GAVE HIGH HOPES OF BEING PICKED UP BY PLANE AT SEVENTY MILES
X THE HIGH HOPES WERE GOOD FOR MORALE BUT FACT REMAINS THAT
WITH BACKGROUND OF SNOW AND LAND ANY INDICATION OF RETURN
PROBABLY WOULD BE NEGLIGIBLE. ATTENTION OF RESCUE PLANE WAS
ATTRACTED BY FILLING RUBBER LIFE RAFT WITH PAPER CARTONS CMA
PIECES OF MANILA LINE CMA PIECES OF PARACHUTES CMA SMALL PIECES
OF WOOD AND GASOLINE AND THEN SETTING IT AFIRE X THIS MADE
EFFICIENT PILLAR OF BLACK SMOKE CMA THAT WITH NO WIND CONDITION
CMA REACHED A HEIGHT OF 300 FEET X LT(JG) BALL CMA PILOT OF
RESCUE PLANE WHICH FIRST SIGHTED MISSING PLANE CMA STATED PLANE
WOULD NOT HAVE BEEN SIGHTED ON THAT SEARCH IF SMOKE SIGNAL HAD
NOT BEEN MADE BT.....121545Z"

"PART TWELVE X PREPARED BY MEDICAL DEPARTMENT X ABLE X WHEN
PLANE CRASHED NO MEDICAL SUPPLIES COULD BE FOUND AT THE TIME
X SEVEN DAYS LATER SULFADIAZINE TABLETS AND SULFANILAMIDE
CRYSTALS WERE FOUND X LTJG LEBLANC WAS THEN GIVEN ONE SULFA-
DIAZINE TABLET EVERY FOUR HOURS FOR THE REMAINING TIME X
MCCARTY AND WARR WERE TREATED BY PUTTING SULFANILAMIDE CRYSTALS
ON THEIR LACERATIONS X BAKER X THERE WAS NO SEVERE LOSS OF
BLOOD FROM LACERATIONS AS BLOOD COAGULATED RAPIDLY IN LOW
TEMPERATURES X CHARLIE X ENOUGH FOOD WAS AVAILABLE TO AFFORD
A SUFFICIENT DIET X AVAILABLE RATIONS INCLUDED CANNED HAM
COMMA CANNED PEACHES COMMA SPAM COMMA PEANUT BUTTER AND CANDY
X BREAD LASTED FOR ELEVEN DAYS X ICE AND SNOW WERE MELTED FOR
DRINKING WATER X DOG X RESCUE PLANES DROPPED ADDITIONAL FOOD
X EASY X THE MAJOR PART OF THE MEDICAL SUPPLIES WERE DESTROYED
IN THE FIRE X THE NORMAL AMOUNT OF MEDICAL SUPPLIES AND EQUIP-

MENT CARRIED IN THE PLANES ARE CONSIDERED ADEQUATE BT"

"THIS IS PART THIRTEEN X NARRATIVE AND MORALE BY LIEUT EVERETT
J LE COMPTE (CHC) FORMERLY PASTOR OF CENTRAL PRESBYTERIAN
CHURCH JOLIET ILLINOIS X DIARIES OF THE DAYS PASSED ON THE ICE
WERE KEPT BY CAPTAIN CALDWELL AND BY CPHOM OWEN MCCARTY X PARA
X AFTER THE SHOCK OF THE CRASH WHICH LEFT ALL DAZED FOR FROM
THIRTY SIX TO FORTY EIGHT HOURS THEY BEGAN TO TAKE STOCK OF
THEIR SITUATION X MUCH OF THEIR TIME AT FIRST WAS PASSED SLEEP-
ING OR JUST SITTING X ROBBINS WAS THE FIRST TO BECOME ACTIVE
AND LATER WAS HELPED BY WARR WHO RECOVERED NEXT X ROBBINS BE-
GAN TO RUMMAGE AROUND THE WRECKAGE FOR FOOD X THE PLANE HAD
DISINTEGRATED TO SUCH AN EXTENT THAT MOST OF THE FOOD SUPPLY
HAD FORTUNATELY BEEN THROWN CLEAR OF THE PLANE BEFORE IT BURST
INTO FLAMES X BY ABOUT TWO OCLOCK ON DECEMBER 31ST HE HAD
FOUND CANS OF APRICOTS WHICH HE SERVED ALL HANDS X ON NEW YEARS
EVE HE SERVED EACH MAN A CUP OF HOT SPINACH SOUP WHICH WAS THEIR
FIRST HOT MEAL X AFTER EATING ALL SEEMED TO FEEL BETTER AND
THEIR SPIRITS BEGAN TO RISE X HOWEVER KEARNS LEBLANC AND MCCARTY
WERE NOT ABLE TO GET UP X PARA X FOR THREE DAYS PARTLY BECAUSE
OF BAD WEATHER AND PARTLY BECAUSE OF SHOCK THEY STAYED IN THE
TUNNEL WHERE ALL EXCEPT KEARNS AND LEBLANC WHO HAD SLEEPING
BAGS SHIVERED WITH THE COLD X GRADUALLY SLEEPING BAGS WERE RE-
TRIEVED FOR THE OTHERS PARA X AS THE DAYS WENT BY THE NECESSARY
WORK PROVIDED ANY WHO COULD GET ABOUT WITH ALL THE EXERCISE
THEY DESIRED X SOON IT BECAME NECESSARY TO PROVIDE SOME FORM
OF DIVERSION FOR THE LONG HOURS OF WAKEFUL WAITING X THIS WAS
NOT EASY X THERE WERE NO BOOKS NO RADIO NO CARDS NO GAMES X
PASTIMES HAD TO BE INVENTED X CHECKERS WERE MADE OUT OF CANDY
CHARMS FOR WHITE MEN AND MALT DISCS FOR BLACK MEN X WHEN THIS
PROVED TO BE ONESIDED CAPTAIN CALDWELL AND WARR TAUGHT THE OTHERS
HOW TO PLAY SALVO AND MANY HOURS WERE WHILED AWAY IN AN ENJOYABLE
MANNER X PARA X MOST OF THE MEN CONFESSED THAT DOWN DEEP IN THEIR
HEARTS THEY CONSIDERED THEIR SITUATION QUITE HOPELESS BUT THAT
CAPTAIN CALDWELL HELD UP THEIR SPIRITS X PARA X THE INSTANTANEOUS
DEATHS OF ENSIGN LOPEZ HENDERSIN ARM AND THE DEATH ABOUT TWO
AND A HALF HOURS AFTER THE CRASH OF WILLIAMS AMM TOGETHER WITH
THEIR BUMPS AND BRUISES CONTRIBUTED TO THEIR LOW SPIRITS X THE
SITUATION WAS BETTERED SOMEWHAT ON SUNDAY WHEN THEY WERE ABLE TO
DIG A GRAVE IN THE ICE IN WHICH THEY BURIED THEIR DEAD AND PLANT-
ED A FLAG AFTER BRIEF FUNERAL SERVICES X PARA X THE SEARCH FOR
FOOD BECAME A HOBBY ALTHOUGH AT FIRST THE MEN COULD NOT SPEND
OVER A HALF HOUR AT A TIME OUTSIDE THEIR CRAMPED SHELTER IN THE
AFTER SECTION OF THE PLANE X ITEMS OF FOOD WERE STILL FOUND UP
TO THE DAY BEFORE THEY WERE SIGHTED X PARA X IT WAS DECIDED THAT
THEIR MEALS WOULD BE TWO A DAY COMMA BREAKFAST AT EIGHT OCLOCK
AND DINNER AT SIX OCLOCK AFTERWHICH ALL WOULD TURN IN X PARA X
THEY IMPROVED THEIR SITUATION FURTHER BY SETTING UP TWO TENTS
NEAR THE PLANE COMMA ONE FOR CAPTAIN CALDWELL AND MCCARTY THE

OTHER FOR ROBBINS AND WARR X KEARNS REMAINED IN THE PLANE
AND IN SPITE OF A BROKEN ARM AND OTHER INJURIES LOOKED AFTER
THE BADLY BURNED LEBLANC X PARA X ALL REALIZED THAT THERE WAS
NO HOPE OF RESCUE AS LONG AS THE WEATHER CONTINUED BAD X THE
FIRST THURSDAY COMMA FRIDAY AND SATURDAY WERE BEAUTIFUL DAYS
IN WEATHER OVER THE AREA WHERE THE PLANE CRASHED AND THEIR
PRAYERS WERE THAT IT WOULD MOVE OUT TO SEA WHERE THE PINE
ISLAND WAS WAITING BEYOND THE ICE FLOES X DESPITE THE FACT
THAT THE WEATHER CONTINUED BAD OVER THE SHIP THEY NEVER GAVE
UP HOPE THAT A RESCUE PLANE WOULD BE SENT X PARA X CAPTAIN
CALDWELL SEEMED NEVER TO SLEEP BUT ALWAYS HAD AN EAR COCKED
LISTENING FOR THE FIRST SOUND OF A PLANE X YET WHEN THE
RESCUE PLANE DID FLY ALMOST OVER THEM THEY WERE ALL INSIDE X
THEY RUSHED OUT ONLY TO FIND IT DISAPPEARING FAST WITH NO
SIGN OF RECOGNITION X THERE WAS GREAT GLOOM IN THE CAMP BECAUSE
THEY HAD BEEN VERY CONFIDENT THEY COULD BE EASILY SPOTTED AND
NOW THEIR HOPES FELL X THEY WERE REASSURED BY CAPTAIN CALDWELL
THAT THE PLANE WOULD BE BACK AND DURING THE HOURS THEY WAITED
THEY MADE READY A SMOKE SIGNAL USING A RUBBER RAFT WHICH THEY
SATURATED WITH GASOLINE AND LIGHTED WHEN THE PLANE RETURNED X
ANXIOUSLY THEY WATCHED WHILE THEY WAVED ANYTHING THEY COULD
FIND X ALMOST IMMEDIATELY THEY SAW THE PLANE TURN AND HEAD
STRAIGHT FOR THEM X IN THEIR JOY THEY DANCED AND CHEERED X
PARA X NOW ALL ANXIETY LEFT THEM AND WITH THE KNOWLEDGE THAT
THEY HAD BEEN SIGHTED AFTER 13 DAYS ALL CARE LEFT THEM AND
THEY KNEW THEY COULD WAIT ANOTHER THIRTY DAYS IF NECESSARY
WERE IT NOT FOR THE INJURED LEBLANC X PARA X THEY HAD NOT
KNOWN THE PRESENCE OF CLEAR WATER ABOUT TEN MILES NORTH OF
THEM X WHEN THE PLANE ASKED THEM IF THEY COULD MAKE THE JOUR-
NEY NORTH THEY HELD A CONFERENCE AND ANSWERED YES BY FORMING
A CIRCLE AND JOINING HANDS ALTHOUGH KEARNS HAD ONLY BEEN ABLE
TO LEAVE HIS SHELTER THE DAY BEFORE X PARA X LEBLANC WAS PLACED
ON THE SLED ALONG WITH CONSIDERABLE STORES AND EQUIPMENT FOR
THEY WANTED TO INSURE AGAINST MISHAP ALONG THE JOURNEY OVER
UNKNOWN TERRAIN X DRAGGING THE HEAVY SLED AND HAMPERED WITH
ROUGH GOING THROUGH THREE FOOT DRIFTS AND CREVASSES TWO TO THREE
FEET WIDE THEY PRESSED NORTHWARD X MANY TIMES THEY WERE FORCED
TO TURN BACK BY IMPASSABLE BREAKS AND CLIFFS BEFORE THEY QUOTE
MIRACULOUSLY UNQUOTE AS CAPTAIN CALDWELL SAID COMMA FOUND A WAY
DOWN TO THE LOWER ICE SHELF X PARA X NOW WITH THE GOAL ALMOST
IN SIGHT A HEAVY FOG SET IN AND THEIR HOPES FELL AGAIN OF EVER
BEING ABLE TO FIND THE PATH LAID OUT BY THE PLANE WITH MARKER
FLAGS X PARA X IT WAS AT THIS POINT THEY WERE SPOTTED BY LT
COMDR HOWELL AND PHOM1 CONGER WHO HAD LEFT THE PLANE BY RAFT
COMMA LANDED ON THE SHELF ICE AND WERE ADVANCING TOWARD THEM
X THEY HEARD THE SHOUT OF GREETING BY THESE ANTARCTIC LIVINGSTONS
AND PRESENTLY SAW THEM STANDING A LITTLE WAY OFF AS THEY THOUGHT
X IT HADNT OCCURRED TO THEM HOW FAR SOUND TRAVELS OVER THE QUIET
ICE WASTES X THEIR JOY GAVE WAY TO GRUMBLING QUOTE THATS RIGHT

MAKE YOURSELVES COMFORTABLE AND WAIT FOR US UNQUOTE X THE
SURVIVORS WERE ALL SET TO GIVE THEIR RESCUERS A GOOD BAWLING
OUT BUT FOUND WHEN THEY REACHED THEM THEY HAD BEEN MOVING ALL
THE WHILE X BY NOW THE FOG WAS SO THICK THEY WOULD LIKELY
HAVE BEEN UNABLE TO GO ANY FURTHER HAD IT NOT BEEN FOR THE
TRACKS LEFT BY THE SLED HOWELL AND CONGER HAD PULLED BEHIND
THEM X PARA X AS SOON AS THE FOG LIFTED ENOUGH THEY STEPPED
OFF THE ICE INTO THE RAFT AND SOON WERE ON THE PLANE X ON THE
WAY DOWN SOME OF THEM HAD BEEN WORRIED ABOUT HOW THE EDGE OF
THE ICE MIGHT BE AND IF THEY WOULD HAVE TO SLOSH THROUGH MUSHY
ICE X WHEN BACK ON THE SHIP THEY STILL MARVELLED THAT THEY HAD
GOTTEN OFF WITHOUT GETTING A FOOT WET X PARA X QUOTE TO BE
SIGHTED FINALLY WAS GOOD ENOUGH BUT TO BE RESCUED AND BACK ON
THE SHIP THE NEXT DAY SEEMS ALMOST TOO MUCH TO BEAR UNQUOTE
MCCARTY REMARKED AND WHILE HE WAS EATING FRENCH FRIES AND
STEAK TOPPED OFF BY ICE CREAM IN THE COMMODORES CABIN HE SAID
QUOTE CAPTAIN CALDWELL PROMISED ME ALL THIS WHEN WE GOT BACK
BUT I NEVER THOUGHT WE WOULD BE EATING IT SO SOON X GOLLY HOW
I LONGED FOR SOME GOOD ICE CREAM WHILE WE WERE ON THAT ICE UN-
QUOTE X PARA X LEBLANC TOLD THE CHAPLAIN AFTER THE SHIPS
DOCTOR HAD MADE HIM COMFORTABLE QUOTE CHAPLAIN DURING THIS
EXPERIENCE IVE MET THE FINEST MAN IVE EVER KNOWN COMMA CAPTAIN
CALDWELL UNQUOTE X THEY ALL REFERRED TO HIM AS THE IRON MAN
AND MOST WONDERFUL LEADER X PARA X THEY HAD THEIR LITTLE JOKE
AT THE CAPTAINS EXPENSE X WHEN THEY STOPPED TO EAT FOOD WHICH
HAD BEEN DROPPED BY THE PLANE TWO AND ONE HALF HOURS OUT ON
THEIR TEN HOUR MARCH COMMA THE CAPTAIN SAID QUOTE NOW MEN DONT
GORGE YOURSELVES UNQUOTE AND THEN ATE A WHOLE CAN OF SPAM HIM-
SELF X PARA X AND KEARNS WHO IN SPITE OF HIS BROKEN ARM AND
BRUISED SHOULDER AND SIDE RUSHED BACK TO THE PLANE TO RELEASE
LEBLANCS SAFETY BELT THUS MAKING HIS RESCUE POSSIBLE SAID OF
ROBBINS AND WARR QUOTE I CANT SAY ENOUGH FOR THEIR COURAGE X
THEIR SPIRIT AND INGENUITY WERE AMAZING UNQUOTE X PARA X ANOTHER
SAID QUOTE WHAT WOULD WE HAVE DONE WITH A CAMERA IF YOU WOULD
HAVE DROPPED IT X JUST LET IT LIE WHERE IT FELL X WE WERE
WORRYING HOW WE WOULD GET OUR SLED DOWN OFF THE ICE SHELF AND
A CAMERA WOULD HAVE BEEN NO HELP X THE SAME WAS TRUE OF A LOT
OF THINGS YOU DROPPED X WE DO APPRECIATE YOUR THOUGHTFULNESS
COMMA HOWEVER UNQUOTE X PARA X THE CONVERSATION THEN RETURNED
TO CAPTAIN CALDWELL AGAIN AND HE SAID QUOTE IT WAS QUITE A
WHILE BEFORE CAPTAIN CALDWELL RECOVERED HIS DIGNITY X YOU SEE
COMMA HE LOST HIS TROUSERS AND UNDERWEAR WHEN WE CRASHED COMMA
TORN OFF HIM X IT WAS TWO OR THREE DAYS BEFORE HE FOUND SOME
UNDERSIZED REPLACEMENTS IN THE WRECKAGE X OH COMMA YES COMMA
WE WERE ALWAYS HAVING OUR JOKES X AFTER FOUR OR FIVE DAYS SOME-
BODY FOUND A MIRROR AND WE ALL SAW OURSELVES FOR THE FIRST TIME
X THAT DAY WE DECIDED TO GROW BEARDS COMMA WE HAD NO RAZORS ANY-
WAY UNQUOTE X PARA X WARR SAID QUOTE WHEN I SAW THE PINE ISLAND
IT WAS ONE OF THE MOST BEAUTIFUL SIGHTS I HAVE EVER SEEN X BY

THE WAY COMMA I WOULD LIKE TO LOOK THIS SHIP OVER FOR THE
NEXT THREE WEEKS X AND DONT ANYBODY SAY ANYTHING ABOUT FLY-
ING UNTIL THAT THREE WEEKS IS UP UNQUOTE X PARA X AS LONG
AS THEY FOUND THEMSELVES ON THE CONTINENT THEY WERE THRILLED
AT ITS AWEINSPIRING SCENERY AND BLEAKNESS AT THE HAUGHTY AND
MAGNIFICENT EMPEROR PENGUINS AND WERE THEY SASSY TOO X AFRAID
OF NOTHING X THEY WERE THRILLED TOO AT THEIR FIRST SIGHT OF
THE MOON AS THEY WERE LEAVING THE ICE X BUT THRILLED MOST OF
ALL TO BE BACK SAFE ABOARD X AMID THEIR SHIPMATES WHO THROUGH
LONG DAYS AND MANY SLEEPLESS NIGHTS HAD DONE EVERYTING POSSI-
BLE BY PRAYER AND HUMAN EFFORT TO EFFECT THEIR RESCUE BT.....
130511Z"

"THIS IS PART FOURTEEN X FLORA AND FAUNA X PRACTICALLY NIL X
ONLY FIVE UNIDENTIFIED BIRDS SEEN AT CAMP FOR PERIOD OF THREE
DAYS X ABOUT TWENTY EMPEROR PENGUINS ON THE COAST X ADELE
PENGUINS SIGHTED IN WATER AND ON FLOES X NO VEGETATION X ONLY
EXPOSED LAND SIGHTED WAS THE MOUNTAIN TOPS IN THE DISTANCE BT....
121545Z".

Shortly after the rescue plane was hoisted aboard, the weather
came down like a wet blanket.

Taking stock of the situation to date we found that part of the
coastline assigned the Group had been delineated. We were left with
only two PBM's and two flight crews. CTF 68 Operation Plan originally
intended we should continue to the eastward, but Admiral Byrd had expressed the desire, which was approved by CTF 68, for this group to
delineate the coast line as far west as Mount Ruth Siple which previously had been sighted from the westward at a distance and plotted at Lat.
73° 15' S., Long. 123° 00' W. We made our plans accordingly, and proceeded with the attempt to discover the Antarctic coastline between Cape Dart
and Mount Ruth Siple.

For the next ten days due to adverse weather it was impossible
to get a plane in the air. Snow, fog, low ceilings, poor visibility,
mixed with high winds and rough seas, plagued our operations. During
this period, sixty hour maintenance checks were made on the two PBM's.

On 18 January, BROWNSON came alongside for provisions and received PINE ISLAND's stateside mail. BROWNSON had been ordered to report to the PHILIPPINE SEA to act as plane guard during the launching
and flight of the six R4D's to Little America. The survivors of the
crashed plane, less Captain Caldwell who remained as Commanding Officer,
U.S.S. PINE ISLAND, were transferred to the BROWNSON for further transfer to the PHILIPPINE SEA and return to the United States. Enroute to
the PHILIPPINE SEA, BROWNSON was fueled by the CANISTEO at her station
200 miles west of the PINE ISLAND.

During all these operations, CANISTEO and BROWNSON were doing their work quietly and efficiently. On station their weather reporting was of great value. They were equipped and trained to act as emergency seadromes which was a great morale booster to the flight crews. Their excellent reporting of ice conditions enabled the PINE ISLAND to change position rapidly by avoiding the annoying loss of time attendant to becoming caught in ice tongues and bays. Their wide range of activity afforded the scientists and observers aboard excellent opportunities to collect and record the data necessary for their projects. They were in there pitching all the time, always in the right spot. They contributed greatly to the successful accomplishments of the group.

On the afternoon of 19 January the sun became visible for the first time in several days, and we had a glimpse of blue sky. The helicopter (HO3S-1) was launched for ice reconnaissance. Purpose of the flight was to locate a suitable operating area for launching PBM aircraft. Drift ice, in which it was not possible to take off or land PBM's, extended twenty miles north of the open pack. North of the drift ice the water was too rough to hoist planes over the side. We searched for a sheltered area of ice-free water. We found none and decided to return to the ship and move the PINE ISLAND westward.

During the 55 minutes absence of the helicopter from the ship, low ceiling and fog closed in about the PINE ISLAND, causing severe icing conditions. The pilot became aware that the rotor blades had commenced to ice up, so he made a deliberate high landing approach to the tender platform. The helicopter began to settle rapidly, and in order to prevent flying into the ship, the pilot turned the aircraft and crashed in the water 40 yards off the port beam of the PINE ISLAND. Equipped with wheel type landing gear, the helicopter began to sink and the cabin fill rapidly with water, temperature 30° F. Difficulty was experienced by both pilot and observer in unfastening the transport type safety belts. With safety belts finally unbuckled the cabin was almost completely submerged. To open the doors would destroy the airpocket, so the pilot butted out the plexiglass cabin door top with his head and emerged, followed closely by the observer. The rescue boat stationed close by hauled the two occupants out of the water in less than one minute, and both were soon in the PINE ISLAND under medical care. Neither suffered injuries or ill effects from the incident. The helicopter was a total loss. It is believed that if it had been equipped with floats it might have been saved.

A despatch was received from CTF 68 suggested that if we moved west to Longitude 120° West, we might find improved weather.

The PINE ISLAND set a westerly course to 120° West. Bad weather continued and we were forced to the north by the pack ice. At 1900 on 21 January we reached Lat. 66° 57' S., Long. 120° W., and changed course to the south. From early morning of the 22nd and throughout most of the

RESTRICTED

day, the winds were high (26 knots) and the seas rough. The ice pack
was encountered at Lat. 67° 15' S., Long. 120° W. As conditions appeared to be better eastward, we proceeded in that direction, skirting the
pack ice in search of a suitable operating area. Many icebergs were
seen along the course and a count of them at one time came to 103, the
majority of which were large tabular bergs.

The morning of 23 January gave indications of improved weather,
the high winds and choppy seas tapered off. We were still hampered by
a ten mile strip of drift ice north of the pack. Clear of the drift
ice the seas were too rough to launch aircraft. The flying weather was
improving; it was imperative we find sheltered water clear of ice for
hoisting out the planes.

In maneuvering for position we sighted a huge iceberg midway in
the drift ice belt. Through the glasses it appeared that in its wake
was an area free of drift ice. PINE ISLAND proceeded to that position,
and to the immense satisfaction of all hands we found we had the answer
to our problem. The lee of this iceberg provided smooth water for
launching, and an ice free water area for take off. Position, Lat. 68°
13' S., Long. 119° 31' W.

Flight quarters were sounded on the afternoon of 23 January, and
at 1919 Mariner George Three departed PINE ISLAND for the Antarctic
Continent. Mission: to pick up the coastline south of our position and
to develop it westward as far as Mount Ruth Siple.

At 2022 Mariner George Two departed PINE ISLAND for the Continent.
Mission: to pick up the coastline south of our position and develop it
eastward as far as practicable.

Both flights were extremely successful. Major mountain ranges
were discovered, as was the coastline between Longitudes 127° 30' West
and 110° 00' West. This was perhaps the most productive flight of the
entire operation. The coastline was much farther south than had been
estimated. It was necessary to fly over 360 miles of pack ice to reach
the coast, and the planes flew as far south as Latitude 74° 15' South
to develop the area.

The planes returned above the overcast to the ship the next
day, the morning of January 24th. During their absence the weather
had closed in. The ceiling was down to 800 feet with solid overcast
up to 8,000 feet. The tender was forced to move clear of the iceberg
so that if the ceiling became zero the planes could make a radio control
let down and landing without danger of flying into the icebergs.
Fortunately, the ceiling held at 800 feet. The planes made instrument
let downs from 8,000 feet, then circled below the overcast until the
tender returned to open water to recover them. George Three landed at
0342 and George Two landed at 0500 on 24 January.

With the planes safely aboard, the PINE ISLAND proceeded eastward to attain a suitable position for the next flights. Our next attempt was to fill in the gap between Cape Dart and the eastern limit of the last flights.

With the tender in a favorable position, preparations for flight operations were made early Sunday morning, 26 January. At 0550 Mariner George Two departed for the continent, followed an hour later by George Three. These planes were highly successful in completing the delineation of the coastline between Cape Dart and Longitude 107° 30' West. The Antarctic coastline to date had been discovered and photographed from Longitude 95° 30' W. to Longitude 127° 30' W.

George Two and Three landed at 1330 and 1430, respectively, 26 January, and were hoisted aboard.

It is interesting to note at this point that these flights on 26 January 1947 were the last flights which were successful in penetrating the unknown areas of the Antarctic Continent. Weather prevented anything but local flights or flights over previously discovered land masses.

For the next three weeks repeated attempts to penetrate the coastline proved unsuccessful.

On 27 January the PINE ISLAND rendezvoused with CANISTEO for refueling at sea. Upon the conclusion of this operation, with these two vessels in company, course was set to the eastward toward the vicinity of Peter I Island for the conduct of flight operations and hydrographic survey.

The CANISTEO was directed on 28 January to proceed independently to 102° West Longitude along the ice pack to act as a weather station and emergency seadrome while the PINE ISLAND continued her attempts to reach Peter I Island.

On 30 January the PINE ISLAND was 85 miles north of Peter I Island and on the edge of the icepack. The weather was poor; however, at 1700 the helicopter with pilot and observer left the PINE ISLAND for two ice reconnaissance flights of short duration.

High winds and bad weather continued until 8 February when the weather cleared sufficiently to warrant launching aircraft. The two Mariners were launched and by 1000 both aircraft were airborne. George Three remained in the vicinity of the PINE ISLAND for flight testing while George Two proceeded eastward to Charcot Island, about sixty miles distant. However, bad weather developed so rapidly the aircraft were recalled and hoisted aboard at 1330.

9 February the BROWNSON rendezvoused with PINE ISLAND. The weather had cleared sufficiently meanwhile so that at 0500 both Mariners were launched for flights 14 and 15, and after they were airborne, mail and provisions were transferred from BROWNSON to PINE ISLAND by boat.

At about 1620 both aircraft landed during light snow flurries in the ice-studded water after having covered a considerable area of coastline. George Two had flown over the Douglas Mountains, the south portion of Marguerite Bay, Alexander I and Charcot Islands, while George Three had photographed the coastline from 78° 15' West Longitude to 70° 15' West Longitude, including the entire west coast of Alexander I Island and the northern and eastern coasts of Charcot Island.

Monday, 10 February, a conference of commanding officers was held at which time plans were made for future operations as follows:

The PINE ISLAND was to lie to and continue attempts to launch aircraft for further reconnaissance near the Palmer Peninsula, while the CANISTEO was stationed to the westward as a weather station and the BROWNSON was to attempt to reach Charcot Island to send a landing party ashore to make observations.

Equipment and personnel required for the operation were transferred to the U.S.S. BROWNSON. The Task Group Commander transferred his flag to the BROWNSON that same afternoon and the BROWNSON set course for Charcot Island, while the CANISTEO remained on station to report weather.

The BROWNSON was successful in reaching within 500 yards of Charcot Island by small boat, where heavy ice with rough seas stopped further progress. The successful reconnaissance of Charcot Island and Alexander I Island is contained in the BROWNSON's report.

PINE ISLAND was ordered to proceed to Marguerite Bay on 11 February. Course was set to the northeast through high seas and wind, and at 0840 on 12 February, the northern coast of Alexander I Island was sighted, distant 40 miles. At 2215 on the same date this vessel reported sighting five small islands in Latitude 68° 45' S., Longitude 72° 13' W., which from their appearance and location were believed to be the Johansen islands.

PINE ISLAND and BROWNSON rendezvoused in the morning of 13 February, both cruising off the southwest coast of Adelaide Island awaiting a favorable change in weather to enter Marguerite Bay.

PINE ISLAND fueled BROWNSON on 14 February during which operation preparations were made to transfer the Task Group Commander to PINE ISLAND by breeches buoy. While attempting the transfer, with the Task Group Commander at mid-span between the vessels, an out of phase roll parted the span between the ships and dropped the Task Group Commander in the water.

By skillful maneuvering the BROWNSON retrieved the Task Group Commander within eight minutes. He was given medical treatment aboard the BROWNSON while the vessels continued the fueling operation.

On 14 February, the Task Group was ordered to rendezvous and proceed in company to the Weddell Sea for operations in that area. Enroute, on 17 February, the Task Group Commander and his staff transferred to the PINE ISLAND by small boat.

Refueling of the BROWNSON and PINE ISLAND was carried out by CANISTEO from 19 to 21 February, and during the following days inclement weather and heavy pack ice prevented flight operations.

Russian whaling vessels consisting of S.S. SLAVA, factory ship, and three steam catcher vessels of about 150 tons displacement were encountered on 26 February. These vessels when asked about ice conditions and weather to the eastward failed to reply with other than their call letters.

On 27 February, the PINE ISLAND and BROWNSON crossed the intersection of the Greenwich Meridian and the Antarctic Circle.

In view of the prospect of suitable weather for flight operations the following day, flight crews were briefed in the afternoon February 28th, and on 1 March at about 1230, when the weather cleared after heavy snow squalls, both aircraft were launched. Weather was extremely bad over the continent with clouds extending from the surface to 15,000 feet, which prevented any exploration over land and restricted flight operations to reconnaissance of ice conditions about 10 miles off the estimated position of the coastline.

Again on 2 March at 0300, preparations were made for flight operations; however, the weather soon closed in forcing cancellation of the proposed flights.

On 3 March the Task Group was ordered to withdraw from the Antarctic and proceed towards Brazil. At the time there was uncertainty as to whether the Group was to visit Rio de Janeiro or some other port in Brazil, in view of objections posed by the Naval Attache at Rio. This problem was resolved in favor of Rio de Janeiro by the sixth of March.

PINE ISLAND provisioned BROWNSON on 11 March. During the following night the wind velocity increased with heavy seas and gusts to forty knots.

BROWNSON fueled from PINE ISLAND during the morning of 14 March, afterwhich the Task Group lay to for five hours to prepare the vessels for entering port. A conference of commanding officers was held on board to discuss honors and ceremonies during the period in port. All commanding officers were directed to bring to the attention of their crews the provision of Atlantic Fleet Letter 28L-46, and to take positive measures to assure good behavior on the part of their crews as representatives of their country in Brazil.

During daylight hours on 15, 16 and 17 March the Task Group lay to completing preparations for entering port, and on 18 March the Task Group entered the harbor of Rio de Janeiro at 1100Z after firing the National Salute to Brazil and a 13-gun salute to Rear Admiral Raul de San-Tiago Dantas, Commander, Destroyer Force. By 1240Z the Group was moored in Baia de Guanabana.

A shore patrol was established, official visits made and received for the following six days.

On Monday, 24 March, the Task Group got underway and stood out of the harbor.

BROWNSON and PINE ISLAND fueled at sea from CANISTEO on 25 March, following which BROWNSON and CANISTEO were ordered to report to type commanders, with BROWNSON taking departure for Norfolk, Virginia, and CANISTEO for Ascension Island. PINE ISLAND proceeded to Cristobal, Canal Zone, at 13.5 knots.

On 6 April, the PINE ISLAND entered the Cristobal breakwater, and proceeded to moor alongside Pier 4, Naval Operating Base, Coco Solo, C.Z., after discharging her two Martin Mariner seaplanes. The ship was underway on 7 April to transit the Panama Canal, and was moored at Berth 4, Balboa, C.Z. PINE ISLAND was drydocked on 8 April for replacement of a damaged port screw and for bottom painting.

PINE ISLAND was undocked on 11 April, and on 14 April reported to Commander Air Force, Pacific Fleet, got underway, and stood out enroute to San Diego, California.

Commander Task Group 68.3 proceeded from Coco Solo, Canal Zone, to Washington, D.C. via Naval Air Transport Service, and reported to Commander Task Force 68 for duty.

The specific accomplishments of the Task Group are covered in detail in the individual ships' reports of Operation HIGHJUMP which have been submitted to the Task Force Commander.

ANNEX ONE (d)

NARRATIVE

U.S.S. PHILIPPINE SEA (CV47)

1.   Orders for the PHILIPPINE SEA to participate in Operation HIGHJUMP were received while the ship was undergoing shakedown operations at Guantanamo Bay, Cuba. Shakedown was cut short and the ship proceeded to South Boston Annex, Naval Shipyards, Boston, Mass., for a one month period of preparation. During this time, urgent items of repair and alterations were accomplished as would normally have been done during post-shakedown availability. Certain preparations for transit of the Panama Canal were also made. Disassembled parts for twenty sleds were received from NSY, Boston, and were assembled and made ready for use by ship's personnel. Several bolts of Byrd cloth were received for the construction of various items of cold weather clothing and equipment. The ship left the yard on 27 December, 1946, for Norfolk.

2.   The ship arrived and docked at NOB, Norfolk, on 29 December. Here were loaded the six R4D airplanes with the major portion of their spare parts and special equipment including the skis. One HO3S1 helicopter was flown aboard while at the dock. In addition, the ship received on board spare crews and spare parts for Operation SEABISCUIT. Approximately 100 tons of miscellaneous equipment for other ships of the Task Force was loaded which had not been on hand when these ships departed from the United States. Two OY-1 planes were received for transfer to the base camp at Little America. Rear Admiral Richard E. Byrd, USN (Ret.) and the crews of the R4D's came aboard.

3.   Departure from Norfolk was taken on 2 January 1947, arriving Colon, C. Z. on 7 January. The ship made the transit of the Canal on 8 January. During transit of Gatun Locks, one electric mule had a power failure which resulted in the ship striking the retaining wall, damaging two 40MM quad gun mounts in the port forward gun tub and putting a large hole (4' X 3') in the gun tub. Also during the transit, a projecting part of one of the forward winches caught on the side wall, damaging the winch beyond immediate repair. The ship reported to Commander, Task Force 68 when transit of the canal was completed. After docking at Balboa, the ship was fueled to capacity and repairs to the gun tub made. A winch was requisitioned and mounted to replace the damaged one. Departure from Balboa was taken on 10 January.

4.   After passing Cape Mala a great circle course was set for Lat 60° South, Long 160° West with the idea of thus by-passing the major portion of the expected Northern limit of ice bergs and then steaming direct for the rendezvous point. Permission was requested and received to proceed at 20 knots since it was probable the base camp would be prepared to receive the planes at the earlier launching date thus made possible. During the passage from Norfolk to the rendezvous point relatively good weather prevailed and advantage was taken of this good sailing to put everything in complete readiness for the launching operations and for off-loading of the cargo. Plane crews checked planes and engines, and loaded the planes for take-off. Loading and equipment carried is given in detail in Annex D, Sec. 7d. The ship's air department mounted the skis on all planes and adjusted them for carrier

take-off (skis were set to ride 3 inches from the deck with tires normally inflated). The two OY-1's were fitted with skis in lieu of wheels and were partially disassembled. Wings and tail surfaces were crated. The cargo, which had been put aboard hurriedly, was segregated, marked, and in some cases repacked to facilitate transfer. The sail loft manufactured tents, sled sails, engine covers, and various items of cold weather equipment (see Annex D, Sec. 2b). The navigators of the R4D's received intensive training and practical work in navigation during the trip, a vital necessity since the pilots selected were almost totally untrained in celestial navigation.

The helicopter was not used for the greater portion of the trip down since it was not desired to impede speed of advance by maneuvering to achieve suitable wind conditions and since any flights made could achieve no useful purpose and might produce some accident which would deny its use when really needed. It was warmed up periodically and kept in condition for flight on short notice. On 22 January in Lat 58° 48' S. Long. 156° 04' West, it was assumed ice bergs could be encountered during the day and the helicopter was scheduled for ice patrol. The plane was spotted forward, just aft of number one elevator. The pilot, when ready, started a normal take-off, hovering a moment just off the deck to determine the amount of pitch and roll to be expected when landing, then without gaining altitude started forward across the port bow. As soon as the plane had cleared the edge of the flight deck, it stopped and started to turn and lose altitude. Apparently the down wash over the port side (wind was on the starboard bow) and the loss of cushioning effect of the deck caused a down motion greater than was expected or could be countered and the plane sank rapidly to near water level, paused there momentarily, then dropped into the water on the port side abreast the island structure. The crew, alerted for this emergency, abandoned ship promptly and inflated their life jackets. The ship turned, stopped, and lowered a life boat which picked up the men in about eight minutes. The plane remained partially afloat for 12 minutes before sinking. The crew suffered only exposure and shock (water temperature 40° F.). There was no evidence of mechanical failure, therefore 100% pilot error was assigned, due to error in judgment and to inexperience.

Ice bergs were first encountered on 24 January. No small bergs or growlers had been sighted and it was not known whether radar reception would give sufficient warning. Therefore during the periods of heavy fog which were subsequently encountered, speed of advance was materially reduced by lying to waiting for visibility to improve.

5.   The CACAPON was sighted on the morning of 25 January also proceeding to the designated rendezvous point and was directed to join. An hour later, at 0400, (+ 12), the NORTHWIND and SENNET were sighted

lying to and all ships joined. A conference of commanding officers
was called on board the PHILIPPINE SEA to outline procedures and to
acquaint all ships with the work to be done, in addition to launching the planes. This involved refueling of all ships from CACAPON
and the transfer of cargo and mail to the other ships from PHILIPPINE
SEA. A number of personnel transfers were also required including
the transfer of survivors of the PBM crash from BROWNSON and other
patients for return to the United States. It was first decided that
SENNET, which required only fueling, would go alongside CACAPON while
lying to, but this proved impracticable due to rolling of both ships
in the long swell which was running. Therefore the entire group got
underway, steaming to the northward with SENNET fueling from CACAPON,
and PHILIPPINE SEA transferring cargo to NORTHWIND. SENNET was detached upon completion of fueling with orders to return to the vicinity of Scott Island. These orders were later modified to include a
sweep to the east in an attempt to determine the southward limit of
free water satisfactory for launching operations. This sweep was not
productive of any satisfactory information due to errors in navigation and the submarine's inability to proceed safely thru the brash
encountered. Loading of NORTHWIND continued throughout the day. The
Burtoning method of transfer was used and proved satisfactory in spite
of heavy rolling by NORTHWIND. However, it was decided that conditions
were such that transfer of personnel and of the OY-1 airplanes and
several other heavy or bulky items of cargo would involve undue hazard at this time. Therefore at 0025 (+12) 26 January cast off transfer lines and and went alongside CACAPON to fuel. BROWNSON, who had
just joined, came alongside PHILIPPINE SEA to transfer survivors.
These two operations were completed by 0230 and course was reversed.
No further operations were attempted during the remainder of 26 January. At 0700, 27 January, sea conditions had improved somewhat, so
NORTHWIND came alongside and received personnel and remainder of cargo.
This was completed by 0945 and NORTHWIND was detached to proceed to Bay
of Whales, scouting the pack enroute for best suitable launching area
and then taking station on track of planes to Little America as rescue
vessel in case of forced landing in the pack. At 1300 BROWNSON came
alongside for transfer of cargo and personnel. This was accomplished
in a very smart and expeditious manner, mainly due to the energetic and
enthusiastic efforts of the crew of BROWNSON. The Burtoning method was
not practicable, so all cargo was passed by personnel carrier lines,
three of which were rigged. BROWNSON cast off at 1600 and the group
then proceeded in company to the Southeastward to the area indicated
by NORTHWIND as most suitable. The following day, 28 January, was spent
proceeding to and in the area selected for launching. BROWNSON scouted
ahead 30 miles to determine the actual position of the bay in the pack
reported by NORTHWIND. CACAPON transferred a patient to PHILIPPINE SEA.
The next day, 29 January, was spent lying to in approximate position
LAT 68° 50' South, LONG 174° 40' West, awaiting favorable weather conditions at Little America. Conditions in launching area were satisfact-

ory with overcast to broken clouds, a large area of clear water and light
variable winds. It had been decided that two planes would be launched
first and remainder would wait until these had landed and reported weather and field conditions. Weather at Little America appeared to be improving throughout the day and planes were kept ready for launching on
short notice. Little America reported "open for flight operations" in
the late evening. The first plane, with Rear Admiral Byrd aboard, was
launched at 2214 with the second following at 2231. Thirty knots speed
thru the water was required to achieve 41 knots of wind over the deck.
The first two planes landed safely and reported satisfactory conditions,
so it was decided to launch the remainder as one group, but to proceed
in pairs after launching. Planes were launched at 0633, 0648, 0708,
0718. The same wind over the deck for the second launch was obtained
with only eighteen knots speed thru the water. All launches were normal
with actual deck runs being very close to those predicted. JATO units
worked satisfactorily, skis did not interfere with take-off or with retracting landing gear, no plane experiences difficulty with swerving on
take-off, nor was any unforeseen difficulty encountered. Two circumstances were very fortunate a relatively large area of ice-free water
was found comparatively far south which permitted the ship to maintain
course and speed for each launching operation, and secondly, suitable
weather at ship and base and along the flight route was encountered
without an undue delay. If the second launch had been delayed for even
an hour, weather at the ship would have prevented take-off and several
days wait would have been required before suitable conditions again existed.

The three ships remained in the launching position until all
planes were in sight of base in case a water landing would be required.
When a report was received that all planes had arrived, course was set
to the Northward and transfer of cargo and personnel to CACAPON started.
BROWNSON was kept in position astern during this operation as life guard
vessel. This operation had been left until the last in order that fuel
requirements of PHILIPPINE SEA for return trip could be more accurately
determined. A possible shortage of fuel for the Task Force existed,
with the result that PHILIPPINE SEA was ordered to return without refueling, although the reserve for this trip was not as great as was desired. Transfer to CACAPON was effected in a normal manner using the
Burtoning method. Operations were complicated, however, by extremely
low visibility and the presence of numerous icebergs. During the $3\frac{1}{2}$
hours taken by this operation several course changes up to thirty degrees were required. Radar showed free lanes satisfactorily and all
course changes were made at the rate of about one degree per minute
with both ships turning simultaneously on voice signal. At 1630, 30
January, the operation was completed, BROWNSON and CACAPON were released and course set for return to Panama, following closely the track of
the outbound trip.

6.   The return trip to Panama was completely uneventful. The
ship conducted routine training enroute, expending 24 of the 25 TDD
drones carried on this cruise for gunnery training. Performance of
the drones was good and great benefit to all batteries was derived
from this type of exercise. The ship arrived Balboa, C. Z. on 18
February 1947. All survivors except Lt. LeBlanc, who could not be
moved, were sent to the United States by air. PHILIPPINE SEA reported
to ComAirLant: duty with Task Force 68 completed. Transit of the Canal
and return to Quonset was routine and normal.

7.   It is felt by PHILIPPINE SEA that its participation in Operation HIGHJUMP was in practically all respects a normal, routine operation. Navigation in areas where ice bergs are present requires caution when low visibility is also encountered since radar performance
is not all that could be desired, particularly as regards detection of
growlers and small ice. Suitable weather would be the determining
factor in any carrier operations in the areas involved whether for transport of planes as in this case or for operation of normal carrier types.
Temperatures encountered throughout were much milder than those existing at the time in the normal operating area of this ship, i.e., the
Newport-Quonset Point area, therefore no assessment from the point of
view of cold weather operations could be made. No difficulties were
encountered in loading, handling, or launching R4D type planes. These
planes could undoubtedly be launched from a carrier without the use
of JATO, but it does provide a desirable safety feature.

CONFIDENTIAL

ANNEX ONE (e)

NARRATIVE

TASK GROUP 68.5

I. Objectives of Base Group (Task Group 68.5)

        The objectives of the Base Group (TG 68.5) were as follows:

        (a) To establish and maintain during the Antarctic summer a temporary base for approximately 300 personnel, including a matted air strip for the operation of aircraft on wheels, on the Ross Shelf Ice in the vicinity of Little America, Antarctica.

        (b) Conduct systematic outward radial air exploration of assigned area of the Antarctic continent.

        (c) Be prepared to carry out rescue operations for aviation personnel forced down in the interior of the continent, including the establishment of an emergency winter camp at Little America to accommodate thirty-five personnel (to be activated only upon orders).

        (d) Carry out assigned projects for training naval personnel, testing material, and amplifying scientific knowledge of the Antarctic.

II. Organization of the Base Group

        The Base Group (TG 68.5) was activated upon arrival of the ships of the Central Group (TG 68.1) at the Bay of Whales. The number of personnel involved varied from day to day due to the necessity for the ships to move out of the bay when sea and wind conditions became unfavorable. All records, pay accounts, etc., were retained on the ships to which the personnel were attached and as many men as practicable lived aboard the ships tied up to the ice when not engaged in their work ashore. After the departure of the ships on 6 February, a total of 197 officers, civilians and enlisted men were based ashore.

        The Base Group was divided into the following units for administration under the Task Group Commander (CTG 68.5), Commander C. M. Campbell, USN:

        (a) Aviation Unit (Comdr. W. M. Hawkes, USN, CTU 68.5.1)
                20 officers, 52 enlisted men.

        (b) Construction Unit (Comdr. C. O. Reinhardt, CEC, USN, CTU
                68.5.2) 1 officer, 27 enlisted men.

        (c) Communications and GPN Crew (Lt. M. M. Hershey, USN)
                5 officers, 17 enlisted men.

        (d) Aerology, scientific and observer Unit (Capt. G. F.
                Kosco, USN) 11 observers, 6 scientists, 4 news
                correspondents and 5 enlisted men.

(e) Photo Unit (Lt. C. C. Shirley, USN)
           1 officer, 10 enlisted men.

(f) Commissary, supply and galley Unit (Lt.(jg) L.D. Wilson
           (SC), USN). 21 enlisted men.

(g) Ground rescue and transportation Unit (Capt. V. D. Boyd,
           USMC). 2 officers, 5 enlisted men.

(h) Medical Unit (Lt.(jg) H. R. Richardson (MC), USN)
           1 enlisted man.

III Narrative of the Base Group (TG 68.5) 16 January, 1947 to 23
February, 1947.

On the 16th and 17th of January, 1947 while the ships of the
Central Group lay to off the entrance to the Bay of Whales small parties
of officers and observers, including CTG 68.5 and Dr. Paul Siple, went
ashore to investigate sites for the Base Camp. The site of Little
America IV was selected and the route over which it would be necessary
to haul supplies from the ships to the camp was laid out and marked with
trail flags. The old camp (Little America III) used on the '39-'41 expedition, was visited to ascertain whether it would be usable as an
emergency base camp in case the emergency base was activated to remain
over the winter night. It was found to be intact with all the buildings
and equipment in good condition.

At 0345 R on 18 January the U.S.S. YANCEY commenced discharging
cargo onto the bay ice. The first items unloaded were the tractors,
trucks and other vehicles needed for transportation. It was found
necessary to bridge a pressure ridge and an open crack in the Bay ice.
The construction detail was divided into two twelve hour shifts so that
the work could proceed as fast as possible.

The JA aircraft on skis was unloaded from the U.S.S. MOUNT
OLYMPUS on 21 January and towed to the air strip. On 22 January a local
photo flight was made with the JA and thereafter frequent flights were made
to make a progressive photographic record of the progress made in building the Base Camp.

A temporary transportation headquarters was established at the
foot of the barrier on the Bay ice with fueling and repair facilities
for all vehicles. Wooden extension tracks had been built on all tractors
to be used on the barrier; tractors without extensions were used for
hauling loads on the bay ice from the ships sides to the foot of the
barrier. A cableway was rigged on the barrier slope to haul sleds up and
down the slope over the crevassed area to speed operations and reduce
tractor traffic.

Messing facilities were set up and the first meal served ashore on 23 January. The total personnel living ashore varied from day to day between a low of 30 and a high of 248 reached during a period when all ships were forced to leave the ice suddenly due to bad weather. Upon the final departure of all ships the number of men based ashore stabilized at 197. This figure was arrived at as the maximum number of personnel that could be evacuated by the icebreaker in one trip. The decision to take the ships of CTG 68.1 out through the ice pack departing the Bay of Whales about 6 February caused a considerable change in plans for the Base Group. The communication facilities planned for the Base had to be greatly increased, all material for the emergency base had to be quickly unloaded and installed at Little America III, work on the projected Marston Mat airstrip had to be discontinued and all fuel and other supplies for the Base Camp had to be unloaded prior to the projected departure of the vessels of CTG 68.1.

It was decided to only unload enough Marston mat for an experimental strip 590 feet long by 150 feet wide. In the meanwhile, the Commander of the Base Group reported that conditions on the airstrip were suitable for landing R4D's on skis. To the North, the PHILIPPINE SEA had been lying to in the vicinity of Scott Island waiting for a favorable moment to launch the R4D's. At 2330 (X) 29 January, 1947 the first two R4D's took off from the carrier, bound for Little America. Not only was it the first time that a plane as large as an R4D had taken off from a carrier but it was the first time that any airplane had ever taken off from a carrier with a combination wheel-ski arrangement. In the first plane, the Officer in Charge of the Antarctic Development Project, Rear Admiral R. E. Byrd, U.S.N. (Ret) was flying as observer. The take-off of the first two planes was successful and for five and a half hours they continued winging their way southward. They passed over the ice breaker NORTHWIND, which had been stationed at the mid-point of the flight, slightly behind schedule. Strong head winds were encountered all the way down. Finally at 0500 (X) they were sighted from Little America and at 0520 the first plane landed. When it slid to a stop, Admiral Byrd was the first one to disembark. His first words of greeting were, "Well, it's good to be 'Home'."

As soon as the news of the success of the first flight was received aboard the carrier, preparations were at once made to launch the remaining four planes. In these, besides their crews, were two correspondents, Mr. R. Nichols and Mr. R. Reuben. The first plane of this group took off at 0800 (X) and shortly thereafter the remaining three were airborne. The same strong headwinds were encountered enroute. About 200 miles from Little America, the last plane ran into trouble. First its gyro went out and it had to rely on its magnetic compass. The weather had started to close in and the sun was no longer visible so its Astro compass was of no use. A short while later its radio went out and many anxious moments were spent by those listening both at Little America and on the U.S.S. PHILIPPINE SEA. At 1332, the first plane of

this group landed on the snow strip at Little America, followed shortly thereafter by two more. But one did not land - it was kept airborne
to help the fourth plane. The fourth plane still had not been heard
from. It was a great relief when a few minutes after the third plane
had landed, radio contact with the fourth plane was made. The plane
reported that it was uncertain of its position and was flying east along
the Barrier. They had evidently been set to the west for the radar on
the MOUNT OLYMPUS picked them up almost immediately and at 1406 they
landed. It was none too soon. The last plane had no sooner landed when
the weather for which the Antarctic has long been famous, closed in.
Thus another chapter had been written in the History of the Antarctic
and in the History of Aviation.

During the next week work at the Base Camp proceeded at a rapid
pace, making use of working parties from the ships present to augment
the manpower available ashore, to complete the preparations necessary
for the camp to operate entirely on its own upon the departure of all
the ships. Tests were completed and preparations made for the R4D airplane reconnaissance flights that were going to be made over the interior
of the Antarctic Continent. As stated previously the planes were equipped with ski-wheel landing gear. After they arrived at Little America,
the wheels were removed and a strip of dural placed over the wheel slot
of the first two planes leaving the other four with open slots. During
the remaining few days until the ships all departed on 6 February numerous flights with various loads were made, not only to familiarize the
pilots with ski landings and take-offs, but also to determine the largest
pay loads that could be taken off with safety from the snow surface of
Little America.

Two disassembled Stinson OY-1 airplanes equipped with skis had
been shipped in from the PHILIPPINE SEA via the U.S.C.G.C. NORTHWIND for
use as general utility and short range rescue planes. One of these was
assembled and made a number of local flights during the next three weeks.

After the departure of the ships on the 6th of February, all
efforts were concentrated on preparing the planes for flight so that
full advantage could be taken of any break in the weather. On the 9th
of February two planes, V-1 and V-2, took off on operational flights to
the southeast with Rear Admiral Byrd aboard V-1. The planes ran into
bad weather with light icing and being unable to climb on top of the
solid overcast, turned back from a point about two hundred miles southeast of Little America and photographed the local area between Discovery
Inlet and Kainan Bay before landing at base. On the 10th of February two
planes, V-3 and V-5, took off on an operational flight to the southwest
with CTG 68.5 aboard V-3. While flying at 9000 feet altitude about two
hundred and forty miles from Little America, V-5 began having engine
trouble with low oil pressure on one engine and the other cutting out
periodically. Both planes returned to base via Discovery Inlet flying
through snow and sleet between Discovery Inlet and the Bay of Whales.

On the first operational flight V-1 and V-2 had 1200 gallons of gasoline aboard and used four Jato bottles apiece. On the second operational flight V-3 and V-5 had 1400 hallons of gasoline aboard and used four Jato bottles apiece. The wheel openings in the skis of these last two planes were left open and seemed to work better than the filled ones of V-1 and V-2 as much less power was required to taxi over the snow surface of the field. On the remainder of the flights, loads up to 1600 gallons of gasoline were taken off without Jato although the usual loading was 1400 gallons and two Jato bottles.

On 14 February V-1 and V-2, with Admiral Byrd in V-1, flew southeast to the vicinity of the Horlick Mountains and the Thorne Glacier, discovering a new range of mountains and photographing considerable unknown area. V-6 and V-3 were launched as soon as the first pair were on their way back to base and their track carried them well to the east of the first pair covering much unknown territory. A solid undercast prevented extending the track of this pair further than five hundred miles. V-1 and V-2 were gassed upon return from the first flight and sent out to the southwest over Wade and Beardmore Glaciers and out into the unexplored area to the southwest of Mount Markham covering the sector out to almost 700 miles from Little America.

Early on 15 February V-3 and V-5 were launched to the eastward where they reached the area south of Mount Walker and discovered and photographed several new mountains in that area.

Late that evening the phenomenal weather still holding, it was decided to send a pair of planes to the South Pole and the area beyond and to the west of the pole. V-1 with Admiral Byrd aboard and V-6 with CTG 68.5 aboard flew to the Wade Glacier, up the 180th Meridian to the Pole, made a wide circle over the pole, went north on the 0° meridian for over sixty miles, then west over sixty miles, and returned to base passing through the area between Wade and Beardmore glaciers. A large amount of polar plateau was explored and several new mountains sighted along the south west slopes of the known range of mountains next to the Ross Shelf Ice.

On 17 February four planes were launched singly to cover the sectors to the southwest in the area south of McMurdo Sound. Engine trouble turned back V-6 and V-1 before getting over the mountains. Weather stopped V-3 but V-2 was able to climb over the range and photograph and discover new mountains on the southwest side of the range and northward toward McMurdo Sound. On his return V-2 sighted many new bays and cracks along the north edge of the Ross Shelf Ice between McMurdo Sound and Discovery Inlet. Being out of film, he requested another plane to be sent out to complete the photography. V-5 was launched but had to turn back before much was accomplished due to lowering visibility west of Discovery Inlet.

On 19 February, V-1 made a local Magnetometer flight with interesting results. The following day two planes, V-3 and V-5, were again launched to cover the southwest sectors but again ran into solid overcast on the Polar Plateau and were forced to turn north where they were able to photograph considerable areas to the north of McMurdo Sound along the mountain range. Later that day, V-1 made a magnetometer flight.

On 21 February, Plane V-3 made an ice reconnaissance hop to the northwest but bad weather limited the range to about one hundred twenty miles. Plane V-6 made an experimental altitude flight locally to try and determine what effects oxygen lack would have on crews in this latitude compared to the effects in temperate zones. Plane V-1 made another magnetometer flight through the Rockefeller Mountains and over Roosevelt Island with very good results.

On 22 February, planes V-2 and V-3 were launched to try and tie in previous discoveries in the southeast sector toward the Horlick Mountains. Bad weather turned both planes back after having covered about 500 miles of the track out. Plane V-1 was launched for a magnetometer flight but experienced a complete engine failure when about eighty miles east of the base and it returned on one engine. The BURTON ISLAND which had completed a survey of the McMurdo Sound area had arrived early that morning and a conference was held between Rear Admiral Byrd and the Task Force Commander. It was decided to cancel further flight operations and evacuate the base.

The planes were secured, headed into the prevailing wind with fabric control surfaces removed and stowed inside the fuselage. Classified communications gear was removed and either destroyed or evacuated on the BURTON ISLAND along with camera gear, essential scientific equipment and the personal baggage of the camp inhabitants. All caches of supplies and other equipment was marked by tall poles and a sketch locating the caches was posted inside the two permanent quonset huts.

All personnel were taken aboard the BURTON ISLAND and a last inspection of the base made by CTG 68.5. The colors were left flying at the mast-head of the flag-pole at the corner of the galley and mess hall and the BURTON ISLAND departed for Wellington, New Zealand at 2300 R 23 February, 1947, with all members of the Base Group safely aboard.

Besides the long range air operations which are completely covered in the Aviation annex of HIGHJUMP report, a great many other things had been accomplished. An experimental airstrip had been laid, an R4D on wheels had taxied on it, an OY-1 on wheels had taken off and landed on it successfully, and other weight supporting and drop tests had been made. Numerous scientific experiments had been conducted such as magnetometer tests, measurement of the velocity of sound through snow and ice, Geiger counter recordings of cosmic rays, etc. These were carried out by representatives and scientists of other government agencies.

CONFIDENTIAL

Tests of a more immediate practical nature, such as operation of
different types of standard construction and transportation equipment,
tests of medical supplies and various types of clothing, and the problem
of maintaining a camp of approximately 200 men on the ice for a period
of one month with only temporary shelter and no outside help, were also
made. Complete accounts of tests made and experiments conducted can be
found in the annexes of the HIGHJUMP report.

IV. Summary of Base Group Accomplishments and Recommendations.

The Base Group accomplished the following tasks during the
thirty-six days ashore on the Ross Ice Shelf at the Bay of Whales:

(a) Unloaded and transported to the camp area a total of 1,800
tons of provisions, fuel, and equipment.

(b) Constructed and put in operation a galley and mess hall
from which over 21,000 hot palatable rations were served.

(c) Constructed an insulated 96' by 20' communication quonset
hut at Little America III with an interconnecting passageway to the buried
buildings of the old camp. Set up long range communication with Washington, D. C. direct by means of rhombic antennae mounted on forty-foot poles.
Stored below, in the food caches, food for thirty-five men for fourteen
months. Stored just outside the quonset hut 50,000 gallons of diesel fuel
for the generators.

(d) Constructed at Little America IV fifty-four pyramidal tents
with wooden decks, and three prefabricated wannigans for living quarters
equipped with diesel oil stores, folding cots with mattresses and sleeping bags. Constructed eleven other tents of various sizes for outdoor
toilets, aerology, photographic stowage and aviation supply purposes.

(e) Constructed a 48' X 20' quonset hut for aviation maintenance
and aircraft communications.

(f) Transported a complete GCA equipment including a power
supply truck to the Air strip, set up and tested the equipment, disassembled it and returned it to its stowage aboard ship prior to the departure of the AKA's on 6 February.

(g) Transported and set up a GPN unit with power supply truck
at the airstrip. Disassembled and transported it for loading aboard the
BURTON ISLAND during evacuation.

(h) Established a sled dog village adjacent to camp area from
which three dog teams were trained. They made trips to the bay ice area
daily to bring back Wedell seals killed for dog food.

Annex I - (e)   - 7 -

CONFIDENTIAL

(i) Operated the eight aircraft of the air unit a total of 300 flying hours doing all maintenance work on them in the open in temperatures that ranged as low as -23° C.

(j) Constructed three hard surface snow runways for ski planes totaling 13,000 feet in length.

(k) Constructed a Marsten Mat landing strip on the snow surface 835' long and varying from 150' to 40' wide for experimental purposes.

(l) Conducted the scientific program ashore as completely as limited time allowed.

(m) Carried out the numerous technical and military projects requested by Bureaus of the Navy and other governmental agencies.

The details of the above accomplishments are contained in appropriate annexes of the Operation HIGHJUMP Report.

Recommendations

The two most important shortcomings of the Base Group were internal communications and personnel transportation. Short range radio voice sets were used of the SCR-610 series but proved inadequate for the purpose due to number of operating personnel needed and maintenance difficulties with the sets. It is recommended that a field telephone set be used in similar future operations. Weasels towing one ton sleds were used for personnel transportation and would have sufficed if there had been about twenty-four available instead of eight. However, it is recommended that for future operations on similar type snow surface, a new weasel be designed to be a little more rugged, eliminate excess weight by removing the amphibious parts and design a light sled with a covered body so that personnel will be protected from the snow thrown by the rubber tracks of the weasel.

ANNEX ONE - (f)

NARRATIVE

U.S.S. MOUNT OLYMPUS (AGC-8)

NARRATIVE OF PARTICIPATION

1. The MOUNT OLYMPUS was assigned to Operation HIGHJUMP in early October, after a period of six weeks in the New York Navy Yard preparing the ship for inactivation in the SIXTEENTH Fleet. During the Period of reactivation much was accomplished. Stores were put aboard, spare parts obtained and a partial overhaul completed and the ship reported to Commander Task Force SIXTY-EIGHT at Norfolk, Va. on November 16, 1946. During the ensuing two weeks, additional stores and equipment were loaded and by sailing time on December 2, 1946, the ship was ready to sail.

2. The voyage from Norfolk to Scott Island via the Panama Canal was uneventful and provided a shakedown cruise for the more than 90% new personnel on board. After arriving at Scott Island on December 30, 1946, the remaining ships of the group refueled while the Coast Guard Cutter NORTHWIND scouted the pack to the southward.

3. At 1530 on the afternoon of December 31, 1946, under a bright sun and calm seas the Central Group of Task Force SIXTY-EIGHT entered the Ross Sea Ice Pack and commenced 15 days of the arduous and hazardous task of navigating the pack. The northern edge of the pack was loose and easily navigable, but by the New Year, the pack was becoming closer and more difficult to negotiate. During the afternoon of January 1, 1947, the group reached a pool of open water in the vicinity of numerous icebergs and very heavy bay ice and lay to while the NORTHWIND scouted for a lead to the south. During the first 24 hours, the MOUNT OLYMPUS had sustained damage to several frames forward and two blades of the propeller were bent. Succeeding days were a repetition of the first day, sometimes laying to in pools and sometimes making fair progress to the southward through the pack. Finally on 11 January 1947, the pack gradually loosened up as southward progress was made and late in the evening of January 14, 1947, the Central Group finally broke through to the open waters of the Ross Sea. At this time additional frames forward had been damaged and all blades of the propellor were bent maximum sustained speed being reduced to 10 knots.

4. At midnight 14 January 1947, the Ross Sea Ice Barrier was sighted dead ahead and after investigating Discovery Inlet, the group proceeded to the Bay of Whales arriving at 0843, 15 January. The NORTHWIND commenced breaking the ice out of the Bay which was frozen over and by 18 January, the Bay was sufficiently clear for the U.S.S. YANCEY to enter and commence unloading. On 22 January, the MOUNT OLYMPUS finally entered the Bay of Whales for the first time and commenced unloading on a 24 hour basis.

5. On 23 January, a northerly wind blew a small iceberg through the entrance to the Bay and all ships had to get underway as the berg was bearing down on the moorings. The Bay was entered again on January 24th and unloading operations continued. By the 27th, the MOUNT OLYMPUS was almost completely unloaded but a strong northerly wind

with heavy snow again forced all ships to get underway and stand out of the Bay. During this storm sections of bay ice broke off. The ship again entered the Bay of Whales on the morning of January 30th and again moored to the bay ice. During the day, Rear Admiral Richard E. Byrd flew in from the PHILIPPINE SEA and came on board. During the afternoon, unfavorable conditions again forced us to leave the bay. On February 2nd the MOUNT OLYMPUS again entered the Bay and moored port side to the U.S.S. MERRICK. We remained moored to the MERRICK until our final departure from the Bay of Whales on February 6th. During this period, unloading was completed and working parties were furnished for the base camp.

6.   At 1848 on February 6th, the MOUNT OLYMPUS got underway and stood out of the Bay of Whales for the last time and departed for Scott Island in company with the YANCEY, MERRICK, and NORTHWIND. The passage out through the pack was uneventful except that on 11 February, the U.S.S. MERRICK lost her rudder in heavy ice and a high wind. The NORTHWIND stood by the MERRICK and the BURTON ISLAND which had joined us on 9 February, escorted the U.S.S. YANCEY and MOUNT OLYMPUS and at 0924 on February 12th, we cleared the pack. The NORTHWIND took the MERRICK in tow and with the U.S.S. YANCEY in company departed for New Zealand on February 13th.

7.   The MOUNT OLYMPUS proceeded to Scott Island and acted as a weather reporting station until February 27th when the BURTON ISLAND rejoined. After the Task Force Commander and his staff together with all Base Camp Personnel had transferred to the MOUNT OLYMPUS, we proceeded to Wellington, New Zealand, arriving on 7 March. After a pleasant stay in Wellington, the MOUNT OLYMPUS departed March 14, 1947, for the United States via the Panama Canal arriving in Washington, D.C. April 14, 1947.

RECOMMENDATIONS

1.   All ships operating in Arctic and Antarctic regions be provided with sufficient boat capacity for all personnel carried, as life jackets, floater nets and navy type life rafts are almost worthless unless personnel can be rescued within a few minutes.

2.   Ships of type similar to MOUNT OLYMPUS expecting to operate in ice pack should be prepared for such operations by taking the following minimum measures:

      (a) Install steel propeller designed for use in ice.
      (b) The stern to be reinforced with concrete.
      (c) Install voids or tanks to provide additional watertight protection for engine rooms and evaporator room.
      (d) Double plate the curvature of the bow from the waterline to the turn of the bilge.

      (e) Provide a collision net

3.   If ships are to be designed for this type of operation, the following are desirable characteristics in addition to incorporating the above.

      (a) As small a turning circle as possible.
      (b) Screw to be submerged as deeply as possible.
      (c) Low free board and reduce superstructure to minimum as wind has a very great effect at the low speeds required in ice operations.

4.   In future operations in ice pack planes should be available to thoroughly scout pack in order that easiest route may be picked and the extent of the pack determined.

15 Nov. Moored at N.O.B., Norfolk, Virginia.

In accordance with Cinclant's dispatch of October 3, 1946 U.S.S. MOUNT OLYMPUS (AGC-8) reported at N.O.B., Norfolk, Virginia, to Commander Task Force 68 for duty.

15 Nov. - 2 Dec. Moored at N.O.B., Norfolk, Virginia.

Moored portside to Pier 3, N.O.B., Norfolk, Virginia. Loading equipment, supplies, stores and embarking civilian observers and personnel of CTF-68.
Replaced boat chocks on forward deck with steel pedestal for Norseman ski plane and chocks for two plane rearment boats.
Replaced grating on fantail for twenty-seven sled dogs.

31 Nov. Moored at N.O.B., Norfolk, Virginia.

Transferred 27 sled dogs from USCG NORTHWIND to this vessel.

2 Dec. Underway from N.O.B., Norfolk, Virginia.

0945 Rear Admiral R.E. BYRD, Officer in Charge Antarctic Development Project, came aboard on official call. 1300 Rear Admiral BYRD left the ship. 1316 Underway from Pier Three (3), N.O.B., Norfolk, Virginia, for Balboa, Canal Zone, with Rear Admiral CRUZEN, CTF-68, OTC, and staff aboard this vessel, in company with U.S.S. PINE ISLAND (AV-12), U.S.S. BROWNSON (DD-868) and USCG NORTHWIND.

3 Dec. 1200 Pos. 32°11.5'N. Lat.,75°03'W. Lon.

Steaming on southerly course in column with U.S.S. MOUNT OLYMPUS guide, in company with U.S.S. PINE ISLAND, U.S.S. BROWNSON, and USCG NORTHWIND.

4 Dec. 1200 Pos. 26°35'N.Lat., 74°51'W. Lon.

Steaming as before. USCG NORTHWIND having trouble maintaining speed of guide, ordered to proceed independently to Balboa, Canal Zone.

5 Dec. 1200 Pos. 20°10'N. Lat., 74°05'W. Lon.

Steaming as before. 0557 U.S.S. PINE ISLAND (AV-12) detached, ordered to proceed to Balboa, Canal Zone independently.

6 Dec. 1200 Pos. Standing out of Canal Zone.

2133 U.S.S. BROWNSON (DD-868) detached, ordered to proceed to Balboa, Canal Zone independently.

RESTRICTED

7 Dec. 1200 Pos. Passing through Panama Canal

1108 Arrived at Colon breakwater and started through Canal astern of the U.S.S. PINE ISLAND (AV-12). 1244 Entered Gatun Locks. 1702 Entered Pedro Miquel Locks. 1803 Entered Miraflores Locks. 1943 Moored starboard side to pier 18, Balboa, Canal Zone.

8 Dec. Moored at Balboa, Canal Zone.

Moored starboard side to pier 18, Balboa, Canal Zone. Receiving stores and equipment aboard.

9 Dec. Moored at Balboa, Canal Zone.
Moored starboard side to pier 18, Balboa, Canal Zone.

10 Dec. 1200 Pos. 08°45'N. Lat., 79°03'W. lon. 1011 Underway from pier 18, Balboa, Canal Zone enroute to Little America, Antarctica, with CTF68 and staff aboard this ship in company with U.S.S. PINE ISLAND (AV-12), U.S.S. SENNET (SS-408), U.S.S. BROWNSON (DD-868) and USCG NORTHWIND.

11 Dec. 1200 Pos. 03°59'N. Lat., 81°57.8'W. lon. Steaming as before. 0800 Executed formation "oboe" of CTF68 Operation Plan No.2-46. U.S.S. MOUNT OLYMPUS in company with U.S.S. SENNET steaming along assigned track in accordance with CTF68 dispatch. 1100 Sighted Mapelo Island (3°59'07"N., 81°34'27"W) bearing 131°T., distance 19 miles. 1900 Retarded clocks one hour to zone plus 6 time.

12 Dec. 1200 Pos. 00°26'S. Lat., 85°04'W Lon. 0750 Crossed the equator at longitude 84°39'W. Traditional equator crossing celebration held and all "pollywogs" initiated as "shellbacks".

13 Dec. 1200 Pos. 04°39.2'S.Lat., 88°40'W.Lon. Steaming as before, U.S.S. SENNET conducting trim dives.

14 Dec. 1200 Pos.09°17'S.Lat., 91°23.5'W.Lon. Steaming as before.

15 Dec. 1200 Pos. 14°04.2'S.Lat.,93°44.5'W.Lon. Steaming as before.

16 Dec. 1200 Pos.18°58.2'S.Lat., 96°32'W. Lon. Steaming as before. 1900 Retarded all clocks one hour to zone plus 7 time. 1925 Sounded Fire Quarters, small fire in starboard boat deck life raft at frame 100. 1936 Secured Quarters.

17 Dec. 1200 Pos. 23°53.5'S., 99°26'W.Long.

Steaming as before. 2130 Commenced taking soundings beginning at 346 fathoms and decreasing slowly until 2143 when sounding was 185 fathoms. From 2153 until 2217 soundings increased slowly from 185 fathoms to 462 fathoms. 2230 Pathometer indicated no bottom. Chart indicated no bank of such depth in this position. 2130 Position 25°49'50"S, 100°39'20"W. 2153 Position 25°54'10"S., 100°41'40" W.. 2217 Position 26°01'50"S., 100°45'30"W..

18 Dec. 1200 Pos. 28°45'S. Lat., 102°22.8'W.Lon. Steaming as before.

19 Dec. 1200 Pos. 33°30'S.Lat., 105°39'W.Lon. Steaming as before.

20 Dec. 1200 Pos. 38°14.2'S.Lat.,109°08'W.Lon Steaming as before.

21 Dec. 1200 Pos. 42°16.2'S.Lat.,112°44.2'W.

0447 U.S.S. CANISTEO (AO99) joined the formation and took station in preparation for fueling exercise. 0825 Commenced making approach on CANISTEO for fueling exercise. 0934 Commenced fueling. 1123 Completed fueling. 1155 Took station astern of CANISTEO while SENNET fueled. 1735 SENNET completed fueling. CANISTEO returning to her station fifty miles on port beam of this vessel.

22 Dec. 1200 Pos. 45°30'S.Lat., 116°48.5'W.Long.

Steaming as before.

23 Dec. 1200 Pos. 49°28.7'S Lat., 121°31'W Long.

Steaming as before.

24 Dec. 1200 Pos. 53°29.1'S.Lat.,127°10.4'W.Long.

Steaming as before.

25 Dec. 1200 Pos. 56°59.4'S.Lat.,133°07.2'W.Long.

Steaming as before. 1900 Retarded all clocks one hour to zone plus 9 time.

26 Dec. 1200 Pos. 61°10.5'S. Lat., 139°49.0'W. Lon.

Steaming as before. 1035 U.S.S. CANISTEO joined formation. 1800 Sighted first iceberg bearing 155°T., distance 18 miles, position 141°22'W., 62°15'S..

27 Dec. 1200 Pos. 63°51'40"S. Lat., 148°01'30"W. Lon.

Steaming as before. 0435 USCG NORTHWIND joined formation. 1630 Opened distance in formation to 1000 yards. 1900 Reatarded clocks one hour to zone plus 10 time.

28 Dec. 1200 Pos. 65°41.9'S. Lat., 159°35'W. Lon.

Steaming as before, in column open order, guide in this vessel in company with U.S.S. CANISTEO (AO-99), U.S.S. SENNET (SS-408) and USCG NORTHWIND. 1145 Commenced getting numerous radar contacts on icebergs of various sizes. Steaming at various courses to avoid icebergs. 1900 Retarded clocks one hour to zone plus 11 time.

29 Dec. 1200 Pos. 66°45.4'S.Lat., 170°51.9'W. lon.

Steaming as before. U.S.S. CANISTEO (AO-99) fueled USCG NORTHWIND and U.S.S. SENNET (SS-408). Crossed the Antarctic Circle.

30 Dec. 1200 Pos. 67°24'S.Lat., 179°48'W. Lon.

Steaming as before. 1044 Sighted Scott Island bearing 244°T. distance 16 miles. 1200 U.S.S. MERRICK (AK-97) joined formation. 1202 USCG NORTHWIND left formation on reconnaisance around Scott Island. 1303 U.S.S. CANISTEO commenced fueling U.S.S. YANCEY, U.S.S. MERRICK, and the U.S.S. SENNET. 1359 Sighted pack ice all around the horizon ahead of this ship. 1422 Commenced steering at various courses and adjusting speed to maintain approximate position 67°48'S., 179°24.2'W.. Upon completion of fueling exercise U.S.S. CANISTEO detached and ordered to proceed to rendezvous with Eastern Group.

31 Dec. 1200 Pos. 67°49'S. Lat., 180°00'W. Lon.

Hove to approximately 12 miles North of pack ice in company with U.S.S. MERRICK, U.S.S. YANCEY, U.S.S. SENNET, and USCG NORTHWIND. 1025 Underway entering into the outer limits of ice pack. 1055 Hove to. Conference of all Commanding Officers of the Central Group aboard U.S.S. MOUNT OLYMPUS. 1327 Rear Admiral CRUZEN, CTF-68 and part of his staff transferred to the USCG NORTHWIND for the passage through the ice pack. Underway in column with USCG NORTHWIND guide, U.S.S. MERRICK , U.S.S. YANCEY, and U.S.S. MOUNT OLYMPUS respectively. Entered ice pack, steering at various courses and speeds to maintain position in column.

1 Jan. 1200 Pos. 69°17.5'S. Lat., 179°44.7'E. Lon.

Underway proceeding through medium pack ice with USCG NORTHWIND guide in company with U.S.S. MERRICK (AK-97), U.S.S. YANCEY (AK-93), and U.S.S. SENNET (SS-408). Steering various courses and speeds to maintain position. Stopped numerous times by pack ice. 1535 Formation lying to while USCG NORTHWIND reconnoiters to the Southward. 1758 Underway shifting to new position in the ice. 1917 Lying to in clear water using various courses and speeds to keep clear of ice.

2 Jan. 1200 Pos. 69°17.5'S. Lat., 179°49.5'E. Lon.

Lying to maintaining position in clear water. 1838 Chief of Staff and Captain MOORE, Commanding U.S.S. MOUNT OLYMPUS, left the ship to attend conference of Commanding Officers with CTF-68 aboard the USCG NORTHWIND. 2035 Chief of Staff and Captain MOORE returned to the ship. 2230 Underway in column in the following order. USCG NORTH-WIND GUIDE, U.S.S. MERRICK (AK-97), U.S.S. MOUNT OLYMPUS (AGC-8), U.S.S. YANCEY (AK-93), and U.S.S. SENNET (SS-408).

3 Jan. 1200 Pos. 69°17.5'S. Lat., 179°27.8'E. Lon.

0400 Forward progress of formation stopped by heavy pack ice. USCG NORTHWIND maneuvering to take U.S.S. SENNET (SS-408) in tow, taking her to the northward to clear water. 1945 Shifted position in ice, lying to.

4 Jan. 1200 Pos. 69°18.0'S. Lat., 179°50.3'E. Lon.

Attempting to shift out position in heavy pack ice. 0800 Situation in vicinity of U.S.S. MERRICK, U.S.S. YANCEY rapidly moving to a critical stage. Two large icebergs moving with the current into the face of the wind. Heavy pack ice moving with the wind opposite the general direction in which the icebergs are moving, piling up pressure ice ahead of the icebergs. U.S.S. MERRICK and U.S.S. YANCEY frozen in solid in the path of the icebergs. U.S.S. MOUNT OLYMPUS present position not in any immediate danger. USCG NORTHWIND requested to return to this vicinity as soon as possible. 1246 Put three experienced men, Dr. Paul Siple, Capt. Boyd, USMC, and Mr. Perkins (Fish & Wild Life representative) on the ice to study ice conditions in view of possibility of moving men on foot over the ice. 1330 USCG NORTHWIND sighted returning to our assistance. 1402 Ice party returned. 1135 USCG NORTHWIND broke U.S.S. YANCEY out of the ice into clear water astern of the icebergs. 1727 USCG NORTHWIND breaking ice around U.S.S. MERRICK.

5 Jan. 1200 Pos. 69°04'S. Lat., 179°45.5'E. Lon..

0045 Underway to form column USCG NORTHWIND breaking ice ahead.
0113 Formed column with USCG NORTHWIND guide, U.S.S. MERRICK, U.S.S.
YANCEY, and U.S.S. MOUNT OLYMPUS respectively. 0328 Hove to with bow
in ice while USCG NORTHWIND proceeds to the North to tow U.S.S. SENNET
(SS-408) back to vicinity of Scott Island.

6 Jan. 1200 Pos. 69°41.8'S. Lat., 179°43.5'E. Lon.

0157 USCG NORTHWIND returned, all ships underway in column
as follows: USCG NORTHWIND guide, U.S.S. MERRICK, U.S.S. MOUNT OLYMPUS
and U.S.S. YANCEY. Underway throughout the day.

7 Jan. 1200 Pos. 70°16.2'S. Lat., 178°18.0'W. Lon..

0400 Reversed base course to return to clear water pool to
Northward. Hull at frame 35 starboard leaking at rate of 1 gallon per
minute. 0825 Lying to in clear water.

8 Jan. 1200 Pos. 70°13.0'S. Lat., 178°19.2'W. Lon.

Lying to. 1942 Chief of Staff and Dr. Paul Siple left the
ship for a conference aboard the USCG NORTHWIND with CTF-68. 2052
Chief of Staff and Dr. Siple returned aboard. 2100 USCG NORTHWIND
left group for reconnaisance of ice pack to the Southwest. Commanding
Officer of U.S.S. MERRICK, O.T.C. of remaining ships.

9 Jan. 1200 Pos. 70°13.0'S. Lat., 178°19.2'W. Lon.

Lying to. 1130 USCG NORTHWIND returned. 1900 USCG NORTHWIND
left group to scout ice pack. 2056 USCG NORTHWIND returned.

10 Jan. 1200 Pos. 70°18.5'S. Lat., 178°17.8'W. Lon.

Lying to 0858 Underway in column with USCG NORTHWIND
guide, and U.S.S. MERRICK, U.S.S. YANCEY, and U,S,S, MOUNT OLYMPUS in
that order. 1517 Lying to with bow in ice.

11 Jan. 1200 Pos. 70°28.4'S. Lat., 178°32.8'W. Lon.

Lying to, 0915 Underway to form column in the following
order: USCG NORTHWIND guide, U.S.S. MERRICK, U.S.S. YANCEY, and
U.S.S. MOUNT OLYMPUS. Underway rest of the day.

12 Jan. 1200 Pos. 71°47.8'S. Lat., 179°09.0'W. Lon.

Underway, steaming as before through ice pack.

13 Jan. 1200 Pos. 73°58.5'S.Lat.,179°41'W.Long.

Underway, steaming as before through ice pack.

14 Jan. 1200 Pos. 76°46'S.,Lat., 178°32'W.Long.

Underway, steaming as before through ice pack. 1300 Formation stopped. U.S.S. MOUNT OLYMPUS took position astern of USCG NORTHWIND. New order in formation as follows: USCG NORTHWIND guide, U.S.S. MOUNT OLYMPUS, U.S.S. MERRICK, and U.S.S. YANCEY. 1345 Rear Admiral CRUZEN, CTF-68 returned aboard U.S.S. MOUNT OLYMPUS. 1352 Proceeded underway in new column order, standard distance 700 yards, standard speed 13 knots. 2130 Entered Ross Sea (Pos. 77°37'S., 173°15'W.).

15 Jan. 1200 Pos. 78°23'S.Lat., 164°00'W.Long.

Underway steaming as before through Ross Sea. 0005 Sighted Ross Sea Ice Barrier ahead, bearing 135°T. 0040 USCG NORTH-WIND and one vessel left formation to explore Discovery Bay. 0110 Reversed course, reformed column and proceeded on East-erly course along Ross Sea Ice Barrier, distance one mile. 0615 Passed Lindberg Inlet on starboard beam, distance one mile. 0828 Approaching entrance to Bay of Whales. All ships proceeding independently. 0843 Hove to off entrance to Bay of Whales. 0930 Rear Admiral CRUZEN,CTF-68 and part of his staff transferred to USCG NORTHWIND. USCG NORTHWIND pro-ceeding into Bay of Whales. Commenced to clear bay of ice. 1345 Helicopter from the USCG NORTHWIND dropped film on fan-tail of this ship. 1744 USCG NORTHWIND standing out of Bay of Whales.

16 Jan. 1200 Pos. 78°22'S.Lat.,164°15'W.Long.

Lying to off entrance to Bay of Whales in company with U.S.S. MERRICK and U.S.S. YANCEY. USCG NORTHWIND in Bay of Whales. 0120 Underway, steaming on course 315°T. for purpose of establishing communications with Task Unit north of ice pack. 0400 Reversed course to 145°T., return-ing to former position off entrance to Bay of Whales. 0800 Members of Staff and party left ship for USCG NORTHWIND which is standing out of Bay of Whales. 0842 USCG NORTHWIND standing into Bay of Whales. 1718 Commanding Officer of USCG NORTHWIND came aboard. 1905 Commanding Officers of YANCEY and MERRICK came aboard. 1943 CTF-68 and Commanding Officers of MOUNT OLYMPUS, YANCEY, MERRICK left ship to go aboard USCG NORTHWIND to observe ice conditions in Bay of Whales. 2058 USCG NORTHWIND standing out of the Bay of Whales. 2119 Captain returned aboard. Commanding Officer of MERRICK and YANCEY returning to their respective ships. Lying to for rest of day.

CONFIDENTIAL

17 Jan. 1200 Pos. 78°23'S.Lat.,164°28'W.Long.

Lying to as before off entrance to Bay of Whales. 2305 Transferred Staff officers and men to the U.S.S. YANCEY (AKA-93).

18 Jan. 1200 Pos. 78°24'S.Lat.,164°03'W.Long.

Lying to as before off entrance to Bay of Whales. 0045 U.S.S. YANCEY proceeded into Bay of Whales in company with USCG NORTHWIND and moored to the Bay ice.

19 Jan. 1200 Pos. 78°27'S.Lat.,164°00'W.Long.

Lying to as before off entrance to Bay of Whales. 0825 Transferred Captain QUACKENBUSH, Chief of Staff, TF-68 and various observer personnel to Base Camp. 1608 Captain QUACKENBUSH returned aboard.

20 Jan. 1200 Pos. 78°27'S.Lat.,164°W.Long.
Lying to as before off entrance to Bay of Whales. 1323 Rear Admiral CRUZEN, Captain MOORE and Captain QUACKENBUSH left ship to go aboard U.S.S. YANCEY for conference. 1530 Rear Admiral CRUZEN, Captain MOORE, and Captain QUACKENBUSH returned aboard. 1628 USCG NORTHWIND standing out of Bay of Whales proceeding to northerly direction for rendezvous with U.S.S. PHILIPPINE SEA (CV-47) north of ice pack.

21 Jan. 1200 Pos. 78°27'S.Lat., 164°10'W.Long.
Lying to as before off entrance to Bay of Whales.

22 Jan. 1200 Pos. Lying to off Bay of Whales.
Lying to as before off entrance to Bay of Whales. 1217 Using various courses and speeds to enter Bay of Whales. 1250 Entered Bay of Whales. 1332 Moored starboard side to ice in Bay of Whales, maintaining regular sea watch in preparation for getting underway. 1600 Commenced unloading ship.

23 Jan. 1200 Pos. Moored in Bay of Whales.

Moored as before in Bay of Whales. Iceberg approaching ships through Bay entrance. 2254 Using various courses and speeds to get clear of Bay ice. 2310 Passed towing hawser over ice to U.S.S. YANCEY to assist that ship in getting free from Bay ice. U.S.S. YANCEY free without our assistance. Hauled towing hawser back aboard. Standing by to assist U.S.S. MERRICK if necessary.

Annex I (f)   - 11 -

24 Jan. 1200 Pos. Lying to off Bay of Whales.

0000 Standing out of Bay of Whales. 0330 All ships out of Bay of Whales. Lying to off entrance to Bay of Whales. 1551 U.S.S. YANCEY re-entered Bay of Whales. 1850 Entered Bay of Whales. 1937 Moored starboard side to ice shelf. This ship, MERRICK, and YANCEY now moored to ice shelf, as before.

25 Jan. 1200 Pos. Moored in Bay of Whales. Moored as before.

26 Jan. 1200 Pos. Moored in Bay of Whales.

Moored as before.

27 Jan. 1200 Pos. Lying to off Bay of Whales.

Moored as before. 0630 Heavy snow storm set in with 25 knots of wind. 0700 Observed Bay ice beginning to crack. Our mooring lines insecure. 0740 Underway, using various courses and speeds to stand out of Bay of Whales. 0810 Damage reported in evaporator room starboard side, taking water at water-line through cracked seam. 0815 By orders of Commanding Officer ship listed 2° to port. 0825 Lying to as before off entrance to Bay of Whales. 0909 U.S.S. YANCEY standing out of Bay of Whales. 0923 U.S.S. MERRICK standing out of Bay of Whales. 0923 U.S.S. MERRICK standing out of Bay of Whales.

28 Jan. 1200 Pos. Lying to off Bay of Whales.

Lying to as before off Ross Sea Ice Barrier. 1030 Corrected 2° list of ship to port; ship now on even keel.

29 Jan. 1200 Pos. Lying to off Bay of Whales.

Lying to as before off Ross Sea Ice Barrier. 2050 Standing in toward Bay of Whales. 2121 U.S.S. MERRICK standing into Bay of Whales. 2324 Using various courses and speeds to re-enter Bay of Whales.

30 Jan. 1200 Pos. Moored in Bay of Whales. Lying to as before off entrance to Bay of Whales. Underway steaming on various courses and speeds to stand into Bay of Whales. 1353 Passed through entrance to Bay of Whales. 1357 Hove to inside Bay of Whales. 1600 Commanding Officers, YANCEY, MERRICK came aboard for conference. 1720 Commanding Officers, YANCEY, and MERRICK left ship. 1725 Standing out of Bay of Whales. 1736 Lying to off Ross Sea Ice Barrier. 1836

Sighted USCG NORTHWIND bearing 283°T., distance 13½ miles.
2013 Standing into Bay of Whales. 2052 Commenced transferring
first mail from USCG NORTHWIND to this ship since departure
from Balboa, Canal Zone.

1 FEB.1200 Pos. Lying to off Bay of Whales.

Lying to off entrance to Bay of Whales. U.S.S. MERRICK
(AK-97), U.S.S. YANCEY (AK-93), and USCG NORTHWIND are moored to ice
in Bay of Whales. 1301 Transferred personnel to Base Camp. 1346
Stood out of Bay of Whales. 1400 Lying to off entrance to Bay of Whales.

2 Feb. 1200 Pos. Lying to off Bay of Whales.

Lying to as before off entrance to Bay of Whales. 1230
Using various speeds and courses to stand into Bay of Whales. 1322
Moored port side to U.S.S. MERRICK (AK-97) in Bay of Whales.

3 Feb. 1200 Pos. Moored in Bay of Whales.

Moored as before, to U.S.S. MERRICK (AK-97).

4 Feb. 1200 Pos. Moored in Bay of Whales.

Moored as before to U.S.S. MERRICK. 1010 Stationed
special sea detail as precautionary measure, while U.S.S. MERRICK
was in process of moving stern closer to ice. 1322 Underwater Demolition Team #4 in charge of Lt. (jg) IVERSON commenced swimming tests,
using special rubber suits, along the starboard side. 1504 UDT-4
secured from swimming test with successful results.

5 Feb. 1200 Pos. Moored in Bay of Whales.

Moored as before.

6 Feb. 1200 Pos. Moored in Bay of Whales.

Moored as before. 1700 Rear Admiral R.H. CRUZEN, CTF-68
and part of his staff of TF-68 left ship to board USCG NORTHWIND.
1845 Rear Admiral R.E. BYRD left the ship for Base Camp. 1848
Underway for Scott Island. USCG NORTHWIND assisting this ship in
getting clear of U.S.S. MERRICK and Bay ice. 1940 U.S.S. MERRICK
(AK-97) and U.S.S. YANCEY, and U.S.S. MOUNT OLYMPUS following in that
order. Speed 10 knots, course 301°T. 2132 Cleared local pack around
entrance to Bay of Whales.

7 Feb. 1200 Pos. 77°29'S. Lat., 174°40'W. Lon.

Steaming as before. 0926 Entered area of freezing water.
1200 Passing through area of medium and large tabular icebergs.
2130 Base course now 340°T. 2155 Commenced taking Fathometer readings.
Depths indicated 152 - 214 fathoms.

CONFIDENTIAL

8 Feb. 1200 Pos. 74°36.5'S. Lat., 178°38'E. Lon.

Steaming as before. 0030 Commenced taking soundings with
fathometer; fathometer indicated depths of 205 - 240 fathoms. Passing
through areas of clear water with occasional large tabular icebergs.
1600 Fathometer indicated depths of 132 - 160 fathoms. 1800 Fathometer
indicated depths of 195 - 213 fathoms. 2318 Sighted U.S.S. BURTON
ISLAND bearing 020°T., distance 12 miles. 2330 Hove to awaiting arrival
of U.S.S. BURTON ISLAND.

9 Feb. 1200 Pos. 71°38'S. Lat., 178°38'E. Lon.

Lying to at southern boundary of Ross Sea Ice Pack awaiting
arrival of U.S.S. BURTON ISLAND (AG-88). 0010 U.S.S. BURTON ISLAND
joined task group. 0025 Received U.S. Mail from BURTON ISLAND. 0208
Underway on course 000°T. through fairly heavy but loose pack ice.
0353 Entered open water with scattered growlers. 0630 Entered ice pack.
1130 Entered thick ice pack.

10 Feb. 1200 Pos. 70°23'S. Lat., 177°57'E. Lon.

Steaming as before through Ross Sea Ice Pack. 0117 All
ships lying to while USCG NORTHWIND freed U.S.S. MERRICK from ice.
0215 Resumed formation. 0236 Lying to while NORTHWIND and BURTON
ISLAND attempt to locate lead through the ice pack. 0725 BURTON
ISLAND breaking us clear. 0825 BURTON ISLAND resumed position in
formation. 0830 Resumed position in column. 1200 Formation course
changed to North. 1614 Lying to in open water while USCG NORTHWIND
scouted the ice pack. 1639 NORTHWIND returned to position in formation
going ahead on various courses and speeds in largely open water, with
some growlers. 1730 USCG NORTHWIND left formation to scout ice pack.
Increasing winds and snow storm decreased visibility greatly. 1800
Visibility reduced to 1000 yards because of heavy snow. 2010 Steering
engine airbound unable to move rudder. Lying to. 2017 Making all
preparations for being towed by USCG NORTHWIND. Repairing steering
engine. 2033 Steering by hand. 2205 Steering control shifted back to
pilot-house. 2206 Gaining position to put bow into ice pack headed
into wind. 2345 Bow into ice approximately 450 yards to starboard of
U.S.S. YANCEY (AK-93).

11 Feb. 1200 Pos. 70°01.5'S. Lat., 177°49'E. Lon.

Steaming as before through Ross Sea Ice Pack. Presently
lying to with bow into ice riding out blizzard and sleet storm, visibility 400 yards. 0045 Visibility increased to 5 miles. 0800 Visibility reduced to one mile. 1520 U.S.S. BURTON ISLAND proceeding Southwest on scouting mission. USCG NORTHWIND proceeding Northward on

CONFIDENTIAL

Scouting mission. 1632 Moving ship to new position 2000 yards
to port of U.S.S. MERRICK. U.S.S. YANCEY moving to new position
700 yards on our port bow. 1827 Formation underway proceeding
on Northerly course, U.S.S. BURTON ISLAND guide, U.S.S. MERRICK,
U.S.S. YANCEY, and U.S.S. MOUNT OLYMPUS. 1902 Sighted USCG
NORTHWIND bearing 008°T.. 1918 USCG NORTHWIND came alongside port
quarter to transfer mail and Admiral CRUZEN's personal effects.
1932 USCG NORTHWIND assumed position as guide. 1934 Steaming
through light ice pack. 2115 U.S.S. MERRICK lost use of rudder as
ice sheared pin holding rudder to rudder post. 2154 This ship
ordered to proceed on Northerly course in company with U.S.S.
YANCEY and U.S.S. BURTON ISLAND. USCG NORTHWIND preparing to take
U.S.S. MERRICK in tow. Pack ice thinning.

12 Feb. 1200 Pos. 67°48'S. Lat., 177°51.5'E. Lon.

Steaming as before through ice pack. 0145 Steaming through
largely clear water with many small and medium sized growlers and occasional large tabular icebergs. Passed through main part of ice pack.
0924 Entered open water with scattered small growlers. 1044 U.S.S.
BURTON ISLAND left formation and proceeded southward to meet USCG
NORTHWIND and U.S.S. MERRICK. 1145 Reversed course, took position
2500 yards on port beam of U.S.S. YANCEY. 1815 Hove to, off edge of
growlers field awaiting arrival of U.S.S. BURTON ISLAND. 1950 Underway at various courses and speeds to shift position clear of icebergs.
2000 Sighted U.S.S. BURTON ISLAND. 2015 Maneuvering to allow boat
from U.S.S. BURTON ISLAND to come alongside, to transfer personnel
to this ship.

13 Feb. 1200 Pos. 68°02.5'S. Lat., 176°53'E. Lon.

Steaming an various courses and speeds as necessary to maintain position outside of ice pack in area of scattered tabular icebergs.
2009 Sighted Scott Island bearing 062°T., distance 7 miles. 2047 Passed
Scott Island abeam to starboard distance 2000 yards. 2117 Stopped,
lying to 5 miles Northeast of Scott Island.

14 Feb. 1200 Pos. 67°18'S. Lat., 179°51.5W. Lon.

Lying to as before off Scott Island. Awaiting return of
U.S.S. BURTON ISLAND from Little America. 0858 Lowered small boat to
scout Scott Island for possible landings. Lt.Comdr. MEAGHER in charge
of landing party, which consists of four officers, three civilians,
and two enlisted men. 1028 Landing party returned. No landings made
on Scott Island. Lying to rest of the day.

15 Feb. 1200 Pos. 67°21'S. Lat., 179°33'W. Lon.

Lying to as before off Scott Island. 1615 Heavy snow storm, visibility decreased to less than one mile. 1720 Visibility now about 10 miles. 1800 Heavy snow storm with wind up to thirty knots, lying to rest of day using various courses and speeds to remain headed into wind.

16 Feb. 1200 Pos. 67°18'S. Lat., 179°33'W. Lon.

Lying to as before off Scott Island. Using various courses and speeds to remain headed into wind, wind about 10 knots. Lying to rest of day.

17 Feb. 1200 Pos. 67°13'S. Lat., 179°59'E. Lon.

Steaming as before in vicinity of Scott Island. 1421 Fired 150 rounds of 50 caliber ammunition for test purposes. 2005 Entered moderate snow storm, visibility reduced to about 3 miles. 2030 Visibility decreased to about 100 yards. 2055 Emerged from snow storm. Visibility opened to about 10 miles.

18 Feb. 1200 Pos. 67°23'S. Lat., 179°57'W. Lon.

Steaming as before in vicinity of Scott Island. 0904 All engines stopped and hove to for repairs in the engine room to the steam throttle valve. Repairs completed, engines now in normal running condition. 1300 Exercised at general drills. 1400 Steaming around Scott Island, distance ½ mile to conduct soundings of adjacent waters. 1439 Making run on iceberg for 50 caliber machine gun drill, expending 500 rounds.

19 Feb. 1200 Pos. 67°23'S. Lat., 179°51'E. Lon.

Steaming as before in vicinity of Scott Island. 1300 Exercised at emergency drills. 1325 Secured from all emergency drills.

20 Feb. 1200 Pos. 67°21'S. Lat., 179°46'E. Lon.

Steaming as before in vicinity of Scott Island. 1300 Exercised at General Quarters. Commenced run on iceberg. 1350 Secured from General Quarters.

21 Feb. 1200 Pos. 67°23'S. Lat., 179°49'E. Lon.

Steaming as before in vicinity of Scott Island. 0130 Heavy fog set in, visibility reduced to 2½ miles. 0200 Steaming through heavy snow flurries. Steaming in fog rest of day.

CONFIDENTIAL

22 Feb. 1200 Pos. 67°23'S. Lat., 179°52'E. Lon.

Steaming as before in vicinity of Scott Island. 1904 Stopped, lying to 9½ miles northeast of Scott Island.

23 Feb. 1200 Pos. 67°30'S. Lat., 179°59'E. Lon.

Lying to as before off Scott Island. 0000 Underway on various courses and speeds to maintain position 4 - 12 miles from Scott Island. 0010 Heavy snow flurries set in, visibility reduced to 50 yards. 1102 Steaming toward northern edge of Ross Sea Ice Pack for purposes of scouting pack ice conditions, in compliance with CTF-68 dispatch T-A-T618 232046Z of February 1947. Steaming through areas of poor visibility with occasional heavy fog.

24 Feb. 1200 Pos. 69°19'S. Lat. 175°00'W. Lon.

Steaming as before. 0825 Entered Ross Sea Ice Pack for scouting purposes. 1118 Left ice pack on course 050°T. and entered area of water free from ice. Resumed steaming in order to scout edges of ice pack. 1340 Steaming through field of tabular icebergs, moderate to large. 1545 Steaming through area of loose pack, heavy pack one mile to port. 1859 Retarded all ships clocks one hour to plus 12 zone time.

25 Feb. 1200 Pos. 68°30.7'S. Lat., 179°53'E. Lon.

Steaming as before. Running through clear water with reduced visibility, encountered heavy fog and occasional rain squalls. 0647 Entered area of freezing water and numerous scattered pieces of ice. 0722 Sighted ice pack dead ahead, distance 6 miles. 1200 Advanced date to Wednesday, February 26, 1947. 1300 Exercised at General Quarters. 2223 Proceeding on northerly course to join U.S.S. BURTON ISLAND with CTF-68 embarked, in accordance with CTF-68 dispatch 260741Z of February 1947.

27 February. 1200 Pos. 68°39'S Lat.,177°27.5'E. Lon.

Steaming as before to rendezvous with U.S.S. BURTON ISLAND. 0700 Steaming through area of numerous large growlers. 0733 U.S.S. BURTON ISLAND reported bearing 157°T., distance 4770 yards by radar. 0740 Sighted U.S.S. BURTON ISLAND bearing 138°T. and 5400 yards distance. 0745 U.S.S. BURTON ISLAND standing in on starboard beam closing distance to 700 yards. 0801 U.S.S. BURTON ISLAND assumed position 600 yards astern guide. Steaming through area of numerous growlers and reduced visibility. 0850 Forced draft blower on No.2 boiler out of commission. Repairs being made. 0859 Engine room reported unable to maintain speed of 10 knots. Stopped engines, lying to in accordance with verbal orders of CTF-68. 0930 U.S.S. BURTON ISLAND scouting area to northeast. 0905

Engine room reported ability to steam at 9.5 knots, 50 RPM. 0914 Using engines and rudder as necessary to maintain steerageway. 0918 All repairs completed, No.2 boiler back on the line. 0920 Using various courses and speeds to gain position astern of U.S.S. BURTON ISLAND. Visibility now about 1000 yards, Formation heading northward to clear water in order to facilitate transfer of personnel from U.S.S. BURTON ISLAND to U.S.S. MOUNT OLYMPUS. 1000 Visibility closing to about 300 Yards, U.S.S. BURTON ISLAND trained searchlight aft to facilitate our following her. 1330 Lying to, to transfer personnel from BURTON ISLAND to this ship. 1146 Rear Admiral R.E. BYRD, Officer in Charge Antarctic Development Project and Rear Admiral R.H. CRUZEN, CTF-68 returned on board. O.T.C. aboard this ship. 1146 to 1600 transferred various personnel of CTF-68 and observers to this ship. 1750 Engines ahead 2/3, 10 knots, 53 RPM, steaming on course 357°T. Underway for Wellington, New Zealand. 1930 Steaming through clear water passing many moderate-sized tabular icebergs.

28 Feb. 1200 Pos. 66°39'S. Lat., 177°27.5'E. Lon.

Steaming as before. Passing through areas of snow squalls and occasional icebergs.

1 March 1200 Pos. 62°33'S. Lat., 177°40.2'E. Lon.

Steaming as before. 0800 Ship beginning to roll heavily. Taking rolls from 15° to 32° to port and starboard. 0802 Changed course to Northeast putting stern into seas. 0944 Changed course to Northwest headed bow into seas. 1405 Changed course to 310°T. Wind abating and seas becoming much calmer. 1436 Reduced speed to 10 knots because of excessive vibration in propellor shaft when screw comes out of water.

2 March 1200 Pos. 59°36'S. Lat., 175°44.5'E. Lon.

Steaming as before. 1500 Entered dense fog visibility 400 yards. 1730 Fog lifted, visibility 8 miles. Running through moderately rough seas.

3 March 1200 Pos. 56°14.5'S. Lat., 176°20'E. Lon.

Steaming as before. Seas becoming gradually calmer.

4 March 1200 Pos. 51°45'S. Lat., 175°43'E. Lon.

Steaming as before.

5 March 1200 Pos. 47°08.5'S. Lat., 175°43'E. Lon.

Steaming as before. 0947 Sighted USCG NORTHWIND bearing 160°T. distance 12.5 miles. 0955 Using various increasing speeds to test effect of vibrations on shaft alley and hull. 1053 Completed test on shaft vibration of alley and hull. 1245 USCG NORTHWIND took position in column 700 yards astern of this ship (guide). 1415 USCG NORTHWIND dropped astern to obtain oceanographic data. 1852 USCG NORTHWIND resumed position in formation.

6 March 1200 Pos. 43°53'S. Lat., 175°15'E. Lon.

Steaming as before. 0921 USCG NORTHWIND left formation to take core samples. 1434 Sighted U.S.S. BURTON ISLAND bearing 305°T., distance 10.5 miles. 1635 U.S.S. BURTON ISLAND took position in column 700 yards astern this ship (guide). 2125 USCG NORTHWIND rejoined formation and took position 700 yards astern U.S.S. BURTON ISLAND.

7 March 1200 Pos. Moored at Wellington, New Zealand

Steaming as before. 0218 Sighted Cape Palliser Light bearing 037°T., distance 25 miles. 0307 Sighted Baring Head Light bearing 353.5° T.,distance 6 miles. 0621 Using various courses and speeds to conform to dredged channel. 0658 Stopped, lowered starboard gangway to take aboard pilot, Captain P.S. PETERSON, RNZN. 0710 Passed Holswell Point Light abeam, distance 450 yards. Pilot at conn. 0729 Moored portside to Aotea Quay, Wellington, New Zealand with six manila hawsers and one wire hawser, all lines tripled. 0752 Secured main engines. 0754 Secured No.1 boiler, No.2 boiler in use for auxiliary purposes. 0756 Pilot left ship. 0835 In accordance with CTF-68 dispatch 015054Z of March 1947 all enlisted men from U.S.S. YANCEY going to the East Coast of the United States were transferred to this vessel. 0902 Received on board fresh provisions. Moored as before rest of day with regular in port watch set. Receiving fresh water and telephone service from the dock.

8 March 1200 Pos. Moored at Wellington, New Zealand.

Moored as before. 1740 Lighted off boiler No.1. 1945 secured boiler No.2.

9 March 1200 Pos. Moored at Wellington, New Zealand.

Moored as before.

10 March 1200 Pos. Moored at Wellington, New Zealand

Moored as before.

11 March 1200 Pos. Moored at Wellington, New Zealand.

Moored as before.

12 March 1200 Pos. Moored at Wellington, New Zealand.

Moored as before.

13 March 1200 Pos. Moored at Wellington, New Zealand.

Moored as before.

14 March 1200 Pos. Moored at Wellington, New Zealand.

Moored as before. 1540 Mr. FRASER, Prime Minister of New
Zealand, came on board for an official visit. 1600 Mr. FRASER
left the ship. Made all preparations for getting underway.
1603 Tug alongside to assist ship in getting away from dock.
Pilot, Captain P.S. PETERSON, RNZN, came aboard. 1637 Underway
for Balboa, Canal Zone in accordance with CTF-68 dispatch 122200Z
of March 1947. Pilot at the conn. Steaming at various courses
and speeds to conform to dredged channel. 1645 Formed column, this
ship guide, USCG NORTHWIND and U.S.S. BURTON ISLAND in that order.
1651 Pilot left the ship. 1947 With Cape Palliser Light abeam to
port bearing 016°T., distance 4.3 miles, took departure on initial
great circle course of 094°T., speed 14 knots, 77 RPM. 2038
U.S.S. BURTON ISLAND and USCG NORTHWIND left formation to proceed
on assigned duty.

15 March 1200 Pos. 41°40'S. Lat., 173°37'W. Lon.

Steaming as before. 1033 Shifted steering control to automatic gyro pilot. 2400 Changed date to 15 March, 1947 to conform
to plus 12 zone description.

16 March 1200 Pos. 41°12.5'S. Lat., 167°46'W. Lon.

Steaming as before. 0100 Advanced ship's clocks one hour
to conform to plus eleven time.

17 March 1200 Pos. 40°43.6'S. Lat., 161°49'W. Lon.

Steaming as before through heavy fog areas, visibility one
mile.

18 March 1200 Pos. 39°32'S. Lat., 156°27'W. Lon.

Steaming as before. Passing through alternate fog and heavy
rain squalls. 1145 Changed from gyro pilot to hand telemotor.

steerage. 1527 Casualty in steering engine room due to extraction of wrong connecting pin; veered off course northward. 1529 Shifted steering to trick wheel in steering engine room and reduced speed to 1/3 ahead. 1535 Resumed steering control in pilot house and changed speed to ahead standard.

19 March 1200 Pos. 38°32'S. Lat., 150°38'W. Lon.

Steaming as before through low overcast and rain squalls and winds from 20 - 25 knots.

20 March 1200 Pos. 37°07'S. Lat., 145°15' W. Lon.

Steaming as before through low overcast and rain squalls.

21 March 1200 Pos. 35°10'S. Lat., 139°16'W. Lon.

Steaming as before through low overcast and rain squalls.

22 March 1200 Pos. 32°45'S. Lat., 133°29'W. Lon.

Steaming as before through low overcast and rain squalls.

23 March 1200 Pos. 30°24'S. Lat., 127°45'W. Lon.

Steaming as before. Sky becoming clear, velocity of wind increasing.

24 March 1200 Pos. 27°26.3'S. Lat., 122°47.5'W. Lon.

Steaming as before. Through calm seas and clear weather.

25 March 1200 Pos. 24°05'S. Lat., 117°57'W. Lon.

Steaming as before.

26 March 1200 Pos. 20°48'S. Lat., 113°16'W. Lon.

Steaming as before. Passing through light rain squalls. 1300 Exercised at emergency drills. 1349 Secured from all emergency drills..

27 March 1200 Pos. 17°33'S. Lat., 108°33'W. Lon.

Steaming as before. 0100 Advanced ship's clocks one hour to conform to plus 7 zone time.

28 March 1200 Pos. 14°05'S. Lat., 104°00'W. Lon.

Steaming as before through intermittent light rain squalls.

CONFIDENTIAL

29 March 1200 Pos. 10°22'S. Lat., 99°34'W.Long.

Steaming as before. 0900 Commander Task Force 68 and Staff held personnel and material inspection. 1130 Secured from Admiral's inspection.

30 March 1200 Pos. 6°54'S.Lat., 95°34'W.Long.

Steaming as before. 0100 Advanced ship's clocks one hour to conform to plus 6 zone time.

31 March 1200 Pos. 3°15'S.Lat., 91°09.5'W.Long.
Steaming as before through intermittent rain squalls.

1 April 1200 Pos. 0°10'S.Lat., 87°33'W.Long.

Steaming as before. 0001 Made radar contact with San Cristobal (Chatham) Island, of the Galapagos, bearing 336°T., distance 54 miles. 0135 Passed San Cristobal Island abeam to port, distance 48 miles. 2028 Electrical fire caused by a short circuit started in passageway B-0301LC. 2035 Fire extinguished.

2 April 1200 Pos. 3°00'N.Lat., 84°04.5'W.Long.

Steaming as before.

3 April 1200 Pos. 5°46'N.Lat., 81°17.6'W.Long.

Steaming as before. 0100 Advanced ship's clocks one hour to conform with plus 5 zone time. 1455 Made radar contact with Punta Mariato, Panama (3300 ft) bearing 002°T., distance 77 miles. 2237 Sighted Cape Mala light bearing 352°T., distance 20 miles.

4 April 1200 Pos. Moored at Balboa, Canal Zone.
Steaming as before. 0715 Passed Toboguille Light abeam to port. 0720 Stationed special sea detail. 0732 Took Pilot on board. 0755 Entered Balboa entrance channel and commenced steaming at various courses and speeds to conform to dredged channel. 0839 With assistance of yard tugs moored starboard to berth 16, Balboa, Canal Zone. 0850 Secured special sea detail. 0855 Pilot left the ship.

5 April 1200 Pos. Moored at Balboa, Canal Zone.

Moored as before.

CONFIDENTIAL

6 April 1200 Pos. Moored at Balboa, Canal Zone.

Moored as before. 0140 SURRATT, T.W., CM3, USN, was drowned
forward of the ship while swimming from boat landing between
piers. Rescue party recovered body at 0345 by use of grappling
hooks.

7 April 1200 Pos. Passing through Panama Canal.

Moored as before. 0500 Made all preparations for getting underway. 0530 Stationed special sea detail. 0554 Pilot came aboard.
0614 Underway to transit the Panama Canal in accordance with the
verbal orders of Commander Task Force 68. 0714 Entered Miraflores
Locks. 0756 Left lock and entered Miraflores Lake. 0812 Entered
Pedro Miquel Locks, and entered Pariso Reach. 1116 Exchanged
passing honors with U.S.S. PINE ISLAND (AV-12) which passed
abeam to port in Pena Blanca Reach. 1233 Anchored in Anchorage
Basin, Gatun Lake to await southward transit of four ships through
the Gatun Locks. 1745 Underway to complete transit of Canal. 1756
Entered Gatun Locks. 1918 Left Gatun Locks and entered Gatun approach. 2013 With Toro Point Light abeam to starboard, bearing
091°T., set first course enroute Cristobal, Canal Zone to Washington
D.C.. 2202 Passed Isla Grande Light abeam to starboard.

8 April 1200 Pos. 12°21'N. Lat., 78°23'W. Lon.

Steaming as before.

9 April 1200 Pos. 17°00.5'N. Lat., 75°59'W. Lon.

Steaming as before. 1901 Passed Navasso Island abeam to port.

10 April 1200 Pos. 22°09.5'N.Lat., 74°41'W. Lon.

Steaming as before. 0407 Passed Cape Maipi Light abeam to port.
1150 Passed Costle Island abeam to starboard. 1334 Passed Fortune
Island abeam to starboard. 1445 Passed Crooked Island to starboard.
1945 Passed San Salvador abeam to port. Passed various southbound
merchant vessels all during the day and night.

11 April 1200 Pos. 27°55'N. Lat., 74°41'W. Lon.
Steaming as before.

12 April 1200 Pos. 33°48'N. Lat., 75°23'W. Lon.
Steaming as before. 1700 Passed Diamond Shoals Light abeam to port.
2140 Steaming through moderate fog.

Annex I (f)   - 23 -

CONFIDENTIAL

13 April 1200 Pos. Steaming up the Chesapeake Bay.

Steaming as before. 0235 Passed Cape Henry Light abeam
to port. Entered inland waters; steaming at various courses and
speeds to conform to dredged channel. 0332 Anchored in Merchant
anchorage in Chesapeake Bay. 0656 Underway, steaming up
Chesapeake Bay to Washington, D.C..

ANNEX I-(g)

NARRATIVE

U.S.S. MERRICK (AKA 97)

Chronological Order of Events.

NARRATIVE OF OPERATIONS

1-8 November 1946 - Upkeep at San Diego, California. During this period all personnel whose enlistments would expire prior to completion of the scheduled operation were transferred. Replacement personnel were received as necessary to bring the personnel strength up to full authorized allowance, plus some additional engineer force ratings. All officers and men were given special physical and dental examinations, including chest x-ray. All excess boats were turned in an necessary requisitions submitted to bring all ship's stores, provisions, spare parts and equipment up to the level of estimated requirements.

9 Nov. - 5 December 1946 - Departed San Diego on 9 November and arrived Port Hueneme on same date. Reported to CTF 68 for duty on 10 November. Commenced loading cargo, provisions, stores and spare parts and installing foul weather protection on bridge wings and lookout stations. Installed six 675-cu.ft. reefers on main deck and one diesel powered motor generator unit to provide AC power for their operation. Received one LCM-5 equipped with keel heat exchanger in exchange for a standard LCM-3. U.S.S. YANCEY departed for Operation HIGHJUMP on 2 December but this vessel was delayed pending receipt of certain items of cargo. Completed loading cargo on 5 December, having received 3,354 long tons. Received all CTF 68 passengers, including CB detachment, Marine LVT Unit, several individual observers and ratings on board. Departed Port Hueneme, California, for Scott Island at 1000, 5 December 1946.

6-13 December 1946 - Steaming independently enroute Scott Island, conducting individual ship exercises. Crossed Equator on 11 December and conducted appropriate "Neptune" ceremonies.

14-21 December 1946 - Enroute Scott Island. On 18 December rendezvoused with YANCEY and CACAPON in Lat. 37°-57'-S, Long. 157°-W. Received 165,308 gallons of fuel oil from CACAPON and transferred mail, stores, movies and two enlisted photographer's mates to CACAPON via breeches buoy. Fueling from CACAPON was conducted without incident. The weather was clear and the sea calm. A speed of 10 knots was maintained throughout the operation. Upon completion of fueling, CACAPON departed to join the Western Task Group and MERRICK and YANCEY proceeded in company as Task Unit 68.1.2. Sighted the first small piece of floating ice in Lat. 49°-40'-S, Long. 158°-50'-W on 21 December 1946.

22-28 December 1946 - Enroute Scott Island in company with YANCEY. On 23 December arrived in reported position of Nimrod Islands and conducted search for same with YANCEY deployed 20 miles on port beam. Although visibility was excellent, no land was sighted, no radar contacts or soundings were recorded (limit of fathometer was 250 fathoms). Resumed course to Scott Island. On 27 December commenced encountering numerous icebergs, large and small. The operation of the surface search (SG-1) radar was extremely satisfactory. All bergs produced a distinct image and

contacts were made at ranges up to 40,000 yards. At one time a total
of 78 separate contacts were clearly visible on the radar screen. At
1830 on 28 December arrived off Scott Island but were unable to see
the islands due to fog. Radar contact was unreliable due to the
large number of icebergs present. At 2010 on 28 December encountered
northern edge of ice pack. YANCEY was deployed to eastward and MERRICK
to westward to scout edge of pack for possible open water channels and
to observe the general characteristics of the ice. To the West of
Scott Island the pack contained heavy concentrations of large tabular
bergs and no open water. From Lat. 56°-S to the Scott Islands the sea
remained calm with only a slight to moderate swell, but the weather
was consistently foggy with only short intervals of fair visibility.
Without the aid of radar it is considered that the navigation of
these waters would have been extremely hazardous and much time
would have been lost.

29 December 1946 - 16 January 1947 - YANCEY and MERRICK continued
scouting northern edge of ice pack until 0100 on 30 December, at
which time departure was made for Scott Island to rendezvous with
CTF 68 and the ships of the Central Group. Sighted Scott Island at
1000 and joined with MOUNT OLYMPUS, NORTHWIND, CANISTEO and SENNET.
Commenced fueling from CANISTEO at 1630 and completed receiving 56,000
gallons of fuel oil at 1845 without incident. The sea was calm and
visibility good. A speed of 5 knots was maintained throughout the
operation. Entered Ross Sea ice pack in Lat. 67°-43'-S, Long. 179°
-57'-E at 1444, 31 December. MERRICK second ship in column astern of
NORTHWIND, followed by YANCEY, MOUNT OLYMPUS and SENNET. Light pack
encountered with much open water. About midnight encountered heavy
close pack and encountered difficulty due to channel closing in astern
of the icebreaker causing stops by individual ships and necessitating
assistance from NORTHWIND. About 1200 on 1 January 1947 sustained
minor damage to hull at water line, port side, frame 32, caused by
striking edge of heavy pack. Ice pack continued very heavy resulting
in many stops for aerial reconnoitering and waiting for wind and currents to loosen the pack or create open channels through which the
ships could pass. On 3 January it was decided that it was unsafe
for the submarine SENNET to attempt to proceed further and the
NORTHWIND departed to escort her back to the open sea in the vicinity
of Scott Island. The three remaining ships were left lying to in
what appeared to be a safe position. At midnight the ship was beset
in ice. A large tabular iceberg was observed to be drifting toward
the ship contrary to the movement of the ice pack. Our position
steadily became worse and attempts to move the ship were made by
alternately dropping the bow anchors to break the ice at the stem
and by dropping heavy camels suspended from the forward booms over
each side. A few rounds were fired into the ice from forward 40 mm
guns but were too far forward to be of any help. As a result of the
above efforts the ship was moved ahead a distance of approximately
160 yards which improved our position to some extent. The timely

return of the NORTHWIND enabled the ship to break out of the ice into
a large open pool in the lee of the berg and eliminate a grave situation. This incident was the only serious condition encountered during
transit of the ice pack. The ice pack varied from open pack of thin
rotted ice to close pack of solid ice up to 15 ft. thick. On 13
January cleared southern limits of pack and entered open water only
sparsely dotted with small bergs and drift ice. Arrived off entrance
to Bay of Whales at 0900 on 15 January and commenced lying to while
NORTHWIND reconnoitered the Bay, breaking up bay ice and shearing
off shelf ice to facilitate mooring of remaining ships.

17 January - 6 February - Entered Bay of Whales at 2000, 19 January
and moored port side to shelf ice, using four 8-inch manila lines
secured to "deadmen" which had been planted in the ice approximately
60 yards from the edge by our advance line handling party who were
landed by boat. On 22 January commenced discharging cargo from
ship directly to ice shelf and continued operations on 24-hour
schedule until departure on 6 February. Twice during this period
it became necessary for the ships to get underway and clear the bay
due to weather and ice drifting into the bay from the sea. Upon
return the ship moored in the same position each time, using the
same "deadmen" as previously. The ice shelf remained intact throughout the entire period. Considerable melting of the ice shelf in the
immediate vicinity of the overboard discharge from main condenser
necessitated warping the ship ahead a few feet in order to discharge
cargo from #3 hold.

6-22 February - Departed Bay of Whales on 6 February enroute to Scott
Island accompanied by MOUNT OLYMPUS, YANCEY and NORTHWIND. Joined
with BURTON ISLAND off southern edge of ice pack at midnight 8 February
in Lat. 72°-42'-S, Long. 179°-04'-E and entered loose pack preceded by
NORTHWIND and BURTON ISLAND and followed by MOUNT OLYMPUS and YANCEY.
About 1600 on 10 February encountered heavy pack and proceeded with
difficulty. At 2116 on 11 February a large piece of heavy ice drifted
into rudder shearing the stock above the rudder and rendering its
further use impossible. Taken in tow by NORTHWIND but cast off due
to heavy weather. During the night the rudder carried completely
away and was lost. The ship drifted with the current until 2000 on
12 February in open pack at which time NORTHWIND resumed tow. While
being towed through ice it was necessary for NORTHWIND to proceed
with extreme caution. BURTON ISLAND maintained continuous reconnaisance in order to utilize most advantageous route. Cleared northern
limits of ice pack on the morning of 13 February and continued toward
Wellington, New Zealand in tow of NORTHWIND. On 16 February heavy
weather was encountered and at 0400 on the 17th the towing cable
parted. Drifted in heavy seas until 2000, 18 February when we were
again taken in tow by NORTHWIND. Our destination was changed from
Wellington to Port Chalmers, New Zealand and we arrived there on the
afternoon of 22 February. Work of fabricating and installing a temporary rudder was commenced on 25 February and completed 21 March.

RESTRICTED

ANNEX ONE (h)

U.S.S. YANCEY (AKA-93)

Table of Contents

NARRATIVE

Page No.

1. INTRODUCTION   1

2. DAILY NARRATIVE   4

    ANTARCTIC SYNOPSIS   17

    SUPPLEMENTARY DAILY NARRATIVE   19

Annex I-(h)   - i -

NARRATIVE - OPERATION HIGHJUMP

1. INTRODUCTION

The following is a summary of events from time of departure from Norfolk, Virginia on October 21, 1946 to time of departure from Port Hueneme, California on December 2, 1946.

Departed Norfolk, Virginia, October 21, 1946.
Arrived Cristobal, C.Z., October 26, 1946; discharged cargo.
Departed Cristobal, C.Z., October 28, 1946.
Arrived San Pedro, Calif., November 5, 1946; discharged cargo.
Departed San Pedro, Calif., November 9, 1946.
Arrived Port Hueneme, Calif. and reported to CTF-68 for duty
  November 9, 1946; discharged cargo November 12 to 15; loaded
  cargo November 18 to December 1.
Departed Port Hueneme, Calif., December 2, 1946 at 1400U.
Joined CTG-68.2 at 0500U December 3, 1946.

During the time from tentative assignment to TF68 in early October to time of departure from West Coast, this vessel accomplished following major items of maintenance and repair.

All weatherdecks chipped and repainted two coats zinc chromate and two coats blue deck.

Holds completely cleaned. Hold drainage system tested.

All P-500 pumps and submersible pumps overhauled and tested.

Painted side one coat haze grey.

Inspected and cleaned out all fresh water tanks.

Cleaned vent systems as practicable.

Sealed evaporators.

Cleaned firesides and watersides of both boilers. Took bridge gauge readings of all bearings. Overhauled instruments of Hayden Board. Procured spare brushes for all motors at Terminal Island

Conducted general cleaning and adjustment Gyro Compass.

Annex I-(h)   - 1 -

Conducted complete electronics check with the assistance of Naval Shipyard, Terminal Island and N.A.R.D., Port Hueneme.

Completely overhauled and rebalanced boiler fan No. 1 with assistance of Naval Shipyard, Terminal Island.

Completely overhauled main exhaust blower for engine room.

Completely overhauled one boat engine.

Broke out towing gear and with assistance Naval Shipyard, Terminal Island modified towing cable to bring up to drawing specifications. Changes have been covered in a letter to the Bureau of Ships.

There were many small items of general maintenance work accomplished in addition to the foregoing. It can be stated that as much ship's force work was accomplished during aforementioned period as during an ordinary two months yard overhaul period. The ship left Port Hueneme in very good material condition and in a good state of preservation to undergo the stormy weather and rigorous operating conditions in the higher southern latitudes.

During this period, the general supply level was brought up to eight months. The principal deficiency in spare parts at time of departure was bearings for the main generators. Only one set of spare bearings for three generators were on board at time of departure. Additional bearings were received via U.S.S. BURTON ISLAND arriving in early February.

During this period a medical and dental examination of all officers and men was conducted with the assistance of the Dental Clinic at Naval Station, Port Hueneme. Some ninety-six officers and men received the necessary corrective dental attention at the Clinic. One man had to be transferred thereto for extensive dental work as he had to be disqualified medically for Antarctic operations due to poor condition of his mouth. Some ten men were transferred to the U. S. Naval Hospital, Long Beach for treatment or because of medical disqualification for this duty. None of these men could be returned to the ship. With the exception of one man, all of these men were received during October when the crew was augmented for the Operation.

At the time of departure from Port Hueneme there were on board the below listed personnel:

Officers	-	14 (Ship's Company)
Officers	-	4 (Staff TF-68)
Enlisted Men Ship's Company	-	223
Enlisted Men CTF68 Flag Complement	-	13
Enlisted Men CTF68 Seabees	-	91
Enlisted Men FFT MT. OLYMPUS	-	4
	TOTAL -	349

At time of departure from United States, the only deficiency in Enlisted men was one Chief Pharmacist's Mate, who joined at sea on December 19 from U.S.S. MERRICK. This vessel was not supplied with engineer ratings to bring complement up to 125% of postwar allowance as recommended by the Task Force Commander. Some of the men transferred to this vessel from 16th Fleet and other Atlantic activities could not have been as a general rule the best available.

The Bureau of Naval Personnel provided a Medical Officer and Radio Electrician in a temporary duty status upon my request and the backing of the Task Force Commander. In addition, there were three officers, one Chief Pay Clerk and two Ensigns Deck Limited, in excess of the regular postwar allowance of nine officers. This complement of fourteen officers was six or seven below that of the U.S.S. MERRICK. The discrepancy comes as result of fleet assignment of the two vessels. An Amphibious Force AKA has over two times as many officers as a Service Force AKA. The above augmentation came only as result of much representation - officially and unofficially - on my part to the Bureau of Naval Personnel. With the exception of the Executive Officers and the Commanding Officer, no officer on board was fully qualified to handle the ship in ice berg waters, in Restricted Waters, and in the Antarctic Ice Pack. This fact, in addition to the fact that the Executive Officer is also the Navigating Officer, worked considerable hardship on both these officers.

The enthusiasm of the men and officers for the Highjump Operation initially was very high. With the arrival of many ratings from the Sixteenth Fleet and elsewhere, with early departure from the Atlantic, and with the subsequent unexpected reassignment of this vessel to the Pacific Fleet on November 9, 1946, I noted a marked decline in enthusiasm. Only a few of the men who were transferred at Port Hueneme seemed to regret the fact that they could not make the trip. On departure from Port Hueneme two men missed the ship. One of these men was considered to be temperamentally unsuited for this operation. I was relieved not to have him along. After departure, I saw a notable improvement in enthusiasm. One man told me that he thought everyone wanted to make the trip, but about half of the crew disliked leaving the United States. I noted splendid manly attitude and enthusiasm of Seabees on reporting on board on December 2, 1946.

Annex I-(h)   - 3 -

The recreational facilities of the ship were augmented considerably by direct purchases from Recration Fund, by surplus supplies obtained from Terminal Island, and by gifts of past issues of magazines and periodicals. Over seven-hundred books were added to the Library. One of the troop officers state rooms was converted to a reading room and library. Several hundred new phonograph records and recordings along with three playing devices were obtained. Twenty-eight movie programs were provided. Several sets of USAFI publications were provided by Terminal Island and Bureau of Naval Personnel. Materials and tools for hobbycrafts, such as carpentry, metal work, square knot work, splicing and rigging, leathercraft, photography were obtained. Some second-hand musical instruments for forming a "hill-billy" band were obtained from Surplus stocks at Terminal Island. A sum of four-hundred and sixty-one dollars ($461.) was expended from Recreation Fund in November for Recreation materials for the operation.

The loading at Port Hueneme was performed entirely by civilian steve-dores. Some opportunity, nevertheless, was available for training ship's personnel. At time of departure, the state of training was considered to be only fair but as good as possible to obtain in the short time available.

This vessel made all preparations for the operation without benefit of additional funds with exception of one thousand ($1000.) provided by Commander Service Force, U.S. Atlantic Fleet for voyage repairs at Terminal Island.

2. DAILY NARRATIVE

Monday, December 2, 1946.

Underway at 1400 SOA 15 knots direct route to join TG-68.2 and to inter-cept Second Track from West on Sheet 4 of TF Track Charts.

Tuesday, December 3, 1946.

At 0500U intercepted track line, exchanged calls with U.S.S. CURRITUCK, changed course to 219°(T) and speed to 14 knots. At 1800U changed course to 207°(T).

Monday, December 9, 1946.

Course 205°(T), speed 14 knots. At 0443 crossed the equator at long-itude 135-10 W.

Tuesday, December 10, 1946

At 0630 changed course to 176°(T). At 1130 changed course to 204°(T) and speed to 15.2 knots. At 2145 changed course to 225°(T). Commenced

Annex I-(h)   - 4 -

RESTRICTED

transit of the passage between HIVA OA and HUA POU of the Marquesas Group.

Wednesday, December 11, 1946.

Course 225°(T), speed 15.2 knots. At 0230 changed course to 213°(T). In view of CTF-68 110232Z December and Alcom 445, each person on board had opportunity to send out a Holiday Message. Some 150 messages were sent to the U.S.S. CURRITUCK for transmission to a shore station.

At 2025 changed course to 215°(T), speed 12.5 knots because of delay in time for rendezvous north of Tuamotus with TG-68.2.

Thursday, December 12, 1946.

Course 215°(T), speed 12.5 knots. At 0610 took position in column astern U.S.S. HENDERSON - order from Van to rear CURRITUCK, CACAPON, HENDERSON, YANCEY - and changed speed to 16.5 knots. At 0933 changed speed to 12 knots and commenced using changes of course transiting passage between MAKEMO and KAUIU Islands. Between 1500-1700 engaged in tactical maneuvers. At 1700 set course 231°(T), speed 11 knots. At 2000 ordered detached from TG-68.2 and directed proceed independently along fourth track from West; reported to CTU-68.1.2 (CO, U.S.S. MERRICK) and set SOA 10 knots to permit MERRICK to overtake prior reaching 40°S. At 2200 changed course to 190°(T).

Friday, December 13, 1946.

Course 190°(T), speed 10 knots on fourth T.F. track from West. At 1800 changed course to 205°(T).

Wednesday, December 18, 1946.

Course 180°(T), speed 9 knots. At 0300 changed course to 270°(T). At 0710 sighted U.S.S. MERRICK. At 0730 commenced using changes of course and speed falling in with MERRICK. At 0815, took course 206°(T), speed 15 knots following MERRICK. At 1142 set fueling course 214°(T), speed 10 knots; MERRICK alongside U.S.S. CACAPON first. At 1708 commenced fueling, completing at 1925 (Zone ∕10). At 1911 (Zone ∕11) set course 213°(T), 8 knots to intercept former track line.

Thursday, December 19, 1946

Course 213°(T), speed 8 knots. At 1300 changed course to 152°(T) and speed 15 knots, joining MERRICK. At 1807 sighted MERRICK bearing 172°(T), distance 15 miles and changed course to 175°(T). At 2030 took position on port beam MERRICK and set course 180°(T), speed 9 knots.

Annex I-(h)   - 5 -

Thursday, December 19, 1946 (continued)

Informed that unit had been ordered to proceed through position 56-20 S., 158-30 W. in order to disprove or verify existence of NIMROD Group of Islands.

Friday, December 20, 1946

A most unusual display of phosphorence was noted after dark, there being many streamers two or more feet in length.

Monday, December 23, 1946.

At 0800 stationed aloft lookouts to search for Nimrod Group of Islands. At 1200 commenced using changes of course and speed circum-navigating the supposed location of Nimrod Island to the eastward. 1400 Results negative. Course 262°(T), speed 14 knots rejoining MERRICK. At 1830 rejoined MERRICK and set course 258°(T), speed 10 knots.

Thursday, December 26, 1946.

Course 258°(T), SOA 9 knots. At 1100 changed course to 190°(T). At 1200 changed speed to 15 knots to expedite arrival at Pack Ice. At 1900 slowed to 7 knots due to heavy fog.

Friday, December 27, 1946

Course 190°(T), speed 7 knots in dense fog. At 0445 changed speed to 15 knots as result improved visibility. At 0625 sighted first ice - a small bergy bit - distance 12000 yards by radar. At 0900 changed course to 185°(T). Used changes of course and speed variously throughout day due to menaces to navigation - ice bergs growlers, and fog.

Saturday, December 28, 1946.

At 2000 sighted pack ice. There were all the conditions of the pack ice of all types, the Antarctic and Snowy Petrels, drop in injection to 31°, smoothening of sea, etc. Later entered pack ice to determine its nature; concluded conditions not favorable for investigation under low visibility conditions prevailing. After penetrating about six miles, turned about at 2400 and retired to Northward.

Sunday, December 29, 1946.

Departing from Pack Ice and investigating conditions. Retired at 0000 due low visibility. Conditions found much like those described in HO 138.

At 0500 sighted Scott Island to Northward. Proceeding to eastward
along edge of pack ice. At 1100 dense fog set in. Resumed operations
at 2300.

Monday, December 30, 1946.

Continuing search to eastward for leads to southward through Pack Ice.
During afternoon fueled from U.S.S. CANISTEO and joined CTF-68 in MOUNT
OLYMPUS, MERRICK, and SENNET. Making preparations to proceed to Little
America.

Tuesday, December 31, 1946.

Lying to 25 miles south Scott Island in company CTF-68 (Also CTF-68.1)
with TG-68.1 (USCGC NORTHWIND, USS MOUNT OLYMPUS (F), MERRICK, YANCEY,
SENNET). TF Commander held conference of Commanding Officers and later
shifted his flag to NORTHWIND. At 1400 commenced transit of ice pack
in column in order NORTHWIND, MERRICK, YANCEY, MOUNT OLYMPUS, and SENNET.

Wednesday, January 1, 1947.

Traversing ice pack as before. In early afternoon necessary to heave to
in "lake" pending improvement in weather conditions and reconnaissance
of pack to southward.

Thursday, January 2, 1947.

Maneuvering as before. 0900 TFC in NORTHWIND departed for reconnaissance
to the Southward. At 1900 CTF-68 helf conference at which it was decided
to move all ships to south westward to a safer position. At 2100 underway.

Friday, January 3, 1947.

Hove to and blocked in ice. Conditions unfavorable for movement. At
0200 set Damage Control watch (1 officer, 1 CPO, 8 men).

Saturday, January 4, 1947.

Hove to as before. Ice and weather conditions steadily growing worse
after 0600. Between 0800 and 0930 sent several messages reporting that
our condition growing serious due to near approach to ice berg. At 1430
NORTHWIND broke path to open water where ship attempted to maneuver under
extremely unfavorable conditions - gusts to 40 knots, large drift ice,
small sea room, pool closing in under SW winds. At 1620 went alongside
ice due inability to maneuver. Requested assistance. At 1725 NORTHWIND
came alongside to take in tow. 1820 Underway with NORTHWIND towing. At

Annex I-(h)   - 7 -

2100 cast off towing due inability of NORTHWIND to make progress to the
Southward in heavy ice. By using speeds up to 12 knots and by accepting
hazards attendant to navigation in very heavy and solid ice, the ship
was able to reach a small pool where she hove to at 0020, January 5,
1947. Inspected propeller and found small bend in each of two blades
occurring as result this experience.

Sunday, January 5, 1947

Hove to in Small Pool awaiting NORTHWIND and MOUNT OLYMPUS to rejoin after
latter is broken out of ice. Those vessels rejoined at 0130 at which time
TG-68.1 less SENNET continued progress to Southward toward Little America.
At 0400 TFC directed MERRICK, MOUNT OLYMPUS, and YANCEY to Heave To. The
TFC departed in NORTHWIND to rejoin SENNET. At 0500 went alongside large
ice floe.

Monday, January 6, 1947

Hove to in company with MERRICK (SOPA) and MOUNT OLYMPUS awaiting return
TFC in NORTHWIND. 0200 CTF-68 in NORTHWIND joined. 0330 Underway to
Southward in column in order NORTHWIND, MERRICK, MOUNT OLYMPUS, YANCEY.
Used speeds up to 10 knots in traversing Close Pack (rotten ice). Progress
represents best to date.

Tuesday, January 7, 1947

Traversing ice pack as before. At 0420 Reversed course and returned to pool
of open water to await improvement in conditions. No leads to Southward
could be seen. The condition is consolidated pack with hummocks. A number
of ice bergs were noted in the area.

Wednesday, January 8, 1947

Hove to as before. Late in day NORTHWIND departed on extended reconnaissance of the ice pack to the Southward.

Thursday, January 9, 1947

Hove to as before. At 1120 NORTHWIND returned. It was decided to remain
in pool until tomorrow.

Friday, January 10, 1947

Hove to as before. At 0800 all ships underway in order NORTHWIND, MERRICK,
YANCEY, MOUNT OLYMPUS on base course 145°(T) at 4 knots. Two PBM's from
TG-68.2 flew over group on air reconnaissance of ice pack to southward. At
1400 hove to due to unfavorable conditions of ice pack as result of increasing pressure between floes. At 1730 secured No. 2 boiler to repair leaky
economiser header gaskets.

RESTRICTED

Saturday, January 11, 1947

Hove to as before. 0615 Completed repairs on boiler No. 2 and put it on the line. At 0915 underway in column NORTHWIND, MERRICK, YANCEY, MOUNT OLYMPUS, on southerly courses; progress slow due to consolidated pack. At 1800 ice conditions seemed to improve slightly with close pack some rotten ice. By 2300 constant improvement in ice conditions noted. Ice now is close pack pancake rotten ice.

Sunday, January 12, 1947

Traversing ice pack as before. At 0300 ran in open pool southern periphery of which surrounded by thick bay ice; headed east in order to reach pack ice again. Radar picked up shelf (4 ft. high) at 1700 yards. At 1100 indications were that pack conditions improving constantly - now close pack rotten ice pancakes, 20 to 30% open water. At 1800 entered close pack apparently as result strong southerly winds blowing during early afternoon. At 2000 ice and conditions again improved. At 2200 encountered close pack pancake ice and progress thereby retarded again. During the day made turns as high as for 9 knots which was considered too high a speed for safe navigation. The ship was subjected to heavy vibrations.

Monday, January 13, 1947

Traversing ice pack as before. 0015 Secured No. 1 boiler to repair leaky economizer header. 0030 Pack deteriorating rapidly now in open pack with much clear water. 0330 Entering very loose pack or drift ice. 0420 Heavy fog set in. *0630 Visibility increased to five miles. *1015 Fog set in. 1128 Fog lifted. 1145 Cut No. 1 boiler back in on the line. 1200 The ship now entered a large area of sea ice differing materially from that encountered over the past twenty-four hours. This ice is best characterized by its heterogenity - loose pack, close pack, drift ice, ice bergs, bergy bits, shelf ice. There were many large pools of water. Generally speaking the ice was loose pack with open water 30 to 80%. At 1630 recorded fathometer sounding of 145 fathoms.

Tuesday, January 14, 1947

Traversing ice pack as before. Conditions of ice are same as described for yesterday except pools are much larger in extent and there is more drift ice in the pack. At 1220 cleared the pack. At 1300 ships lying to for CTF-68 to shift flag to MOUNT OLYMPUS. At 1400 underway, standard speed 13 knots, course 140°(T) in order NORTHWIND, MOUNT OLYMPUS, MERRICK, YANCEY - clear water ahead. At 1840 entered heavily packed floe and cleared at 1930. At 2000 entered floe of loose pack ice and cleared at 2119, at which time took speed 12 knots. 2200 Entered open pack ice and cleared at 2300, at which time resumed standard speed.

Wednesday, January 15, 1947

Enroute Bay of Whales in column in order NORTHWIND, MOUNT OLYMPUS (CTF-68), MERRICK, YANCEY on course generally 145°(T), speed 12 knots slowing as required while traversing areas of open pack ice. At 0030 sighted shelf ice or barrier at 20,000 yards bearing 150°(T) believed to be Discovery Inlet (Picked up by SA & SG Radars at 14,000 yards). DR position checked within 4 miles of navigational fix at 0048. At 0040 directed to lie to while CTF-68 in MOUNT OLYMPUS investigates inlet. 0142 Again formed column and proceeded on easterly course at 12 knots for entrance to Bay of Whales. At 0830 sighted entrance to Bay of Whales. At 0900 directed by CTF-68 to lie to while NORTHWIND investigates condition inside Bay.

Thursday, January 16, 1947

Lying to as before off entrance to Bay of Whales. Commanding Officer visited Bay of Whales in NORTHWIND and considered conditions therein unfavorable for operating this vessel at that time.

Friday, January 17, 1947

Lying to as before. At 2130 directed to make preparations to enter Bay of Whales. Receiving personnel from MOUNT OLYMOUS and MERRICK up to midnight.

Saturday, January 18, 1947

Standing by to enter Bay of Whales. At 0015 following NORTHWIND into Bay of Whales. At 0108 due to sudden sharp right turn and to restricted sea room damaged two propeller blades while backing full speed to avoid collision with large bergy bit. 0120 Went alongside shelf ice. 0340 Commenced discharge of cargo as directed by CTF-68 Staff representatives. Vessel lying nicely alongside ice even with winds up to 20 knots.

Sunday, January 19, 1947

Moored to shelf ice Bay of Whales discharging cargo. At 1200 records indicate 400 tons of cargo out. Transportation of cargo from dock side to dumps is a difficult problem due to softness of snow and no tendency to compact. Under the circumstances the progress is good. 2055 U.S.S. MERRICK stood in and moored to shelf ice to westward.

Monday, January 20, 1947

Moored to shelf ice Bay of Whales, discharging cargo from two hatches. At 0300 gusts up to 20 knots from North. All appearances are that shelf ice will deteriorate under these conditions if they persist for any length

Monday, January 20, 1947 (continued)

of time. At 0830 under continued swell conditions shelf broke off for
an area to eastward 500 ft. x 100 ft. - shelf ice still satisfactory for
mooring. At 1200 records indicate 475 tons of cargo discharged. 1400
The Task Force Commander came aboard for conference with members of his
staff attached temporarily to this ship and commanding officers. 1500 The
Task Force Commander left the ship. 1630 NORTHWIND departed for rendezvous
with PHILIPPINE SEA North of the Pack.

Tuesday, January 21, 1947

Discharging cargo in Bay of Whales as before. 0515 Vance WOODALL, seaman
second class, U.S. Navy, met accidental death while handling cargo on shelf
ice alongside No. 1 hatch. At 1200 estimate 590 tons cargo discharged to
date.

Wednesday, January 22, 1947

Discharging cargo in Bay of Whales as before. At 0900 Board met in
connection with Investigation of accidental death of Vance (n) WOODALL,
seaman second class, U.S. Navy. At 1200, 727 tons cargo discharged to
date. At 1430 Chaplain MENSTER from U.S.S. MOUNT OLYMPUS conducted
Divine Service in memory of the late Vance WOODALL. It is my under-
standing that this was the first Mass Service of Adoration on record
on the Antarctic continent.

Thursday, January 23, 1947

Discharging cargo in Bay of Whales as before. At 1200 - 872 tons cargo
discharged to date. At 2000 The Board of Investigation convened because
of death of Vance WOODALL, seaman second class, adjourned, investigation
completed. During day Dr. SIPLE and Navigating Officer determined width
of Narrows between East and West Capes to be 675 feet by use of Sextant
Angles and other observations. At 2335 Task Force Commander ordered this
ship to proceed out of Bay due to ice berg drifting through entrance en-
dangering all vessels.

Friday, January 24, 1947

Making preparations to clear shelf ice. 0210 Cleared pack ice surrounding the ship and headed for entrance of Bay of Whales. 0230 Passed through
the Narrows between West and East Capes heading seaward. 0300 Conducted
test to determine vibrational effect of bent propeller blades. Excessive
vibration set in at 65 RPMs ahead. There was no appreciable vibration at
50 RPMs astern. 0330 MERRICK and MOUNT OLYMPUS stood out of Bay of Whales.
All ships lying to off entrance. 1100 U.S.S. MERRICK returned to moorings
in Bay of Whales. 1530 Proceeding into Bay of Whales. 1655 Moored starboard side to shelf ice. 1845 U.S.S. MOUNT OLYMPUS stood in and moored.

Saturday, January 25, 1947

Moored to shelf ice Bay of Whales; Base Camp personnel not unloading cargo from this ship. The crew generously donated ninety-seven dollars and forty five cents ($97.45) to "March of Dimes".

Sunday, January 26, 1947

Moored to shelf ice, Bay of Whales; Base Camp personnel not unloading cargo from this ship. Perfect morning - cloudless sky, flat calm bay, balmy winter weather. Holiday routine enjoyed by all. 1800 Commenced discharge U.D.T. ammunition

Monday, January 27, 1947

Moored to shelf ice in Bay of Whales discharging ammunition. 0300 Stopped discharge ammunition due to snow storm (approximately 40 tons off loaded and delivered to Ammo Cache). Total cargo discharged to date 970 tons. 0730 All ships making preparations to clear Bay of Whales due to increasing Northerly winds, this rendering Bay untenable. 0850 Underway following MOUNT OLYMPUS. 0909 Cleared the Narrows of Bay of Whales. 1000 MOUNT OLYMPUS, MERRICK, YANCEY, maneuvering in open formation on northerly and southerly courses off entrance to Bay of Whales. Fresh winds and snow storm continued throughout day. Visibility at times 1000 yards.

Tuesday, January 28, 1947

Maneuvering off entrance Bay of Whales as before. No notable moderation of weather until 2100. At 2140 sent LCM in to Bay of Whales with supplies and personnel for tent camp. 2330 LCM returned.

Wednesday, January 29, 1947

Lying to off entrance of Bay of Whales as before. Weather moderating slowly; light snow intermittently during forenoon; afternoon beautiful winter day.

Thursday, January 30, 1947

Lying to as before off entrance to Bay of Whales. 0500 sighted first wave of two R4D airplanes over Little America. 0740 Sent in LCM to Bay of Whales with personnel and supplies for Base Camp. 1950 Stood in to Bay of Whales and moored to shelf ice at 2040.

Friday, January 31, 1947

Moored to shelf ice in Bay of Whales; U.S.S. MERRICK also present. 1350 U.S.S. MOUNT OLYMPUS stood into Bay and commenced lying to. 1500 Commenced reloading material not required at Base. 1600 The TFC held conference of Commanding Officers and Officers of his Staff, after which flagship stood out. 1940 USCGC NORTHWIND stood in and moored to shelf ice.

Saturday, February 1, 1947

Moored to shelf ice in Bay of Whales reloading vehicles as Base Camp sends them to ship's side. With constantly falling barometer the weather began to worsen; by 2000 wind velocity was 40 knots with gusts to 60 knots; lowest temperature recorded 10°F.

Sunday, February 2, 1947

Moored to shelf ice in Bay of Whales. Early morning winds of over 40 knots from S.E. experienced. With 8 lines out and strain carefully equalized, no difficulty was experienced staying alongside. Fortunately, the wind direction was such as to minimize break-up of shelf ice. With high wind and low visibility it would have been touchy getting out of the Bay of Whales. At 0500 with barometer rising weather began to moderate. Loading and unloading cargo intermittently throughout the day. At 1300 U.S.S. MOUNT OLYMPUS stood in and moored alongside U.S.S. MERRICK.

Monday, February 3, 1947

Moored in Bay of Whales as before standing by to reload cargo.

Tuesday, February 4, 1947

Moored in Bay of Whales as before reloading cargo as it becomes available.

Wednesday, February 5, 1947

Moored in Bay of Whales as before reloading cargo as it becomes available.

Thursday, February 6, 1947

Moored in Bay of Whales as before reloading cargo as it becomes available. During past few days have furnished approximately 100 man days assistance to Temporary Camp in form of working parties (41 man days yesterday). 1300 Completed reloading equipment mostly trucks, tractors, sleds, spare airplane engines and propellers, airplane jacks, etc. 1900 Ships getting underway in following order for Scott Island, NORTHWIND (CTF-68 temporary flagship), MOUNT OLYMPUS, YANCEY, MERRICK. 2005 This ship cleared Bay of

Whales. 2045 Formed column in order Van to rear NORTHWIND, MERRICK, YANCEY, MOUNT OLYMPUS, speed 7 knots using various courses between West and West Northwest. Encountered heavy ice off entrance to Bay of Whales. At 2215 Changed standard speed to 10 knots.

Friday, February 7, 1947

Enroute Scott Island as before. Standard speed 10 knots, course generally West to West Northwest. At 1630 changed course to 310°(G). During day passed a number of ice bergs and bergy bits; sea otherwise partically free of ice. At 2130 changed course to 340°(G). At 2300 changed course to 000°(G).

Saturday, February 8, 1947

Enroute Scott Island as before. At 1000 changed course to 015°(G). Observations indicate Gyro error at high latitudes (75-78 S) approximately 3°W on N-S headings and 12°W on E-W headings. Beautiful weather today. 1400 Changed course to 020°(G). At 1940 changed course to 345°(G). 2320 Sighted U.S.S. BURTON ISLAND 10 miles to Northward; stopped, commenced lying to in order to transfer mail and supplies from BURTON ISLAND.

Sunday, February 9, 1947

Lying to as before. 0250 Formed column in order Van to rear NORTHWIND, BURTON ISLAND, MERRICK, YANCEY, MOUNT OLYMPUS and went ahead on northerly course at 5 knots. 0317 Entered close pack ice 6 to 8 feet thick. 0341 Entered open water speed 5 to 10 knots; many bergy bits in area. 0640 Entered loose pack ice. 0915 Rosary Service conducted by LTJG Victor C. SZCZEPKOWSKI, USNR. 1000 Protestant Lay Service conducted by Chief Machinist Edwin F. STEINFELD, USN. 1200 Entered area of close pack Bay ice 5 to 8 feet thick, 10-20% open water. 1700 Entered open pack mostly open water. 2000 Entered area close pack. 2330 Entered area of consolidated pack and heavy bay ice; necessary lie to while NORTHWIND investigated conditions.

Monday, February 10, 1947

Lying to as before. 0300 Directed by Task Force Commander to clear area to Southward. 0800 Entered area of close pack 3 to 8 feet thick rotten ice. 1000 Entered area of loose pack ice 1 to 3 feet thick. 1600 Entered large pool. 1630 All ships lying to while NORTHWIND investigated area of consolidated pack to Northward. 1800 Barometer dropped .09" in past hour, wind increased to 26 knots and wind veered from N.E. E.; blizzard suddenly in progress; all ships ordered to be prepared heave to. 2050 Bow came against large floe in the pack, course 90°; hove to turning over 20-25 rpm during night; winds up to 35 knots with gusts to 45 knots.

Tuesday, February 11, 1947

Hove to as before. 0300 with wind velocity rapidly decreasing and with rate of fall of barometer decreasing weather commenced to moderate. 2005 Formed column order NORTHWIND, BURTON ISLAND, MERRICK, YANCEY, MOUNT OLYMPUS preparing to head Northward; strong winds from Southward. 2020 MERRICK became fouled in heavy ice and subsequently damaged rudder necessitating her being taken in tow. 2250 CTF-68 directed this vessel to take charge of U.S.S. BURTON ISLAND and MOUNT OLYMPUS and proceed out of pack; formed column order BURTON ISLAND, YANCEY, MOUNT OLYMPUS and proceeded at six knots on generally northerly course; during night experienced winds of 45 knots with gusts to 55 knots.

Wednesday, February 12, 1947

Proceeding through pack ice with wide leads on northerly course. 0930 Cleared pack ice at 68-07 S. - 177-12 E. 1040 Directed BURTON ISLAND join CTF-68; MOUNT OLYMPUS and this vessel lying to and maneuvering on northern extremity of pack. 2030 BURTON ISLAND rejoined for purpose transfer personnel to MOUNT OLYMPUS and upon completion returned to join NORTHWIND and MERRICK.

Thursday, February 13, 1947

Lying to as before with MOUNT OLYMPUS in company. 1100 Towing group cleared the pack. 1230 Reported to Captain THOMAS, USCGC NORTHWIND as CTU-68.1.2 in accordance CTF-68 despatch 132223Z. 1350 Formed column in order YANCEY, NORTHWIND, MERRICK (in tow), heading for Wellington, New Zealand. 1420 Set course 359°(T); building speed up slowly ; at 1640 speed 8.3 knots. Beautiful weather today. Task Force Commander shifted Flag to BURTON ISLAND; MOUNT OLYMPUS headed for Scott Island. Except for few bergs water clear of ice. 1900 Retarded clocks one hour. 2215 Increased speed to 11 knots.

Saturday, February 15, 1947

There was no Friday this week as date advanced one day. Enroute to Wellington, New Zealand on course 359°(T), speed 11 knots, as part of TU-68.1.2 (YANCEY, NORTHWIND, MERRICK in tow). 0940 Changed course to 356°(T). 1400 Conducted vibration test; made 15 knots 82 turns without difficulty and with tolerable vibration; maximum sustained speed reported as 13 knots. 2210 Commenced snowing. 2256 Reduced speed of formation to 10 knots due to heavy load on towing gear of NORTHWIND.

Sunday, February 16, 1947

Enroute Wellington, New Zealand as before, course 356°(T), speed 10 knots in low visibility due to snow later becoming drizzle. 0355 Reduced speed to 8 knots due to sea conditions becoming less favorable as result westerly winds about 20 knots. 0915 Catholic Rosary Services conducted

by LTJG Victor C. SZCZEPKOWSKI, USNR. 1000 Protestant Service conducted
by Ensign Gordon M. COLEMAN, USNR. 1035 increased interval on NORTHWIND
to 2,000 yards and commenced laying oil slick; sea conditions worsening.
2021 Base course changed to 344°(T); ship rolling heavily; changing speed
and course as required to keep station.

Monday, February 17, 1947

Enroute Wellington, New Zealand as before. Course 344°(T) using various
courses and speeds to keep station on NORTHWIND. 0025 Reported to CTU-68.1.2
that this vessel was rolling violently (45°) and suggested that we head up
into wind; changed course to 315°(T). 0120 Changed course to 270°(T); winds
60 knots, seas rough and confused; at about 0200 towline parted and MERRICK
adrift. 0510 Made turn to port rolling up to 45° with sea astern and headed
for MERRICK to lay oil slick. 0652 Reported to CTU-68.1.2 that even pumping
to stopl hove to for remainder of day keeping in visual contact with MERRICK.

Tuesday, February 18, 1947

Hove to as before with TU-68.1.2 using various courses and speeds to keep
in visual contact of MERRICK which is adrift. During afternoon weather began
moderating slowly. 2000 MERRICK in tow; formed column normal order; course
337°(T) building up speed.

Wednesday, February 19, 1947

Underway as before in company TU-68.1.2 in order YANCEY, NORTHWIND, MERRICK
in tow, course 337°(T), speed 8-10 knots. During early morning wind shifting
through North to East of North and barometer commenced to fall very slowly.
0900 LTJG Victor C. SZCZEPKOWSKI, USNR, conducted Catholic Service (Ash
Wednesday). 0943 Changed course to 015°(T) to head into slight sea, that is
forming as result new storm estimated to be located between position and
Campbell Island. 1200 Changed course to 030°(T). 1700 Fog set in. 1900
Changed course to 350°(T). 2210 Fog lifted.

Thursday, February 20, 1947

Underway as before in company with TU-68.1.2 enroute Port Chalmers,
New Zealand in order YANCEY, NORTHWIND, MERRICK in tow at speed 10 ⅟ knots
on course 350°(T). 1050 Increased speed to 12.2 knots. 2400 Changed
course to 319°(T).

Friday, February 21, 1947

Underway as before in company with TU-68.1.2 enroute Port Chalmers, New
Zealand in order YANCEY, NORTHWIND, MERRICK in tow at speed 12 ⅟ knots, course
319°(T). 0915 Reduced speed to 10.5 knots due to heavy strain on NORTHWIND's
towing cable. 1722 Increased speed to 12 ⅟ knots. 2045 Changed course to
311°(T).

Saturday, February 22, 1947

Underway as before in company TU-68.1.2 course 311°(T), speed 12 ⊀ knots. 0821 Changed course to 319°(T). 0834 Changed speed to 13 knots. 1500 Commenced using changes of course and speed preparatory to taking on pilot and entering port. 1705 Moored starboard side to south side George Street Wharf, Port Chalmers, New Zealand.

Sunday, February 23 to Friday, February 28, 1947

At Port Chalmers in the Otago District of South Island, New Zealand in company U.S.S. MERRICK.

The following is synopsis of principal events during period in the Antarctic:

ANTARCTIC SYNOPSIS

December 27, 1946	- Sighted first ice at 0625 U at latitude 62-30 S., 173-28 W. - a small bergy bit.
December 28, 1946	- Sighted Pack at 2000 U at position (DR) 67-37 S., 179-23 E.
December 29-30, 1046	- Investigating conditions of ice pack by radar and by observation from crow's nest to eastward from longitude 179-30 E. to vicinity of the 176° W. meridian. Afternoon December 30, fueled from U.S.S. CANISTEO after rendezvous with Task Force Commander.
December 31, 1946	- At 1400 Xray entered pack at 67-47 S., 179-53 W.
January 14, 1947	- At 1200 Xray left pack at 76-42 S., 177-40 W. Width of pack 550 miles.
January 15, 1947	- At 0030 Xray sighted Discovery Inlet.
January 15, 1947	- At 0630 Xray sighted Bay of Whales. Distance steamed from Port Hueneme to Bay of Whales 8309 miles.
January 18, 1947	- Entered Bay of Whales and commenced discharge of cargo. Served as headquarters ship for TF-68 personnel connected with erection temporary camp until January 23, 1947.
February 1, 1947	- Commenced reloading equipment not required at Temporary Camp.
February 6, 1947	- Completed reloading. Departed Bay of Whales for operating area to North of the Ice Pack.
February 9, 1947	- Entered Pack Ice at 0317 Xray at 72-35 S., 178-57 E.
February 12, 1947	- Departed Pack Ice at 0930 Xray at 68-07 S., 177-12 E. Width of pack 275 miles.

February 13, 1947   — Formed towing unit, TU-68.1.2, Captain THOMAS in NORTHWIND senior and at 1350 Xray set course for Wellington, New Zealand in column in order YANCEY, NORTHWIND, MERRICK (in tow). Perfect weather.

February 14, 1947   — Friday was skipped.

February 15, 1947   — Sighted last ice berg latitude 64-01 S., Longitude 175-52 E.

February 17, 18, 1947 — Riding out storm. U.S.S. MERRICK adrift. 2000 M February 18 set course for Port Chalmers, New Zealand as destination changed.

February 22, 1947   — Arrived Port Chalmers, New Zealand.

Miles steamed since 2 December 1946 - 10620 miles.
Fuel used since 2 December 1946   - 424440 gallons.
Fresh water used since 2 December - 765820 gallons.
Fresh water distilled since 2 December - 721420 gallons.

SUPPLEMENTARY DAILY NARRATIVE FROM MARCH 1 TO APRIL 17, 1947

Saturday March 1 to Tuesday March 4, 1947

At Port Chalmers, New Zealand.

Wednesday, March 5, 1947

At Port Chalmers, N.Z. 0700 Got underway for Pago Pago, Samoa. 0806 Cleared entrance and set course 046°(T), speed 13 knots. 1911 Changed course to 040°(T).

Friday, March 7, 1947

Underway as before. 0000 Changed course to 023°(T). 2400 Retarded date one day having crossed 180th meridian during early afternoon.

Friday, March 7, 1947

This is a repeat day having shifted to Zone ≠ 12 time. Underway as before. 0830 Reduced speed to 10 knots to permit securing boiler No. 2 for repairs. 2200 Completed boiler repairs. 2300 Increased speed to 13 knots.

Saturday, March 8, 1947

Underway as before. 0000 Advanced clocks one (1) hour to Zone ≠11 time.

Tuesday, March 11, 1947

Underway as before. 0800 Changed course to 012°(T). 1400 Arrived Pago Pago, Samoa (distance from Port Chalmers 2126 Miles).

Wednesday, March 12 to Wednesday, March 26, 1947

At Pago Pago, Samoa loading general cargo. Completed loading at 1600 Xray March 26th, having taken on board approximately 1400 tons GSK surplus material destined for Pearl Harbor. Ship's force engaged in loading operations furnishing dockside and hatch details.

Thursday, March 27, 1947

Departed Pago Pago, Samoa at 0830, Xray with YTL-153 in tow, SOA 10 knots.

Friday, March 28, 1947

Enroute Pearl Harbor as before course 020°(T).

Saturday, March 29, 1947

Underway as before except SOA 9.3 knots. At 1130 reduced speed to 7.8 knots in view of receipt of dispatch from ComServPac stating that he considered SOA 10 knots excessive.

Sunday, March 30, 1947

Underway as before except SOA 7.2 knots. 0830 Stopped for excutive officer and party to inspect tow. They found everything including shaft locking device to be in very good condition. 0900 Went ahead at SOA 7.5 knots. 0930 Ensign COLEMAN conducted Protestant lay services. 1030 LTJG SZCZEPKOWSKI conducted Catholic Rosary Services. 2000 Changed course to 023°(T).

Tuesday, April 1, 1947

Underway as before. 0400 Slowed to SOA 6 knots due to light head seas. 0700 Changed course to 030°(T). 1000 Changed course to 035°(T) and SOA to 3.2 knots due to moderate head seas. 1900 Changed course to 040°(T).

Monday, April 7, 1947

Underway as before except course 035°(T) SOA 3.1 knots. The drift due to wind and current is over 3.5 knots.

Monday, April 14, 1947

Underway as before. 0930 Arrived Pearl Harbor with YTL-153. (Total 2286 miles).

ANNEX ONE - (j)

NARRATIVE

U.S.S. BURTON ISLAND

1.   The U.S.S. BURTON ISLAND was commissioned at the Naval Shipyard, Terminal Island, San Pedro, California on 28 December 1946. Outfitting and provisioning ship for Operation HIGHJUMP was begun on 30 December 1946. During the precommissioning period 1 October 1946 to commissioning all plans had been formulated and material and provisions ordered so that after commissioning, it remained only a matter of getting the material on board. Loading of provisions and stores was completed on 10 January 1947, except for items of cargo for the task force which continued to arrive until the time of departure. Much of this cargo was for ships of the Eastern and Western Groups and in the absence of specific instructions to the contrary, was taken aboard even though it was known these ships would not be contacted in the Antarctic.

2.   After loading, during the period 10-15 January the ship conducted at sea training underway, running the measured mile, obtaining tactical data, and exercising at aircraft training. Training was completed and fuel and provisions topped off on 15 January 1947 and at 0800 on that date the ship reported to Commander In Chief, Pacific Fleet and Commander Training Command, Pacific, for duty, ready in all respects for sea. Orders were received directing the ship to report to Commander Training Command, San Diego Group, for shakedown during the period 16 January - 7 February 1947. Knowing this was not the intentions of Commander Task Force SIXTY-EIGHT, a dispatch was sent to him informing him of the circumstances and requesting instructions.

3.   The ship departed Los Angeles Harbor at 0700, 16 January for San Diego, California and reported to Training Group, San Diego, California. It was decided that Training Group San Diego would conduct an inspection of the ship and if the ship was found ready for sea, orders would be issued for it to report to Commander Task Force SIXTY-EIGHT for duty. The inspection was held during the forenoon of 17 January 1947. As a result of the inspection the ship was ordered to report to CTF 68 for duty and departed San Diego at 1530, 17 January 1947 for Little America. Speed of 14 knots was set and the great circle course to Scott Island was laid down and followed.

4.   The trip southward was made without unusual incident. Numerous minor engineering deficiencies developed during the first two weeks of the trip but were speedily repaired and at no time was the ship delayed by them. On the whole the ship and ship's personnel preformed remarkably well considering the short period available for training and indoctrination.

5.   On 5 February in approximately Latitude 62° S, Longitude 168° W. the first iceberg was sighted. From then until the pack was encountered icebergs were constantly in sight. It was found the SU radar did not pick up the Antarctic icebergs at the ranges that a

Annex I-(j)   - 1 -

similar unit picked up Arctic icebergs. It is believed this is due to
a difference in the density of the bergs and to the fact that Antarctic
bergs are not as high as those encountered in the Arctic.

6.   The northern edge of the ice pack was encountered in
Latitude 68° 21' S. Longitude 175° 15' W. and in accordance with orders
from CTF 68, course was changed to the westward to scout the edge of
the pack, heavy pack was encountered during the forenoon of the next
day, 7 February, and appeared to get steadily heavier as the ship proceeded westward. This fact was reported to CTF 68 and orders were
received to proceed southward along the 179° E. Meridian. The ship
worked southward through ice varying from close heavy pack to pancake
ice until clear water was reached in Latitude 70° 40' S. and Longitude
178° 52' E. At 2200 on 8 February the vessels of the Central Task
Group were joined in Latitude 72° S. Longitude 179° 15' E. and cargo and
mail for these vessels was delivered.

7.   At 0125 on 9 February the Central Task Group proceeded northward to clear the pack ice. The group proceeded northward without untoward incident until at about 1900 on 11 February the U.S.S. MERRICK
broke her rudder stock by drifting into a heavy floe. At 2200 this
vessel was ordered to proceed with U.S.S. YANCEY and U.S.S. MOUNT
OLYMPUS to clear water, while the U.S.C.G.C. NORTHWIND stood by the
U.S.S. MERRICK. The trip northward clear of the pack was completed at
0900, 12 February 1947, without incident and at 1045, BURTON ISLAND
reversed course to rejoin NORTHWIND and MERRICK. At 1430, rejoined
NORTHWIND and MERRICK, then NORTHWIND came alongside to transfer
passengers. Upon completion of transfer, BURTON ISLAND proceeded
northward to transfer passengers to MOUNT OLYMPUS. This task was
completed at 2200 and again course was set to the southward to rejoin
NORTHWIND and MERRICK. Rejoined at 0130, 13 February. Proceeded to
act as scouting vessel to guide NORTHWIND with MERRICK in tow through
loose pack. At 1100 all ships were clear of pack.

8.   At 1325, 13 February Rear Admiral R. H. Cruzen, (CTF 68)
shifted his flag to BURTON ISLAND and at 1340, set course to the
southward and proceed at 14 knots enroute McMurdo Sound, Antarctica.

9.   At 1850 on 15 February made sight contact with Mt. Melbourne
and proceeded southward toward Drygalski Ice Tongue which was reached
at 0330 on 16 February. Took departure and headed for McMurdo Sound
which was entered at 2100 same day. At 2336 encountered solid bay ice
in vicinity of Inaccessible Island and lay to with bow in edge of ice.
The ship remained in McMurdo Sound until 2000 on 20 February when departure for Little America was taken. During the stay in McMurdo
Sound, reconnaissance flights were made of surrounding area for possible
landing areas for planes and ships. The camp sites of Scott's two
expeditions were visited and found to be in a remarkable state of

Annex I-(j)   - 2 -

preservation considering the length of time since they were established. The helicopter was damaged during a reconnaissance flight to Scott's camp on Hut Point, Ross Island, but was repaired and flown back to the ship.

10.   The ship arrived off the entrance to the Bay of Whales at 0532, 22 February 1947. At 0626, ship moored alongside bay ice in Bay of Whales, to evacuate personnel of base camp. At 0328 on 23 February, all personnel and equipment to be evacuated were on board and the ship got underway to proceed northward clear of pack. An uneventful trip was made and at 2350, 25 February the ship was clear of the ice pack—a record run.

11.   The following morning, 26 February, the U.S.S. MOUNT OLYMPUS was joined and Rear Admirals Cruzen and Byrd, and the majority of personnel, evacuated from base camp were transferred. Upon completion of transfer of personnel, departed Antarctica for Port Chalmers, New Zealand to transfer cargo to the U.S.S. MERRICK. Arrived Port Chalmers, 1700, 4 March 1947 after a very rough voyage, during which the ship rolled 51°. Transferred cargo and at 1700, 5 March, got underway to join U.S.S. MOUNT OLYMPUS and U.S.C.G.C. NORTHWIND to proceed to Wellington, New Zealand. Joined up at 1600, 6 March and at 0700, 7 March entered Wellington harbor.

12.   Departed Wellington, New Zealand, 1600, 14 March 1947, enroute Pago Pago, Samoa in company with U.S.C.G.C. NORTHWIND. Arrived Pago Pago, Samoa, 0930, 19 March 1947. Departed Samoa, 1800, 19 March 1947 enroute San Pedro, California. Nothing worthy of comment occured during this trip. Arrived San Pedro Harbor, 1600, 31 March 1947. Reported to Commander In Chief, Pacific Fleet and Commander Service Force, Pacific Fleet for duty.

ANNEX ONE-(1)

NARRATIVE

U.S.S. CURRITUCK (AV-7)

NARRATIVE AND PREPARATIONS PRIOR DEPARTURE ON OPERATION

1.   Situation.

        Prior to receipt of the orders to participate in the operation, the CURRITUCK had been alongside a dock in a maintenance status for a period of months, but was now in the process of being reactivated for duty on the Asiatic Station. The acute personnel situation then current in the Navy by reason of the demobilization fully affected this vessel. Of prime concern was the Engineering Department where the inexperienced personnel were encountering numerous difficulties with all phases of the plant. The ship was to continue to be handicapped by critical personnel shortages throughout the entire operation.

2.   Ship Employment.

        The period 3 - 16 October was utilized in undergoing a curtailed Underway Training Program for reactivated ships under the supervision of the Underway Training Command, San Diego. On 16 October the ship conducted successful tests in the use of shipboard radar for controlling instrument landings of seaplanes under zero conditions. The procedure developed at this time proved satisfactory and was not modified with further experience. On 17 October the ship sailed for the U. S. Naval Shipyard at Hunters Point, San Francisco, arriving the next day. In addition to urgent repairs and overhauls, a helicopter platform and additional transmitters for aircraft communications were installed during yard availability. On 14 November the ship departed from the shipyard for San Diego, arriving the 16th—encountering some engineering difficulties enroute. The next week the ship was at anchor in order to give the Air Department its initial training in tending PBM seaplanes loaned for this purpose. On 23 November the ship got underway, rendezvoused with the Task Group destroyer and conducted fueling exercises. Upon completion the ship held a full power run. During the final week and until departure on 2 December, the ship was moored alongside the dock at North Island receiving supplies and making final preparations. On 28 November Captain Charles A. Bond, USN, reported aboard to assume duties as ComTaskGroup 68.2. During this week the aviation detachment and staff personnel reported aboard. The aircraft also arrived, three PBM's one HO3S-1, one HOS-1, and SOC-1.

3.   Preparation.

        It was realized, of course, that realistic planning and meticulous preparation should be made before venturing on an Antarctic expedition about which little was known and during which no outside aid could be expected. Insofar as was possible the efforts of all departments were directed towards accomplishment of the following obvious but essential objectives for preparedness:

A. Personnel on board sufficiently in advance and to be trained and rehearsed in all phases of expected operations.

B. Sufficient number of competent technicians on board.

C. Actual drill with and development of satisfactory procedures for anticipated operations.

D. Complete testing and satisfactory check out of all equipment through whole range of operation, accurately calibrated as required.

E. A full allowance of spares and special equipment.

F. Complete data maintained.

Although little time was available, most equipment and procedures were tested to some extent by the personnel assigned to their operations.

As noted, fueling at sea and seaplane tending was rehearsed, radio direction finders and other radio and navigation equipment were calibrated or compensated.

The correction of engineering deficiencies required the utmost effort before sailing, although the performance of the Engineering Department during the operation was excellent.

In the matter of personnel, the ship was unable to obtain all required ratings and supplies and spares were being received up to the last hour of sailing with a number not arriving on time.

Liaison - Contact was established early with the tanker and the destroyer. Meetings were held with the several Department Heads, and this vessel arranged to carry stores and provide services for the other ships as required. The other ships were provided with Jato units, seaplane buoys, gasoline, and instructions and procedures to enable them to act as emergency seadromes. This vessel arranged to carry the spare propellers for the destroyer.

Research and Study - Implementing the information and recommendations received from Commander Task Force 68 and the Navy Department concerning sub-arctic conditions and operations, local libraries were searched for all volumes pertaining to the Antarctic, but useful information obtainable was sparse. Officers in the vicinity who were known to have had duty in Arctic zones were interviewed. Information and recommendations were evaluated for their application to this vessel; special material was requisitioned as considered advisable and an ice bill drawn up. Classes for officers and men were held to study available cold weather operation reports and instructions were given in appropriate subjects with assistances from various sources.

Welfare and Recreation - The crew was given physical examinations to determine individual fitness. Material and facilities for an excellent recreation program were obtained through energetic effort. Individual personnel requirements were taken care of to maximum extent practicable before sailing.

NARRATIVE OF CURRITUCK ON OPERATION HIGHJUMP

1.   Enroute initial operating area off Balleny Islands, Antarctica - CURRITUCK with the CACAPON and HENDERSON of Task Group 68.2 departed from the San Diego area 2 December 1946. The ships followed parallel tracks fifty miles apart to obtain sounding data. Enroute the helicopter was flown on three days when weather and sea conditions were favorable. The group rendezvoused the 12th to transverse the Tuomotu Islands, the helicopter being sent ahead to scout for reefs in the little frequented passage. CACAPON fueled the CURRITUCK the 13th and again on the 17th. The HENDERSON also rejoined at this time to effect transfer of personnel and material, and after fueling resumed her track line.

The "Roaring Forties (and Fifties)" were crossed with propititious weather and on 23 December the HENDERSON joined. That same day the first iceberg was sighted in latitude 63-05 South and longitude 174-09 East. Immediately thereafter many icebergs were sighted and for the succeeding ten weeks they were constant companions. This day was bright and clear, and the sudden entry into a vast, dead world of grotesque, multishaped bergs produced a bizarre inpression.

2.   Operations at Antarctica. - The first airplane operations were held the next day, 24 December. The helicopter was flown in the morning to scout and a PBM was hoisted out for a three hour test hop in the afternoon. This was the first time the ship had hoisted a PBM at sea and it was at once apparent that hoisting operations in still water provide little preparatory training for the much more critical problem of hoisting in the open sea. During this hoisting operation and those immediately following it, a continuous and searching analysis was made of all phases of plane handling. Since good seaplane operating weather in Antarctica was usually reckoned in hours, the problem was to reduce all plane handling times to a minimum except crane operating time and that of actual fueling from the ship's side, which were, of course, uncontrollable. Efficient organization, team work, timing, and "know how" evolved steadily until it was believed all bugs had been removed and all unnecessary delays eliminated. Time was eventually cut almost two thirds and planes were hoisted in a roll of slightly over $3°$ on a side, and a wind of seventeen knots, which is considered limiting. Hoisting out in more than a 15 knot wind or a $1\frac{1}{2}°$ roll is not recommended for beginners.

After the first flight dense fog closed in making it possible for the ship to celebrate Christmas undisturbed. On 26 December the continental ice pack was sighted for the first time. On this morning during a helicopter flight CAVU conditions were changed by fog to zero zero in a matter of minutes. The helicopter was landed aboard after some tense moments by means of directing it to follow the rim of the ice pack into which the ship had stuck her bow. That afternoon a PBM took off but was forced to return due to bad weather. The 27th and 28th were foggy but the sea was calm and on the 28th the CURRITUCK moored loosely to the CACAPON to fuel. The CACAPON and HENDERSON then took their weather stations, the former about four hundred miles to the north, and the destroyer the same distance to the west. The rest of December was spent in dense fog, moving frequently to clear drifting bergs.

As the ship gained experience in Antarctic navigation, it was soon found that the biggest menace was the growler, a large chunk of ice with too little area above the surface to be picked up readily with radar. Although frequently large enough to do substantial damage to the hull, their greatest danger was damage to the ship's bronze propellers. The ship navigated among bergs at night and in thick fog at 5 to 10 knots, the consideration being whether visibility was such that growlers would be seen in time to turn. Bergs were shown by radar with fidelity (the radar was kept in excellent operating condition) and the ship maneuvered in and out among them easily. At one time as many as 120 bergs were visible on a 15 mile scope. Later in the season the bergs began to break up and growlers became an even worse menace.

The CURRITUCK was still near the Balleny's New Years Day and found satisfactory flying weather. The first mapping flight of about seven hours was flown, the helicopter also flying. It might be added here that the usual procedure after a flight was launched was for the ship to steam so as to keep up with good weather which would be of short duration at a single spot. The ship was thus continuously looking for good weather and for ice bays in the pack ice for wind protection, being guided in the former by the aerologist's recommendations.

On the 2nd both PBM's accomplished long mapping flights for the best day's work in the Antarctic to date. Both PBM's again mapped on the 4th, one mapped on the 5th and also on the 6th. Operations were eminently successful and a substantial portion of the area assignment had been completed by this time.

On the 6th the ship received orders to proceed east to Scott Island in latitude 69° and longitude 179° E to scout for the Central Group which was having difficulty breaking through the Ross Sea ice pack to Little America. On the 8th a PBM attempted to scout for the Central Group but was turned back due to bad weather. The SOC was flown this date. On the 10th the ship arrived near Scott Island. Both PBM's scouted for the Central Group on the 11th and 12th under generally poor weather conditions. The helicopter and the SOC also flew, the latter flying to Scott Island and scouting the thickly strewn ice covered area. Duty having been completed, the ship then proceeded westward to her assigned area looking for favorable operating weather. Often the weather was good but the northerly swell was running too strongly and the ice bays did not provide refuge from the swells. In this area adjacent to the magnetic pole, the magnetic compasses were of no value whatsoever. The second or auxiliary Mark 18 gyro compass was of great value, but should be cut into all repeaters to be of full value. The importance of the fathometer in these poorly charted waters is also obvious if any progress is to be made. On the 21st wind under the rotor blades of the helicopter bent them upward putting it out of commission. By the 22nd the ship was in longitude 140° East and weather was good this date. Two PBM's accomplished long mapping flights. During these flights the CACAPON joined and fueled the ship. The CACAPON then proceeded to a rendezvous with the PHILIPPINE SEA, carrying mail for home. While hoisting aboard, one PBM's wing tip was damaged when it came into contact with the side of the ship. Weather was poor for the next few days and a flight was not made until the 26th at longitude 134° East. The damaged wing tip was replaced in the meantime. Again on the 27th and 28th both planes flew photographic missions. The SOC was also flown. At this time the ship was off the Shackleton Ice Shelf at 124 degrees East. It was during these flights that unfrozen lakes or "oases" were discovered. Also it was in this area that the largest icebergs were sighted, one estimated at more than seven miles long. Great numbers of seals and whales were seen on or adjacent to the pack ice. The final flight in January was on the 30th.

The CURRITUCK launched one PBM the first of February in longitude 120° East. On the 2nd both planes flew missions from 115° East. On the 4th the CURRITUCK fueled the HENDERSON and transferred stores. After fueling the seas became rough and the weather became worse. Ship handling in heavy seas was normal. The sea was kept on the bow and the speed was adjusted to wave period to give best results. The ship rides well down wind, but turning into the wind should be made early if there is reason to expect an increase in wind and seas, since turning across the trough could jeopardize the planes secured on deck.

The days were now growing noticeably shorter and colder. Trouble was being increasingly experienced by freezing of the circulating water of the boats. During this time flight operations were often scheduled but the weather conditions forced their cancellation. On the 8th the CURRITUCK fueled from CACAPON. After fueling winds increased to about fifty knots and the ship lay to the next two days. On 11 February both PBM's completed photographic missions. During their absence the five inch guns were fired at ice bergs for test of fuzes and training. Having photographed the adjacent area the CURRITUCK moved westward the 12th. The next day in longitude 93° East, both PBM's made successful flights. On the 16th the ship had reached 65° East looking for favorable weather enroute. The HENDERSON joined and was fueled from CURRITUCK on the 17th. On the 18th the weather was still poor and the CURRITUCK continued to 40° East. Snow storms were encountered, reducing the visibility to zero. Finally, on 22 February conditions improved and both PBM's were launched on photographic missions, one reaching 14° East, the Westernmost limit of exploration. The helicopter was repaired by this time and also flew. The weather again deteriorated and the CURRITUCK now turned east in search of better conditions. Heavy winds tore off the port aileron of one PBM. At noon of the 25th mountains on the mainland were seen from longitude 54°. The 26th one PBM flew a mission while the aileron of the other was repaired. It so happened that the area over the continent that would have been assigned the second PBM was closed in. Both planes flew the next day. February 28th the ship was in longitude 74° East.

On the first of March both PBM's made their last flight over the continent. The helicopter flew that day also. At this time new ice was forming on the water, and on the planes during takeoff. Boat engines readily froze. The temperature hovered around 15° F. and it was concluded that seaplane operations with present equipment were definitely impracticable below this. Weather was unfavorable for flying on March 2nd, and on the 3rd the CACAPON joined and fueled, all ships departing thereafter independently across the fifties and forties for Sydney, Australia. At this time the weather conditions were in an auspicious phase for the crossing, but a succeeding storm caught up with the ship and on the 9th during a 32 degree roll (35 degrees maximum reached) of the ship, the spare PBM without wings located aft on the fantail fell over the side, its beaching gear fittings having crystallized. The fuselage of a second PBM was twisted during the storm, rendering it unflyable.

The ships rendezvoused the 12th in Bass Strait and proceeded to Sydney for a six day visit. Departing the 20th the CURRITUCK fueled from CACAPON and proceeded independently to the Canal Zone and Norfolk, orders having been received to go direct to the East Coast for deactivation rather than returning first to San Diego.

ACCOMPLISHMENTS (STATISTICAL)

1.   Ship Performance.

        (a) Miles steamed - 29,198. Days at Sea - 127.
        (b) Fueling at sea from tanker - No. times - 7.
        (c) Fueling Destroyer at Sea - No. times - 2.
        (d) Casualties or other damage sustained by ship - None.

2.   Aircraft Operations.

   (a)   Number of Flights, PBM   - 36.   Total hours - 248.3.
   (b)   Number of Flights, HO3S-1 - 27.   Total hours - 21.3.
   (c)   Number of Flights, SOC-1 - 3.   Total hours - 6.2.
   (d)   *Losses during Operations - None.
   (e)   Damage sustained during above operations - One PBM
         with tip damaged (quickly repairable) during one re-
         covery, and slight hole (also quickly repairable)
         punched in side of PBM by boat during hoisting in
         another recovery.

         *During a storm while enroute Sydney after conclusion
         of operations, one PBM was lost over side and the other
         two damaged in varying degrees.

3.   Aircraft Photography.

   (a)   Antarctic continental area photographed: 46,618 sq.miles.
   (b)   Coastline photographed from, 167°20' East to 14°00'
         East less following sections: (150°58' to 144°38'),
         (87°44' to 79°53'), and (49°57' to 56°20').

GENERAL COMMENTS AND RECOMMENDATIONS

1.   It is felt that this type ship by reason of its large cargo,
provision, and living spaces plus plane handling facilities is ideally
suited for extended survey missions, either arctic or tropical.

2.   The morale during the operation was excellent. Large quantities of recreational gear were carried, the most important being movies
and a hobby shop. These were augmented by books and music. There
was little time, inclination or space for athletics. It is believed,
however, that the main interest of the men was in the operations and
in the satisfaction of doing their jobs well. Many worked as much as
thirty-six hours without rest in order to keep the planes in commission so that a plane would never be prevented from going on a mission.
It is believed, incidentally, that opportunity was taken of every possibility which existed for a successful flight. This was largely due
to the almost infallible aerological team on board. Complete reliance
was placed in them by all concerned. Station weather ships, of course
were a must.

3.   Regular ship's routine during the long days was maintained
by setting clocks off zone time to have sunrise about 0700-plane
hoisting time.

4.   The helicopter was little used, but should be carried on
exploratory missions since it can be invaluable under certain conditions. The SOC was a nuisance--it couldn't fly when the PBM's
couldn't and just added complication to the flight deck.

5.   The food was excellent and canteen supplies were carried in sufficient quantity to last out the operation. To conserve manpower, reduce waste, simplify accounting and reduce expense to officers, all personnel without exception were placed on the general mess. For long steaming periods with the present personnel shortage this is strongly recommended. Officers' mess of course are privileged to add small delicacy items as and if desired.

6.   It is desired to emphasize strongly that well qualified technicians are essential in radio and electronics. That equipment must work constantly at peak efficiency if any progress is to be made with safety in the ice and over sketchily surveyed waters. Expert maintenance and repair personnel are far more to be desired than auxiliary equipment.

7.   The use of ice bergs to provide a lee for seaplane operations should not be counted on. Long deep swell produced the worst and most frequent hoisting problem and a berg unless aground will not help. As the ship developed hoisting technique, it arrived at a stage where hoisting was possible under any condition which was satisfactory for seaplane water operations. If the berg assists hoisting under worse conditions, the plane is still without a warm-up and take-off area, in addition to which winds in lee of a berg are dangerously confused. The use of bergs to provide a lee in emergency should be kept in mind and their use when grounded is recommended at any time. Under all conditions care must be exercised not to get in irons alongside as it must be remembered that the ship is limited in freedom of movement during hoisting and fueling of the planes. If the berg is drifting faster than the ship, serious damage might easily result in getting clear.

8.   Ice pack was found to smooth wind chop to a marked degree and pack bays were sought and used. Here again, however, no protection from swell can be expected.

                                        JOHN E. CLARK

ANNEX ONE - (m)

NARRATIVE

U.S.S. CACAPON (AO52)

CONFIDENTIAL

OBJECTIVES:

The objectives of this command, set forth in CTF 68 Operation Plan 2-46 and annexes thereto briefly were as follows: (a) To support the general plan for inward radial exploration of Antarctica by tender-based aircraft, (b) to carry out assigned naval and scientific projects, (c) to train personnel and test material in the frigid zone, (d) to amplify existing knowledge of hydrography along the route to be traversed, (e) to supply fuel to the Western Task Group and to such other ships as might be designated. An objective complementary to the latter was to train personnel in and to perfect techniques of fueling at sea by the Elwood method.

NARRATIVE:

On 30 September 1946 the ship first learned that it might participate in the expedition. Participation was confirmed on 8 October. The then commanding officer instituted timely measures to procure for the ship the materials and alterations essential to operations in regions of extreme cold. Subsequent commanding officers prosecuted the program so that when this writer took command on 29 November, 1946, preparations were almost complete. The only outstanding item was procurement of personnel and materials necessary to the institution of a hobby-craft program.

Fog delayed the sailing of this ship for several hours on 2 December. The delay prevented early rendezvous with TG 68.2, but enabled the ship to receive late arriving personnel and materials which had been ordered. Rendezvous was further delayed by a casualty to the #4 spring bearing on the starboard shaft. Errors in machining of the spare bearing introduced problems of fitting which were not overcome for fifty-six hours.

Rendezvous with Task Group 68.2 was made at 110120Z December, 1946. Communication with CTG 68.2 could not be established by TBS due to a defective insulator and antenna. Details of the difficulties encountered are set forth in Annexes ABLE and CHARLIE of the CACAPON report.

The first fueling at sea by the Elwood method for this ship took place on 11 December with the HENDERSON cooperating. Handling of the various details incident thereto was very awkward. The next and succeeding fuelings at sea were marked by continued improvement in the seamanship displayed by all hands. A list of fuelings and/or other transfer operations at sea is attached hereto as Appendix ONE.

After fueling the HENDERSON on 11 December, this ship took station as directed by CTG 68.2. Rendezvous was made again on the 17th, after which, this ship proceeded generally northeast to meet the

Annex I-E   - 1 -

MERRICK and the YANCEY. After fueling these ships, the CACAPON proceeded to rejoin Task Group 68.2 in the vicinity of the Balleny Islands.

Difficulty with the SG-1 radar was first experienced on 19 December when it became inoperative due to a defective tube. The difficulty was finally resolved on 27 December 1946, by personnel on the staff of CTG 68.2.

Icebergs were first sighted at Latitude 61-20 S. Longitude 176-00 E. at 241601Z December 1946. In the absence of effective surface search radar, the long hours of daylight were a source of comfort to this command.

This ship rejoined the Task Group on 26 December 1946. The HENDERSON was fueled alongside. Foul weather prevented fueling the CURRITUCK until the 29th on which date this ship departed to take station approximately 400 miles northwest of the CURRITUCK, there to serve as a weather station and as a possible emergency base for planes should their parent vessel become fog or snow-bound.

While patrolling the station northwest of the CURRITUCK, this ship had two emergency calls from the HENDERSON for medical assistance. At these times and on one other occasion this ship transferred fuel and replenished stores of the HENDERSON. On the last occasion, 21 January 1947, this ship took her outgoing mail for further delivery to the PHILIPPINE SEA.

Rendezvous with the CURRITUCK was made on 22 January 1947, on which date an attempt was made to transfer 1500 gallons of luboil from own ship's stock. A 1½" hose was used but proved ineffective due to the viscosity of the luboil. The operation was of some value, however, for it necessitated operating this ship on one engine while the transfer was being attempted. After picking up mail from the CURRITUCK, this ship proceeded east to rendezvous with CTG 68.4.

Rendezvous was made with CTG 68.4 in the PHILIPPINE SEA at 251420Z January 1947. The commanding officer accompanied by the First Lieutenant and a U. S. Army Chief Warrant Officer, a member of the previous U. S. Antarctic Expedition, boarded the PHILIPPINE SEA where all met the Officer-In-Charge of the Project. The commanding officer and the First Lieutenant with similar officers on the PHILIPPINE SEA discussed proposed means of effecting transfer of the heavy loads destined for Task Group 68.2 and mutually agreed that "Burtoning" would be more feasible than the provision whip method. "Burtoning" was later effectively used to effect the transfer of more than 23 tons of gear.

While awaiting take-off of the R4D planes, this ship fueled the SENNET, the BROWNSON and the NORTHWIND, and transferred a patient to the

PHILIPPINE SEA. Two days prior to the take-off, this ship was instrumental in establishing radio communication between the base at Little America and the carrier. After the take-off of the planes, this ship effected transfer of stores and passengers from and to the PHILIPPINE SEA without untoward incident, and thereafter proceeded generally westward to rejoin Task Group 68.2.

The trip west was night-marish. Much pack ice and many icebergs were encountered. To further complicate the absence of effective radar, a storm of great intensity was encountered for three days.

Rendezvous with CTG 68.2 in the CURRITUCK was effected on 8 February 1947. Stores, mail, passengers, fuel and luboil were transferred after which the ship proceeded to rendezvous with the HENDERSON. Similar services, except for luboil transfer were rendered and this ship proceeded to station approximately 400 miles northwest of the CURRITUCK.

Approximate station was regained on 11 February. Station was difficult to maintain due to preventive maintenance and to actual engineering casualties which prevented this ship from having full boiler power on the line.

On 28 February this ship had a gyro failure while fueling the HENDERSON. No personnel casualties were sustained but two span wires, two fuel hose messengers and two sections of 4" fuel hose were lost. New gear was rigged, and the fueling was resumed five hours after the mishap. Steps were taken to insure against repetition of similar accidents.

The ship proceeded generally westward to Longitude 29-30 E. in obedience to orders of CTG 68.2. It was on this westward trip that the greatest concentration of icebergs was observed. At one time this ship, on the A scope and the PPI, had over two hundred large icebergs within a ten mile radius. (This count did not include bergs of 100-300 tons whose rounded contours would not reflect with sufficient intensity to maintain an image on the PPI.) The large bergs were of unusual shapes and sizes, probably the result of having overturned on GRIGG or BANZARE BANK.

In compliance with instructions from CTG 68.2, this ship had made preparations to participate in a proposed expedition to the oasis discovered on the continent. However, weather and other circumstances forced abandonment of the project.

After reaching 29-30 E., orders were received to make easterly courses. Due to weather and other circumstances, CTG 68.2 announced abandonment of plans to send an expedition to the oasis which had been discovered on the continent. On 3 March made rendezvous with and fueled

CURRITUCK and HENDERSON. Soon after completion of the latter, CTG 68.2 announced his intention to proceed Sydney.

Enroute Sydney this ship encountered heavy weather, lost one life raft and had several feet of small steam piping torn away from the forward well deck.

On 11 March this ship entered Bass Strait and fueled HENDERSON on easterly courses. The CURRITUCK joined up on 12 March and on signal from CTG 68.2, all ships anchored northeast of Wilson promontory. CTG 68.2 held a conference of commanding officers and discussed plans for entry, shore leave and liberty.

Enroute to Sydney the commanding officer advised the crew on expected behavior. While at Sydney the behavior of this crew was uniformly good. Only ten infractions of discipline were recorded, the most serious being an over-leave of two days duration. No officers or men were late returning from the last shore leave or liberty.

Prior to departure from Sydney all members of the staff of CTF 68 and CTG 68.2 doing temporary duty on this ship were transferred to the CURRITUCK. This ship received personnel destined for West Coast ports.

This ship was underway from Sydney at 1400, 20 March, cleared the harbor and joined up on CURRITUCK when the latter was clear. Heavy weather was encountered that evening and the next day to such degree that fueling scheduled for 21 March was not attempted until 23 March. On the latter date this ship fueled the CURRITUCK, after which the latter left the formation to proceed Panama, while this ship and the HENDERSON proceeded toward San Diego.

Enroute San Diego this ship held intership drills with the HENDERSON, fueled the latter on 25 and 31 March. On the latter occasion this ship transferred personnel and gear destined San Diego. After completion of the last fueling the HENDERSON was ordered to proceed San Diego, while this ship set course for San Pedro in obedience to orders from CTF 68.

The remainder of the trip was without incident. No shipping was encountered except a small schooner rigged yacht which was observed in Latitude 23-55 N. 131-30 W., at 051825Z April 1947. This ship entered Los Angeles Harbor, San Pedro, California and anchored in berth ABLE 8 at 081600Z April 1947.

ANNEX ONE (n)

NARRATIVE

U.S.S. HENDERSON (DD785)

The HENDERSON was designated by ComDesPac on 14 September, 1946 for participation in special cold weather operations in the Antarctic. At this time the vessel was in a maintenance status at San Diego, California, and had on board a complement of 15 officers and 123 men.

No further information was received relative to this assignment until about 1 October, 1946 when CTF 68 Ser. 05 dated 23 September, 1946 was received. CNO Conf. Ltr. op33/hcc QG4 Serial No. 065p33 dated 26 August, 1946 was listed as an enclosure to this letter but was inadvertenly omitted when mailed.

The present Commanding Officer reported on board to relieve Command on 5 October, 1946 and at this time there was no information available as to the general concept of the proposed cold weather operation. Inspection of the ship upon relieving of Command revealed that during the time the HENDERSON had been in a maintenance status spare parts and other equipment had not been kept up to full allowance. However, immediate steps were taken to requisition and obtain these items.

About 15 October, 1946 CTF 68 Serial 036 dated 9 October, 1946 was received giving preliminary information on Operation HIGHJUMP. This was the first information received relative to types of ships this vessel would be operating with and the general concept of the proposed operation. Also paragraph 5 of this letter definately indicated that all special cold weather clothing would be procured and issued to the various ship by the Task Force Commander. Upon receipt of this same reference Commander Destroyer Squadron THIRTEEN took immediate steps to exchange personnel who did not have six months obligated service from 1 November, 1946.

On 28 October, 1946 the HENDERSON was ordered to San Francisco, Calif. Area for plane guard duties with the USS BOXER (CV21) and returned to San Diego, California, on 9 November, 1946. At this time the ship's complement was 17 officers and 191 men. Eight critical ratings were ordered to the HENDERSON from ComDesPac for temporary duty during this period.

The HENDERSON returned to San Diego, Calif. on 9 November, 1946 and went alongside the USS DIXIE for a period of two weeks for routine tender overhaul. During the period alongside the tender the ship began taking on stores and provisions. At the same time bathythermograph equipment was installed by NEL San Diego, California. Racks for forty helium bottles were manufactured and installed by the tender.

On 9 November, 1946 CTF 68 serial 0102 of 24 October, 1946 was received directing individual ship to procure their own cold weather clothing. Requisitions were promptly submitted to NSD San Diego, California, for this clothing, and no difficulty was experienced in obtaining required amounts in the desired sizes.

On 12 November, 1946 the Staff Supply Officer for Task Force 68 came aboard and gave considerable helpful information on expediting procurement of stores and supplies, as well as giving instruction in how to properly wear winter clothing.

The USS CURRITUCK returned to San Diego, California, on 15 November and upon her arrival a conference was held between the Commanding Officers and all heads of departments.

The HENDERSON reported to CTF 68 for duty on 20 November, 1946.

After leaving from alongside the tender on 23 November, 1946 the HENDERSON proceeded to sea to rendezvous with the USS CURRITUCK and conducted fueling-at-sea operations. Upon completion of this operation, the HENDERSON returned to port and moored to Pier 3, U. S. Naval Station, San Diego, California, for installation of rescue basket and equipment. While alongside the pier more provisions, stores and special equipment were received aboard.

The ship got underway on 27 November, 1946 and proceeded to Fuel Dock, San Diego, California, to take on special BuOrd equipment (MkIV depth charges), Ammunition and fuel; upon completion returned to pier 3 U. S. Naval Station for completion of installation of rescue baskets and equipment.

Upon completion of installation of rescue baskets and equipment on 29 November, 1946, the HENDERSON returned to her normal mooring at Buoy 20.

Monday 2 December 1946: 1200 - Underway from buoy # 20 for fueling dock, San Diego, California. 1345 - Underway from fueling dock, proceeding out of harbor. Passed sea buoy "1A", set course 210° (T), speed 19 knots, to rendezvous with Task Group. 1718 - Arrived at rendezvous. Proceeded independently.

Tuesday 3 December: 0540 - Sighted Guadelupe Islands, bearing 212° (T), distance 40 miles. 0600 - Stopped for bathythermograph readings. 1240 - Changed course to 208° (T), speed 14 knots. 1800 - Stopped to take bathythermograph readings and twice daily hereafter.

Friday 6 December: Base course 206° (T), speed 15 knots. Set all clocks back one hour to conform to plus 9 zone time.

Saturday 7 December: About 1800 - wind increased to force 8.

Sunday 8 December: 1305 - Stopped to take B. T. readings and allow Neptunes Rex and his court to come aboard. 1321 - Resumed base course 204° (T), speed 15 knots. 1200 - 1600 Took first rawin. Sky overcast entire day.

Monday 9 December 1946, 0213 - Crossed equator at 132° 41' W. 1658 - Port engine stopped for repairs . Starboard engine making turns for 20 knots. 2030 - Repairs completed on port engine, all engines ahead 15 knots.

Tuesday 10 December: 1045 - Change course to 238° (T) to intercept the CACAPON and CURRITUCK. Change course to 223° (T) speed 18 knots to intercept CACAPON and CURRITUCK.

Wednesday 11 December: 0050 - Target bearing 201° (T), range 64,400 yards on S. G. radar. 0057 - Target bearing 270° (T), range 90,000 yards S. G. radar. 0150 - Sighted Fatu Hukir of the Marquesas Islands bearing 182 (T), range 17 miles. 0310 - Sighted Hiva-oa Island, Marquesas group bearing 153° (T), range 19.5 miles. Stopped at 0604 for one hour due to loss of water suction. Underway again set course 215° (T), speed 25 knots. Made radar contact CURRITUCK and CACAPON bearing 228° (T), distance 16 miles. 1115 commenced fueling from CACAPON. Went along starboard side of the CURRITUCK to transfer WHITE, F. V. MM2, 224 86 00, USN, for instruction in photography. 1722 Took station 2,000 yards ahead of the CURRITUCK, base course 210° (T), speed 16.5 knots

Thursday 12 December: 0110 - Made radar contact on YANCEY (AKA93) bearing 204° (T) range 16 miles. 0925 - HENDERSON, CURRITUCK, CACAPON and YANCEY, in that order, started passage through the Tuamotus Archipelago. CURRITUCK launched helicopter to search for hidden reefs. Passed Philipps Island, Saken, and Hiti Island, in that order. From all indications Saken and Hiti Islands are about two (2) miles further west than our charts indicate. 1015 - Sonar picked up reef bearing 185° (T) range 2800 yards. Held tactial drill with HENDERSON as guide. Secured from tactical drill set base course 321° (T), speed 11 knots. 1700 - Set clocks back one (1) hour to conform with plus 10 zone time. Changed base course to 244° (T), speed 16 knots. Proceeded independently to resume course along designated track.

Friday 13 December: Commenced issuing winter clothing. Passed through intermitten rain squalls; heavy overcast all day.

Saturday 14 December: 0013 - Radar (SG) contact on Ile Tabvai, bearing 185° (T) range 40 miles. Passed island to port bearing 120° (T) 23, 400 yards. Held Captain's inspection of personnel, messing and berthing spaces. Heavy overcast all day.

Sunday 15 December: Changed course to 211° (T) speed 16 knots.

Monday 16 December: Test fired two 20mm mounts in the afternoon. 1700 - Set ship's clocks back one (1) hour to conform with plus 11 zone time. 2200 - c/c to 192° (T) to rendezvous with the CACAPON. 2300 - c/s to 13 knots. The sky was overcast all day, wind light, with a heavy swell.

Tuesday 17 December: Sighted the CACAPON at 0415, bearing 114° (T) range 25,000 yards. Refueled from CACAPON on base course 215° (T) speed 12 knots. Sighted the CURRITUCK at 0750 bearing 155° (T) range 15 miles. Pursuant to verbal orders of C. O. USS CACAPON, Dr. R. F. Dietz of the Navy Electronics Labrotory, reported aboard for temporary duty. 1010 - Completed refueling. At 1100 went alongside starboard quarter of the CURRITUCK, base course 215° (T) speed 12 knots. WHITE, F. V., MM2, 224 86 00, USN returned aboard, by breechers buoy and aircraft crane, having completed temporary duty on the CURRITUCK. 1112 - Exercised in operation of the air-sea rescue basket equipment. At 1230 set course 251° (T) speed 16 knots to resume designated track. Changed course to 219° (T). Passed over a sea mountain during the night. Fathometer rose from 2900 to 700 fathoms.

Wednesday 18 December: 0915 - All engines stopped due to loss of vacuum. 0940 - Commenced making turnsfor 10 knots on port engine. By 0945 - had regained vacuum and set speed at 18 knots. Changed course to 217° (T) speed 17 knots. Visibility poor all day.

Thursday 19 December: Commenced 30° sonar ssarch on either bow. 2206 c/c to 232° (T).

Friday 20 December: Force of wind 6, visibility good with a low and middle cloud coverage. Crossed the 180th meridian west bound at 1240 in latitude 52° 55'S. 1917 - Stopped all engines due to water in the fuel oil. 2045 - Engineering casualty corrected, resumed base course and speed. 2215 - c/c to 199° (T) speed 16 knots.

Sunday 22 December: 0800 c/c to 184° (T). Picked up whales on the sonar gear at ranges from 800 to 1000 yards. 2130 - c/c to 169° (T).

Monday 23 December: 0145 - c/c to 090° (T). 0200 - c/c to 000° (T). 0214 Radar contact bearing 020° (T) range 24,800 yards, c/c to 020° (T). 0217 - Sighted the CURRITUCK on base course 212° (T) speed 16 knots. 0830 - Begain circling the CURRITUCK at various speeds for calibration fortheir R.D.F. gear. Sighted first icebergs at 1315. Radar picked them up at a range of 22,000 yards. Fifteen minutes after the first two were sighted we were in a large field of them. Steered various courses and speed to clear icebergs. 1600 - Completed passage through field of ice bergs, set course 225° (T). 1700 - Set clocks back one (1) hour to conform with minus 11 time zone. 1931 - c/c to 220° (T).

Tuesday 24 December: Parted company with the CURRITUCK, proceeded on duty assigned in accordance with previous instructions, using various courses and speeds to pass clear of ice bergs. Our general directions to clear icepack is N.W. 1800 - Ran into heavy snow squalls followed by heavy fog. Slowed to 5 knots. Sonar proved invaluable in detecting growlers, pack ice and ice bergs. Growlers could be detected at ranges of 1,000 to 2,500 yards. Ice bergs were picked up at 5,500 yards and on one occasion at 7,100 yards. Radar had trouble picking up growlers and pack ice. Large and small bergs could be detected at great ranges which was of great assistance in navigating in vicinity of the pack ice. Magnetic compass showed deviations up to 131° W. We are now in the region of continuous daylight. Retained in the fog for rest of day. Maximum visibility, 2,200 yards.

Wednesday 25 December: Christmas Day. Visibility poor ranging from 50 yards to 1,500 yards. Sea calm, with light wind. Continued to get excellent information on ice from radar and sonar.

Thursday 26 December: Running in and out of fog continually. Visibility never increasing over 4,000 yards. Steering various courses and various speeds to clear ice bergs and pack ice. The general heading was W.S.W. The B.T. observations showed a "Peter" pattern most of the time which accounts for the excellent results obtained with sonar equipment. Set course 090° (T) and speed to correspond to visibility to effect rendezvous, with the CACAPON. 2130 - Changed course to 161° (T).

Friday 27 December: 0240 - Arrived at rendezvous position, commenced steaming in a two mile square attempting to contact the CACAPON. Made contact with the CURRITUCK on voice radio late in the morning. Strength one (1). Fog continued. Visibility ranging from 300 to 1,500 yards. Average speed 5 knots. Made voice radio contact with CURRITUCK again about 1430. Radar had picked up the CURRITUCK and the CACAPON earlier in the day, but it was impossible to distinguish them from all the ice bergs in the vicinity, since both ships were lying to in the vicinity of ice bergs. Laid to in the fog for about 2 hours. 1437 - Moored starboard side to the CACAPON. Pursuant to verbal orders of Commander Task Group 68.2, Arbuthnott, J., Jr. 716 60 22, V6, was transferred to the CACAPON for Temporary Additional Duty for about one (1) month. Completed fueling from CACAPON at 1950. Set course 000° (T), speed 5 knots, on route to assigned station 300 miles to westward of refueling rendezvous .

Saturday 28 December: 0205 - c/c to 270° (T). Sun broke through occasionally. Visibility averaging 10 miles. Force of wind four. 1930 - Sighted several "Killer" whaling boats. 2029 - Passed Japanese factory ship Nisshin Maru #1 operating 5 small whaling boats.

Sunday 29 December: 0730 - Changed course to 180° (T). Another day of poor visibility, never increasing over 4 miles, and light winds out of the W.N.W. and W.S.W. Continued to steam on station in a four (4) mile square for the remainder of the day.

Monday 30 December: Visibility averaging from 5 to 7 miles. Winds varying from force 1 to force 6 from E.N.E. to E.S.E.

Tuesday 31 December: 0400 - c/c to 180° (T) speed 5 knots. Visibility from 5 to 7 miles low and middle cloud coverage - wind force of 3 from E.N.E. and E.S.E.

Wednesday 1 January: Patroling station 300 miles to westward of CURRITUCK acting as weather station. Steering on north and south heading for approximately twelve (12) hours at a time. Visibility ranging from three (3) miles to 400 yards.

Thursday 2 January: Conditions same as preceeding day. The sun shines faintly through the overcast each day for an hour or two. The horizon is always poor but the running fixes have never been further than 15 or 20 miles from the D.R.

Friday 3 January: On station 300 miles to westward of the CURRITUCK. 0945 - Chief Pharmacist mate reported an acute case of appendicitis on board. Changed course to 000° (T), speed 20 knots. Notified Commander Task Group 68.2 of situation and requested immediate rendezvous with the CACAPON. The CACAPON's last posit report indicated they were 300 miles to the north of us. 1300 - Set clocks ahead one (1) hour to conform to minus 12 zone time. 1530 - Changed course to 044° (T). 1902 - Changed course to 014° (T). 1945 - Sighted CACAPON bearing 020° (T), range 10 miles. Moored starboard side to CACAPON. Pursuant to BuMed form "G" the following men were transferred to the CACAPON for treatment. KYTE, E. J., S1, 567 39 62, USN, MOORE, G. R., F1, 347 27 98, USN, MILLER, D. L., S1, 798 37 17, USN. Completed refueling about 2300. Set course 218° (T), speed 12 knots for operating area along 147° E. Longitude in vicinity of ice pack. It was noted that ice bergs were more numerous at refueling position than further south in our previous operating area.

Saturday 4 January: En route to operating area along 147° E. Longitude in vicinity of ice pack. Visibility poor with intermitten snow flurries. Arrived on station at approximately 1500, c/c to 180° (T) speed 12 knots to look for ice pack. Arrived at ice pack at 2145 in vicinity of 65° 15' S. The ice pack was very different from any observed before. The ice was jammed in tight and the edge had a very distinct outline. Several bergs over 200 feet in height could be seen deep within the pack. B.T. readings showed a marked change from a positive to a negative gradient. Visibility was good with a low cloud coverage - sea calm with no drift ice of any kind. Radar picks up pack ice at a range of 12,000 yards. 2200 - c/c to 000° (T), speed 3 knots.

Sunday 5 January: 0817 - c/c to 180° (T). Visibility average maximum 10 miles. 1230 - c/c to 225° (T). Commenced swinging ship to

CONFIDENTIAL

compensate magnetic compass. Took an extremely long time for compass
to settle down. Compensation was not completed. The approximate
distance from South Magnetic Pole was 175 miles.

Monday 6 January: 0015 - Set course 000° (T), speed 3 knots.
0513 - c/c to 180° (T). 0955 - Stopped 1,000 yards off ice pack to
take B.T. readings. Weather and sea same as proceeding day. Commenced
swinging ship to compensate magnetic compass. 1735 - Completed
swinging ship. Had greatest difficulty in compensating on SSE and
SSW headings. 1800 - c/c to 020° (T).

Tuesday 7 January: Steaming singly as part of Task Group
68.2 on assigned station along the Antarctic ice pack at longitude
147° E. 0400 - c/c to 180° (T). 0905 - c/c to 090° (T). 1600 -
c/c to 260° (T). 1636 - c/c to 300° (T). 1700 - Fog closed in, visibility reduced to 500 yards. 1947 - Fog lifted, visibility increased
to 4,000 yards.

Wednesday 8 January: 0200 - c/c to 090° (T). Intermitten
fog throughout the day. Visibility never increased over 5 miles.

Thursday 9 January: Visibility poor, moderate sea, and
light wind. CPhM reported an emergency medical case on board. 1211 -
c/c to 000° (T), speed 18 knots to effect rendezvous with the CACAPON
250 miles to the north. c/c at 1500 to 002° (T). c/c to 013° (T).
2111 - Made radar contact with CACAPON bearing 066° (T), range 26,000
yards. c/c to 066° (T), speed 20 knots to rendezvous with tanker
which is lying to. While moored alongside tanker to transfer emergency
medical case the ships rolled together caving in sides of 40MM mount
#41 and #43. Transferred CROSS, R. Jr., SC1, 269 75 19, USN to
CACAPON for treatment, authority BuMed form "G".

Friday 10 January: Refueling from CACAPON. Completed refueling at 0200. Set course 185° (T), speed 11 knots for operating
station on 147° E. longitude in vicinity of ice pack. Visibility poor -
maximum 2 miles, wind force 3, swell confused, averaging from 3 to 5
feet. c/c from 184° (T) to 150° (T) at 1300. 1800 - c/c to 180° (T).
Arrived in vicinity of ice pack at 2400.

Saturday 11 January: Wind of force 3 - visibility poor,
maximum 5 miles, swells average about 4 feet. Steaming on north-south
courses to remain on station - speed 3 knots.

Sunday 12 January: On station along 147° E. meridian in
vicinity of ice pack. Steaming north and south courses to remain
on station, speed 3 knots. Swells confused averaging 10 feet high.
Visibility bad, maximum 2 miles closing in to 1000 yards. Wind, force
5 from N. W.

Monday 13 January: Wind of force 2 from N.W. Swells averaging 5 N.W. Average visibility one (1) mile. Received orders from CTG 68.2 to move westward 300 miles from present position. c/c to 270, speed 4 knots.

Tuesday 14 January: Course 270° (T), speed 4 knots. Wind changing from force 4 to 7. Predominately from the east. Swells averaging 5-8 feet from the east. Maximum visibility ½ mile. Commenced snowing lightly in early part of afternoon. Changed to heavy snow in late afternoon and continued for remainder of day.

Wednesday 15 January: Course 270° (T), speed 4 knots. Crossed magnetic equator about 0600 at 64° 25' S. Distance from south magnetic pole approximately 200 miles. Wind died down after 0600 to a velocity of 12 knots, from the N.E. Swell averaged about 6 feet from the East. Visibility increased after 0600 to eight (8) miles.

Thursday 16 January: Average force of wind 3 from the N.E. Average visibility was 5 miles. Arrived on station and contacted ice pack at 64° 45' S. Commenced steaming on east and west course to remain on station, speed 3 knots.

Friday 17 January: On station in vicinity of 136° E. meridan and 64° 30' S Latitude heading into sea and wind on course 060° (T) through 100° (T). Wind of force 6 and 7 from 090° (T). Swells between 10 and 12 feet from 090° (T). Average visibility 1 mile. Light snow in early evening changing to heavy around 2100.

Saturday 18 January: Swells 20 to 28 feet high from the east. Wind of average force 7 from E.S.E. and at times reaching a maximum velocity of 40 knots. Average visibility was half a mile. Snowed continuously all day with extremely heavy snow late in the evening. 1900 - c/c to 360° (T), speed 4 knots. TDT (RCM) antenna broke loose from the mast. Holding bolts gave way due to continuous rolling of ship. The barometer dropped from 29.32 to 28.76 in twenty four hour period.

Sunday 19 January: On assigned station in vicinity of ice pack near 136° E. Longitude. Course 280° (T), speed 4 knots. Average wind of force 3 from E.S.E. Swell was confused and about 5' high. Average visibility about 1 mile. 1400 - c/c to 180° (T). Continuous snow. Sun broke through the snow around 1800. c/c to 090° (T), speed 3 knots.

Monday 20 January: Course 090° (T), speed 3 knots. Obtained two sun sights in latter part of morning to give first sights for fix in three (3) days. c/c to 270° (T). Obtained another sun sight and LAN at 1515 to verify morning fix. 2200 - c/c to 090° (T). Average force of wind 2 from E.S.E. average visibility 15 miles. Height of swell from 3 feet to 5 feet from N.S. intermittent snow flurries the entire day.

Tuesday 21 January: 0444 - Sighted CACAPON bearing 023° (T), range nine miles. Commenced fueling from CACAPON on base course 030° (T), 5.5. knots. Received supplies from and discharged mail to CACAPON. Pursuant to BuMed form "G" GILLESPIE, R. V.,WT3, 342 66 97, USN. DE LOS RIOS, L. B. RDM2, 325 30 26, USN, WERDER, R. A., F1, 347 27 98, USN. Were transferred to CACAPON for treatment. Pursuant to original orders from Director of Scripps Institution of Oceanography, MANN, H. J., Civilian, was transfered to the CACAPON. KYTE, E. J., S1, 567 39 62 USN, and MOORE, G. R., F1, 347 27 98, USN, were received aboard for duty from the CACAPON, treatment having been completed. 1300 - Completed refueling, set course 250° (T), speed 5 knots. Average wind force 5 from E.S.E., visibility 8 miles, average swells of 5 feet from E.S.E., barometer steady. 2200 - Received orders from Commander Task Group 68.2 to take new station 300 miles distance from the CURRITUCK bearing 300° (T). Changed course to 338° (T), speed 5 knots.

Wednesday 22 January: c/c to 310° (T). 1600 - Arrived on station c/c to 270° (T), speed 3 knots. Average wind force 4 from E.S.E., visibility 15 miles, swells 5 feet from E.S.E. Snowed intermittently during the afternoon.

Thursday 23 January: On station 300 miles bearing 300° (T) from the CURRITUCK. c/c to 285° (T). 1300 c/c to 270° (T). 1700 - c/c to 115° (T). 2000 Average wind for today of force 2 from S.E. visibility 5 miles, swell 5 feet from E.S.E.

Friday 24 January: Average wind of force 5 from E.S.E., visibility 8 miles, swell of 7 to 10 feet, from E.S.E. continuous light snow through afternoon and evening.

Saturday 25 January: Patroling station 300 miles to the W.N.W. of the CURRITUCK. 0600 - Received orders to proceed westward at 10 knots. c/c to 270° (T), speed 10 knots. Average wind of force 5 from E.S.E., a 10 foot swell from E.S.E. visibility of 5 miles, light continuous snow. Received word that the CURRITUCK was moving westward at 7 knots to 130° E. Longitude and we were to adjust station accordingly.

Sunday 26 January: Proceeding to station 300 miles to the W.N W. of the CURRITUCK. Average wind of force 3 from the East. 5 foot swell from E.S.E. visibility of 5 miles, light continuous snow.

Monday 27 January: On station 300 miles to the W.N.W., of the CURRITUCK. Weather average visibiltiy 8 miles, wind of force 3 from E. shifting to N.W. and then back to N.E., swell of 4 feet from E. by S.E. light snow through out morning. 1830 - Received word that CURRITUCK was moving west to vicinity of 125° E. Longitude and to adjust station accordingly. c/c to 285° (T), speed 7 knots.

Thuesday 28 January: Weather visibility 25 miles, average wind force 4 from S.E., swells of 3 feet from E.S.E., weather generally was cloudy with broken skies.

Wednesday 29 January: On station 300 miles W.N.W. of the CURRITUCK. 1616 - c/c to 5 knots, proceeding west to new operating area. Weather wind S.E., force 4, visibility 12 miles, 5 foot swells from E. with secondary swells from N.E. and S.E. Light snow showers during morning. The barometer commenced dropping in the early morning and by midnight had reached 29.13 inches.

Thursday 30 January: 1040 - c/c to 270° (T), speed 7 knots upon receiving word that the CURRITUCK was moving westward to 1150 E. Longitude. Weather, visibility 20 miles, wind of force 4 from E.S.E. 4 foot swell from E. The barometer continued to drop like a rock reaching a new low of 28.52 inches. Excellent weather prevailed

Friday 31 January: Proceeding to new station along 105° E. Longitude, 300 miles to the W.N.W. of the CURRITUCK. Weather overcast with light snow flurries, visibility 15 miles wind of force 3 shifting from S.E. to N.W., and back to E. 4 foot swells from N.W. and E. There was a marked increase in the number of bergs in this area. The storm passed to the N.E. of us. Barometer rose as steadily as it had dropped yesterday.

Saturday 1 February: Weather, wind from the E.S.E., force 4, visibility 15 miles, there were two opposing swells of about 4 feet, one from the east and the other from the north. Sky was overcast the entire day.

Sunday 2 February: On station 300 miles W.N.W. of the CURRITUCK. 1700 - Set all clocks back one (1) hour to conform with minus 11 zone time. Weather, wind of force 3 from N.E., 3 foot swell, confused, visibility 15 miles, observed light intermittent rain during morning. Ice bergs remain numerous.

Monday 3 February: 1430 - Received orders to rendezvous with the CURRITUCK (AV7) to refuel. c/c to 100° (T) speed 10 knots. Weather wind N.E. becoming E.N.E. force 5, sky overcast with precipitation south of ship all day, 4 foot swells from N.E., visibility 15 miles.

CONFIDENTIAL

Tuesday 4 February: En route to rendezvous with the USS CURRITUCK (AV7). Sighted the CURRITUCK bearing 160° (T) range 11 miles. c/c to 180° (T) speed 15 knots. 1540 - Laying to in lee of CURRITUCK. Captain left ship for conference with Commander Task Group 68.2. Commenced receiving small stores, provisions and supplies by boat from CURRITUCK. 1600 - Three men and one officer went to CURRITUCK for dental treatment. Fifteen men left the ship for a recreation trip to (AV7). 1824 Captain returned to the ship. 1915 - The recreation party returned to the ship. Underway on base course 125° (T) speed 6 knots for fueling, 2115 - Commenced fueling from CURRITUCK.

Wednesday 5 February: 0030 - Completed fueling. Set base course 295° (T). Speed 12 knots for assigned station 300 miles to W. N.W. of the CURRITUCK. Weather, light snow with occasional light fog, wind E.S.E., force 5, visibility 10 miles reduced to 1 mile in fog, swell of 5 feet from E.

Thursday 6 February: Steering various courses and various speeds to clear ice bergs. 1300 - c/c to 270° (T), speed 10 knots after receiving orders to move five (5) degrees further west. Weather wind from E.S.E. of force 3 with very light winds in evening. Swell of 5 feet from East winds decreasing to 2 feet in evening, visibility 6 miles. Encountered light snow showers and patches of fog through out the day. 2300 - c/s to 4 knots. Numerous ice bergs. Barometer dropping.

Friday 7 February: On station 300 miles to W.N.W. of the CURRITUCK. Weather, wind of force 6 from the East, visibility 3 miles, Swells 8 feet in early morning increasing to 20 feet in the evening from East. Overcast with continual light snow. Barometer steadied up for about three hours then commenced dropping again. 2400 - Barometer read 28.91 inches.

Saturday 8 February: Barometer dropped to 28.80 inches. Observe rolls between 20 and 30 degrees. Weather, wind of force 6 with gusts up to 40 knots from E.S.E. The weather was overcast with continuous light snow and intermittent light fog. Barometer began to steady down about 1800. By 2400 the storm was abating.

Sunday 9 February: On station 300 miles W.N.W. of the CURRITUCK. Weather, overcast, becoming scattered after 1800. Visibility 20 miles, wind from S.E. force 5, swell from E.S.E. of 8 feet.

Monday 10 February: 0542 - Sighted CACAPON visually bearing 110° (T), speed, range 15 knots. Took station 500 yards astern of the

CACAPON. c/s to 5 knots. Commenced refueling, base course 090° (T), speed 8 knots. Pursuant to verbal orders of Commander Task Force 68.2, ARBUTHNOTT, J. Jr., ETM2 716 60 22, USN, returned aboard and resumed his regular duties having completed temporary additional duty on board the CACAPON. 1140 - Completed taking on supplies and transferring of mail. Completed rueling, set course 130° (T), speed 15 knots for assigned station along Antarctic ice pack approximately 300 miles to the westward of the CURRITUCK. 1700 - Set ships clocks back one (1) hour to conform to minus 10 zone time. Weather, overcast clearing a little in evening, wind from S.S.W. force 5, visibility 20 miles, easterly swell of 10 feet.

Tuesday 11 February: 0425 - Sighted factory ship ARISTOPHANES from Capetown. Weather overcast in morning with snow and fog, clear skies during afternoon, average visibility 20 miles decreasing to 1 mile during snow and fog. Wind shifting for W. to N.E. then S. and back to W. in the afternoon.

Wednesday 12 February: 1700 - Set all ships clocks back one (1) hour to conform to minus 9 zone time. Weather, visibility 20 miles in morning decreasing to average of 3 miles..in the afternoon during fog and light snow. wind force four from S.W. swell of 2 feet from W. over all weather was overcast with light snow and fog. Fog becoming closer in late evening, decreasing visibility to 150 yards. Had communication with one of our planes, Baker One, this afternoon. They were 63 miles to the east of us. Bergs plentiful.

Thursday 13 February: Steaming on various courses in a westerly direction. Set all ships clocks back one hour to conform to minus 8 zone time. Weather, fog until 0500, light snow beginning at 0900 and changing to light rain about 1700, visibility variable 1/4 to 5 miles with an average of about 2 miles, wind N.E. force five, swell N.N.E. 4 feet.

Friday 14 February: Set ships clocks back one (1) hour to conform with minus 7 zone time. 2045 - Crossed the Antarctic circle southbound in Longitude 73° 02' E. Weather, occasional light fog accompanied with very light rain, visibility 6 miles, wind W.N.W., force 3, veering to N.N.E. force 5 in early afternoon, swell from N.W. of 5 feet.

Saturday 15 February: Weather, wind from E.S.E. force 7 with gusts to 35 knots, visibility of 3/4 mile. Swells from east averaging 18 feet and reaching a height of 25 feet. Barometer 28.60 inches. The sky obscured with continuous light snow and high winds.

Sunday 16 February: On westerly course in vicinity of Antarctic ice pack. Weather, visibility 3,000 yards, wind E.S.E. average force 6 increasing to force 7 in the late afternoon, swell from E.S.E., average height 12 feet increasing to 20 feet in the late afternoon. Continuous moderate snow with intermittent light fog with high sea. Barometer 29.60 inches.

Monday 17 February: 1900 - Sighted the CURRITUCK bearing 300° (T) range about 2,000 yards in heavy snow storm. Commenced fueling from CURRITUCK, base course 320° (T), speed 6 knots. Weather intermittent light snow with occasional rain, visibility average 2 miles, wind S.E. force 7 decreasing to force 5 late in the afternoon. Swell of 10 feet from E.S.E.

Tuesday 18 February: Base course 320° (T), speed 6 knots. 0040 - Completed fueling from the CURRITUCK. Set course 270° (T), speed 12 knots for operating area in vicinity of 40° E. Meridian. 1430 - Sighted ship on horizon bearing 260° (T), range about 20 miles, ship identified as a Norwegian ship, Antarctic. Weather swell average 2 feet from E., visibility 25 miles, wind from E. force 4, overcast in morning with scattered clouds in the afternoon.

Wednesday 19 February: On assigned station to west of the CURRITUCK. Weather, visibility 25 miles, wind of force 2 from W., swell of 3 feet from N.W.

Thursday 20 February: En route to assigned station on approximately 300 miles to the west of the CURRITUCK, course 270° (T). 0345-Observed a strong Aurora Australis for about two hours. Weather cloudy varying from overcast to a scattered unstable air Mass, visibility 20 miles, wind of force 2 from W.N.W., swell of 2 feet from N.W.

Friday 21 February: On station west of the CURRITUCK. 1700 Set ships clocks back one (1) hour to conform to minus 6 zone. Weather scattered to broken skies with a few snow showers, visibility 25 miles, no swell during the morning one from the S.W. in the evening of about 4 feet, wind average force 3 from N.W. shifting to W. then to S.

Saturday 22 February: 0900 - Received orders to steam eastward at seven knots, c/c to 090° (T). Weather, scattered clouds becoming overcast about 1600, visibility 30 miles decreasing to 15, wind of force 4 from W. shifting to N. and increasing to force 5, swell of 4 feet from S.S.W.

Sunday 23 February: Weather, overcast with continuous light snow, wind from N.E. force 5, visibility 5 miles, swell was confused of 6 feet height.

Monday 24 February: On station to westward of the CURRITUCK.
No ice bergs in this vicinity. Weather, overcast with an occasional
light snow or rain. Wind of force 3 from N.N.E., visibility 10 miles,
swell from W. of 12 feet.

Tuesday 25 February: 0900 - Conducted test firing of 20MM.
Exercised crew at G.Q. Conducted test firing of 5" V.T.'s. 1700 -
Conducted test firing of 40MM. Weather, overcast with light snow,
wind of force 4 from N.E., visibility 8 miles, swell of 8 feet from E.

Wednesday 26 February: Steering various courses and using
various speeds to clear brash ice. Conducted test firing of 5" mounts
#1 and #2. Observed ice pack in Longitudes 53° E. and 54° E. approx-
imately 65° 45' S. 1445 - Sighted land of continent (Enderby Land)
bearing 149° (T). Distance 45 miles. Weather, overcast with light
intermittent snow, the visibility 10 miles, wind from E. force 5 swell
of 4, confused but mostly from N.

Thursday 27 February: 0947 - Conducted test firing 5"/38
battery. 1530 - Received orders to proceed to fueling rendezvous at
64° S 66° E. Set course 080° (T) speed 15 knots. Weather, overcast
with occasional light snow, wind from S., force 6, sea swell of 5 feet,
and average visibility of 10 miles.

Friday 28 February: Sighted CACAPON (AO52) bearing 110° (T).
Range 20 miles. 1100 - Fueled from CACAPON. Speed 10 knots. 1234 -
CACAPON suddenly veered sharply to the starboard. Own ship had on 25°
right rudder but was unable to keep up. Parted both hose and all lines.
There were no casualties to personnel or own ships equipment. Accident
due to gyro failure on the CACAPON. 1255 - Set course 090° (T) speed
12 knots while CACAPON rerigged for fueling. 1625 - Base course 075°
(T) speed 10 knots, commenced receiving fuel. 1830 - Completed fueling. Set course 270° (T). speed 3 knots. Weather, overcast becoming
scattered in afternoon, wind from S. force 4, S.E. swell of 5 feet,
visibility 25 miles.

Saturday 1 March: On station 300 miles to the W.N.W. of the
CURRITUCK, course 270° (T), speed 3 knots. Received word that our
operation in the Antarctic were finished and to head for a rendezvous
at L. 63° 45'S 85° E. Set course 090° (T), speed 15 knots. Weather
heavy snow, visibility 3/4 mile. Wind from E.N.E., force 7, N.E. swell
of 18 feet. Observed Aurora Australis from 0215 to 0400, there was no
noticable effect on operation of ship. Our maximum roll, 50° with
many others in the forties.

Sunday 2 March: En route to rendezvous. Weather, overcast

becoming scattered in afternoon wind from W.N.W. force 4, visibility 20 miles, a swell of 6 feet.

Monday 3 March: En route to rendezvous with CURRITUCK and CACAPON. 0300 - Sighted CURRITUCK and CACAPON visually. Took station astern, base course 050° (T), speed 6 knots. CURRITUCK commenced re-fueling from CACAPON. 1330 - Took station along CACAPON to receive fuel, base course 090° (T), speed 12 knots. 1800 - Completed fueling. CACAPON departed, we remained in company with the CURRITUCK. Base course 110° (T), speed 13 knots, scattered clouds, visibility 20 miles, swell of 4 foot from N.W.

Tuesday 4 March: In company with the CURRITUCK. Course 110° (T), speed 13 knots. Keeping station 2,500 yards astern of the CURRITUCK. Scattered clouds, visibility 25 miles 3 foot swells from N.W.

Wednesday 5 March: In company with the CURRITUCK. Base course 075° (T), speed 16.5 knots. 0200 - Set all ships clocks ahead one hour to conform with minus 7 zone time. 1500 - Received orders to proceed independently at high speed through the roaring 40's and 50's. c/s to 22 knots. c/c to 061° (T). Steaming great circles route to N.W. entrance to Bass Strait. Weather broken to overcast with a few snow showers. Wind of force and from S.S.W., visibility 20 miles, N.W. swell of 5 feet.

Thursday 6 March: En route to N.W. entrance to Bass Strait. c/s to 16 knots. 0100 - Passed last iceberg to port. 0118 - c/s to 10 knots. 0200 - Set ship's clocks ahead one hour to conform to minus 8 time zone. 0400 - c/c to 057° (T). 0434 - c/s to 20 knots. 2200 - c/c to 049° (T). Weather, mostly cloudy with light snow in early morning, visibility 25 miles, swell of 10 feet from W. wind from W. of force 5.

Friday 7 March: En route to N.W. entrance to Bass Strait course 049° (T), speed 20 knots. c/c to 046° (T). c/c to 045° (T). c/s to 14 knots. Weather, overcast with light continuous rain, wind from N. force 4, visibility average 8 miles reducing to 1½ at times. N.W. swell of 7 feet.

Saturday 8 March: En route N.W. entrance to Bass Strait. Course 045° (T), speed 14 knots. 0200 - Set ship's clocks ahead one hour to conform to minus 9 zone time. Weather, overcast with light rain in morning, clearing rapidly after 1500, wind from W.N.W. backing to W.N.W., force 6 average visibility 8 miles. N.W. swell of 10 feet.

Sunday 9 March: Weather overcast with high winds, rough seas and heavy rain showers, visibility 6 miles except in rain, wind from N.W. of average force 7 with gusts reaching 60 knots, swell of 15 feet reaching heights of 30 feet.

Monday 10 March: 1400 - Sighted King Island bearing 100° (T), range 26 miles. 1700 - Proceeded to anchor N.E. of King Island with Cape Wickham light bearing 270° (T), range 5 miles in 10 fathoms of water. Weather, broken skies in early AM, clearing in PM. Visibility 20 miles, N.E. swell of 16 feet decreasing to 4 feet upon approach to land. Wind from W.N.W. force 4.

Tuesday 11 March: 0815 - Underway and joined CACAPON as she entered the strait. Base course 088° (T), speed 10 knots. 1105 - Commenced fueling from the CACAPON. 1425 - Completed fueling. 1500 - Took station 700 yards bearing 135° relative. Course 088° (T), speed 5 knots. Weather mostly clear with few scattered clouds, wind from N.E. force 5, swell from E.N.E. of 3 feet, visibility 20 miles. 0200 - Advanced ships clocks 1 hour to conform to minus 10 zone time.

Wednesday 12 March: 0205 - Sighted CURRITUCK bearing 260° (T), distance approximately 7 miles. 0500 - CURRITUCK took station ahead of formation and assumed guide, 0955 - Anchored N.E. of Wilson Promontory on Longitude 147° E. 5 miles off coast in 11 fathoms of water. 1035 - Captain left the ship for conference on CURRITUCK. 1100 - CACAPON anchored in vicinity. 1215 - Heavy winds set in from westward, force 6. 1225 - Commenced dragging anchor moved to 75 fathoms. 1415 - Captain returned to the ship. 1457 - Underway in column formation, CURRITUCK, CACAPON and HENDERSON in that order. Set course 073° (T), speed 15 knots.

Thursday 13 March: 1555 - Pursuant to BuMed form "G" SHIELDS, P. T. MM3, 659 66 02, USN was transfered to the CURRITUCK for treatment. 1600 - Took last rawins. 1630 - Set course 030° (T), speed 5 knots in formation. 1835 - Passed the H.M.A.S. BELLANA (Cruiser) and the H.M.A.S. QUIBERON (Destroyer).

Friday 14 March: Making all preparations for entering port Jackson Harbor, Sydney, Australia. CURRITUCK fired 21 gun salute to the nation of Australia. Salute answered from shore battery. 0852 - CURRITUCK fired 13 gun salute to Rear Admiral H. B. Farncomb RAN, Commanding Australian Squadron. 1030 - Moored port side to CACAPON in berth #2, Woolloomooloo Bay, Sydney, Australia.

Saturday, Sunday, Monday, Tuesday, Wednesday, Moored Sydney.
  15   16   · 17   18   19

Thursday 20 March: 1330 - Pursuant to orders of Director of Scripps Institution of Oceanography, Mr. Herbert J. Mann, civilian scientist came aboard, from the CACAPON for transportation to San Diego, California. 1347 - Underway from mooring. 1600 - On station 1,000 yards with CURRITUCK formation guide. Set base course 096° (T), speed

15 knots. Weather, overcast, visibility 18 miles, wind from S.E., force 6, swell from S.E. of 9 feet.

Friday 21 March: Weather, scattered clouds, S.E. wind shifting to S. force 6 rising at times to force 7, S.E. swell of 12 feet, visibility 15 miles.

Saturday 22 March: 0200 - Set ships clocks ahead 1 hour to conform with minus 11 zone time. Weather same as proceeding days with wind and sea dropping after 2200.

Sunday 23 March: 1600 - CURRITUCK parted company en route to east coast by way of Panama. Weather, scattered clouds with no wind or swell.

Monday 24 March: 0200 - Advanced ships clocks one hour to conform to minus 12 zone time. Weather same as proceeding day.

Tuesday 25 March: 1200 - retarded ships clocks 24 hours to conform to plus 12 zone time. Changed date to Monday 24 March 1947. 1350 - Crossed 180th Meridian eastbound in Lat. 22° 54' S. 2357 - c/c to 047° (T). 0900 - Commenced refueling from CACAPON. 1105 - Completed fueling.

Tuesday 25 March: 1700 - Passed Late Island of the Vavau group abeam to starboard distance 20 miles. 1830 - Passed Fanua Lai of the Vavau group abeam to starboard distance 5 miles.

Wednesday 26 March: On station 2,000 yards ahead of CACAPON base course 047° (T). 0200 - Set ships clocks ahead one hour to conform to plus 11 zone time. 1400 - Sighted Tutuial Island bearing 034° (T), distance 50 miles. 1715 - Passed 10 miles east of Pago Pago, Samoa. 1805 - Sighted Tau Island of the Monua Group bearing 080° (T), distance 55 miles.

Friday 28 March: 0145 - c/s to 14 knots due to boiler trouble on CACAPON.

Saturday 29 March: 0200 - Advanced clocks one (1) hour to conform to plus 10 zone time:

Sunday 30 March: 0315 - Crossed equator northbound in Long. 156° 14' S.

Monday 31 March: Took station on port beam of CACAPON for refueling. 1130 - Completed refueling having received 102,160 gallons. Pursuant to verbal orders of Commanding Officers of U.S.S. CACAPON (AO52) the following men were received aboard for transportation to

CONFIDENTIAL

San Diego, California: Lt.Comdr. L. L. Clark, USNR. Mr. J. Gibbs,
Dr. H. E. Dietz, and Doctor Hopkins civilian scientists from N.EL.,
San Diego, California. 1148 - Pursuant to orders of CTF 68, parted
company with CACAPON.

     Wednesday 2 April: 0200 - Advanced ship's clocks one hour
to conform to plus 8 zone time.

     Sunday 6 April: 0524 - Sighted Los Coronados. Entered
San Diego Bay channel. 1000 - Moored port side to U.S.S. PERKINS
at buoy #27, San Diego, California. Reported to ComDesPac for suty.

ANNEX I (o)

U. S. S. PINE ISLAND (AV-12)

Table of Contents

NARRATIVE

1. Preliminary Preparations.

After official notification that the PINE ISLAND would participate in Operation HIGHJUMP, a two months availability period was given
in NSY at Portsmouth, Virginia. Along with needed repair work and installations, a helicopter deck was installed forward of the pilot house,
an innovation unique in seaplane tender construction. After entering
the Navy Yard on September 13, 1946, all hands carried out a strenuous
period of preparation, with an overload of work undertaken by all hands
because of an acute shortage of personnel. However, as work progressed, more personnel were assigned to the ship, so that by the end of
the yard period on November 13, practically the full allowance for
Operation HIGHJUMP was aboard and being indoctrinated in their shipboard duties.

Leaving the yard on November 13, the PINE ISLAND proceeded to
the Deperming Station for a routine check and then on to NOB, Norfolk
the same day. From the 13th to the 18th was spent in loading stores
and continuing with preparations for sea, and on the 18th the ship proceeded to Yorktown, Virginia, for loading ammunition. This operation
was completed on November 22. Little time was available for needed
indoctrination of all hands in actual practice for unde way air operations, although a short drill was carried out with a PBM from NAS,
Norfolk, on the afternoon of the 22nd while operating in the Chesapeake Bay. Magnetic compasses were also calibrated at the same time.

Arriving back at NOB, Norfolk, at dusk on the 22nd, the PINE
ISLAND anchored out and went alongside Pier 3 at NOB early the following morning, 23 November. From the 23rd to the 2nd of December, an
intensive schedule of loading stores, aircraft, small arms ammunition,
fueling ship and receiving additional personnel was carried out. It
was felt that an additional two weeks for practical operations at sea
would have been highly desirable and beneficial at this time, but this
could not be accomplished because of the time limit of the operation
schedule.

2. Norfolk to Panama.

At 1300 on December 2nd, 1946, the ship got underway in ac-
cordance with current sortie plan and proceeded out of the Chesapeake
Bay entrance for rendezvous with the U.S.S. MOUNT OLYMPUS, flying the
flag of Rear Admiral Cruzen. At 1600 course was set for Panama, Canal
Zone, on course 140 degrees T, speed 15 knots, in column with the MT.
OLYMPUS, U.S.C.G.C. NORTHWIND, and the destroyer, U.S.S. BROWNSON.

The cruise to the Canal Zone was uneventful; the time enroute
was utilized in routine shipboard training and exercises. Crooked
Island Passage was navigated during the mid and morning watch of 5
December 1946, but with clear visibility and calm seas, no difficulty
in passage was experienced.

At 0600 on 5 December, after clearing Castle Island, the PINE
ISLAND was granted permission to proceed independently to Colon in
order to reach there in sufficient time to launch her PBMS in preparation for transit through the Canal. At 1100 on the 5th, Cape Maysi
point, southwestern point of Cuba, was rounded and course was set to
pass five miles to port of Navassa Island. At 1800 Navassa Island
was passed abeam to starboard and direct course was set for Colon
for ETA at 0800, December 7th.

On the afternoon of December 6th a special CIC drill was conducted with PBM aircraft attached to VPB-74 based at Coco Solo, Canal
Zone, permitting CIC personnel to work out special exercises dealing
with low visibility control of aircraft.

Isla Grande light was sighted at 0500 on December 7th. The
PINE ISLAND entered the breakwater at Colon at 0800, and anchored immediately afterwards for discharging aircraft and receiving Canal
pilots aboard. Underway at 1100, the ship proceeded through the Canal
with no difficulties and moored at Pier 1, Naval Submarine Base, Balboa, at 1837. The first leg of the voyage to the Antarctic had been
completed.

3. Panama to Operating Area.

Underway from Balboa at 0900 on 10 December, the PINE ISLAND
took aboard it's two PBM aircraft outside the Pacific entrance to
the Canal and then proceeded to rendezvous point. Rendezvous with the
Central Group and the other units of the Eastern Group was effected at
2300, and the PINE ISLAND took station number 5 in column open order.
At 0800 on December 11, the Task Force broke up into independent units
taking stations on tracks at 50 mile intervals with the PINE ISLAND on
the easternmost track. At 1100 Malpelo Island was passed close abeam
to port at a distance of one mile; this was the last land sighted until
the first flights over the Antarctic Continent.

Proceeding ever southward, the outer domain of Neptunus Rex
was entered at 1600 on December 11, and to the dismay of the many pollywogs aboard, Davy Jones made his official visit at 1630. Full preparations had been made by the Shellbacks to properly initiate the landlubbers, and though a very auspicious beginning was made, the plans for
continued initiations and full ceremony had to be suspended because of
unforseen ship repair work, which did not allow time for full initiation
ceremonies.

The Equator was crossed at 0600 on the morning of the twelfth
at longitude 82 47 W, and the pollywogs breathed thankful sighs of
relief when the official announcement was made by the Captain that time
did not allow for further ceremonies.

The days immediately following crossing the Equator were ones to be enjoyed by all hands. Fair and calm weather prevailed and days were spend in routine ship training and exercises. Preparations were made for entering the "Roaring Forties", including the construction of a wooden water shield on the forward part of the helicopter deck to give added protection to the helicopter in the anticipated coming rough weather. At 0600 on December 17th, rendezvous was effected with the CANISTEO and BROWNSON for fueling in latitude 22-30 South and Lon. 97-50 W.

Following refueling operations, the Eastern and Central Groups, including the CANISTEO, proceeded westward to the vicinity of Scott Island, while the PINE ISLAND and the BROWNSON proceeded south on Longitude 99 30 West.

On December 18th, the BROWNSON came alongside the starboard quarter to receive provisions and upon completion of this operation was assigned Station 30 miles on the starboard beam of the PINE ISLAND. Both ships proceeded southward conducting search for Swain's Island, reported in position 100 West Longitude and 59 South Latitude.

The dreaded "Roaring Forties" were entered at 1200 Tare time on December 20th but none of the expected rough weather was encountered. At 1800 on December 21st, the first of the wild-life of the Antarctic was encountered in the form of small flocks of petrels which were to become commonplace from there on. On December 23rd during the forenoon watch, the first whale sightings were recorded in Latitude 58 South and Longtitude 99 40 West. The reported vicinity of Swain's Island was passed with no landfalls; weather was clear, visibility unrestricted. Several cloud formations on the horizon gave illusions of land formations, and these typical formations could have well given the old time navigators the same illusions. Swain's Island was marked off as non-existant.

Up until this time, ice had been expected to be sighted daily, but it was not until 0730 Tare on December 24th that the first iceberg was sighted on the horizon in Latitude 62-56 South and Longitude 99-50 West. Because of the non-existance of ice, north of this latitude, a late break-up of the ice pack was expected. Refueling of the BROWNSON was accomplished in the forenoon watch of the 24th, upon completion of which the BROWNSON took up her previous station.

Icebergs became commonplace after the initial sightings, and from the occasional pieces of brash ice passed, the northern limit of the drift ice was expected to be encountered soon.

4. Operating Area (First Phase)

At 0000 on December 25th, the northern limit of the loose pack ice was sighted, tending generally in a southwesterly direction, with many icebergs on the outer edge and within the pack. Course was set in a southwesterly direction. to scout the outer edge of the drift ice, but at 0300 further progress south was impracticable and the ship was stopped in Latitude 67-10 South and Longitude 101-20 West. At 1100 the helicopter was launched for an ice reconnaissance flight, with the Task Group Commander as observer, but no openings in the open pack, sufficient for seaplane operations, were observed further south. The ship hove to in the vicinity of a large iceberg about 1000 feet long and 300 feet high, and holiday routine was declared for the crew to enjoy Christmas Day as best they could when so far away from the usual atmosphere of Christmas.

On December 26, weather continued generally unfavorable for flight operations, but it was decided to hoist out one PBM for a test flight. At 0830 the plane was hoisted out, but during the fueling operation, one of the assisting boats damaged the port wingtip float and the plane was hoisted back aboard. All flight operations were cancelled until more favorable weather. Still in the vicinity of the large iceberg, which had become surrounded by the outer rim of the drift ice, the creation of an artificial seadrome was attempted by maneuvering the ship upwind of the drift ice and then drifting back across to clear the ice from the area. This was of little value, however, as the ice closed in more rapidly than it could be cleared out. At 1630, 3 rounds of five inch were fired into the iceberg from a range of 3000 yards, but if the iceberg had been expected to collapse everyone was disappointed, as the impact of the projectile was hardly noticeable.

On December 27th, the weather continued unfavorable for flight operations with heavy fog lying over the area. By the afternoon of the 28th, the weather showed indications of improving, but the water was still too rough for operations. An attempt was made to take the ship inside the pack ice, but after about five mile penetration with continued low visibility, course was reversed and the ship took station to the north of the pack, to await improvement in the weather.

The following day, the 29th of December, weather seemed favorable for flights at 0700 and one plane was readied for flight. However, by the time the plane was ready to go into the water, snow squalls reduced the visibility to zero and the plane was left suspended on the hook. The weather steadily improved so that by 1200 fueling of the PBM on the hook was commenced, and upon completion at 1240 was cast off. The first flight to the Antarctic Continent was started at 1305 with Lt. Comdr. Howell, PPC, and Captain Dufek as observer. This first flight reported favorable weather for mapping operations over the continent in the vicinity of Cape Dart, so PBM number 2 was launched and started on the second flight to the continent at 1835. Lt.(jg) Ball was PPC of the second flight.

The first flight returned to the ship at 2305 and although indications of a slight deterioration in the weather was noticed, it was decided to send out a third flight. Lt. LeBlanc was PPC of the third crew, and Captain Caldwell accompanied the flight as observer. Shift of flight crew personnel was made on the water and after checking and refueling, the third flight for the continent departed at 0244 on December 30th.

Flight 2 returned to base at 1541 and was immediately hoisted aboard.
The weather became increasingly unfavorable, and flight 3 enroute to the
continent was reporting low ceiling and visibility. At 0608 radio contact was lost with flight 3 at plotted position at Latitude 71-24 South
and Longitude 99 30 West, and all radio circuits were alerted for possible transmissions. The ETA of Flight 3 was 1245 on 30 December, and as
that time drew nearer, the conditions of no communications, low ceiling
and visibility, accentuated the anxiety which was growing among all the
officers and crew as to the fate of the flight. 1245 passed with no further contact with flight 3; lost plane procedures were instituted, and
the one remaining assembled PBM was placed in readiness for a search
flight as soon as the weather became favorable. Bad weather prevailed
throughout the 31st.

5. Rescue operations.

No one felt the spirit of the New Year, and a general feeling of
impatience began to prevail when there seemed to be no sign of the weather
lifting. Hourly messages were being broadcast to the missing PBM on all
radio circuits, and perhaps it was the feeling that something was being
left undone which brought the request from members of crew to the Chaplain,
asking that a nightly prayer be offered in behalf of the missing plane and
its crew members.

The New Year dawned with little outward prospect of the weather
clearing. Slight improvement began in the weather about midmorning, but
by the time the PBM was over the side, a dense fog had covered the area,
and the PBM with two rearming boats alongside secured to the stern of the
ship by a 300 foot line. Misfortune struck again in the early morning
hours of the midwatch on January 2nd, when the waterborne PBM astern of
the ship swung into the side of the ship and damaged the port wingtip
deicing boot and aileron. It was immediately hoisted aboard for survey of
damage, and after consideration of time element involved, it was decided
to start immediately assembling the spare PBM on board.

The next two days were spent in strenuous effort on the part of
the Air Department personnel in preparing the two remaining planes for
flight operations and both planes were reported ready for test flights on
the morning of January 5th. No break in the weather had occured in the
meantime. The weather improved slightly during the forenoon watch, and
both planes were hoisted over the side. But again the break in the weather
failed to hold, and again misfortune struck as the planes were hoisted back
aboard. Most unfavorable weather prevailed with heavy swells coming in
from astern and parallel to the ship. During the hooking on of the second
plane, the foul weather pendant carried away, falling forward on the plane.
The former was bent near the leading edge of the wing and four holes were
torn in the hull; the largest above the bent former being about a foot long
and one inch wide, and the other three about two inches in diameter. The
weather cleared in the afternoon of the fifth, and the assembled PBM was

RESTRICTED

again hoisted over the side for a test flight. The test was satisfactory, and with continued improvement in the weather, the plane was gassed, and departed on the first rescue and search flight to the Antarctic Continent at 1900. Weather in near the continent was bad with low ceiling and visibility, and after a negativesearch over the last reported position of the lost plane, covering 100,000 square miles of territory, the search plane returned to the ship because of increasingly bad weather.

At 1130 on January 6th, the same PBM again departed on the second rescue and search flight, but was forced to return because of unfavorable weather with negative results, and was hoisted aboard at 2015.

On January 7th, the PINE ISLAND was joined by the CANISTEO and BROWNSON and a routine transfer of supplies was made between the vessels. In the afternoon, both planes were again in comission and were hoisted out for test flights, but weather was unfavorable for extended flights, and both planes were hoisted aboard after local flights. On January 8th, the weather seemed to have taken a definite turn for the better, but by the time a plane was hoisted out and airborne, snow squalls and increasingly bad weather forced the plane to return to the ship.

The following day, one plane was sent on a local weather flight which reported very unfavorable weather towards the continent, and at 1115 it was recalled to the ship. In the meantime opportunity was taken to refuel from the CANISTEO, and a very successful operation was conducted with the ships lying to and drifting with the wind. The CANISTEO, upwind from the PINE ISLAND, drifted at a slightly slower rate. The waterborne PBM was hoisted aboard at 2015, and flight operations were secured for the day.

With no decided break in the weather, Commander Task Group 68.3, Captain George J. Dufek, decided on the following day, January 10 to move 100 miles to the west in search of more favorable operating conditions. The new station, in Latitude 67 00 South and 104 00 West, was reached at 1830 on January 10th, and after sending out the helicopter on an ice reconnaissance flight which reported no possible openings further south in the pack ice, it was decided to lay to north of the pack ice and wait for more favorable weather.

Early January 11th, the weather began to improve, and Aerology, for the first time in days, indicated that the weather might hold for two or three days at least. Flight Quarters were sounded at 0430 and one PBM, Lt. (jg) Ball, PPC, was hoisted over the side, becoming airborne for the continent at 0700. Weather improved as the plane proceeded toward the south, and at 1124, word was received that the scene of the crash had been located about eight miles inland on the Antarctic Continent. The second PBM, Lt. Comdr. John Howell, PPC, was hoisted over the side at 1130 and was loaded with various items of survival gear for the surviving members of the crashed PBM. It became airborne for the continent at 1415.

ANNEX I(o) - 6 -

In the meantime further word was received from the PBM at the scene of the crash that there were six survivors of the crash with three of the crew members killed; Ens. M. A. Lopez, W. L. Hendersin, AMM1, and F. W. Williams, AMM1. Survival gear was dropped, and the survivors were directed to proceed overland to a bay of open water about eight miles from the crash. This plane was forced to depart from the area for base before contacting the second plane because it was running low on fuel supply. The second plane had little difficulty, however, in locating the survivors and after a survey of the situation, Lt. Comdr. Howell asked and was granted permission to land in the water and wait for survivors.

What followed after that has been told and retold again. Only a magnificent display of individual courage and endurance kept the survivors going. The ship with great relief and thankfulness received the word at 0730 on January 12th that all members of the survivors were safely aboard the plane, which subsequently became airborne for the ship at 0830.

The rescue plane was waterborne at 1044 in Latitude 67 00 South, Longitude 104 20 West, and was hoisted aboard at 1125. Thus ended one of the most memorable and trying periods for all hands, and an immediate holiday was declared by the Executive Officer, to reward the crew for many long weary hours spent during the rescue operations.

6. Operations North of Cape Dart.

From January 12th to January 17th, unfavorable weather persisted and advantage was taken of this period to give the crew a well earned rest. On the 17th, the BROWNSON rendezvoused with the PINE ISLAND and both ships proceeded southwest in search of more favorable weather for transfer of survivors and supplies to the BROWNSON, which was to effect a rendezvous with the PHILLIPINE SEA. This transfer was accomplished on January 18th and the BROWNSON departed the area for scheduled rendezvous.

On January 19th, another near catastrophe was narrowly averted when the helicopter crashed in the water on its landing approach after an ice reconnaissance flight. However, both occupants, Captain Lufek and Lt. Comdr. Sessums were quickly rescued by a crash boat standing by near the ship, and outside of cold exposure, escaped without injuries.

At 0400 on January 20th, the PINE ISLAND proceeded northwest, skirting the ice pack, in search of more favorable weather conditions. The northern edge of the pack was skirted along the 67 degree parallel of latitude, to longitude 120 west, and then course was set to the south. Heavy weather had in the meantime opened new leads in the ice pack and at 1600 on January 22nd, the ship lay to on the edge of the ice pack, having achieved its greatest southing to date, in latitude 69 13 South and longitude 119 34 West.

Weather improved and at 1800 on January 23rd, both PBM's were hoisted over the side, the first plane taking departure for the continent at 2009 and the second at 2042. Both planes had successful flights to the continent and were hoisted aboard in the early morning of January 24th at 0430 and 0545 respectively. Prior to termination of this flight, terminal weather had deteriorated and a let down on instruments of 8000 feet was required and heavy snow fall commenced with and continued after landing.

Flight operations in this area were made extremely difficult by the existing areas of brash ice and heavy swells near the pack, and it was decided to move back eastward to longitude 106 west, and course was set to northeast. At 0730 on January 24th, course was changed to 090 T at 1615 to skirt the northeast edge of the ice pack along the 67 degree parallel.

At 0500 on January 25th, course was changed to 150 to head farther south toward the continent, and at 1430 scattered areas of drift ice were encountered which gradually increased until the northern edge of the ice pack was encountered at 1530. All engines were stopped at 1620 to lie to awaiting favorable weather for flight operation, having reached the farthest point south to date in Latitude 68 40 South and 106 17 West.

On January 26, with favorable weather, both planes were hoisted out at 0445. The first plane departed on a photographic and mapping mission to the Antarctic Continent at 0630 and the second at 0721. In the middle of the forenoon watch, the SOC was hoisted out for a local flight and the remaining helicopter on board was flown from the seaplane deck to the helicopter deck. This was the first time that all four planes on board were in the air simultaneously. The two PBM's returned from successful flights at 1330 and 1430 respectively, and both were hoisted aboard by 1500. The completion of these two flights marked the end of operations in the Cape Dart area, and the decision was made to move to the eastward to Peter I Island and then on to Marguerite Bay where it was hoped a suitable anchorage could be found to resume mapping of the continent. Course was set to the northeast at 1530 on January 26th to rendezvous with the CANISTEO for refueling operations in Latitude 66 45 South and Longitude 105 00 West. The PINE ISLAND was fueled from the CANISTEO in the morning of January 27th, and both ships continued in company for Peter I Island.

7. Operations Between Peter I Island and Marguerite Bay.

The pack ice was encountered in 67 50 South and 99 00 West, and the ship was forced to skirt the edge of the pack to the northeast. The northern limit of the pack was cleared at noon on January 28th in Latitude 66 15 South and Longitude 95 30, and course was set to the east in increasingly rough seas. It was apparent that Peter I Island was inaccessable at this time of the year with the pack extending approximately 90 miles to the northward. Easting was continued by the PINE ISLAND until 2000 on January 29th, and in Longitude 93 30 West, course was set south to reach the pack ice in hopes of finding suitable weather for continuation of flight operations.

The CANISTEO was detached during the evening watch to take up
weather station to the west. Heavy concentrations of large tabular bergs
and drift ice were encountered in Latitude 67 46 South and at noon on
January 30th the ship lay to waiting for an improvement in the weather.
The helicopter was launched on the afternoon watch to search for possible
leads in the ice to allow further movement to the south, but engine
trouble developed and it was forced to return immediately to the ship.
The ship lay to in this position throughout the 31st in a heavy fog and
when by noon on February 2nd, there was no improvement in the weather,
course was set to the southeast. Contact with heavy pack ice was made
about 20 miles to the southeast and the ship commenced skirting the
pack to the northeast. Dense fog and heavy seas prevailed throughout
the 3rd, and course was set to the north and east heading into the seas.
The last of the drift ice was cleared in the morning watch in Latitude
66 04 South and Longitude 88 30 West. Slow progress, at 5 knots, was
continued to the northeast. The wind abated during the midmorning watch
of the 4th, but heavy fog persisted and the ship hobe to at 0640 Roger
time.

Easting was continued in a variable weather and sea combination
of fog and snow and icebergs until the 79th meridian of longitude
was reached at 2200 on the 5th of February. At this time course was set
to the south in search of the ice pack and more favorable weather. A
southerly course was maintained throughout the night of the 5th with increasingly better weather and seas. A small concentration of bergs and
brash ice was encountered in Latitude 66 30 South and 79 00 West on
the 6th of February, but no indications of the pack were in evidence.
Speed was increased to 15 knots, and course was continued south. The
continental shelf was crossed at 1730 R on the 6th with the fathometer
shallowing off rapidly from 1900 fathoms to 250 fathoms. The pack was
met at 1900 in Latitude 69 15 South and 77 West with a huge concentration of bergs lying in the direction of Charcot Island. Course was set
to the southwest to skirt the pack and was continued to 69 46 South and
79 00 West. This was the southernmost point reached by the PINE ISLAND
throughout the cruise.

The ship lay to north of the pack at 2200 to await improvement
in the weather. Continued snow squalls prevented flight operations on
February 7th, but on the morning of the 8th, both PBM's were hoisted
over for mapping flights to cut in the coast between Marguerite Bay and
where mapping had been discontinued to the east of Cape Dart. However,
weather over the continent was unfavorable and both planes returned and
were hoisted aboard in a snow squall after only two hours in the air.

The BROWNSON joined the PINE ISLAND during the midwatch of the
9th bringing long awaited mail from the States. Weather became favorable for flight quarters in the early morning and both planes were hoisted out and were airborne by 0830 Roger.

RESTRICTED

The weather steadily deteriorated throughout the afternoon and both planes were advised to return to the base. The two planes joined up over the continent and returned in company, reaching base at 1620. Snow squalls were forming in the area, the last plane getting down in restricted visibility. Both planes were hoisted aboard without incident.

On February 10th, Commander Task Group 68.3, Captain Dufek, shifted his flag to the BROWNSON and the BROWNSON departed the area at 1645 for Charcot Island where an attempt was to be made to put a landing party ashore.

On February 11th, orders were received to proceed to Marguerite Bay and course was set to the northeast. A heavy concentration of growlers, drift ice, and bergs was encountered to the north in Latitude 69 15 South through which the ship had to proceed with heavy seas and wind "to contend with". Course was continued to the northeast, and at 0840 on February 12th, the northern coast of Alexander 1st Island was sighted, distant about 40 miles. Appearing much closer than it actually was, the rugged and broken coast line of high snow-covered peaks and mountain ranges stood out in bold relief above the fog layer near the base of the coast line. This was the first land of the Antarctic sighted by personnel of the ship (with the exception of the Aviators), and it provided an excellent view of the awe-inspiring white wastes of the Antarctic.

At 2215 a group of five small islands were sighted in Latitude 68 41 South and Longitude 72 13 West and from their appearance and position they were believed to be the Johansen Islands. The positions of these islands were accurately plotted by the Navigator as a celestial fix was obtained at the time of the sightings.

Rendezvous with BROWNSON was effected early on February 13th, and both ships cruised north to the southwest of Adelaide Island, waiting for improvement in the weather conditions to enter Marguerite Bay. At midnight on February 13th, course was set toward the eastern tip of Alexander First Island and by 0800 the ice shelf was approached within 10 miles. At this time course was changed to the east to enter Marguerite Bay.

Preparations were made to fuel the BROWNSON and course was set to the north while carrying out the operation. In the process of transferring Captain Dufek from the BROWNSON to the PINE ISLAND by means of the breeches buoy, an unexpected surge of the ships caused the carrying line to part as the Commodore reached the center of the span. The Commodore was catapulted literally into the icy water between the two ships. Without hesitation, the BROWNSON did a full left turn to port and in a superb example of shiphandling and seamanship, Captain Dufek was aboard the lifeboat of the BROWNSON in the record breaking time of seven minutes from the time he was catapulted into the water. Fortunately the Commodore suffered only a minor head injury and for the second time during the cruise, he had another narrow escape from the waters of the Antarctic. The fueling operation was completed without further incident and course was set to the northeast for the west of Adelaide Island.

8. Operation in Weddell

At 0240 Zebra, orders were received from Commander Task Group 68.3 to discontinue operations in the Marguerite Bay area and to proceed around the tip of the Palmer Peninsula to the Weddell Sea. Accordingly, course was set to the northwest to effect a rendezvous with the oiler, CANISTEO, in Latitude 66 00 South and Longitude 70 00 West. The CANISTEO joined the formation at 1500 Roger and course was set for the Weddell Sea.

Progress around the Palmer Peninsula was slow due to high winds and heavy seas. A vibration was noticed in the port shaft of the PINE ISLAND at speeds above 12 knots, and it was believed that there was a possibility of a damaged propeller, caused by proceeding through the heavy ice on February 11th.

On February 17th, Commander Task Group 68.3 transferred his flag back to the PINE ISLAND south of the Shetland Island and course was set east to pass north of the South Orkney group of islands. After rounding the Orkney Islands, the task group was split, each ship proceeding to a newly assigned station on Latitude 66 00 South.

Large concentrations of bergs were encountered in Latitude 63 20 South and Longitude 38 40 West. On February 21st, rendezvous was effected with the CANISTEO during the morning watch of the 21st, and fueling operations were completed during the afternoon. Heavy pack ice was encountered at 1600 Peter at Latitude 63 40 South and Longitude 39 00 West, and slow progress was continued to the eastward in company with the CANISTEO, the BROWNSON being used to scout ice conditions to the south.

The CANISTEO was detached on the 22nd to take up a weather station 50 miles to the northeast of the PINE ISLAND, and the Task Group continued slowly eastward along the 64th parallel of Latitude in search of suitable aircraft operating conditions. Weather continued unfavorable throughout, with overcast skies, fog, and snow flurries.

An attempt on the 23rd to get farther south in the Weddell Sea failed as the heavy pack was encountered in Latitude 64 46 South and Longitude 27 00 West. The pack was skirted to the north and east. After clearing the pack, course was set to the east and on the 24th to the southeast, in an attempt to get close to the Antarctic Continent for flight operations. Brash ice and drift ice were encountered again on the 25th in Latitude 67 00 South and Longitude 16 00 West, and course was set again to the east. At 1100 Z on the 26th, the Russian whaler,

SLAVA, and three killer boats were sighted in Latitude 66 50 S and Longitude 15 30 W. Identification was established by radio - no information on ice or weather was forthcoming. Three other ships were sighted about an hour afterwards but no identification was made. The area seemed to abound with whales as continuous sightings were made while passing through this area.

Heavy pack, brash, and drift ice were encountered in Latitude 66 55 South and Longitude 08 39 West and was skirted northeastward to Latitude 66 32 South at which time course was set to 090. At 2100 Zebra on February 27th, the ship passed through the intersection of the Zero Meridian and the Antarctic Circle and progress was made to the eastward. Course was again changed to the southeast on the 28th and then south so that by 2000 Zebra on the 28th, a position in Latitude 68 14 South and 07 27 East had been reached. Few bergs were encountered in this area, and the sea was calm and glassy. At 2000 Zebra, course was changed to 210 degrees T. The pack was encountered on this course in Latitude 69 20 South and 03 00 West and was skirted to the West for a suitable operating area. Weather continued to improve and shortly before noon, flight quarters were sounded. Both planes were hoisted out in the early afternoon with excellent operating conditions existing in the immediate area, but with unfavorable weather towards the Continent to the south. The ship's position at this time was approximately forty miles off the charted coast of Queen Maud's Land, but no land was visible nor were any radar contacts made. Realistic illusions of mountain peaks were made by cloud formations but all indications were that at least no large mountain ranges existed within 100 miles of the ship's position.

The planes were unable to get over the Continent as a cloud layer starting at 500 feet fifty miles from the ship and rising to 13,000 feet southward existed in the vicinity of the Continent. A small group of islands were reported with reservations by one of the planes in Lat. 70 00b S and Long. 02 35 S, but their existance is doubtful because of the existance of so many lrge bergs in the area which may well have been mistaken for islands. Failing to reach the continent, both planes scouted the ice conditions to the east and west and then returned to base and were hoisted aboard.

On March 2nd, another attempt was made to carry out flight operations, but rapidly developing snow squalls in the entire area brought about the cancellation of all preparations, and it was decided to move away from the pack and proceed northward. While skirting the pack to the northward, virgin ice was observed to be forming on the water's surface, and at 1100 Z, March 3rd, the Commander Task Group 68.3 ordered the group to cease operations, withdraw northward from the area, and when clear, to set course for Rio de Janeiro, Brazil, at best sustained speed.

Departure from the Antarctic was taken at 0800 Z March 4th, at position Lat. 62 37 S and Long. 07 15 W; a great circle course was set for Rio to arrive on 1100Z March 18th. Many bergs, one of which was two miles long, with several large concentrations were encountered to Lat. 51 30 S and scattered bergs to 50 30 S. Heavy winds and seas were met at Lat. 51 30 S during the night of March 7th, but abated by the afternoon of the 8th. Continued further heavy weather was expected through the "Forties", but arrival in Rio was not expected to be delayed. After six days of shore leave and liberty in Rio, course was to be set for the Canal Zone and then to the new home port of the PINE ISLAND, San Diego, California. Arrival in San Diego would complete a cruise of 24,000 miles for the PINE ISLAND with 98 continuous days at sea and 128 days total under way since departure on Operation HIGHJUMP december 2, 1946. The equator had been crossed twice on opposite sides South American Continent, the Antarctic circle crossed several times, the Greenwich Meridian transversed at the intersection of the Antarctic Curcle, Cape Horn had been rounded, and the South American continent had been circumnavigted, taking departure on the west side and returning again through the east. Starting out ninety percent landlubbers, the ship ended the cruise with a well-seasoned, salty crew.

ANNEX ONE - (p)

NARRATIVE

U.S.S. CANISTEO (AO99)

I. PREPARATION FOR OPERATION HIGHJUMP.

The CANISTEO arrived Norfolk, Va., 21 October and at 0937 moored at Craney Island to discharge cargo. At 0955 Captain Kirten reported to ComServLant to obtain any available pertinent information concerning our availability in preparation for Operation HIGHJUMP. About 1530 Captain Kirten returned with information that the ship would moor outboard of the USS AMPHION (AR13) at pier 7, NOB, for availability until 15 November, the date designated for our reporting to CTF 68 at Norfolk.

At 0910, 23 October, the ship moored port side to the USS AMPHION at pier 7, NOB, and preparation for forthcoming operation commenced. Information from Service Force revealed that our crew complement would be in accordance with post-war allowance and arr_ angements were made to procure 100% allowance. The Captain called a conference of all officers and discussed all available information concerning Operation HIGHJUMP. We were informed that TF 68 would make a cruise to the Antarctic in search of scientific data during the short Antarctic summer. The Bureau of Standards would install oceanographic equipment for the study of the ocean bottom and sea water during the entire cruise. All instructions from CTF 68 were discussed and responsibility of each project assigned. Procurement of heavy winter clothing, renewing of salt water lines in engine spaces and lagging of exposed water lines were considered ship's priority number one. The installation of scientific equipment was established as Service Force and NavShpYd Norfolk responsibility. The Supply Officer was instructed to obtain supplies for an eight month cruise. The repair force from the USS AMPHION commenced work on engine space piping. The electronics and ordnance forces started work on routine inspection and repair of our equipment. The fire-room was secured and cleaning of boilers commenced. Steam flushing and fire main water being furnished by the USS AMPHION.

At 1400, 8 November, the Electronics Officer from NavShpYd, Norfolk, Captain Pryor, accompanied by Lieutenant Commander Satter-field, Service Force Electronics Officer, came on board to inspect the spaces tentatively assigned for installation of ionospheric and oceanographic equipment. The space amidships was considered in-adequate for operation of oceanographic equipment and the space on the superstructure deck, port side aft, was selected pending approval of Dr. Hough. The potato locker was selected for conversion to an operations room. The space on the main deck selected for ionospheric installations was considered too low for proper antenna construction. The 40mm clipping room on starboard side of the 02 deck amidships was designated for ionospheric installations pending approval of personnel from Bureau of Standards.

CONFIDENTIAL

At 2000, 9 November Mr. Utz and Mr. Kral from the Bureau of Standards reported aboard. A portion of the ionospheric equipment accompanied them and was placed aboard ship on 10 November. The clipping room on 02 deck was satisfactory but space considered inadequate necessitating the additional assignment of the port clipping room at same frame and level.

At 0400, 11 November a conference of repair officers from the USS AMPHION, engineers from the NavShpYd, Norfolk, Bureau of Standards personnel, Drs. Hough and Barnes from Woodshole Institute and Lieutenant Commander Satterfield from Service Force was held aboard the CANISTEO. Plans for installation of both ionospheric and oceanographic equipment were made and responsibility assigned.

At 1105, 14 November Lieutenant L. L. Edwards, USN reported aboard under orders from CNO for temporary duty in connection with the ionospheric program.

On 15 November, the CANISTEO reported to CTF 68 for duty. The tender availability was extended to 22 November due to delayed progress of work and arrival of equipment.

On 19 November dock trials were conducted alongside the USS AMPHION. Tests were satisfactory.

At 1100, 21 November CTG 68.3, Captain Dufek, and staff Commanding Officers of the USS PINE ISLAND and USS BROWNSON came aboard for a discussion of Operation HIGHJUMP.

22 November at request of CTG 68.3 the availability of the CANISTEO alongside the tender was extended to 27 November, tentative date of our departure.

25 November received orders from CTF 29 to depart Norfolk to Aruba, 27 November. Load Aruba and arrive Canal Zone prior 8 December to report CTF 68 for duty. Spare propellers for the USS PINE ISLAND, USS BROWNSON and USS CANISTEO were loaded and secured for sea on cargo deck. 1300 Captain W. Kirten, Jr. relieved of command by Captain E. K. Walker. Mr. W. N. Reith and Mr. H. M. Ikerd, radio engineers from Naval Research Laboratory reported aboard for duty in connection with ionospheric project.

27 November at 0937 departed Norfolk for Aruba in accordance with CTF 29 dispatch 251614Z.

3 December stood into St. Nicholas Bay, Aruba and moored port side to finger pier. Loaded 92000 barrels NSF and 17990 barrels diesel fuel in 13 hours. Seventy-five percent of the crew

enjoyed liberty until midnight. The Lago Oil Company sponsored a
beach picnic, baseball game and dance especially for the ship.

4 December at 0900 we departed Aruba and set course for Cristobal, Canal Zone.

5 December arrived Cristobal Harbor at 0615 and proceeded to
Pier 9, Cristobal. Discharged seven enlisted Navy passengers and
.topped off with fresh and frozen provisions. Fifty percent of the
crew were permitted to go on liberty. Almost all hands bought the
usual souvenirs and sampled the usual night life.

6 December at 0555 cast off lines and prepared to transit the
Panama Canal. The ship entered Gatum Locks at 0715 and completed
passage through locks at 0845. Experienced almost continuous heavy
rain showers on entire transit of canal. Arrived Pedro Miguel Locks
at 1240 and departed Miraflores Locks at 1419. We then proceeded and
moored port side to Peir #1, Naval Ammunition Depot, Balboa.

On Sunday, 8 December the U.S.C.G. icebreaker NORTHWIND moored
alongside to starboard.

On Monday, 9 December Dr. Raymond Gilmore reported aboard for
duty as a biological observer and collector. At 0900, the Commanding
Officer attended a CTF 68 conference on board the flagship, USS MT
OLYMPUS. This was the last meeting of all the commanding officers of
the task force. (Comment by CTF 68; Only half the ships of the Task
Force were present).

All hands enjoyed port and starboard watch liberty during the
four day lay-over, while final arrangements were being made for the
long voyage ahead. Stores were topped off where necessary. Fueling
conferences were held with the other ships of the task force and all
hands had their last taste of civilization ashore for a few months
to come. Task Group departure was scheduled for 1000, 10 December,
but a steering casualty delayed our departure until 1608 on 10 December, when we departed Balboa. After dropping off the harbor pilot,
we set course and steamed toward the Antarctic.

II. ENROUTE ANTARCTIC.

11 December ship entered Domain of Neptunus Rex. Davey Jones
came on board in the evening and served summons to approximately 155
uninitiated Pollywogs and gave notice of events to take place the
following day.

12 December at 0800, his Royal Highness, King Neptune and
his Royal Party came aboard and conducted a solemn but

energetic initiation of all pollywogs.

13 December through 16 December held numerous emergency and casualty drills while good weather continued. Evening school classes in Algebra, Psychology, English, Auto Mechanics and Spanish were organized. The hobby craft program was also set in motion with all hands, taking an active interest in leather working and model making. Training of all personnel was accelerated with full advantage being taken of many excellent training films aboard.

17 December fueled the USS PINE ISLAND and the USS BROWNSON in that order and exchanged movies and "traded" various needed items. We acted as middleman by obtaining stores and provisions from the PINE ISLAND via a provision whip and later transferring the same to the BROWNSON via the same method while fueling her. Sent one enlisted man to the PINE ISLAND for dental treatment while the PINE ISLAND was alongside fueling. Transfer to and from the PINE ISLAND accomplished by means of a breeches buoy. Completed fueling at sea operation at 1415. Elwood Method of fueling used quite successfully despite inexperienced fueling crews on all ships. Resumed assigned station and re-set course for Antarctic rendezvous.

21 December joined the USS MT. OLYMPUS and the USS SENNET to fuel them. Successfully fueled the MT. OLYMPUS in moderately heavy seas. Fueled the SENNET after considerable difficulty with jury rig for hauling in and securing hose on board the SENNET. Considerable amount of the delay was attributed to the rough seas that were growing worse rather than better. From mistakes that were made on board both the SENNET and this vessel during the operation, a new plan was devised for any fueling of the SENNET in the future. This plan involved utilizing the submarine's midships mooring cleats as fair leads, rather than their small and obviously too weak pipe davit. Completed fueling operation at 1745 and resumed south-southwesterly course.

22 December through 24 December took advantage of generally good weather to continue general exterior maintenance and training program. During past three weeks a detail of eight men had been lagging all steam and fresh water piping on weather deck.

25 December all hands celebrated a merry but not white Christmas. Although in latitude 60° South, weather still mild with air and sea water temperatures averaging 40°.

26 December rendezvoused with the USS MT. OLYMPUS and USS SENNET and formed column formation at 1110. Encountered our first taste of Antarctic weather as heavy broken fogs set in, reducing visibility to as low as 200 yards. Radar was relied upon to keep proper stations. All hands thrilled at sight of iceberg, first material indication that we were approaching the Antarctic Circle.

CONFIDENTIAL

27 December at 0450, the U.S.C.G. NORTHWIND joined column formation. Encountered first touch of sub-freezing weather with fog and generally low visibility continuing throughout the day.

28 December, due to continued fog with resulting poor visibility, interval between ships in formation was increased to 1000 yards, on suggestion of this vessel's Commanding Officer. This somewhat relieved the tension of watch standers on the bridge, who for the past three days had been trying to keep station astern of the NORTHWIND, an apparently difficult vessel to control in anything but a calm sea. Sighted numerous icebergs, necessitating maneuvering formation to avoid them. At 1140 amidst a virtual sea of icebergs, formation wormed its way across the Antarctic Circle. Visibility never better than 6000 yards. Air and sea temperature hovered just above freezing.

29 December continued picking way through icebergs and even more numerous "growlers". Fog patches continued at times to cut down visibility. At 1000 sighted large ice field to port and maneuvered to avoid same. At 1300 commenced fueling the U.S.C.G. NORTHWIND. Successfully completed fueling at 1700. At 1745 the U.S.S. SENNET came alongside to fuel. Completed fueling SENNET at 2150. The new fueling rig planned and adopted after the first refueling was highly satisfactory. Supplied the SENNET with ice cream and freshly baked bread. At 2200 resumed station in column formation.

30 December with visibility varying from 0 to 10 miles, Scott Island and Haggett's Pillar were sighted at 1043. Our formation rendezvoused with the USS YANCEY (AKA93) and the USS MERRICK (AKA97). Our ship broke formation at 1430 and commenced fueling the YANCEY, followed by the MERRICK. Completed fueling operation at 1830 after making many course changes including a 180° turn with refueling vessels alongside to clear numerous icebergs. Movies and New Year's greetings were exchanged. With a "Well done" from the Task Force Commander, took departure from Central Task Group and proceeded to join Eastern Task Group in the vicinity of Peter I Island.

31 December, with air temperatures remaining below freezing most of the day, visibility increased to the maximum. Continued steaming enroute to Peter I Island, and made preparations for ringing in the New Year.

1 January 1947 celebrated New Year's Day amidst heavy seas and strong southeast winds of 30 to 35 knots intensity that continued throughout the day. Air temperatures hovered around freezing. Visibility continued excellent. Dr. Gilmore, the naturalist accompanying us, prepared to take a whale census while we passed through the internationally observed whale sanctuary to the eastward.

Annex I (p)   - 5 -

2 January winds diminished slightly, averaging approximately 25 knots, and diminishing to 8 knots by midnight. Visibility continued excellent until evening, when fog set in, reducing visibility to 500 yards.

3 January, visibility continued poor due to intermittent heavy fog patches. At 2000 encountered the northern limit of the ice pack. Ship was maneuvered so as to skirt well clear of pack ice. This was difficult inasmuch as the SU radar was operating sporadically and could not be depended on to give any length of accurate operation.

4 January, visibility continued very poor but no ice encountered for the first time since taking departure from Scott Island. Our Medical Officer reported that skin infections, respiratory infections and common colds and ailments had dropped off noticeably upon arrival in Antarctic waters. However, appetites were inversely proportionate, necessitating an increased ration for all hands. The sales and consumption of candy bars from the ship's store more than doubled when cold weather arrived.

5 January, we were forced to skirt an extensive ice pack. Many whales were sighted since leaving Scott Island and were logged with an accompanying description by Dr. Gilmore.

6 January we were forced to make passage through several miles of heavy broken ice to reach rendezvous with the destroyer BROWNSON. We moored BROWNSON alongside and fueled her in calm seas. However, long heavy swells made it necessary to tend all available fenders between both ships continuously. At completion of fueling got ship underway and continued toward rendezvous with the USS PINE ISLAND.

7 January, rendezvoused with PINE ISLAND in early morning and hove to close aboard. Commanding Officer attended ComTaskGroup conference on the PINE ISLAND.

8 January spent the day lying to in company with the PINE ISLAND at edge of ice pack in the Bellingshausen Sea. Weather excellent and sea smooth; man overboard drills were held.

9 January got underway and moored alongside PINE ISLAND to fuel her. At completion of fueling stood clear and resumed station lying to close aboard PINE ISLAND.

10 January got underway to take station about 150 miles to the northwest of the PINE ISLAND and act as weather station and emergency sea drome for the PINE ISLAND's efforts to search for and rescue downed PBM crew. Encountered considerable ice enroute and arrived on

station early evening. Hove to about 5 miles south of ice pack.

11 January through 16 January was spent lying to on station just clear of ice pack to our south. Often we were forced to get underway to remain clear of heavy ice pack. Received news of rescue of Mariner PBM #1 crew on the morning of the 12th. All hands anxiously followed the running account of the rescue through the radio messages intercepted from both the rescue plane and the PINE ISLAND. Very heavy NNE winds sprung up on Tuesday, the 14th, and continued through the next day, finally dying down on the 16th when the wind shifted to the Southwest. The monotony of lying to was broken up by several "excursions" with #1 motor launch to the ice pack. A giant iceberg was "boarded", specimens of many species of birds were obtained and one seal was killed and brought back to the ship. Many pictures were taken and to all the men able to go on the trip this was a welcome break in the monotony of shipboard life.

17 January, late in the evening, got underway to shift position 100 miles to the westward and continued duty as weather station and emergency sea drome.

18 January, after spending the night skirting a scattered icepack in a light fog, we arrived on station and resumed duties lying to.

19 January got underway and prepared to fuel the USS BROWNSON. Fueled the BROWNSON, who rendezvoused with us, early in the morning. Commenced fueling operation at 1000 and completed at noon. Our last mail for home was transferred to the BROWNSON for further transfer to the USS PHILIPPINE SEA, the first available transportation to the U. S. After the BROWNSON's departure we resumed duty lying to on station.

20 January through 22 January, continued lying to but were often forced to maneuver to stay clear of the ice pack. After expecting to find close to 0° F. temperature in the Antarctic, all hands are still surprised at continued mild weather. The heavy weather clothing that was issued has, to date, proved more than adequate.

23 January, got underway to take newly assigned position relative to the USS PINE ISLAND.

24 January - Arrived on station and hove to off ice pack to the south. Resumed duties as weather station and emergency sea drome.

25 January, continued lying to clear of ice pack to our south.

26 January, got underway in late afternoon to rendezvous with USS PINE ISLAND. Seas smooth but intermittent fog banks restricted visibility.

CONFIDENTIAL

27 January, rendezvoused with USS PINE ISLAND at 0500 and prepared to fuel her. At 1000 commenced fueling PINE ISLAND. After completion of fueling operation at 1300 we took station astern of PINE ISLAND and proceeded in open order to the eastward. Constant maneuvering was necessary both to keep station on PINE IS-LAND and to avoid ice. Visibility that was alternately bad and then worse added to the ever present danger of ice. Our radar was invaluable in locating icebergs both large and small, and in keeping station on the guide ship ahead.

28 January, continued bad weather made ice evasion increasingly difficult. In late evening we were detached from company with the PINE ISLAND in order to proceed to new position and resume duties as weather station and emergency sea drome.

29 January, weather cleared as we continued underway to new weather station position.

30 January, encountered heavy ice pack and hove to on station.

31 January, we were forced to get underway several times so as to stand clear of shifting pack and small bergs as wind shifted and increased in strength.

1 February through 2 February, continued lying to in the Bellingshausen Sea. Wind increased in strength throughout the day, reaching a high of 40 knots from the east at midnight of the 2nd. Kept ship underway at 1/3 speed to maintain safe position relative to wind and sea. It also became necessary to shift ballast in order to remove excess rolling moments.

3 February, high winds from 30 to 40 knots in intensity continued throughout the day. Frequent maneuvering was necessary to avoid drifting ice.

4 February, continued underway to new station. Wind decreased in strength as the ship continued to the south. We were forced to maneuver continuously in order to avoid irregular ice packs.

5 February, winds decreased to from 10 to 16 knots. Continued moving to avoid scattered ice enroute to new station.

6 February, the wind moderated and heavy snow set in limiting visibility to several thousand yards. Hove to in mid-afternoon just clear of ice pack in the eastern Bellingshausen Sea.

7 February, got underway again and made preparations for refueling the USS BROWNSON on her return from her rendezvous with the

CONFIDENTIAL

USS PHILIPPINE SEA. Spent entire morning refueling the BROWNSON
alongside. Dr. D. F. Barnes, representative of Woodshole Institute,
was hove on board via breeches buoy to carry out hydrographic research during remainder of HIGHJUMP Operation. We also transferred
approximately 30 tons of supplies from the BROWNSON along with 38
bags of mail from home. The latter was afforded an eager welcome
by all hands. At about noon after completion of the fueling operation,
the BROWNSON set course for rendezvous with the USS PINE ISLAND and
we continued underway to regain and maintain station.

8 February we continued lying to in calm seas with excellent
visibility.

9 February through 11 February; got underway in the evening
of the 9th to proceed to newly assigned position. Intermittent
snow and fog reduced visibility on the 10th and continued through
the 11th. Considerable maneuvering was necessary to avoid occasional
icebergs.

12 February through 13 February, continued steaming singly
to our new position. We were forced to steam at reduced speed because of ice conditions and poor visibility.

14 February, with improved visibility we continued steaming
south toward Charcot Island. At 2000 hove to 40 miles north of
Charcot Island, amid scattered ice.

15 February, received orders in the early morning and got
underway to proceed to rendezvous with PINE ISLAND and BROWNSON on
their way north around the Palmer Peninsula to the Weddell Sea. In
the middle of the morning watch passed Mount Gaudrey Adelaide Island,
visible 53 miles to starboard. Met up with the PINE ISLAND and
BROWNSON in mid-afternoon and took station in line formation.

16 February through 18 February, continued steaming in company
with the PINE ISLAND and BROWNSON in line formation. On the 17th,
formation was changed to column because of poor visibility.

19 February, in the early afternoon, took departure from the
PINE ISLAND and the BROWNSON and proceeded independently.

20 February, rendezvoused with the BROWNSON in the early
morning and refueled her between 0900 and noon. After completion
of fueling we continued on course and the BROWNSON returned to her
station. We stopped in the afternoon to take oceanographic soundings.

21 February, rendezvoused with the PINE ISLAND in the early

morning and prepared to refuel her at 1000. Completed refueling operation at 1300 and took station on the PINE ISLAND's port quarter. We continued in company with the PINE ISLAND to the southeast of the Weddell Sea.

22 February, in the early morning, we proceeded on orders to take station 50 miles north of the PINE ISLAND. After arriving on new station continued on course paralleling the PINE ISLAND's.

23 February, we continued on a southerly course to keep relative station on the PINE ISLAND. Much maneuvering was necessary to avoid small scattered icebergs.

24 February, proceeded to take new station 150 miles to the northeast of the PINE ISLAND and act as weather station and emergency sea drome while PINE ISLAND awaited satisfactory flying conditions.

25 February through 26 February, spent alternately lying to and steaming underway to keep on station 150 miles northeast of PINE ISLAND.

27 February, spent morning lying to. In the afternoon we got underway in an easterly direction to maintain position on the PINE ISLAND.

28 February, steaming all day on easterly and then southerly courses to maintain position on PINE ISLAND. We stopped in the late evening for oceanographic soundings and then held "swing ship" to compensate compasses.

1 March completed compensating compasses and headed west. Acting as a weather station.

2 March, alternately lying to and steaming in position 150 miles northeast of PINE ISLAND and acting as weather station and emergency sea drome.

3 March, at 0020 commenced joining up with the PINE ISLAND and BROWNSON to take departure from Antarctic on way to Rio de Janeiro. Stopped in the evening for oceanographic soundings.

III. ENROUTE RIO DE JANEIRO

4 March, steaming in line formation with PINE ISLAND abeam to port 50 miles and BROWNSON abeam to port 100 miles on northeasterly course. Stopped in afternoon for oceanographic readings and while lying to we had a minor engine room breakdown when the fuel oil service pump cut out.

5 March, steaming in line formation through area of numerous icebergs necessitating a great deal of maneuvering. Held "swing ship" in afternoon to calibrate magnetometer.

6 March, the USS BROWNSON left her station to join up with us for fueling and we sighted her at midnight. She took up position on our port quarter at a distance of 1500 yards.

7 March, numerous icebergs continue necessitating various course changes in northeasterly direction. Commenced fueling BROWNSON in morning and completed transfer by noon at which time the BROWNSON departed to join PINE ISLAND.

8 March through 13 March, steaming on northeasterly course 50 miles on starboard beam of PINE ISLAND. During this period we cleared all ice regions and concentrated on cleaning and painting the ship in preparation for our arrival in Rio de Janeiro. We stopped daily for oceanographic soundings.

14 March, joined up with the PINE ISLAND and BROWNSON. We steamed in course formation with the PINE ISLAND leading, CANISTEO second and BROWNSON astern of us.

15 March through 17 March, spent these three days steaming in column at night and lying to during the day to complete cleaning and painting in preparation for entering Rio de Janeiro harbor on 18 March. We sighted land in the evening of the 17th, 50 miles distant.

18 March, got underway on the mid-watch and entered the harbor in the morning while in column astern the PINE ISLAND with the BROWNSON astern of us. We were anchored and had the "in port" watch set by noon.

19 March through 23 March, anchored in harbor of Rio de Janeiro, Brazil in company with TG 68.3 for purposes of liberty and recreation. Daily in port routine for foreign port carried out. While here we received orders to proceed to Ascension Island upon being detached from TG 68.3.

24 March, we got underway in the morning in column in order of PINE ISLAND, CANISTEO and BROWNSON and proceeded northeast along coast of Brazil the rest of the day.

IV. ENROUTE ASCENSION ISLAND

25 March, made preparations for fueling early in the morning and at 0818 the PINE ISLAND was alongside to port for fuel. We completed fueling her shortly after noon and the BROWNSON came alongside

immediately after. We completed fueling the BROWNSON at 1406 and were immediately detached from TG 68.3 whereupon we departed on a course for Ascension Island.

ANNEX ONE -(q)

NARRATIVE

U.S.S. BROWNSON (DD 868)

Table of Contents

ANNEX ONE –(q)

NARRATIVE

U.S.S. BROWNSON (DD 868)

Table of Illustrations

PHASE I - PREPARATORY PERIOD
(28 September 1946 to 2 December 1946)

The U.S.S. BROWNSON was immobilized at Bath, Maine, due to the lack of personnel, when information was received on 28 September, 1946, from ComDesLant to the effect that we had been designated to participate in the HIGHJUMP project, and were to be in such material condition as to permit extended operations away from repair facilities by the tentative departure date of 1 December 1946. A few essential repairs were accomplished with the aid of the Bath Iron Works, but only preliminary planning could be carried out until the ship was mobilized on 31 October, when intensive preparations were initiated which continued with unabated vigor until the time of our departure from the U. S.

On 31 October we got underway from Bath for Portland, Maine, where we carried out two half-days of independent ship exercises in Casco Bay. After mooring alongside the tender SHENANDOAH on 2 November, change of command was effected. The tender availability was utilized primarily to accomplish urgent repairs on all electronics equipment and secondarily to accomplish necessary hull or machinery repairs and to commence work on winterized lookout stations. The excellent and unlimited cooperation of SHENANDOAH personnel enabled us to bring all electronic equipment up to operating standards.

Taking departure from CASCO BAY on 7 November for New London, Connecticut, we reported to ComSubLant on 8 November for operation with the Submarine Training Group and carried out two days of exercises with submarines before departing for Norfolk, Virginia on 13 November. We arrived NOB, Norfolk on 14 November. The following day we reported to CTF 68 by dispatch and shifted to a berth at Norfolk Naval Shipyard, Portsmouth, Virginia where certain special installations were to be made for the operation.

The period from 15 November to 1 December was designated as a preparatory period for Operation HIGHJUMP. It is significant to note that in this period of 18 days there were eight holidays for the civilian-manned shore establishment, leaving only 10 effective working days. Consequently, long hours of work on part of officers and crew were necessary which involved some confusion and loss of effort. Fortunately, however, the cooperation of Navy Yard personnel in making installations and repairs was excellent. Throughout this period we also drew stores from NSD, Norfolk - an operation which continued up to the very moment of our departure.

The personnel situation at this time was extremely unstable and our complement quite unbalanced. Although at the time excessively over allowance in certain rates, acute shortages existed in others. Lack of suitable opportunity to carry out required medical examinations further hampered crystalization of an organized crew by keeping us in doubt as to who would be making the trip. Large numbers of key personnel had been released due to impending discharges and even up until the last week personnel were still arriving on board for several days stay who were disqualified for the operation due to impending discharges. This fact alone added greatly to the burden of making preparations.

Preparations were further handicapped by inadequate or delayed dissemination of some information as to plans, projects, and requirements for the operation. Too limited distribution of information to activities concerned also hampered preparations.

On Friday, 29 November, we fueled from a barge at the dock in the shipyard. Finally, at 1143 Monday, 2 December, 1946, we got underway from our berth at the Norfolk Naval Shipyard and stood down the Elizabeth River enroute to rendezvous with other units of the task force outside the Virginia Capes; anchoring just long enough off Lamberts Point to receive a late delivery of 11 Mk 14 depth charges from an ammunition barge. Although it had often appeared that we might not be completely ready to participate in Operation HIGHJUMP, we passed through the Capes with the knowledge that we were adequately prepared and feeling that although minor deficiencies might come to light which would embarrass us, they would not prevent us from the successful accomplishment of our mission.

PHASE II - PASSAGE TO PANAMA
(2 December, 1946 to 10 December, 1946)

At 1540 Monday, 2 December, 1946, we rendezvoused with other ships of the task force sailing from NORFOLK, and formed column in the following order: MOUNT OLYMPUS (AGC 8), PINE ISLAND (AV 12), BROWNSON (DD 868), and NORTHWIND (WAG 282). A storm was reported off Cape Hatteras and the ship was rolling considerably when at 1810 we experienced a steering engine casualty. A man on the steering engine room watch had knocked against a bus tie on the steering panel, thereby stopping the steering motor. Electricians corrected the difficulty and steering control was regained immediately. At 1845, loss of make-up feed suction due to an error in sounding by messenger made it advisable to reduce speed and shift to cold suction. The deficiency was soon corrected, however, and machinery was not endangered. Both casualties were attributed to inexperienced personnel.

On Wednesday, 4 December, at 0907 the duty boatswain's mate discovered smoke coming out of the hatch leading to the 'midships storeroom, Compt. B-201-A. Fire Quarters was sounded and a preliminary investigation revealed the compartment filled with smoke and intense heat, making it necessary to use salt water to keep bulkheads adjacent to fuel tanks cool. Thick smoke prevented the fire party, equipped with RBA units, from determining the exact location of the fire until the compartment had been cooled and smoke partially withdrawn. The fire was then isolated to S.D. stores room 2-110-B-1. Sludge and foreign matter made it impracticable to use submersible pumps for the removal of excess water so an educator connected to the fire main was rigged which functioned satisfactorily except for slight difficulty encountered in keeping the suction clear. After the fire was extinguished an attempt was made to salvage as much material as possible. Material was washed with fresh water, dried thoroughly, and, where necessary, coated with preservative. The dry provisions were water soaked and unusable except those contained in vacuum packed cans. Subsequent examination revealed that the hydraulic line of the depth charge release mechanism had ruptured, contributing to the intense heat which made the fire difficult to extinguish. Damage to ships structure was negligible except for burned insulation on overhead cables.

The NORTHWIND, having had trouble keeping up with the group, left formation at 2104, Wednesday, 4 December. At 2207 we passed San Salvador Island light abeam to port, distance 10 miles. Shortly after 0500, Thursday, 5 December, we steamed through Crooked Island Passage. At this point the PINE ISLAND left formation to proceed independently. During the morning we held drills with the air-sea rescue equipment and about 1100 we sighted Cuba as we started through the Windward Passage. The next evening, Friday, 6 December, at 2133 the MOUNT OLYMPUS was forced to drop behind and head into the sea to perform an emergency appendectomy. Consequently, we received orders to proceed independently.

We had used the period of passage to PANAMA to good advantage by completing organization bills, assigning personnel to battle and emergency bill stations, conducting preliminary training and shifting men between divisions as necessary to round out the ship's organization. This turned out to be quite a job since 75% of the officers and crew were relatively new aboard the BROWNSON.

At 0700, Saturday, 7 December, we sighted the Isthmus and at 1017 stopped in the vicinity of the PINE ISLAND just inside the breakwater to pick up our pilot and LT. BAILEY, Representative of Naval Research Laboratory, assigned to CTG 68.3's staff. We entered the Gatun Locks at 1055, where, at 1220, we received on board 14 civilian members of the Federal Auditing Board for the Panama Canal Commission for whom arrangements had been made by the Marine Supt. of the Canal to make the transit with us. We cleared the Mira Flores Locks at 1636, completing our passage through the Canal. Shortly, thereafter, we moored to our berth at the Panama Railways Dock at Balboa, Canal Zone.

The following three days were a hectic period of last minute preparations until we got underway early Tuesday morning, 10 December, for passage to the operating area.

PHASE III – PASSAGE TO OPERATIONS AREA.
(10 December 1946 to 25 December 1946)

At 0855 Tuesday, 10 December 1946, we got underway from our berth at Balboa, Canal Zone, and stood out into the Gulf of Panama where we stopped for several hours to practice radar controlled seaplane landings with the Mariners from the PINE ISLAND. While the PINE ISLAND remained behind to hoist in and secure for sea, we rejoined the other units of the force, forming column on the MOUNT OLYMPUS, NORTHWIND #2, BROWNSON #3, SENNET #4 and heading south. About 0500 the following morning the PINE ISLAND moved into her station astern of the SENNET until 0800, when the ships fanned out to take station on individual parallel track routes to facilitate taking of hydrographic data. Distance between ships was 40-60 miles.

As our southerly course brought us deep into tropical waters, all hands were granted welcome permission to go over the side for a swim. For several days during our two hour stops for oceanographic soundings, with armed men and lifeguards on the torpedo deck and in the whaleboat to act as shark watch, we all enjoyed this privilege. Morale was also increased at this time by receipt of orders from CTF 68 to rendezvous with the PHILIPPINE SEA in the Ross Sea in late January. – This meant the receipt of mail!

On the 14th and 16th we test fired 20 MM and 40 MM mounts without casualty.

December 17th, we received 82,700 gallons of fuel oil and 8 tons provisions from the CANISTEO. Our relatively green crew came through with flying colors on this, the first fueling operation at sea. During this operation, Mr. Barnes, civilian oceanographer, was transferred to the CANISTEO by breeches buoy to give instructions on taking of oceanographic data. Later the same day, at 2045, the floor of the sea rose suddenly from 2000 fathoms to 265 fathoms in about 8 miles, depth of 265 was recorded for 3 miles, then the bottom dropped rapidly to normal depth in about 4 miles. The rise was assumed to be an uncharted high spot and unofficially named the "Brownson Plateau" - location 25-03 S, 97-41W.

At 1300 we came up on the starboard quarter of the PINE ISLAND to transfer a radar spare part. It soon became apparent that they were planning to send us some provisions so we rigged the span line to a pad-eye on mount #1. Halfway through the operation, the tension on the line began to pull the pad-eye loose and the span line had to be cast off. Not desiring to delay any longer, it was decided to conclude the operation at that point.

On 21 December we received orders to make a slight change in station to enclose the most probable area of Swain's Island. Ground swells had increased in magnitude giving us a steady roll of 20 to 30 degrees. Everything was lashed down securely as we approached the area in which the OpOrder warned we might "expect to encounter some of the roughest weather in the world". Constant presence of three or four albatrosses, however, calmed the fears of our superstitious shipmates. At 0710 we passed over an uncharted pinnacle at 600 fathoms, mean bottom at this position, 45-13S, 100-34.5W, was 2000 fathoms; base extended north-south for distance of 9.5 miles.

At 2145 on 23 December we passed the plotted position of Swain's Island in clear weather. No land was sighted or picked up by radar. Our fathometer track consistently showed uniform mean bottom; several cloud formations gave a strong impression of land masses.

The day before Christmas found us well into the Antarctic region. At 0800, as we approached the PINE ISLAND for fueling and provisioning, we sighted our first iceberg; from then on they became quite numerous. Transfer of 93,000 gallons fuel required 8 hours because of low delivery rate of PINE ISLAND's pumps (12,000 gal per hour). The CANISTEO with her rate of 1800 gal/minute had transferred approximately the same amount in less than one hour.

We had now arrived in the operating area after a successful passage profitably employed in training and further shaking down.

The Executive Officer and engineering officer had gone through the OpPlan, CTF 68 project manual, special letters from Bureaus to BROWNSON and special letters on operation HIGHJUMP to determine projects specifically assigned to BROWNSON plus those general projects which might be carried out. Upon determination of the applicable projects, a card index was set up in which projects were outlined and reference material noted. Project responsibility was then assigned to specific officers and individual conferences were held with officers concerned to discuss and stress type of report desired. We were now ready to begin our work.

PHASE IV - FIRST PERIOD OF OPERATIONS
(25 December 1946 to 19 January 1947)

Early Christmas morning we sighted pack ice and spent the remainder of the day maneuvering to avoid it. The large bergs.

appeared quite frequently now with bergy bits covering most of the
area outside the pack. By 0800 we had encountered several small floes
on a base course of 245°T. As the pack which we were paralleling on
our starboard hand slowly developed before us we were forced to alter
our course southward, watching all the time for an opening to slip
through to the west. We made one unsuccessful try before sighting a
lead at 0930 through which we managed to pass by stopping all engines
and coasting to avoid damaging the propellers. It was clear sailing
on the base course for a while but by 1015 we sighted pack ice dead
ahead, once more forcing us to bear southward. At 1130, finding ourselves working around to the southeast with fog closing in, we decided
to back track in an attempt to round the northern edge of the field.
By 1300 we had sighted an opening to the west which developed to be
clear for about fifty miles before closing in once more. It soon
became apparent that we had about reached the limit of our southward
progress and that we must be content to work back and forth slowly,
waiting for the pack to break up and trying at the same time not to
lose any ground.

The fog cut our visibility down to less than 2000 yards but the
ice blink gave us an additional 500 yards or so which helped considerably. We maintained a rough chart of the ice pack on the DRT in the
pilot house which gave a general picture of our progress and was helpful to the oncoming watch in that it gave them a picture of the situation. Injection temperature was about 31° which resulted in about a
quarter-inch of ice on the intake.

For three days we moved back and forth on numerous courses
and speeds between latitudes 66-45S and 66-54S and longitudes 107-
45W and 111-38.7W trying to continue southward to our assigned
station - at 70°S on the 110°W meridian. During this period we
crossed the antarctic circle five times. At 0215 on the morning of
the 26th our DRA went out of commission and remained so, with the
exception of a two hour period 1000 until 1200. Since the sun never
set it was impossible to fix our position by star sights and a constant overcast made it extremely difficult to take any sun sights.
Consequently, for 18 hours we had little knowledge of our exact
position. Shortly after 0200 on the 28th we started south once more
and about 1100 we sighted our first seal on an ice floe close aboard
to port.

We pushed on southward until 2000 Saturday, 29 December, when
we ran into close pack, heavy fog, and snow, forcing us to reverse
our course and head back to clear water. Acting as an emergency aero-
drome and weather station for the PINE ISLAND, then about 150 miles
to the east of us, it was necessary for us to remain in an area
sufficiently clear of growlers for a PBM to land. Sunday the overcast lifted completely for the first time since before Christmas;

the unlimited ceiling and visibility contributed greatly to a rise in
the spirit among all hands. To the Navigator it meant a chance to
definitely fix our position with both the sun and the moon visible
for sights; to the Gunnery Officer it presented an opportunity to
run a complete horizon check with the main battery.

When we received word from the PINE ISLAND Monday, 30 December,
that flight operations had commenced, we started circling a large
clear area (9 miles by 6 miles) bounded by four large icebergs. By
approaching within 500 yards of several we were able to inspect them
closely; two were particularly worthy of mention, one for its construction, the other for its size. The first had a large archway formed at
one end with two large beautifully formed peaks 125 feet high alongside. In the center was a small pool of deep blue water, the color
undoubtedly resulting from a reflection of the blue glacial ice of
which the berg was composed. The second, without doubt the largest
seen to date, was quite rectangular in shape which made it easy to
compute its displacement. By measuring its dimensions with the help
of a stadimeter, pelorus, and radar we found it to be 2300' X 900' X
100' and conservatively estimated its displacement to be upward of
20 million tons - in the vernacular of our crew - "many ice cubes".

Our pleasant state of affairs came to an abrupt end, however,
upon receipt of word from the PINE ISLAND that PBM George 1 on flight
#3 piloted by LT JG LE BLANC with Capt. CALDWELL, skipper of the PINE
ISLAND, aboard was overdue and weather about the PINE ISLAND was
rapidly closing in. George 1 had taken off at 0428 Thursday morning
with fuel for twenty-one hours on a ten hour flight to photograph and
explore the Demas Mountains and coastline of Cape Dart to the south
of the PINE ISLAND. Reporting every half-hour, his last report had
been received at 0606 at which time he was 10 miles from land with
sufficient clear water below for a landing. Since that time nothing
had been heard except unidentified fragments of voice transmission on
channel Dog or Charlie at 1525. Meanwhile, a heavy fog had settled
over the PINE ISLAND making rescue flights impossible not only because
of reduced visibility, but also because the fog was heavily laden with
ice crystals which would quickly form ice on the leading edge of the
wing of any plane brave enough to attempt to fly through it and force
it to land. We radioed CTG 68.3 suggesting that a platform be
constructed on our fantail to accomodate the helicopter, the help of
which would, we believe, enable us to push through the ice pack to
the Eights Peninsula.

On 6 January we rendezvoused with the CANISTEO for fueling.
With an unusually calm sea, it was decided to moor along side the
CANISTEO to expedite transfer of fuel and materials. The operation
was highly successful. A slight break in the weather allowed one
plane to get off from the PINE ISLAND which covered an area eleven
thousand one hundred square miles centered approximately at last
plotted position of missing plane with negative results. Zero ceiling
over mountain tops prevented inland search.

CONFIDENTIAL

The following afternoon we rendezvoused with the PINE ISLAND and CANISTEO, bringing all units of TG 68.3 together for first time since the CANISTEO departed with the Central Group on 17 December for the Ross Sea entrance. CTG 68.3 requested the commanding officer to come on board PINE ISLAND at which time we received orders to get under way at 2000 and push southward through a lead plotted by air reconnaissance to take up station on line of bearing from PINE ISLAND to Cape Dart where we were to act as weather and advanced communications station for the search planes. Just before getting under way, Doctor R. M. GILMORE of the Department of Interior came on board from the CANISTEO to make the trip down into the pack with us for wild life research.

We got under way at 2000 and headed due south into the pack until the evening of the 9th when we reached the limit of our southern penetration at 68-13S and headed west, speed about 1½ knots because of ice coverage which varied from 50% to 80%. The next morning we sighted our first penguin, an Emperor about 4 feet high. He not only appeared to be unconcerned with our presence but also put on quite a show for us - waddling around on his feet, skimming about on his belly, rolling and tumbling on the snow, and making a general fool of himself, much to the delight and amusement of all hands. That afternoon we test-fired the 5" mounts, #2 and #3, firing four rounds per barrel at a large iceberg, range 1700 yards. The projectiles seemed to make very little visible impression on the ice.

On 11 January it was 12 days since we had last heard from George 1. Several flights had started out but only one reached the search area, and even he was forced to turn back by bad weather after a short search. The weather that morning was greatly improved and George 2 took off at 0649. At 1116 we intercepted the message "Mariner George 1 burnt wreckage and live men at 71-03S, 98-47W". George 2 reported men were eight miles from water suitable for PBM landing. Meanwhile, George 3 was dispatched, arriving on the scene just as George 2 was forced to turn back for fuel. We sighted George 3 14 miles to the west of us at 1430 from our position 100 miles in the pack ice between the PINE ISLAND and Cape Dart. We established communications on the TDQ, wished them "God-speed", and retained contact until just before they arrived over the scene.

While awaiting further developments on the rescue operation we sighted a seal on an ice flow and shot it with a Springfield '03 rifle. We brought it on board for Dr. Gilmore to inspect. It was a Ross Seal which weighed 227 pounds and measured 5' 9" in length. Doctor Gilmore saved the skin, skull and flippers to take back with him and about 40 pounds of seal meat which we later ate - very tasty.

George 3 landed at 1930 and sent two men ashore in a rubber
life raft to aid the survivors who were walking the eight miles to
the shore line. While waiting to take the men on board, George 3
found it necessary to taxi around quite frequently to prevent the
formation of ice in the landing area. Around 0100 a heavy fog closed
in temporarily obscuring the activities ashore. We spent many anxious
moments until the word finally came through that the fog had lifted,
survivors loaded aboard, (0656) and George 3 was off the water (0824)
on her way back. At 0940 George 3 passed within sight of us, landing
at the PINE ISLAND at 1043 — rescue operations completed 24 hours
after survivors were first sighted. It was with some disappointment
that we learned that the survivors had not been able to receive any
of the morale boosting messages sent out by CTG 68.3.

On 12 January we discovered a bulge along a seam 6' below the
water line at frame #52 in 5" magazine A-409-M where our beam approaches its maximum width. The hull plate was forced in one and one-half
inches, horizontal axis 2', vertical axis 1½'. Additional damage 3'
forward of minor consequence (along same horizontal line). Rivets
were not damaged, no leaks were apparent, and a thorough examination
revealed no other areas affected. Vertical frame members were bent
but no shoring was deemed necessary at that time. Frequent inspections
were planned to insure against leakage or rivet failure.

The next evening we received a storm warning and immediately
started to retire to the north until morning when we received an "all
clear" and returned to a southwesterly course. We test-fired 5" mount
#1, 40 MM, and 20 MM during the day. That evening (14 January), we
received orders to proceed northward clear of the ice to facilitate
repairs to a progressive leak under the bonnet of the main steam
guarding valve in our forward engine room. As we headed north, the
wind, which had been steady at 20 knots for 36 hours, began to freshen,
giving us considerable trouble in maneuvering to avoid ice floes before
we finally cleared the pack shortly after 2400. Work was immediately
commenced on the guarding valve, being completed 44 hours later. When
repairs were nearly completed, we received orders to rendezvous with
PINE ISLAND for provisioning. Course was set for rendezvous which
we reached about 1600, 17 January.

Although we had planned to provision from the PINE ISLAND
the evening of the 17th, fog conditions made it necessary to postpone
the operation until the following morning. Consequently, at 0800 on
the 18th, with fog still present we commenced provisioning by boat.
Upon completion of provisioning just before noon, we brought five
survivors of the wrecked PBM (Capt. Caldwell remained on the PINE
ISLAND) aboard for transfer to the PHILIPPINE SEA. At 1158 we took
departure from the PINE ISLAND for the CANISTEO from whom we fueled
at 1000 the following day. During the operation, Dr. Gilmore returned
to the CANISTEO via breeches-buoy. By 1210 we had completed fueling
and were on our way to Ross Sea.

During the passage to the operation area and the first period
of operations we had given basic instruction on - all armament, including test firing; tests to be run; general quarters stations; and
emergency bills. We were now ready to commence the advanced phase of
our operational training program - gunnery practices, full power runs,
general perfection of emergency drills and battle practices. In addition we had also established an ESO program with classes for the
completion of high school educations, mathematics, physics, psychology
and life, and languages.

PHASE V - PHILIPPINE SEA INTERLUDE
(19 January 1947 to 7 February 1947)

At 1210 on the 19th of January we cast off all lines from the
CANISTEO and set course for the rendezvous at 67S 175W in accordance
with CTG 68.3 181809Z directing BROWNSON to rendezvous with PHILIPPINE
SEA to transfer survivors and receive mail and stores for the Group.
Under orders to scout the ice pack enroute, we skirted the pack until
0600 the following morning when, having reached the southern limit of
open water at 68-02S 115-35W, we set a great circle course for the
rendezvous point. We continued to make ice and weather reports to
CTF 68 and CTG 68.3 throughout the remainder of the five day trip,
which was uneventful except for frequent periods of rough weather
during which we made every effort to make the ship ride as easily as
possible in view of the serious condition of Lt.(jg) LeBlanc.

On 24 January at 1500, we sighted the SENNET in column astern
of the NORTHWIND. Reaching the rendezvous at 1706, we reported to
CTG 68.4 for duty and thereupon received orders to scout southward
to determine the northern limits of the ice pack between 175W and
165W in preparation for launching planes. At this time PHILIPPINE
SEA was about eleven hours north of the rendezvous, beset by fog.
We skirted the pack to 68-53S where we encountered brash and drift
ice heavy enough to impede carrier operations. Consequently, having
requested and received permission to return to rendezvous for transfer
of Lt. (jg) LeBlanc to the PHILIPPINE SEA, at 1130 on the 25th we
circled approximately 50 miles to the east to determine the eastern
limit of our lead and then headed north.

Saturday evening, 25 January, we sighted the PHILIPPINE SEA
at 2315, and immediately made preparations for the transfer of
personnel and stores. Taking station on the port quarter of the
PHILIPPINE SEA at 2355, distance 75 feet, we transferred stores
first to test our rig. Each time we moved into a particularly favorable position we sent a man over; first the able bodied survivors
in a breeches buoy, then Lt. (jg) Kearns with a broken arm in a
special steel chair, and finally Lt. (jg) LeBlanc in a stretcher.

Shortly thereafter the wind freshened and snow increased with a result-ant loss of visibility making it necessary to secure the exercise at 0230, 26 January. Several bags of mail had been transferred, however, so the majority of the officers and crew stood anxiously by while it was sorted, hoping for at least a few letters before turning in for a well earned rest. During the remainder of Sunday, 26 January, the Task Group steared on various courses in the area awaiting improved weather to complete the transfer of materials and flight operations.

At 0815 Monday, 27 January, we came alongside the CACAPON for about 2 hours to take on 77,634 gallons of diesel oil. That afternoon at 1255 we came alongside the PHILIPPINE SEA once again to resume the transfer of personnel and stores, which had been discontinued early Sunday morning. Knowing that we had approximately 20 tons (it later turned out to be about 30 tons) to transfer, we rigged two lines for-ward; one to the pad-eye on 5" mount #2, one to a set of pad-eyes on the bridge, and a third line amidships. Two of the rigs were standard but the one to 5" mount #2 was novel in that each end of the span line, which passed through a large block secured to a pad-eye on our mount, was tended by a steam winch. A large hook was then secured to the span line instead of to a free running trolley as is the usual practice. Hence as one winch took in on the span line, the other winch payed out, thus moving the hook from one ship to the other. Each time the ships rolled the line became taut and during the first attempt to transfer approximately a 1.5 ton load in a cargo net it pulled our bow danger-ously close before the pad-eye failed, dropping the entire load into the 50' of swirling water between the two ships. The carrier personnel managed by quick action to haul the net aboard and salvage the cargo. Nevertheless, we soon had the station in operation again by securing a 3/8" cable to a deck stanchion, passing the cable up over the top of the mount, and then attaching the span line to the cable with a quick releasing pelican hook. All three lines led to the forward hangar deck from which we received a steady flow of cargo for 2½ hours. A fairly heavy sea time and again doused the "O" Division men amidships with icy salt water.

Upon completion of transfer of cargo, 28 men were transferred — CANISTEO 1, PINE ISLAND 8, BROWNSON 19. While this was being accomplish-ed the C.O. was called to the inter-ship phone and talked for several minutes to Admiral Byrd. The gist of the Admiral's remarks was some-what as follows - "I have been here in the background watching with considerable interest the progress of operations and have been pleased to follow the activities of the BROWNSON. You are doing a fine job - keep it up. Please inform your officers and men of my commendation for the good job they are doing." The C.O. wished Admiral Byrd and his companions good luck in the forthcoming flight operations to Little America. At the conclusion of the day's operations the C.O. passed the Admiral's remarks to all hands over the P. A. system.

Although the actual transfer was completed at 1545, there still remained a large job to be done. Immediately after supper several large working parties turned-to to sort and re-stow all the cargo. We put a portion of the stores below, then lashed the remainder down topside. This proved to be unsatisfactory, however, so the next morning more working parties struck every possible crate below, filling every available spot.

For the next two days we steamed around in formation waiting for the weather to clear. During the interlude we made one more ice recco trip, this time reaching 69-03S where we encountered the NORTHWIND from whom we received two bags of mail which we delivered to the PHILIPPINE SEA late Tuesday evening. At 1925 on 29 January we commenced preparations for 30 knots; by 2200 we were on station 2000 yards astern of the PHILIPPINE SEA making 32 knots. At 2214 the first plane took-off in a cloud of smoke caused by the JATO units. The second plane took-off 17 minutes later. As these two circled us before heading southward, we gradually slowed down with orders to stand-by to launch the other four planes upon the safe arrival of the first two at Little America. The last four were finally launched at about 15 minute intervals commencing at 0633, 30 January 1947.

At 1252 on the 30th we took station 800 yards astern of the PHILIPPINE SEA and CACAPON to act as safety ship during their transfer of supplies and personnel. At 1406 the PHILIPPINE SEA informed the Task Group - "For your information we have received word that all planes have landed safely on Little America. Congratulations on your very able assistance" - to which we replied - "Thank you. Congratulations on the successful accomplishment of your mission. It was a pleasure to participate in this unique operation." At 1637 we received the following TBS transmission from CTG 68.4 - "Temporary duty completed. Carry out basic orders. Official orders will follow. Give Captain Caldwell our regards and best wishes for his recovery. Well done." Accordingly, we set course to rejoin TG 68.3.

Bad weather limited us to 8 knots for the first few hours after our departure from TG 68.4. About 2000 on Thursday, 30 January improving weather conditions permitted an increase of speed and resumption of ice pack scouting. On 2 February at 1058, upon receipt of CTG 021828Z, we discontinued ice scouting and stood to northeast to clear pack and continue eastward in area north of pack limits.

Except for occasional periods of poor weather the trip was uneventful until 0744, 7 February, when we sighted CANISTEO hull-down on the horizon. As we rejoined the Eastern Group, we made preparations for fueling and the transfer of supplies - it was good to see an old friend again.

PHASE VI - TASK GROUP FLAGSHIP
(7 February 1947 to 19 February 1947)

At 0838, Friday, 7 February, we started our approach on the CANISTEO. As we slowly moved alongside we gradually discerned familiar faces and at 0913 the first line went across to begin once again an operation which had by this time become almost second nature to us. In the arms of one of the CANISTEO's officers we spied with envy a small Adelie penguin. One hour after the commencement of fueling and provisioning at 0935, having considerable difficulty maintaining proper distance with a quartering sea and wind, we opened distance too far when the wind suddenly freshened, breaking the fuel hose and spraying oil over our starboard side. While passing over the fuel hose we transferred Mr. Barnes, civilian oceanographer, and one chief petty officer to the CANISTEO for duty. By 1134 the second hose was connected enabling us to complete the operation at 1235 having received on board 111,756 gallons of fuel oil.

Upon taking departure from the CANISTEO we steamed on a south-easterly course for 3 hours until, at 1600, we encountered the pack which forced us to change course to northeast, north, and finally north-west before we eventually rounded its northern tip at 2217.

At 0200, Saturday, 8 February, we headed southeast until just before noon when we stopped for about an hour at CTG's direction to act as weather station. Upon getting underway at 1215 we stood to the eastward until at 1400 we turned south on the final leg of our trip to rejoin the PINE ISLAND. During this period we received word that George 2 and 3 were airborne but prior to their departure on coastal mapping flights bad weather developed, forcing them to return. George 2, however, completed a short flight to Charcot Island - a flight which was to have greater significance for the BROWNSON at a later date.

Sunday, 9 February, we sighted the PINE ISLAND at 0128 and hove to at 69-59.3S 78-34W to await daylight to commence transfer of supplies. Lying to in the lee of the pack at the southern tip of a large lead, we were completely surrounded by 30 to 100 icebergs, some in the open water but the greater number embedded in the heavy pack ice which lay on three sides of us. It was interesting to watch the water on our lee side as it slowly began to freeze. Numerous spots of calm water which were freezing were also visible. For the first time in many weeks the sky was clear with beautiful cloud formations providing a splendid backdrop for the impressive array of icebergs.

The PINE ISLAND had launched two flights by 0825 on Sunday when we commenced the transfer of supplies and personnel. A steady north wind made it necessary to maneuver quite frequently, thereby delaying operations. With 23 tons of material to be discharged and

20 tons of supplies to be received we had rigged two receiving stations to port and three discharging stations to starboard. At 1150 operations were discontinued due to the impending return of one plane because of bad weather over the continent. At 1158, however, the plane was ordered to make a local flight so we resumed work until 1412 when both planes returned. We moved into the lee of an iceberg while they were hoisted aboard the PINE ISLAND, then resumed operations for the second time at 1745. By this time our clear weather had disappeared, being replaced by a rather heavy snow squall. Consequently, it was with no regret that we completed the transfer at 1846 and hove-to to await further orders from CTG 68.3.

During one of the flights it had been observed that it would be possible to proceed by ship to the northern coast of CHARCOT ISLAND, where it was hoped a small boat landing could be affected. That evening CTG 68.3 requested approval from CTF 68 to take the BROWNSON and attempt a landing in CHARCOT. The approval was received at 0049 Monday, 10 February, and by 0802 the commanding officer was on his way to the PINE ISLAND for a conference. The Captain returned at 1152 and shortly thereafter additional materials for the proposed landing operation, including sleds, skis, sleeping bags, flags, special clothing, and an extra motor whaleboat and portable fathometer arrived from the PINE ISLAND. We put our boat in the skids and hoisted the extra boat on our falls. At 1530 CTG 68.3, Captain G. J. DUFEK and four members of his staff came aboard, breaking his flag. By 1541 we were underway for CHARCOT ISLAND, 55 miles to the east.

CHARCOT ISLAND was sighted bearing 120°, 35 miles, at 1800 that evening. At 2100 and 2200 we put motor whaleboats #2 and #1 respectively over the side. At 2135, the landing party composed of the Commodore, the C.O., Lt. (jg) Warfield and CPHOM Ryan, plus the boat's crew of Mountz, BM1, Wiley, S1, and Finstein, MM1, shoved off to attempt a landing. Soon after leaving the ship it was found that the portable fathometer was inoperative, so some few minutes were lost when they stopped to unrig it. Progress in the boat was very slow, their path being impeded by ice floes of various sizes. On approaching to within about 500 yards of the shore line they encountered shifting loose pack, compacted by the wind and sea, composed of floes of such sizes that it was seen they could not reach the shore. So, reluctantly the party returned to the ship. MWB #2 was hoisted aboard almost immediately (2225) and MWB #1 was hoisted aboard at 2245. Consequently, at 2310 we hove-to for the night with intentions of making another attempt the following morning.

After lying-to all night in heavy fog and frequent snow squalls, awaiting better weather which never came, at 0830, Tuesday, 11 February, we got underway to investigate CHARCOT's northern coast, seeking an area suitable for small boat landings. Since the off shore area was jammed with pack ice and bergs which barred all access to the northern coast, a return trip was made to the southwest, still seeking a sheltered area in the lee of the island. Encountering solid shelf ice at 1450 at 69-47S, 75-53W we retraced ourprevious course to northeast where course was set for ROTHSCHILD ISLAND and ALEXANDER I ISLAND, intending to return to CHARCOT when the wind had shifted. This intention, however, was never realized.

Wednesday morning, 12 February, we investigated the area northwest of ROTHSCHILD ISLAND and ALEXANDER I ISLAND just off the HAVRE MOUNTAINS. It appeared that instead of being an island, ROTHSCHILD's is actually a peninsula extending out to the westward from ALEXANDER I ISLAND. During the day we followed the coastline of ALEXANDER I around to the northward, doubling back and forth frequently to permit staff personnel to photograph coastline while we plotted it using bearings, ranges and heights obtained with the Mk 37-53 Director. Several times we attempted to maneuver into favorable position for a small boat landing but each time the attempt was thwarted by heavy swells, decreasing visibility, and for increasing winds. Early in the afternoon as we rounded the northwest extremity of ALEXANDER I we sighted the JOHANSEN ISLANDS at 1400, bearing 340°, 5 miles, located at 68-53S, 72-39W. At 1500 we sighted an uncharted rock bearing 000°, 10 miles, located at 68-52S, 72-21W. A second uncharted rock bearing 010°, 16 miles, was sighted at 1845, location 68-27S, 71-52W. A final uncharted rock was sighted at 1847, bearing 060°, 6 miles, location 68-39S, 71-47W.

Steaming slowly in uncharted waters likely to be dotted with shoals and reefs, we kept the fathometer in operation continuously with the operator sending depths to the bridge every 30 seconds. At 2140 prudence dictated we back full on both engines as the depth dropped below 15 fathoms. Distance and size were difficult to estimate in this region. Our course lay within 8 to 10 miles of the shoreline but the distance never appeared to be more than 3 or 4 miles. Rocks on the shore line judged to be 150' high proved to be 850' high. Peaks and ranges which appeared to be just back from the shoreline invariably turned out to be 20 or 30 miles away. Bare rock was visible, but the majority of the peaks were covered with snow and ice.

Early Thursday morning, 13 February a storm began to blow up so we headed on a northerly course to ride it out at about 5 knots. Wind and seas increased throughout the day giving us rolls as great as 40° at times. To keep the wind and seas about 2 points on the starboard bow for optimum riding conditions we found it advisable to keep a 25 turn differential on our screws i.e. port engine making 50 revolutions and starboard engine making 25. By 2200 the wind began to slacken and weather reports indicated that we could hope for better weather. Consequently, we changed course to 160° for the entrance to Marguerite Bay.

At the entrance to Marguerite Bay Friday morning, 14 February, with weather conditions unsuitable for flying CTG decided to refuel us while we were still in ice-free water and at 1142 we commenced our approach on the PINE ISLAND.

Fueling and transfer of supplies was commenced at 1216. In the meantime the Commodore had decided to go over to the PINE ISLAND for a conference with Captain Caldwell during the operation. We rigged for the exercise in our usual manner by securing a 3/8" wire cable to a chock on the port side of the foc's'le and passing it up over 5" mount #2 where its fore and aft movement was checked by leading it through a shackle secured to a pad-eye. To this wire strap we shackled a quick releasing pelican hook which was to take the PINE ISLAND's provisioning span line. After testing the rig first with several loads of supplies, Captain G. J. DUFEK, CTG 68.3, had been started across when a large swell caused both ships to roll in opposition making the span line dangerously taut and causing Captain DUFEK to strike the left side of his head on an overhead structural member of the trolley. As the ships rolled toward each other the PINE ISLAND took up the slack with a steam winch to prevent the TGC from getting wet. Again the ships rolled out of phase parting the span line at 1227 with a snap like the shot of a gun and dropping Captain DUFEK from a height of approximately 25' into the water at a point about midway between the two ships. He came to the surface once still strapped in the special steel chair that had been used, than disappeared from sight. A few seconds later, however, he reappeared, free of the chair with his life jacket inflated, and floating rapidly aft. The men in the fueling party acted so quickly in casting off their lines that the open end of the fueling hose, still spurting oil, landed in the water close to the Commodore as he floated by.

By this time we were already angling away from the PINE ISLAND, coming around to make a recovery. The shafts had revved up to 250 turns (about 23 knots) before the order was given, "all engines back full." We came to a stop 30 yards from the Commodore and it was only a matter of minutes until he was hoisted into the whaleboat at 1235. At 1238 Captain DUFEK was brought on board the ship; rescue operations completed 11 minutes after the span line had parted. From Captain Caldwell we received, "That was the best piece of work I have ever seen." Under the ministrations of the Medical Department, and thanks to his rugged condition, the Commodores' recovery was rapid.

At 1310 we resumed fueling and completed the operation at 1302, having taken on board 58,970 gallons of fuel oil. We then fell in astern of the PINE ISLAND and at 2238 pursuant to CTG 68.3's 150338Z we set course to round the PALMER PENINSULA for operations in the Weddell Sea. Weather reports had indicated that we were in for a spell of bad weather with no possibility of flight operations for at

least four days. In view of this it had been decided to forego the
Marguerite Bay operation and start immediately for the Weddell Sea.
At 2400 we moved out to our assigned station 10,000 yards on the
starboard beam of the PINE ISLAND.

Between 0100 and 0700 Saturday, 15 February, the barometer
dropped .42 inches to 28.28. Wind and seas increased throughout the
day. At 1545 we reached the rendezvous where the CANISTEO joined us,
taking her station 10,000 yards on the port beam of the PINE ISLAND.
As the storm increased we regretted the fact that, steaming in formation,
we could no longer slow to our best riding speed. Throughout the night
we were taking solid water up to mount #1 with spray over the bridge,
which thoroughly drenched the watch. The after lookouts also fared
badly with spray running over the gun deck aft of #2 stack. For all
practical purposes, our fan-tail was awash; all hands were cautioned
to use the inside passageway.

In accordance with the oceanographer's suggestion, fathometer
tapes were marked every 15 minutes with zebra time correct to the
nearest five seconds, latitude, longitude and range and bearing of
other ships.

Sunday the storm abated and Monday, 17 February, at 2000 we
passed 400 miles due south of Cape Horn in calm seas. Tuesday morning,
18 February, dawned clear and bright so the Commodore decided to return
to the PINE ISLAND; this time, however, by boat. Accordingly, at 1527
CTG 68.3 shifted his flag and staff to the PINE ISLAND.

At 2000 that night the wind freshened with gusts up to 35 knots.
Shortly thereafter we sighted the largest iceberg of the trip - $6\frac{1}{2}$
miles long. By Tuesday morning, 18 February, we were hitting 35° and
37° rolls quite frequently; at 0800 we rolled 42°. Waves breaking over
our starboard side constantly caused considerable concern regarding the
4 drums of aviation gasoline lashed amidships. One stanchion had
already carried away when the weather moderated sufficiently to repair
the damage and relash the drums. At 2200 we established radar contact
on the SOUTH ORKNEY ISLANDS bearing 136°, 73 miles and checked our
position for about two hours by this means until they dropped out of
range behind us.

Finally on Wednesday, 19 February, gradually we turned southward into the Weddell Sea to commence the final period of our operations.

PHASE VII - IN THE WEDDELL SEA
(19 February 1947 to 3 March 1947)

After almost a week of heavy seas, the weather had moderated
sufficiently by the morning of 20 February to allow us to go along-

side the CANISTEO for fueling. Consequently, at 0930 we commenced our
approach. Fortunately, we had very few supplies to transfer because
the spray running over the foc's'le froze quickly, sheathing both the
forward part of the ship and the men working there in a coat of ice. A
covering of slushy ice made the hauling lines difficult to handle and
the continuous roll of the ship made footing insecure on the icy deck.
Having received on board 54,248 gallons of fuel oil, we completed the
operation at 1116 and at 1555 set course for our station at 65S, 36W.
Late in the afternoon another storm blew up during which we hit the
heaviest roll of the trip, 50°. Heavy seas and high winds continued
throughout the night, leaving the entire forward part of the ship thinly
coated with ice. During darkness we slowed to steerageway using a 35
turn differential on our screws to keep the seas on our bow.

By Friday, 21 February, the state of the sea had returned to
normal but we now found ourselves faced with a new problem. The length
of darkness was increasing each night. With a constant overcast which
made the nights pitch black and a steady, cold, biting south wind, it
became necessary to shorten the topside watches to two hours, with the
exposed lookouts being relieved every twenty minutes. The inability to
distinguish icebergs and growlers made it necessary to slow to steerageway each night and head north while awaiting daylight. We sighted the
northern limits of loose pack at 1247 and commenced ice recco to the
east remaining well clear of the pack. Throughout the afternoon we
conducted gunnery exercises, withdrawing to the northeast that night
during darkness.

With the first light the next morning, 22 February, we resumed
our southing. For the next six days we continued scouting the pack
and firing gunnery exercises, gradually working our way southeastward
toward the Greenwich Meridian but retiring to the northward away from
the ice each night upon the approach of darkness. During this period,
on Monday, 24 February, the task group was ordered to take formation
in the shape of a triangle with the PINE ISLAND at the southern vertex,
CANISTEO 100 miles to the northeast, and BROWNSON 150 miles to the
northwest. In this formation we continued to the southeast in search
of a suitable area for launching aircraft but bad weather plagued us
constantly. Everyone was primed to leave the area and head north for
Rio but the PINE ISLAND was hoping to get off at least one good flight
before we concluded operations.

Finally, on Wednesday, 26 February, the weather was CAVU for
the first time in many weeks and Thursday morning at 0705 we received
word that the PINE ISLAND had commenced launching aircraft. Weather
and sea conditions deteriorated, however, and flight operations were
cancelled. We were ordered to take station 100 miles west of the
PINE ISLAND and at 1200, Friday, 28 February, we crossed the Greenwich
Meridian at the Antarctic Circle.

Two flights were launched Saturday, 1 March, but bad weather over the continent forced each to return. Accordingly, we were again ordered southwest for ice recco and weather reporting. During the afternoon and evening we encountered numerous scattered fingers of growlers which gradually forced us to change course to the left until we were heading southward when darkness made it necessary to discontinue scouting. At daylight, Sunday, 2 March, we resumed our reconnaissance. We changed course to the eastward at 0336 when the pack prevented further southern progress, and commenced skirting the pack. Our southernmost point (68-40S, 01-18W) was reached at 0430 when course was again changed to northeast. At 0530 it appeared that, except for occasional fingers, the main edge of the pack extended on a line from our position to the PINE ISLAND's position 100 miles to the east and south where she was lying to in preparation for flight operations. Accordingly, at 0530 we retraced our course to the westward. Ice conditions indicated that close pack could be expected 5 miles south of our course. At 0800 we came around to a northwesterly course and about 1000 found a bay 10 miles long and 5 miles wide suitable for aircarft operation, which we reported to CTG 68.3.

Throughout the morning we encountered considerable pancake ice varying from filmlike ice to an extensive coverage of pancakes. At 1040, with pancake coverage increasing rapidly, we changed to a northerly course to clear the ice area. This was accomplished at 1245.

Heading west again at 1400, we immediately encountered a filmlike coverage of from 50% to 80%. As we proceeded westward the crystals of the filmlike ice gathered together to form the small circular pancakes. Gradually these small units collected to form large pancakes up to 6 feet in diameter with the area between cakes covered with a light slush. At 1445 with 100% coverage we changed course to NNW, gradually veering around to north and increasing speed to 17 knots to clear the area as expeditiously as possible. The increase in speed at this time was permitted by the fact that the area was notably free from growlers or other old ice, the entire coverage being composed of new ice in the state of formation. Between 1400 and 1600 the temperature had dropped 4° and we had no desire to risk being caught in the ice at that late date.

The composition of the ice and the speed at which it was forming indicated that two more days with temperatures below 25° F would probably find the area entirely iced in. Although little ice blink was visible because of clear weather and small cloud coverage, that which was present indicated that the main edge of the pack lay to the westward. An increasing number of growlers and brash added further weight to this assumption.

At 1810 we cleared the pack but continued northward to insure that we were definitely clear of the ice, since by then, with southerly winds from the continent, the temperature was still dropping and we could practically see the ice forming before our eyes. We were all mighty thankful when the ice was definitely behind us for had darkness overtaken us we would have been forced to reduce speed to about 5 knots. Even that speed might have been dangerous because the icebergs and growlers which were hard enough to see when silhouetted against the black water at night would have been doubly hard to discern against the background of newly formed ice.

We were still steaming north at 2255 when CTG 68.3 advised CTF 68 that because of unfavorable conditions he had decided reluctantly to discontinue operations. Shortly thereafter, at 2318, CTG 68.3 ordered TG 68.3 to discontinue present operations and set course for Rio de Janeiro, Brazil, at 12 knots with BROWNSON 50 miles on port beam and CANISTEO 50 miles on starboard beam of PINE ISLAND. Later, at 0930, we received from the Task Group Commander, "Upon conclusion of operations in the Antarctic I am proud to say to every officer and man in this group 'well done!'."

PHASE VIII - ROLLING DOWN TO RIO
(2 March 1947 to 24 March 1947)

For two days after receiving orders to discontinue operations, we steamed steadily northward. During the first day we maintained station 50 miles on the port beam of the PINE ISLAND, but at 1743 Tuesday, 4 March, in anticipation of fueling and provisioning, our station was changed to 25 miles on the starboard beam of the PINE ISLAND and we immediately set course to comply with that order. At 0647 on Thursday, 6 March, we changed course to rendezvous with the CANISTEO who was maintaining station 50 miles on the starboard beam of the PINE ISLAND. Neither ship, however, had been able to fix its position for 3 or 4 days, and consequently, we found nothing but empty ocean upon reaching what we believed to be the rendezvous. During the forenoon we steamed back and forth over the area trying to compensate for various errors of navigation, both our own and CANISTEO's, with negative results. It now seemed quite paradoxical that, after experiencing little difficulty in rendezvousing throughout the entire operation, we should miss completely when out in the wide open spaces. Since neither ship had RDF equipment, we constructed a jury rig consisting of about 25 turns of small wire wound lengthwise around a cardboard box. This unit was mounted on a small boom connected to a galvanometer, and trained manually while MO's were being sent out from the CANISTEO. Meanwhile, the CANISTEO had evolved a similar rig and was enabled to give us a course to steer. By means of this

CONFIDENTIAL

makeshift RDF unit we obtained an approximate bearing on the CANISTEO, which confirmed her date. With this information we changed course to head in her direction. That night, with unlimited visibility and a ceiling approaching 2000 feet, we arranged for each ship to train its searchlight for a period of 5 minutes every half hour. On the second attempt at 2130 we sighted the reflection of the CANISTEO's light on the clouds slightly off our starboard bow. Shortly thereafter we picked her up on the radar.

At 0742, Friday, 7 March, we arrived on station 1000 yards astern of the CANISTEO and at 0818 commenced our approach. Fueling was commenced at 0903 and completed at 1152. Having received on board 122,033 gallons of fuel oil, we cast off all lines at 1205 and set course to rendezvous with the PINE ISLAND.

Shortly after rendezvousing with the PINE ISLAND at 1730, we received a storm advisory and took station to ride it out. During the night we had gusts up to 62 knots and swells up to 47' high, probably the worst weather of the operation to date. By Sunday morning, 9 March, the storm had abated but the seas were still too high for provisioning. Consequently we took station 5 miles on the port quarter of the PINE ISLAND to await calmer seas. Early Monday morning, 10 March, we moved into position to commence our approach. It was decided, however, to delay the operation another day since we were still rolling quite heavily.

By this time we were about 40°S with the weather becoming very pleasant. The unusual sight of the sun and blue skies for days at a time resulted in a marked rise in morale among all hands. At 0827 Tuesday, 11 March, we commenced our approach on the PINE ISLAND and, at 0910, began receiving supplies. We cast off all lines at 1120 and set course for our station 50 miles on the port beam of the PINE ISLAND, test firing the 20 MM enroute.

The next two days were uneventful until 2206, Thursday, 13 March, when we changed course to rendezvous with the PINE ISLAND for fueling. This was desired in order to lighten her for propeller repairs. From our station 1000 yards astern, we commenced our approach on the PINE ISLAND at 0858, Friday, 14 March. We completed the operation at 1325, having received on board 63,982 gallons of fuel oil. The CANISTEO having joined us earlier in the morning, all three ships hove-to at 1420 and commenced cleaning ship's sides. While we were thus engaged, the Group Commander called a conference of Commanding Officers on board the flagship and advantage was taken of this trip to return the PINE ISLAND's motorwhaleboat to her. At 1750 we resumed base course and speed.

Saturday, 15 March, the task group lay-to from 0800 to 1740 to continue cleaning. Sunday, 16 March, the PINE ISLAND and CANISTEO hove-to to paint ship's sides from 0700 until 1800. During this period we patrolled the area at 1.5 knots and continued cleaning since we did not have sufficient paint aboard for the sides. From 1423 until 1730 we circled the PINE ISLAND at 10,000 yards, transmitting MO's for RDF calibration. At 1810 we sighted land bearing 000°T. That night we lay-to again for six hours before getting underway at 0400 Monday, 17 March, on the final leg of our trip to Rio.

Still a little ahead of schedule, we lay-to for 7 hours Monday night, getting underway in column (PINE ISLAND, CANISTEO, BROWNSON) at 0305 Tuesday, 18 March, for the harbor entrance. At 0800 the column started up the channel which provides such an impressive entrance to Rio. At 0841 we passed the Santa Cruz fortress 500 yards abeam to starboard. At 0900 we received the pilot and Lt. Paulo Moreira de Silva, Brazilian Navy, aboard. Shortly thereafter the PINE ISLAND fired a 21 gun salute to the Republic of Brazil and a 13 gun salute in honor of Rear Admiral Dantas, Commander Brazilian Destroyer Force. Both salutes were immediately returned, and at 0927 we moored to a buoy ——. Rio at last!

Just before our arrival in Rio we received the following message from the Task Group Commander - "Our arrival in Rio marks the end of a long arduous cruise that has been successfully completed. Each officer and man can be rightfully proud of the part he played in contributing to that success. Your devotion to duty under hazardous and trying conditions has been in keeping with the high standards expected of our Navy. I am proud of you and I wish you all a very pleasant and happy stay in Rio."

On the afternoon of our arrival, Tuesday, 18 March, calls, which had been previously arranged were made on various Brazilian and U.S. officials. This proved to be quite a pleasure and an honor for the commanding officer who at this time was introduced to the Brazilian Minister of the Navy, the Minister of Foreign Affairs, and the Minister of Aeronautics among others. The following morning all commanding officers called on Admiral Guilhobel, Director of the Navy Yard. By way of return, that afternoon a number of Brazilian officials and the American charge d'affaires were piped aboard the PINE ISLAND to return their official calls.

Early Thursday, 20 March, the British light cruiser, HMS SHEFFIELD, was perceived quietly standing into the harbor at Rio. Shortly thereafter, as she was easing into her berth at the Navy Yard, the PINE ISLAND fired a salute to her flag officer, Vice Admiral Sir William Tennant, R.N. That afternoon a very pleasant luncheon was given at the University Club for Commanding Officers and Brazilian Liaison Officers. Friday at 0940 official calls were made on the British in HMS SHEFFIELD, and the calls were returned that forenoon aboard the PINE ISLAND as before.

CONFIDENTIAL

Saturday, 22 March, the Commanding Officer, Executive Officer, and Medical Officer joined other officers from the Task Group for an inspection of the Navy Yard. Following this, they were entertained at a luncheon, given by Rear Admiral Guilhobel, the Director of the Navy, at which the senior U. S. Naval Officer present was Rear Admiral Leland P. Lovette, Chief of the U.S. Naval Mission to Brazil. Saturday afternoon a group of the ship's officers attended a garden party at the Naval Club given in honor of Vice Admiral Tennant. Sunday, the last day of our visit, we were guests of the Rio Jockey Club for a very enjoyable afternoon at the races.

Several other entertainments were provided during our stay such as a trip to Corcovado, a trip to Sugar Loaf, and a very successful dance for the enlisted men. In addition, all officers were kindly accorded the privileges of the Naval Club during this period.

Probably the most impressive action taken in our behalf, however, was the very fine practice of detailing a Brazilian Liaison Officer and an official car for each Commanding Officer. In our case specifically, Lt. Paulo Moreira de Silva gave unstintingly of his time and did everything in his power to make our stay enjoyable.

PHASE IX - HOMEWARD BOUND
(24 March 1947 to 25 March 1947)

Having made all preparations for sea, at 1015 Monday, 24 March, we got underway from our buoy and stood out through the Rio harbor. As we took departure from the Santa Cruz Fortress at 1115, a beautiful array of clouds shrouded Corcovado and the surrounding mountains to form a striking background for our last look at Rio.

We steamed in column until Tuesday morning, 25 March, when the PINE ISLAND went alongside the CANISTEO to refuel. As soon as this had been completed, we commenced our approach on the CANISTEO and began fueling at 1238. Having received on board 51,912 gallons of fuel oil, at 1405 we cast-off all lines. In accordance with CTG 68.3 251148Z, we were then relieved of present duties and reported to CINCLANT and COMDESLANT for operational control. Pursuant to COMDESLANT 261710Z we set course for Norfolk, Virginia. As we gradually steamed away from the CANISTEO's side for the last time, she sounded a hearty farewell blast on her whistle amid much waving and shouting indicative of the strong feeling of comradeship between the two ships.

With the PINE ISLAND and CANISTEO heading for Panama and Ascension Island respectively, and slowly fading out of sight behind us we bring this narrative and our part in Operation HIGHJUMP to a close with a feeling of pride in our accomplishments and the knowledge that we have obtained a wealth of experience which will be of value to the Navy and to ourselves in future years.

PHASE X - STATISTICAL HIGHLIGHTS OF OPERATION HIGHJUMP

BROWNSON sailed from Norfolk, Virginia, in company with other ships of the force, on 2 December, 1946 and returned to that port on 3 April, 1947. During that period she steamed 28,772 miles, of which 21,457 miles were steamed continuously. She was in port on two occasions, for three days from 7 to 10 December in Balboa, Canal Zone, and for six days from 18 to 24 March, 1947 in Rio de Janeiro, Brazil. She was underway a continuous period of 98 days. Some of the more important statistics concerning BROWNSOM's participation in operation HIGHJUMP are tabulated herewith.

From 1100, 2 December 1946 to 0800, 8 April 1947.

```
Total days underway - - - - - - - - - - - - - - - - - 118
Total miles steamed - - - - - - - - - - - - - - - 28,772
Total days not underway - - - - - - - - - - - - - - - 9
Fuel used underway - - - - - - - - - - - - - - 1,079,916
Fuel used not underway - - - - - - - - - - - - - 18,332
Number of times refueled at sea - - - - - - - - - - - 11
Number of times refueled in port - - - - - - - - - - - 1
Maximum speed made - - - - - - - - - 32 knots 325 RPM
Minimum speed made (not lying to) - - 1 knot  15 RPM
Days out of sight of land - - - - - - - - - - - - - - 62
```

12/12/46	Crossed equator at longitude 83°23.7'W
12/26/46	First crossed Antarctic Circle at Longitude 110°56.8'W
3/1/47	Crossed Antarctic Circle at Greenwich Meridian
	Crossed the Antarctic Circle 36 times.
2/17/47	Rounded Cape Horn.
1/27/47	Farthest west - - - -- 67°50.3'S 177°04'W
2/28/47	Farthest east - - - - - -66°58.3'S 04°39.6'E
2/9/47	Farthest south - - - - 69°59.3'S 78°34.1'W

Meteorological conditions, extremes encountered below Lat. 55°S

1/24/47	Maximum temperature - 40°F, Lat. 67°S, Long. 174°50'W
2/21/47	Minimum temperature - 20°F, Lat. 63°S, Long. 38°33'W
3/2/47	Minimum Seawater temperature - 29°F, Lat. 67°58'S, Long. 03°15'W
3/7/47	Maximum wind force - 62 knots from 300°T dir. Lat. 51°S, Long. 25°W

Oceanographic conditions, extremes encountered below Lat. 55°S.

3/4/47 Deepest water - 2840 fathoms, Lat. 61°36'S, Long. 11°18'W
1/26/47 Shoalest water - 720 Fathoms, Lat. 66°24'S, Long. 173°34'W (outside of bays, harbors, which were traversed).

Land Sighted

2/10/47 Charcot Island, Antarctica
2/11/47 Rothschild and Alexander I Islands.
2/13/47 Adelaide Island
2/14/47 Palmer Peninsula

Gastronomic Conditions

Provisioned ship 2 times in port
Provisioned ship 7 times at sea
Provisions consumed - 36.6 tons
Provisions consumed - 244 pounds per man
Largest item of use - flour. 12,600 pounds consumed.
Smallest item of use - Chili powder. 16 ounces consumed.

PERSONNEL STATISTICS:

	OFFICERS	ENLISTED MEN	OBSERVERS (civilian)
On departure	16	264	1
Maximum	18	293	2
On Return	16	283	1

MEDICAL STATISTICS:

Upper respiratory disease decreased rapidly from 44 to 23 after two weeks and decreased almost to zero after one month in the Antarctic.

There were no serious illnesses during the operation.

Plate No. 1

First Iceberg - 2 Miles on Port Beam

Plate No. 2

Ice Blink on the Horizon.

Plate No. 3

We went through it.

Plate No. 4

Fueling at sea from PINE ISLAND.

Plate No. 5

Fueling at sea from CANISTEO.

Plate No. 6

Cargo for the PINE ISLAND on the Fantail.

Plate No. 7

Cargo for the PINE ISLAND coming over from the PHILIPPINE SEA.

Plate No. 8

Transfer of Personnel - BROWNSON to CANISTEO.

Plate No.9

Transfer of Personnel - PHILIPPINE SEA to BROWNSON.

Plate No. 10

Lt. (jg) LE BLANC (in stretcher) and other survivors coming aboard.

Plate No. 11

PINE ISLAND launching Aircraft.

Plate No. 12

Charcot Island.

Plate No. 13

Charcot Island.

Plate No. 14

Alexander I Island.

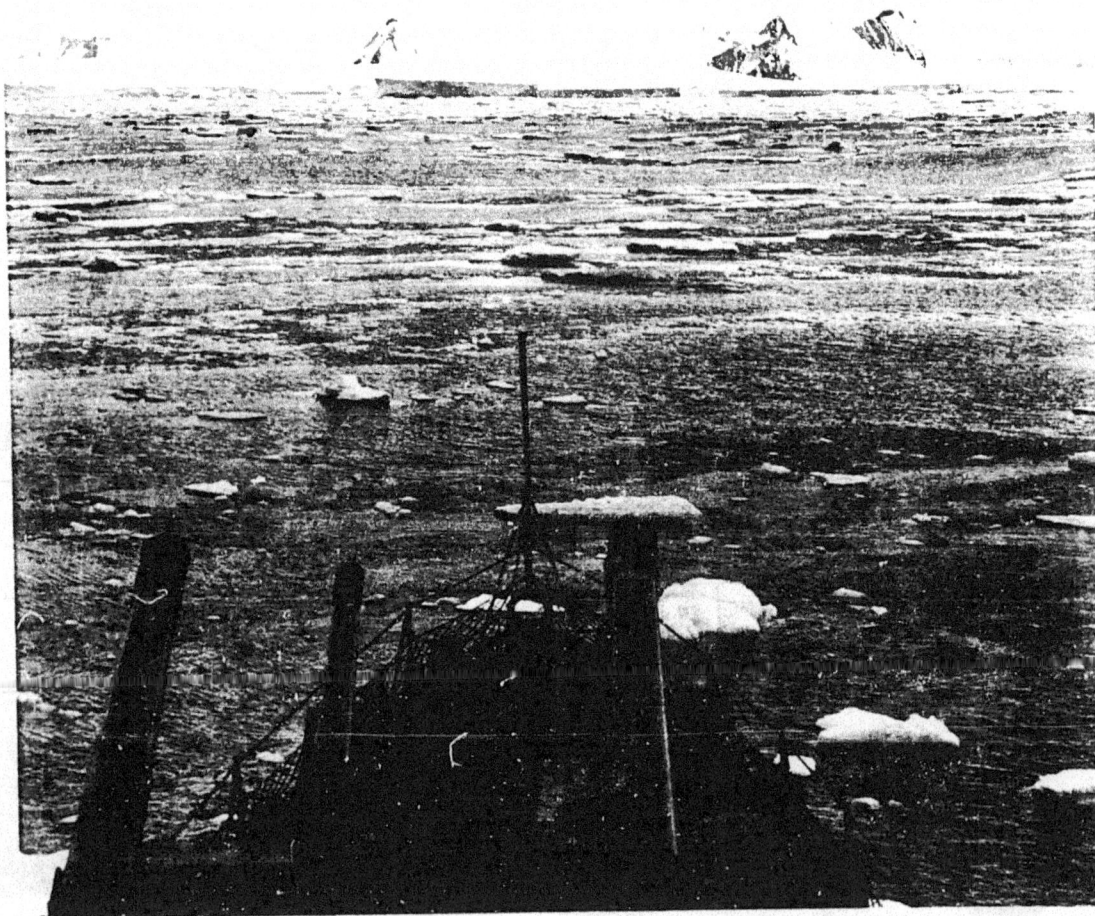

Plate No. 15

Rothschild Island dead ahead

Plate No. 16

Heavy ice formed on the Forecastle.

ANNEX TWO

PHOTOGRAPHIC REPORT

OPERATION HIGHJUMP

ANNEX TWO (a)

Table of Contents

ANNEX TWO (a)

Table of Illustrations

ANNEX TWO (b)

Table of Contents

ANNEX TWO (b)

Table of Illustrations

ANNEX TWO (c)

Table of Contents

ANNEX TWO (c)

Table of Illustrations

ANNEX TWO (a)

TASK FORCE SIXTY EIGHT

PHOTOGRAPHIC SUMMARY

AND

TASK GROUP 68.1

PHOTOGRAPHIC REPORT

ANNEX TWO (a)

INTRODUCTION

Prior to Operation HIGHJUMP, there were no set standards for photographic operations in extremely cold weather. Therefore, in the anticipation that this report may be of value in planning for any future operations of its kind in the Arctic or Antarctic, many details have been included not only in the achievements, but in errors, observations, performance of equipment and proficiency of personnel, etc., that would, under normal operating conditions, be omitted.

I. OBJECTIVES

The primary photographic objective of Operation HIGHJUMP was the reconnaissance survey of the unexplored coastal and continental areas of the continent with the tri-metrogon camera installation. The secondary objective was the survey of certain coastal and island areas requested by the Hydrographic Office. In carrying out these photographic objectives effectively, other aerials, stills, and motion pictures in color and black and white of the operational and training aspect were required. These all presented problems in equipment, personnel, and in actual operations and organization, which will be reported on in detail in the various Task Group reports immediately following this summary.

II. AIRPLANE ALLOCATIONS:

The Task Force was organized into three main operational groups; the Central, Eastern, and Western Groups. For exploration and photographic survey, the Central Group was equipped with six R4D-5 airplanes. The other two groups with three PBM-5 seaplanes each. Each of these groups was augmented by lighter airplanes and helicopters for short exploratory flights and for scouting purposes as follows:

Central Group

One (1) JA-1 (Norseman)
Two (2) Helicopters
Two (2) J2F-6 Amphibians

Eastern and Western Groups

One (1) SOC airplane
Two (2) Helicopters

III. AIRPLANE INSTALLATIONS:

None of these lighter airplanes were to be equipped with any photographic installations; however, small scout hand-held reconnaissance cameras were provided. The R4D-5 airplanes were to be completely equipped with the tri-metrogon camera installations as well as oblique, still, and motion pictures, and certain other cameras to record altitude (both pressure and radio), time, and written data simultaneously with each set of tri-metrogon photographs taken. The R4D-5 installations were made at the Assembly and Repair Department, Naval Air Station, Quonset Point, Rhode Island; the PBM-5 installations at the Assembly and Repair Department, Naval Air Station, Norfolk, Virginia.

The Task Force Sixty-Eight Photographic Officer, because of previous experience, was requested to visit each of these assembly and repair departments at various times by the cognizant Bureau of Aeronautics' representative to offer any suggestions and criticisms that might be helpful in expediting the satisfactory completion of the installations. During these visits, it was stressed by this officer, that in addition to a good technical installation, all camera hatches were to be sealed against wind-blast to protect the camera operator against severe frost-bite. Considerable changes were made in the PBM tri-metrogon and oblique installations after they were begun as a result of these visits. Unfortunately, because of weather and remoteness to Task Force Headquarters, visits to Quonset Point were not as frequent as they should have been. Consequently, there were several discrepancies in the tri-metrogon installations of the R4D-5's. The hatches were never satisfactory. The oblique photographs were masked off to such an extent that they were rendered less valuable for the purpose intended, although still usable. This ultimately required the removal of the wind-blast seal in order to have an adequate unobstructed camera view. The PBM installations, however, both tri-metrogon and oblique, were very satisfactory except for a minor modification to permit leveling tri-metrogon cameras. This installation is an excellent standard for future installations in that type airplane.

IV CAMERA MOUNTS

The tri-metrogon mounts installed in R4D-5 and PBM-5 airplanes were not engineered primarily for those airplanes. Actually the mounts are the N.A.S. San Diego, Local Change 113 for the F6F (Hellcat). When the F6F was originally fitted with the tri-metrogon cameras in 1943, it was found necessary, because of lack of space, to install one of the oblique K-17 6-inch cameras in a reverse position to afford room for the electric-drive motor. This resulted in the film travelling in the direction of flight in the vertical and one of the oblique cameras, while film travel in the other oblique was in the opposite direction. This difference in the direction of film travel made marking or study of a set of three rolls of negatives a very awkward operation. Also, there was no provision for leveling the tri-metrogon cameras in the F6F airplane except by leveling the airplane. The Bureau of Aeronautics directed that the F6F tri-metrogon installation be installed in the R4D-5 and PBM-5 airplanes of Task Force Sixty-Eight without modification.

It would have been very desirable to install the tri-metrogon camera mount so that the film travel in all cameras would be in the same direction. It is believed that the Task Force airplanes were large enough to permit this modification to the F6F San Diego Local Change 113. Also, a means of leveling the cameras should have been provided in these airplanes, as flight characteristics do not permit the leveling and trimming of the R4D and PBM airplanes when they are heavily loaded. The F6F San Diego Local Change 113 mount was installed in the R4D airplanes, not only without modification, but in addition, reversed, which caused the film in two cameras to travel in the opposite direction to the line of flight, instead of only one as in the F6F. At first, this caused considerable confusion to the Photogrammetrist and his assistants. After it was determined which way the film traveled in all the cameras, it was less confusing, but it was still awkward to handle the rolls of negatives when marking or identifying landmarks on the film.

It was found on 1 December 1946, prior to departure of the Task Force on 2 December, that none of the calibrated K-17 6-inch aircraft camera case-drives, which were all that were delivered upon request to the U.S.S. MOUNT OLYMPUS, would fit into the R4D mounts, as the pins for holding the cameras in the proper position would not fit into the recesses of the oblique view finder since they were out of line about 1/8 inch. Fortunately, however, there were enough uncalibrated cameras at N.A.S.D., Norfolk, which would fit. Thus it was necessary to exchange all the calibrated cameras for the uncalibrated cameras at the last instant before sailing. This action required calibration after return to the U.S.; unfortunately, two sets of cameras were jettisoned and their calibration can not be made. Instead of using the F6F installation without modification, the specifications for the installation and camera angles should have been stipulated to the various assembly and repair departments and a mount built from these specifications. It is recommended that, in the future, adapters be furnished with all tri-metrogon mounts to facilitate using either type camera.

V. SURVEY CONTROL PROBLEMS

It was realised immediately that the best known method of accurate controlled aerial survey, that of establishing field control points by surface parties, was completely out of the question in the Antarctic on Operation HIGHJUMP. It would have entailed many months of working in the field by terrestial survey parties to establish these points and mark them suitably to record in the photographs. It was remotely possible to establish a few control points along some of the coast line if time permitted; this possibility could not, however, be relied upon. The best alternative to obtain any control at all was to endeavor to tie all the photographs or rather strips of photographs that were to be taken, into old fixes in the picture, and operate the cameras, with proper overlap, out to the end of the extent of the range of the airplane or to the end of the flight. The cameras were to be operated all the way back and were to include some well established point before being turned off. This would be reconnaissance survey at its best unless some instrumental or electronics method could be utilized in addition to the navigator's various sun lines against time. Many methods were discussed with Hydrographic Office representatives. Radio, the most desirable, had to be discarded because of lack of bases suitably situated for obtaining navigational fixes. The best that could be done was to use what fixes the navigator could obtain by use of the Astro-compass, by plotting various sun lines across the flight track and tying geographical points obtained in photographs to these meager navigational fixes.

VI.   MODIFIED GREMLIN RECORDER

It became immediately apparent that accurate time, in order to determine position, must be furnished with each set of photographs taken. The K-17 6-inch aircraft cameras used in the tri-metrogon installation do not have clocks in them; therefore, it was decided to modify an instrument used at Bikini in Operation CROSSROADS to record time simultaneously with each set of photographs taken of the bomb blast, which for lack of a name, was called a Gremlin Recorder. A Gremlin Recorder is the combination of two F-56 aircraft cameras; one (1) F-56 20-inch drive and cone mounting an F-56 8½-inch lens, with the instruments to be recorded located the proper distance in front and illuminated for photographing. It was decided to install several additional instruments in this recorder. A photograph of these instruments with each set of photographs taken by the tri-metrogon would be very useful. Installations included: (1), an accurate watch, (2), a pressure altimeter, (3), an inclinometer, and (4), an SCR-718 radio altimeter. The Bureau of Aeronautics authorized the Gremlin Recorders to be modified at the Assembly and Repair Department, N.A.S., Norfolk, Virginia. Many installations and photographic problems prevented the inclusion of the SCR-718 in these recorders. Twelve of these recorders were completed and delivered to the Task Force. Detailed reports on the operation of these recorders will appear in the various Task Group reports following this summary.

VIII. AERIAL SURVEY MATERIAL

Except for the number of aircraft cameras required and other standard aerial photographic equipment, it was extremely difficult to estimate the amount of sensitized material needed for the primary photographic objectives of the operation. The basic factors necessary to estimate film for any aerial survey project, are based on how much territory is to be surveyed. Once the size of the territory is known, the problem is relatively simple, and one which is familiar to every aerial photographer. These first factors were known, but because the elevation of the terrain in the unexplored areas was not known, the problem remained indeterminate. It was, of course, very desirable to fly the airplanes 20,000 feet above the terrain. This was impossible for the PBM's as their service ceiling is near 15,000 feet or more and the elevation of the terrain that was known in the interior of the continent in places exceeds 10,000 feet and some mountains are 15,000 feet or more above sea level. It was finally decided that the Eastern Group and the Western Group airplanes would fly at 13,000 feet if possible, and the Central Group airplanes 20,000 feet true altitude. It was estimated that the Central Group would be able to fly a total of twenty-four radial flight sectors, weather permitting, from the Base at Bay of Whales extending 750 miles from Base and return. It was also estimated that the Wing Groups, even though with one-half as many airplanes each, by commencing operations earlier and continuing later than the Central Group, could each fly an equal number of flight miles. The total number of nautical miles thus estimated was 108,000 miles. With all the unknown factors and uncertain weather conditions considered, it was decided to base the amount of film needed on these estimates and the fact that with oxygen, the airplanes should be able to fly at least 5,000 feet above the terrain. These assumptions established a basis for the film, chemicals, paper, and other material etc. for the survey operations. Because the number of flights anticipated did not materialize, there was a considerable amount of film in excess. Due to insufficient space on the U.S.S. BURTON ISLAND to transport all material when that vessel evacuated the Base at the Bay of Whales, the following material was left stored in the Quonset Hut at the Emergency Base at the Bay of Whales:

294	Rolls	$9\frac{1}{2}$" x 200'	Super XX	Film aero
24	Rolls	$9\frac{1}{2}$" x 75'	Tri-X	Film aero
13	Rolls	$9\frac{1}{2}$" x 75'	Infra-red	Film aero
12	Rolls	7" x 18'	Super XX	Film aero

IX MISCELLANEOUS MATERIAL

The following miscellaneous material was also left stored in the Quonset Hut at Bay of Whales (Emergency Camp).

147 Dozen 4x5 Ansco daylight color film.
 10 Gross 10x20 paper.
  2 Safe lights - 8x10 hangar type.
  1 Model "J" Aerial film dryer.
  2 Smith film developing units (9½).
150 1 gal. cans D-76 developer.
 50 1 gal. cans D-19 developer.
  1 10" trimmer.
  1 9x18 Contact Printer (Argon).
  2 Immersion heaters   (110V.).
  2 8 x 10 trays   (enamel).
  2 11 x 14 trays   (enamel).

X DIFFICULTIES ENCOUNTERED

Because of low altitudes necessitated by removal of oxygen equipment prior to take-off from the PHILIPPINE SEA, the inability to reinstall, and the high elevation of the Polar Plateau, several flights expended film before the end of their flight. In some instances, the altitude of the airplane above the terrain was 1700 feet or less. Extra rolls of film were provided but it was too cold (minus 20 to 40 degrees Fahrenheit) to unload and reload film in flight. Six (6) rolls of film were loaded in Flight Number Seven Able (7A), resulting in frost-bitten fingers. It was, of course, necessary to load film bare handed. This procedure was so slow and painful and since no better system could be improvised, it was not attempted on any later flights. On all flights, however, all available spare magazines were carried.

XI PHOTOGRAPHIC PERSONNEL

The photographic personnel were experienced aerial photographers and were all very anxious to do an excellent job; but the airplanes were so cold, since the camera compartments were not properly sealed against wind-blast, that it was not possible to do any work bare-handed, except for very short intervals, which were frequently necessary in making notes. It was necessary to move about frequently and because of the distance between cameras, electrically heated flying suits were not practical. The photographer usually was so involved in the operation of the tri-metrogon cameras that there was seldom time for operating the oblique K-17 12-inch cameras. The 16mm. motion picture cameras became known as the Pilot's camera, and considerable Kodachrome footage was obtained with this camera operated by the pilot or co-pilot on nearly all flights. It was a simple matter to keep these motion picture cameras operating at sub-zero outside air temperatures because of the heat inside of the Pilot's compartment.

XII PILOTS

When it was found that the pilots assigned to Operation HIGHJUMP were not experienced photographic pilots, Captain John H. McElroy, U.S.N., who was assigned collateral duties with the Task Force Staff to assist in planning for the photographic operation, went to N.A.S., Norfolk, Virginia, and gave a series of lectures to the crews. Captain McElroy did a commendable job in the short interval of time that could be spared by the crews for these lectures and indoctrination in photography. There was not sufficient time taken however, for the crews to gain enough photographic air experience. It must be remembered that the shortest course of instruction to qualify a pilot for photographic reconnaissance flying during the war was six (6) weeks of intensive and continued lectures, and photographic flying. It is, therefore, strongly recommended that for any future operation similar to Operation HIGHJUMP, where aerial photography is of such paramount importance, all pilots be thoroughly trained and experienced photographic pilots. It is believed that superior photographic coverage would have been obtained if a photographic squadron had been assigned to duty with this Task Force.

XIII ACCOMPLISHMENTS

Total survey flights	28	Total K-17 6" (Tri-met)Neg.		16,924
Total F-56 Gremlin Neg.	4,178	Total K-17 12" Kodacolor"		35
Total F-56 8¼ Neg.	200	Total F-56 8¼" "	"	22
Total Radar Alt. 35mm. Neg.	1,553	Total 50'Mag. " 16mm. "		19

XIV PERSONNEL

The important role that photography was to play in Operation HIGHJUMP necessitated an officer in charge of photography on the Staff. This officer was assigned 10 October 1946, and immediately commenced the task of organizing the Photographic Department. After considerable study of the photographic requirements, it was determined that the following additional personnel were needed:

One (1) Officer on the Staff in charge of motion picture photography
One (1) Photographic Officer for each of the three Task Groups.
One (1) Motion picture specialist officer or enlisted man, for each of the two Wing Groups.

Prior to the assignment of the Staff Photographic Officer, CinCLantFlt and CinCPacFlt had been requested to assign a photographer's mate who was also a qualified aircrewman to each of the twelve Task Force airplanes. A determined effort was made to obtain skillful, experienced color and black and white motion picture specialists for the three main operating groups; but, unfortunately, the required number were not available in the Navy. A request was submitted to the Marine Corps and two officers were assigned for motion picture work. In addition, a similar request was submitted to the Army, and four (4) enlisted motion picture specialists were assigned. Only one Navy photographer's mate could be obtained who had specialized in color photography. Thus it was clear that the photographic complement of Operation HIGHJUMP was to be general, all around Navy photographer's Mates generalizing in all fields but specializing in none. It was possible, however, to select a nucleus of experienced men; especially from the higher rates who were versatile but rusty in some fields and refresh them while enroute to the Antarctic. The complement was assigned as follows:

> Officer-in-Charge of Photography (Staff)
> One (1) Lt. U.S.N. in MOUNT OLYMPUS
> Officer-in-Charge Motion Pictures (Staff)
> One (1) 1st.Lt. U.S.M.C. in MOUNT OLYMPUS
> Central Group Photographic Officer.
> One (1) Lt.(jg) U.S.N. in MOUNT OLYMPUS
>
> Photographic Officer - Western Group
> One (1) Lt.(jg) U.S.N. in CURRITUCK
> Motion Pictures - Western Group
> One (1) C.W.O. U.S.M.C. in CURRITUCK
>
> Photographic Officer - Eastern Group
> One (1) Chief Photographer in PINE ISLAND

It was obvious that the biggest task to be accomplished was in the Central Group. This Group had to transit the ice pack to reach the Bay of Whales, moor to the bay ice, unload two AK's, haul material, construct a base and airstrip on the ice shelf, operate and support six (6) long range reconnaissance airplanes.

Photographs, in both motion and stills, were required by all branches of the Armed Forces of all phases of these operations. The fact that the operations of the Central Group were to be completed and the Base evacuated in less than two (2) months was indicative of a short but intense period of operation. The two Wing Groups had three (3) long range airplanes and no base to build. Hence, the ratio of assignment of personnel was 2-1-1 for the Central and Wing Groups respectively. The total complement of photographic personnel assigned was as indicated on the following page:

Central Group

Three (3) officers (2, USN; 1, USMC)
Sixteen (16) Photographers' Mates
Four (4) Photographers' Mates (Aircrewmen)
Two (2) Photographers (Marine Corps)   .
One (1) Photographer's Mate (Ships company)
Two (2) Photographers, motion picture (U.S. Army)
One (1) Photographer's Mate (in BURTON ISLAND)

U.S.C.G.C. NORTHWIND

One (1) Chief Photographer (U.S.C.G.)
One (1) Photographer's Mate (U.S.C.G.)
One (1) Photographer's Mate (U.S.N.)

Total - four (4) officers, twenty-eight (28) men for Central Group.

Western Group

Two (2) officers (1, U.S.N.; 1, U.S.M.C.)
Sixteen (16) Photographers' Mates, U.S.N.
One (1) Photographer, motion picture, U.S. Army

Total - Two (2) officers, seventeen (17) men for Western Group.

Eastern Group

One (1) officer, U.S.N.
Fourteen (14) Photographers' Mates, U.S.N.
One (1) Photographer, motion picture, U.S. Army.

Total - One (1) officer, fifteen (15) men for Eastern Group.

Grand total of photographic personnel for Task Force Sixty-Eight -
Six (6) officers and fifty-seven (57) men. (The roster of Task
Force Personnel appears in the appendix).

XVI POLICY

Because of the limitation of personnel, especially those
qualified in the more skillful fields, it was an immediate
necessity to ascertain the qualifications of every man and commence
a refreshing and training program enroute to the Antarctic. It
was found that some of the men who had been in large organizations
such as; Naval Photographic Center, Operation CROSSROADS,
Photographic Squadrons, Interpretation Squadrons, and Intelligence
Centers, had been assigned to one type of work so long in those

organizations, that proficiency in other fields was seriously lacking. Some of these photographers had graduated from the Photographic School several years previously but had not operated a motion picture or still camera for such a long time, that they were not up-to-date on the operation of the latest cameras. All of the officers and chief petty officers were given to understand that they must become proficient in the use of all types of aerial, motion, and still cameras, and also laboratory technique. For instance, there was not an officer or man in the Central Group that could crank a Mitchell Motion Picture camera proficiently. This was important because experience in the Antarctic had proven to the Staff Photographic Officer, that in cold temperatures, these cameras could not be depended upon to operate electrically. Some of these men had once been excellent in various fields of photography years before or while in school, but during the war years when specialists were so prevalent in all large organizations of the Navy, certain ones had been assigned administrative, laboratory, plant, or aircrew assignments so long that most of their photographic ability as operating photographers in the field with cameras was gone. Fortunately, all hands were most willing to knuckle down and work to regain or better their skills.

The general policy was, and justly had to be, after the men were shaken down to various fields or refreshed to get the pictures first at all costs, then process and file them later. This accounts for not obtaining names of personnel, home town addresses, etc., which were highly desirable and was accomplished in a number of instances; but in general, there was not time for this, except at the expense of missing some important part of the operation which had to be photographed as it occurred.

The Officer-in-Charge of Photography, who had been relegated to strictly administrative positions for the last six (6) years, frequently operated motion or still cameras; otherwise, some important aspect of the operation would not have been photographed. This also applies to the Officer-in-Charge of Motion Picture Photography, who often operated an Eyemo camera.

XVII BASE OPERATIONS

The Staff Photographic Officer, Lieutenant C.C. SHIRLEY, transferred to the U.S.S. YANCEY (AK93) at 2200, 16 January 1947, with the following listed photographic officers and men to photograph the entry of that vessel into the Bay of Whales, and subsequently, unloading activities, and the construction of the Base on the ice shelf:

1st. Lieut. H.H. ANGLIN, U.S.M.C.

WEED, A.D.	CPHOM
JOHNSON, E.E.	CPHOM
MEDING, J. (N)	PHOM1
RIZZOLLA, L.M.	PHOM1
MALONE, T.H.	PHOM1
PETERSON, R.F.	PHOM2
SACK, N.F.	PHOM2
POLLACK, J.M.	PHOM3
WALTERSDORF, J.M.	PVT.,U.S.A.
SHIMBERG, J. (N)	PVT.,U.S.A.

These men were divided into two (2) twelve (12) hour shifts to obtain twenty-four (24) hour coverage of unloading and construction activities. One group was headed by Lt. Shirley, the other by Lt. Anglin.

XVIII. PHOTOGRAPHIC MATERIAL TO U.S.S. YANCEY

2	Eyemo's complete with case plus 12 volt motor.
4	400' magazines for Eyemo.
2	Mitchell's complete with 8-400' magazines.
2	Cine Specials complete with 2-100' magazines each.
6	Auto-load Speedsters.
3	Speedgraphics complete with flash.
1	Graflex.
5	Medalist's
2	Kodak 35mm.'s.
2	Mitchell heavy duty tripods.
3	Professional Junior tripods.
4	Exposure meters.
1	8½ F-56 with magazine.
2	K-20's, one equipped with focusing mount.
18	Graflex typecut film holders.
4	6 volt batteries.
1	12 volt aircraft battery
60	Rolls 400' Super XX 35mm. B&W.
20	Rolls 100' 35mm. B&W.
100	Rolls 100' 16mm. Kodachrome.
150	Magazines 50' 16mm. Kodachrome.
100	Packs 4 x 5 B&W film.
5½	Doz. 4 x 5 Kodachrome.
20	Rolls 620 Ansco color.
30	Rolls 35mm. Kodachrome for Kodak 35mm.
5	Rolls 7" x 125' B&W for F-56 8½"
4	Rolls 5½"x 20' B&W for K-20
80	Number 5B flashbulbs.
88	Number 5 flashbulbs.
12	Rolls 5½"x 9' B&W for K-20.

In the meantime, the following listed personnel remained on board the U.S.S. MOUNT OLYMPUS, under the direction of Lt.(jg) R.C. TIMM, CTG 68.1 Photographic Officer, to process, handle, and file negatives and prints and in general, operate the Central Group's photographic laboratory:

BOWE, O.F.   412 02 12 CPHOM

HAYDEN, L.H.	263 56 79	PHOM1	NAWODYLO, W.H.	300 75 06	PHOM1
TURNER, W.R.	262 96 93	PHOM1	GILLASPY, J.L.	557 40 29	PHOM3
TEIGAN, B.(n)	382 81 58	PHOM1	PATTERSON, R.H.	968 56 56	PHOM3

As soon as the U.S.S. YANCEY nosed into the bay ice immediately astern of the U.S.C.G.C. NORTHWIND, Lt. Anglin and a party went onto the bay ice to obtain as many views as possible of the mooring operations; the remainder of the personnel covered the operations from the ship.

The electric motor of the Mitchell camera, operated by Lt. Shirley, slowed down to half speed; it was immediately removed and the camera hand-cranked.

XIX   PHOTOGRAPHIC ACTIVITIES ON THE ICE

During the first few hours after the ship completed mooring, unloading operations moved at such a rapid pace that it was necessary to utilize all hands of the photographic party to obtain proper coverage, instead of one shift turning in. Important transportation equipment, already on the whips, went over the side from four different places at the same time and it was important to obtain coverage of all this equipment as it hit the ice. Various pieces were behaving differently and all branches of the Armed Forces wanted photographs of it. The motor transport that did not bog down, soon began to haul material to a safe distance away from the edge of the ice. It was soon obvious that the Photographic Department was going to need transportation to keep up with the operations.

The following morning, 18 January, a Weasel was assigned to the Photographic Department. The elecrically operated Mitchell was mounted on the bow of the Weasel and one (1) of each of the following cameras was kept in it, in a ready condition at all times; Eyemo, Speedgraphic, Speedster, and Medalist. In the meantime the U.S.S. MERRICK arrived and commenced unloading operations. If it had not been for the Weasel, there would have been very poor coverage by this time as operations were moving so fast and over such a large territory, that it would have been impossible to move heavy cameras, or even personnel, from place to place fast enough.

Coverage was quite satisfactory up to date by this time to permit a visit to the Base of the United States Antarctic Service Expedition 1939 - 1941. During the filming of some interiors in the old camp, one of the Eyemo cameras froze up at a temperature of minus 26 degrees Fahrenheit. It was noted, that as cameras were brought to the surface, lenses fogged over from condensation in the warmer atmosphere on the surface of the shelf ice.

All of the exposed motion picture film and still negatives were to be sent back to the United States via the NORTHWIND, which was now ready to depart for a rendezvous with the U.S.S. PHILIPPINE SEA, north of the ice pack. Shelby, PHOM1 was recalled from the NORTHWIND to augment the force of photographers on the ice. By this time camp construction was well underway, which necessitated a headquarters for the photographic unit there as well as at the side of the ships. Until a photographic tent could be erected, one of the unoccupied pyramidal tents was used.

The U.S.S. MOUNT OLYMPUS arrived and moored to the ice on the morning of 20 January. On 21 January, all of the ships unmoored and left the Bay of Whales for the safety of the open Ross Sea, because of the turbulent ice and wind conditions. All of the photographers, however, moved up to the Base to continue coverage of construction operations and moving of supplies from the bay ice to the Base. The ships returned and moored again on 22 January and continued unloading operations. By this time, complete coverage of mooring and unmooring had been obtained, but it was desirable, if possible, to repeat coverage of all operations for documentary purposes, as it might be needed. Also, it was desirable to be ready to cover any accidents which might occur during an operation the magnitude of mooring a ship to the ice.

Coverage was obtained of Divine Services which were held upon completion of the Base. The generator available permitted the use of only 3,000 watts of light; consequently, Shelby made interiors of the church service with the Mitchell at f2.3 at 24fps. On 27 January, the two (2) twelve (12) hour shifts were discontinued as most of camp construction and unloading was complete and good coverage obtained. Accordingly, a crew was organized under Lt. Anglin to obtain various subjects in motion and still pictures of camp activities; living conditions, etc.. The crew assigned for this purpose was as follows:

MALONE, T.H.	PHOM1	(motion pictures)
WALTERSDORF, J.M.	PVT.	(motion pictures)
SHIMBERG, J. (N)	PVT.	(motion pictures)
PETERSON, R.F.	PHOM2	(still pictures)
RIZZOLLA, L.M.	PHOM1	(still pictures)

Lt. Shirley and the following personnel obtained documentary and general coverage of construction activities and commenced to prepare material for the arrival of the R4D-5's:

WEED, A.E.	CPHOM		MEDING, J. (N)	PHOM1
JOHNSON, E.E.	CPHOM		SHELBY, A.D.	PHOM1
PATTERSON, R.H.	PHOM3		POLLACK, J.M.	PHOM3

By the afternoon of 22 January, most of the personnel on the ice were sunburned, some quite severely, except those with good beards. Sack, N.F., PHOM2 was relieved by Teigan, B., PHOM1 and sent back to the MOUNT OLYMPUS to recuperate from sunburn.

The morning of 30 January, the first two R4D airplanes arrived, and shortly afterward, it was decided that the thin-skinned ships of the Central Group must leave the Bay of Whales and clear the ice pack and Ross Sea before ice conditions would prevent their leaving. Only enough personnel were to remain on the ice that could be evacuated on the one (1) icebreaker which would take them off later, after completion of the Aerial Survey Program.

It was directed that only one photographic officer and four (4) men in addition to the six (6) in the flight crews, could remain during that period and that all other photographic work was to be subjugated or stopped, if necessary, to support the Aerial Survey Program. Fortunately, one (1) more excellent photographer was obtained when Commander W.M. HAWKES, Commanding Officer of the R4D unit, permitted Lt. A.E. STEIN, USNR to remain. Lt. Stein arrived with the R4D unit which he had photographed in 16mm. color since the unit was organized. It was highly desirable that each man be selected as carefully as possible for versatility, experience, willingness, initiative, and devotion to duty, because at this point 10 photographers and 2 photographic officers had to support the photographic requirements of six R4D airplanes. This included flying on survey missions, and accomplishing all the other photography possible until they were evacuated. Consequently, the following men were selected to remain on the ice from the Central Group:

			From the R4D Unit (TG68.5.1)		
BOWE, O.F.	CPHOM		HUFNER, F.C.	CPHOM	
WEED, A.E.	CPHOM		SWAIN, K.C.	PHOM1	
MALONE, T.H.	PHOM1		MCDONALD, W.L.	PHOM1	
RIZZOLLA, L.M.	PHOM1		JANSSON, C.L.	M/SGT.	USMC
TEIGAN, B. (N)	PHOM1		BALDWIN, G.E.	SGT.	USMC

All efforts were now turned to rigging the airplanes with cameras and photographic equipment. At the same time, photographic coverage in motion and still pictures was being made of the removal of the wheels from the airplanes and as much coverage as possible of all operations connected with the air program, such as; fueling, maintenance, pre-heating and starting engines, as well as activities connected with construction and research connected with the airstrip, bearing and loading capacity of the snow and shelf ice surfaces for airplane operations. The photographers were determined to photograph all of the subjects required by the Operation Plan, if possible, in addition to the Aerial Survey, despite the fact that the policy had been changed to eliminate all but the Aerial Project, if both could not be accomplished simultaneously.

The first flight was made and the tri-metrogon cameras operated to determine the proper exposure setting, and to test mechanical operation for possible malfunctions. Prior to departure of the ships, the following material was put ashore in anticipation that the United States Antarctic Service Expedition 1939 - 1941 Laboratory at West Base could be activated and that a small amount of processing could be done there. It was well known that cameras, especially those with mechanisms as complex as aircraft cameras, are bound to break down or develop malfunctions even in moderate climates, that are sometimes never discovered until the film has been processed. A camera with a defective shutter or a magazine which may begin overlapping exposures might be used on several important flights before it is discovered, unless the film can be processed and inspected frequently. Upon the return of the first flight, it was important that the film be developed to determine the proper exposure to be used on all subsequent survey flights and to check operation of equipment.

It was doubtful, with the limited personnel available, if any processing could be done after flight operations had begun. Consequently, a party loaded the necessary materials and equipment into a Weasel and went to West Base to develop the film. Considerable time was required to clean out the coal stove in the Science Building and melt enough snow for mixing chemicals. It was soon apparent that the best that could be accomplished was to develop a short test strip from each roll and return to the Base with the information prior to the take-off of any flight of consequence. The idea of processing any more film was abandoned as it had taken thirty-six hours (36) to process a short test strip from four rolls of film. The proper exposure was determined to be 1/300 sec. at f.6.3 on bright, clear days. If a force of about four additional men had been available, heat could have been maintained all the time in the Laboratory Building and subsequent processing would have been possible.

Many other conditions beyond the control of the photographic officer also adversely affected the photographic coverage. Extreme cold reduced note-taking, overcast restricted altitudes, as did lack of oxygen, continually changing terrain both flat and mountainous, as well as varying altitudes change intervals. Minor things, such as poor briefing facilities also were handicaps. The foregoing is not offered as excuses for possible poor results, but to point out the difficulties encountered, which, because of the "unknown" were very difficult to overcome.

XX PHOTOGRAPHIC PROJECTS

(A) Projects Numbers 1 and 2.

For tri-metrogon survey of interior, coastline, and islands of Antarctica, see Chart Number 1, in the Appendix for appropriate coverage. In connection with these two projects, the various operating groups made the following flights and photographs:

CENTRAL GROUP	WESTERN GROUP	EASTERN GROUP
28 flights	26 flights	17 flights
21,000 Aerial neg.	40,763 Aerial neg.	8,198 Aerial neg.

It is anticipated that two (2) 9 by 9 inch contact prints of each of these negatives will be made on double weight, waterproof, non-shrinkable paper as expeditiously as possible by the Naval Photographic Center, Anacostia, D.C., whose photographic complement will be augmented by the staff photographic complement of CTF 68 upon arrival in the United States.

(B) Projects Numbers 3 through 14.

Individual letters and reports will be forwarded to the various bureaus, offices, and other agencies who requested coverage of certain projects. In all instances, it is believed that more than ample photographic coverage was obtained in still and motion pictures in both black, white, and color. These bureaus, offices, and other agencies will be advised from time to time by CTF 68 when still and motion pictures are available for viewing by appointed representatives.

XXI AIR OPERATIONS

Air operations commenced as soon as all of the wheels were removed from the airplanes. While standing-by for flights, the aircrew photographers assisted in ground photographic coverage of all types; consequently, in many cases, when a flight was ordered, the photographers were not fresh. Because of the weather, very short notice was usually given and very seldom was it possible for the photographers to turn in for a few hours of rest immediately prior to a flight. When weather conditions became favorable, the flights took-off immediately or as soon as airplanes could be prepared. In some instances, when the photographers took-off, they had been working long periods without rest, carrying heavy motion picture cameras or

Annex 2 (a)

doing other equally strenuous work. Upon return from flights, it was necessary for each photographer to unload all of his film, place it in cans properly marked, and in general, prepare the airplane in the event of short notice for another flight. Most of the time, other members of a returning flight crew had turned in for a complete period of rest and begun another work period before the photographers were able to turn in.

The last flight was made on 21 February 1947. During the period of air operations, twenty-eight (28) flights and approximately 21,000 negatives were made, exclusive of local flights made in the JA-1 and OY-1 airplanes. For future photographic operations in either the Arctic or Antarctic Operation HIGHJUMP where it is necessary to obtain extensive photographic coverage in motion and still pictures in addition to an aerial survey program, it is strongly recommended that the following be adhered to:

(1) A larger complement of photographic personnel should be provided. Airplanes with installations as extensive as those on this operation should be manned by two (2) photographers.

(2) More adequate pre-flight planning as to exactly what territory is to be photographed. Each crew must be briefed thoroughly immediately prior to each flight, and interrogated immediately afterwards.

(3) Provide oxygen for higher level operation.

(4) Process film as it is exposed.

(5) Provide a larger complement of personnel. Recommend twenty-five (25) men for the operation of six (6) airplanes and a laboratory, in addition to other photographic requirements the magnitude of Operation HIGHJUMP.

(6) Seal camera compartment against wind-blast and heat to about plus forty-five (45) degrees Fahrenheit.

(7) Install Gremlin recorder in camera compartment.

(8) Install radio altimeter recorder, a clock, and a compass in camera compartment.

(9) Modify Gremlin recorder to accommodate a 9 by 9 inch magazine and 250 exposures.

(10) Install tri-metrogon cameras so that film travel in all three cameras is in the same direction in relation to airplane's heading.

(11) Improve oblique camera hatch in R4D-5's to afford easier access.

(12) Install storage space for spare loaded magazines.

(13) Provide viewing ports on each side of camera compartment.

On 22 February 1947, all personnel were evacuated from the Base by the U.S.S. BURTON ISLAND. Because of limited space on the ship, it was directed by the Central Group Commander that only valuable instruments and exposed film was to be evacuated.

Consequently, the following equipment and exposed film was loaded on the BURTON ISLAND along with enough unexposed film for coverage of the BURTON ISLAND'S passage through the ice pack:

```
21  K-17 6"
 4  K-17 12" aircraft cameras
 2  F-56 8¼ aircraft cameras
 6  F-56 8¼ Gremlin recorders
 2  K-20 aircraft cameras
 3  Mitchell motion picture cameras
 3  Cine Special 16mm. motion picture cameras
 5  Eyemo motion picture cameras
 5  Speedster 16mm. motion picture cameras
 5  Medalist cameras
 2  70DA 16mm. motion picture cameras
 2  Kodak 35mm.
 5  Speedgraphics
 1  Graflex
 1  8 x 10 view
 2  Cine magazine, motion picture
 2  Cones, aircraft, complete with lens and
        shutter K-17  12".
```

XXII JETTISONED CAMERAS

While flying an R4D-5 airplane, BuNo. 12415 about sixty (60) miles east of the Base on 20 February 1947, on a magnetometer flight, 1st. Lt. E.D. PITMAN, USMC, ordered the following listed aircraft cameras jettisoned when an engine failed and there was some delay in feathering the propeller:

```
Four   (4) K-17 6" aircraft cameras
Eight  (8) A5A aircraft camera magazines
One    (1) View finder
```

XXIII SUMMARY OF AIR AND GROUND OPERATIONS

During the period from the departure of the Central Group ships on 6 February 1947, until 23 February 1947, ten (10) photographers' mates and two (2) photographic officers accomplished the following:

(a) Exposed 39,500 feet of motion picture film.
(b) Made 21,000 aerial negatives.
(c) Took 900 still negatives.

Aerials, motion and still pictures were taken of the transit of the BURTON ISLAND through the ice pack.

Because of heavy swells, no material other than personal equipment could be transferred from the BURTON ISLAND to the MOUNT OLYMPUS after rendezvous with that vessel north of the ice pack. The following listed photographic personnel who were evacuated from the Base were transferred to the MOUNT OLYMPUS:

Lt. C.C. SHIRLEY   Lt. A.E. STEIN

BOWE, O.F.   CPHOM   RIZZOLLA, L.M.   PHOM1
WEED, A.E.   CPHOM   SWAIN, K.C.   PHOM1
JANSSON, C.L.   M/SGT. USMC   MCDONALD, W.L.   PHOM1
HUFNER, F.G.   CPHOM   TEIGAN, B. (N).   PHOM1
MALONE, T.H.   PHOM1   BALDWIN, G.E., SGT. USMC

        These officers and men were immediately organized and
began the task of bringing the files up to date. At New Zealand,
the exposed film and photographic material left on the BURTON
ISLAND was transferred to the MOUNT OLYMPUS, except for the
following which that vessel transferred to the MERRICK:

8   Radar cameras APS 15
6   Complete with scope and (2) magazines (planes)
2   Complete with no scope and (1) magazine (ship)
7   Complete with no scope and (1) magazine (PHILIPPINE SEA)
1   70DA 16mm. motion picture cameras.
1   Medalist
2   Cine magazine 16mm. motion picture
6   GSAP cameras
2   GSAP bore sighting tools
1   Model "J" Smith aerial dryer
1   Gremlin Recorder less camera
24 Dark slides A5A magazines
6   Dark slides F-56 magazines

        Immediately after departure of the MOUNT OLYMPUS from
New Zealand, the photographic personnel were organized into two
(2) twelve (12) hour shifts, working seven (7) days a week in an
attempt to complete processing all aerial and still film, and to
complete filing all stills and print sufficient photographs
for completion of Task Force reports before reaching the Canal
Zone.

XXIV.   MOTION PICTURE SECTION

        At a Staff conference held on 3 November 1946, when
objectives of the entire operation were fully discussed, it
became apparent that a feature length motion picture of
considerable value to the Armed Forces and of interest to the
public could be produced in addition to historical, technical,
and training films. The initial problem was to photograph the
operation in a manner to insure continuity in recording a
running story involving the activities of thirteen ships and
4,000 men over a period of six months. The general requirements
were written into the Operation Plan outlining certain motion
picture footage which would tend to weld together a series of

unrelated technical pictures into feature length motion picture in both color and black and white. Special emphasis was placed upon obtaining newsreel coverage highlighting the activities of the entire operation. Therefore, the motion picture would necessarily consist of the types of coverage previously mentioned taken in such a manner that any one type would compliment the others. The inability of the Navy to furnish motion picture specialists necessitated the Task Force to request qualified motion picture cameraman from the Army and Marine Corps. One additional photographic officer (Chief Warrant) USMC with motion picture experience, and four U.S. Army motion picture technicians were obtained. These motion picture specialists were distributed in the Task Force in a manner to insure professional coverage from the beginning and to act as instructors, if necessary, in training other assigned photographic personnel in the method of coverage for production and newsreel footage. The interest shown, and the ability demonstrated in obtaining motion picture coverage by all photographic personnel in the Central Group was most commendable. Since there were no public relation personnel in any capacity attached to motion picture photography, it became, from the beginning, the duty of the photographers not only to take pictures, but to plan sequences; lay out the story both in written form and to record commentary information, and at the same time keep in mind the continuity to last over a period of six months. Only by all hands exercising great zeal and paying strict attention to duty could this program be successfully carried out.

During the first part of November, in compliance with a Task Force request, Commander C.H. CLARK, Officer in Charge of Training Films, Navy Department, called a conference of various Bureau personnal to discuss training film requirements on the Operation. The Task Force Photographic Officer and Motion Picture Officer attended this conference. As a result of this meeting held in the Office of Public Information, many additional requests for desired motion picture coverage were discussed. Also, a promise was exacted from the Office of Public Information to furnish wire recorders for field use. Two recorders were placed aboard the MOUNT OLYMPUS under the supervision of Task Force Communications. These were unable to be removed to the ice shelf because of their continuous use in recording radio broadcasts, etc..

The first motion picture coverage of Task Force Sixty-Eight began on 17 November 1946, when the Naval Photographic Center complied with a Task Force request to photograph the activities of Task Force personnel engaged in training as sled dog handlers near Tamworth, New Hampshire, and to establish background footage pertaining to the dogs that were taken on the expedition. This coverage extended to the transfer of personnel and sled dogs from the Chinook Kennels to Boston and thence to Norfolk, and terminated when the Task Force departed Norfolk on 2 December 1946.

About the middle of November, an outline of motion pictures to be obtained prior to the departure of the Task Force for the Antarctic was distributed to photographic officers of the command ships and to the Office of Public Information. This outline was designed to place before the public a preliminary introduction to the Task Force and its objectives through the medium of the newsreels. When advised by the Task Force, the Office of Public Information notified all newsreel companies of Task Force activities and locations. A number of representatives of these companies participated in covering the operation until the ships' departure from Norfolk and San Diego. As a result of these efforts, subsequent reports indicate that the Task Force received wide-spread newsreel publicity throughout the United States and some of this footage was shown in foreign newsreels.

From a photographic standpoint, whether successful or not, the definite departure in motion picture procedure in this operation from war time principles to peace time necessities should be discussed. Heretofore, the Office of Public Information had headed motion pictures with experienced scenario writers, directors, and photographers on a Naval operation of any consequence, and ordinarily, several newsreel companies would be represented. However, this Task Force was to rely entirely upon services of general photographic officers and enlisted photographers plus four Army motion picture cameramen to film one of the most comprehensive motion pictures ever undertaken by the service. Through the efforts of interested parties outside the Task Force, one official pamphlet pertaining to motion pictures was received just prior to departure Norfolk. Some well known elementary policies were discussed in this pamphlet. Although these instructions were well received and studied by all photographers, it was found that they were, in effect, restatements and slight enlargements pertaining to subjects and policies previously outlined in the Task Force Operation Plan. General conditions in the Antarctic and operational details involved, which this pamphlet should have embraced in detail but did not, can only be written by one with comprehensive Antarctic experience.

When the Motion Picture Officer reported to the MOUNT OLYMPUS at Norfolk, 27 November 1946, it was discovered that the motion picture equipment was aboard but some film had not been received. The inability of the Naval Supply system to make final deliveries of film quantities in speed groups ordered caused concern. This resulted in the redistribution of film in the Task Force where possible. The substitution of speed groups of the majority of 35mm. film received was too high for quality results under photographic conditions that were to be encountered in the Antarctic. After unsuccessful attempts to obtain quantities of 35mm. film at Panama, a division of 400' stock was affected with the PINE ISLAND group which had received only a small amount of its original order. By conserving this film, it was anticipated that both the Central Group and Western Group might have enough to last until another supply could be furnished by the PHILIPPINE SEA which was ordered by dispatch for distribution later to all command ships. The motion picture cameras were checked for repair and accessories were inventoried. Some minor maintenance was necessary on the Eyemo and Mitchell type cameras, but all were in running condition within a short time. The Cine Special and Speedster type cameras were found to be in good condition from the beginning.

Motion picture coverage of the loading and preparations for departure were made on board and in the vicinity of the various ships. Enroute to Scott Island via the Panama Canal, numerous phases of shipboard activities were filmed and a constant schooling of personnel in the handling of motion picture equipment and methods of coverage conducted. The high-lights recalled of the trip consisted mainly of canal transit, stay in Panama, reunion of the three Husky puppies with their mother aboard the MOUNT OLYMPUS at Panama after being stolen in Norfolk, crossing the line ceremony, refueling at sea, Christmas, first icebergs encountered, demonstration and issuing of cold weather clothing, and navigating through fog and icebergs. Short scenes of personnel activities from Norfolk to Scott Island were taken in an effort to create a "transition" of the gradual change in weather, the preparations for transiting the ice pack, and at the same time, planning and photographing sequences designed to combine and hold together in one continuous story the highlights mentioned above. The first whale was sighted 24 December, but was not close enough to the ship to photograph. Although every effort was made to photograph whales and bird life, very little, if any, presentable footage was obtained of these subjects while enroute to the Antarctic.

Upon entering the iceberg and sea ice area on 26 December, a photographic watch was established on the MOUNT OLYMPUS and maintained throughout the entire time the Task Force slowly progressed through the ice pack to the Ross Ice Shelf and the Bay of Whales which was reached 15 January 1947. This proved to be a cold and uncomfortable vigilance for all photographers, but the cameras were manned enthusiastically and often when one was relieved of the regular watch, he obtained another camera and proceeded to stand an unofficial watch for hours at a time. By this method, it is believed that the story of the ice transit has been thoroughly and efficiently photographed both in color and black and white.

By the time the rendezvous of the ships of the Central Group was affected at Scott Island, 31 December 1946, photographic personnel showing the most interest and adaptability in using motion picture cameras were temporarily assigned to take motion pictures. These photographers, totaling five, in addition to the two Army technicians, were drilled daily in many phases of motion picture cameras and especially the value of employing a variety of lenses, angles, and distances; the importance of slating and writing up data sheets; the selection of events concerning an activity, which was the most important to photograph; the trick of anticipating action in a given set of unrehearsed circumstances and previously placing themselves at vantage points.

The Staff Motion Picture Officer, the two Army cameramen, and one still photographer transferred with the Flag from the MOUNT OLYMPUS to the NORTHWIND on New Year's Eve, 1946, to obtain coverage of transit through the ice pack from the ship. Both color, black and white motion pictures and still pictures were taken from the air as well as from aboard the NORTHWIND during the fifteen days the Central Group worked its way through the ice pack. A constant watch was maintained by these four photographers during the transit. The regular working hours of all hands was between the hours of 0600 until 2400, after which time, one man was left on watch and would employ any or all cameras if necessary. In the event that more help was considered necessary, one or more of the remaining three photographers would be called to assist. Almost every night these men had to be ordered to go off watch and turn in. Their enthusiasm was so great, that they insisted on staying on deck constantly.

The arrangement of coverage on the MOUNT OLYMPUS and NORTHWIND constituted excellent long distance team coverage for photography as it afforded reverse angles in the difficult problem of filming the story of the icebreaker clearing a path for the other ships, and the method of extricating ice-bound ships from two angles.

Both still and motion pictures were made of difficulties surrounding the experiences of the submarine SENNET and its eventual enforced retirement from the Task Force. Reverse angles were obtained from each ship, that is from the NORTHWIND and the SENNET. It is believed that every conceivable phase of the ice pack transit of the Central Group was thoroughly photographed. A boom was rigged over the side to obtain a better view of the bow of the icebreaker in action cutting a path through ice, so thick that often the NORTHWIND would "stall".

14 January 1947, the Central Group ships broke into navigable waters of the Ross Sea. The Flag returned to the MOUNT OLYMPUS late in the afternoon of the 14th. All exposed film was taken to the MOUNT OLYMPUS for packing and shipping

at the first opportunity. The next day, the Motion Picture
Officer, one Army camerman, and one still photographer
returned with RAdm Cruzen and others of the Staff to the
NORTHWIND to enter the Bay of Whales. This proved to be one
of the most singular tasks of the entire trip for the NORTH-
WIND and consequently, afforded excellent photographic
subjects. The bay was frozen over solid with bay ice, ranging
from five to ten feet thick. The NORTHWIND began the task of
breaking and clearing out huge sections of this ice to afford
the Central Group's ships ample space to enter the bay and moor.
The first party on the ice consisted of four staff and Observer
Officers from the MOUNT OLYMPUS. These officers were photographed as they left the NORTHWIND for the shelf ice in search
of a suitable site for a landing strip and camp. Three aerial
(helicopter) flights were made on this date, from which both
motion and still pictures were taken of the entire area as well
as showing the NORTHWIND breaking up and clearing the ice out of
the Bay of Whales. Also, one MOUNT OLYMPUS photographer and
three NORTHWIND photographers went onto the bay ice and photographed the landing party as well as the actions of the NORTH-
WIND clearing the bay of ice. On the evening of the 17th of
January, the NORTHWIND had the Bay of Whales sufficiently cleared
to permit the YANCEY to enter and moor without incident.
Consequently, the Staff Photographic Officer, the Motion Picture
Officer, and eight photographers transferred from the MOUNT
OLYMPUS to the YANCEY for this operation. These eight photographers
and two officers covered many aspects of operations on the ice
with motion and still pictures from 17 January to 6 February,
when some of them were shifted from the camp site to the ship in
order to evacuate the MOUNT OLYMPUS, YANCEY, and MERRICK from the
Bay of Whales and the Ross Sea before freezing conditions became
serious.

In discussing briefly the personnel for this operation,
it is pointed out that the number of personnel was far below that
which the motion picture coverage required. These men, operating
under extremely adverse field conditions, put in consecutive
working hours which would ordinarily require two and one half
times that number of men employed under average conditions. Thirty
consecutive hours without rest was not unusual, with a maximum
of fifty-six hours recorded for one CPHOM and fifty-two for one
PHOM1. Because of the long hours, the cold and fatiguing conditions,
after photographers had willingly and voluntarily remained on the
job, their efficiency was somewhat diminished after the first
twenty-four hours. When men became fatigued so that results of
achievements might be affected, they covered activities of less
importance and a photographer more refreshed, when available,
assumed the duties of the first cameraman. To the reader who
may not be familiar with the numerous and simultaneous projects
requiring motion picture photography at the Base and vicinity,
it might be surmised that the eight men and two officers would
be sufficient for covering all operations without working

so many consecutive hours. However, because of working under
normal factors of Antarctic conditions, such as; low temperatures,
lack of communications, scarcity and slowness of transportation,
the rapid development of engineering and technical projects in
widely separated areas, the photographic personnel, in order to
obtain sequence and continuity were required to be on the alert
and patrol the entire area continuously, much in the manner of
an established sentry patrol. Coupling the above with the fact
that continuous daylight prevailed, and that part of these men
were shooting still pictures and parallel coverage when possible
with both 16mm. Kodachrome and 35mm. black and white pictures,
it can be readily understood that a shortage of personnel prevailed. It must also be kept in mind that an effort was maintained to record all motion picture coverage from the standpoint
of obtaining newsreel footage where applicable and feature
production and technical information on all footage. All motion
picture coverage was made from all three standpoints. The
results of this endeavor will be interesting, especially when
viewed from the fact that these photographers had, at the beginning of the operation, only elementary knowledge of motion pictures.
Although it is to be hoped that the objectives were attained, the
important part at this time is the fact that these men showed
keen interest, personal initiative, and pride of profession in
their voluntary willingness to forego sleep and rest so that no
desirable motion picture footage would be lacking upon completion
of this operation. The admirable characteristics shown by these
men are worthy of the highest praise.

XXV MOTION PICTURE FILM

The bulk of the motion picture film ordered in October
1946, was not received until delivery was made via the
PHILIPPINE SEA and NORTHWIND, arriving in Little America 31
January 1947. The enforced conservation of the 100 ft. stock
up to this delivery date will be evident in the scarcity of
scenes and the shortened sequences in the former and the lack
of general quality of exposure of the 400 ft. stock of high
speed film. These could cause the final production to be somewhat inferior in quality production than was anticipated.

The amount of motion picture film left at the Base seems
so excessive that it is felt necessary to include the following
information. The Central and Eastern Groups left Norfolk without
receipt of any 35mm. by 400 ft. motion picture film. However, the
Central Group received 208 rolls of speed group 100 instead of
speed group 50 via NATS in the Canal Zone, which was equally
divided with the Eastern Group. The Chief of Photographic Services
was immediately requested to send additional motion picture film

to all groups via the PHILIPPINE SEA which was to depart Norfolk
in early January. Again speed group 50 was requested, because
the Central Group did not have neutral density filters to use
with speed group 100, and it was doubtful if either of the other
groups did. An excessive amount of 35mm. by 400 ft. speed group
100 was received by the Central Group. All speed group 50
received via the PHILIPPINE SEA was used, except the 200 ft. rolls.
Consequently, the following listed film was left at the Base
because of lack of transportation:

428 rolls 400' by 35mm.		Speed group 100
91 rolls 200' by 35mm.		Speed group 100
188 rolls 200' by 35mm.		Speed group 50

XXVI   SUPPLY

The inability to deliver quantities of sensitized stock
on sixty days' notice indicates that, since the cessation of
hostilities, such stock is probably not accumulated in large
amounts as was the case during the war. Therefore, it is
recommended that, when possible, more time be allowed Supplying
Agencies in accumulating and delivering stock to peace time
operations of such wide scope as Operation HIGHJUMP.

XXVII   MOTION PICTURE CAMERAS

Only one of five (5) Eyemo cameras performed adequately
in temperatures below plus ten degrees Fahrenheit, and this one
(1) failed to operate at about zero degrees Fahrenheit. The
primary difficulty experienced, with the exception of temperatures,
was not new or indigenous to Antarctic conditions. On this
operation, as well as many others, it has been found that the
35mm. Eyemo collects an excessive amount of emulsion on the pressure
plate, resulting in "emulsion scratches" and the slowing and
choking down of the cameras. It is understood that the Bell and
Howell motion picture company has manufactured a new type pressure
plate which eliminates this trouble. It is recommended that, if
available, these plates be supplied to all ships and stations
now using 35mm. Eyemo and that future camera issues carry this
special plate.

XXVIII   BASE CAMP PHOTOGRAPHIC HEADQUARTERS FOR USE IN THE ANTARCTIC

The Base camp headquarters for the Central Group
on Operation HIGHJUMP consisted of two (2) tents; one seventeen
(17) ft. by twenty (20) ft., wall tent used as an operational
tent, and one (1) fourteen (14) ft. by fourteen (14) ft. wall
tent used as a storage tent only. The main value of getting
material under housing is to prevent digging it out of drifted

snow every time something is needed which causes a loss of time, a great amount of unnecessary work, and a possible loss of valuable material.

The following is a description of a serviceable photographic headquarters storage and working space for a unit on the ice where it is necessary to use tents. One (1) twenty ft. by forty ft.,(20' x 40') circus type, three pole tent, with two layers of flooring and about ten (10) inches of air space between them for better heat insulation. The walls of this tent should have two by four inch skeleton bracing completely around the inside of the tent, high enough from the floor, about four (4) feet, to install one width of plywood. This skeleton bracing and plywood liner is necessary to brace the tent and also serve as an insulator against cold. There should be a false ceiling constructed of unbleached muslin or similar material installed in the tent to serve as a light and heat reflector, as well as an insulator. An entrance should be constructed at each end of the tent. One end of the tent to be used for camera storage, the center for film and miscellaneous equipment, and the other end to be utilized as a work-shop and dark-room. The latter section is the only section to be heated. The dark-room, about six (6) ft. by ten (10)ft. can be constructed on one side of the room and the work-shop on the other. A larger, but the same type of stove as used on Operation HIGHJUMP, should be installed in this end of the tent. The necessity for a larger stove is not only for adequate heat for comfort, but also for holding a container large enough to melt snow to obtain water for the dark-room processing. This will facilitate a better and more thorough coverage of all photographic coverage projects. A 15 KW 110 Volt generator is also necessary for a unit of this type, not only for lighting, but to furnish power for shop tools, film dryers, etc..

XXIX   PHOTOGRAPHIC TRANSPORTATION IN ANTARCTICA

A photographic unit based on the ice, as was that of the Central Group on Operation HIGHJUMP, should be equipped with transportation, independent of the regularly assigned transportation unit. The field of coverage is so great and the necessity of having photographers in several places at once, makes transportation as important to a base photographic unit as its cameras.

The first day on the ice, the photographic unit was fortunate enough to secure and retain a Weasel for transportation, with the exception of one week, for the entire operation. There were only eight vehicles for personnel on the operation. After several of them had broken down, it was necessary to recall all vehicles and enter them into a transportation pool with assigned drivers. It was then up to the Photographic Officer to try to anticipate the necessary photographic coverage for twenty-four hours in advance in order to insure transportation at the proper time. As a result, there were several important events that had to be reenacted in order to get the necessary coverage, causing hardship for all concerned.

After the ships of the Central Group had left the Bay of Whales enroute to Scott Island, the transportation problem eased up again, and the photographic unit was again fortunate in securing transportation. The photographic work progressed with greater efficiency and a greater field of coverage was obtained in general.

The type of vehicle used on Operation HIGHJUMP for personnel transportation and light cargo, was the Army "Weasel" Specification M29C-Cargo Carrier (refer War Department Technical Manual TM9-772). This type vehicle proved highly satisfactory. Photographic coverage as obtained would not have been possible without the Weasel.

(a) A 35mm. Mitchell Tripod was mounted on the front of the Weasel affording camera elevation of about ten (10) feet from the surface of the snow. With the Mitchell mounted in this manner it not only afforded better coverage because of the elevation, but far greater coverage in a large field of activity by being able to move the Weasel with the Mitchell camera in a mounted position. Although the Weasel is an excellent vehicle for an operational photographic unit in the Antarctic, it is recommended that the following modifications be made:

(a) Install a solid top to accommodate a working space for a motion picture camera and operator.
(b) Remove all excess gear from the inside of the cargo compartment and install racks for spare film and cameras.
(c) Install a magazine loading dark-box on the engine cover to accommodate magazines as large as the K-18. The door of this box should open outward to facilitate using the box while standing alongside the Weasel.
(d) Install a 12 volt battery with generator, powered by the Weasel engine, with outlets enough to accommodate at least two cameras.
(e) Install a 5 KVA generator on the stern deck for 110 V. AC. to accommodate the high-speed camera motor and facilitate using several lights for interior motion pictures inside of tents, buildings, etc., where no other power is available. It is strongly recommended that at least one, and if possible, two of these vehicles be assigned permanently to any photographic unit that is based on ice for operations. It is also recommended that each of these vehicles be equipped with the Army M-1, one (1) ton cargo sled.

XXX   REPORT ON SUB-ZERO OPERATION OF CAMERAS

(a) K-17 6 inch (Tri-metrogon)

The type cameras used in the R4D aircraft for reconnaissance survey were new and unused. The cameras were received in Norfolk; checked, cleaned, de-lubricated, and re-lubricated with a limited amount of ANG-3A grease and AN-O-6A oil. One shim was removed from the armature shaft of the case drive motor to give more clearance between the end of the armature and housing. This was done to prevent binding when operating in sub-zero weather, as two different types of metals contract different amounts. This proved highly successful as no malfunctions occurred in the operation of case drives. The shutter wind and trip lever coupling assemblies were not checked for clearance between coupling shafts and housings, and as a result, several of these assemblies froze up at sub-zero temperatures. In some instances, the shutters slowed down to a speed of approximately one (1) second. This difficulty was overcome in every camera as it occurred at the Base, by removing the shutter wind and trip lever coupling assemblies and increasing the clearance between the coupling shafts and housings by using emory and crocus cloth. After increasing the working tolerances, the cameras operated perfectly at minus forty (-40) degrees Fahrenheit. Because of the lack of shop facilities and sufficient personnel, it was impossible to prepare all of the cameras as mentioned above after the first malfunction; consequently, there were recurrences of slow shutters.

It is recommended that working tolerances of close-fitting moving parts of cameras of this type be made larger when they are to be used in sub-zero temperatures; and that cameras be de-lubricated and re-lubricated with a minute amount of ANG-3A grease and AN-O-6A oil. If old, well-worn cameras are used, all that is necessary is to remove one shim from the motor armature shaft and re-lubricate with a slight amount of the above specified grease and oil.

(b) K-17 12 inch

The K-17 12" cameras were old and well-worn when received but after being placed in service, cleaned; de-lubricated and re-lubricated with a slight amount of ANG-3A grease and AN-O-6A oil, they operated perfectly at the lowest temperature encountered (-40) degrees Fehrenheit.

(c) F-56 8¼ inch (hand-held oblique)

After receiving these cameras in Norfolk, they were cleaned, de-lubricated and re-lubricated with a slight amount of ANG-3A grease and AN-O-6A oil, after which they operated perfectly both on the surface and in the air.

(d) GREMLIN RECORDER (F-56 20in. cone and drive with
F-56 8¼"lens)

These cameras were assembled and installed by the
Assembly and Repair Department at Naval Air Station, Norfolk, but
were not checked or re-lubricated by this unit, because they were
reported to have been made ready for sub-zero temperatures. The
only malfunctioning was the shearing of the taper pins in one (1)
shutter spring assembly. It is not known if this was caused from
continued use or the possibility of a freely-moving assembly
working against a slightly-bound assembly caused by sub-zero temperatures. It is believed that the taper pins had crystalized.

(e) F-56 Magazines

These magazines developed the following malfunctions:
(1) One (1) magazine was found to have been received on board one
half (½) turn out of time; resulting in no vacuum at the time of
exposure.
(2) One (1) magazine was returned from a flight with a sheared taper
pin in the take-up assembly.
(3) Another magazine sheared a stud in the spring clutch assembly.

(f) Aerial Cameras - General Recommendations for.

It is strongly recommended that all aerial cameras,
regardless of type, when they are prepared for use in sub-zero
temperatures, be given greater working tolerances between close-
fitting moving parts especially where two (2) or more different
types of metal are working together. This conclusion was derived
from the fact that the only malfunction caused directly by low
temperatures, was with the new cameras, which in this instance,
was the K-17 6 inch camera. All other cameras were old and had
been used extensively and all close-fitting, moving parts were
worn enough to permit free operation; consequently, they did not
freeze up in sub-zero temperatures.

XXXI   STILL CAMERAS

(a) Speedgraphics (4 x 5)

These cameras proved very unsatisfactory in low
temperatures. At plus ten (10) degrees Fehrenheit, the shutters
became sluggish, and to make them function, it was necessary to
advance the shutter speed selectors to 1/400 sec. to obtain a
working speed of approximately 1/75 sec. The focal plane shutters
of these cameras operated efficiently at zero (0) degrees Fahrenheit

but at any lower temperatures, the efficiency dropped considerably. It is strongly recommended that a special camera, similar to the combat graphic be designed with the following shutter features for use in an Antarctic operation :

(1) A shutter designed with as few working parts as possible.
(2) Shutter speeds of 1/50, 1/100, 1/200, and 1/400 of a second, are all that are required in an Antarctic operation.

It is believed that a very successful design would be a shutter similar to one in some box cameras with a strong enough scissor spring to operate the shutter at 1/400 sec. and a retard pallet as in the aerial camera shutter to reduce speed to 1/200, 1/100, and 1/50 sec. This type of shutter would also eliminate the cocking mechanism. A contact point flash synchronizer could very easily be adapted to this type of shutter.

(b) Graflex

The operation of the focal plane shutter type camera could be used in sub-zero weather if stronger springs were used for curtain and tension springs although the more versatile speedgraphic with the shutter recommended in the previous paragraph, would be all that would be necessary for a 4 x 5 camera.

(c) Kodak Medalist

This type camera was not used extensively, except by one photographer, who used it for all stills. The Medalist proved very satisfactory at the lowest temperature (-23°F.) encountered on the ground at the Base. The Medalist is a fine supplementary still camera and could be given to trail parties and other activities to cover events where photographers could not be present. It is suggested that the Model Two (2) be used however, as the improvements in this camera make it more desirable than Model One (1).

(d) Kodak "35"

The Kodak "35", although not very extensively used, proved to be, like the Medalist, a handy still camera for those other than official photographers for B&W and color; and a very handy cover-up color camera for an official photographer to carry when shooting B&W stills.

XXXII   MOTION PICTURE CAMERAS

(a) 35mm. Mitchell

The only malfunction of this type camera was in the

large new type 12 volt Mitchell motor. This motor would only operate the camera from 12 to 18 frames per second at temperatures of plus fifteen (15) degrees Fahrenheit. It is strongly recommended that the small old type 12 volt Mitchell motor be used in sub-zero weather. This motor operated the Mitchell camera efficiently at the lowest temperature encountered. The friction head tripod is not satisfactory for sub-zero operation. It is recommended that the gyro head tripod be used.

(b) 35mm. Eyemo

These cameras proved very unsatisfactory for sub-zero operations. At temperatures as high as plus fifteen (15) degrees Fahrenheit, they would not operate at 24 frames per second, and eventually stall completely.

(c) 16mm. Cine Special

This camera was not satisfactory in sub-zero temperatures since it began to slow down at minus three (3) degrees Fahrenheit. It is recommended that this camera be fitted with a turret-head to accommodate at least three (3) lenses, and a 12 volt motor for power instead of the spring.

(d) 16mm. Bell and Howell Auto-load Speedsters

The auto-load had a tendency to freeze up at the lower temperatures, but could be relied upon for efficient operation at minus fifteen (15) degrees Fahrenheit. They proved to be highly successful "quick fill-in" 16mm. cameras.

(e) Recommendations for Motion Picture Cameras

For sub-zero operation and for a wide field of coverage, when transportation is at a premium as it was on Operation HIGHJUMP, it is highly recommended that a small portable 12 volt motor drive, quick-load, magazine type 35mm. camera be designed to accommodate at least 100 ft. of film. It is also recommended that this quick-load magazine be designed similar to the auto-load Speedster or the Cine Special, so that it would not be necessary to thread film into the camera in sub-zero temperature.

XXXIII   SECURITY OF EQUIPMENT AND MATERIAL

The proper security of valuable cameras, film, and material, constituted a major problem in the Antarctic. The best security possible on Operation HIGHJUMP was a storage tent with a door which was kept locked, and this was not adequate security. Before the erection of the tent, material was usually stored in a cache on the ice which afforded no security whatsoever. Consequently, photographic material and equipment was found broken into on several occasions, and a portion of it was missing. On future operations, it is suggested that strong-boxes be constructed for each photographer. Equipment and material could be issued and stowed in the strong-box before landing on the ice. Of course, it would be very important to erect a tent or other proper shelter as soon as possible for storage of these boxes and for operational convenience against blizzards and drifts. Kits similar to cruise boxes should be constructed for storage and security of film when it is issued, and later when it is exposed.

XXXIV   RADAR CAMERAS

Radar cameras were distributed to the following ships of Task Force Sixty-Eight for obtaining photographs of weather, icebergs, and other obstructions to navigation:

U.S.S. MOUNT OLYMPUS	(AGC-8)	U.S.S. HENDERSON	(DD-785)
U.S.S. CURRITUCK	(AV-7)	U.S.S. BROWNSON	(DD-868)
U.S.S. PINE ISLAND	(AV-12)	U.S.S. SENNET	(SS-408)
U.S.S. CANISTEO	(AO-99)	U.S.S. BURTON ISLAND	(AG-88)
U.S.S. CACAPON	(AO-52)	U.S.C.G.C. NORTHWIND	(WAG-282)

XXXV   TECHNIQUE AND HINTS ON CAMERA OPERATION

(a) Never breath on lenses, as breath will condense and freeze and it is very difficult to remove ice satisfactorily in sub-zero temperatures. The same precaution applies to eye-pieces and focusing screens. Form the habit of breathing through the mouth when using a Graflex and keep the mouth outside of the hood. It is very difficult to clean a lens outdoors in the normal manner, as heat transmitted from the hand through the lens paper causes condensation and icing of the lens surface. The hand should be insulated with a mitten when cleaning a lens in sub-zero weather.

(b) Never take a warm lens out to photograph a blizzard or snow storm as the drifting snow will melt upon contact with the warm lens surface. If a cold lens is used, the snow will bounce from the surface and cause no ill effects whatever.

(c) All diaphragm leaves must be free of oil and grease and the index control ring should be made as free as possible.

(d) It is best to keep all of the cameras for outdoor use stored at outside temperatures. In sub-zero weather, if a cold camera is taken into a warm building, condensation will immediately form. Considerable time is required for thawing and drying before it may be used again, either inside or outside. If a camera must be taken indoors, it should be insulated to permit a gradual thawing. On the other hand, no harm is done by taking a warm camera outdoors if there is no drifting snow or snowfall.

(e) Keep bare skin of face and fingers away from the unpainted metallic surfaces of cameras in sub-zero weather.

XXXVI PUBLIC INFORMATION PICTORIAL SUMMARY

Following the issue of the Navy Department press release announcing the 1947 Antarctic Development Project, an invitation was extended by the Pictorial Section of the Office of Public Information to all the major still picture outlets to participate on either individual or pool basis. At the time, the Motion Picture Section invited all major newsreel companies to send representatives. In view of the extended period of the Operation and the expense of maintaining a representative in the field, none of the still or motion picture companies elected to participate. There was general agreement among the companies that extensive Navy plans to cover the Operation eliminated competitive advantage. Metro-Goldwyn-Mayer expressed an interest in making a feature or featurette from Navy footage. Mr. Fred Sparks performed a dual function as reporter and photographer for Colliers and Look Magazines, but his status aboard was that of a correspondent.

Complete working-press still and motion picture coverage of pre-departure and departure activities of the Task Force was obtained. Special Navy coverage was requested and supplied.

Enroute Panama, ships of the Central and Eastern Groups were requested to obtain as many candid portraits and individual action close-ups of key officer and enlisted personnel as possible prior to arrival. Approximately three hundred fifty of these plus a selection of pictures of general news interest were forwarded by air to Washington, for hometown and general release, from Panama.

Enroute back to the U.S., prior to arrival in Panama, a three-hour daily, except Sunday, radiophoto schedule was initiated with Washington and maintained, except for occasional lapses due to atmospheric conditions until 6 March. Radiophoto units in San Francisco, Honolulu, and Guam participated in the schedules and frequently relayed pictures to Washington, when conditions precluded direct contact. A total of one hundred ninety pictures, which are in effect, a picture history of the highlights of the activities of the Central Group of Task Force Sixty-Eight,

were transmitted during this period. This figure is broken
down by months:

December - 62   January - 73 February - 48   March - 7

            To expedite release to the public, all films, still
and motion pictures in black and white and color, exposed up
to the time of the arrival of the U.S.S. PHILIPPINE SEA in
the vicinity of Scott Island was placed aboard that carrier
for return to the United States. This shipment included
photography from all units of the Task Force. A complete
file of all radiophoto prints transmitted up to that time was
forwarded also, so that transmission quality could be judged.

            In the course of the Operation, advantage was taken
of occasional rendezvous of units from different groups to
affect the transferring and forwarding of pictures to the flagship for radio transmission. Pictures of the PBM crash
survivors and of a helicopter mishap are cited as examples.

            On the return voyage, picture releases were prepared
and issued at the two ports of call, Wellington, New Zealand,
and Panama.

            More than 4,000 contact prints, representing the
black and white still coverage of the Operation were mounted
on file cabinet size cards, captioned and classified by subject
by the photographic staff. This is regarded as an ideal presentation
of photographic material for quick inspection. This file was
flown to Washington from Panama to facilitate screening by the
working-press. A selection of approximately four hundred contact
prints were supplied the Pictorial Public Information Officer
and will be made into a similar file for permanent retention in
the Office of Public Information.

XXXVII   FILM

   (a) Motion Picture

            Brittleness of film from cold and dehydration
necessitates extreme care when loading and threading a motion
picture camera. If the camera is not loaded exactly right, the
film will break.

            There is a tendency to load and thread a camera rapidly
because of the necessity to use bare hands, and this is
conducive to carelessness. It is desirable to use skin-tight,
cotton, silk, or rayon gloves for loading, as they will prevent
the skin from adhering to the unpainted metallic parts. They

offer very little protection from cold and until the cameraman becomes proficient at speedy loading, he will have to stop several times to warm his hands.

Because of dehydration, it is best not to load an excessive amount of film in advance. It should remain in sealed containers as long as possible.

There is no apparent loss of emulsion speed because of cold.

(b) Film Pack

Film pack is the ideal film for professional size still photography. More of it can be carried, and it is more readily loaded and unloaded than cut film. With very little care in pulling the tabs, no breakage will occur. The film packs should be sealed about six (6) to a package in an airtight container to prevent dehydration until immediately before using. Another good feature about film pack is that each sheet is numbered, which facilitates identification from written references after it is processed. Cut film does not always bear sheet numbers. The greatest disadvantage of cut film is the fact that it may become necessary to unload and reload outdoors in a changing bag, which is most miserable when the temperature is minus thirty (-30) degrees Fahrenheit or colder. This kind of loading operation once started, has to be completed before the hands can be warmed. After several loadings of cut film, under these conditions, there will be no skin left on the finger tips from handling the unpainted steel film septums.

(c) Exposures

The amount of actinic light is very deceiving, and normal exposure is almost impossible without a light meter. There is much more reflected than incident light on an overcast day on the shelf or bay ice. This is because the bottom of the overcast is white and reflects most of the light back to the surface again.

On clear days a higher light meter reading is obtained from the snow surface than from the sky. It is impossible to obtain a reading with a Weston or General Electric Meter by pointing it at the snow surface, unless the sun is lower than about ten (10) degrees altitude. The indicating needle on these meters will swing completely off the scale when they are pointed at the white surface, if the sun is higher. It has been found that a normal reading may be obtained when the meter reading is taken in a shadow on the surface on a sunny day, and from the object to be photographed on an overcast day. For further information on an overcast day, see Appendix I in this report.

XXXVIII   ANTARCTIC LIGHT

(a) Color Temperature

To determine the color temperature of light in the Antarctic under various light conditions, a Harrison and Harrison Color Temperature Meter was used, and both Ansco color and Kodachrome film was exposed using various correction filters. Considerable information should be gained when resulting transparancies are compared with the meter readings obtained to determine the composition of the spectrum in Antarctica.

(b) Ultra-Violet

Several tests were made to determine the amount of ultra-violet light over the continent. All film exposed for these tests has been returned for control processing and when resulting negatives are compared with collected data, it is anticipated that the amount of ultra-violet light in the spectrum will thus be determined.

XXXIX   TASK FORCE PHOTOGRAPHIC ACCOMPLISHMENTS

Central Group

35mm. black and white motion picture footage taken.	120,700 ft.
16mm. Kodachrome motion picture footage taken.	41,400 ft.
Black and white stills.	3,414
Color stills.	1,000
Aerials	41,000

Western Group

35mm. black and white motion picture footage taken.	25,250 ft.
16mm. Kodachrome motion picture footage taken.	19,600 ft.
16mm. black and white motion picture footage taken.	1,500 ft.
Black and white stills.	1,694 ft.
Color stills.	486
Aerials	50,559

Eastern Group

35mm. black and white motion picture footage taken.	27,400 ft.
16mm. Kodachrome motion picture footage taken.	7,550 ft.
Black and white stills.	1,263
Color stills	113
Aerials	8,298

In addition to the above, one or more prints were made from all negatives.

All motion picture footage has been screened, identified, and filed at the Naval Photographic Center, Naval Air Station, Anacostia, D.C..

All still negatives, except those made by Coast Guard personnel on board the U.S.C.G.C. NORTHWIND, have been placed in the Bureau of Aeronautics files at the Naval Photographic Center. The negatives made by the Coast Guard are on file at U.S. Coast Guard Headquarters in the Treasury Building, Washington, D.C..

Aerial survey negatives are on file at the Naval Photographic Center.

APPENDIX I

WHITE DAYS

The so-called "white days" exist in the Antarctic over the ice on days when it is overcast. On these days it is impossible to distinguish any irregularities on the surface, no matter how irregular they may be, unless there happens to be discoloration, which sometimes exists in pressure ice in a bay area, caused by algae or diatones prevalent in sea ice and in some pressure ice in the various bays. Another good name for these overcast days for the surface travelleris "stumbling days". On these days, a foot traveler without skis will stumble over the slightest irregularities, such as sastrugi which is usually plentiful, especially on the barren and otherwise smooth surface of Shelf or Plateau Ice.

These white days are most disappointing to the photographer. It is impossible to photograph the surface on a white day. Photographs made of persons or objects on such days give the illusion of the subject hanging in space, or of a print that has been thoroughly bleached except for the subject which is darker than the surrounding and background territory.

There are no conventional size objects on the Antarctic Continent when one is away from the Base, such as telephone poles, fences, trees, etc., to lend scale to a photograph. This also lends to the confusion on a white day.

After some thought on the subject of white days, there is no mystery involved whatever. The reason one cannot see the surface is simply because there are no shadows. The surface is all one color, white. Unless there is undiffused sunlight to cause the irregularities on the surface to cast shadows, the ice surface cannot be seen. Just imagine a large white enclosed area, say a hundred feet square with one slightly raised area in the center about one foot high, and all of the illumination is from above and it is evenly distributed and diffused. The raised portion will not be perceived by sight and it is impossible to show the raised portion photographically. One might say it could be done if the observer were at a low enough angle. However, extend the white area upwards now several feet high, and then it resembles a white bowl of milk and the raised surface still cannot be seen. These white days are disappointing to the novice photographer, for at first he will try to make his prints darker until finally they are almost black, and invariably a dirty-white, gray looking print will result in trying to obtain detail. The photographer has been taught that there must be detail or it is not a photograph. He is also taught (except for color photography) that photography is "Highlights and Shadows". All this may be temporarily forgotten when trying to photograph the surface of an ice sheet on an overcast or "white day".

One of the best illustrations of this is from an aerial photographic mission made with tri-metrogon cameras by a plane of Operation HIGHJUMP, numbered Flight 14, over the Ross Ice Shelf. The Ice Barrier occasionally appears in some photographs (The Barrier is the front or cliff of the Ice Shelf). But, in the photographs in which only the ice shelf appears, it is all white, with no detail whatever, and it is truly a darkroom technician's dilemna. This particular roll of negatives were printed and reprinted several times and then finally given up as being "just no good", when in reality, several good sets of prints had been obtained of the entire roll. Fortunately, the Staff Photographic Officer happened to enter the laboratory when the whole crew had given up in thorough disgust and informed them that they had some excellent photographs taken on a white day.

Another unusual thing about a white day (overcast), is the fact that there is more light prevalent on the surface than there is on a clear, bright, sunshiny day, when the sun is at an equal elevation. This is a fact that is readily observed by a photographer using an exposure meter.

The reason for this is understood after some thought. Light penetrating through the overcast and striking the white surface is almost entirely reflected back by the white snow surface. After being reflected by the snow, the light is reflected by the white bottom of the overcast back to the snow surface. This action is repeated over and over again, thereby, building up the intensity of light until it reaches a maximum.

On Operation HIGHJUMP an attempt has been made to measure this build up. An exposure meter was used to take hourly observations on the ice shelf, simultaneously with readings taken in the vicinity, just outside of the Bay of Whales, over the Ross Sea. The reason is that those made over the sea water will indicate less light intensity because the dark sea will absorb most of the light; whereas, just the opposite is the case over the ice shelf. A comparison of these intensities will show the amount of build-up. As yet these readings have not been compared to measure the exact difference of intensities but, a difference definitely exists. There is more light on an overcast day on the ice in Antarctica than there is when it is clear and unlimited.

APPENDIX II

ROSTER OF PHOTOGRAPHIC OFFICERS

Lt. C.C. SHIRLEY 177286 USN	Officer in Charge Photography
Lt. A.E. STEIN USNR	Photographer R4D and Central Group
Lt. E.C. BRAUER USN (ret.)	Photographic Historian
lst. H.H. ANGLIN 012189 USMC	Motion Picture Officer
Lt. (jg) R.C. TIMM USN 319547	Photographic Officer CTG 68.1
CHPHOT E.F. MASHBURN USCG	Photographer Officer NORTHWIND
Lt. E.P BROWN USN 309612	Photographic Officer CTG 68.2
CWO R.L. CHAPPEL USMC	Motion Picture Officer CTG 68.2
CHPHOT H.D. FORD USN 319878	Photographic Officer CTG 68.3

ROSTER OF PHOTOGRAPHERS

Central Group

BOWE, O.F.	412 02 12	CPHOM	McDONALD, W.L. 372 30 07	PHOM1	
WEED, A.E.	380 83 21	CPHOM	MEDING, J. (N) 300 95 23	PHOM1	
JOHNSON, E.E.	266 21 36	CPHOM	PETERSON, R.F. 807 54 69	PHOM2	
HUFNER, F.G., Jr.	268 76 63	CPHOM	SACK, N.F. 300 19 50	PHOM2	
HAYDEN, L.H.	263 56 79	PHOM1	ZIMMERMAN, P.R. 655 69 56	PHOM2	
TURNER, W.R.	262 96 93	PHOM1	GILLASPY, J.L. 557 40 29	PHOM3	
MALONE, T.H.	287 29 63	PHOM1	GORDON, C.D. 623 43 15	PHOM3	
SWAIN, K.C.	723 06 08	PHOM1	POLLACK, J.M. 567 35 07	PHOM3	
TEIGAN, B. (N)	382 81 58	PHOM1	WALTERSDORF, J.M. 43052217	USA CORP.	
NAWODYLO, W.H.	300 75 06	PHOM1	SHIMBERG, J. (N) 12103976	USA CORP.	
RIZZOLLA, L.M.	402 59 71	PHOM1	BALDWIN, G.E. 924547 USMC	SGT.	
			JANSSON, C.L. USMC 278437	M/SGT.	

U.S.S. BURTON ISLAND (AG-38)

COPE, H.F.	891 31 19	PHOM3

U.S.C.G.C. NORTHWIND (WAG-282)

SHELBY, A.D.	382 40 98	PHOM1
EICHORN, D. (N)		PHOM2

WESTERN GROUP

SHIRLEY, Q. (N)	381 22 20	CPHOM	PAZ, H.J.	382 96 38	PHOM2
GOSSARD, G.C. Jr.	380 90 93	CPHOM	DAVIS, M.C.	336 80 46	PHOM3
McGRADY, E.D.	265 80 85	CPHOM	MILES, R.A.	225 86 66	S1PHOM
HARGREAVES, R.B.	412 13 01	CPHOM	SAUNDERS, R.J.	798 32 03	PHOM3
DIEGLMAN, E.D.		PHOM1	GARAN, E.M.	269 01 38	PHOM1
BLAKENEY, A.A.	356 69 80	PHOM1	FOSTER, H.C.	12251153 USA	CORP.
WHITNEY, I.A.	411 13 27	PHOM1	WARRINGTON, W.H.	759 26 14	PHOM2
PIDGEON, E.C.	338 02 64	PHOM1	ELLIS, E.E.	869 73 97	PHOM1
MOHAUPT, H.E.	329 02 64	PHOM1			

EASTERN GROUP

LITZ, A.K.	295 38 55	CPHOM	LEVKO, G. (N)	238 82 31	PHOM1
RYAN, A.E.	328 70 35	CPHOM	O'CONNOR, J.J.	311 77 48	PHOM1
FILBY, A.L.	393 36 41	CPHOM	BEARMAN, F.O.	329 43 68	PHOM2
MAHAFFEY, J.S.	368 31 90	PHOM1	BULBUR, E.R.	579 57 16	PHOM2
PAYNE, J.B.	657 19 51	PHOM1	SIMPSON,	579 20 84	PHOM3
CONGER, R.R.	410 76 72	PHOM1	WALSH, R.W.	202 49 11	PHOM1
BAKER, T.W.	552 11 15	PHOM1	ZINBERG, E. (N)	42273520 USA	CORP.
LOWE, W.L.	223 87 25	PHOM1	*McCARTHY, O. (N)	413 28 87	CPHOM

*(Transferred to U.S. after PBM crash)

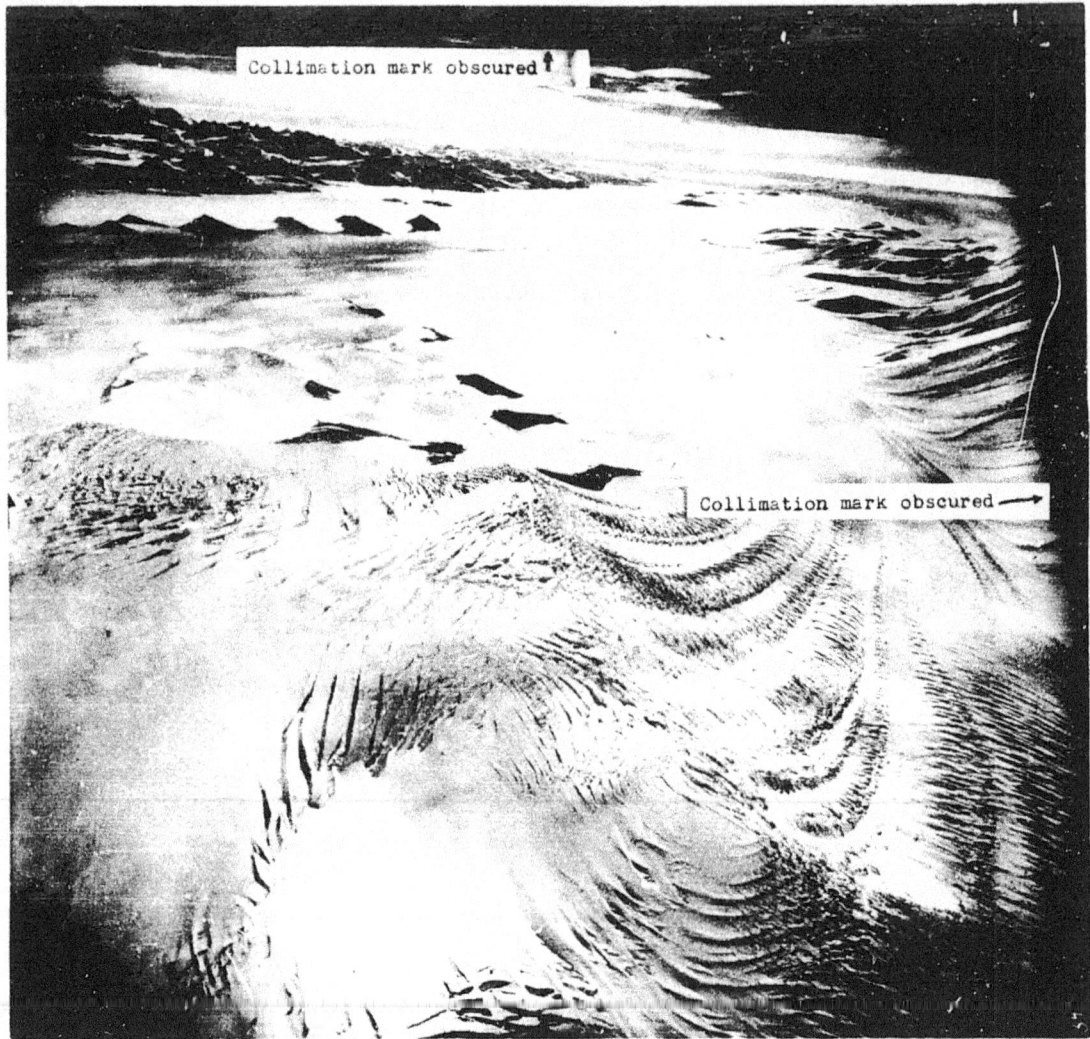

- Collimation mark obscured (top)
- Collimation mark obscured (right)

Plate No. 1

Oblique Photograph Taken from R4D-5 by K-17 (6") tri-metrogon
Camera Showing extent of Masking Caused by Camera Hatch.

Plate No. 2

M29C Cargo Carrier (Weasel) in Use as a Photographic Vehicle.

Plate No. 3

M29C Cargo Carrier (Weasel) in Use as a Photographic
Vehicle in the Bay of Whales.

Plate No. 4

Gremlin Recorder.

Plate No. 5

Annex 2 (a)   Gremlin Recorder Showing Access to Instruments.

Plate No. 6

Adapter for Adaption of APS/15 Radar
Camera to SCR-718C Radio Altimeter.

Plate No. 7

SCR-718 C Radio Altimeter with Necessary Parts
Removed for Adaption of APS/15 Radar Camera.

Plate No. 8

SCR-718 C Radio Altimeter with Adapter for APS/15 Radar
Camera Attached.

Plate No. 9

SCR-718 C Radio Altimeter with Telescope of APS/15 Attached.
(Side View)

Annex 2 (a)

Plate No. 10

SCR-718 C Radio Altimeter with Telescope of APS/15
and Bracings attached (Rear View)

Plate No. 11

SCR-718 C Radio Altimeter and APS/15 Radar Camera Completely
Assembled for Recording Altitude.

Plate No. 12

Photographic Operations Tent, Bay of Whales,
Antarctica.

ANNEX TWO (b)

TASK GROUP 68.2

PHOTOGRAPHIC REPORT

I. TASK GROUP PHOTOGRAPHIC PERSONNEL

1. PERSONNEL AND SUPPLY

The Commander Task Group 68.2 Photographic Personnel reported aboard the U.S.S. CURRITUCK (AV-7) on 18 November 1946, 14 days prior to sailing on 2 December 1946.

An effort was made to give each man of this unit flight experience so as to qualify as many photographers as possible in actual flight experience in trimetrogon photography in the Antarctic. The men gained much experience in aerial motion picture and hand-held oblique photography, also experience in obtaining the proper information for marking and filing of aerial photographs after each flight.

2. TASK GROUP PHOTOGRAPHIC SUPPLIES:

The photographic supplies were received eight days prior to sailing for Antarctica. This short length of time prevented this unit from making a thorough inventory before departure. However, an inventory was held as soon as possible and it was found that several items were missing. Also, equipment with direct current motors was received instead of the alternating current equipment that had been ordered. With sufficient personnel, a complete inventory of the photographic material could have been accomplished and most of the missing items procured from NASD, San Diego. The ship was also short of personnel and was busy loading ship's supplies. Therefore, it was necessary for only nine photographers to accomplish in one week the highly commendable job of handling this bulk of material without assistance.

In addition to the small space in the laboratory and the refrigerated film stowage, five unused bunkrooms were made available for stowage of photographic material. The material was segregated into the following categories: In the first of the two largest compartments were cameras, washers, printers and other bulky items such as cases of flash bulbs, negative preservers, developing tanks, etc.; in the second, hypo, aerial film, movie film and color processing kits. The three smaller compartments were used for stowage of chemicals, glassware, jugs, graduates and contact, enlarging and sonne roll paper. The compartments were fitted with wooden slat doors and hasps, thereby permitting them to be locked. The compartments were easily adapted for storing gear by removing the bunks and by utilizing the various lockers and drawer spaces for small articles. All gear was easily accommodated in the spaces assigned to photography and by using bunk hangers and stanchions, material was easily secured for rough seas.

All wooden boxes were saved along with excelsior and other packing material, for use in re-transporting any gear not used or being returned. Such foresight proved wise as the ship had very little lumber to spare for crating or boxing. A small hand truck (made for galley use) was used to great advantage in handling supplies and it is suggested that several be made to fit normal hatches encountered aboard ship as they save many hours of labor and, in some instances, prevent damage to material in heavy cases.

At the end of flight operations all supplies, cameras, print washers, etc. were inventoried and restored in the various photographic supply compartments and secured for heavy seas. All equipment and material to be turned in were inventoried and listed for return to stock.

II. AERIAL CAMERA INSTALLATION.

This section introduces the good and bad features of all the cameras and mounts used in the aircraft with their related equipage. Detailed information on the problems, mechanical failures, modifications and recommendations on all the cameras and mounts will be found in the Camera Repair Section III with the operational difficulties of the motion picture cameras which are also covered in the Motion Picture Section VI.

1. TRI-METROGON CAMERAS

The K-17's operated exceptionally well in the low temperatures encountered by the Western Group. Cold weather lubricating oils and greases were used and only two mechanical failures occured; sheared gear trains in one camera and a cracked shutter case in another camera. Because the change of shutters would affect the calibration, the camera was removed intact and a spare was installed in its place for the duration of the operation. However, the same magazines were continued in use with the replacement cameras.

2. A5A MAGAZINES

The A-5-A's performed almost as trouble-free as the K-17 cameras, and in proportion to their extensive use the number of mechanical failures was very small. Information on their use, mechanical operation, and recommendations is included in the Camera Repair Section of this report.

3. TRI-METROGON CAMERA MOUNTS

This installation, used in the PBM-5 aircraft, was permanently installed at a 0° deck angle at Norfolk, Virginia. Due to the 3°, nose high, flight characteristic for maximum engine efficiency, all photographs have from 3 to 6° tilt. If this type mount is to be used on other operations, it is suggested that it be installed so as to be adjustable for correction of tilt, or installed at an angle in proper relation to the cruising attitude of the plane when heavily loaded.

The mount was found to be tailored for uncalibrated cameras of the late "44" series that were drawn by the A&R Norfolk. In attempting to install calibrated cameras shipped to the U.S.S. CURRITUCK, it was discovered that these cameras were of an earlier "44" series, and would not fit without modifications being made to the mounts. However, it was decided that the lesser of the two evils would be to use the uncalibrated Norfolk cameras and not change the mount.

The ideal arrangement would be to have the tri-metrogon cameras in the bow. This would allow the photographer to see ahead as well as beneath, and shorten travel and communications, as well as make for greater warmth.

4. VACUUM

The vacuum system functioned very satisfactorily throughout the entire operation.

5. VIEW FINDERS

The Fairchild Model F-5 Vertical Viewfinder served the purpose during the operation, but it is felt that much more accuracy and less photographer fatigue could be gained by using one of the design that is covered in the Camera Repair Section of this report.

6. TRI-METROGON HATCHES

The general construction of the tri-met camera hatches was very good, although the bolts for securing the vertical camera hatch cover should be approximately one inch longer and the wing nuts should be larger.

7. GREMLIN RECORDING CAMERA

The F-56 Gremlin Recorder functioned quite well mechanically for about the first half of the operation and then mechanical failures became increasingly numerous. Detailed information regarding the failures, repairs and recommended modification are thoroughly covered in the camera repair section of this report.

8. CAMERA CONTROL PANEL, PBM-5

The Control Panel functioned very satisfactorily throughout the entire operation. The only change made was to add a warning light which indicated during the take-up of film in the Gremlin Recorder magazine.

9. RADIO ALTIMETER AND AIRBORNE CAMERA

The type A Recording Camera operated very satisfactorily. The only failure occured when one magazine failed to take-up film, due to a tight bushing on the take-up spindle. Because of the congested area in which the watches were installed, the stems of several were broken while being removed for re-setting. Details are contained in the camera repair section.

III. PERSONNEL

It is strongly recommended that two photographers be assigned to each flight crew for it is impossible for one photographer to ful- full all the photographic requirements on a photographic mission. Assigning the second photographer to the flight crew rather than utili- zing a different laboratory man for each flight gives smoother coordination in the air.

IV. CAMERA REPAIR

It is stated in the operation plan that "all tri-metrogon photo- graphy will be accomplished with K-17-6" aircraft cameras calibrated by the Bureau of Standards."

The aircraft received on board were equipped with cameras issued in Norfolk, Virginia that were not calibrated. The calibrated cameras were received on board in separate cases and when unpacked and checked it was found that at least three of the cameras had been disassembled since the date of calibration. It was further found that the nuts holding the cones to the case drives were loose. Still further some of these calibrated cameras did not fit the mounts in the aircraft. The camera mounts in the aircraft were made for cameras with case drives of 44-600 series or later. Because of the above discrepancies the calibrated cameras were not used on this operation.

Case drives of the 44-600 series or later and cones of the 43 series were assembled in as closely matched sets as possible. The match- ing was according to the focal lengths in millimeters. For example; set No. 1 (in plane B-3) consisted of port camera 152.8 millimeters, star- board camera 152.7 millimeters, vertical camera 152.2 millimeters and spare camera 152.9 millimeters. Each plane carried a spare camera for use in the event of a breakdown. On two occasions these spare cameras were used. The field data sheets for tri-metrogon photography note these changes and the exact exposures taken by each camera. Camera No. 6 in set No. 2 (in plane B-1) was replaced by spare camera No. 7 on 9 January 1947. Camera No. 6 was removed because of a damaged shutter housing. Damage was appar- ently from internal parts of shutter and the camera was not disassembled, for the lack of calibration date.

A set of four (4) magazines was used with each camera. In the instances when the spare cameras were installed the same set of magazines were used with the replacement camera. Notations of the magazines used were always made on the Field Data Sheets.

The filters used were of the sunflower type. Tests were made before the first photographic mission to determine the f. stop at which the sun- flower image would appear on the film. It appeared at f.11 therefore all missions were flown with lens aperatures larger than f.11. The filters were not removed from the cameras at any time during the operation.

It is suggested that sunflower filters for use with aerial kodocolor be made.

Some of the missions were photographed when the sun angle was lower than 10° and on several occasions a reflection from one of the diaphram control gears registered on the film.

The most serious K-17 defect was in the shutter gear chain on the wind and trip mechanism. The support that serves as bearing surfaces for the shafts is of cast aluminum and apparently under low temperatures contracts to a greater degree than the steel shafts, causing the shafts to bind and freeze (See Plate 1 and 2). This was first noted on camera No. 4 on 2 February 1947 after approximately 2,500 cycles of operation. The result was that the camera was slow in tripping and, in one instance, did not trip with the other two cameras for a period of ten exposures. When this condition was discovered all cameras were checked, and two other cameras were found to have the same condition to a lesser degree. It is suggested that these shafts be seated in ball or roller bearings.

Another defect which is present in all K-17, K-18 and K-19 type aircraft cameras is the magazine locking slide which is actuated by an eccentric pivot shaft. This shaft does not have sufficient leverage and when the magazine is not seated properly it is very easy to force the shaft out of its recess, thus forcing the slide up in the center and usually breaking it. It is recommended that magazine locks similar to the F-56 be installed but in the reverse manner by placing the studs on the magazine and the locking lever on the camera (see Plate 3).

Camera No. 1, after 3,737 cycles of operation, had stripped all teeth off the bevel or miter gear which transfers power from the motor coupling. (See Plate 4). Inspection of the drive did not disclose any other mechanical trouble. The sea level temperature at the time of take-off was 28.4° F with 86 percent humidity. Due to the fact that the drive assembly is practically a sealed container it is possible that when the camera cooled to minus 0.4°F condensation formed and froze on portions of the drive.

A complete new drive assembly was installed and the camera operated with out trouble the remainder of the operation.

Cameras and lenses were often covered with a heavy coating of frost when the aircraft descended. It was necessary for the cameras to warm up before any photographs could be taken from low altitude. Frost would form on the lenses as fast as it was wiped off.

The K-17 cameras as a whole performed remarkably well on this operation and it is believed that it is the best camera for Antarctic Operations that the Navy has.

A5A MAGAZINE

The loaded A-5-A Magazines were used in sets of four (4) for each camera. The magazines containing exposed film were removed and placed in the film developing room for unloading and reloading.

During the rapid descent of the aircraft, cameras and magazines were sometimes covered with frost, depending upon the humidity at sea level. This frost continued for a few minutes after they were brought into the warm air of the ship. Frequent inspection of the magazines' mechanism showed little evidence of rust, however, the dark slides that were tinned had a tendency to rust around the handles.

The seating surfaces of the magazines were scarred and chipped by handling on and around the tri-metrogon camera mount. The collimation marks in the magazines were damaged by parts of the camera mounts; this was due to the fact that the magazines were attached to the cameras with the dark slides out. The mount could be simplified and the parts that caused this damage could be eliminated thus making it much easier to attach and remove magazines with the dark slides in (See Plates 7 and 8 on tri-met mount).

The seating surfaces of the magazines should be chemically blackened the same as the seating surfaces on the 44 series case drives. This processing makes the metal more resistant to corrosion.

Dark slides became very difficult to insert and remove from the magazines. This was caused by starting the dark slides in at a slight angle, thereby gouging the track slightly on first one side and then the other. This action increased each time the dark slide was inserted, finally reaching the point where it was extremely difficult to insert or remove. This could be overcome by rounding or beveling the leading corners of the dark slide a little more.

The bearings on both the takeup film spool pivot shaft and on the metering roller are exposed to the inside of the magazine. On two occasions these bearings were found to have accumulated a sufficient amount of dirt and film chips to stop their action (See Plates 5 and 6). This occurred more readily on the metering roller bearing because of its lower position and close proximity to the film as it travels through the magazine. This could be remedied by using sealed bearings or dirt shields.

On one occasion the magazine failed to advance film . It was found that the locking nut on the set screw adjustment for the metering lever had loosened and the lever was in constant engagement with the metering gear.

Three magazines sheared the taper pin in the bevel gear on the top of the main drive shaft. One failure was the result of dirt in the bearing on the takeup spool pivot shaft. No apparent reason could be found for the other two failures.

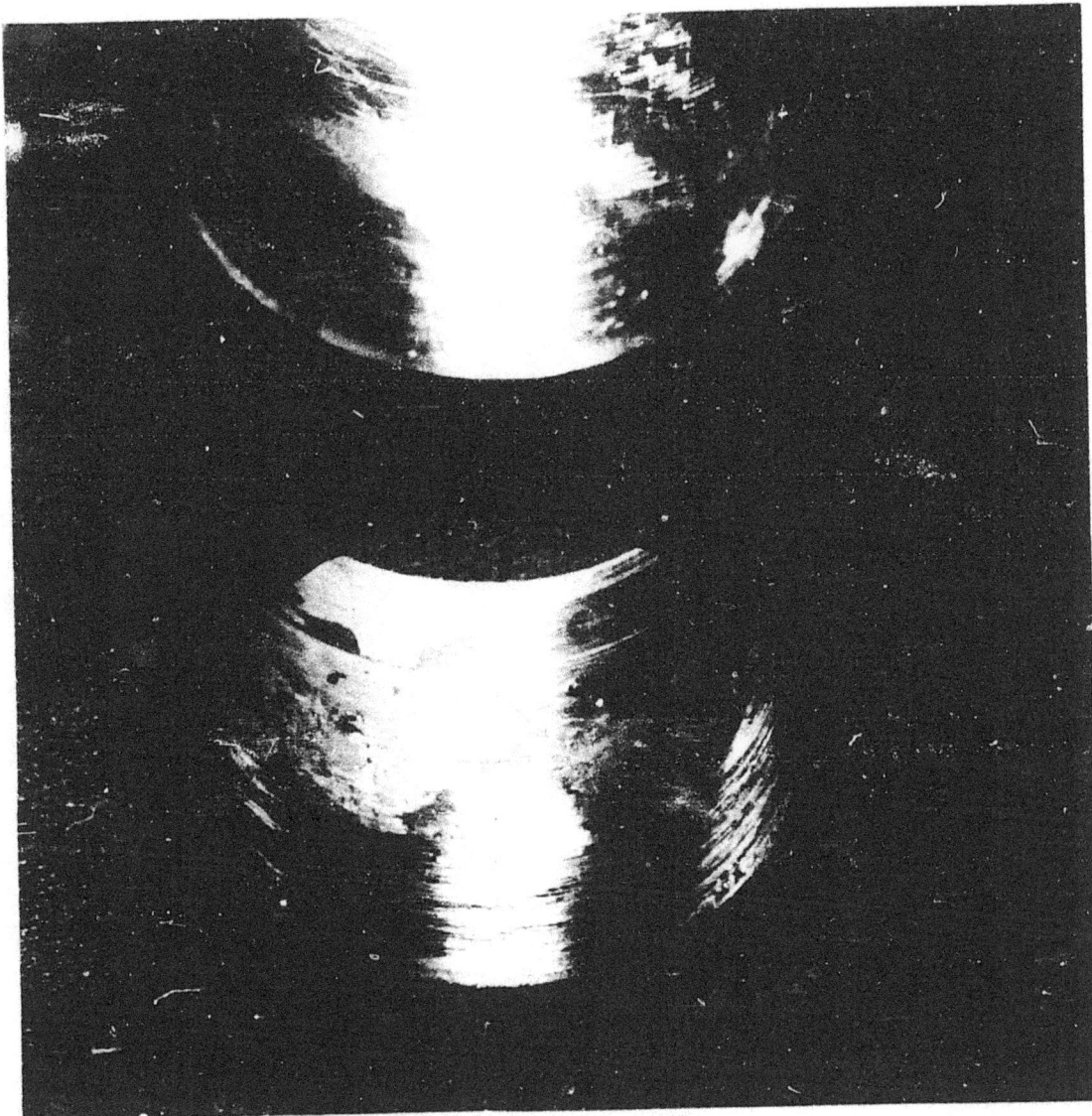

Plate No. 1.

Shutter wind and trip gear chain
casting, K-17-6" Metrogon shutter.

Plate No. 2.

Shutter wind and trip gear chain,
K-17-6" metrogon shutter.

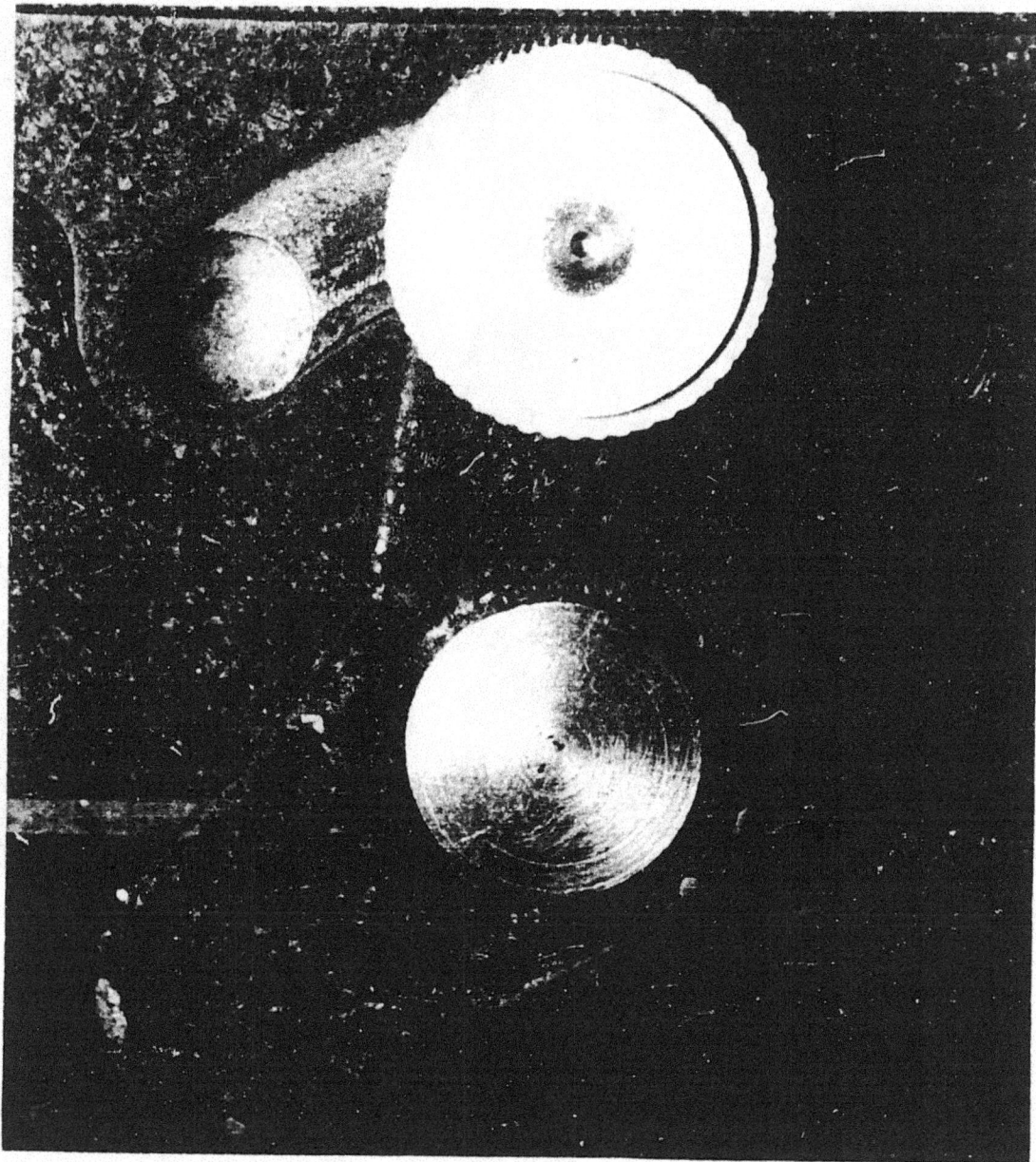

Plate No. 3.

F-56 magazine lock.

Plate No. 4.

Intermediate bevel gear for motor drive
chain in K-17 case drive.

Plate No. 5.

Metering roller bearing,
A-5-A magazine.

Plate No. 6.

Takeup spool pivot shaft
bearing, A-5-A magazine.

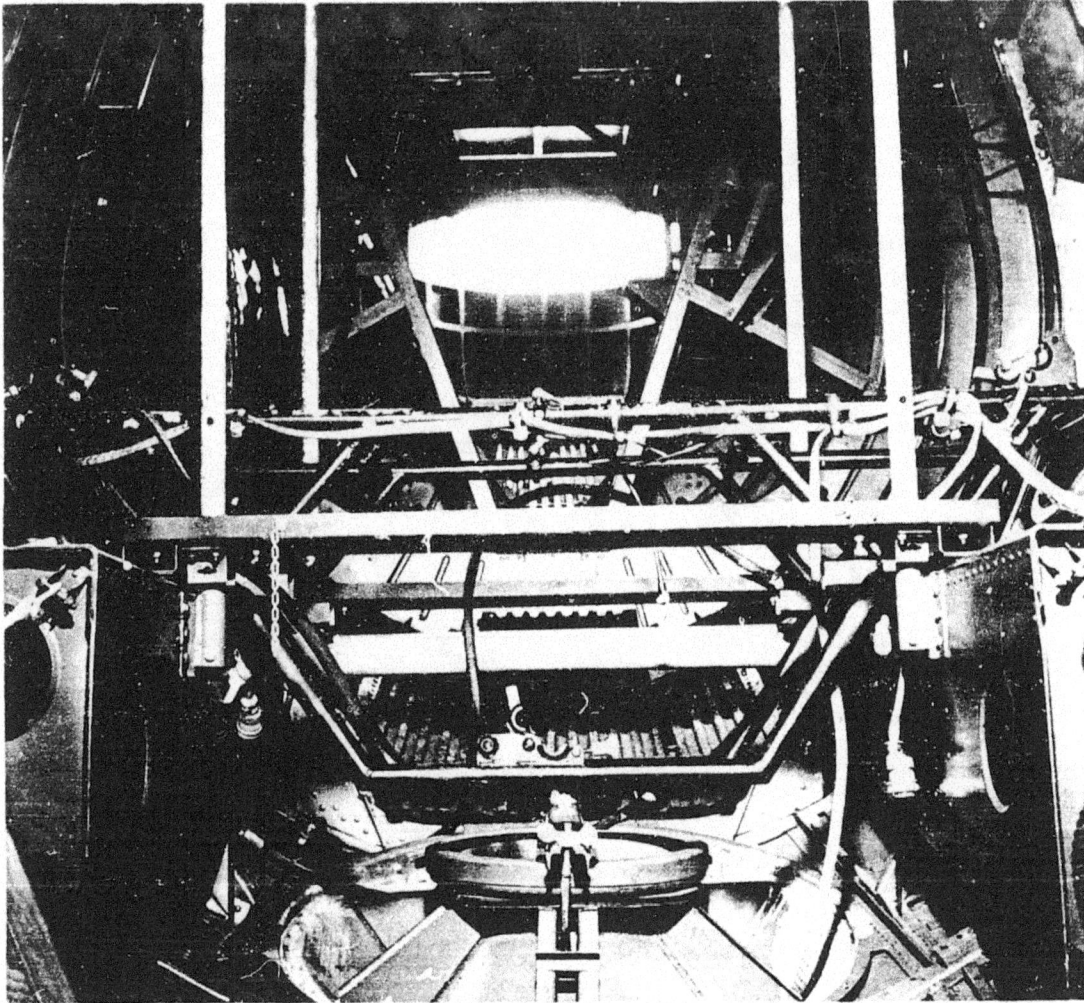

Plate No. 7.

Tri-metrogon camera mount for PBM-5

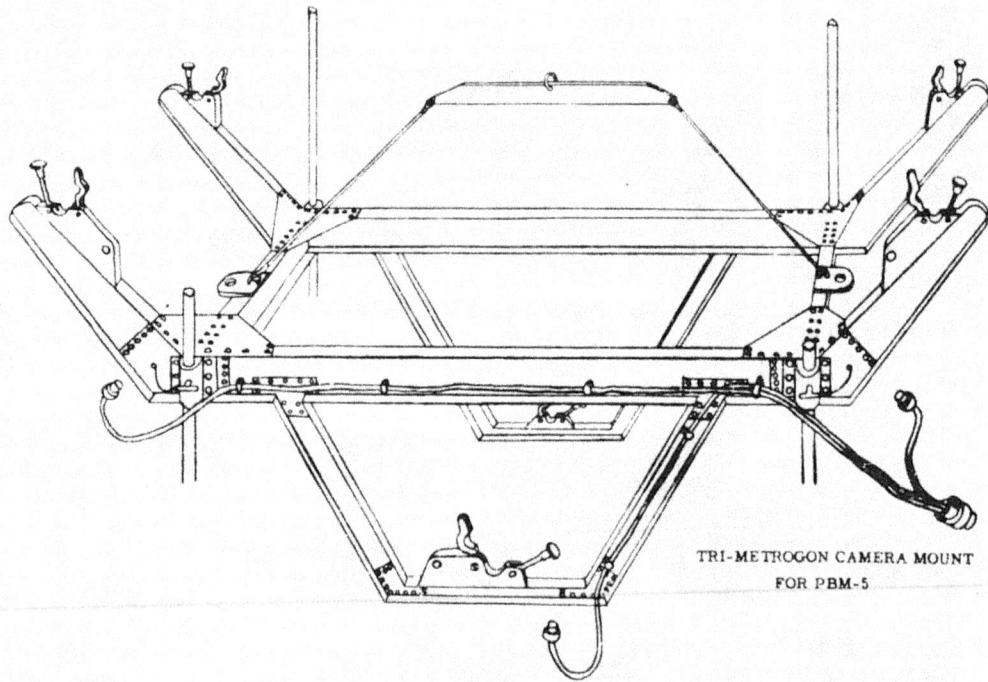

TRI-METROGON CAMERA MOUNT
FOR PBM-5

Plate No. 8.

Tri-metrogon camera mount, recommendations for.

The metering system in one magazine failed to free itself after the proper amount of film had been advanced. No mechanical troubles were found and the magazine functioned properly on the next mission. Because of the fact that the magazine had been stored in the aircraft for a number of days before the flight, the humidity in the mechanism chamber could possibly have condensed forming ice as the aircraft reached colder levels. This possibly locked the metering system preventing it from releasing thereby allowing film to be advanced during the entire wind cycle. Three magazines locked after being brought into the ship, so that film could not be advanced by turning the wind coupling. No mechanical trouble could be found and the magazine operated on the next mission without trouble. This could be explained by the fact that all moisture on the magazines froze until they had been inside the ship and allowed to thaw for a period of about fifteen minutes.

One magazine had faulty metering due to a scored shaft around which the metering clutch spring grips. This scoring caused the spring to hold when the metering lever engaged the metering gear. This was remedied by replacing with new parts.

It is recommended that a film advance light be installed similar to the one on the 42 series F-56 magazines. This light would enable the photographer to keep a constant check on his film and magazine operation.

The mechanical failures in relation to the number of exposures made, shows that the A-5-A magazine is well adapted for cold weather operation.

TRI-METROGON CAMERA MOUNT

The Tri-Metrogon camera mounts used on this operation were constructed at Naval Air Station, Norfolk, for cameras of 44-600 series cases, or later. It was found that the calibrated cameras, which were of an earlier series, would not fit the mounts. The mounts are of tubular steel construction (See Plate 7), with braces across the top which obstruct the placing on and removal of magazines from the cameras. The power cables for the cameras are attached to the mount with metal clamps which scar and chip the seating surfaces of the magazine. The design of the mount necessitates the attaching of the magazines with the dark slides removed, which exposes the fiducial marks and subjects them to damage while positioning the magazine.

It is recommended that consideration by given to a mount similar to the one shown in Plate 8. It is believed that a mount of this type constructed of I-beams would be as strong, and much more accessible than the type used on this operation. The power cables and vacuum lines could be fastened to the inner surfaces of the I-beams, thereby protecting them from damage.

The mounts installed in the PBMs could not be corrected for tilt which varied from approximately three to six degrees. The four upright posts which guide the mount could be hinged at the base and fastened to a carriage on the overhead. This carriage should be movable forward and aft to compensate for the aircraft's angle of flight.

FAIRCHILD MODEL F-5 VERTICAL VIEWFINDER

The model F-5 viewfinder was used in conjunction with all tri-metrogon photography. Numerous defects were noted, and it is believed that a much more suitable viewfinder could be constructed. Due to the 10" lens used on the Model F Viewfinder it has a very restricted area of view in comparison with the 6" Tri-Metrogon camera, and this is especially noticeable when flying over irregular coastlines. After watching the viewfinder for a short length of time, the photographers were subjected to temporary blindness upon turning to observe the operation of the cameras, due to glare on the terrain below.

It is recommended that consideration be given a viewfinder of the type shown in Plate 9. This viewfinder incorporates a 6" metrogon lens for comparative coverage and a moveable filter to reduce the intensity of the snow glare. The viewing glass could be also calibrated for longer focal length lenses. It would be necessary to change the location of the view-finder port in the PBM-5 type aircraft to accommodate this viewfinder.

GREMLIN RECORDER (F-56)

The F-56 Gremlin Timer consisted of an F-56 20 inch case and cone with an 8.25 inch lens and shutter. Its purpose was to record the baro-metric altitude, Greenwich Civil Time, turn and bank indicator, and data card. It was operated by the same B-3-B Intervalometer that tripped the tri-metrogon cameras.

Taper pins seemed to be the weak points in this camera. On two occasions the pin in the wind rod coupling that is attached to the drive, was sheared off. No contributing mechanical failure could be found as a cause for the pins to shear. This occurred after approximately 2,500 exposures.

The Gremlin Timer, Case No. 42-953 in PBM 5 "DAKOR ONE", after approximately 8,500 operating cycles since date of manufacture, broke down completely. The wind coupling (See Plate 10) on the spring housing (See Plate 11) was being cut by the shim between it and the housing. This finally caused the coupling to freeze, which in turn twisted the wind rod (See Plate 12), and sheared the taper pin in the coupling on the spring housing. The faulty skim (See Plate 13) appears to have been forced on the spring housing bushing tearing up the inside edge on one side.

The shutter was disassembled at this time, and it was found that the teeth on the snubber and retard segments were badly worn (See Plates 14 and 15) Shutter springs were also fatigued beyond the point of safe operation.

It is recommended by the Fairchild Corp. that these cameras be given a major overhaul at 10,000 cycles of operation. If the case driven counters

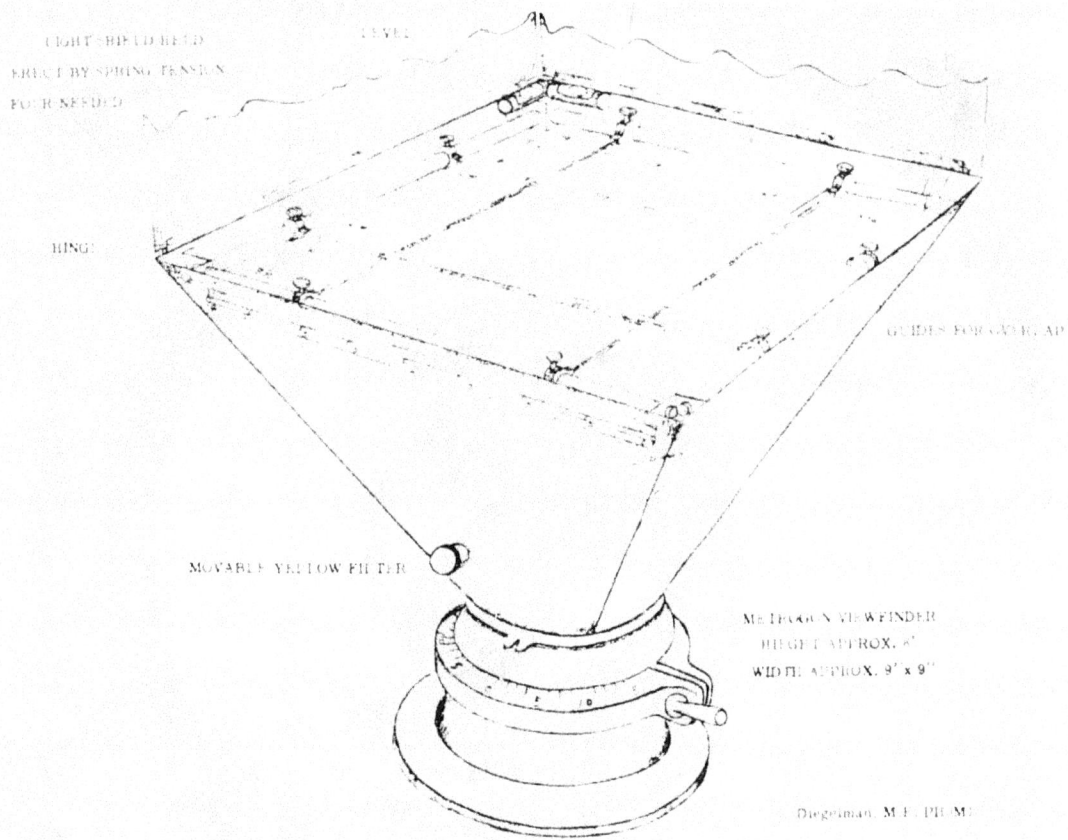

LIGHT-SHIELD HEED ERECT BY SPRING TENSION
FOUR NEEDED

LEVEL

HINGE

GUIDES FOR OVERLAP

MOVABLE YELLOW FILTER

METROGON VIEWFINDER
HEIGHT APPROX. 8"
WIDTH APPROX. 9" x 9"

Diegelman, M.E., PH.M1

Plate No. 9.

Metrogon viewfinder, recommendations for.

Plate No. 10.

F-56 shutter spring housing wind coupling cam.

Plate No. 11.

F-56 shutter spring housing.

Plate No. 12.

F-56 wind rod.

Plate No. 13.

F-56 shutter spring housing

Plate No. 14.

F-56 8.25 inch shutter retard pallet and retard segment.

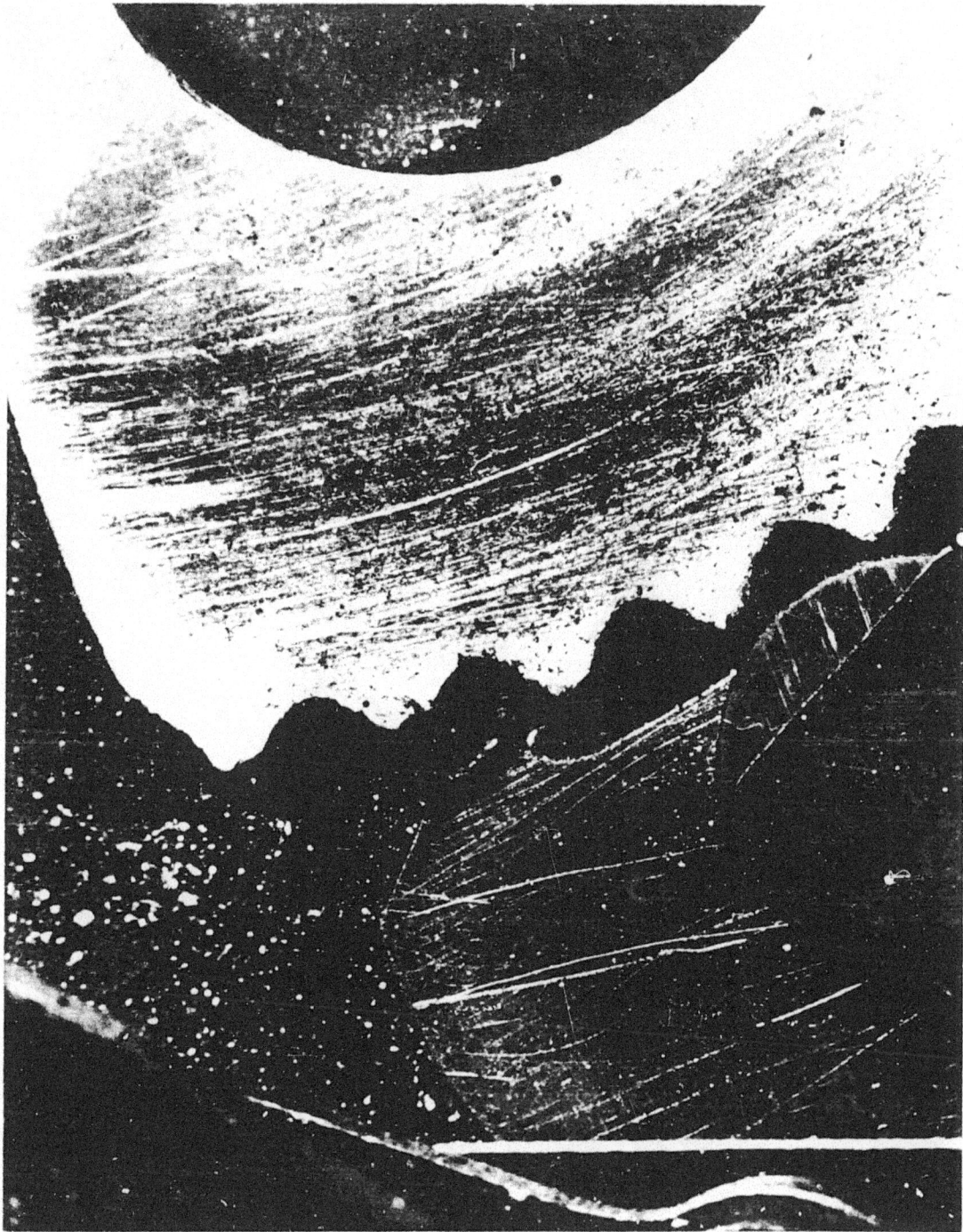

Plate No. 15.

F-50 3.25 inch shutter retard pallet and retard segment.

Plate No. 16.

F-56 magazine maindrive shaft bearing.

had not been re-set since manufacture, cameras were beyond the point of safe operation at approximately 6,000 exposures. Possibly the rapid changes in temperatures and humidity on the flights contributed to these breakdowns; however, the K-17 cameras held up very well under the same conditions.

F-56 MAGAZINE

The F-56 Magazine was used on both the Gremlin Timers and Obliques.

Taper pins and vacuum pistons were the causes of the troubles encountered. The F-56 magazine and camera supposed to be cycled one complete operation by hand before switching to electric operation. This was complied with on this operation, and was not the cause of the taper pin failure. The taper pin in the bevel gear on the main driveshaft sheared off on three occasions. The magazine when cold and when fully loaded seemed to be too great a load stress for the taper pin to withstand.

The main bearing on the magazine driveshaft was found on three occasions to be fouled with dirt, paint chips, and gummed grease (See Plate 16). This foreign matter was picked up during the handling of magazines in the aircraft and aboard ship. The moveable connection which travels up and down in this shaft permits this foreign matter to work up into tne bearing seat.

The vacuum pistons and cylinders gave the most trouble. Due to the difference in casting structures and the rate of contraction in sub-normal temperature, the pistons were binding in their downward travel during the wind cycle (See Plate 17). When the piston completely froze, the rocker arm which actuates the piston exerted sufficient pressure to form indentations in the rocker arm bearing surface on the piston (See Plate 18). This caused the pistons to sluff or score the cylinder walls, usually on only one side. All the pistons showed signs of excessive wear on the center guide post. This wear occurred on the base of the post on one side (See Plate 19) and at the top on the opposite side (See Plate 20) denoting that the pistons were not traveling straight. The bulk of the trouble occurred after each magazine had cycled approximately 2,000 exposures. Toward the last of the expedition's tri-met flights one or sometimes two magazines would be inoperative because of frozen or stiff pistons. Five (5) magazines per plane were needed for actual coverage due to the unbalanced proportion of 250 exposures per A-5-A magazine and 200 per F-56 magazine.

The remote position of the Gremlin Timer did not permit a close watch on the magazine operation. A film advance light was installed so that the photographer could watch its action from his position aft with the tri-metrogon cameras.

Magazine number 42-3998 had pulled the clutch spring, on film take-up pivot gear completely free of its locking bolts (See Plate 21). It is believed that this was caused by the film being stuck or frozen to the flippers or film guides. No other reason could be found because the film advanced freely upon opening the magazine.

RECOMMENDATION FOR F-56 GREMLIN RECORDER

The Gremlin timers used on this operation incorporated barometric altimeter, navigator's watch, turn and bank indicator, and data card. A separate camera was used to record the radio altimeter.

It is recommended that a Gremlin timer be constructed in such a manner as to include a radio altimeter, 24-hour navigator's clock, barometric altimeter, deck angle indicator, turn and bank indicator, and data card. It would be necessary to use two lenses and two shutters, one to record the radio altimeter, and one to record the other instruments. This unit would eliminate the necessity for a separate radio altimeter camera, and would give a larger negative of the radio altimeter. It is suggested that the two lenses be of approximately 5" focal length, and that the shutters be solenoid-operated and of Packard type. The shutter for recording the radio altimeter could be adjusted by use of a B-3-B Intervalometer similar to the one referred to in the Type A Recording Camera section of this report.

TYPE "A" RECORDING CAMERA

The Type "A" Recording Camera was received on board with instructions to use it for recording the Radio Altimeter every sixty seconds while the aircraft was in flight

Due to the lack of plugs for the camera it was necessary to build a different type receptacle box. This box, shown in Plate 23, contains two receptacles; one for camera power, lights and heater units; and one for intervalometer. The intervalometer plug furnished power for the intervalometer which in turn furnished tripping power and film advance power. The duration of exposure was determined by the trip cam in a B-3-B intervalometer. The shutter was held open by the camera solenoid for the duration of time in which the intervalometer trip lever was resting in the low portion of the trip cam, thus holding the tripping contacts closed. The trip cam rotates at a rate of one (1) r.p.s., therefore in order to obtain the required exposure the trip cam in the B-3B was ground down as shown in Plate 24. This enabled the tripping contacts to be held closed for a period of approximately 3/4 of a second. A 50 Ohm resistor was wired in series with the recording lights to decrease intensity. The exposure was approximately 3/4 of a second at f2.3. This system worked without a failure during the entire operation on PBM-5 Baker Three.

The same system was installed in PBM-5 Baker One but due to the lower intensity of the Radio Altimeter tube the exposure was not sufficient.

The negatives made on the trip do not show the painted numerals on the dial.

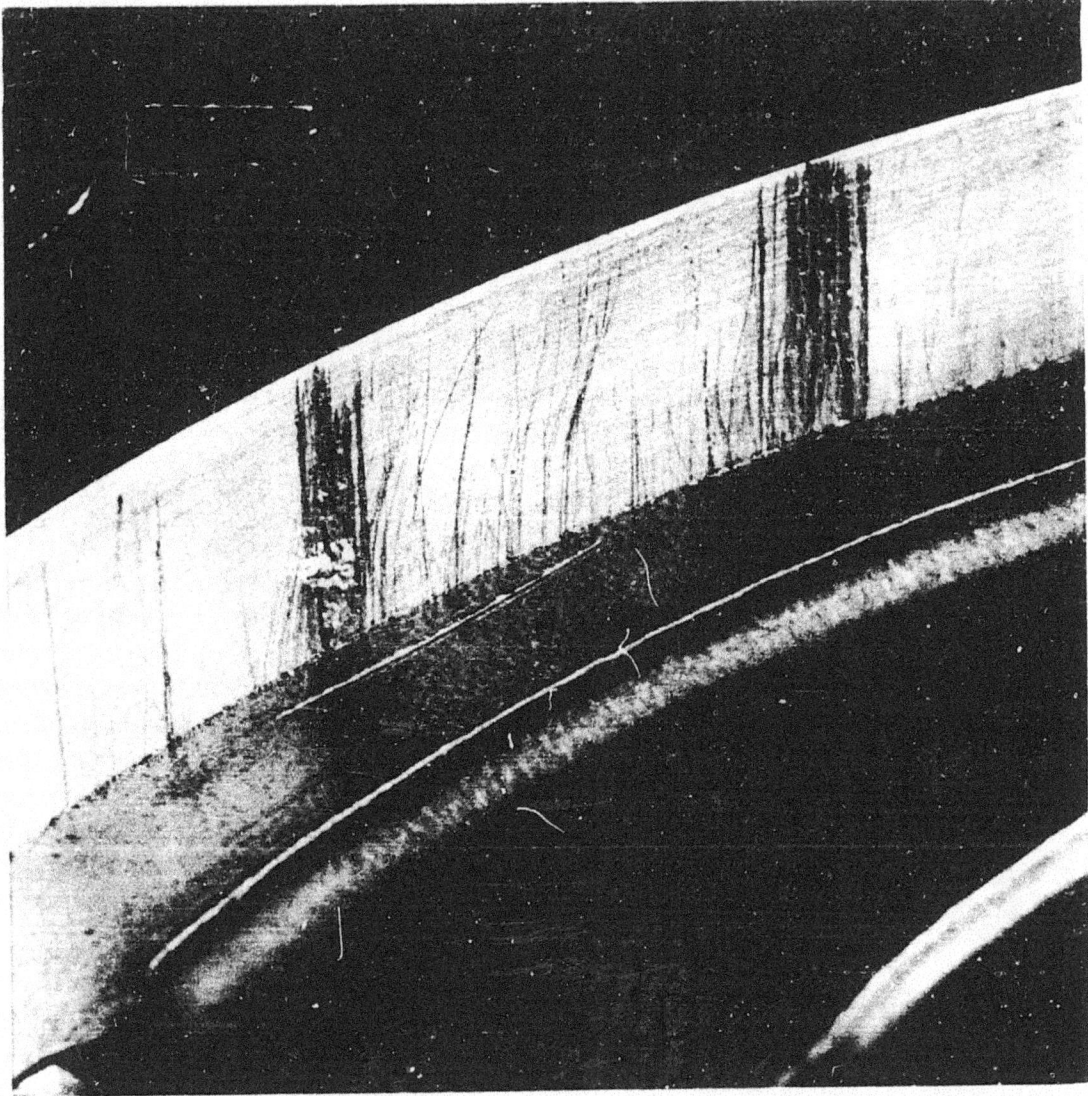

Plate No. 17.

F-56 magazine vacuum assembly cylinder wall.

Plate No. 18.

F-56 magazine vacuum piston

Plate No. 19.

F-56 magazine vacuum piston guide post.

Plate No. 20.

F-56 magazine vacuum piston guide post.

Plate No. 21.

F-56 magazine takeup spool, pivot
shaft and clutch spring.

Plate No. 22.

F-56 magazine metering roller gear
and metering cam gear.

Plate No. 23.

Type "A" Recording camera mounted on radio
altimeter powered by B-3-B intervalometer.

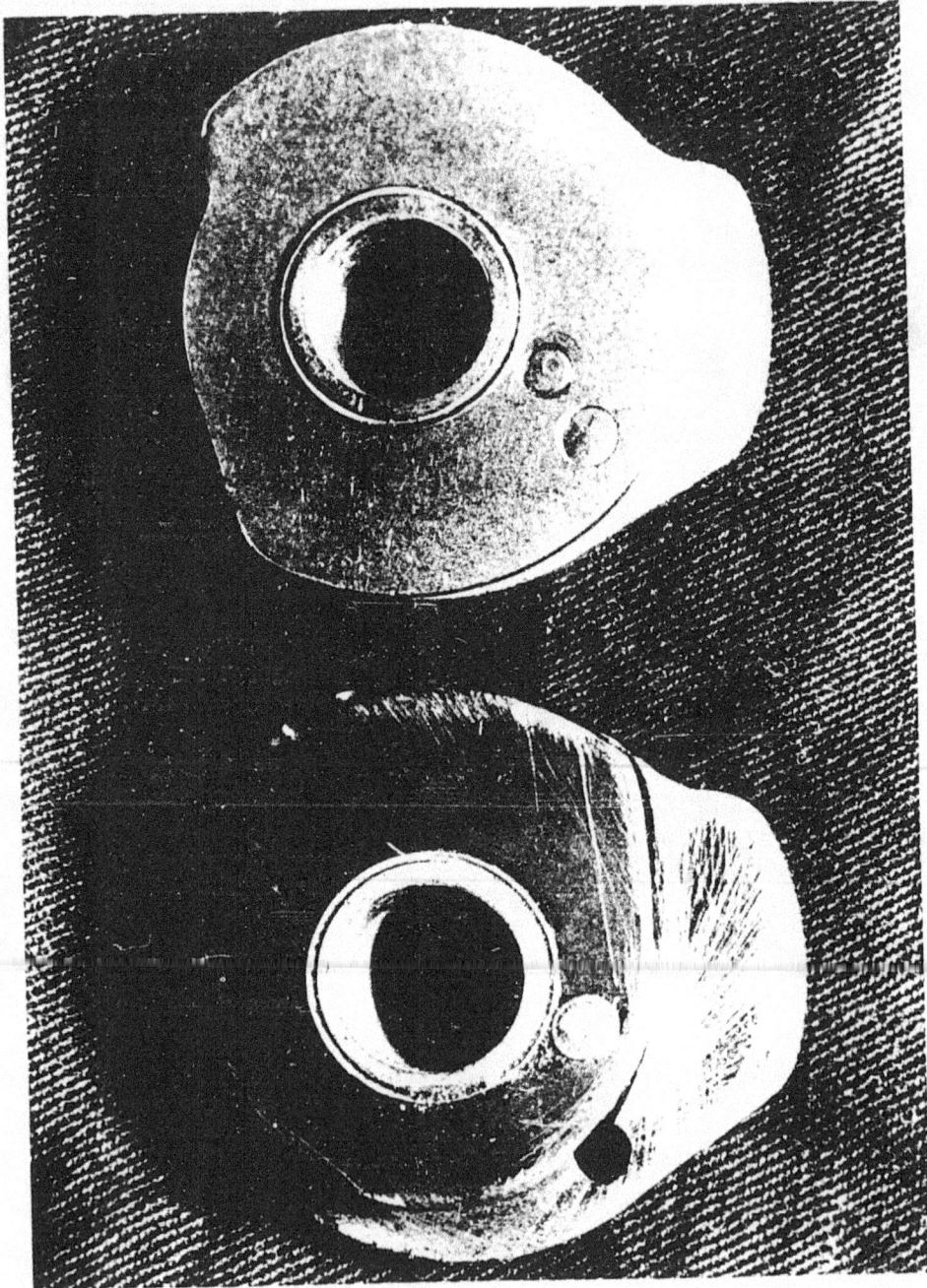

Plate No. 24.

Modified trip cam B-3-B intervalometer.

The calibrations on the scope of the altimeters will not record both the altitude blip and the calibrations simultaneously. Therefore the negative of the blip should be enlarged to a readable size, and a transparent template made of the calibrations on the altimeter scope, (See Plate 25). This transparent template is then laid on top of the print containing the blip to obtain a reading of the altitude.

All altimeter negatives have a ghost image which is inherent where transparent mirrors are employed as they are in the radio altimeter telescope and recorder. The ghost images could be overcome by using front surfaced mirrors; the mirror between the viewing end and the scope should be moveable for the purpose of viewing scope, and so mounted that when released it will return to normal operating position. This would be possible on the altimeter for it is not necessary to view the scope at all times.

The four Recording Cameras worked perfectly throughout the entire operation.

The watch stems were twisted off on four occasions. It is believed that smaller winding knobs would remedy this failure.

One magazine failed to operate (No. 0355). The trouble was found to be a tight bearing on the take-up spindle. This bearing is press fitted into its support (See Plate 26) and seemed to have been forced in far enough to bind on the shoulder of the shaft. By forcing the bearing back slightly it operated throughout the rest of the operation without any trouble.

The fasteners on the cover plates for the seat of the magazines were broken on all magazines (See Plate 27). It is necessary to lift the cover straight off the magazine to prevent bending these friction fasteners. If they are removed one end at A time, as was usually the case, these fasteners were bent and finally would snap off (See Plate 28). It is recommended that a different type cover in the form of a dark slide be used. The magazine also has a type of hinge fastening that is not reliable. The pin that holds the two parts of the hinge together is held in place by two small clips (See Plates 29 and 30). These clips are easily broken or knocked off in handling. Because the hinges projected away from the magazine, they are subjected to bending and thereby springing of the cover could easily occur. It is suggested that they be replaced by a piano type hinge..

K-20 AIRCRAFT CAMERA

The K-20 operated with very little trouble. Its main use was as a color test camera and as a miscellaneous shipboard and small boat camera. It was taken aloft on three flights and subjected to temperatures of minus 19° centigrade. On two occasions the pressure plates did not release. This was due to lack of lubrication on the locking shafts and releasing fins on back of the piston. Locking shafts and releasing fins were oiled with ANO-6 oil and placed back in operations with out any further trouble.

The CNO color tests called for the use of ultra violet and "Harrison and Harrison" color correction filters. A quick change filter holder was constructed on the K-20 (See Plates 31 and 32) so that the filter could be easily swung out of the lens path for comparative exposures with various types of filters, or without filters.

PORTABLE AERIAL FILM DEVELOPING KIT TYPE D-1

All aerial developing was accomplished with the Type D-1 Developing kit. Six new kits were received and performed efficiently for approximately two thousand two hundred (2,200) feet of film. After loading on the reel, each roll of film was given a pre-wash in water before development was started. Due to the extreme dryness of the film it abosrbed approximately one third of a gallon of the pre-wash thus causing the film to swell. This caused pressure to be exerted on the core of the reel, bending the top portion into a cone shape causing it to bind on the shaft and closing the slot in which the locking lever is actuated; thereby preventing the unlocking of the film clamp (See Plate 33).

This defect was overcome by attaching a disk to the top end of the reel similar to the one on the lower end (See Plate 34). This disk braced the end of the reel and also prevented the film from climbing up the reel during processing. This climbing is not a common defect but will occur occasionally. The modification was made on one reel and proved satisfactory with both 7½ inch and 9 inch film.

The second defect noted was the failure of the reel to make a complete shift after it had reached the end of the film. This was especially noticable when the reel was operated by motor. The trouble was due to the loosening of the change of direction gears in their stainless steel carriage (See Plate 35). This condition was remedied by pressing the gear carriage so that it was tighter on the main wind gear.

SMITH AUTOMATIC FILM DRYER, MODEL "J" AND HEATING UNIT MODEL "J".

The Smith Automatic Film Dryer, Model "J", was inefficient. Four units were used, three with Smith Model "J" Heating Units. These four units were not sufficient to dry one mission's film before the next mission went out. An hour and a half was the approximate time required to dry one two hundred (200) foot roll of film. Tests were run on these dryers before we reached the area of operation and at that time no defects were noted. When the film from the first mission had started through the dryers, the gears on the film rollers began to loosen and fall off. This defect is common with the Model "J" film dryer because these composition gears are fastened to the rollers with only glue. The defect was more prevalent on this operation due to the extreme dryness of the air. It was remedied by fastening the gear to the roller by means of three (3) wire brads (See Plate 36.)

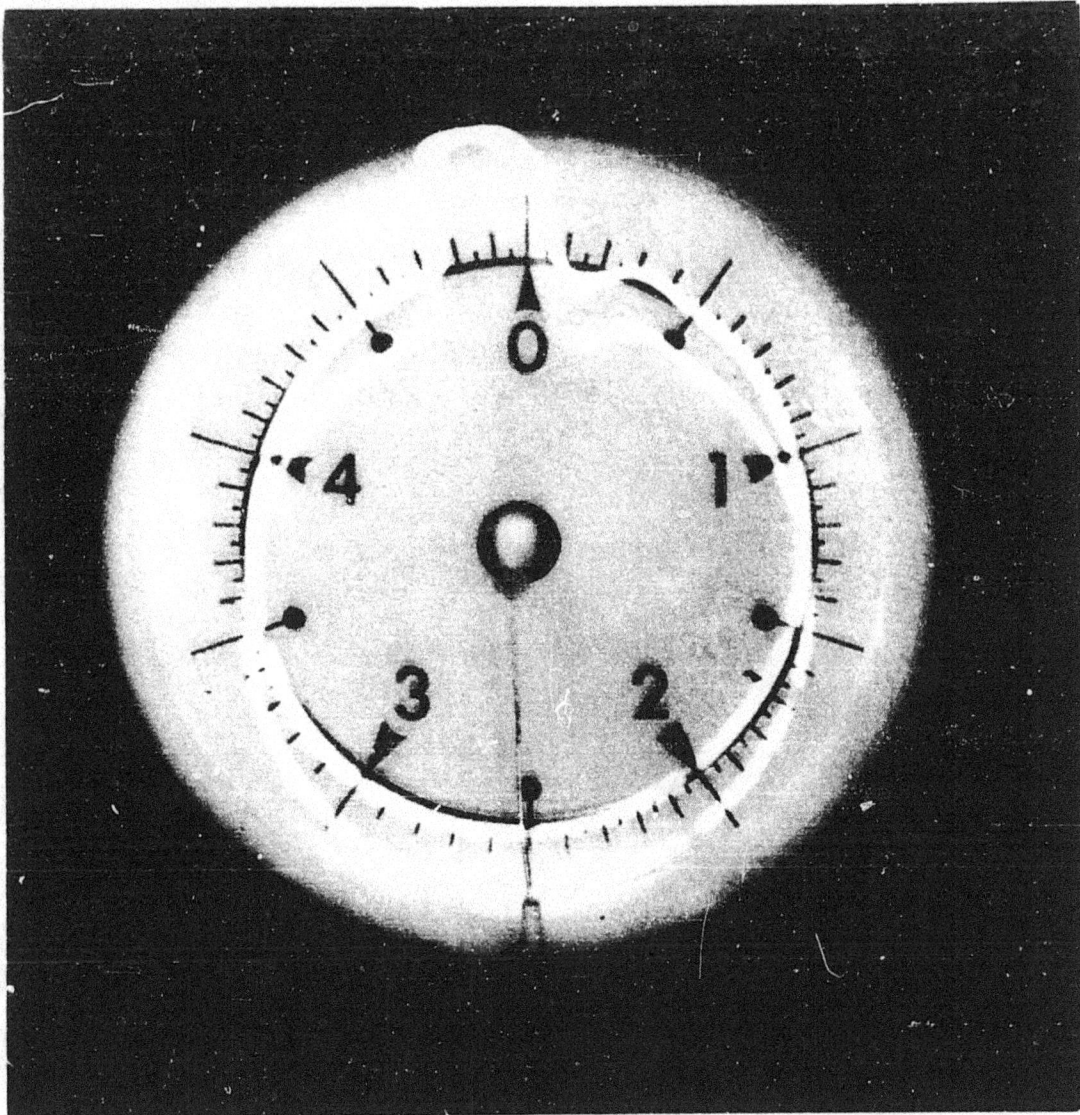

Plate No. 25.

Composite print of Radio Altimeter Scope image and grid

Plate No. 26.

Takeup spool shaft bushing type
"A" recording camera magazine.

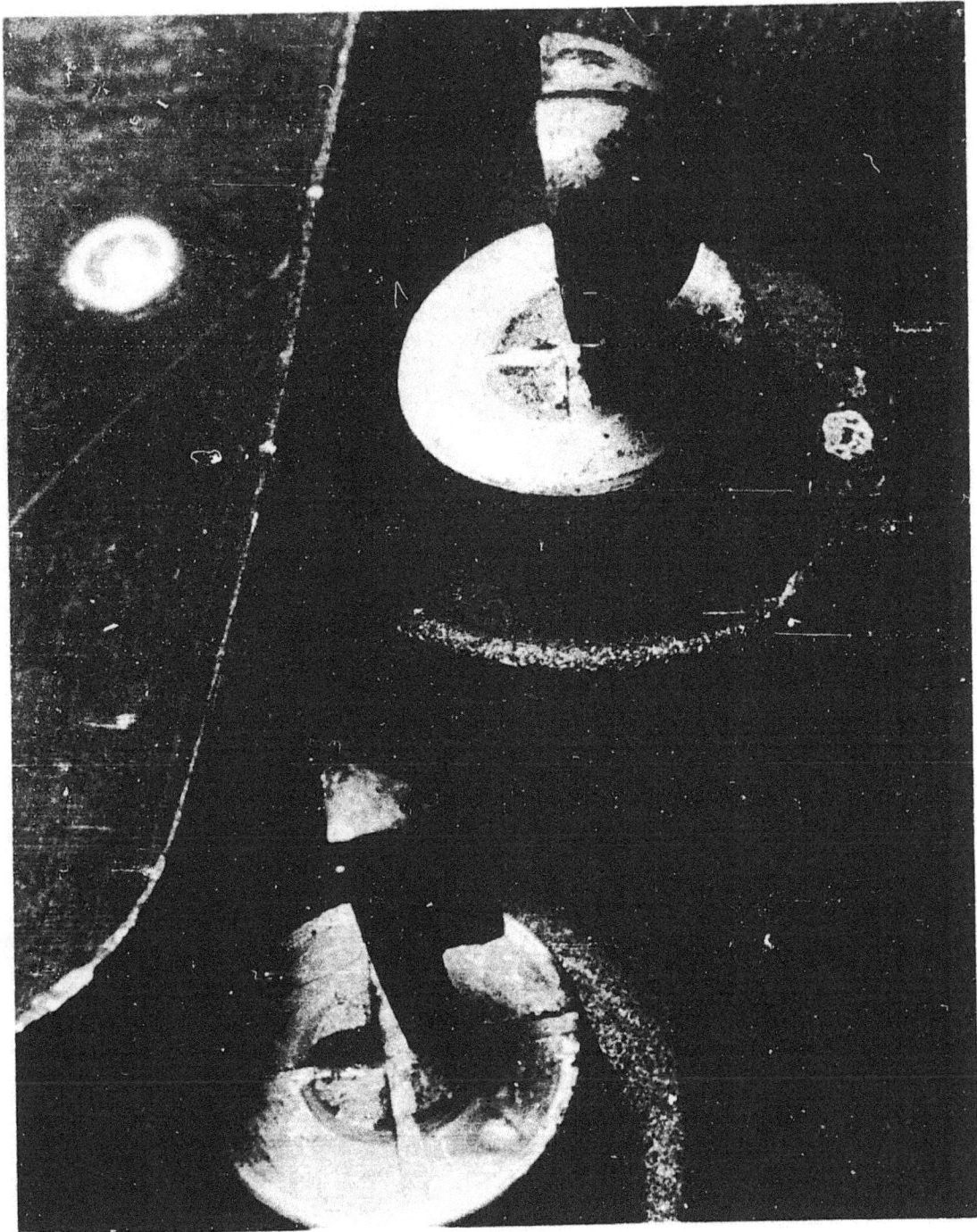

Plate No. 27.

Cover fasteners type "A" recording camera magazine.

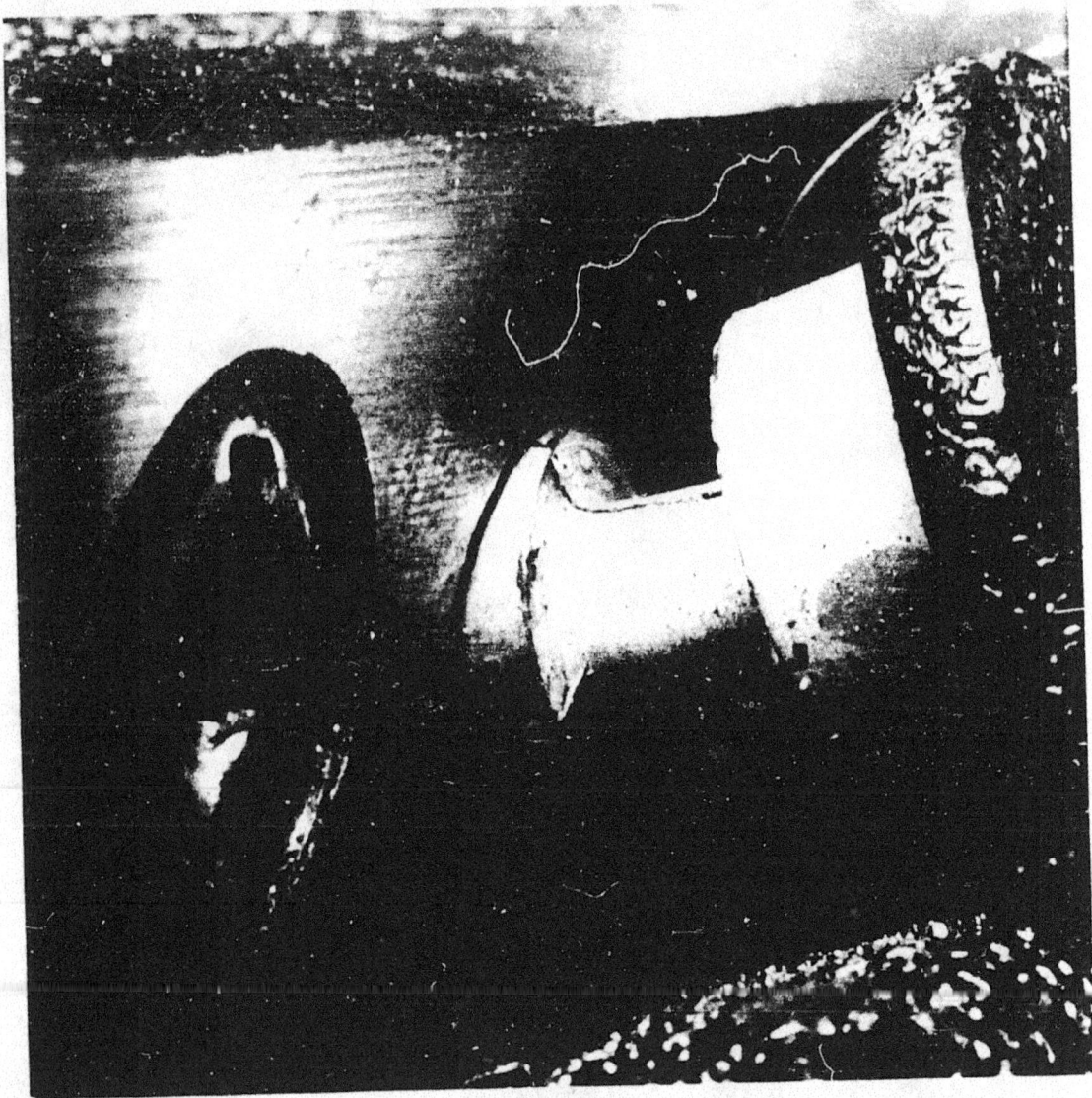

Plate No. 28.

Cover fasteners type "A" recording camera magazine

Plate No. 29.

Hinge pin type "A" recording camera magazine.

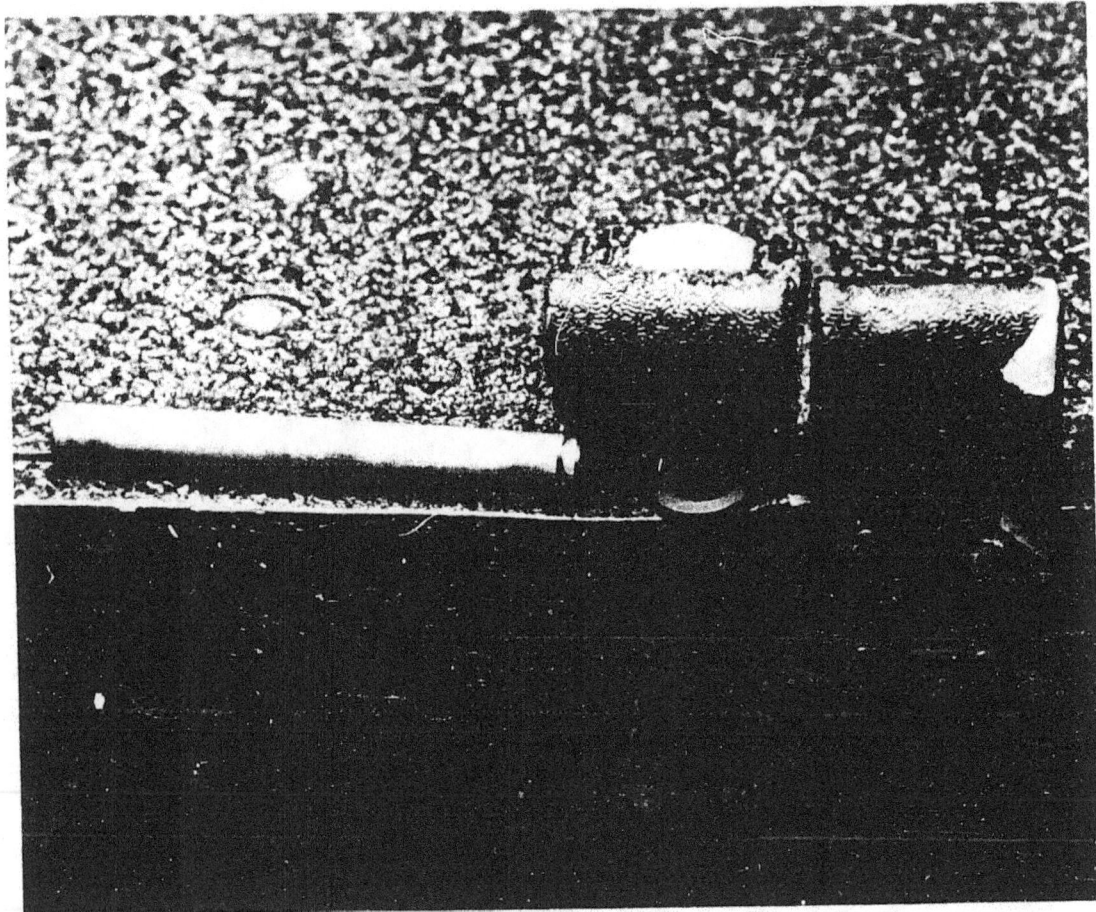

Plate No. 30.

Hinge pin type "A" recording camera magazine

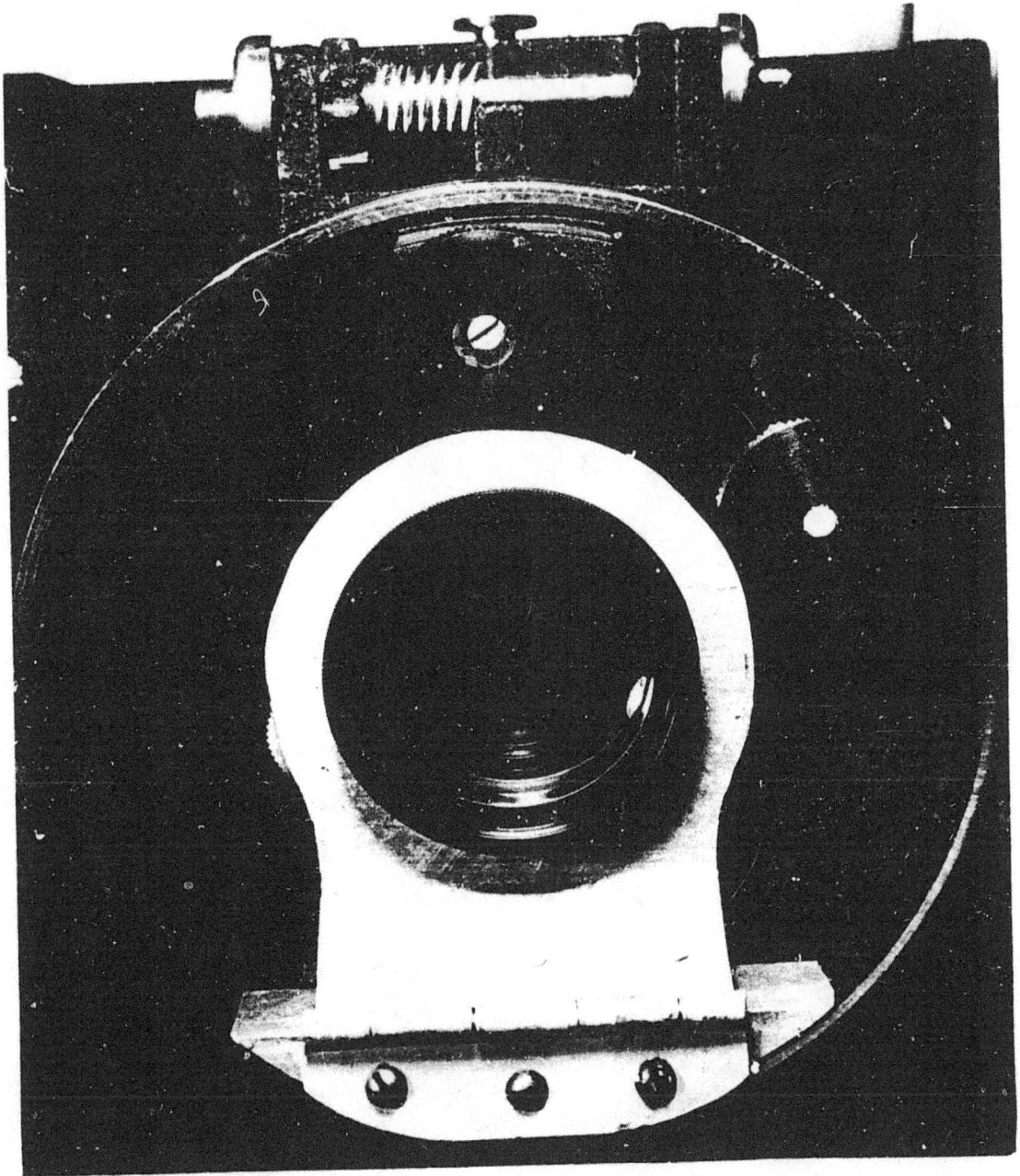

Plate No. 31.

Filter adapter, K-20 camera

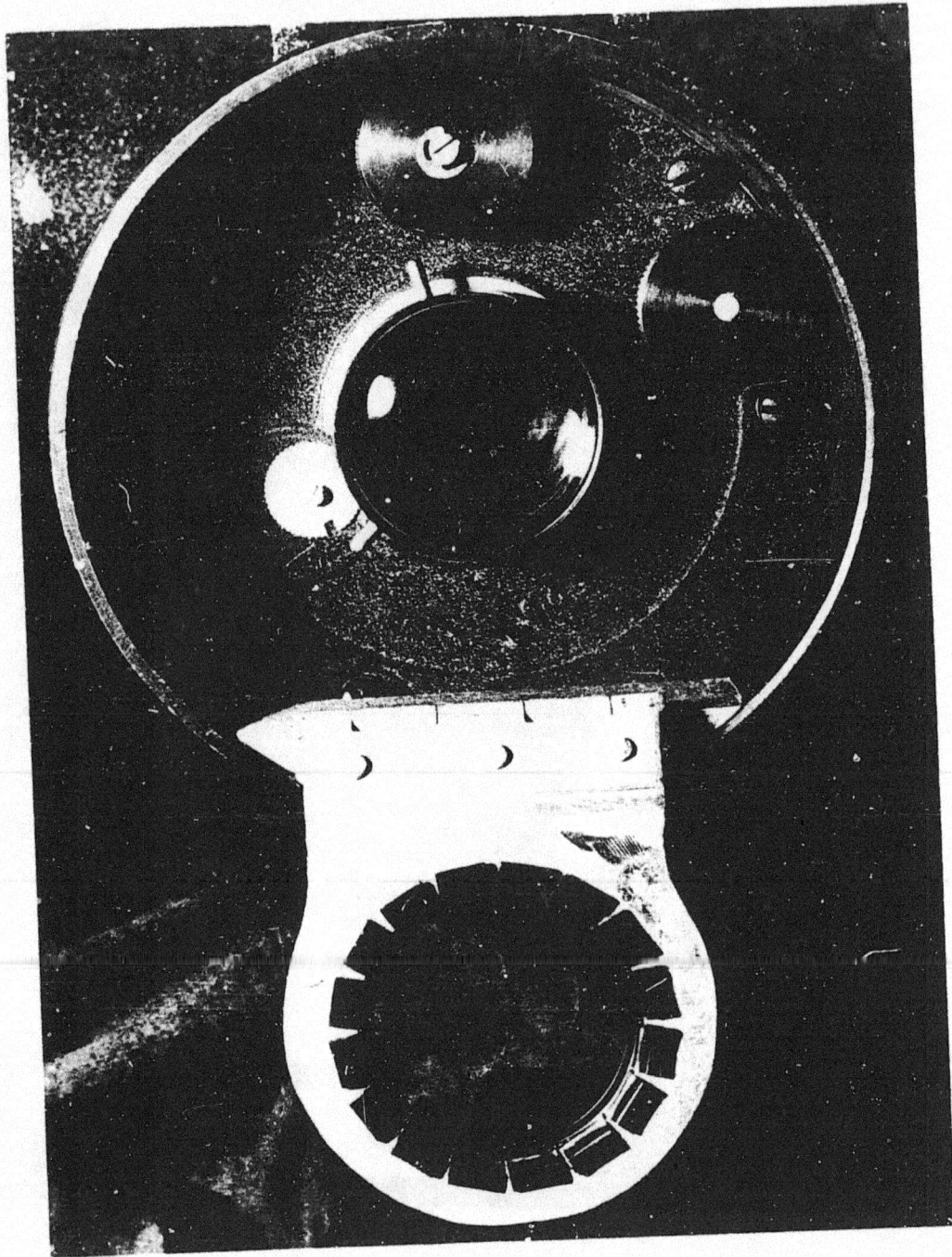

Plate No. 32.

Filter adapter, K-20 camera

- 44 -

Plate No. 33.

Type D-1 portable aerial film developing kit.

Plate No. 34.

Type D-1 portable aerial film developing kit.

Plate No. 35.

Type D-1 portable aerial film developing kit.

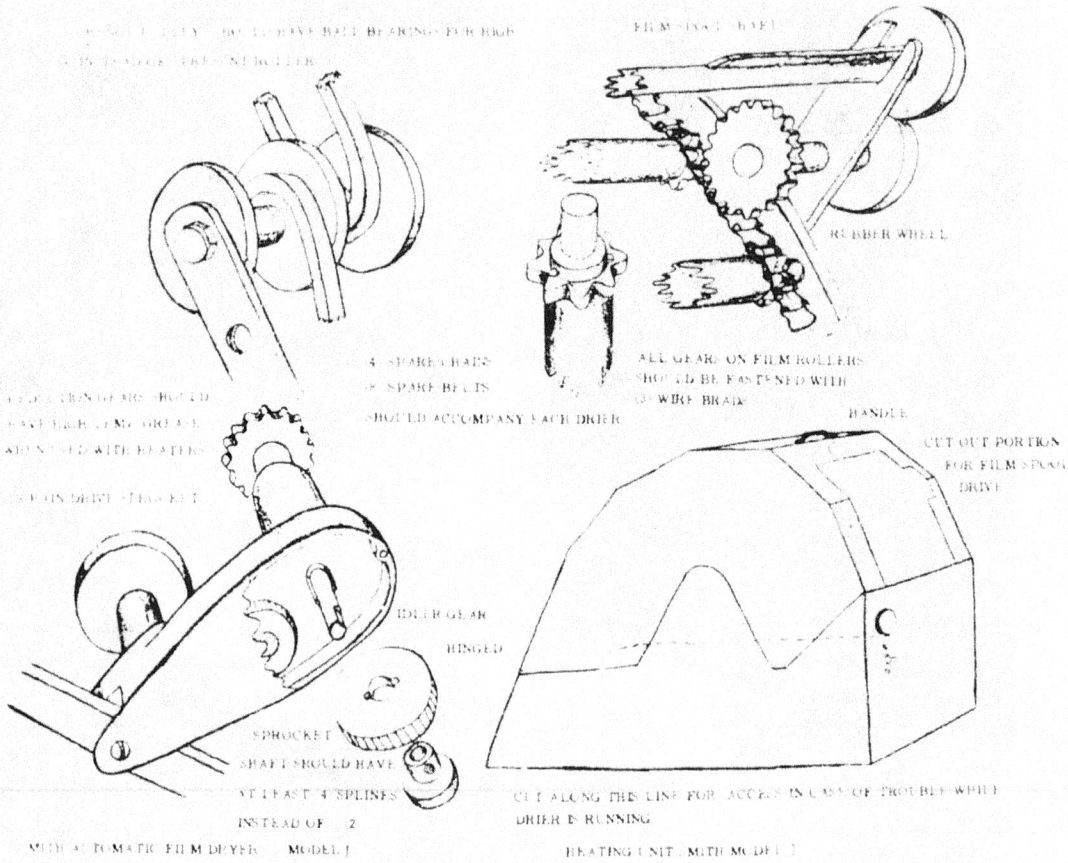

Plate No. 36.

Smith Automatic Film Dryer, Model "J",
Heating Unit, Recommendation for.

The second defect was in the film roller chains. This chain, on five (5) occasions, wound itself around the drive sprocket. The cause for this action was the fastening of the sprocket drive (See Plate 36). This drive was supported by one bolt on one end and a loose fitting adjusting bracket on the other was allowed to wobble as the dryer operated. This action would cause the chain to bind on the sprocket. The chain binding on the sprocket would then start to wind around the sprocket again. This would stretch the chain links out of shape and if not detected immediately, would break the chain. This defect was remedied by attaching a supporting bracket across the outside of the sprocket drive assembly.

The third defect noted was the type of grease in the sprocket drive assembly. When the dryer was used with the Model "J" Hearing Unit the grease in the assembly melted and ran out. This was remedied by packing the assembly with high temperature grease.

The fourth defect noted was in the speed change pulleys. These pulleys were mounted on roller type bearings. Because of the high temperature and speed at which they operated, two bearings wore out. This was remedied by replacing the bearings with sealed ball bearings.

The fifth defect was the speed regulator belts. These belts operated at a high rate of speed and were usually worn beyond use, after one hundred (100) hours of operation. Spare belts should accompany each dryer.

The sixth defect noted was the film take-up spool drive wheel. This wheel, after approximately seventy (70) hours of operation, was worn beyond use. It is recommended that this wheel be replaced by a sprocket (See Plate 36, thereby doing away with the direct chain drive on the wheel. The direct chain drive causes the excessive wear.

The seventh defect noted was the drive shaft for the chain sprocket. This shaft has two splines that mate with the drive gear. Their purpose is to permit the shaft to be pushed in, thus disengaging the splines stopping the chain drive sprocket. These splines are sometimes not fully engaged and slip in and out causing them to chip. Four splines are recommended instead of the present two. The knob that adjusts the shaft is fastened by a set screw that loosens and permits the shaft to disengage. The adjusting knot should either be fastened by a straight pin, or a holding screw placed at the end of the shaft rather than on the side.

The heating Unit performed efficiently throughout the operation. The only objectionable feature noted was the inaccessibility to the dryer in the event of a film jam. It is recommended that the Unit be constructed in two (2) parts. The lower portion should contain the heating elements, indicator light and switch. The top portion should be hinged in the rear so that it could be raised to permit access to the dryer (See Plate 36).

GUN SIGHT AIMING POINT CAMERA, TYPE AN-N6A.

The type AN-N6A Gun Camera was used for supplementary 16-mm motion picture coverage on Tri-metrogon flights. Of the two cameras used, one performed throughout the operation without mechanical failure; the other camera was being tested at different frames per second when the shutter became entangled with the gear chain (See Plate 37). This failure is not uncommon with the Bell and Howell gun camera. It is believed that the Fairchild AN-N6 Gun Camera has a superior type shutter, in that it is constructed of a complete circular cone shaped disc, thereby giving support across the shutter's opening. This support is necessary when the camera is operating at sixty-four (64) frames per second.

Both cameras were placed in operation with factory lubrication and it was not deemed necessary to lubricate either at any time. The heating elements performed efficiently throughout the operation. It was found that all camera failures were due to jammed film in the Type G magazines.

EYEMO MODEL Q

Two cameras were received on board in the following very poor condition:
(a) In need of lubrication, (b) full of dirt and film chips, (c) Scratched aperture plates.

The cameras operated on the spring motor until temperatures of $59^{\circ}F$ were encountered. After completely overhauling and relubricating with type ANO-6 oil, the cameras would operate by electric motor at temperatures as low as minus $4^{\circ}F$. It is believed that the reason for the cameras freezing at this temperature, is the type of governor used. This governor is preset at the factory and existing instructions state that it is not to be disassembled.

The camera release mechanism on the Model "Q" Eyemo is practically inaccessible and is so constructed that it causes it to bind after short operational use. It was almost impossible to operate this type of release with the heavy winter gloves provided for this operation. One modification in the form of a trigger release was constructed and found highly satisfactory (See Plates 38 and 39). An addition could be made to this modification in the form of an electrical microswitch which could be installed directly behind the trigger thus eliminating the need for a switch on the power cable. (Plate 40) shows the exact size and shape of the parts installed and (Plate 41) shows their relative position.

MITCHELL, HIGH SPEED 35MM AND FRICTION HEAD TRIPOD

Two Mitchells were received on board and only one was in operating condition when received. The positioning posts were out of time with the film advance claw in the defective camera, and due to the need for only

Plate No. 37.

GSAP Camera Shutter

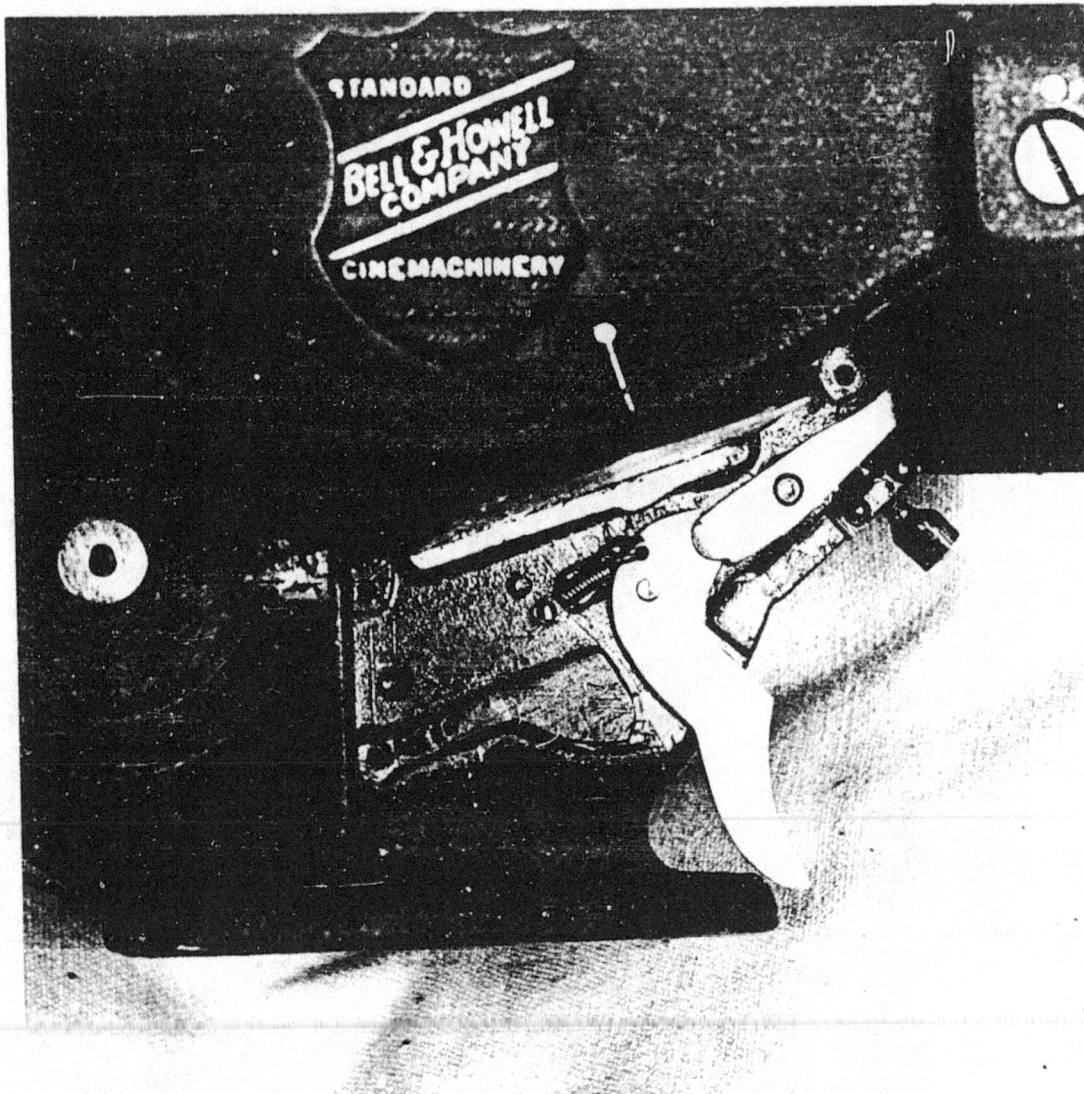

Plate No. 38.

Modified trigger release for Model "Q" Eyemo.

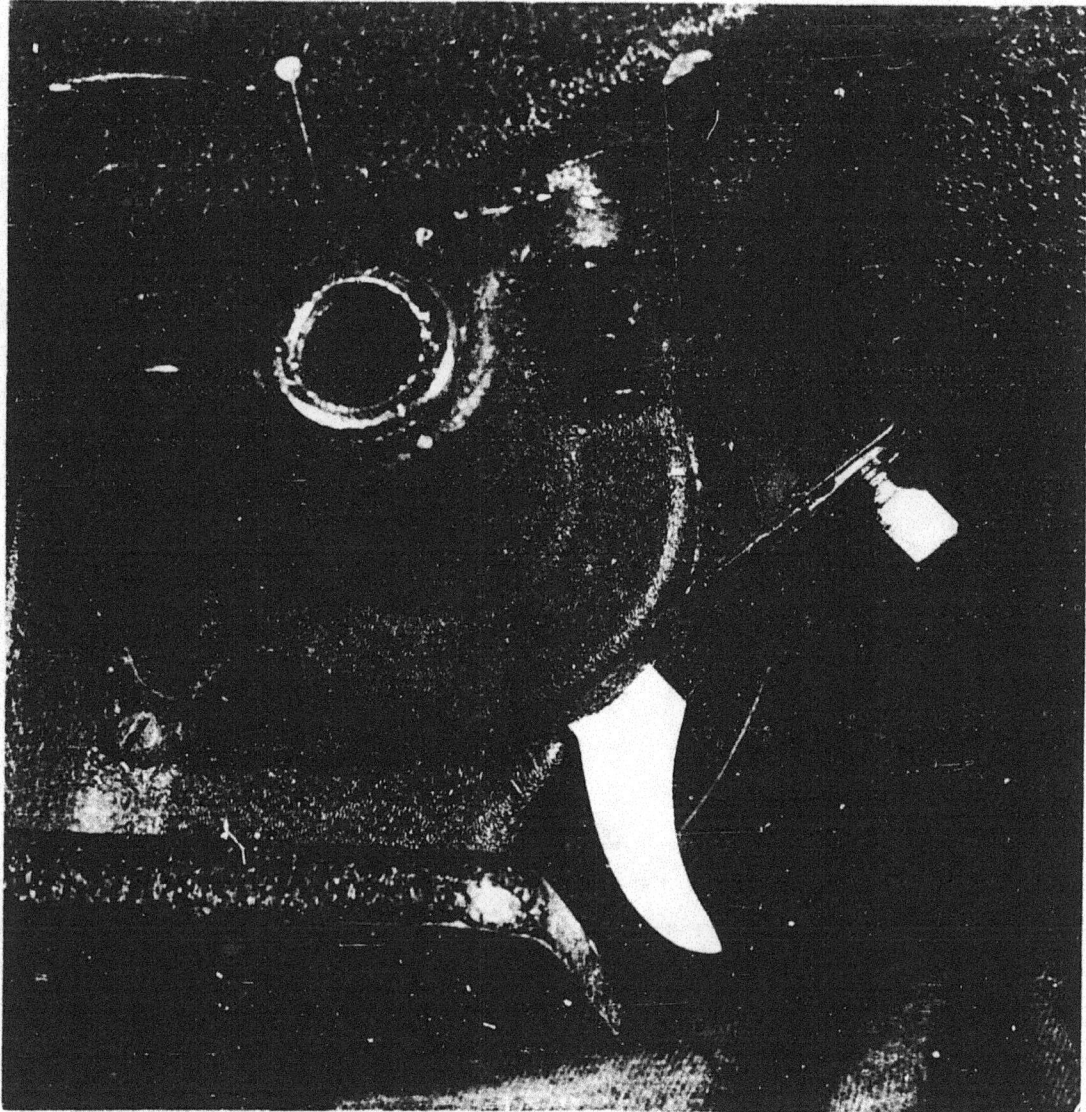

Plate No. 39.

Modified trigger release for Model
"Q" Eyemo.

Plate No. 40.

Trigger for modified release on Model "Q" Eyemo.

one camera during the operation, no attempt was made to re-time it.

The first aerial mission on which the Mitchell was used, temperatures ranged from 28.4°F to minus 23.8°F. The camera was powered by four 12-volt batteries, and froze up completely after a temperature of minus 15.8°F was reached.

Tests were made on shipboard using the aircraft's 24-volt power supply, and it was found that the camera operated without overheating its 12-volt motor. The camera and motor drive assembly was completely overhauled and lubricated with ANG-3A grease. It was also necessary to clean and lubricate the diaphragm actuating rings and the lens focusing rings with ANO-6 type oil. The positioning pin in the base of the camera, which locks it in the focusing and operating position, sometimes froze in the retracted position. This was remedied with proper lubrication. After this overhaul, and with the use of 24-volt power supply, the camera operated without any mechanical defects. However, it was extremely difficult to thread the camera without breaking the film or freezing the operators hands.

The Mitchell friction head tripod was found to be inoperative at 5°F. The reason for this was the hardening of the grease in the disc-type friction parts. It was necessary to completely disassemble this head and re-lubricate with type ANG-3A grease. After this change in lubrication the tripod functioned without trouble.

It is recommended that all Mitchell cameras that are to be used on aerial missions be equipped with 24-volt motors, and that all cameras and tripods be given winterized lubrication when tools and equipment are available.

AERIAL MOTION PICTURE CAMERA, RECOMMENDATIONS FOR.

The motion picture cameras used were found to be lacking in numerous respects. The Mitchell camera performed satisfactorily, but due to its bulk and weight, it was very difficult to handle, necessitating extreme care when the camera was moved about. Loading the Mitchell camera while in flight was very difficult because dryness and brittleness of the film. Invariably it was necessary to remove gloves in order to load the camera

The Cine Special performed exceptionally well under all conditions, but it has numerous special attachments and devices which, to this type of photography, are absolutely of no value. In aerial operation, and , especially while in foul weather clothing, some of these attachments would change adjustment during operation and ruin all exposures until this change was noticed.

The Bell & Howell Filmo Speedster was found unreliable in this operation. Of the six cameras used on aerial flights only one was found to operate reliably at all times. Four were found to operate sporadically, and one would not operate unless kept warm inside flight clothing. The spring motor on this camera is not sufficient for the average scene. The desirable features of this camera are: fast magazine loading, light weight, and compactness.

The Model "Q" Eyemo is not suitable for aerial operation because of small magazine capacity and chamber loading. It also freezes quickly in cold weather operation.

It is recommended that the desirable features of each camera be incorporated in one camera designed mainly for aerial use.

(1) This camera should be of the magazine load type with a capacity of one hundred feet for 16mm and two hundred for 35mm.

(2) It should be operated by either a spring motor or 24-volt electrical motor. The spring motor should be wound with a ratcheting type charging handle similar to that used on automatic guns.

(3) It should incorporate a three lens turret with the viewfinder elements mounted beside their respective lenses and viewed through a prism arrangement over the top of the camera.

(4) A filter ring similar to the one used in the Mitchell camera should be installed behind the three lens turret.

(5) The opening for the film magazine chamber should be in the rear of the camera similar to the Filmo Speedster and GSAP Camera.

(6) The film advance claw should be of a type similar to that used in the High Speed Mitchell camera, but modified to engage the film from the front of the magazine.

(7) The magazine sprocket drive should be engaged by the photographer through a positive lever system.

(8) The handles to this camera should be similar to those used on most aerial still cameras and the trigger should be placed above the right handle and operated by the right thumb. The handle on the right side should be placed on the rear portion of the camera, and would also serve as the charging handle. The handle on the left side should be mounted on the forward portion when the camera is used without a mount, and made detachable for installation on the rear portion when used on a mount.

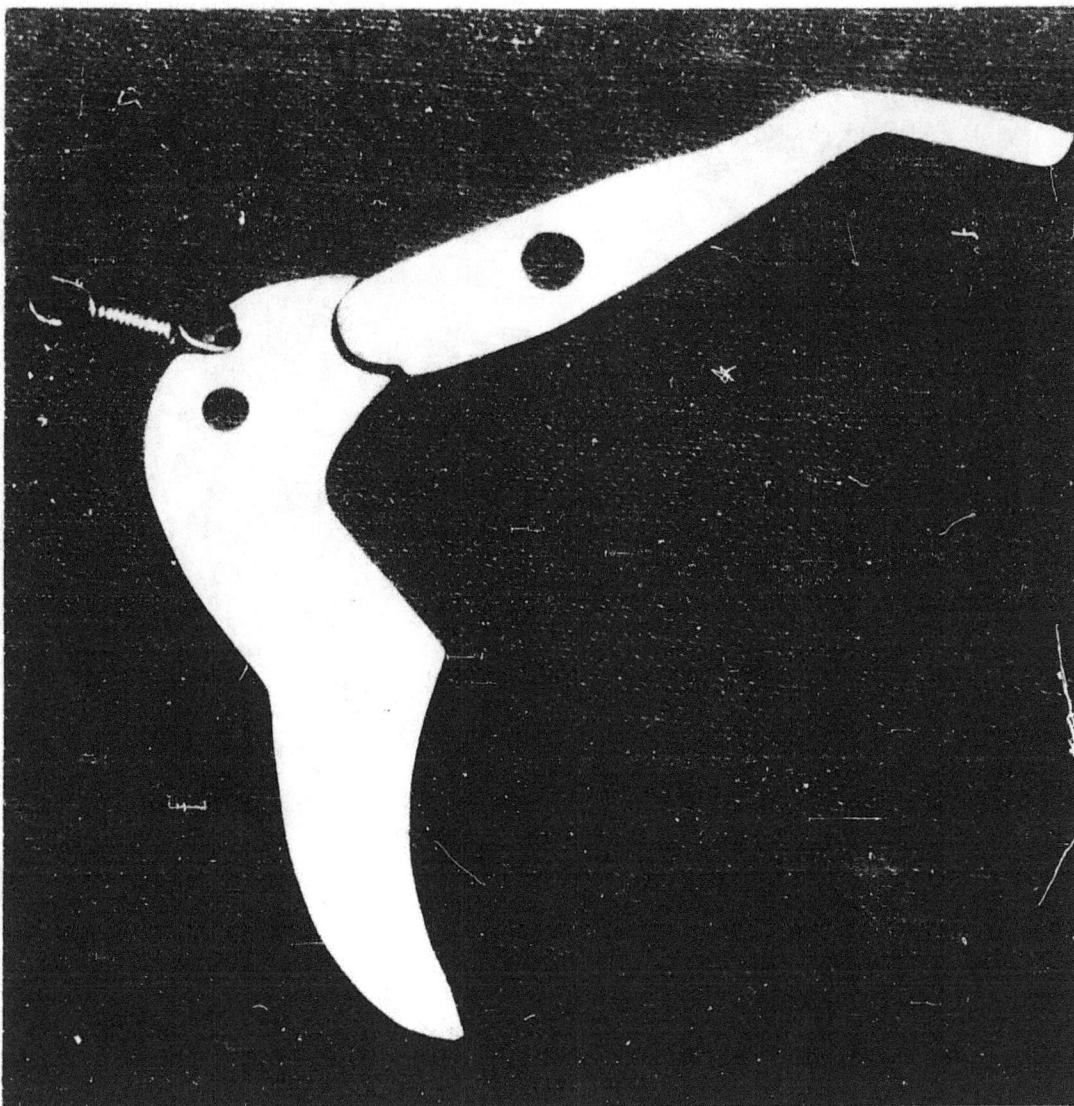

Plate No. 41.

Modified trigger release for Model "Q" Eyemo

Plate No. 42.

VC Radar with modification to mount the Abrams
Recording Camera Adapter, USS HENDERSON (DD-785).

(9) In place of a frames-per-second setting knob, a tachometer and speed adjustment knob should be substituted. This would permit accurate operation or adjustment regardless of temperature changes.

SPEED GRAPHIC

Speed graphics were used for shipboard, plane handling boat, and aerial photography. Speed Graphics were equipped with both Supermatic and Graphex type shutters. These shutters were mounted with both Ektar and Wollensak coated lenses. It was found that the Supermatic shutter with the solenoid type synchronizers were not as dependable for flash synchronization as the Graphex type shutter. The reason for this was that the solenoids lagged when operated in extreme cold. The lag was evident with the use of either the three or the five cell flash guns. The Graphex type shutter was subjected to temperatures as low as minus 16.6°F and still operated satisfactorily. It was sometimes necessary to place the batteries inside the foul weather clothing to keep them warm enough to insure operation when either type shutter was used.

Tests were requested to be performed on coated lenses to determine the susceptibility to cold weather operation. Because of the limited number of cameras on board this test was not performed as recommended by the requesting agency. The coated lenses on the Speed Graphics (that were constantly used) were subjected to extreme cold temperatures during normal operation over long periods of time and did not show any visible signs of deterioration.

These cameras were equipped with KALART range finders model E. It was found that at temperatures below minus 10°F, two of these range finders were not accurate. These range finders should have more working tolerances, so that the weight of the mirrors will cause them to fall when operating in low temperatures. The focal plane shutters on these cameras were very seldom used but functioned allright when used. With the exception of the above discrepancies the speed graphics were reliable.

GRAFLEX

The Series "D" Graflexes used on this operation performed satisfactorily until temperatures of 68°F were encountered. These cameras are lubricated at the factory with a grease that appears to have a heavy parafin base. This lubricant is quite suitable for average temperatures, but will harden to a soap-like consistency when low temperatures are encountered. This lubricant hardening was first noticed on the moveable mirror shafts and tripping mechanism. It is believed that the action of the focal plane shutter, due to its rubberoid coating, was retarded when colder temperatures were reached, but no accurate means were available for testing the shutter speed. It was found necessary to increase the tension on the movable mirror spring in order to overcome the lag in tripping action. After the lubrication was changed to type ANG-3A grease and tension increased on the mirror spring, this camera operated more successfully. It is doubtful wheather this camera would operate in temperatures lower than 23°F.

ABRAMS ADAPTER FOR RADAR RECORDING CAMERA

(a) Abrams recording camera adapters were received on board both the U.S.S. HENDERSON (DD-785) and the U.S.S. CURRITUCK (AV-7). The units were used to record VC radar Repeater (modified) on board the HENDERSON and the VC-1 on board the CURRITUCK.

(b) On board the CURRITUCK modifications were made to adapt the Abrams camera mount to the SG-1-B radar indicator. It was believed that better results would be obtained from the Indicator than from the VC-1 repeater. The camera was used on the SG-1-B until it was considered to interfere with the operation of the radar. It was then changed to the VC-1 repeater where it was used for the rest of the operation. This permitted changing from SK to SG radar by means of selector switch rather than moving the camera each time.

(c) On board the HENDERSON difficulties were encountered in adapting the camera mount to the 12 inch scope on the VC-1 repeater. It was necessary to construct an adapter plate to support the mount as shown in Figures 42, 43 and 44. With the camera so mounted, it did not cover the entire scope, but covered a sufficient amount to be considered adequate. A more desirable mount would have been one which raised the camera approximately six inches higher, and thereby enabled the entire scope to be photographed.

IV. ALTERATIONS OF WARRANT OFFICERS MESSROOM PANTRY TO AERIAL NEGATIVE PROCESSING, DRYING AND MARKING ROOMS

The Warrant Officers Messroom and Pantry were obtained for conversion into a processing laboratory, film drying and marking room. The loose gear and fixed equipment such as chairs, tables, cabinets and electrical appliances were of general use in the conversion and little had to be removed.

In the Warrant Officers Pantry were three metal benches (one with a sink with cold and hot running water faucets), one electric range and oven, one 8.5 cubic foot electric refrigerator and numerous dish, cup and glass racks. Electrical outlets were few but overhead lighting was adequate (See Plate 45.)

Both the benches and the sink were utilized. One bench on the after bulkhead was used for the loading and unloading of magazines and for the loading of film onto the Smith developing reels for processing. The bench on the port side of the forward bulkhead was utilized for general work and for the passing of the processed film through the serving window to the dryers in the finishing and marking room. The long bench along the forward bulkhead that contained the sink was converted into the processing bench with a few minor alterations (See Plate 45).

In the conversion of the bench to processing, twelve (12) inch and one (1) inch pieces of one (1) inch angle iron were welded to hold nine (9) 9½-inch Smith Developing Tanks (See Plates 46 and 47). Across the front of the bench, strips of light iron six (6) inches high were welded to hold any water or solutions that should splash or overrun the tanks from going over the side on to the deck. At the same time, the open end of the splash shields could be closed off and that section filled with cold water around the tanks to serve as a cooling basin for the solutions in the tanks (See Plate 47). The cold and hot water lines running into the sink of this bench were maintained with a slight alteration to the cold water line. This line was continued to run to the bench section on the starboard side of the sink. Three spigots were added to take hoses.

AERIAL PROCESSING FINISHING, MARKING AND DIFFICULTIES ENCOUNTERED

Exposed magazines removed from the aircraft on the seaplane deck were brought down one deck and all the way forward to frame 29 to the processing room, practically from stern to bow. The film trailer was then marked for identification after winding a few exposures through the magazine, by pulling the dark slide and scratching the necessary information on the film. It was then, placed in film cans marked and taped, and allowed to sit and gradually thaw out to approximately room temperature. Magazines with exposed film were often received with a temperature of freezing or below, having been subjected to temperatures of minus 13°F to 22°F while airborne. Upon completion of unloading and checking of magazines, the faulty ones were turned over to camera repair for checking, overhauling or replacing. The good ones immediately reloaded, marked and returned to their respective aircraft ready for operations.

V. FILM DRYING.

Four dryers proved to be insufficient for the amount of film being processed. The Model "J" Aerial Film Dryer proved to be the biggest setback in the processing and finishing operation. This was due to many design faults. Light construction and constant high speed operation resulted in the breakdown and faulty operation of most of the dryers. The speed of the dryer also proved to be quite slow and the film was constantly becoming a backlog in the darkroom. During the first few weeks of operation the dryers were constantly breaking down, requiring the constant vigil of one man and the continual services of a repair man. After a few weeks of reinforcing, overhauling and altering, the dryers began to operate with less trouble and could run at full capacity without trouble.

STARTER PLATES

For a positive identification between tri-metrogon aerial survey runs, a Starter Plate was manufactured and used. This plate was a strip of aluminum approximately two inches wide and eight inches long with the word "Start" perforated on it. Prior to each run the starter plate was inserted in the dark slide slot of the magazine and a few exposures made. This would result in the image of the starter plate and the word "Start" showing clearly on the exposures.

By the use of the starter plate system the maneuvering of the plane on one wing and the photographer making a few exposures at that time was eliminated. This saved considerable time by enabling the pilot, photographer and crew after each run to settle down and commence the next run as soon as possible.

The use of the starter plate also aided the film markers to positively identify runs in the process of marking, thus saving time in that phase of the operation. In this way they did not have to take too much time in discarding, marking and identifying exposures between each run.

The only disadvantage of this system is that the photographer may fail to remove one or more of the four plates before starting the next run. On only two occasions did this occur. In these two cases the exposures were good except for the small area covered by the plate.

The use of these starter plates proved very valuable and was highly successful to this unit during the survey operations.

VI STILL PHOTOGRAPHY

1. Speed Graphic

Speed Graphics with the Graphex Shutter and the Supermatic Shutter were used and in most cases operated satisfactorily. The synchronization of the Supermatic Shutter with the solenoid type synchronizer was not as dependable as the Graphex Shutter.

Graphex flash attachment operated especially well except when it was exposed to temperatures of approximately 15°F. The batteries were affected by this low temperature and it was necessary to put them inside foul weather clothing for warmth, to insure operation.

Suggestions and Recommendations:

That on future operations where cameras are exposed to salt spray, rain, cold weather and the possibility of rough handling, tests should be conducted using the Combat Speed Graphic with flash and range finder equipment.

K-20 AIRCRAFT CAMERA

The K-20 with focusing ring attachment was used extensively and proved to be of great value. It is fast in operation, light in weight and carries a desirable number of exposures. It was used in all kinds of weather, in boats and in planes. As an all around out door camera it would be hard to find a better one.

Suggestions and Recommendations:

The K-20 camera should be used on all future operations. It should be lubricated with the proper oils and greases before being used in cold weather. Special locations for lubrication on the K-20 camera are the retracting fins on the back of the piston, the locking shafts which holds the pressure plate down and the actuating disc in the drive assembly.

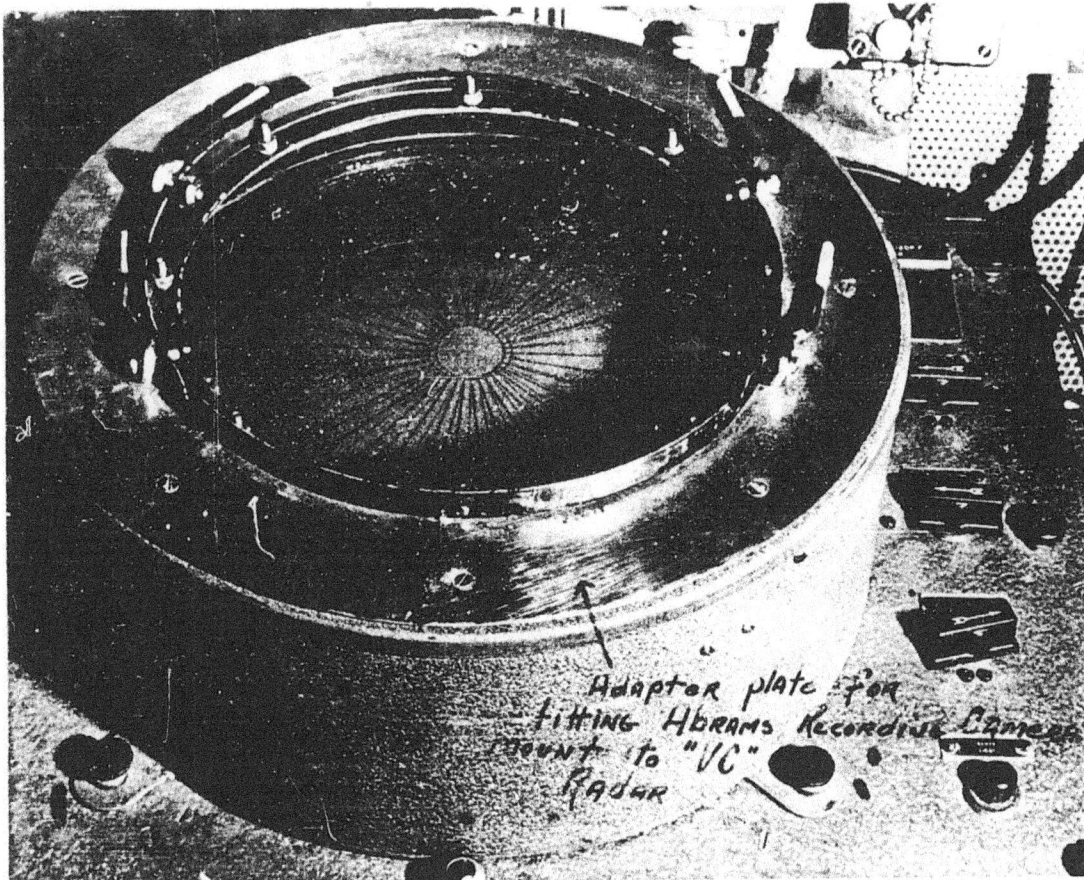

Plate No. 43.

VC Radar with modification to mount the Abrams
Recording Camera Adapter, USS HENDERSON (DD-785)

Plate No. 44.

VC Radar with modification to mount the Abrams
Recording Camera Adapter, USS HENDERSON (DD-785)

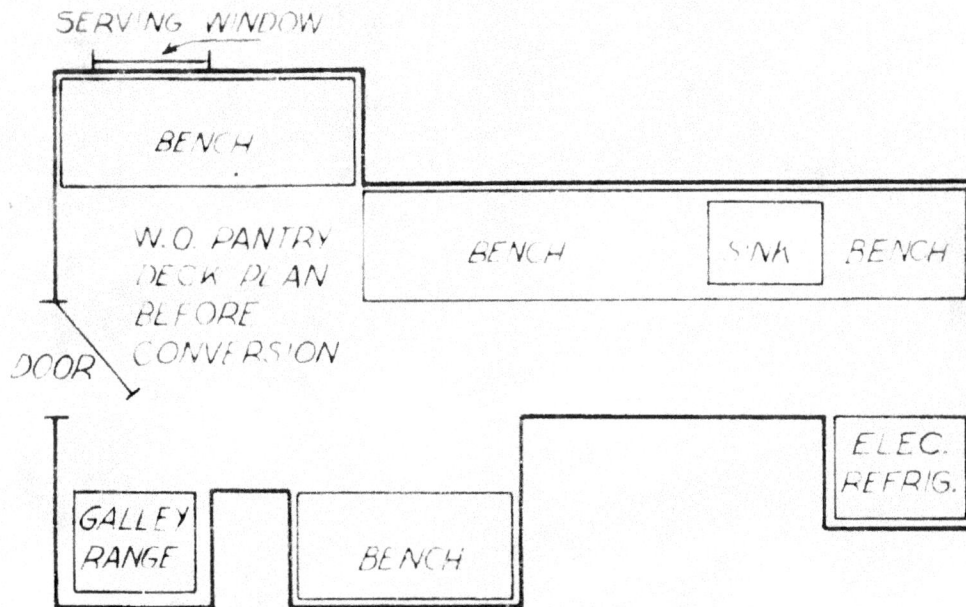

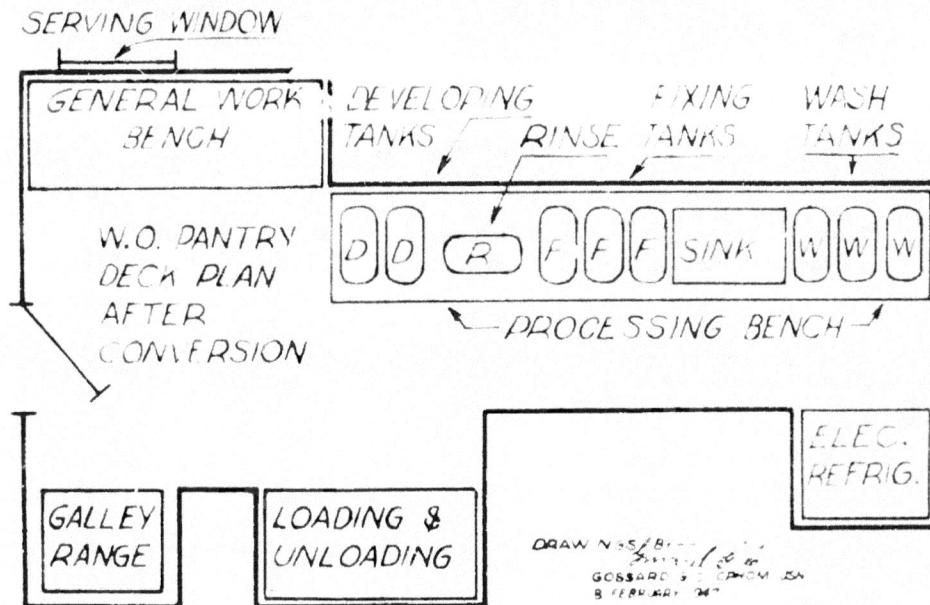

SERVING WINDOW

BENCH

W.O. PANTRY DECK PLAN BEFORE CONVERSION

DOOR

BENCH   SINK   BENCH

GALLEY RANGE

BENCH

ELEC. REFRIG.

SERVING WINDOW

GENERAL WORK BENCH

DEVELOPING TANKS   FIXING TANKS   WASH TANKS

RINSE TANKS

W.O. PANTRY DECK PLAN AFTER CONVERSION

D D   R   F F F   SINK   W W W

PROCESSING BENCH

ELEC. REFRIG.

GALLEY RANGE

LOADING & UNLOADING

DRAWN SS/B..........
GOSSARD ....
8 FEBRUARY 2...

Plate No. 45.

Drawing of floor plan of W.O. Pantry showing conversion
for aerial film processing and loading.

Plate No. 46.

View of angle irons installed on W.O. Pantry sink board
to prevent Smith Aerial Film Developing Tanks from shifting.

Plate No. 47.

View of Aerial Film Developing and fixing installation in W.O. Pantry showing arrangements of tanks and alteration to sink.

Plate No. 48.

View of aerial film washing system installed in W.O.
Pantry showing fresh water lines and sink alterations.

Plate No. 49.

General view of W.O. Pantry as
altered for aerial film processing.

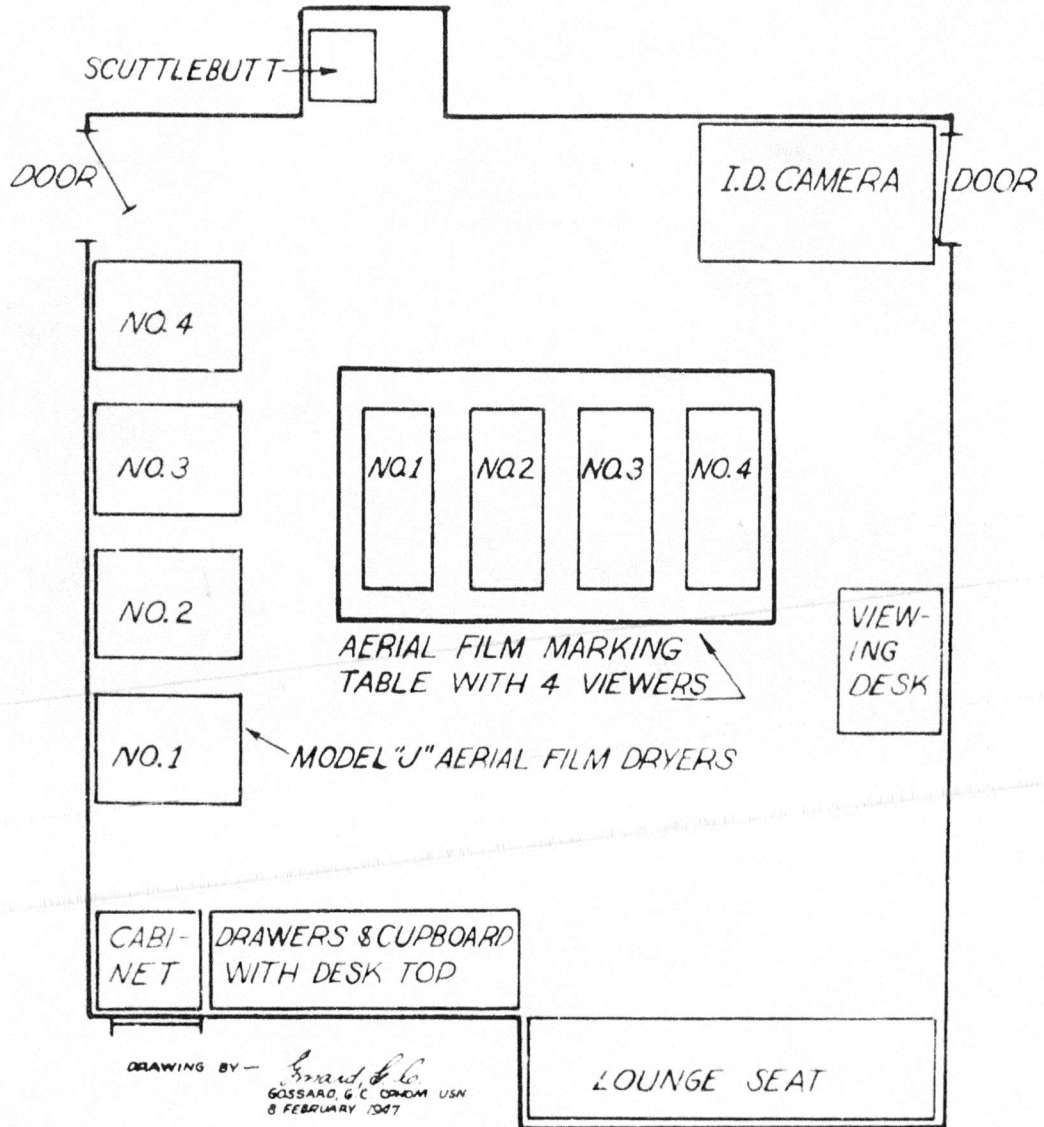

W.O. MESSROOM DECK PLAN
AERIAL FILM FINISHING & MARKING

SCUTTLEBUTT

DOOR

I.D. CAMERA   DOOR

NO. 4

NO. 3

NO. 2

NO. 1

NO.1   NO.2   NO.3   NO.4

AERIAL FILM MARKING
TABLE WITH 4 VIEWERS

VIEW-
ING
DESK

MODEL "U" AERIAL FILM DRYERS

CABI-
NET

DRAWERS & CUPBOARD
WITH DESK TOP

DRAWING BY — Gossard, G C CPHOM USN
8 FEBRUARY 1947

LOUNGE SEAT

Plate No. 50.

Drawing of floor plan of W.O. Messroom showing conversion
for aerial film finishing and marking.

Plate No. 51.

Aerial film drying and marking
arrangement in W.O. Messroom.

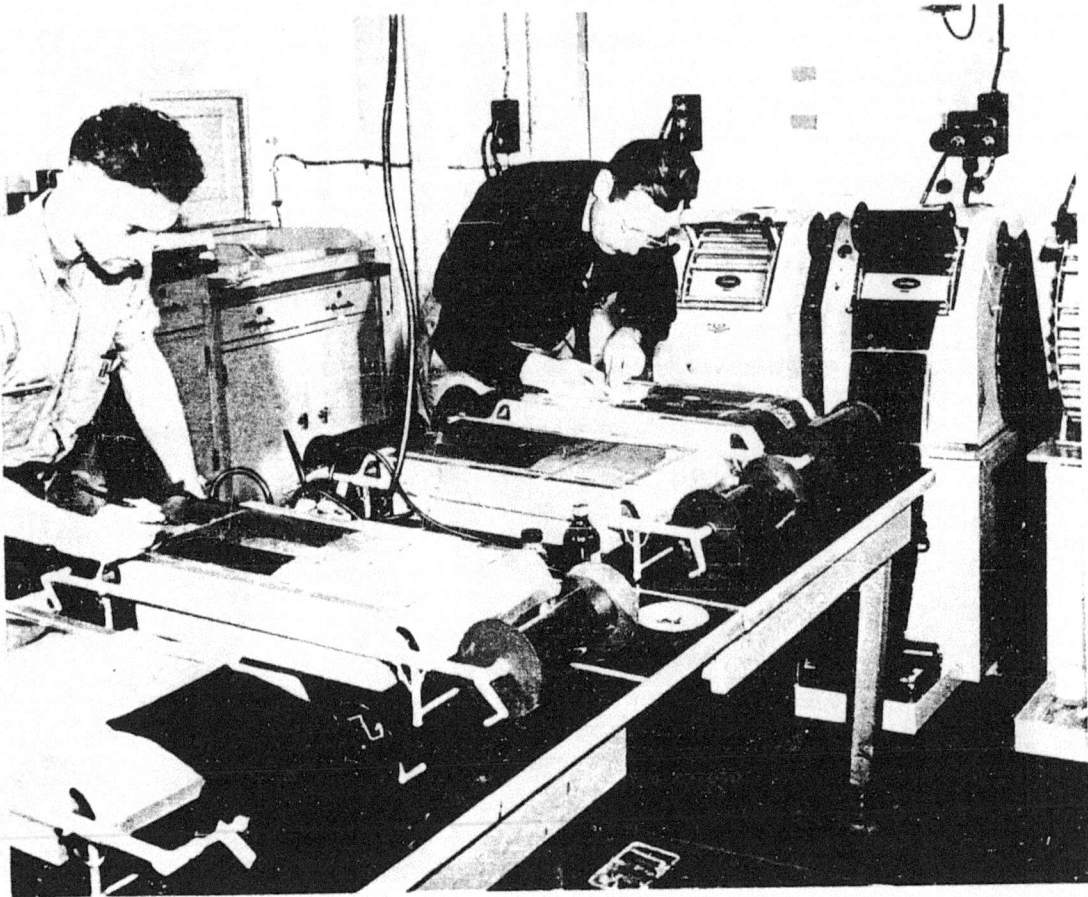

Plate No. 52.

Aerial film drying and marking
arrangement in the W.O. Messroom.

Plate No. 53.

Aerial film drying and marking
arrangement in the W.O. Messroom.

MEDALIST

The Medalist was used very little due to the availability of other cameras with a greater number of exposures. The Medalist jammed on the 7th or 8th exposure, causing undue trouble in returning to the laboratory for unloading order to save the film.

Suggestions and Recommendations

That the Medalist be eliminated from this type expedition; no substitute is required.

GRAFLEX

The Graflex was used but not to great advantage. In cold weather the mirror slowed down and at times completely stopped, causing the camera to be abandoned for outdoor use.

F-56 AIRCRAFT CAMERA

The F-56 was used aboard ship for photographing cloud formations, Antarctic phenomena, and surface views of mountain peaks in the ice-pack.

Suggestions and Recommendations:

That an infra-red focusing post be included with the F-56 camera, making it possible to use the F-56 in carrying out tests and reconnaissance missions with infra-red.

FILM PACK

Film Packs were used throughout the operation and were successful. The film itself maintained its sensitivity when the film was exposed 24 to 72 hours to the weather with the temperatures ranging between 14° to 25°F. No cracking or checking of the emulsion was encountered as a result of brittleness. The Film Pack tabs were difficult to separate when wearing five finger winter aviation gloves but could be parted with not too much loss of time.

Suggestions and Recommendations:

Film Packs be used in all outdoor photography in the Antarctic.

CUT FILM

For indoor photography, where it is possible to operate without gloves, operation with cut film was convenient. Outdoors where it is impossible to remove gloves for operating and attaching the holder to the camera, it is quite difficult.

Suggestions and Recommendations:

Cut film be used for indoor photography and photographic tests only.

KODACOLOR

There were very few days that could be called ideal for color photography but in almost every case where Kodacolor was used, good results were obtained.

Suggestions and Recommendations:

Kodacolor be used in the Antarctic, and further tests be conducted using Harrison and Harrison color correction filter.

ANSCO COLOR

Very little success was experienced with this film. Indoor use of blue flash bulbs with daylight film gave fair results. When used outdoors there was a predominance of red or ultra-violet. In development, fraying of the edges occurred unless the film was re-exposed under water.

Suggestions and Recommendations:

Further experiments be carried out using the Harrison and Harrison color correction filters for compensating for the predominance of red in the film or the Antarctic light. That re-exposure of the film be carried out under water.

GLOVES

Nylon or rayon gloves were not received by this unit, making it difficult to operate the cameras. At times it was necessary to remove the five fingered winter flying gloves to make an adjustment on the camera, thus causing unnecessary exposure to the hands.

Suggestions and Recommendations:

That special care be taken to include nylon or rayon glove inserts. Also, that a warm close fitting glove be used over the inserts making it possible to adjust the major parts of the camera without removing the outer glove.

FILTERS

Filters are of the utmost importance in Antarctic color photography. They are important in black and white photography when it is desired to correct or over correct the sky. The H. and H. color correction filters were used and tested to a certain degree but not thoroughly enough to determine how effective they were on all types of color film at different geographical localities and times of the day.

UV-15, UV-16, and UV-17 filters were tested with Ansco Color film but were abandoned because of the predominance of red that resulted.

The G, 25-A, minus blue and K-2 filters were used for black and white film. The G and the minus blue gave more normal correction, therefore were used more frequently.

Suggestions and Recommendations:

That a 23-A filter be tested with panchromatic film. Also that a C-5 filter series Wratten VI be made available for further testing in the Antarctic.

EXPOSURE METERS

The General Electric Exposure Meter was the only one available to the Western Group. The performance of this exposure meter at all times was as accurate as could possibly be expected.

Suggestions and Recommendations:

That the General Electric and the Weston Meters both be included on future expeditions so that comparative tests may be made.

FLASH BULBS

The 25-B, 2-B, Press-40, Press-5, and Number 3 Flash Bulbs were used. All bulbs performed with a low percentage of failures and were indispensable for direct and fill-in lighting. Very few bulbs failed to operate, regardless whether they were being used inside or outside, in low temperatures. It is believed the cold weather had little or no effect on the bulb itself.

Suggestions and Recommendations:

Care be taken to keep the batteries for the flash gun as warm as possible by keeping them inside foul weather clothing. The use of an electronic type flash, having portable batteries for carrying over the shoulder, making it possible to strap them around the body inside the foul weather clothing, could be the answer to Antarctic flash photography. The batteries would have to be of a design to fit inside foul weather clothing and curved to fit the body, as an aid in carrying for long periods of time.

VII PHOTOGRAPHIC TESTS

Some of the difficulties encountered, besides cold weather, in performing photographic tests for C.N.O. were: the scarcity of men, the absence of the proper film and the small number of days photographically available for this type of photography.

One Chief Photographer's Mate and one Photograph's Mate second class were assigned to this detail along with their other duties (such as the responsibility for all still coverage for Task Group 68.2, second photographers in the PBM-5's and laboratory duties).

Black and white out-of-date film was a constant source of trouble and part of the color film arrived too late to be utilized to the best advantage. Infra-red film was not used because cameras of the proper size did not have infra-red focusing posts.

The normal day in the Antarctic is overcast with a high reading in light value. For close-up photographs of planes, ships, and icebergs, the light value was high and good results were obtained. In the photographs taken out over the ice-pack and water, the ice, water and sky blended together causing a flat negative, even with the use of filters. The abnormal day when it would have been possible to run tests, it would also be good weather for flying and the photographers were necessarily assigned to higher priority tasks making it impossible to perform these tests in the manner suggested.

Suggestions and Recommendations:

Any activity requiring tests involving non-standard equipment should furnish the equipment, material, and personnel required.

VIII. NEGATIVES AND TRANSPARENCIES TAKEN FOR VARIOUS ACTIVITIES

AEROLOGICAL

Aerological Black and White and color stills of weather phenomena and equipment in use aboard the U.S.S. CURRITUCK (AV-7).

Negative numbers AAW 347, 350, 351, 352, 353, 354, 355, 356, 357, 358, 359, 361, 389, 390, 407 and 408.

One roll of color film K-18, marked: Aerological Supplementary color vertical and horizontal cloud formation Supplementary Roll No. 1 dated 1-12-47.

One roll of Black and White. K-18 film marked Aerological Special Black and White Vertical and Horizontal cloud formations Roll No. 1 dated 1-12-47.

PANORAMIC

Panoramic photographs from surface vessels of coast line or islands. Negative numbers AAW 450, 451, 452.

BUREAU OF SHIPS, HELICOPTER

Bureau of ships requirements. Helicopter installation facilities. Negative numbers AAW 391, 392, 393 and 394.

ELECTRONICS, Chief of Electronics.

Black and White photographs of modified electronic equipment. Negative numbers AAW 164, 165, 166, 180, 182, 229, 198 and 199.

RADAR

12 Rolls of Shipborne Radar Recording Camera Film taken on U.S.S. CURRITUCK and one (1) roll of film from the U.S.S. HENDERSON was turned over to Lt. Comdr. R.L. Hildebrand, USNR, Electrical Engineer, Task Group 68.2.

PHOTOGRAPHIC INSTALLATIONS. Chief of Bureau of Aeronautics.

Photographic equipment installed in PBM-5. Negative numbers AAW 163, 180, 182, 183, 187 and 229.

HELICOPTER OPERATIONS.

Bureau of Aeronautics Black and White and color transparency stills of helicopter operations. Negative numbers, AAW 3, 6, 8, 27, 158, 362, 363, 364, 365, 366, 367, 368, 369, 370, 391, 392, 393, and 394.

IX MOTION PICTURES

It is felt that the operations of Task Group 68.2. were adequately covered in motion pictures, and that an interesting documentary story was obtained in color and Black and White.

However mechanical and structural deficiencies of the motion picture cameras were many, and several scenes that were impossible to duplicate were probably lost because of camera malfunctions.

Motion picture cameras when received were in very poor condition. Most of them were stamped OPERATION CROSSROADS, and upon inspection some were found to be out of time. Gear drive boxes and magazines still contained heavy lubricants mixed with particles of sand. It was obvious that few, if any, were cleaned or checked for mechanical failures prior to issue for use on OPERATION HIGHJUMP. One Cine Special camera bore a tag marked "Do not use - no good".

Detailed mechanical discrepancies and modifications are listed in the Camera Repair Section of this report.

EYEMO

The Eyemo was the most unreliable motion picture camera aboard. Of the two received, only one could be used outdoors in cold climate, and then was under constant repair. When first tested both cameras would fail on spring power at temperatures of approximately plus 59°F., and motor power at plus 50°F. By polishing down the aperture plate and lubricating with low temperature oils, one Eyemo would operate at about minus 0.4°F. with motor power only, while the other could not be improved despite all efforts made. Fortunately, colder weather was not too often encountered.

Neither camera would operate while in flight where temperatures of from minus 0.4°F. centigrade to minus 23.8°F. were encountered.

MITCHELL

Of the two Mitchells received, one was out of time, and because of the overload of camera repair work and their being no need for its services, no attempt was made to place it in commission.

The Mitchell was not used to any great extent because none of the 400 ft. motion picture stock ordered had been received prior to leaving San Diego, Calif., and by the time the U.S.S. PHILIPPINE SEA arrived south with our requested supplies, most of the 35-millimeter shipboard coverage had been completed. However, its bulkiness and weight were also reasons for its little use aboard ship. Shortage of outdoor bulkhead electrical receptacles necessitated the use of batteries for power source, making the combined weight of the equipment about 160 pounds. It was very difficult for one man to carry this equipment from one section of the ship to another, with adequate assurance of shifting to a more advantageous position in time to catch some desired action.

In flight however, after certain modifications were made, the Mitchell was the only 35-millimeter M.P. camera that could be used with any degree of success.

In the first attempt at 35-millimeter work in the air, four (4) 12-volt portable batteries were used as power source because of the 24-volt electrical system in the plane. The batteries were placed in the area of the port waist hatch and were subjected to approximately the same temperature, as the cameras. A high hat was designed to carry the camera on either of the two waist gun mounts. The temperatures reached at different times of day and different altitudes were:

0630	Minus 28.4°F	28 F.P.S.	Camera normal temp.
0730	Minus 28.4°F	22 F.P.S.	After takeoff.
0900	Minus 18°F.	8 F.P.S.	14,000 feet alt.
1000	Minus 23.8°F	2 F.P.S.	16,800 feet alt.
1030	Minus 5.8°F.	0 F.P.S.	11,000 feet alt.

At approximately 1400 feet altitude the lens focusing rings, aperature rings and focusing knob on the view finder became frozen and inoperative.

Upon return to the ship, the camera was completely de-oiled, cleaned, and relubricated with low temperature lubricants. A 12-volt line direct to the waist hatch from the plane's batteries was installed in order to rectify any possible independant battery power loss from low temperature.

Another flight was made with approximately the same results, so it was decided to use a direct 24-volt line on the 12-volt camera motor, and replace the high hat installation in the waist hatch gun mount for a tripod set up on the center line of the deck in order to eliminate the wind blast. The results of this change proved satisfactory, with 2,000 feet of film exposed, although the tripod legs and spider took up all the available athwartship space in the waist, causing a bottleneck for the transfer of tri-metrogon magazines from storage to the tri-metrogon camera position.

During time the 24-volt power source was used, the 12-volt motor did not spark out or become excessively warm during operation. The friction clutch on the motor was set wide open in order to obtain 24 frames per second.

GUN CAMERA

The Gun Camera performed in excellent style mechanically. The only difficulties encountered were from jamming magazines. Cold weather and the tight loop method of threading magazine film is conducive to film breaks. Because it has only one fixed focus lens, and can be operated only by electricity, the Gun Camera's uses are limited. It is however an excellent camera for the purpose designed.

CINE SPECIAL

Of the four (4) Cine Special cameras and eight (8) magazines received, two cameras and four magazines failed mechanically during the first phases of the operation. It is believed however, that the Cine Special is the best of the movie type cameras received for all purpose work. It operated at all temperatures encountered, the lowest being minus 23.8°F, without noticeable lag.

Focus stop pins were sheared on two of the 15 millimeter lenses which may result in some footage being out of focus.

Mechanical failures were due mostly to irreplaceably worn claws which put three magazines permanently out of commission.

EXPOSURE METER

The General Electric Meter was used exclusively throughout the operation and was considered thoroughly reliable. At times accurate readings were difficult or impossible to make depending on the subject.

Light reflection from the ice pack was extraordinarily great, and in the case of a PBM-5 taking off or landing, the average water reading was about 6 foot candles. 3 to 5 degree upward change in meter angle however, would bring the needle against the 70 foot candle pin, so a happy medium, favoring slight under exposure for color film was used. The average lens aperture opening used on outdoor scenes at 24 f.p.s. was f.8.

A frequent topic of conversation was the possibility of adding another light factor to a meter for extreme light. It is felt that it would be of more use in Antarctica than the now used "Hood Off" element for measuring weak light values.

RECOMMENDATIONS

It is the general opinion that the standard motion picture cameras used by the Navy today are not suitable for the many varied uses in freezing climates, nor do they give positive assurance of consistently good mechanical operation in the field under low temperature conditions. Both in structure and design, they lack too many essential qualities necessary for cold weather photography. Almost all of them are good for the purpose designed, but it is believed that one type can be built to incorporate all of the good features of each into an all-climate camera. This camera, it is felt, should be of combat design, of as light weight and compact structure as possible for portability, and definately a magazine load type. A Mitchell, Cine Special or, Eyemo cannot be threaded with any amount of speed or assurance when heavy mittens are worn, and to remove them places the cameraman in danger of severe frost bite at extremely low temperatures.

Many features of the present day cameras could be eliminated to make room for more important appliances that would serve a better purpose. The single frame exposure, the rewind unit, and the degree opening lever are a few units on the Cine Special that are of little or no use to a field cameraman. The wind handle is too long, and often hits the speed knob while cranking, thereby changing the frames per second speed. By merely brushing the camera against clothing it is found that the degree opening lever would change to various positions, and the rewind handle would fall away from the camera because of a poor locking device. The footage speed indicator window could be replaced with a tachometer, which is considered all-important for work where frames per second speed will vary with temperature.

A three lens turret similar to the Filmo Auto Master could be adopted for quick lens changes. The finder elements should be placed above or along side their respective lenses so that the lens and view finder element change is made simultaneously.

The view finder should be hooded, because many times the sun is directly behind the photographer and glare from it blinds out the window view entirely, very often causing the photographer to lose sight of his action.

Making the many necessary filter changes was a lengthy and clumsy problem when wearing heavy mittens. Filters should be of glass construction, and a disc containing at least four (4) receptacles for various types of filters should be situated between the shutter and the lens position of the camera. Similar to the Mitchell, it could be of rotary design that facilitates a rapid choice and change of filters.

In a modification of an Eyemo, it was found that a pistol grip trigger method of starting was most suitable. The pistol grip could be placed beneath the camera in such a manner that it could be adjusted and locked to suit the individual photographer's shooting position.

Time and lack of necessary equipment prevented experimentation on installing heating units in gear drive boxes to prevent freezing of the assembly. The problem of controlling metal contraction and expansion to prevent the jamming of a camera remains to be solved. In some cases, regardless of lubricants, it is believed this contraction of metal parts was the cause of most difficulties.

It is believed that the above recommended features could be built into 16-millimeter and 35-millimeter cameras of identical design, each to carry not less than 100 feet of magazine film.

ANNEX TWO (c)

TASK GROUP 68.3

PHOTOGRAPHIC REPORT

I INTRODUCTION

This report presents the photographic objectives and accomplishments of the Eastern Task Group, with the problems encountered, action taken, and recommendations.

Recommendations similar or identical to those of the Central or Western Groups have been omitted.

II OBJECTIVES

Primary: Tri-metrogon reconnaissance survey of the continental area, coastline, and island areas of Antarctica, from longitude 145 West to as far East as operations would permit. Secondary: To obtain complete still and motion picture documentary coverage (in Black and White, and color) of the operational and photographic requirements of various Bureaus and other Governmental agencies.

III AIRCREWMEN

Prior to flight the cameras were run through several operating cycles to insure proper working condition. A check was made to insure that lenses and filters were clean, and that the shutter and diaphragm were set for light conditions expected. The navigation and stop watches were drawn from the Squadron Navigation Officer, and the navigation watch was installed in the Gremlin recorder. The date, name of the photographer and flight number was recorded on the data card provided in the recording chamber of the radio altimeter, radar camera and gremlin recorder. All clocks were set on GCT. The contents of the spare parts kit were checked. The check-off list was signed and turned in prior to departure.

As soon as the crew secured from their take-off positions, the photographers installed the plexiglass hatches in the waist and set up the handheld oblique camera. One photographer took station in the waist; the other set up the tri-metrogon cameras, installed the viewfinder, and inserted markers in magazines.

When the area to be photographed was reached, the first photographer manned the tri-metrogon station and the second photographer manned the oblique waist station. Both remained at stations until the area was photographed. On return flights to the ship the tri-metrogon cameras were secured after leaving the coast but the oblique station was not secured until the flight landed at the ship.

The photographer recorded as accurately as practicable the GCT of photographs taken, true heading, drift, ground speed, and barometric altitude of the plane. This information was obtained from the pilot or navigator. Entry was made on the data sheet to show from which side of the aircraft oblique photographs were made, indicating the relative bearing of the subject when possible.

Prior to landing the plexiglass hatches were removed and the waist hatch secured. Tri-metrogon hatches were checked to insure that they were properly secured and watertight.

After the plane was hoisted on deck the photographers passed magazines with data sheets to the waiting processing team. After each flight and upon securing the aircraft, the photographic aircrewmen reported any discrepancies in photographic equipment, or any deviation from the normal procedure prescribed for making runs and recording data.

Between flights photographic aircrewmen assigned to flight crews worked with other members of the plane crew making the plane ready for the next flight. The photographers' main concern being photography, they were responsible that cameras were cleaned and in good mechanical working condition. After work in the aircraft was completed photographers worked in the laboratory.

IV   AIR OPERATIONS

Prior to departure from the United States pilots, navigators and aircrewmen were given training in photography. Installation of tri-metrogon camera mounts and Gremlin recorders was completed in PBM aircraft and a recording apparatus for photographing the radio altimeter (SCR-718) once each 60 seconds during survey flights was installed.

While enroute to the Antarctic lectures were conducted for pilots, navigators, and photographic aircrewmen on overall requirements, their individual responsibilities, procedure for making mapping runs, identification and marking of negatives, and photographer's check-off list. The radio altimeter recording apparatus installation was completed and tested, aerial cameras and magazines were cleaned, winterized and tested, standby aircrewmen were familiarized with the operation of tri-metrogon cameras, radar scope recording camera, and radio altimeter recording apparatus.

V   LABORATORY

Prior to transfer of TF-68 photographic personnel to the USS PINE ISLAND the Photographic Officer of this Task Group visited the ship to estimate additional space to be required, changes, alterations and additions necessary for photographic installations. In addition to the photographic laboratory proper and the sensitized cold storage, the following spaces were assigned to photography:

(1) W.O. Mess and Pantry for use in aerial film processing, marking, Sonne printing and aerial camera storage.
(2) Admiral's and W.O. Stores for use as storage for chemicals, printing paper, and small photographic equipment.

(3) Officers' bunk room number 4 for storage of large equipment and the bulk of photographic material.
(4) Stateroom number 104 for storage of camera trunks, small
photographic equipment not in use, and hand held aerial
cameras.
(5) Stateroom number 101 for movie office and storage of movie
film and cameras for quick access.
(6) Aviation Instrument Repair shop for camera repair.
(7) Flag Plot for TG Commander, Hydrographic and Photographic
Officers' office and work space.

VI   ACCOMPLISHMENTS

(1) Stills.
1376 still photographs were made and filed by the Eastern
Group of which 1263 were Black and whites (85% being 4 by
5 inches), 87 Kodacolor and Ansco, and 26 Kodachromes.
(2) Movies.
42,000 feet of motion picture film were exposed during the
operation of which 35,550 feet were 35-mm black and whites,
5,950 feet 16-mm Kodachrome, and approximately 500 feet
16-mm black and whites.
(3) Aerials.
8,298 aerial negatives were made and processed; 514 K-17
obliques, 5,763 Tri-Metrogon, and 1,921 Gremlin timer
negatives.
(4) Photographic Flights.
Twelve photographic flights were made averaging 8.25 hours
per flight a total of 99 hours. The longest and shortest
photographic flights were 12.4 and 4.2 hours respectively.
(5) Aerial Film Processing.
An aerial film processing log was kept for recording work
accomplished and time required.
The following is a brief summary of accomplishments for
one processing period flights Nine and Ten.
24 Jan 47 - 0500
    Film received from flight Nine (9):
    6 rolls Tri-Met, 2 rolls Gremlin timer, 1 roll oblique,
    1 roll 35 mm radio altimeter film, and 1 roll 35 mm
    radar scope film.
    0600 Test strip completed from oblique camera; processing
    started.
    0630 Received film from flight Ten (10):
    6 rolls Tri-Met, 2 rolls Gremlin timer, 1 roll oblique,
    and 1 roll 35 mm radio altimeter film.
    0800 two rolls from flight 9 processing (Power failure
    of film dryer delayed work ½ hour and damaged one roll
    of film).
    1200 Commenced marking film from flight 9.
    1700 Flight 9 completely processed.
25 Jan 0500 Flight 9 completely marked. Flight 10 completely
processed.
    0730 commenced checking flight 10 for marking. Dark room
    ready for Sonne printing. (Power failure in W.O. Pantry

delayed Sonne printing $7\frac{1}{2}$ hours).
1030 Commenced marking flight 10.
1200 Processed Radio Altimeter and Radar Film; flights 9 and 10.
1500 Commenced Sonne printing (strip printing).
1900 Finished marking flight 10.
26 Jan 0230 Both flights finished - job complete.
0900 Laboratory ready for next flight (field day held, chemicals mixed, etc).

Comments

$45\frac{1}{2}$ hours were required to process 18 rolls of film (14,200' rolls and 4,125'), 3 rolls 100' 35 mm movie film, mark aerial film, and make one (1) Sonne print from 18 rolls. This included approximately 8 hours lost due to power failures.

(6) Photographic Prints
Photographic Prints made from above negatives are listed below:

(1) 7 inch Sonne roll prints (Approx 7 x 7")	18,720
(2) 9 inch Sonne roll prints (Approx 9 x 9")	16,900
(3) 4 x 5 inch prints	3,360
(4) 5 x 7 inch prints	375
(5) 8 x 10 inch prints	7,547
(6) 10 x 10 inch prints	3,500
(7) 10 x 20 inch prints	1,075
(8) 11 x 14 inch prints	875
(9) 18 x 22 inch prints	125
	52,477

VII DIFFICULTIES ENCOUNTERED AND RECOMMENDATIONS.

Shipboard Personnel

It was found that the number of photographic personnel assigned were not sufficient to carry out photographic requirements.

When processing aerial film it was necessary to stop all other photographic work and use all available men in two twelve hour shifts to expedite completion of aerial survey work.

VIII SHIPBOARD PERSONNEL.

The following photographic complement is suggested as necessary on an AV when operating two PBM airplanes on a similar operation.

One Photographic Officer, four CPhoM's, six PhoM1, ten PhoM3, four Seamen Photo Strikers, and one Yeoman (Second class or above.).

When supporting six to twelve aircraft the complement should be increased as follows:

One Photographic Officer, four CPhoM's, Nine PhoM1, fifteen PhoM2 or PhoM3, six Seamen Photo Strikers and One Yeoman Second Class or above.

IX   PHOTOGRAPHIC AIRCREWMEN

During flights over the Antarctic Continent one photographer could not efficiently operate the tri-metrogon cameras, shoot supplementary oblique cameras, and record essential data necessary for accurate compilation of all photographs.

A second photographer was assigned using stand-by photographic aircrewmen from the supporting personnel. This increased efficiency within the aircraft during flights but at the same time cut laboratory processing and completely stopped work on several projects to which these men were assigned.

It is recommended that in future operations of this nature two PhoM's be assigned each plane crew with one stand-by PhoM for each three aircraft. These photographers should be in addition to the supporting shipboard personnel listed above.

X   PILOTS

In many instances mapping procedure and instructions were not followed. Common errors were: Changing course during mapping runs, changing altitude during runs, and failing to overlap the previous run. This is attributed to the fact that pilots were not thoroughly trained photographic pilots.

XI   PHOTOGRAPHIC OFFICERS

Aerial survey operations would be more efficient if photographic officers were given a period of training in photogrammetry. This would familiarize the photographic officers with the compilation of tri-metrogon photographs and their translation into charts. The officers would gain necessary information to properly plan and accurately evaluate work of this type.

XII   CAMERA PROBLEMS

(1) K-20 aircraft cameras: These cameras were received in poor condition requiring a major overhaul before they could be relied upon. All K-20's in this Task Group were manufactured by Folmer Graflex Co., but the spare parts were for

Fairchild models. Theoretically these parts are inter-
changeable, but it was found that this was true only in
major assemblies.

(2) K-17 Aircraft Cameras: The winding clutch in one K-17
case drive broke due to metal fatigue. This camera was
placed back in commission by cannibalizing a calibrated
K-17 set, as no spare parts for these cameras were received.

(3) Gremlin Recorder: The shutter assembly in one recorder
was bent when received and jammed beyond repair. It was
evident that this timer had not been tested before delivery,
for such a major discrepancy would have been discovered.
No photographs could be made with the shutter in such a
condition.

(4) Gremlin Recorder Magazine (F-56): During one flight an
F-56 magazine sheared a taper pin on the take-up spool
drive. The magazine was repaired and placed back in
commission.

(5) The 35 mm Eyemo Motion Picture Camera: Considerable
trouble was encountered with the Eyemo cameras. With four
cameras it was impossible to keep more than one in operation at a time. The bearings of the cameras received, as
well as those previously on board, were worn to such an extent that it was impossible to use them until all bearings
were replaced. This condition is attributed mainly to lack
of proper lubrication and proper maintenance by previous
custodians.

(6) Mitchell Cameras: Two Mitchell motion picture cameras were
received. One camera had a burned out buckle switch; the
other was received with magazines belonging to a newer
model camera and with a turret missing. The buckle switch
could not be repaired or replaced, so it was necessary to
wire around the switch in order to operate the camera, thus
eliminating an important safety feature. Both cameras had
25 mm lens but had no flanges for mounting them. One camera
was kept in commission by cannibalizing the other one.

(7) Radio Altimeter Recording Camera. This camera functioned
satisfactorily and is considered essential to aerial survey
where ground control is impossible. It is recommended that
this camera operate simultaneously with the survey cameras
and so wired that it can be operated continuously when the
survey cameras are turned off.

XIII AIRCRAFT

The dome light installed in the tunnel of PBM aircraft was inadequate. Additional lights were installed.

XIV LABORATORY PROBLEMS

(1) Hypo.

Atkinson prepared fixing bath had many impurities causing small spots on the film. After this was discovered all fixing baths were mixed with hypo crystals.

(2) Developer.

A large shipment of Atkinson low contrast developer (51-D-118-100) was received. Many cans were rusted through, oxidized and deteriorated, and were discarded as unreliable.

(3) Temperature Control of Water.

Water from the fresh water tanks was too cold for use. (Approximately 40°F). There was one hot water spigot within the photographic laboratory which supplied water to the film developing room.

(4) Aerial Film Developing Outfits.

The Smith Aerial Film Developing Outfits, (18-D-155, 18-D-156 and 18-D-176) were not adequate to fulfill the demand made upon them. The reels provided (18-D-155) were not properly designed to operate under the load of $9\frac{1}{2}$"x 200' film. All Smith reels and motors provided were inoperable in a short while. The drive shafts slipped continually in the rubber shock absorbers which at first would not allow the motors to reverse and finally become so loose it was impossible to crank the film through by hand.
The Army type B-5 Developing Outfit, Army stock number 8900-219150, 115-volt, 90-watt is recommended.

(5) Aerial Film Dryers.

The Smith Model "J" Aerial Film Dryers (18-D-796) were found entirely too slow in operation. Drying of aerial film created a considerable bottleneck in processing. In addition, the rollers of the three dryers were impregnated with wax. All efforts of removal, including boiling, sanding, and soaking in benzine were of no avail. The dryers continuously deposited patches of wax on the back of all film.
The Army type A-10, Army stock number 8900-237860, 115-volts or 115-230-volts, 3000-watts, aerial film dryer is recommended.

(6) Sonne Printers (18-P-24575).

The two Sonne printers were out of commission when received. All switch handles were broken off, frames of both printers were bent, and one printer was missing a major part of the negative supply spool brake. With two printers enough parts were available to keep one in commission.

(7) Sonne Print Dryer.

A modification was made on a Pako Liberty Model matte dryer to provide an automatic take-up for rolls of Sonne prints. The matte dryer was superior to the Smith Aerial Film dryers for the drying of Sonne prints. It is also considerably faster and the prints are not subjected to as much strain. See Plate 12.

XV   CONCLUSION

There were many photographic tests and projects carried out

by all Groups, but because of the scientific or technical nature, this material is not included in this report. All of this material has been forwarded to CNO (OP-55P) for final analysis.

Plate No. 1

Accommodation rack in PBM-3 for spare AA magazines.

Plate No. 2

Flag Plot – TG Commanded, Photographic
& Hydrographic Office and work space.

Plate No. 3

Photographic Laboratory - Finishing Room - A-303-1L.

Plate No. 4

Printing Room — Contact and Enlargement
— Photographic Laboratory (A-303-1L).

Plate No. 5

Developing Room (Color and B&W)
Photographic Laboratory (A-303-1L).

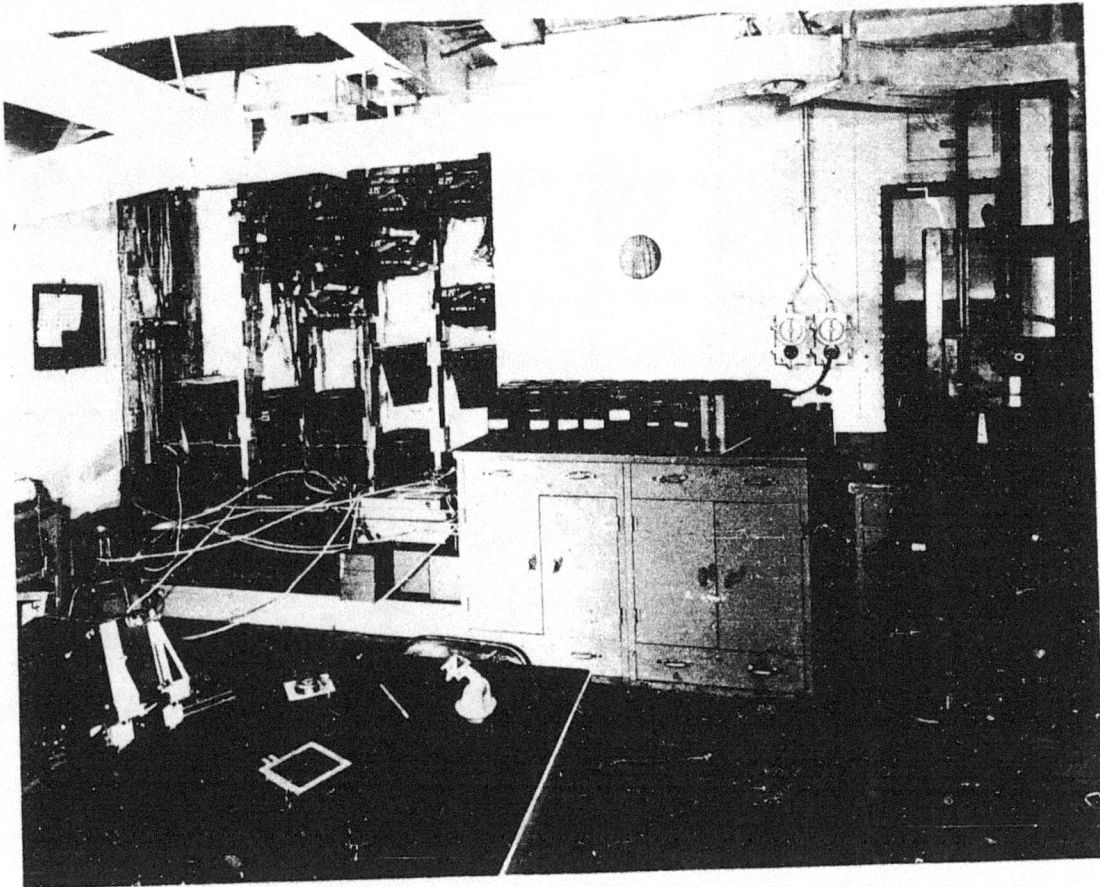

Plate No. 6

Aerial Finishing & Aerial Camera Storage - W. O. Mess.

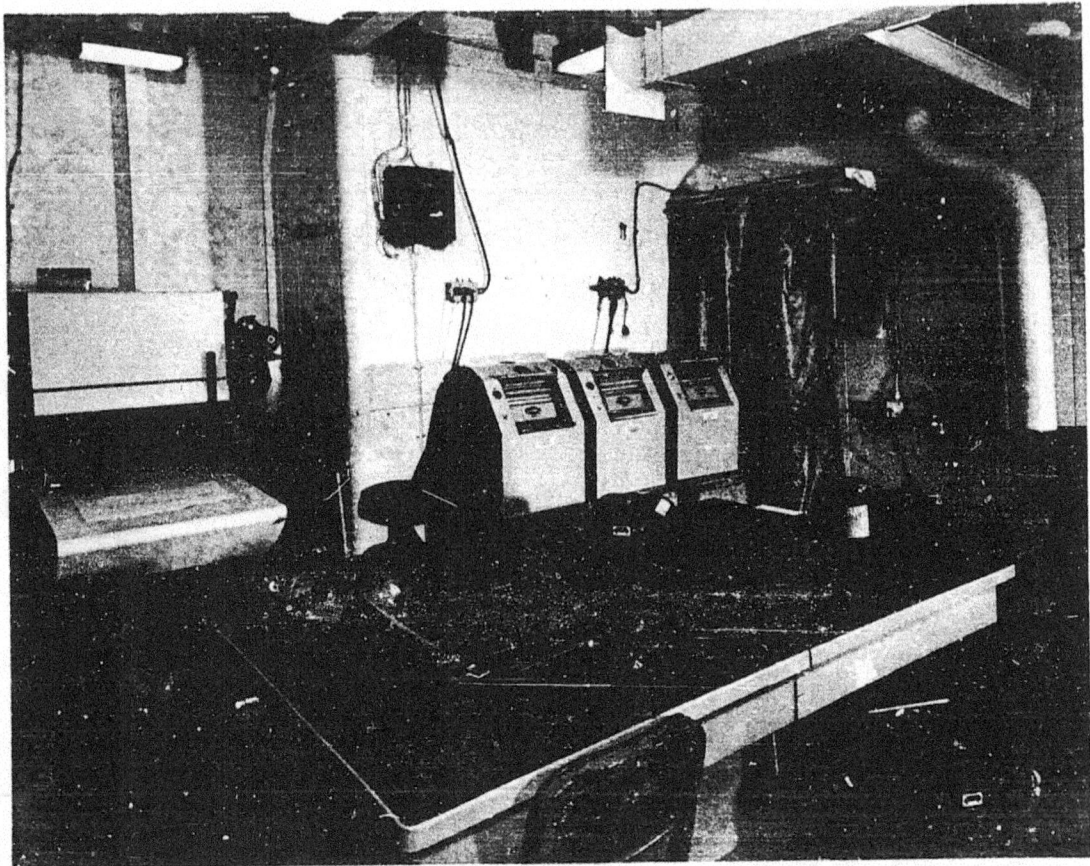

Plate No. 7

Aerial Finishing – W. O. Mess.

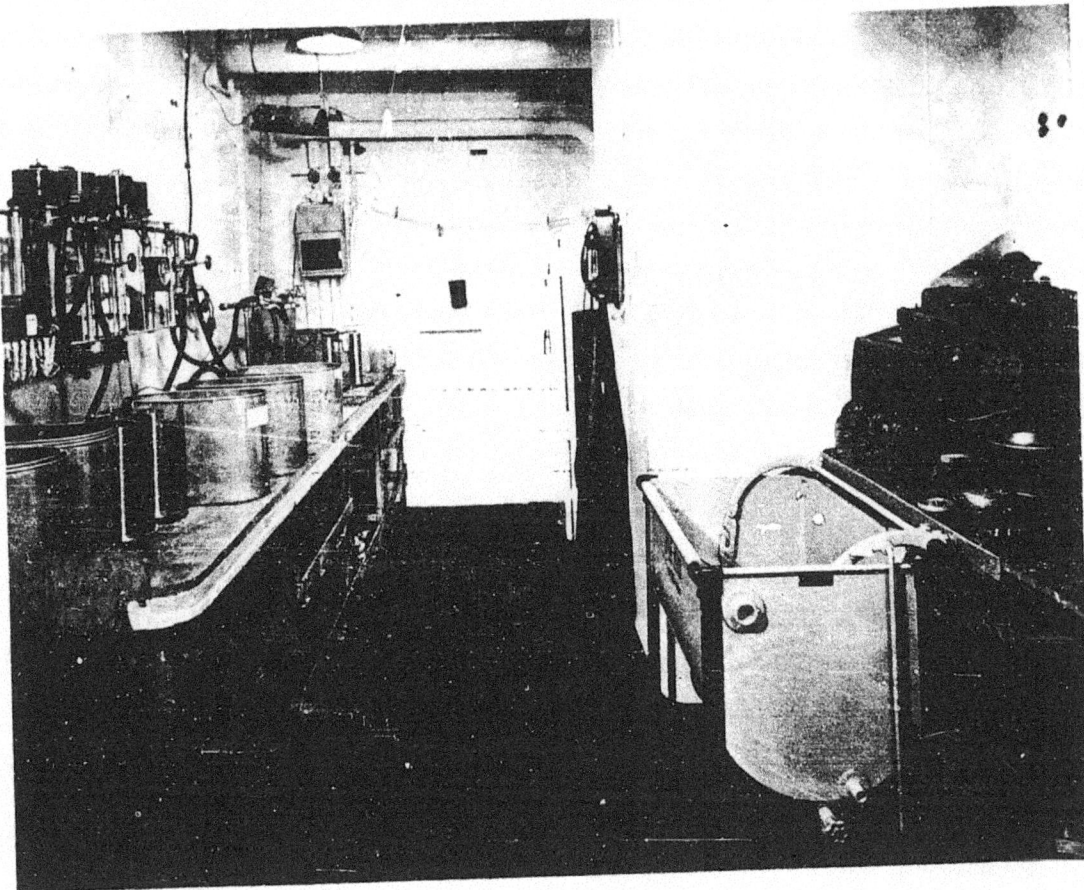

Plate No. 8

Aerial Film Developing & Sonne Printing
- W. O. Pantry.

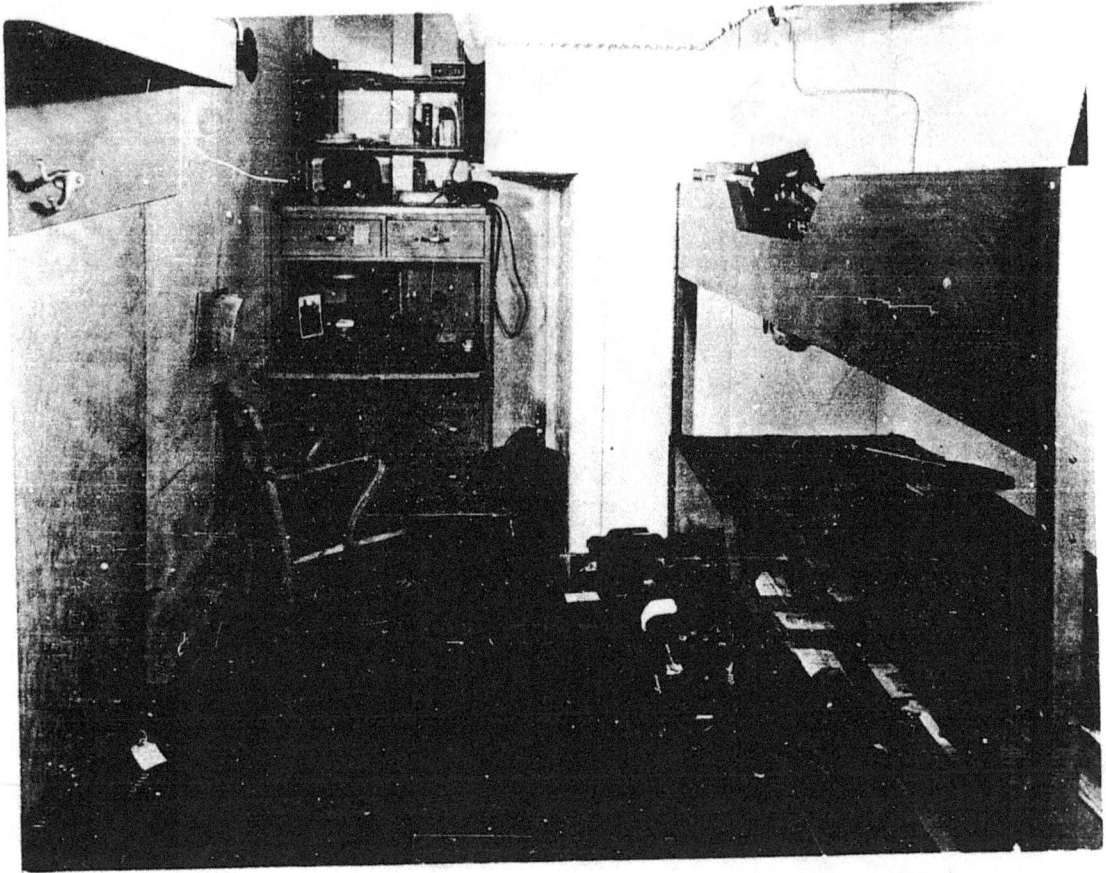

Plate No. 9

Movie (Office) Storage (Stateroom 101).

Plate No. 10

Camera Repair.

Plate No. 11

Photographic Coverage — Officer's Bunk Room No. 4).

Annex II-...   - 1. -

Plate No. 12

Attachment for Matte dryer for drying Sonne prints.

Plate No. 13

Altitude Recording Apparatus Installed
in PBM Aircraft of Eastern Group.

Ph'grammetry

ANNEX III

PHOTOGRAMMETRY

Table of Contents

ANNEX III

PHOTOGRAMMETRY

Table of Illustrations

I. INTRODUCTION

The Annex concerning photogrammetry is treated somewhat differently than the other Annexes because the activities resulting from the photogrammetric and cartographic activities of Operation HIGHJUMP constitutes a program of several years duration. For this reason it is not possible to give thoroughly qualitative findings in these pages. However, the first phase or the "Field Program" has been completed and while complete, detailed, qualitative analysis is not available, a comprehensive report on the activities which took place and numerous specific recommendations are presented herewith.

II. THE OBJECTIVES

A. To obtain aerial reconnaissance mapping photography of as much of the coastal, continental, and pack-ice regions of the Antarctic as practical within the limits established by available equipment, time, and weather. Detailed preferences, which generally favored little or totally unknown areas, were established by the Hydrographic Office and the Naval Photographic Services.

B. To obtain along with the reconnaissance mapping photography, sufficient air and ground control, consistent with the equipment and time available, to provide a basis for the construction of relatively accurate maps and charts of the Antarctic.

C. To make operational tests of photogrammetric methods, procedures, and equipment in an unknown area with a minimum of ground control.

D. To provide operational photographic reconnaissance training under conditions peculiar to polar areas for aviation personnel, especially pilots, navigators and photographers.

III. PLANNING AND PREPARING FOR PHOTOGRAMMETRIC OPERATIONS

No photogrammetrists were assigned duty in the Task Force until after operations had begun, therefore all plans and preparations for photogrammetric activities on Operation HIGHJUMP were designed and executed by various members of the Staff, with advice from the Hydrographic Office. There were no Naval photogrammetric Officers available for duty. The billet for staff Photogrammetric Officer was filled by a reserve officer who reported for duty to the Staff, Task Force 68 as it passed through the Canal Zone on its way south.

While much preparatory work had been completed, no method is practicable, as yet, by which ground control of the aerial photography can be secured in the Antarctic on such short notice.

Note: Refer to Annex Two for more detailed information concerning the planning and preparation of photogrammetric operations and the design, use, and performance of all mapping cameras and associated equipment.

Between the Canal Zone and Little America, the Photogrammetrist familiarized himself in detail with what had previously transpired and studied the aerial photography taken on previous expeditions, planned tentative flight lines based upon the range of the aircraft, probable number of flights, and areas of priority, and studied the locations and accuracy of previous ground control.

Discussions were held between the Staff Photogrammetric Officer and other members of the Staff and observers concerning the possibilities of obtaining ground control with the equipment available. After considerable thought and interchanges of views, it was established that within the time required and with the equipment at hand, ground control could not be obtained.

Operations in Task Groups 68.2 and 68.3 began on 24 December 1946 approximately one month and a half before similar operations commenced in Task Group 68.5 based at the Bay of Whales. Flight information was dispatched as it occurred to CTF 68 and transferred to specially prepared logs, charts, and overlays. Among the types of information placed on charts were the indicated flight tracks, photo coverage, exploration and discovery, changes in coastline, and the daily positions of the Seaplane Tenders.

IV. PHOTOGRAMMETRIC FIELD OPERATIONS IN THE ANTARCTIC

A. Location of the Base

The Bay of Whales, site of three previous United States Expeditions, was chosen as the site for the base camp and airfield of the Central Group. One of the determining factors in locating the base at Little America was the knowledge that if the Bay of Whales was accessible to the icebreaker, it would be possible to unload the necessary cargo for camp construction, remove this heavy cargo to the ice shelf, and find a suitable location for an airfield nearby. Unfortunately, however, the Bay of Whales is in the center of a relatively well-explored area in the Antarctic. This factor meant that the aircraft had to fly 400 miles before reaching the area in which the reconnaissance photography was to be performed, and to return over that same 400 miles after the mission had been accomplished. This fact considerably decreased the effective area to be photographed. For example, twelve missions averaging 4.2 hours each never did get out of known territory either because of weather changes, mechanical difficulties, or because the particular mission did not warrant a trip of more than 400 miles away from base.

B. Office Space and Security

Upon establishing the airfield, quarters were assigned the Staff Photogrammetrist and the Squadron Navigator in the already overcrowded Quonset hut provided for aircraft maintenance. Drafting and chart tables were built, electric lights rigged, and storage areas and shelves for charts and equipment were installed.

Effective use of the quarters for photogrammetric, cartographic, and navigation operations was hampered by use of the same space for briefing of the crews, by the operations duty officer, and by all hands as a general refuge from the cold.

Security for classified material and for the chronometers and other valuable navigation instruments was provided by use of padlocked parachute bags.

After eighteen flights had been completed, photogrammetry was moved to a large tent which provided ample space for all photogrammetric and cartographic field office activities. The temperature in this hut was seldom above 50°F. even with the oil stove turned to its maximum. Such temperatures made working with acetate ink and metal drafting instruments upon cellulose acetate a very slow and difficult process. Also this space was considerably removed from the airfield and made contact with the navigators, pilots, and photographers difficult, since there was no camp telephone system available.

C. Photographic Reconnaissance Aircraft

Six R4D-5 aircraft were used by the Central Group as photographic reconnaissance aircraft. While these planes were of pre-war design, they had many advantages not shared by some of the more modern designs. However, in so far as exploration and reconnaissance were concerned these aircraft also had several important disadvantages. They did not have a long enough range, nor were they able to fly sufficiently high to make a practical tri-metrogon reconnaissance of the 10,000 foot high polar plateau and mountains. The average ground speed of approximately 120 knots increased the time necessary to be in the air. Most important, however, was the limited carrying capacity. After loading the hull fuel tanks, emergency gear, camera assemblies, and a crew of five members, it was not safe to place additional crew members and their equipment aboard considering the planned range. This prevented the use of two additional crew members whose presence would have contributed to a more successful operation: (1) A second photographer to help manage the assembly of eight cameras, from six to eight of which were designed for simultaneous action; and (2) A trained technical observer to operate the wire recorder and to establish complete control information necessarily neglected by the various crew members, each of whom was assigned to perform a part of it, in the interest of paying full attention to their regular duties to get the plane out and back successfully.

D. Pilots

The naval aviators selected as R4D photo reconnaissance pilots for Operation HIGHJUMP did not possess the requisite training and experience necessary for such an operation. With but two exceptions, none of these officers had previously flown aerial photographic flights. A sufficient number of pilots with a combination multi-engine and photo-mapping background could not be obtained. A serious effort was made to train the officers selected but the minimum requisite time necessary for this purpose was not available before the sailing date. Both the quality and quantity of reconnaissance photography obtained could have been materially increased by the selection of experienced photo pilots.

E. Navigation Aids

The Navigators were considerably handicapped by a total lack of many of the navigational aids considered a necessity in ordinary naval aviation. It was planned to use as navigational aids, the GPN, the specially prepared Inverse Mercator charts, and the radar and radio from the U.S.S. MOUNT OLYMPUS. However, the GPN could not be grounded in the ice and its signals were frequently not picked up until the base was within sight. The charts were ruled and numbered by hand for flying the grid system and served as good plotting sheets, but the planemetric and topographic details were so inaccurate they could only be used as a general guide. The navigators were so accustom-ed to accurate charts that it was difficult to make them believe that sometimes they were right and the chart was wrong. The MOUNT OLYMPUS was forced to retire from the Ross Sea by ice conditions and its long range radio and radar were not available for use in connection with the reconnaissance program. The magnetic compass could not always be relied upon. Thus the only tools at the command of the navigator for use in establishing control data for the photography as well as for the safety of the plane, consisted of an astro-compass and a chart with good navigation and terrestrial grids but inaccurate detail.

F. The Photographers

Ten of the twelve photographers in the Central Group also acted as aerial photographers. The fact that these men had been well trained in their duties is evident from the excellent quality of their work. Their work was not perfect, however, but repetition of imperfections in later flights was caused by the lack of a photo-graphic laboratory at the base, where such errors would have been discovered and corrected. Sample errors committed included an oblique camera which was accidently stopped all the way down to F.22, and the failure to insert some sort of marker in the tri-metrogon and gremlin cameras to mark the beginning and end of runs for correlation of the port, vertical, starboard, and gremlin photographs.

The photographic situation which adversely effected photo-grammetry was the fact that the R4D's were equipped with too many cameras for the single photographer allowed in the crew. As a result, the oblique, movie, and radio altimeter cameras as well as the field data sheets, suffered at the expense of operating the tri-metrogon assembly. The supplementary photography and the field data sheets are especially important to the photogrammetrist since it is the combination of these and the navigators records that makes the aerial photography useful for mapping purposes.

G. Photogrammetric Flight Performance

According to the Operations Plan, mapping missions were to be flown at an altitude of 10,000 feet above the terrain. When the aircraft left the U.S.S. PHILIPPINE SEA all unnecessary gear including oxygen equipment was removed to insure a safe take-off. Later it was impractical to replace this oxygen equipment. Without the oxygen the aircraft were able to fly at 10,000 feet above the shelf ice but averaged approximately only 2000 feet above the 10,000 foot high plateau.

Tri-metrogon photography is not considered practical at altitudes less than 5,000 feet and is usually flown from 10,000 to 25,000 feet above the terrain. The 2,000 foot relative altitude considerably limited the amout of land photo-mapped in each photograph as well as on each photographic flight, and also caused the expenditure of a considerably larger amount of film than would have been necessary to map the territory had higher altitude flights been possible.

Photographs of mountainous areas and rugged terrain taken at these low relative altitudes will therefore be very difficult to process, since the difference in elevation between mountain ridges and valleys in any one photograph will sometimes be greater that the difference in elevation between the mountain ridges and the aircraft. This means that working out scales for individual photographs, and even sections of individual photographs will involve extra time and additional technical difficulties.

H. The Effect of Antarctic Weather upon Photographic Reconnaissance.

The lack of a sufficient number of weather stations, lack of detailed knowledge of the climatic habits of the Antarctic, and a paucity of weather records made prognostication of flying weather very difficult. The effect upon photographic reconnaissance was felt in many ways. Weather came in "bunches". Several good days were very suddenly followed by many bad ones. During the good days, the air and ground crews wore themselves out to the point of exhaustion trying to take advantage of the twenty-four hours of daylight each day. There was no time for interrogation or reworking navigation logs while the details were still fresh.

All too frequently a plane on an assigned flight line was forced to turn off that line because of inclement weather, or clouds which prevented photography. The investment in time and effort which had placed the aircraft that far along was too great to waste, however, so in most cases the plane turned and traveled to an area of acceptable weather and photo-mapped the terrain there. This caused a constant jumbling of flight lines and helped cause an undue amount of photo reconnaissance in certain areas in relation to other, non-photographed areas.

When photographs were taken with clouds or haze above the aircraft, the resulting photography was frequently not of mapping quality. (See Appendix to Annex II: "White Days") When photographs were taken with clouds or haze under the aircraft, it was frequently impossible to differentiate between the white haze and the white snow showing through the breaks in the clouds. Sometimes important photography was taken during cloudy days, for example, the aerial photographs of previously uncharted mountains emerging through thick undercast at 12,000' altitude.

I. Laboratory Facilities.

The lack of laboratory facilities at the base caused difficulties. As mentioned previously, some errors were constantly repeated since they were not discovered until the film was finally processed. Air crews could not be intelligently interrogated by use of the processed photography until after the ships left New Zealand, weeks after the flights were made. By this time the incidents of individual flights had become hazy and crews were not able to answer detailed questions. Similarly, the navigators did not get an opportunity to check their charts against the photography until after all the flights had been completed.

J. Bay of Whales Mapping Project.

Many aerial photographs were taken over the Bay of Whales. These included vertical photographic runs at 10,000 and 2,000 feet, hundreds of hand-held oblique photos, and a tri-metrogon photo circle. Representatives of the Hydrographic Office, the Coast and Geodetic Survey, and the War Department calculated the new geographical position of the old base line and measured the directions and speeds of the shelf ice movements.

From this data it will now be possible to make an excellent map of the Bay of Whales as of February 1947 and, with some degree of certainty, to project a map as to how it may appear at any given date within the next few years.

During the last Antarctic Summer the geographic position of the Base Camp established at the Bay of Whales was determined to be: 78° 26' 09" South Latitude 163° 55' 16" West Longitude This position is believed to have moved more than 8300' in the seven years since 1940.

V. SUMMARY OF ACCOMPLISHMENTS

A. Aerial Reconnaissance Mapping Missions and other Flights.

	Mapping Flights	Weather Rescue and Test Flights	Total Flights
Eastern Group- - - - - - - - 10	10	11	21
Central Group- - - - - - - 28	28	18	46
Western Group- - - - - - - 26	26	8	34
Total- - - - - - - - - - - 64	64	37	101

B. Approximate Number of Hours Spent in the Air.

Eastern Group- - - - - - - 137
Central Group- - - - - - - -260
Western Group- - - - - - - -228
Total- - - - - - - - - - - - - - -625

C. Approximate Number of Aerial Reconnaissance Photographs for Mapping Purposes.

Eastern Group- - - - - - - -9,000
Central Group- - - - - - - 21,000
Western Group- - - - - - - 40,000
Total- - - - - - - - - - - - - - -70,000

D. Number of Aviation Personnel Trained in Polar Photographic Reconnaissance.

	Pilots	Navigators	Photographers
Eastern Group- - - - - - - 6	6	2	4
Central Group- - - - - - - 19	19	7	10
Western Group- - - - - - - 9	9	3	16
Total- - - - - - - - - - - 34	34	12	30

E. Preliminary Estimate of Approximate Number of Square Miles Visible to Occupants of the Aircraft.

Eastern Group- - - - - - -675,000
Central Group- - - - - - -700,000
Western Group- - - - - - -125,000
Total- - - - - - - - - - - - - - - 1,500,000

F. Preliminary Estimate of Approximate Number of Square Miles Discovered.

1. Total Estimated   350,000 Sq. miles
2. Total Possible   700,000 Sq. miles

G. Coastline Investigated.

Approximately 60% (by longitude) of the Antarctic coastline
was photo mapped by aircraft of Task Force 68. This coastline
measured some 5500 miles by airline connecting each degree of longitude and did not include any large areas of shelf ice. A quarter of
this coastline was sighted for the first time by personnel of Operation
HIGHJUMP. Forty percent had been sighted before but charted incorrectly
or, as in some cases, the previous mariners had plotted shelf ice thinking it to be coastline. Only thirty-five percent of the coastline
investigated corresponded to the charts and navigation of Task Force
68. In addition a considerable amount of the Antarctic Pack Ice was
explored. Many of the Shelf ice barriers, were photographed including the 400 mile Ross Barrier.

H. Other Geographic Discoveries.

Aside from the hundreds of peaks seen for the first time in
the mountains south and west of the Ross Ice Shelf, at least 18 other
mountain ranges or groups of mountains and 10 or more individual mountains of importance were discovered by members of Operation HIGHJUMP.
Some of these mountains average between 15,000 and 20,000 feet. The
new maps will show numerous glaciers, nunataks and skerries along the
coastline as well as 12 newly discovered (or enlarged) bays and 9 capes.

Unusual features explored, included a series of dry glacial
valleys continuing tarns and ice falls in Victoria Land and two so-
called "Oasis" near the Indian Ocean Coast. The latter consisted of
bare rock areas as much as 20 miles on a side completely surrounded
by the usual ice topography. Each "Oasis" contained several lakes
of various colors, probably caused by the algae in the water. Some
of the lakes were frozen and some not. One of the PBM aircraft
landed in a lake and took water samples. The bare rock was not
examined but did not contain visible vegetation although lichens
may not have been visible at that distance. There was no evidence
of thermal activity in these areas.

The Ross Ice Barrier, and the Bay of Whales area in particular,
was photographed in order that changes in the position of the ice front
and rates of movement of the various sections of Shelf ice could be
determined. New tension cracks were discovered in the barrier. The
Bay of Whales was found to be considerably smaller than on previous
expeditions. This movement had been discovered before, but the
actual rate of closing was determined this time to be between 4.5 and
5 feet a day. As a matter of fact the already narrow entrance to the
Bay of Whales closed in by 200 feet (more than 1/5 of its width) during
the six weeks the Central Group occupied the area. The walls of shelf
ice guarding the entrance will probably close this Antarctic winter
causing a pressure ridge and the breaking away of a tabular berg thus
providing a new entrance to the Bay of Whales.

Our knowledge of the polar plateau and ice cap was increased by several flights of the Central and Western Groups. The pole had only been approached from the Ross Ice Shelf. It has now been established that there are no mountains within at least 180 miles of the South Pole in a clockwise direction from 50° W. to 150° E. longitude. Completing the circle from 150° E. to 50° W. longitude mountains appear at the extremity of this 3° radius, many of which will be charted for the first time by means of HIGHJUMP aerial photography.

This great ice cap is believed to continue north 100° and 150° W. longitude almost to the very coastline at elevations of 8500'or higher. Most of this area has never been seen except the south and east, sectors which were seen by members of the Central Group and the north sector over which personnel from the Western Group flew.

Aviation personnel of the Western Group deduced from their flights in its vicinity, that the South Magnetic Pole had migrated to the north and west of where it is indicated on H.O. chart 2652. However, this data is not certain since there was no physicist or special magnetic equipment aboard the aircraft.

Detailed exploration by aerial photography was carried on in the mountainous areas south and west of the Ross Shelf Ice. The tall peaks in these areas had been discovered by previous explorers operating from the Ross Shelf Ice and from the Beardmore and Thorne Glaciers. Now many of the lesser peaks and valleys which were in defilade from these explorers have been discovered and photographed.

Important work was performed in confirming locations of physical features which had not been thoroughly investigated on previous expeditions. Some features, however, had been incorrectly located in relation to the charts and navigation of the HIGHJUMP aerial explorers. It is quite probable, for instance, that Mount Siple, an important land mark, confirmed by this expedition to be 15,000' high, will be relocated considerably to the south and west of its present position on the map. Similarly, the Noville Mountains and Cape Dart must be relocated. In some instances features previously on the map were proven to be non-existant. The Eastern Group proved that a large portion of George Getz Shelf Ice just did not exist and the Western Group finally settled the doubtful existance of Thorshammer Island, by flying over the location of that non-existant feature.

I. Mapping By Use of the Aerial Magnetometer.

A geo-physicist from the U.S. Geological Survey operated an Aerial Magnetometer synchronized with the tri-metrogon mapping cameras. This instrument records intensity and area of magnetic bed rock. Magnetometry recordings confirmed the known presence of burried Roosevelt Island and helped confirm the presence of islands thought to be burried under the Ross Shelf Ice and causing such formations as Kainan Bay. By the same method, evidence was given to indicate one such burried island does not exist. The Eastern shoreline of the Ross Sea is covered over by the Shelf ice and its exact location is not known. The magneto-meter established evidence that it is probably further to the east at least between latitudes 81° and 82° South.

J. Summary: It is believed that because of the quality and quantity of aerial reconnaissance photography with the resulting maps to be made by the photogrammetrists, that the knowledge of the areal geography of the Antarctic Region has been advanced more by the U. S. Naval Expedition, 1946-1947, than by any other expedition, in spite of the short time of this operation. Had more time been available for the proper preparation of trained photographic reconnaissance groups and the construction of a runway, the quality and quantity of that reconnaissance could have been materially increased.

VI. THE CARTOGRAPHIC PROGRAM

The work of many previous expeditions has been lost because there was no agency prepared to receive the raw data upon the return of the explorers, analyse that data, and publish the results. The material usually ended in rough manuscript form in the archives or in the files of some government or private office. This time a program has been prepared in advance to publish the scientific and cartographic data.

The Chief of Naval Operations had designated the Hydrographic office as the central clearing house and coordinating agency for Operation HIGHJUMP hydrographic, scientific, and mapping data. To help finance this program the office of Naval Research has alloted the Hydrographic office an initial sum of $100,000.

The Hydrographic Office does not have the space and equipment necessary to make a rapid tri-metrogon assembly of the 70,000 photo-graphic exposures. Furthermore, the money allotted may not be used to pay Navy Department salaries. For these reasons the Hydrographer, has contracted with the Aeronautical Chart Service for the services of the Tri-metrogon Section, Topographic Branch of the U.S. Geological Survey to do the following work on the Operation HIGHJUMP photography:

    a. Indexing, of tri-metrogon photography.
    b. Evaluation, of tri-metrogon photography.
    c. Compilation, by photogrammetric methods of planimetric and topographic data at a scale of 1:500,000 of Antarctic Coastal areas and other photographed areas of special interest to the U. S. Navy.
    d. Furnish compilation sheets and negatives for Base Preliminary Maps.

The Hydrographic Office has furnished, through the Naval Photographic Center, one set of 70,000 contact prints suitable for indexing and evaluation purposes. In the near future a set of contact prints of good photographic quality on double-weight waterproof paper will be

RESTRICTED

provided via the same channels.

During June, 1947, representatives of the Task Force, Hydrographic Office, Aeronautical Chart Service, and U.S. Geological Survey thoroughly investigated control data and map information necessary for photogrammetric compilation.

The Aeronautical Chart Service has the option of compiling maps by photogrammetric means from the photographs of the Continental Interior. Credit for the photography must be accorded to the U.S. Navy.

The Staff Photogrammetric Officer has been designated Liaison officer between the various Naval and other government agencies working on the cartographic program. In this capacity he is coordinating the activities of these agencies under the direction of the Head Engineer of the Hydrographic Office.

The Photographic Interpretation Center will detail aerial photo interpreters to aid in the interpretation of planemetric and topographic data and photogrammetrists to aid in the solution of any unusual polar photogrammetric problems.

The U.S. Geological Survey will assist by plotting maps based upon the work of the aerial magnetometer and with the geological interpretation of the aerial photographs.

The Hydrographic Office will supply the oceanographic data.

It is estimated that the photogrammetric and cartographic compilation period prior to the publication of the new maps and charts will take a minimum of two years time. The $100,000 initial allotment will have to be supplemented in order to complete the planned production of sailing and aeronautical charts, sailing directions and aerological and other scientific information.

VII. ANTARCTIC PLACE NAMES IN RELATION TO TASK FORCE SIXTY EIGHT.

The important natural features discovered by personnel of Task Force 68 must be named before the publication of the new maps and charts. However, since for the most part it is not known just what features have been actually discovered until the photogrammetric compilation of planemetric and topographic data has been completed, this naming will not take place until that time.

The Board on Geographic Names, has the responsibility for all place names appearing on maps and in publications of the U.S. government. Anyone may submit a proposal for a name. The final decision will be made by the Board based upon its "Statement of Policy Covering Geographical Names in Antarctica", a copy of which is attached to this Annex as Appendix A.

Annex III   - 11 -

Generally speaking, this policy provides for three categories of importance of natural features and three categories of importance of personnel connected with Antarctic Exploration. Features of the first category may be named for personnel of the highest category and so forth. Any member of Task Force 68 or anyone who has assisted in the analysis of the technical data derived from the expedition is eligible for at least a third order feature, such as a mountain to be named after him. This imposes no obligation on the government to name features after any particular individual, nor to give names to unimportant geographical features where names would be of little use, merely for the sake of naming them.

Unacceptable names include those suggested because of relationship or friendship, those of pets, those which advertise commercial products, or those of personnel of high rank or prominent position unless otherwise qualified.

A number of proposals for names of features have been received from various members of the Task Force by the Staff Photogrammetric Officer who also acted as Expedition Geographer. These names, along with others, will be submitted to the Board with the recommendation that the sponsors of the names, rather than the names they sponsored, be used for naming appropriate features.

Appendix A to Annex III

STATEMENT OF POLICY COVERING
GEOGRAPHICAL NAMES IN ANTARCTICA

These policies are for the guidance of the Board in deciding cases and for the guidance of explorers and others in proposing names for natural features in Antarctica.

The problem of geographic nomenclature is different for Antarctica than for any other part of the world. It has no permanent settlements. Even in the explored portions of the continent many of the features are unnamed, and still others have never been seen by man. Antarctica has been visited and explored by the nationals of many nations, who, by their heroic efforts to broaden man's knowledge of this land of ice and snow, have fully demonstrated the international nature of the world of science. Names, therefore, will be considered without reference to the nationality of the person honored.

Under the policy here set forth, decisions on Antarctic names will be based on priority of application, appropriateness, and the extent to which usage has become established. The grouping of natural features into three orders of magnitude, with corresponding categories of persons according to the type of contribution which they have made, is intended to provide the greatest possible objectivity in determining the appropriateness of a name. It does not, however, exclude the use of other than personal names when appropriate. Non-personal names are discussed under a separate heading.

Types of Natural Features

First-order features
    Plateaus
    Coasts
    Regions or "lands"
    Extensive mountain ranges
    Ice shelves
    Large glaciers
    Seas
    Major submarine deeps, ridges, plateaus, or swells

Second-order features
    Peninsulas
    Mountain ranges, except the most extensive
    Great or prominent mountains
    Glaciers, except the largest
    Large bays
    Gulfs
    Prominent capes
    Islands
    Straits or passages
    Harbors
    Extensive submarine reefs, shoals, or shallows

Third-order features
    Glaciers   )
    Bays   (except the greater or more prominent ones
    Capes   )
    Points
    Coves
    Rocks
    Minor shore features
    Cliffs
    Minor mountains and hills
    Nunataks
    Anchorages
    Parts of these features
    Submarine reefs, shoals, and shallows of small extent.
    Camp or camp sites and depots (not natural features and not
        necessarily permanent).

Features having special significance or prominence in geographic discovery, scientific investigation, or the history of Antarctic may be placed in the next higher category than their magnitude alone would warrant.

RESTRICTED

Scheme for Application of Personal Names to these Features.

First-order features

The leader or organizer of an expedition to Antarctica.

Persons who have made discoveries of outstanding significance in Antarctica, or leaders of field parties, or captains of ships, that have made such discoveries.

Persons who, through their work with Antarctic expeditions, have made outstanding contributions to scientific knowledge or to the techniques of Antarctic exploration.

A person who has provided the major financial or materials support to an expedition, thereby making such an undertaking possible.

Second-order features.

Persons whose outstanding heroism, skill, spirit, or labor has made a signal contribution to the success of an expedition.

Persons who have made important contributions in the planning, organisation, outfitting, or operation of expeditions to Antarctica.

Ship captains or leaders of field parties of such expeditions.

Persons whose contributions to the knowledge of the Arctic either have advanced our knowledge of Antarctica or have expanded the possibilities of Antarctic exploration.

Persons who have made outstanding contributions to equipment for polar exploration.

The directors or heads of learned societies that have given significant support or made material contributions to Antarctic exploration.

Persons who by substantial contributions of funds or supplies have made possible an Antarctic expedition.

Persons who have done outstanding work in the utilization of data, identification of specimens, or interpretation of the results of Antarctic exploration.

Third-order features

Persons who have assisted in the work of organizing or conducting Antarctic exploration, or who have assisted in analysis of information gathered in the course of such exploration.

Members of expeditions, including ship-based personnel.

Persons whose contributions to knowledge in their respective fields have facilitated the discovery, recognition, identification, or recording of Antarctic phenomena.

Persons who have made material contributions in any form to Antarctic expeditions, and who have by their words or actions demonstrated an interest in furthering scientific exploration rather than in seeking commercial exploitation of such contributions.

The Application of Non-personal Names.

In accord with the tradition of Antarctic exploration, it is considered appropriate to apply non-personal names to natural features. Examples of non-personal names are:

1. Names which commemorate events (e.g., Scott's "Arrival Bay" and Ross' "Possession Island").

2. Names of ships from which discoveries have been made (e.g., "Discovery Inlet" and "Peacock Bay").

3. Names of organizations which have sponsored, supported, or given scientific or financial assistance to Antarctic expeditions. (e.g., "Royal Society Range," "Admiralty Range," "Banzare Coast.")

4. Names which are peculiarly descriptive of the feature named. (e.g., "Deception Island"). Descriptive names which are not unique, nor particularly appropriate, and for which there are likely to be duplicates are, however, undesirable.

5. Any other non-personal name which because of its acknowledged importance occupies a major role in Antarctic exploration or Antarctic history.

Names in the above categories may be appropriately applied to a feature in any order of magnitude with which there is association.

Criteria of Appropriateness

Newly proposed names will be considered for features of the first-, second-, or third-order, as described above, in the light of their appropriateness, as evidenced by the following factors arranged in order of weight:

1. Chronological priority of discovery, naming, or other relevant action.

2. Actual association of the person, ship, organization event, etc., with the feature.

3. Association of the person, ship, organization, event, etc., with Antarctic exploration.

4. Contribution of the person to the knowledge of Antarctica.

5. Association of the person, ship, organization, event, etc., with other polar exploration.

6. Contribution of the person to relevant fields of knowledge.

7. Extent to which financial or material contributions have contributed to the success of an expedition, or to the collection of valuable scientific data.

8. Previous recognition through a geographic name in Antarctica.

    a. To prevent confusion, it is considered advisable, in the future naming in Antarctica, to apply the name of one person or the names of persons having the same surname, to no more than one feature of a kind.

9. The possibility of ambiguity or confusion with names already in use.

    a. The duplication of names already in current usage is undesirable, and, except in special cases, is to be avoided.
    b. Since descriptive names are often ambiguous and easily duplicated, they should be avoided, unless a descriptive name is peculiarly appropriate.
    c. The duplication in Antarctica of names well known in other parts of the world is undesirable even though qualified by adjectives such as "new", "south", and "little".

Names already in use will be considered in the light of:

1. Appropriateness, as outlined above;

2. Wideness of acceptance, as evidenced by use in scientific and popular map and other literature. Usage which is considered sufficiently fixed and/or unanimous may be accepted as valid grounds for approval of a name which would not otherwise qualify.

Fields of Knowledge Pertinent to Antarctica

The following is a list of fields of knowledge in which outstanding contributions may be considered justifications for commemoration in an Antarctic place name. It is to be considered neither exclusive or exhaustive, and no order of priority is intended.

1. Navigation and astronomy

2. Oceanography and hydrography

3. Surveying, photogrammetry, and cartography

4. Meteorology and climatology

5. Geodesy and geophysics

6. Glaciology and ice physics

7. Radio, radar, and allied fields

8. Geology, volcanology, and seismology

9. Geography

10. Botany and its subdivisions

11. Zoology and its subdivisions

Recommended Language and Form

In keeping with long established policies based upon trends in the normal evolution of geographical names, consideration will be given to brevity, simplicity, and unambiguity in selecting the form of names derived by these procedures.

1. The application of full names and/or titles of persons will be considered appropriate only when required to avoid ambiguity, duplication, or other confusion.

2. The names of organizations, ships, and other non-personal names, when unduly long and cumbersome, will ordinarily be used in some shortened, though intelligible, form.

3. English generics will be used, and titles will be translated where their use is required.

Inappropriate Names

Names in the following categories will not be considered, unless otherwise appropriate according to the principles stated herein, or unless such names are widely and firmly established as of the date of approval of these principles.

1. Names suggested because of relationship or friendship.

2. Names of contributors of funds, equipment, and supplies, who by the nature and tone of their advertising have endeavored to capitalize or to gain some commerical advantage as a result of their donations. This would not include advantages resulting from testing of donated equipment under Antarctic conditions. In cases of doubt, the decision shall be in favor of the individual whose name has been proposed.

3. The names of products, sled dogs, or pets will ordinarily not be considered as appropriate for application to natural features in Antarctica.

Board on Geographic Names
July 13, 1946.

VIII. SUGGESTIONS AND RECOMMENDATIONS

The following suggestions and recommendations are submitted as a guide for use in planning future operations.

Adequate Photogrammetric Personnel

Photogrammetric billets should be provided with respect to the quantity, quality and kinds of aerial photographic mapping to be performed. In the case of an operation similar to HIGHJUMP it would be preferable to have one trained photogrammetrist with each task group. In addition there should be a task force staff photogrammetric officer and several enlisted assistants, some with photographic and some with drafting or cartographic experience. There is no regular rate for photogrammetric personnel in the Navy. They were formerly designated as Specialist X or Specialist P. There were no photogrammetric personnel in the Navy available for assignment during HIGHJUMP preparation.

Supply of Photogrammetric Personnel

There should be a naval organization responsible for furnishing trained officers and men for photogrammetric use as required. It is recommended that photographic officers in the Navy and the Marine Corps be regularly assigned to the Photographic Interpretation Center for training in photogrammetry.

Planning Period

For as extensive an operation as HIGHJUMP, it is suggested that the planning period for photogrammetric operations be lengthened to a minimum of six months and preferably a year or longer. The research on available control, the selection of cameras and related equipment, the designing of data sheets and records, the selection of a suitable combination of aircraft, and the outfitting of the planes all require a reasonable amount of time.

Selection of the Base

The shore bases should be selected with regard for the accessibility to supply ships, the availability of air operation facilities, and the geographical relationship to the actual area most important to photograph.

In polar operations, and particularly in the Antarctic, floating bases such as seaplane tenders should be accompanied by an icebreaker. The addition of this vessel would increase the effective range of the photographic survey aircraft from two hundred to six hundred miles by allowing the tender to launch its seaplanes from positions south of the pack ice. It would also permit terrestrial photogrammetry and ground control parties.

Physical Layout of the Land Base

Quarters for photogrammetry should be established close to the air operations quarters in order to facilitate briefing, interrogation, and technical observation. It is essential that the quarters for navigation and photography be within the same immediate area, and that the ready rooms for pilots and air crewmen be within reasonable distance.

Photogrammetric Space Required

For mapping operation of HIGHJUMP proportions, both shore and ship bases should have approximately 150 square feet of unobstructed floor space devoted to photogrammetric purposes. This room should be equipped with the appropriate necessary equipment.

Photographic Laboratory

The presence of a photographic laboratory at the base of operations is necessary to insure proper photographic mapping coverage.

Selection of Aircraft

Photographic reconnaissance and mapping aircraft should be selected for two primary uses. These uses and the basic criteria relative to photogrammetry by which the aircraft should be chosen for each function are listed below:

1. Survey Aircraft.

   a. Ability to take off and land on surface selected by expedition.
   b. Sufficient range to cover areas to be mapped.
   c. A ceiling of 20,000 feet, to make exploratory photography practicable over high elevation terrain.
   d. Large enough to carry the emergency, camera, and scientific gear, necessary crew, two photographers, and a technical observer.

RESTRICTED

    e. It is suggested that a plane similar to the P2V might be
       conformed for such purposes. A pressurized cabin would
       be an advantage over oxygen gear.

2. Control Aircraft

    a. Ability to take off or land on ice or snow.
    b. Sufficient range to cover area for which control is to
       be obtained.
    c. Just large enough to carry one set of tri-metrogon cameras,
       emergency gear for two, and magnetic and surveying instru-
       ments.
    d. Crew to consist of one photographic pilot and one geographic
       surveying engineer, both with navigation experience and
       training.
    e. It is suggested that the TBM might be redesigned for this
       purpose to operate from a shore base, fly to the desired
       point, land and take the geographic position, and return
       to the base.
    f. Helicopters could also be designed for this purpose as
       based upon ice breakers or protected seaplane tenders
       operating inside the pack ice. Control would be limited
       to coastal points by this system.

Selection of Aviation Personnel

The pilots selected should be trained photo-mapping pilots, with experience in flying actual mapping photography as opposed to war time photographic reconnaissance. If the aircraft are designed for co-pilots, only one-half of the pilots selected need meet this classification.

The navigators selected should be experienced in navigation without the aid of radio beams and accurate charts. In addition they should pass a thorough course of instruction in the problems peculiar to polar navigation.

Qualified Technical Observers in Each Aircraft

A qualified technical observer should accompany each flight as a member of the aerial photographic crew. This man should be trained in photogrammetry with a background in geography, cartography, geology, or geomorphology and would serve to assemble, organize, and correlate all control and descriptive data accrued by individual members of that flight. This photogrammetric observer would operate the wire recorder: advise the plane commander concerning the value of alternate flight lines; advise the aerial photographer concerning which portions of the terrain to photograph, the altitude for best mapping photography and the kinds of supplementary photography most useful in individual cases. At the end of the flight, it would be the duty of this photogrammetric observer to collect the navigation charts and logs, the photographic data sheets, the pilot's logs, the wire recorder spools, and his own notes and sketches. He would be responsible to see that the navigator and the photographer reworked their figures together and in his presence, if reworking was needed. He would view the photographs and chart the area covered by them. He would maintain a record of the statistics of each flight. And he would be responsible for the preservation of this data until it reached the rear echelon at which point he would be instructed to make it available to the agencies which prepare the maps and to assist those agencies in placing the topographic and planimetric detail on the maps.

Design of Logs and Data Sheets in Advance

Before the expedition leaves the United States the types of maps to be produced should be considered in relation to the kinds of photography which are to be undertaken and a series of appropriate log and data sheets must be devised to allow the maximum information to reach the rear echelon photogrammetrists and cartographers.

Those whose duties include keeping of one or more of these logs and data sheets should be trained in the meaning and importance of each column.

Data Sheet designed for Supplementary Cameras

A special photographic data sheet should be designed for aerial motion picture cameras which are used to supplement tri-metrogon photography. Exact GCT time and the angle of shooting in relation to line of flight must be recorded if the photography is to serve as an aid to interpretation and mapping.

Radar cameras, radio altimeter cameras, and other supplementary cameras also require special data sheets to obtain full value from the photography. A chronometer should be set in all cameras photographing instruments.

Use of Planned Flightlines and Alternates

Flightlines should be drawn during the planning stage of the operation upon the best aerial navigation charts available. In the case of the polar regions these charts should be gridded and numbered for flying by the grid method. Care should be exercised that either the vertical or horizontal grid lines are also rhumblines.

Flightlines over unexplored territory are difficult to draw since there is no knowledge of the type of terrain or its elevation above sea level. They are more difficult to fly because of the absence of landmarks and navigation aids. Yet it is essential that a practical set of flightlines be planned and followed in a systematic fashion if acceptable mapping photography is to be secured. When weather conditions during flight make it impractical to continue on one

flightline, the pilot should change his course to a first or second
alternate which has been prepared in advance for his navigator. Only
in the event that all courses are weathered in or if there are instruments or mechanical failures, should the pilot fly a course of his
own choice.

Instruction of Air Crews in Geography of Area

In the photomapping operations of partially explored areas all
flying personnel should be instructed in the geography of the area.

Geographic Observations during Exploritory Flights

Members of exploratory photo-reconnaissance missions should
include a description of the local geography of each flight for use
by the rear echelon cartographers. This information could be secured
either by including a trained observer in the crew or by training the
crew members to fill out prepared forms in addition to their other
duties while in flight.

Briefing and Interrogation

Briefing and interrogation should be complete for reconnaissance
flights in unknown territory. Suitable briefing quarters should be
installed in which there is sufficient seating capacity for all personnel
who may be required to be in the air at one time. A large table and a
chalk-board should be provided. Neither the briefing before nor the
interrogation after the flights should be rushed. It might pay divi-
dends to provide hot coffee and sandwiches, especially during the post-
flight interrogations.

It is important that the crews be briefed and interrogated
systematically. The crews should recognize these to be as much a part
of the flight as the actual operations in the air.

It is also important that the crews be briefed and interrogated
as a unit instead of individual conferences with the plane commander
and the navigator and omission of the remainder of the crew.

Inverse Mercator Charts

The Inverse Mercator Chart is a form of transverse Mercatorism
in which the equator of the fictitious grid extends around the earth
from pole to pole along the 90° meridians. This grid alone, however,
is insufficient since it shows no true geographical positions, and is
therefore usually over printed on a normal polar system of meridians and
parallels. Five such charts of Antarctica were developed by the
Hydrographic Office and submitted in quantity to Task Force Sixty Eight
before operations commenced. These charts were used for navigation by
Task Group 68.5 and the following recommendations are submitted.

RESTRICTED

(1) The inverse Mercator grid should be printed for each ½ degree of latitude and longitude. This will eliminate inaccurate hand gridding by navigators who are flying a grid system.
(2) Over print the inverse Mercator grid in a different color for each of the four polar quadrants, as an aid in flying the grid system.
(3) Establish letter values as well as fictitious number values for either the latitude or longitude.
(4) Extend the quadrants or sheets to include all areas south of 65°S. for the Australian and African Quadrants, all areas south of 70°S. for the American and Pacific Quadrants, and special charts for the Palmer Peninsula and all areas south of 82° S.
(5) The inverse Mercator grid should be drawn true or have light dotted lines showing the true positions of the meridians in order to possess the navigation value of great circles.
(6) Supply a number of charts equal to a minimum of three times the number of flightlines appearing on any quadrant.

Geographic Detail on Polar Aeronautical Charts

At the present time, personnel unacquainted with the minute details of the history of Antarctic exploration have not the ability to determine what parts of the charts are really reliable and what parts represent conjecture.

Therefore the topographic and planimetric detail on aeronautical charts of the polar regions should be indicated in such a manner that the reliability of the information is expressed along with its supposed geographic position.

There are several methods of doing this. It may be practicable to use a system of heavy, medium, and light solid, dashed and dotted lines. Various colors could be used. Straight letters versus reverse slant or reverse italics is another possibility. A key chart in the legend would be a solution. All definitely fixed points should be indicated by an appropriate symbol.

The areas explored should be illustrated in a more qualitative manner to differentiate between those areas relatively well known and those areas merely "glimpsed thru a rift in the clouds".

Navigation Aids

It is impossible to make flights of 1500 miles in a polar region by crossing dead-reckonning lines with sun lines for "fixes" and return with an accurate flight track chart. And without an accurate flight track chart, the photography is almost valueless.

Drift meters are frequently useless since there are no objects in the white surface by which to judge drift. The magnetic compass will

RESTRICTED

not perform well in all these regions and variation changes rapidly.
Meridians are so close together that the true course of a plane flying
a straight line (or great circle) is constantly changing unless it
is due north or south. Landmarks for the most part do not exist.

For all these reasons, it is essential to good photographic
reconnaissance that all navigation aids such as Loran, Radar, and radio
be installed where ever possible. Loran stations could be established
along the shore of each quadrant. Fixes from any two of these stations
crossed with a sunline would be a sufficient "fix" for exploratory
mapping purposes.

Gyro-Compass

A gyro compass should be installed in front of the co-pilot as
well as the pilot in order to eliminate navigation errors caused by
parallax From the co-pilots' position in the R4D it was not possible
to read the gyro compass within two degrees.

Establishment of Ground Control

It is most necessary to establish ground control for accurate,
precision mapping. The complete absence of this on Operation HIGHJUMP
at once reduced the aerial photography from mapping to merely reconnaissance in value. Although ground control presupposes frequent positions
of accurate geographic location, it would be possible to produce suitable maps and charts of a desert area like Antarctica with a fraction
of the number of points ordinarily required.

It is suggested that a means of providing ground control be
worked out in advance of any future operations. Methods may involve
sledging or amphibious tractor parties, specially equipped aircraft
as previously mentioned, possibly the use of a zenith-nadir camera,
or an icebreaker landing control parties at various points along
the coast.

Gremlin Photography

It is recommended that the cognizant naval organization be
instructed to develop a recording camera for use in obtaining readings
from various instruments each time the tri-metrogon cameras are tripped.

This new "Super-Gremlin" would have the following features:

(1) The same number of exposures as the K-17, 6" Tri-metrogon
    cameras.
(2) 9 X 9 or 9 X 18 film exposure
(3) A divided instrument panel containing:
    a- Pressure Altimeter
    b- Thermometer (to minus 60°F)
    c- Inclinometer for tilt

d- Inclinometer for tip
e- Chronometer
f- Gyro-compass
g- Magnetic compass (?)
h- Indicated Air Speed
i- Data Card
j- Radio Altimeter
k- Possibly a radar scope

Provision should be made for this device to function without tri-metrogon cameras when flying over an undercast.

Location of Photographer in Airplane

It would be desirable to mount the tri-metrogon cameras near the nose of the airplane, if the type construction permits. This would allow the photographer use of a plastic nose window to see what terrain would be passing under his camera so he could adjust the controls in advance. It would also be easier to heat the photographic compartment, to converse with the others in the crew, and it might eliminate wing tips in the oblique photography.

Tri-Metrogon Mount

The tri-metrogon mount should be specifically designed for the plane in which the cameras are to be installed. Benefits of such changes in design would be:

(1) Proper orientation of the starboard camera.
(2) Ability to insert magazine with dark slide in place to keep the calibration marks intact.
(3) A non-rigid mounting so that the entire mount may be adjusted for tilt.

The photographic officer has submitted new designs to eliminate the present feature which effect the photogrammetric value as well as the photographic quality of the exposures.

Use of the Wire Recorder

The benefits from the use of the wire recorders from the few flights on which they were properly used make these instruments valuable accessories on photographic and exploratory missions. It is recommended that one of these instruments be installed in each survey aircraft; it is suggested that the aviation personnel concerned be instructed in the simple mechanics involving its use and that they be given a check list of the kinds of items to record.

Relative Altitude of Survey Aircraft

It is recommended that the Aerial Photographic reconnaissance mapping aircraft remain at a relatively constant altitude of 10,000 feet above the terrain. When this is impracticable it is recommended that the aircraft maintain not less than 5000 feet altitude above the terrain. These altitudes will require the use of oxygen equipment or pressure cabins.

Operation of the Plane and Crew as a Unit.

It is recommended that the aircraft and crews be selected at an early period during the planning operations and be given considerable experience in working together as a unit while performing actual missions similar to those planned for the operations. Six weeks of photo flight practice as a unit should be required in order to eliminate the "rough-spots".

Policy Regarding Flying Personnel

Space is at a premium in aerial survey planes. Only those most qualified to produce the information require should be allowed to go on such missions. To insure this when the Task Force is operating in separate groups, the Task Force Commander's established policy indicating flight crews, scientifically trained observers and passengers, regardless of rank, should be communicated to the personnel concerned.

THE U S NAVAL ANTARCTIC EXPEDITION 1946

INDICATED FLIGHT LINES

RESTRICTED

ANTARCTIC CONTINENT

TG 683
TG 682

TG 683
TG 685

TG 683
TG 682

TG 683
TG 682

ACCURACY OF FLIGHT LINES IS DEPENDENT UPON CODED TRANSMISSION
OF DATA AND POLAR NAVIGATION ERRORS RESULTING FROM INABILITY
TO ESTABLISH TRUE GEOGRAPHIC POSITIONS DURING THE FLIGHTS

THE NUMBERS INDICATE THE TASK GROUP AND INDIVIDUAL FLIGHT

THE COASTLINE ON THIS BASE MAP IS NOT ACCURATE SEE
DISCOVERY MAP FOR COASTLINES ESTABLISHED BY TASK FORCE 68.

SUBMITTED 12 MARCH 1947

John H. Roscoe, Jr Lt USNCR
Staff Photogrammetric Officer

SCALE
0   100   200   300
NAUTICAL
MILES

Plate No. 2

Chart of indicated flight tracks.

Annex III

- 6 -

POSITIONS OF SEAPLANE TENDERS

U S NAVAL ANTARCTIC EXPEDITION 1946-47

TASK FORCE 68

TASK GROUP 68.2 - U.S.S. CURRITUCK - IN EASTERN HEMISPHERE
TASK GROUP 68.3 - U.S.S. PINE ISLAND - IN WESTERN HEMISPHERE
TASK GROUP 68.8 - LITTLE AMERICA - AT 78°28'S 163°55'W

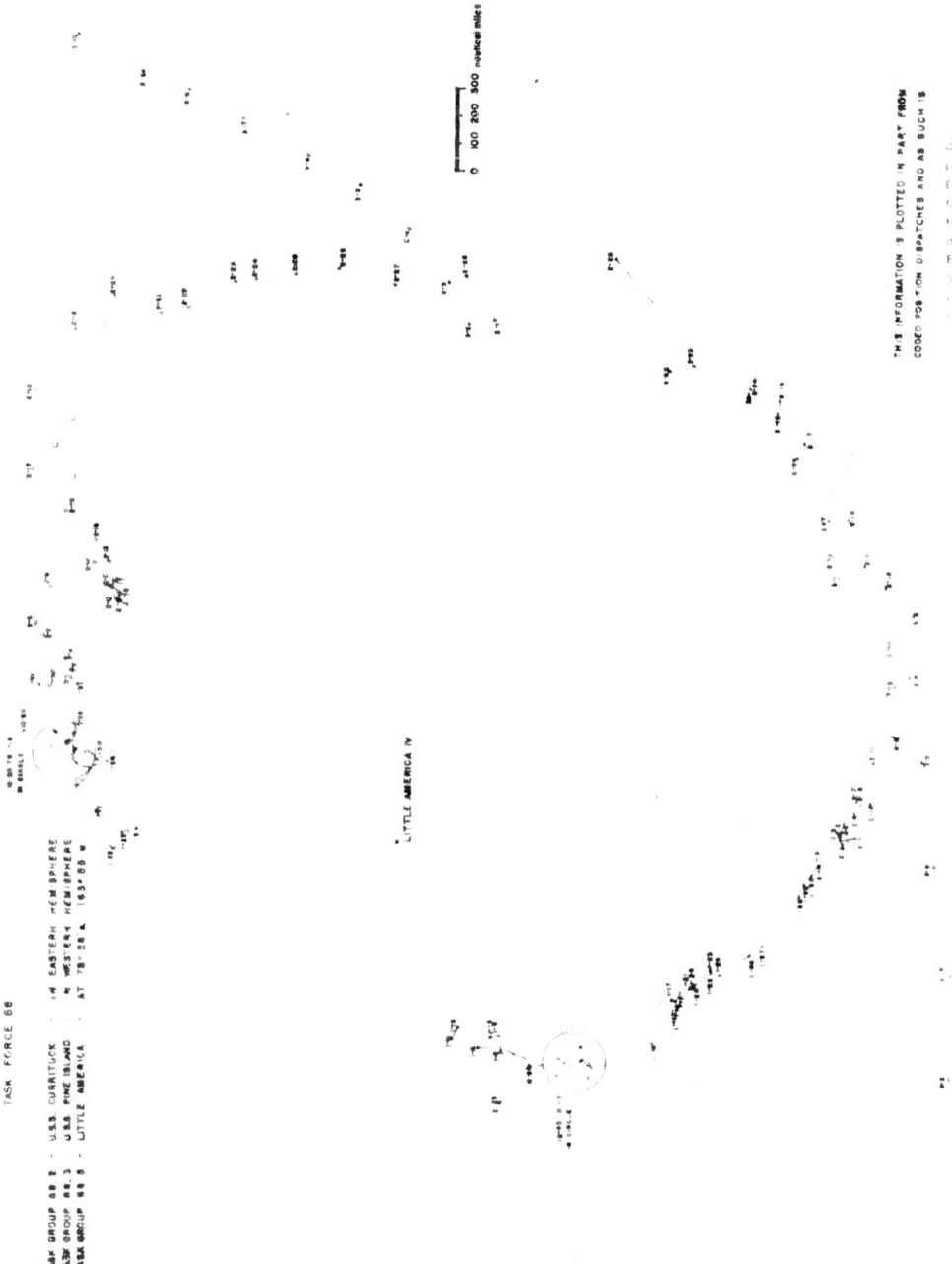

LITTLE AMERICA IV

0   100   200   300   nautical miles

NUMBERS INDICATE THE DATE THE SEAPLANE
TENDERS WERE AT EACH SPECIFIED LOCATION

SUBMITTED 8 MARCH 1947

JOHN H. ROSCOE Lt. USNR
Staff Photographic Officer

U.S. NAVAL ANTARCTIC EXPEDITION 1946–1947

DISCOVERY and EXPLORATION

RESTRICTED

1. TWO SMALL ISLANDS, EXPOSED ROCK, ELEVATION 500
2. MT SIPLE RELOCATED HERE, 15,000' ELEVATION CONFIRMED
3. OPEN WATER WEST AND SOUTHWEST OF MT SIPLE INDICATES GEORGE GETZ SHELF ICE NON-EXISTANT IN THIS LOCALITY.
4. AND 5. HIGH MOUNTAIN SIGHTED HERE FROM DISTANT AIRCRAFT
6. TWO HIGH MOUNTAINS, APPROXIMATELY 16,000'
7. MOUNTAIN RANGE 9,000', PLATEAU TO SOUTH 8,000'
8. LARGE FIRN FIELD INLAND FROM COAST FROM 121 TO 128 W., 2,000'
9. MOUNTAIN, 35 MILES INLAND, FROM 117 30 TO 118 42 W., 5,000'
10. FIVE MOUNTAINS, ELEVATION 3,000', CENTERED AT 73 14 S 111 30
11. MOUNTAIN RANGE, ELEVATION 3,000', EXTENDS ALONG 110 W.
12. "X-RAY MOUNTAIN RANGE", ELEVATION FROM 2,500' IN WEST TO 15,000' PEAK OF MOUNT X-RAY AT THE EASTERN EXTREMITY
13. MOUNTAIN RANGE, 35 EXPOSED PEAKS, 85 MILES LONG, ELEVATION RISES FROM 2,500' IN THE NORTH TO 5,000' IN THE SOUTH.
14. FIVE MOUNTAIN PEAKS, ESTIMATED ELEVATION 6,000'
15. FIVE SMALL ISLANDS, EXPOSED LAND, 400 YARDS LONG, 700' HIGH
16. THIS COASTLINE IS SNOW-COVERED WITH PATCHES OF BROWN LAND EXPOSED. OPEN WATER ALONG SHORE INSIDE OF PACK ICE.
17. ISLANDS AND GLACIERS DISCOVERED HERE. NORTH PART OF PENINSULA DEFINED BY OPEN WATER, WEST COAST DIFFICULT TO LOCATE.
18. TWO PARALLEL MOUNTAIN RANGES EXTEND APPROXIMATELY EAST-WEST ACROSS THE PENINSULA. (ROVILLE MOUNTAINS RELOCATED)
19. SEVERAL ISLANDS DISCOVERED IN THIS AREA.
20. MONTIQUE PEAK SIGHTED, ESTIMATED 3,000', BUT TOP IN CLOUDS.
21. OPEN WATER ON NORTH COASTS OF ALEXANDER FIRST AND CHARCOT IS
22. ICE COVERS WILKINS STRAIT JOINING ALEXANDER FIRST AND CHARCOT
23. SOUTHERN PORTION OF MARGUERITE BAY ACCESSIBLE TO SHIPS.
24. AND 25. SIGHTED MOUNTAIN HERE.
26. LOCATION OF DOUGLAS RANGE AND OTHER MOUNTAINS ON ALEXANDER FIRST ISLAND ARE CORRECT AS PREVIOUSLY CHARTED.
27. ADDITIONAL DATA SECURED VIA AERIAL PHOTOGRAPHY CONCERNING SPEED AND DIRECTION OF MOVEMENT OF SECTORS OF ROSS SHELF ICE.
28. KAINAN BAY FORMED BY SUBMERGED ISLAND.
29. STRONG MAGNETOMETER IRREGULARITY INDICATES SUBMERGED ISLAND OR VOLCANIC DIKE UNDER SHELF ICE AT THIS POINT.
30. CONFIRMED PRESENCE SUBMERGED ISLAND.
31. MAGNETOMETER CONFIRMS [illegible] OF [illegible] ROOSEVELT ISLAND.
32. SUBMERGED ISLAND HERE (MAGNETOMETER)
33. SUBMERGED ISLAND THOUGHT TO BE HERE IS EITHER NON-EXISTANT OR [illegible] MENTARY ROCK STRUCTURE.
34. EAST COAST OF ROSS SEA [illegible] COVERED UNDER ICE COVER.
35. [illegible] ACTIVE SNAKE-LIKE BELT OF DISTURBED ICE
36. MOUNTAIN GROUP WITH PLATEAU TO SOUTH.
37. HIGH MOUNTAIN RANGE WITH FOOTHILLS TO NORTH
38. MOUNTAIN RANGE, ELEVATION [illegible], WITH SADDLE PASS
39. MOUNTAIN RANGE, ELEVATION APPROXIMATELY 13,000
40. DISCOVERED GLACIER DESCENDING FROM POLAR PLATEAU.
41. INTERIOR AND UPPER REACHES OF [illegible] GLACIER EXPLORED. MOUNTAINS AND TRIBUTARIES TO [illegible] GLACIER DISCOVERED.
42. EXPLORED MOUNTAINS BETWEEN WADE AND BEARDMORE GLACIERS.
43. SMALL GROUP OF MOUNTAINS APPROXIMATELY 10,000' LOCATED HERE.
44. EXPLORED [illegible] MOUNTAINS OF BEARDMORE AREA.
45. REVISITED THE SOUTH POLE [illegible] FROM [illegible]
46. DISCOVERED CHANGES IN ICE [illegible] TENSION CRACKS PRESSURE, ETC.

47. EXPLORED DRY GLACIERS, ICE LAKES, [illegible] AND FALLS, [illegible] POSTPILE, ETC. HERE
48. EXPLORED AND MAPPED ENTIRE WESTERN AND CENTRAL PORTION OF MOUNTAINS BORDERING [illegible] ROSS ICE SHELF. NOTHING BUT POLAR PLATEAU VISIBLE [illegible] OF MOUNTS.
49. [illegible] FEATURELESS TO EXTENT OF VISIBILITY.
50. [illegible] MAPPED, PEAK ELEVATION [illegible]
51. [illegible] STURGE ISLAND 9,500' [illegible] MAPPED.
52. MOUNTAINS [illegible] BETWEEN CAPES CHEETHAM AND WILLIAMS, HIGHER MOUNTAINS TO THE SOUTH AND A VERY HIGH ROLLING PLATEAU INLAND.
53. RENNICK BAY EXTENDS INLAND TO 71 30 S. [illegible] STEEP MOUNTAINS UP TO 8,000'.
54. SCATTERED LOW MOUNTAINS IN THE VICINITY OF ARCHER'S POINT.
55. OATES COAST LINED WITH MOUNTAINS UP TO 10,000' ELEVATION.
56. ROLLING ICE PLATEAU AVERAGING 6,000' IN ELEVATION.
57. SEVERAL NEW ISLANDS AND GLACIERS FOUND ALONG THIS RUGGED TERRAIN COASTAL AREA.
58. SOUTH MAGNETIC POLE MAY HAVE MOVED HERE (INEXACT AIRCRAFT COMPASSES).
59. ICE CAP ELEVATION 8,500' AND FEATURELESS EXCEPT FOR ROLLS, FEW SHARP RISES.
60. FEATURELESS ICE CAP AREAS.

61. ICE CAP ELEVATION 8,500 AND ABSOLUTELY FEATURELESS.
62. VALLEY [illegible] WATER [illegible] FROM BEYOND [illegible] THE SEA
63. LOOSE PACK, EASY ACCESS TO THE COAST WITH AN ICEBREAKER.
64. SOLID PACK WITH NO LEADS FROM DAVIS BAY TO CAPE DECOUVERTE
65. DENSE PACK [illegible] OPEN [illegible] OF WATER IN SOLID PACK
66. LOOSE PACK [illegible] COLLECTIONS OF [illegible]
67. [illegible] LOCATED HERE.
68. [illegible] BAY [illegible] TO BE MUCH DEEPER THAN PREVIOUSLY KNOWN
69. ICE CAP ELEVATION 8,500'. NO MOUNTAINS OR GLACIERS VISIBLE FROM HERE

70. LOOSE PACK, NAVIGABLE BY ICE BREAKER AT ANY POINT.
71. OPEN WATER ALONG COAST AS FAR OUT AS VISIBILITY ([illegible] MILES).
72. MANY SMALL ISLANDS AND MANY NUNATAKS ALONG COAST, NO MOUNTAINS.
73. ACTUAL COASTLINE THIS AREA DOES NOT AGREE WITH EXISTING CHARTS.
74. OPEN WATER IN DAVIS SEA FROM 92 E TO THE SHELF ICE.
75. ICE CAP RISES TO A GREAT ELEVATION WEST OF 115 E.
76. ICE CAP LESS THAN 1,000' ELEVATION IN THIS AREA.
77. TWO LARGE GLACIERS HERE.
78. ICE CAP FORMS DOME AT THIS POINT, RISING TO 5,000'.
79. ICE CAP ELEVATION 2,700'.
80. OUTCROP OF BLACK EARTH (POSSIBILITY OF COAL?)
81. 110 E MERIDIAN DEEPLY EMBAYED.
82. GLACIER, [illegible] AND OUTCROPS DISCOLOR GLACIER AND ITS BERGS
83. LARGEST GLACIER IN GROUP, SHEER DROP OF 1,000'
84. AND 86. GLACIER.
85. EXCELLENT LANDING FIELD ACCESSIBLE TO PROTECTED SHIPS
87. DISCOVERED NARROW ICE TONGUE.
88. SEVERAL NUNATAKS HERE.
89. "BUNGER'S OASIS", 20 MILE CIRCLE OF ICE FREE HILLS 500' AND CONE SHAPED, MANY COLORED LIQUID LAKES, SUITABLE FOR LANDING [illegible] PLANE.
90. DENMAN GLACIER EXTENDS SOUTH TO 67 35, RIMMED BY 5,000' MOUNTAINS
91. ICE CAP ELEVATION 6,000.
92. MOUNTAINS SIGHTED HERE PROTRUDING SEVERAL THOUSAND FEET OVER ICE CAP
93. ICE CAP ELEVATION 8,300'.
94. ICE CAP ELEVATION 9,000'.
95. NUNATAK DISCOVERED HERE.
96. LARGE GROUP OF MOUNTAINS.
97. ICE CAP ELEVATION ABOUT 8,000'.
98. PROMINENT MOUNTAIN RANGE.
99. PROMINENT MOUNTAIN RANGE.
100. SORSDAL GLACIER MUCH LONGER THAN DESCRIBED.
101. SOUTH COAST OF MACKENZIE SEA IS OPEN WATER.
102. SHELF ICE TWO HUNDRED FEET HIGH.
103. MOUNTAIN INDICATED HERE ON EXISTING CHARTS, DOES NOT EXIST
104. ICE CAP ELEVATION 20 MILES [illegible] IS 3,500. ASCENT CONTINUES.
105. EDWARD VIII GULF MUCH LARGER THAN CHARTED, HAS SPLIT GLACIER.
106. SCOTT RANGE 6,000', TOP OBSCURED
107. MOUNTAIN RANGE.
108. LARGE GLACIER DISCOVERED HERE.
109. MAX ELEV. ALONG THIS LINE IS 4,000'.
110. GLACIER AND SHELF ICE TO THE NORTH.
111. THORSHAMMER ISLAND IS NON-EXISTANT.
112. THIS PENINSULA ACTUALLY IS SHELF ICE.
113. SIGHTED MOUNTAIN RANGE HERE.
114. LOWER AND LESS WELL DEFINED MOUNTAIN RANGE.
115. MOUNTAIN RANGE 13,000?, ICE CAP TO NORTH 5,000'.
116. PAYER GROUP OF MOUNTAINS MISPLACED. THE PLANE FLEW NEARBY IN GOOD WEATHER BUT DID NOT SIGHT IT.
117. LOCATION OF ICE TONGUE CONFIRMED.
118. OPEN WATER TO OCEAN, EXCEPT FOR VERY LOOSE PACK.
119. PREVIOUSLY KNOWN COASTLINE REMAPPED AND CONFIRMED. ABOUT HALF OF THIS COAST HAS OPEN WATER INSIDE LOOSE PACK ICE.
120. NUNATAKS ALONG EDGE OF COAST.
121. ACTUAL COASTLINE HERE LIES 30-TO-45 MILES SOUTH OF THAT PLOTTED ON EXISTING CHARTS. THE FORMER COASTLINE WAS ACTUALLY THE ICE BOUNDARY AS DEMONSTRATED BY THE AIRCRAFT RADIO ALTIMETER.
122. CONSOLIDATED PACK OFF COAST. CLOUD COVER FROM 0 TO 14,000' OVER THE CONTINENT PREVENTED EXPLORATION.
123. SHELF ICE EXTENDS NORTH OF COAST TO 69 55 S BETWEEN 03 AND 04 E
124. PROBABLE ROCK (GARBLED WORD), APPARENTLY OF VOLCANIC ORIGIN.
125. PROMINENT MOUNTAIN RANGE SIGHTED HERE.
126. MOUNTAIN RANGE SIGHTED HERE.

NOTE: THE COMMENTS [illegible] HEREON ARE EXCERPTS FROM CODED DISPATCHES, FROM [illegible] OF AIR CREWMEN, OR FROM CASUAL EXAMINATION OF [illegible] PHOTOGRAPHIC PROOFS (TASK GROUP 68.5 ONLY). AT THIS DATE THE MAPPING PHOTOGRAPHY HAS NOT BEEN PREPARED OR EXAMINED.

THIS PRELIMINARY [illegible] SUBMITTED 18 APRIL 1947.

JOHN H. ROSCOE, 1ST LT., USMCR
STAFF PHOTOGRAMMETRIC OFFICER

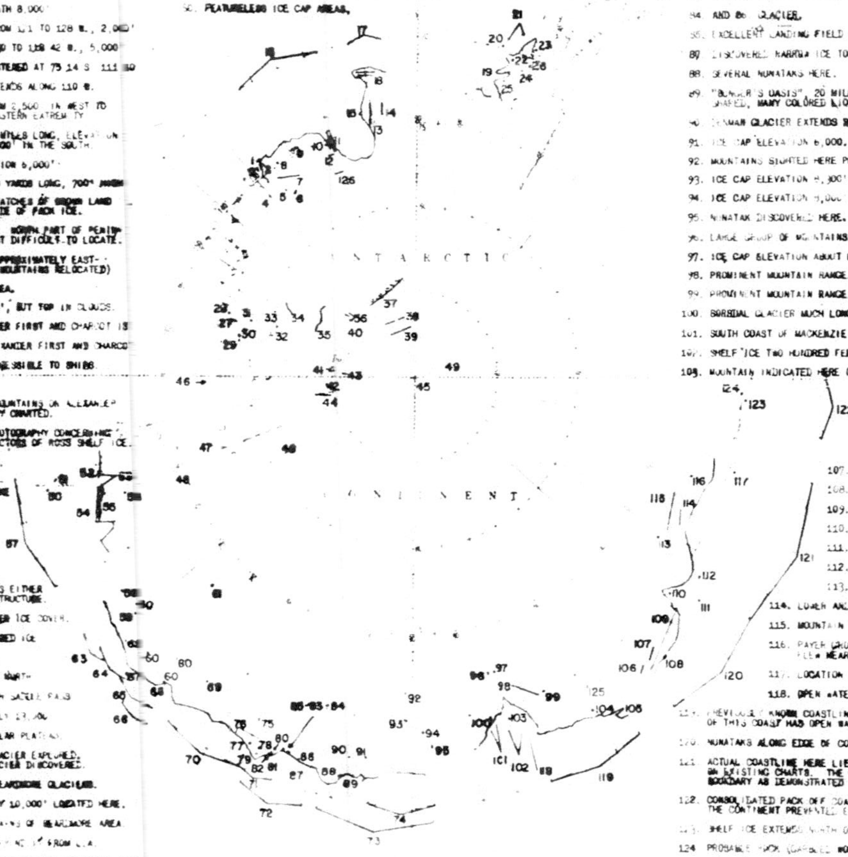

RESTRICTED

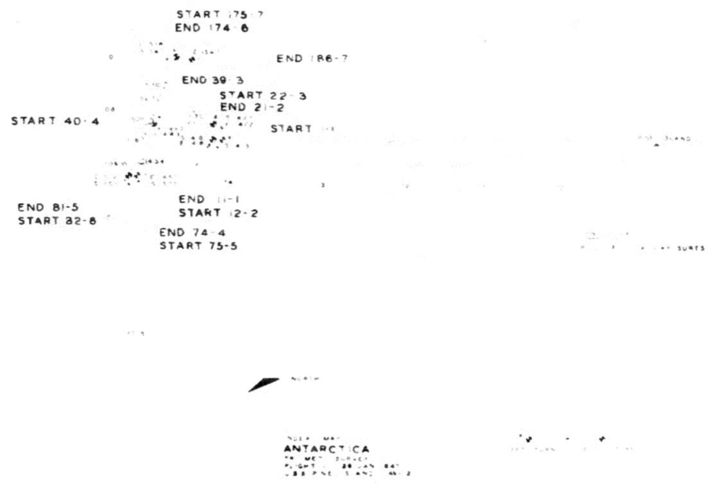

START 175-7
END 174-6

END 186-7

END 39-3
START 22-3
END 21-3
START

START 40-4

END 81-5
START 82-8

END 11-1
START 12-2
END 74-4
START 75-5

ANTARCTICA

Plate No. 4

Typical Tri-Metrogon Index Map prepared by Task Group 68.3 on Flight No. 11.

Annex III

- 30 -

FIELD DATA SHEET

TRIMETROGON PHOTOGRAPHY

PROJECT _____

FOR
Port CAMERA   Camera No _____   Cone No _____   Lens No _____   Magazine No _____
Stbd CAMERA   Camera No _____   Cone No _____   Lens No _____   Magazine No _____
VERTICAL CAMERA   Camera No _____   Cone No _____   Lens No _____   Magazine No _____

CALIBRATED DATA
Port CAMERA   Date _____   Calibrated FL _____
Stbd CAMERA   Date _____   Calibrated FL _____
VERTICAL CAMERA   Date _____   Calibrated FL _____

REMARKS _____

ROLL	FILM MARKED FROM	FILM MARKED TO	GCT START OF RUN	GCT END OF RUN	EXPOSURE INTERVAL TIME	LOCATION	GROUND SPEED Knots	TRUE HEADING	DRIFT	RATE	ALTITUDE BAR	ALTITUDE CR	ABOVE TERRAIN	FLYING HGT
1	1	11	1413	1413	20		126	280°					9,600	
2	12	21	1413	1442	21		124	90°					9,600	
3	22	39	1424	1425	21		127	240°					9,600	
4	40	74	1445	1450	20		138	112°					9,600	
5	75	81	1500	1505	20		133	120°					9,600	
6	82	174	1505	1505	20		142	280°					9,600	
7	175	194	1513	1514	20		133	010°					9,600	

PHOTOGRAPHERS NAME _____

Plate No. 5

Field data sheet for Tri-Metrogon Photography prepared on flight No. 11 by Task Group 68.3.

AERIAL DATA SHEET
TASK FORCE SIXTY-EIGHT

DATE _____

DATA SHEET NO. _____

FLIGHT NO. _____

PILOT _____

NAVIGATOR _____

PHOTOGRAPHER _____

PLANE NO. AND TYPE _____

CAMERA NO. _____

TYPE OF FILM USED _____

RUN NO	NO ALT	ALT ABOVE TERRAIN	LOCATION	TRUE COURSE	GCT START RUN	GCT END RUN	EXP INT	NO EXP	FILTER USED	MAG NO	F L	SHUTTER SPEED	F STOP	REMARKS

CONTINUED ON REVERSE SIDE

Plate No. 6

Aerial data sheet for supplementary oblique photography pre aerial on
flight No. 11 by Task Group 61.3.

Annex III

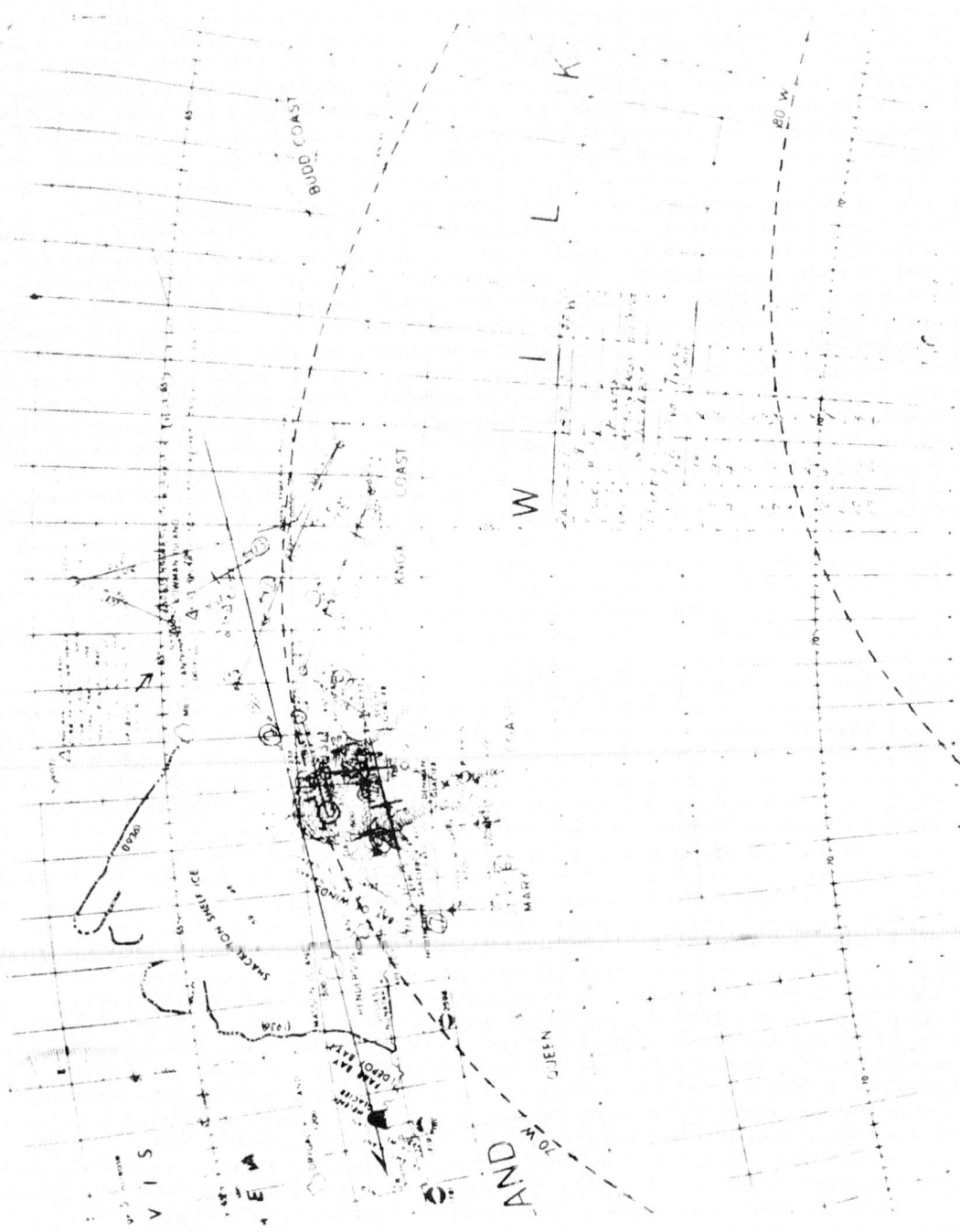

Plate No. 7

Tri-Metrogon index chart prepared by Task Group 68.2 on flight No. 19.

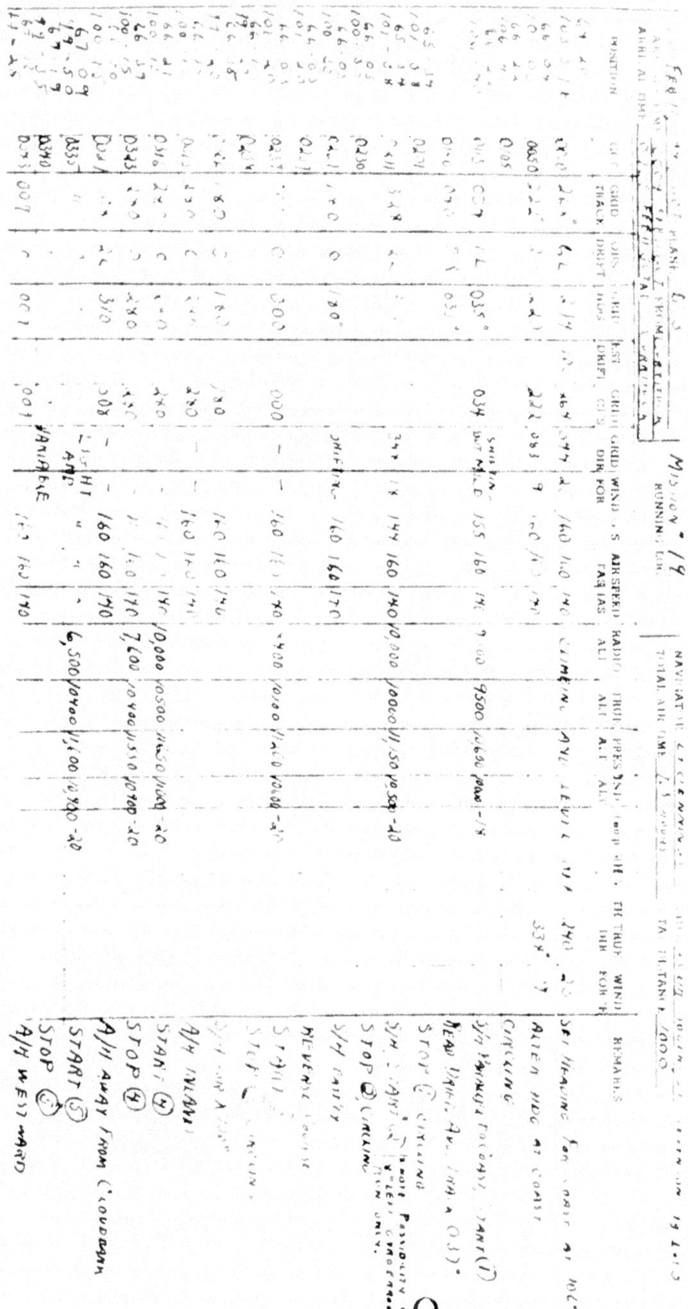

Plate No. 8

Navigators Data sheet prepared by Task Group 68.2 on Flight No. 19.

U. S. NAVAL ANTARCTIC EXPEDITION 1946-47

TASK FORCE 68

PHOTOGRAPHIC RUNS

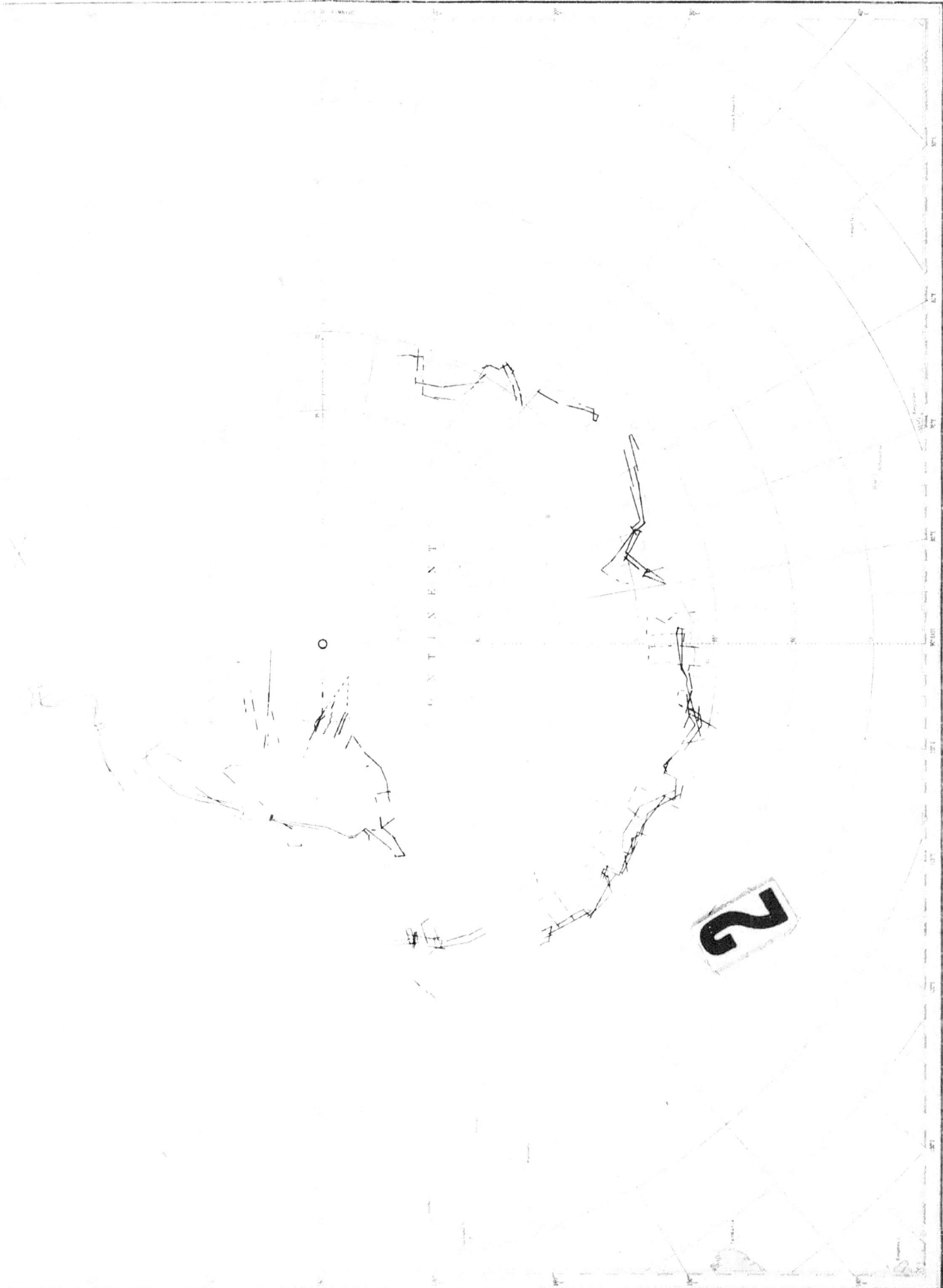

CONTINENT

O

2

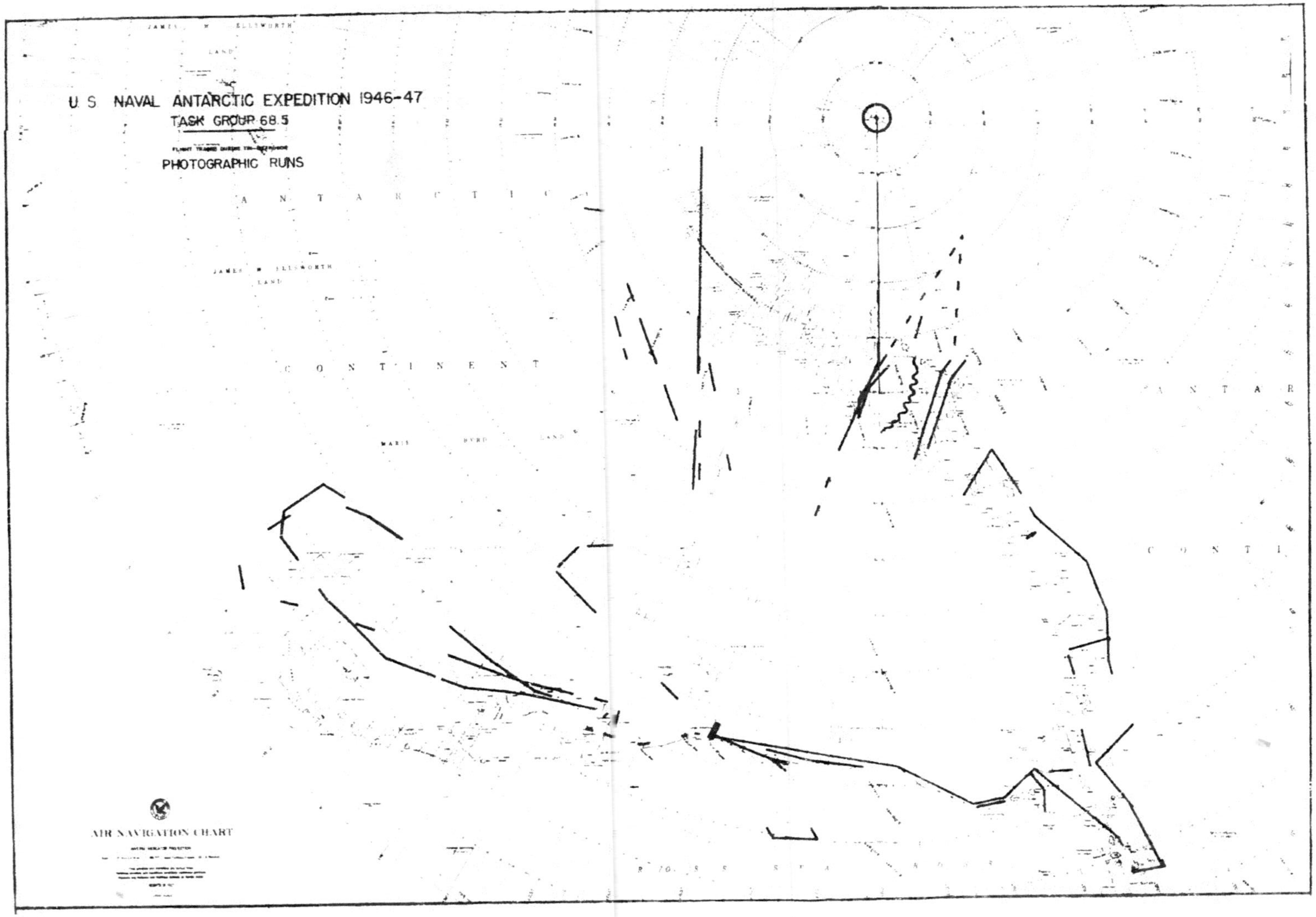

U S NAVAL ANTARCTIC EXPEDITION 1946-47

TASK GROUP 68 5

PHOTOGRAPHIC RUNS

Plate No. 9

Tri-Metrogon Photographic runs of Task Group 68.5

- 35 -

Annex III

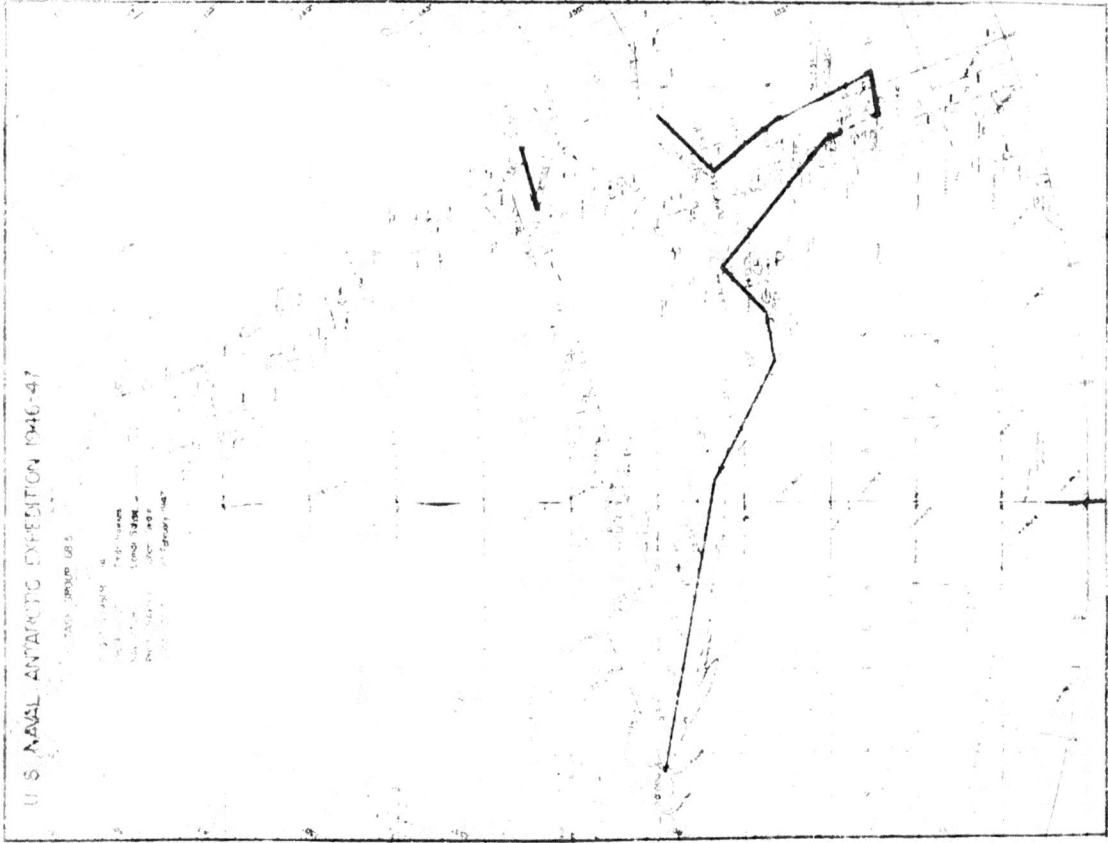

U.S. NAVAL ANTARCTIC EXPEDITION 1946-47

Figure No. 11

DATE Feb 20, 1947 PLANE (V)(V) BuNo 7767 Cmdr Hawkes, Lieut Anderson Lt Cmdr. Salyer

L.A. DEP. 2237 2235

DEP. 0937 Lit le America 110 hrs 1327 naut. mi.

RUNNING LOG

Position											Remarks
Little America	2237	/								2250	Take Departure
Red V-6	2250	074	0°		A.b	Climb	-10	110	13	26	2320 Climbing
Red V-4	2320	074	0°		130	5000	-15	125	30	65	2330 Above clouds
Red U-4	2330	134			130	5000	-15	125	10	21	2345 Above clouds
Red V-3	2345	104			130	5000	-16	125	15	32	2358 Above clouds
Red V-3	2351	074			130	5000	-15	125	6	8	0015 Above clouds
Red V-1	0015	074			130	5000	-15	125	19	41	0115 Above clouds, Sighted Mt. Erebus
Blue D-21	0115	072	2r		131	9000	-15	117	60	1N	0200 Over Mountains
Blue E-20	0200	074	0°		131	9000	-15	117	45	98	0231 Object Pt. Head North
Blue I-19	0231	155			134	10800	-20	117	31	79	0300 Above clouds
Blue J-21	0300	155			135	10800	-20	119	29	65	0305 Circled at Object Pt.
Blue V-22	0313	226	0°		135	10800	-20	112	5	8	0400 Hd for Mts & reload cameras
Blue I-23	0418	140			145	11000	-20	112	13	31	0440 Photo'd Prince Albert Mts.
Blue J-25	0440				145	11000	-20	125	41	81	0515 Photo'd Prince Albert Mts.
Blue K-27	0515				138	12500	-20	116			0540 Object Pt. Circled
Blue J-27	0540	331			138	12800	-20	116			0605
Blue I-25	0606	287									Over McMurdo Sound
Blue F-24	0630										
											Depart for Little America from McMurdo via the Ross Ice Barrier. Photo'd all along edge of Barrier under poor light conditions.
Little America	0930										

Plate No. 10

Navigators running log of Flight 1, Task Group 6.8.

FIELD DATA SHEET

TRIMETROGON PHOTOGRAPHY

PROJECT _____

SHEET ___ OF _2_

Flight 14

FOR:

	Camera No	Cone No	Lens No	Magazine No
RIGHT CAMERA	44-435	44-469	MS-92)	43-12149
LEFT CAMERA	44-444	43-184	Mag-er888	43-3402
VERTICAL CAMERA	44-531	42-4553	MS-139	43-2134

CALIBRATED DATA:

	Date
RIGHT CAMERA	NOT CALIBRATED
LEFT CAMERA	Calibrated F.L.
VERTICAL CAMERA	Calibrated F.L.

REMARKS Pilot Commander Hawkes
Navigator lt. Cdr. Salver
Co-Pilot lieutenant Anderson
Radioman Nyhan
Technical Observer First lieut. Rosco

RUN	ROLL	FILM MARKED FROM	FILM MARKED TO	G.C.T. START OF RUN	G.C.T. END OF RUN	EXPOSURE INTERVAL (TIME)	LOCATION	GROUND SPEED MPH	TRUE HEADING	DRIFT	DATE	ALTITUDE BAR REG	TEMP REG	ALTITUDE ABOVE TERRAIN	RADAR FIX TIME	EXP NO OR NOS.
1	1R	1	71	1400	1423	22	7b 40'S 162 8	120	274		2/21/44	10800	10800	8000		
1	1V	"	"	"	"	"	"	"	"		"	"	"	"		
1	1L	"	"	"	"	"	"	"	"		"	"	"	"		
1	1G	"	"	"	"	"	"	"	"		"	"	"	"		
2	1R	72	198	1525	1600	22	S E E F L I G H T C H A R T				10800	10800	8000		
2	1V	"	"	"	"	"					"	"	"		
2	1L	"	"	"	"	"					"	"	"		
2	1L	72	293												

N O T E: GREMLIN TIMER USED 7 EXPOSURES

PHOTOGRAPHERS NAME ___Swain, K. C. FbOW 1/c___

Plate No. 13

Tri-metrogon field data sheet on flight 14 Task Fook 00...

- 39 -

Flight of Thursday   20 February 1947
Airplane # 17197
Plane Cdr. Hawkes, Cdr.
Pilot Anderson, Lt.
Co-Pilot Salyer, Lt. Cdr.
Radio Nyhan, ARM 1/c
Photo Swain, PHOM
Observ Roscoe, Lt.   All Times G.C.T.

2235   Off Little America (1135 Local)
        Grid Hdg 074 Cruising 5000 ft. temp - 10 deg cent.
        Barom. Pres. 29.10
2330   On instruments during climb to top overcast. Light to
        moderate ice encountered at 10000'. Changed course 60
        deg to stbd in attempt to find clear area nearer bar-
        rier.
2345   Chgd to Grid Cus 104 Deg.
2351   To grid cus 074. Port Aft fuel tank on.

21 Feb 1947
0020   Sighted humps in clouds in far distance believed to
        be the Western Range.
0035   Sighted first mountains to stbd bearing 30 deg. Mts.
        Erebus and Terror sighted at 50 deg. relative to Stbd.
0142   Plenty mountains in sight both to port and stbd extend-
        ing thru overcast.
0152   Over foothills. Crevasses to port. Hull tanks on.
0204   High snow and glacier-covered irregular mountains ahead.
        Mt. McClintock abeam on port hand.
0206   Radar altitude 7500 plane altitude 10280
0207   7000   10280
0210   4000   10300
0212   2700   10400
0249   Radar altitude averages 2300-2500 feet, airplane 9900.
        Plateau height about 7600 feet.
0325   Radar 4000 Plane 10900
0326   4500   10900 Grid hdg 224 flying behind the
        Western Range — Entire plateau solid overcast with top
        at 9000 plus
0332   Took 16 mm. movies of Western profile of Western Range
        12 feet film.
0345   In this vicinity all surface ice noted to be clear when
        on Eastern side of low ridges. That on west side is all
        snow covered.
0348   North edge of Ross Island noted to be directly ahead with
        Grid hdg 224.
0352   Cameras on altitude 11000
0353   16 mm film of dry Valley showing well-defined rock
        strata.

                         Plate No. 14

           Pilots Log of flight 14 Task Group 68.5.

0355	To grid hdg 226
0400	Circled to change Tri-Met Camera Packs
0408	Contacted V5 on VHF. Advised V5 to Proceed north and cover east face of Range as far as Terra Nova Bay if possible.
0412	Requested Altimeter setting from Burton Island.
0416	Magazines O.K. Cameras on to heading 140 grid at 0416 Cameras set for radar altitude of 6000 feet account irregular terrain.
0419	Altimeter setting 29.11 (Same as at L. A. on takeoff)
0426	Radar alt 6700 Plane 11900
0433	16 MM of Rock pinnicles -- then out of film
0441	Chg cus to?
0443	Radalt 5300 Plane 12400
0444	Vertical and Port Cameras off. nothing except flat Plateau to port with no distinguishing features.
0516	Advised Alpaca of position. Few isolated peaks, not very high, visible to Northwest. High range visible to Northeast estimated not in excess of 100 miles. At bottom of chart and fuel more than half expended.
0525	Passing over dull Maroon-colored mountains - Trimets still in action. Peculiar rounded bare surfaces -- May be tops of cirques (this inserted by Lt. Roscoe)
0532	Circled to load Gremlin, resumed 330 Grid.
0547	Weather received from Base 500' ceiling unlim visib. Advised Gremlin and k17 not on since reloading.
0605	Turned to 287 grid to return to base. Sighted Erebus.
0628	Over Burton Island at 5000.
0641	Passing Terror.
0643	Passing Cape Crozier. Proceeding along Barrier for photo survey of edge. Port oblique on.
0705	Over cove in barrier for vertical shots.
0937	On chocks L.A. (2237 local)

Plate No. 15

Pilots log of Flight 14 Task Group 68.5, (Continued)

Plate No. 16

Navigators running log on flight No. 11, Task Group 68.3

UNITED STATES DEPARTMENT OF THE INTERIOR
BOARD ON GEOGRAPHICAL NAMES

ANTARCTIC NAME PROPOSAL

NAME PROPOSED   BUNGER'S OASIS

DESCRIPTION Kind of feature ROCK & TARN AREA   Lat 66° 27' S Long 100° 42' E

_____ nautical miles distant from   XX N of Scott Glacier, S & E of Shackleton Shelf XX

                                                    in a   direction

   Map Reference (air chart, H.O chart, map title, etc   H.O. 2562, H.O. (BA) 3171, AAF LRAN Charts,
WILKES LAND, ETC.

   Identifying Characteristics (size, shape, length, width, height, etc   as much as 20 miles on a side with
a decadent glacier to the west and ice cap on the remaining sides which rises
to the south and east, ice and then pack ice to the north. Lakes 200-250 feet high.

   Photo Reference (vertical, oblique, other) Flights Eighteen and Nineteen of Task Group 68.2
See Photographs submitted.

   Materials Submitted   TRI-METROGON AND COLOR AERIAL PHOTOGRAPHS as attached.

SUPPORTING DATA Reason for Choice   Lt. Cmdr BUNGER commanded the patrol bomber from
which the ice free area was discovered. Two days later Cmdr. BUNGER landed
his aircraft in one of the lakes therein. Subsequent news dispatches have
made this name one of common usage, even though it is not technically an oasis.
   Date discovered, seen, recorded, mapped, etc First discovered 11 February 1947, landed 13 Feb.

   By whom Lt. Cmdr. BUNGER, USN and crew of PBM, BAKER ONE of TASK GROUP 68.2

   Personal Information (of honoree)   DAVID ELI BUNGER
                                1110 G Avenue, Coronado, California

   Expedition UNITED STATES NAVAL ANTARCTIC EXPEDITION 1946--1947 (HIGHJUMP)

   Supporting Data Submitted (surveys, charts, photos, other)
        Motion Pictures and descriptions by aerial explorers.

                                                    to be returned   X
                                                    not to be returned _____

SUBMITTED BY Name   John H. Roscoe
   Address   Task Force 68, US.S Navy
   Rank or official duties First Lieutenant, USMCR   Date 1 June 1947

                    DO NOT WRITE IN SPACE BELOW

   CODE _____   DATE RECEIVED _____

   CASE SECTION _____   PROMULGATION _____

RG 42-5-5/47-1000 Mult

Plate No. 17

Sample form for Antarctic Name Proposal.

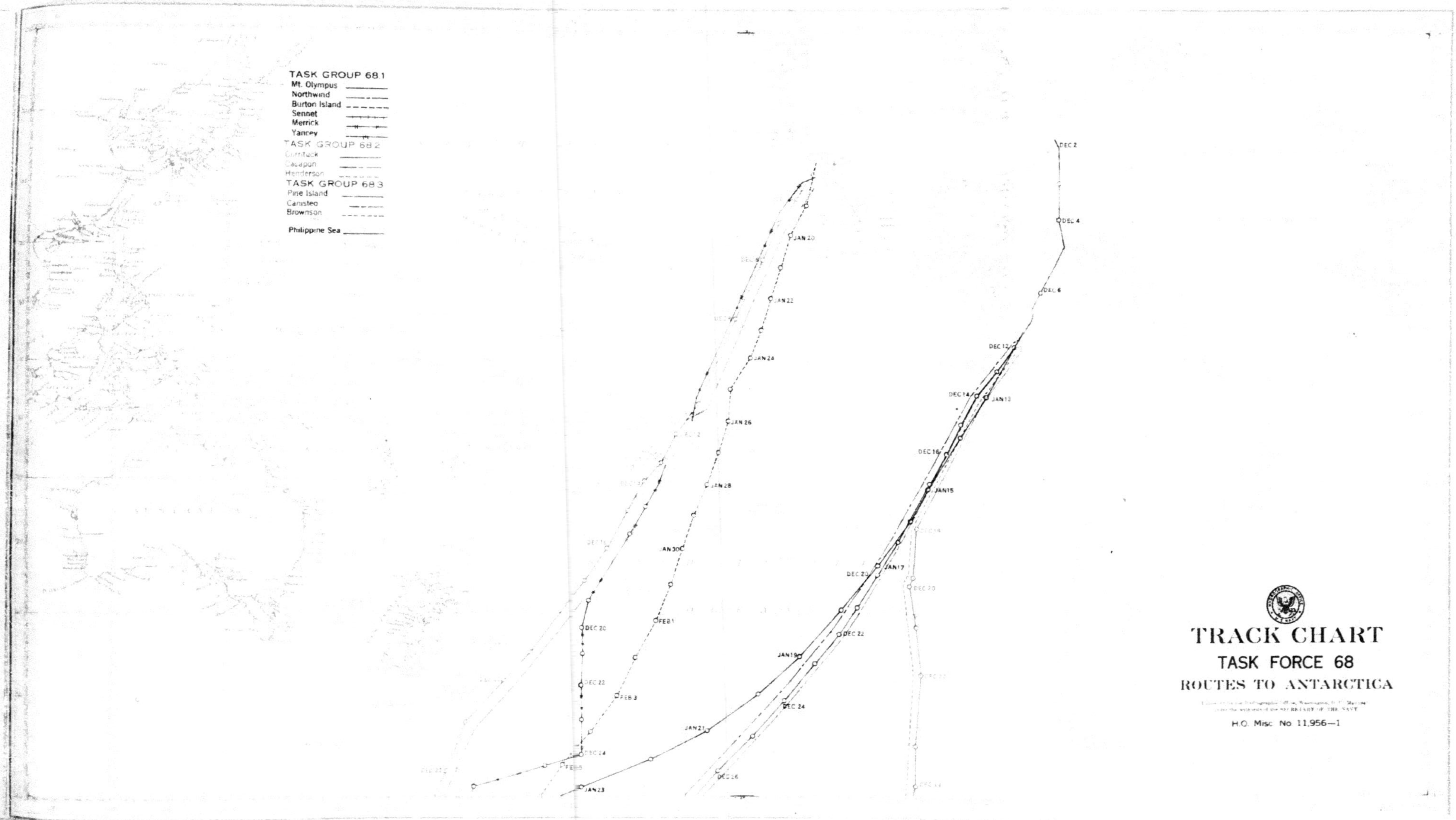

TRACK CHART
TASK FORCE 68
ROUTES TO ANTARCTICA

H.O. Misc. No 11,956–1

TASK GROUP 68 1
Mt. Olympus
Northwind
Burton Island
Sennet
Merrick
Yancey
TASK GROUP 68 2
Cacapon
Henderson
TASK GROUP 68 3
Pine Island
Canisteo
Brownson

Philippine Sea

DEC 2
DEC 4
DEC 6
DEC 10
DEC 12
DEC 14
DEC 16
JAN 12
JAN 15
JAN 17
DEC 22
DEC 21
DEC 20
DEC 24
JAN 19
JAN 20
JAN 22
JAN 24
JAN 26
JAN 28
JAN 30
FEB 1
FEB 3
DEC 20
DEC 22
DEC 24
JAN 23
JAN 21
DEC 26

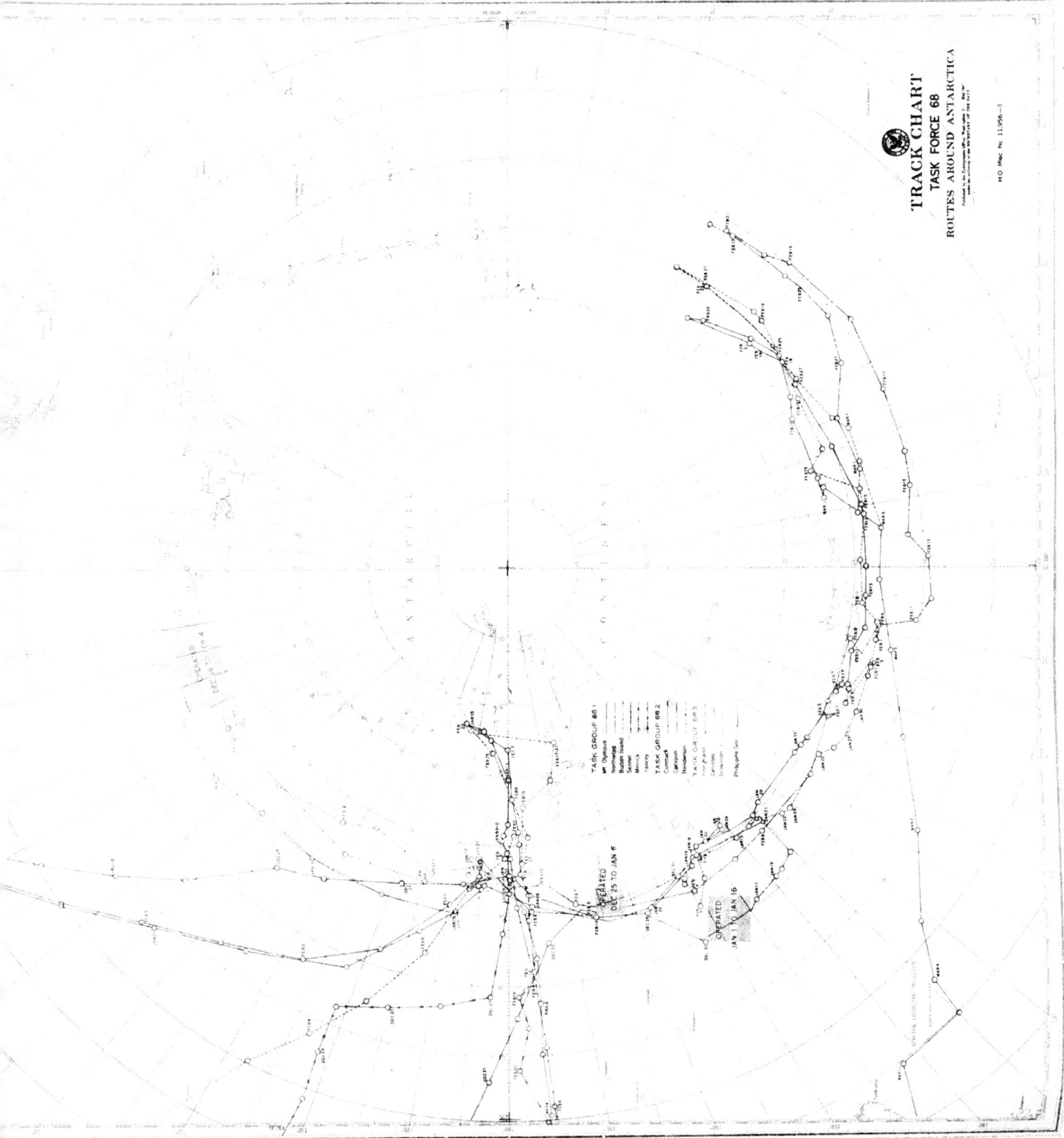

TRACK CHART
TASK FORCE 68
ROUTES AROUND ANTARCTICA

H.O. Misc. No. 11,956-3

TRACK CHART
TASK FORCE 68
ROUTES FROM ANTARCTICA

H.O. Misc No 11,956-2

TASK GROUP 68.1
Mt Olympus
Northwind
Burton Island
Sennet
Merrick
Yancey

TASK GROUP 68.2
Pine Island
Canisteo
Brownson

Philippine Sea

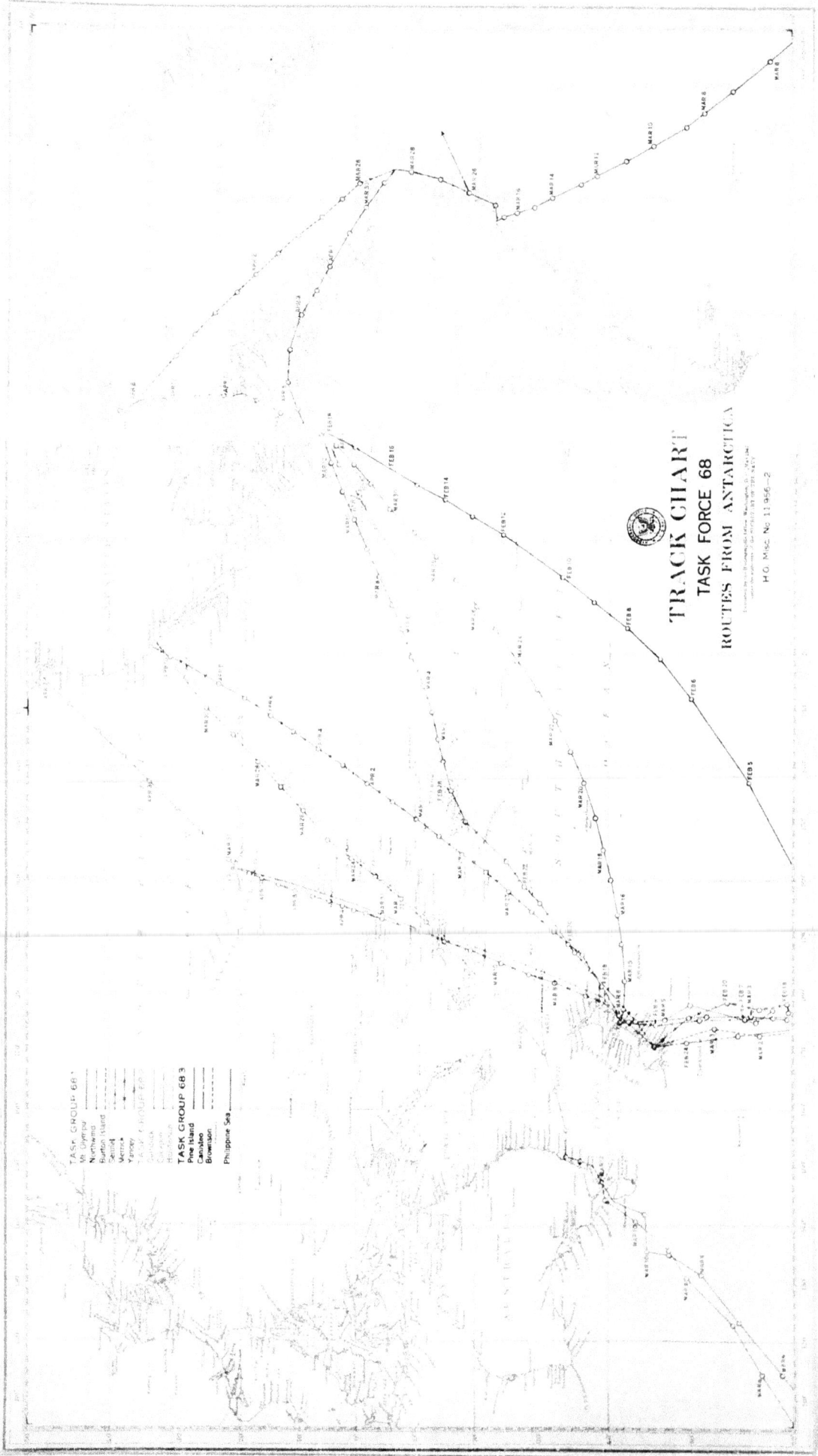

DEPARTMENT OF THE NAVY
COMMANDER
U.S. FLEET FORCES COMMAND
1562 MITSCHER AVENUE SUITE 250
NORFOLK, VA 23551-2487

5720
Ser N01P1(2013-13)/003
February 14, 2013

Dear ████████████:

Thank you for your Freedom of Information Act request dated October 19, 2012, originally sent to the Defense Technical Information Center (DTIC) at Fort Belvoir, VA. During the initial processing of this request by the DTIC, a document entitled "U.S. Navy Antarctic Development Project 1947: Report of Operation HIGHJUMP. (Volume 1)" was identified requiring Navy review. This document was forwarded to the Department of the Navy Privacy Act/Freedom of Information Act Policy Branch Office (DNS-36), which further forwarded it, and your request, to U.S. Fleet Forces Command (USFF) for action. Your request was received on January 29, 2013.

Following a thorough review of this document by various subject matter experts at USFF, it was determined the information in this document was fully releasable. Consequently, it is released to you in its entirety and, due to its size, is provided as enclosure (1) on CD-Rom. The original classification of CONFIDENTIAL was changed to UNCLASSIFIED by the Armed Services Technical Information Agency on January 13, 1955. Any residual classified markings throughout the document have been lined through to avoid confusion regarding the document's classification.

I am the person responsible for this determination. Please contact Ms. Linda Alvers at (757) 836-3630 or at linda.alvers@navy.mil if you require further assistance.

Sincerely,

J. E. CAMPBELL
By direction

Encl: (1) Responsive document on CD Rom

Copy to:
Defense Technical Information Center
  8725 John J. Kingman Rd, Suite 0944
  Ft Belvoir, VA 22060-6218
Serial file
Case file

9781608880591